Actuarial Theory for Dependent Risks

Actuarial Theory for Dependent Risks

Measures, Orders and Models

M. Denuit
Université Catholique de Louvain, Belgium

J. Dhaene
Katholieke Universiteit Leuven, Belgium and Universiteit van Amsterdam, The Netherlands

M. Goovaerts
Katholieke Universiteit Leuven, Belgium and Universiteit van Amsterdam, The Netherlands

R. Kaas
Universiteit van Amsterdam, The Netherlands

John Wiley & Sons, Ltd

Telephone (+44) 1243 779777

Email (for orders and customer service enquiries): cs-books@wiley.co.uk
Visit our Home Page on www.wiley.com

Other Wiley Editorial Offices

John Wiley & Sons, Inc., 111 River Street, Hoboken, NJ 07030, USA

Jossey-Bass, 989 Market Street, San Francisco, CA 94103-1741, USA

Wiley-VCH Verlag GmbH, Boschstr. 12, D-69469 Weinheim, Germany

John Wiley & Sons Australia Ltd, 42 McDougall Street, Milton, Queensland 4064, Australia

John Wiley & Sons (Asia) Pte Ltd, 2 Clementi Loop #02-01, Jin Xing Distripark, Singapore 129809

John Wiley & Sons Canada Ltd, 22 Worcester Road, Etobicoke, Ontario, Canada M9W 1L1

Wiley also publishes its books in a variety of electronic formats. Some content that appears in print may not be available in electronic books.

Library of Congress Cataloging in Publication Data

Actuarial theory for dependent risks / M. Denuit … [et al.].
p. cm.
Includes bibliographical references and index.
ISBN 0-470-01492-X (acid-free paper)
1. Risk (Insurance)—Mathematical models. I. Denuit, M. (Michel)

HG8781.A35 2005
368′.001′51—dc22

2005043709

British Library Cataloguing in Publication Data

A catalogue record for this book is available from the British Library

ISBN-13 978-0-470-01492-9 (HB)
ISBN-10 0-470-01492-X (HB)

Typeset in 10/12pt Times by Integra Software Services Pvt. Ltd, Pondicherry, India
Printed and bound in Great Britain by Antony Rowe Ltd, Chippenham, Wiltshire
This book is printed on acid-free paper responsibly manufactured from sustainable forestry in which at least two trees are planted for each one used for paper production.

Contents

Foreword xiii

Preface xv

PART I THE CONCEPT OF RISK 1

1 Modelling Risks 3

1.1 Introduction 3
1.2 The Probabilistic Description of Risks 4
1.2.1 Probability space 4
1.2.2 Experiment and universe 4
1.2.3 Random events 4
1.2.4 Sigma-algebra 5
1.2.5 Probability measure 5
1.3 Independence for Events and Conditional Probabilities 6
1.3.1 Independent events 6
1.3.2 Conditional probability 7
1.4 Random Variables and Random Vectors 7
1.4.1 Random variables 7
1.4.2 Random vectors 8
1.4.3 Risks and losses 9
1.5 Distribution Functions 10
1.5.1 Univariate distribution functions 10
1.5.2 Multivariate distribution functions 12
1.5.3 Tail functions 13
1.5.4 Support 14
1.5.5 Discrete random variables 14
1.5.6 Continuous random variables 15
1.5.7 General random variables 16
1.5.8 Quantile functions 17
1.5.9 Independence for random variables 20
1.6 Mathematical Expectation 21
1.6.1 Construction 21
1.6.2 Riemann–Stieltjes integral 22

1.6.3 Law of large numbers 24
1.6.4 Alternative representations for the mathematical expectation in the continuous case 24
1.6.5 Alternative representations for the mathematical expectation in the discrete case 25
1.6.6 Stochastic Taylor expansion 25
1.6.7 Variance and covariance 27
1.7 Transforms 29
1.7.1 Stop-loss transform 29
1.7.2 Hazard rate 30
1.7.3 Mean-excess function 32
1.7.4 Stationary renewal distribution 34
1.7.5 Laplace transform 34
1.7.6 Moment generating function 36
1.8 Conditional Distributions 37
1.8.1 Conditional densities 37
1.8.2 Conditional independence 38
1.8.3 Conditional variance and covariance 38
1.8.4 The multivariate normal distribution 38
1.8.5 The family of the elliptical distributions 41
1.9 Comonotonicity 49
1.9.1 Definition 49
1.9.2 Comonotonicity and Fréchet upper bound 49
1.10 Mutual Exclusivity 51
1.10.1 Definition 51
1.10.2 Fréchet lower bound 51
1.10.3 Existence of Fréchet lower bounds in Fréchet spaces 53
1.10.4 Fréchet lower bounds and maxima 53
1.10.5 Mutual exclusivity and Fréchet lower bound 53
1.11 Exercises 55

2 Measuring Risk **59**

2.1 Introduction 59
2.2 Risk Measures 60
2.2.1 Definition 60
2.2.2 Premium calculation principles 61
2.2.3 Desirable properties 62
2.2.4 Coherent risk measures 65
2.2.5 Coherent and scenario-based risk measures 65
2.2.6 Economic capital 66
2.2.7 Expected risk-adjusted capital 66
2.3 Value-at-Risk 67
2.3.1 Definition 67
2.3.2 Properties 67
2.3.3 VaR-based economic capital 70
2.3.4 VaR and the capital asset pricing model 71

2.4 Tail Value-at-Risk 72
2.4.1 Definition 72
2.4.2 Some related risk measures 72
2.4.3 Properties 74
2.4.4 TVaR-based economic capital 77
2.5 Risk Measures Based on Expected Utility Theory 77
2.5.1 Brief introduction to expected utility theory 77
2.5.2 Zero-Utility Premiums 81
2.5.3 Esscher risk measure 82
2.6 Risk Measures Based on Distorted Expectation Theory 84
2.6.1 Brief introduction to distorted expectation theory 84
2.6.2 Wang risk measures 88
2.6.3 Some particular cases of Wang risk measures 92
2.7 Exercises 95
2.8 Appendix: Convexity and Concavity 100
2.8.1 Definition 100
2.8.2 Equivalent conditions 100
2.8.3 Properties 101
2.8.4 Convex sequences 102
2.8.5 Log-convex functions 102

3 Comparing Risks **103**

3.1 Introduction 103
3.2 Stochastic Order Relations 105
3.2.1 Partial orders among distribution functions 105
3.2.2 Desirable properties for stochastic orderings 106
3.2.3 Integral stochastic orderings 106
3.3 Stochastic Dominance 108
3.3.1 Stochastic dominance and risk measures 108
3.3.2 Stochastic dominance and choice under risk 110
3.3.3 Comparing claim frequencies 113
3.3.4 Some properties of stochastic dominance 114
3.3.5 Stochastic dominance and notions of ageing 118
3.3.6 Stochastic increasingness 120
3.3.7 Ordering mixtures 121
3.3.8 Ordering compound sums 121
3.3.9 Sufficient conditions 122
3.3.10 Conditional stochastic dominance I: Hazard rate order 123
3.3.11 Conditional stochastic dominance II: Likelihood ratio order 127
3.3.12 Comparing shortfalls with stochastic dominance: Dispersive order 133
3.3.13 Mixed stochastic dominance: Laplace transform order 137
3.3.14 Multivariate extensions 142
3.4 Convex and Stop-Loss Orders 149
3.4.1 Convex and stop-loss orders and stop-loss premiums 149
3.4.2 Convex and stop-loss orders and choice under risk 150
3.4.3 Comparing claim frequencies 154

3.4.4 Some characterizations for convex and stop-loss orders 155
3.4.5 Some properties of the convex and stop-loss orders 162
3.4.6 Convex ordering and notions of ageing 166
3.4.7 Stochastic (increasing) convexity 167
3.4.8 Ordering mixtures 169
3.4.9 Ordering compound sums 169
3.4.10 Risk-reshaping contracts and Lorenz order 169
3.4.11 Majorization 171
3.4.12 Conditional stop-loss order: Mean-excess order 173
3.4.13 Comparing shortfall with the stop-loss order: Right-spread order 175
3.4.14 Multivariate extensions 178
3.5 Exercises 182

PART II DEPENDENCE BETWEEN RISKS **189**

4 Modelling Dependence **191**

4.1 Introduction 191
4.2 Sklar's Representation Theorem 194
4.2.1 Copulas 194
4.2.2 Sklar's theorem for continuous marginals 194
4.2.3 Conditional distributions derived from copulas 198
4.2.4 Probability density functions associated with copulas 201
4.2.5 Copulas with singular components 201
4.2.6 Sklar's representation in the general case 203
4.3 Families of Bivariate Copulas 204
4.3.1 Clayton's copula 205
4.3.2 Frank's copula 205
4.3.3 The normal copula 207
4.3.4 The Student copula 208
4.3.5 Building multivariate distributions with given marginals from copulas 210
4.4 Properties of Copulas 213
4.4.1 Survival copulas 213
4.4.2 Dual and co-copulas 215
4.4.3 Functional invariance 216
4.4.4 Tail dependence 217
4.5 The Archimedean Family of Copulas 218
4.5.1 Definition 218
4.5.2 Frailty models 219
4.5.3 Probability density function associated with Archimedean copulas 220
4.5.4 Properties of Archimedean copulas 221
4.6 Simulation from Given Marginals and Copula 223
4.6.1 General method 223
4.6.2 Exploiting Sklar's decomposition 224
4.6.3 Simulation from Archimedean copulas 224

4.7 Multivariate Copulas 225
4.7.1 Definition 225
4.7.2 Sklar's representation theorem 225
4.7.3 Functional invariance 226
4.7.4 Examples of multivariate copulas 226
4.7.5 Multivariate Archimedean copulas 229
4.8 Loss–Alae Modelling with Archimedean Copulas: A Case Study 231
4.8.1 Losses and their associated ALAEs 231
4.8.2 Presentation of the ISO data set 231
4.8.3 Fitting parametric copula models to data 232
4.8.4 Selecting the generator for Archimedean copula models 234
4.8.5 Application to loss–ALAE modelling 238
4.9 Exercises 242

5 Measuring Dependence **245**

5.1 Introduction 245
5.2 Concordance Measures 246
5.2.1 Definition 246
5.2.2 Pearson's correlation coefficient 247
5.2.3 Kendall's rank correlation coefficient 253
5.2.4 Spearman's rank correlation coefficient 257
5.2.5 Relationships between Kendall's and Spearman's rank correlation coefficients 259
5.2.6 Other dependence measures 260
5.2.7 Constraints on concordance measures in bivariate discrete data 262
5.3 Dependence Structures 264
5.3.1 Positive dependence notions 264
5.3.2 Positive quadrant dependence 265
5.3.3 Conditional increasingness in sequence 274
5.3.4 Multivariate total positivity of order 2 276
5.4 Exercises 279

6 Comparing Dependence **285**

6.1 Introduction 285
6.2 Comparing Dependence in the Bivariate Case Using the Correlation Order 287
6.2.1 Definition 287
6.2.2 Relationship with orthant orders 288
6.2.3 Relationship with positive quadrant dependence 289
6.2.4 Characterizations in terms of supermodular functions 289
6.2.5 Extremal elements 290
6.2.6 Relationship with convex and stop-loss orders 290
6.2.7 Correlation order and copulas 292
6.2.8 Correlation order and correlation coefficients 292
6.2.9 Ordering Archimedean copulas 292
6.2.10 Ordering compound sums 293
6.2.11 Correlation order and diversification benefit 294

6.3 Comparing Dependence in the Multivariate Case Using the Supermodular Order 295
6.3.1 Definition 295
6.3.2 Smooth supermodular functions 296
6.3.3 Restriction to distributions with identical marginals 296
6.3.4 A companion order: The symmetric supermodular order 297
6.3.5 Relationships between supermodular-type orders 297
6.3.6 Supermodular order and dependence measures 297
6.3.7 Extremal dependence structures in the supermodular sense 298
6.3.8 Supermodular, stop-loss and convex orders 298
6.3.9 Ordering compound sums 299
6.3.10 Ordering random vectors with common values 300
6.3.11 Stochastic analysis of duplicates in life insurance portfolios 302
6.4 Positive Orthant Dependence Order 304
6.4.1 Definition 304
6.4.2 Positive orthant dependence order and correlation coefficients 304
6.5 Exercises 305

PART III APPLICATIONS TO INSURANCE MATHEMATICS 309

7 Dependence in Credibility Models Based on Generalized Linear Models 311

7.1 Introduction 311
7.2 Poisson Credibility Models for Claim Frequencies 312
7.2.1 Poisson static credibility model 312
7.2.2 Poisson dynamic credibility models 315
7.2.3 Association 316
7.2.4 Dependence by mixture and common mixture models 320
7.2.5 Dependence in the Poisson static credibility model 323
7.2.6 Dependence in the Poisson dynamic credibility models 325
7.3 More Results for the Static Credibility Model 329
7.3.1 Generalized linear models and generalized additive models 329
7.3.2 Some examples of interest to actuaries 330
7.3.3 Credibility theory and generalized linear mixed models 331
7.3.4 Exhaustive summary of past claims 332
7.3.5 A posteriori distribution of the random effects 333
7.3.6 Predictive distributions 334
7.3.7 Linear credibility premium 334
7.4 More Results for the Dynamic Credibility Models 339
7.4.1 Dynamic credibility models and generalized linear mixed models 339
7.4.2 Dependence in GLMM-based credibility models 340
7.4.3 A posteriori distribution of the random effects 341
7.4.4 Supermodular comparisons 342
7.4.5 Predictive distributions 343
7.5 On the Dependence Induced by Bonus–Malus Scales 344
7.5.1 Experience rating in motor insurance 344
7.5.2 Markov models for bonus–malus system scales 344
7.5.3 Positive dependence in bonus–malus scales 345

7.6 Credibility Theory and Time Series for Non-Normal Data 346
7.6.1 The classical actuarial point of view 346
7.6.2 Time series models built from copulas 346
7.6.3 Markov models for random effects 348
7.6.4 Dependence induced by autoregressive copula models in dynamic frequency credibility models 349
7.7 Exercises 350

8 Stochastic Bounds on Functions of Dependent Risks 355

8.1 Introduction 355
8.2 Comparing Risks With Fixed Dependence Structure 357
8.2.1 The problem 357
8.2.2 Ordering random vectors with fixed dependence structure with stochastic dominance 358
8.2.3 Ordering random vectors with fixed dependence structure with convex order 358
8.3 Stop-Loss Bounds on Functions of Dependent Risks 360
8.3.1 Known marginals 360
8.3.2 Unknown marginals 360
8.4 Stochastic Bounds on Functions of Dependent Risks 363
8.4.1 Stochastic bounds on the sum of two risks 363
8.4.2 Stochastic bounds on the sum of several risks 365
8.4.3 Improvement of the bounds on sums of risks under positive dependence 367
8.4.4 Stochastic bounds on functions of two risks 368
8.4.5 Improvements of the bounds on functions of risks under positive quadrant dependence 370
8.4.6 Stochastic bounds on functions of several risks 370
8.4.7 Improvement of the bounds on functions of risks under positive orthant dependence 371
8.4.8 The case of partially specified marginals 372
8.5 Some Financial Applications 375
8.5.1 Stochastic bounds on present values 375
8.5.2 Stochastic annuities 376
8.5.3 Life insurance 379
8.6 Exercises 382

9 Integral Orderings and Probability Metrics 385

9.1 Introduction 385
9.2 Integral Stochastic Orderings 386
9.2.1 Definition 386
9.2.2 Properties 386
9.3 Integral Probability Metrics 388
9.3.1 Probability metrics 388
9.3.2 Simple probability metrics 389
9.3.3 Integral probability metrics 389

9.3.4 Ideal metrics 390
9.3.5 Minimal metric 392
9.3.6 Integral orders and metrics 392
9.4 Total-Variation Distance 393
9.4.1 Definition 393
9.4.2 Total-variation distance and integral metrics 394
9.4.3 Comonotonicity and total-variation distance 395
9.4.4 Maximal coupling and total-variation distance 396
9.5 Kolmogorov Distance 396
9.5.1 Definition 396
9.5.2 Stochastic dominance, Kolmogorov and total-variation distances 397
9.5.3 Kolmogorov distance under single crossing condition for probability density functions 397
9.6 Wasserstein Distance 398
9.6.1 Definition 398
9.6.2 Properties 399
9.6.3 Comonotonicity and Wasserstein distance 400
9.7 Stop-Loss Distance 401
9.7.1 Definition 401
9.7.2 Stop-loss order, stop-loss and Wasserstein distances 401
9.7.3 Computation of the stop-loss distance under stochastic dominance or dangerousness order 401
9.8 Integrated Stop-Loss Distance 403
9.8.1 Definition 403
9.8.2 Properties 403
9.8.3 Integrated stop-loss distance and positive quadrant dependence 405
9.8.4 Integrated stop-loss distance and cumulative dependence 405
9.9 Distance Between the Individual and Collective Models in Risk Theory 407
9.9.1 Individual model 407
9.9.2 Collective model 407
9.9.3 Distance between compound sums 408
9.9.4 Distance between the individual and collective models 410
9.9.5 Quasi-homogeneous portfolios 412
9.9.6 Correlated risks in the individual model 414
9.10 Compound Poisson Approximation for a Portfolio of Dependent Risks 414
9.10.1 Poisson approximation 414
9.10.2 Dependence in the quasi-homogeneous individual model 418
9.11 Exercises 421

References **423**

Index **439**

Foreword

Dependence is beginning to play an increasingly important role in the world of risk, with its strong embedment in areas like insurance, financial activities, safety engineering, etc. While independence can be defined in only one way, dependence can be formulated in an unlimited number of ways. Therefore, the assumption of independence prevails as it makes the technical treatment easy and transparent. Nevertheless, in applications dependence is the rule, independence the exception. Dependence quickly leads to an intricate and a far less convenient development.

The authors have accepted the challenge to offer their readership a survey of the rapidly expanding topic of dependence in risk theory. They have brought together the most significant results on dependence available up to now. The breadth of coverage provides an almost full-scale picture of the impact of dependence in risk theory, in particular in actuarial science. Nevertheless, the treatment is not encyclopaedic. In their treatment of risk, the emphasis is more on the ideas than on the mathematical development, more on concrete cases than on the most general situation, more on actuarial applications than on abstract theoretical constructions.

The first three chapters provide in-depth explorations of risk: after dealing with the concept of risk, its measurement is covered via a plethora of different risk measures; its relative position with respect to other risks is then treated using different forms of stochastic orderings. The next three chapters give a similar treatment of dependence as such: modelling of dependence is followed by its measurement and its relative position within other dependence concepts. While illustrations come mainly from the actuarial world, these first two parts of the book have much broader applicability; they make the book also useful for other areas of risk analysis like reliability and engineering. The last three chapters show a stronger focus on applications to insurance: credibility theory is followed by a thorough study of bounds for dependent risks; the text ends with a treatment of risk comparison by using integral orderings and probability metrics. An asset of the book is that a wealth of additional material is covered in exercises that accompany each chapter.

This succinct text provides a thorough treatment of dependence within a risk context and develops a coherent theoretical and empirical framework. The authors illustrate how this theory can be used in a variety of actuarial areas including among others: value-at-risk, ALAE-modelling, bonus-malus scales, annuities, portfolio construction, etc.

Jozef L. Teugels

Katholieke Universiteit Leuven, Belgium

Preface

Traditionally, insurance has been built on the assumption of independence, and the law of large numbers has governed the determination of premiums. But these days, the increasing complexity of insurance and reinsurance products has led to increased actuarial interest in the modelling of dependent risks.

In many situations, insured risks tend to behave alike. For instance, in group life insurance the remaining lifetimes of husband and wife can be shown to possess a certain degree of 'positive dependence'. The emergence of catastrophes and the interplay between insurance and finance also offer good examples in which dependence plays an important role in pricing and reserving.

Several concepts of bivariate and multivariate positive dependence have appeared in the mathematical literature. Undoubtedly, the most commonly encountered dependence property is actually 'lack of dependence', in other words mutual independence. Actuaries have so far mostly been interested in positive dependence properties expressing the notion that 'large' (or 'small') values of the random variables tend to occur together. Negative dependence properties express the notion that 'large' values of one variable tend to occur together with small values of the others. Instances of this phenomenon naturally arise in life insurance (think, for instance, of the death and survival benefits after year k in an endowment insurance, which are mutually exclusive and hence negatively correlated), or for the purpose of competitive pricing. Note that, in general, a negative dependence results in more predictable losses for the insurance company than mutual independence. The independence assumption is thus conservative in such a case. Moreover, assuming independence is mathematically convenient, and also obviates the need for elaborate models to be devised and statistics to be kept on mutual dependence of claims.

There is only one way for risks to be independent, but there are of course infinitely many ways for them to be correlated. For efficient risk management, actuaries need to be able to answer the fundamental question: is the correlation structure dangerous? And if it is, how dangerous is the situation? Therefore, tools to quantify, to compare and to model the strength of dependence between different risks have now become essential.

The purpose of this book is to provide its readership with methods to:

- measure risk
- compare risks
- measure the strength of dependence
- compare dependence structures
- model the dependence structure.

To illustrate the theoretical concepts, we will give many applications in actuarial science.

This book is innovative in many respects. It integrates the theory of stochastic orders, one of the methodological cornerstones of risk theory, the theory of risk measures, the very foundation of risk management, and the theory of stochastic dependence, which has become increasingly important as new types of risks emerge.

More specifically, risk measures will be used to generate stochastic orderings, by identifying pairs of risks about which a class of risk measures agree. Stochastic orderings are then used to define positive dependence relationships.

The copula concept is examined in detail. Apart from the well-known correlation coefficient, other measures of dependence are presented, as well as multivariate stochastic orderings, to evaluate the strength of dependence between risks. We also emphasize the numerous connections existing between multivariate and univariate stochastic orders.

In the third part of the book, we discuss some applications in actuarial mathematics. We first review credibility models. In these models, past claims history not only of the risk itself, but also of related risks, is used to determine the future premium. This method is based on the serial correlation among the annual claim characteristics (frequencies or severities) induced by their sharing a common random effect, and on the correlation between 'related' risks caused by a similar effect. We describe the kind of dependence induced by credibility models, and establish numerous stochastic inequalities showing that the classical credibility construction pioneered by Bühlmann produces very intuitive results.

Secondly, we will derive bounds on actuarial quantities involving correlated risks whose joint distribution is (partially) unknown or too cumbersome to work with. Our focus will be on stop-loss premiums and Value-at-Risk.

Next, we will present probabilistic distances, and show the close connection between this theoretical tool and stochastic orderings. In particular, the relevance of probabilistic distances for the analysis of dependent risks will be demonstrated.

This book complements our *Modern Actuarial Risk Theory* (Kaas *et al.* 2001), which only scratches the surface of the material found here. Since the traditional actuarial risk theory assumes independence between the different random variables of interest, the present book may be thought of as an advanced course on risk theory dropping this hypothesis.

The target audience of this book consists of academics and practitioners who are eager to master modern modelling tools for dependent risks. The inclusion of many exercises also makes the book suitable as the basis for advanced courses on risk management in incomplete markets, as a complement to Kaas *et al.* (2001).

Sometimes, we will give proofs only under simplifying assumptions, in order to help the reader understand the underlying reasoning, bringing out the main ideas without obscuring them with mathematical technicalities. Some proofs are omitted. Appropriate references to the literature will guide the readers interested in a more thorough mathematical treatment of the topic.

Insurance markets are prominent examples of incomplete markets, since the products sold by insurance companies cannot be replicated by some financial trading strategy. We firmly believe that this book should be of interest not only to actuaries but more generally to traders aware that perfect hedges do not exist in reality. The main effect of accounting for market incompleteness has indeed been to bring utility theory back into pricing. More generally, it should bridge quantitative finance and actuarial science.

We would like to thank the Committee on Knowledge Extension Research of the American Society of Actuaries for financial support, under grant 'Actuarial Aspects of Dependencies in Insurance Portfolios'. Thanks also to Virginia Young, the scientific referee of our project, for her careful reading of earlier drafts of the manuscript, and her invaluable advice on matters mathematical and stylistic.

We express our gratitude to Paul Embrechts, Christian Genest, Alfred Müller and Moshe Shaked for having read (parts of) the manuscript, and for the numerous remarks they made. We also thank Professors Frees and Valdez for kindly providing the loss–ALAE data set used in Chapter 4, which were collected by the US Insurance Services Office (ISO).

Michel Denuit is grateful for the financial support of the UCL Fonds Spéciaux de Recherche (under projects 'Tarification en assurance: Vers une nouvelle approche intégrée' and 'Nouvelles méthodes de gestion des risques assurantiels et financiers') and the Belgian Fonds National de la Recherche Scientifique (Crédit aux Chercheurs 'Dépendances entre risques actuariels et financiers'). This work was also partly supported by the contract 'Projet d'Actions de Recherche Concertées' nr 98/03–217 from the Communauté Française Wallonie-Bruxelles.

Jan Dhaene and Marc Goovaerts acknowledge the financial support of the Onderzoeksfonds K.U. Leuven (GOA/02 'Actuariële, financiële en statistische aspecten van afhankelijkheden in verzekerings- en financiële portefeuilles').

Finally, we would like to express our gratitude and appreciation to all those with whom we have had the pleasure of working on problems related to this book: Hélène Cossette, Christian Genest, Hans Gerber, Angela van Heerwaarden, Bart Kling, Claude Lefèvre, Etienne Marceau, Alfred Müller, Marco Scarsini, Mhamed Mesfioui, Moshe Shaked, Sergei Utev, Shaun Wang and Virginia Young.

Michel Denuit
Jan Dhaene
Marc Goovaerts
Rob Kaas

Louvain-la-Neuve, Leuven and Amsterdam

Supplementary material for this book can be found at http://www.actu.ucl.ac.be/staff/denuit/mdenuit.html

PART I
The Concept of Risk

Certum est quia impossible est
Tertullian, AD 200

1

Modelling Risks

A risk can be described as an event that may or may not take place, and that brings about some adverse financial consequences. It is thus natural that the modelling of risks uses probability theory. The basics of probability theory are briefly reviewed in this first chapter, with special emphasis on multivariate tools, such as random vectors and related quantities. The material introduced here will be extensively used throughout the book.

1.1 INTRODUCTION

Much of our life is based on the belief that the future is largely unpredictable. We express this belief by the use of words such as 'random' or 'probability' and we aim to assign quantitative meanings to such usage. The branch of mathematics dealing with uncertainty and randomness is called probability theory. Together with statistics, it forms the basis of actuarial science.

In a broad sense, insurance refers to the business of transferring (totally or partially) the economic impact of unforeseen mishaps. The central notion in actuarial mathematics is the notion of risk. A risk can be described as an event that may or may not take place, and that brings about some adverse financial consequences. It is thus natural that the modelling of risks uses probability theory, with the concepts of random events and random variables playing a central role.

This first chapter aims to lay the mathematical foundations for the modelling of insurance risks. We begin by describing the classical axiomatic construction of probability theory. Probability spaces are carefully defined. Subsequent sections deal with random variables, distribution functions, quantile functions, mathematical expectations, etc. Emphasis is put on mutual independence and random vectors.

We also list several transforms, such as the hazard rate, the mean-excess function, the Laplace transform, the moment generating function as well as the probability generating function. These transforms will be used in the next chapters to characterize partial order relations defined on sets of distribution functions.

The final sections of this chapter are devoted to very particular dependence structures, extreme in some sense to be specified later on: comonotonicity and mutual exclusivity. The former corresponds to perfect positive dependence: all the random variables can be written as

Actuarial Theory for Dependent Risks M. Denuit, J. Dhaene, M. Goovaerts and R. Kaas

non-decreasing transformations of the same underlying random variable. They thus 'move in the same direction', are 'common monotonic' – hence the name. On the other hand, mutual exclusivity can be seen as a very strong negative dependence concept. In this case, just a single random variable can be positive (and the others then have to be equal to zero). These two structures will be widely used in later chapters.

An excellent introduction to probability theory can be found in Chow and Teicher (2003). The book by Barlow and Proschan (1975) contains many results involving reliability concepts. A detailed account of comonotonicity can be found in Dhaene *et al.* (2002a,b).

1.2 THE PROBABILISTIC DESCRIPTION OF RISKS

1.2.1 Probability space

In probability theory the starting point is a 'probability space'. The usual phrase at the beginning of a stochastic model is (or should be): 'Let $(\Omega, \mathcal{F}, \Pr)$ be a probability space ...'. Such a general approach to probability plays a fundamental role in the theory, and it is not our intention to recall all definitions and axioms, which can easily be found in any textbook on probability theory. We shall confine ourselves to concepts and results used in this book. The three ingredients of a probability space are a universe Ω, a sigma-algebra $\mathcal{F}$ and a probability measure Pr. We briefly review each of these notions in this section.

1.2.2 Experiment and universe

Many everyday statements for actuaries take the form 'the probability of A is p', where A is some event (such as 'the total losses exceed the threshold € 1 million' or 'the number of claims reported by a given policyholder is less than 2') and p is a real number between 0 and 1. The occurrence or non-occurrence of A depends upon the chain of circumstances under consideration. Such a particular chain is called an experiment in probability; the result of an experiment is called its outcome and the set of all outcomes (called the universe) is denoted by Ω.

The word 'experiment' is used here in a very general sense to describe virtually any process of which all possible outcomes can be specified in advance and of which the actual outcome will be one of those specified. The basic feature of an experiment is that its outcome is not definitely known by the actuary beforehand.

1.2.3 Random events

Random events are subsets of the universe Ω associated with a given experiment. A random event is the mathematical formalization of an event described in words. It is random since we cannot predict with certainty whether it will be realized or not during the experiment. For instance, if we are interested in the number of claims made by a policyholder belonging to an automobile portfolio in one year, the experiment consists in observing the driving behaviour of this individual during an annual period, and the universe Ω is simply the set

$\mathbb{N} \equiv \{0, 1, 2, \ldots\}$ of the non-negative integers. The random event $A =$ 'the policyholder makes at most one claim' is identified with the pair $\{0, 1\} \subset \Omega$.

As usual, we use $A \cup B$ and $A \cap B$ to represent the union and the intersection of any two subsets A and B of Ω, respectively. The union of sets is defined to be the set that contains the points that belong to at least one of the sets. The intersection of sets is defined to be the set that contains the points that are common to all the sets. These set operations correspond to the words 'or' and 'and' between sentences: $A \cup B$ is the event realized if A or B is realized and $A \cap B$ is the event realized if A and B are simultaneously realized during the experiment. We also define the difference between sets A and B, denoted as $A \backslash B$, as the set of elements in A but not in B. Finally, $\overline{A}$ is the complement of the event A, defined as $\Omega \backslash A$; it is the set of points of Ω that do not belong to A. This corresponds to negation: $\overline{A}$ is realized if A is not realized during the experiment. In particular, $\overline{\Omega} = \emptyset$ where $\emptyset$ is the empty set.

1.2.4 Sigma-algebra

For technical reasons, it is useful to consider a certain family $\mathcal{F}$ of random events, that is, of subsets of Ω. In practice, $\mathcal{F}$ can be chosen so that this limitation is not restrictive in the sense that virtually every subset of interest is sufficiently regular to belong to $\mathcal{F}$. The family $\mathcal{F}$ has to be closed under standard operations on sets; indeed, given two events A and B in $\mathcal{F}$, we want that $A \cup B$, $A \cap B$ and $\overline{A}$ are still events (i.e., still belong to $\mathcal{F}$). Technically speaking, this will be the case if $\mathcal{F}$ is a sigma-algebra, as defined below.

Definition 1.2.1. A family $\mathcal{F}$ of subsets of the universe Ω is called a sigma-algebra if it fulfils the three following properties:

P1 $\Omega \in \mathcal{F}$;

P2 $A \in \mathcal{F} \Rightarrow \overline{A} \in \mathcal{F}$;

P3 $A_1, A_2, A_3, \ldots \in \mathcal{F} \Rightarrow \cup_{i \geq 1} A_i \in \mathcal{F}$.

∇

The properties P1–P3 are quite natural. Indeed, P1 means that Ω itself is an event (it is the event which is always realized). P2 means that if A is an event, the complement of A is also an event. P3 means that the event consisting of the realization of at least one of the A_i is also an event.

1.2.5 Probability measure

Once the universe Ω has been equipped with a sigma-algebra $\mathcal{F}$ of random events, a probability measure Pr can be defined on $\mathcal{F}$. The knowledge of Pr allows us to discuss the likelihoods of the occurrence of events in $\mathcal{F}$. To be specific, Pr assigns to each random event A its probability $\Pr[A]$; $\Pr[A]$ is the likelihood of realization of A. The probability of A is a numerical measure of the likelihood that the actual outcome of the experiment will be an element of A.

Definition 1.2.2. A probability measure Pr maps $\mathcal{F}$ to $[0, 1]$, with $\Pr[\Omega] = 1$, and is such that given $A_1, A_2, A_3, \ldots \in \mathcal{F}$ which are pairwise disjoint, that is, such that $A_i \cap A_j = \emptyset$ if $i \neq j$,

$$\Pr\left[\cup_{i\geq 1} A_i\right] = \sum_{i\geq 1} \Pr[A_i];$$

this technical property is usually referred to as the sigma-additivity of Pr. ∇

The properties assigned to Pr in Definition 1.2.2 naturally follow from empirical evidence: if we were allowed to repeat an experiment a large number of times, keeping the initial conditions as equal as possible, the proportion of times that an event A occurs would behave according to Definition 1.2.2. Note that $\Pr[A]$ is then the mathematical idealization of the proportion of times A occurs.

We can associate a probability space $(\Omega, \mathcal{F}, \Pr)$ with any experiment, and all the questions associated with the experiment can be reformulated in terms of this space. It may seem reasonable to ask for the numerical value of the probability $\Pr[A]$ of some event A. This value is deduced from empirical observations (claims statistics recorded by the insurance company in the past, for instance) and is often derived from a parametric model.

1.3 INDEPENDENCE FOR EVENTS AND CONDITIONAL PROBABILITIES

1.3.1 Independent events

Independence is a crucial concept in probability theory. It aims to formalize the intuitive notion of 'not influencing each other' for random events: we would like to give a precise meaning to the fact that the realization of an event does not decrease nor increase the probability that the other event occurs. The following definition offers a mathematically unambiguous meaning of mutual independence for a pair of random events. Nevertheless, we will have to wait until formula (1.3) to get an intuitive meaning for this concept.

Definition 1.3.1. Two events A and B are said to be independent if the probability of their intersection factors into the product of their respective probabilities, that is, if $\Pr[A \cap B] = \Pr[A]\Pr[B]$. ∇

Definition 1.3.1 is extended to more than two events as follows.

Definition 1.3.2. The events in a family $\mathcal{A}$ of events are independent if for every finite sequence $A_1, A_2, \ldots, A_k$ of events in $\mathcal{A}$,

$$\Pr\left[\bigcap_{i=1}^{k} A_i\right] = \prod_{i=1}^{k} \Pr[A_i]. \tag{1.1}$$

∇

The concept of independence is very important in assigning probabilities to events. For instance, if two or more events are regarded as being physically independent, in the sense that the occurrence or non-occurrence of some of them has no influence on the occurrence or non-occurrence of the others, then this condition is translated into mathematical terms through the assignment of probabilities satisfying (1.1).

1.3.2 Conditional probability

Independence is the exception rather than the rule. In any given experiment, it is often necessary to consider the probability of an event A when additional information about the outcome of the experiment has been obtained from the occurrence of some other event B. This corresponds to intuitive statements of the form 'if B occurs then the probability of A is p', where B might be 'March is rainy' and A 'the claim frequency in motor insurance increases by 5 %'. This is called the conditional probability of A given B.

Definition 1.3.3. If $\Pr[B] > 0$ then the conditional probability $\Pr[A|B]$ of A given B is defined to be

$$\Pr[A|B] = \frac{\Pr[A \cap B]}{\Pr[B]}. \tag{1.2}$$

∇

The definition of conditional probabilities through (1.2) is in line with empirical evidence. Repeating a given experiment a large number of times, $\Pr[A|B]$ is the mathematical idealization of the proportion of times A occurs in those experiments where B occurred, hence the ratio (1.2).

Let us now justify the definition of conditional probabilities by means of the ratio (1.2). As mentioned earlier, conditional probabilities correspond to situations where additional information is available; this information is reflected by the fact that an event B is realized, and implies that only events compatible with B have a positive probability (hence the numerator $\Pr[A \cap B]$ in (1.2)) and that B is given probability one (being the new universe, hence the denominator $\Pr[B]$ in (1.2)).

With Definition 1.3.3, it is easy to see from Definition 1.3.1 that A and B are independent if, and only if,

$$\Pr[A|B] = \Pr[A|\overline{B}] = \Pr[A]. \tag{1.3}$$

Note that this interpretation of independence is much more intuitive than Definition 1.3.1: indeed, the identity expresses the natural idea that the realization or not of B does not increase nor decrease the probability that A occurs.

1.4 RANDOM VARIABLES AND RANDOM VECTORS

1.4.1 Random variables

Actuaries are often not interested in an experiment itself but rather in some consequences of its random outcome. For instance, they are more concerned with the amounts the insurance company will have to pay than with the particular circumstances which give rise to the claims. Such consequences, when real-valued, may be thought of as functions mapping Ω into the real line $\mathbb{R}$.

Such functions are called random variables provided they satisfy certain desirable properties, precisely stated in the following definition.

Definition 1.4.1. A random variable (rv) X is a measurable function mapping Ω to the real numbers, that is, $X : \Omega \to \mathbb{R}$ is such that $X^{-1}((-\infty, x]) \in \mathcal{F}$ for any $x \in \mathbb{R}$, where $X^{-1}((-\infty, x]) = \{\omega \in \Omega | X(\omega) \le x\}$. ∇

Henceforth, rvs are denoted by capital letters: for example X. They are mathematical formalizations of random outcomes given by numerical values. An example of an rv is the amount of a claim associated with the occurrence of an automobile accident. The rv X can be represented as in Figure 1.1: X has a specified value $X(\omega)$ at every possible outcome ω in the universe Ω.

In words, the measurability condition $X^{-1}((-\infty, x]) \in \mathcal{F}$ involved in Definition 1.4.1 ensures that the actuary can make statements such as 'X is less than or equal to x' and quantify their likelihood.

Of course, some rvs assume values in subsets of $\mathbb{R}$ rather than in the whole real line. The set of all the possible values for an rv X is called the support of X and is formally defined in Definition 1.5.10.

1.4.2 Random vectors

In this work, we will be mainly concerned with the impact of a possible dependence among risks. For this purpose, we have to consider rvs simultaneously rather than separately. Mathematically speaking, this means that random vectors are involved: the outcomes of most experiments that will be considered in this book will be n-tuples of real numbers. The n-dimensional Euclidean space of all n-tuples of real numbers will be denoted by $\mathbb{R}^n$, that is, $\mathbb{R}^n$ consists of the points $\boldsymbol{x} = (x_1, x_2, \ldots, x_n)^t$ where $x_i \in \mathbb{R}$, $i = 1, 2, \ldots, n$. By convention, all vectors will be written in bold and will be considered as column vectors, with the superscript 't' for transposition.

Let us now formally define the concept of random vectors.

Definition 1.4.2. An n-dimensional random vector $\boldsymbol{X}$ is a measurable function mapping the universe Ω to $\mathbb{R}^n$, that is, $\boldsymbol{X} : \Omega \to \mathbb{R}^n$ satisfies

$$\boldsymbol{X}^{-1}\big((-\infty, x_1] \times (-\infty, x_2] \times \cdots \times (-\infty, x_n]\big) \in \mathcal{F}$$

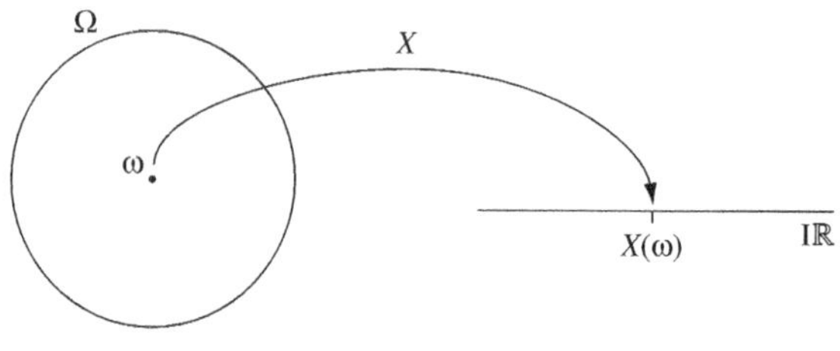

Figure 1.1 The random variable X

for any $x_1, x_2, \ldots, x_n \in \mathbb{R}$, where

$$\begin{aligned}&\boldsymbol{X}^{-1}\big((-\infty, x_1] \times (-\infty, x_2] \times \cdots \times (-\infty, x_n]\big)\\&=\Big\{\omega \in \Omega \Big| \boldsymbol{X}(\omega) \in (-\infty, x_1] \times (-\infty, x_2] \times \cdots \times (-\infty, x_n]\Big\}.\end{aligned}$$

∇

Again, the measurability condition allows the actuary to consider the event 'each X_i is less than or equal to the threshold x_i, $i = 1, \ldots, n$'.

Such a random vector $\boldsymbol{X} = (X_1, X_2, \ldots, X_n)^t$ is in fact a collection of n univariate rvs, $X_1, X_2, \ldots, X_n$, say, defined on the same probability space $(\Omega, \mathcal{F}, \Pr)$. Random vectors are denoted by bold capital letters: $\boldsymbol{X}$, for example. A bold lower-case letter $\boldsymbol{x}$ means a point $(x_1, x_2, \ldots, x_n)^t$ in $\mathbb{R}^n$, and $\mathbb{R}^n$ is endowed with the usual componentwise order, that is, given $\boldsymbol{x}$ and $\boldsymbol{y}$ in $\mathbb{R}^n$, $\boldsymbol{x} \leq \boldsymbol{y}$ ($\boldsymbol{x} < \boldsymbol{y}$) means that $x_i \leq y_i$ ($x_i < y_i$) for $i = 1, 2, \ldots, n$. In an abuse of notation, we will often denote

$$[\boldsymbol{X} \leq \boldsymbol{x}] = \boldsymbol{X}^{-1}\big((-\infty, x_1] \times (-\infty, x_2] \times \cdots \times (-\infty, x_n]\big)$$

and interpret the event $[\boldsymbol{X} \leq \boldsymbol{x}]$ componentwise, that is,

$$[\boldsymbol{X} \leq \boldsymbol{x}] = [X_1 \leq x_1, X_2 \leq x_2, \ldots, X_n \leq x_n] = \bigcap_{k=1}^{n} [X_k \leq x_k].$$

1.4.3 Risks and losses

In a broad sense, insurance refers to the business of transferring (totally or partially) the economic impact of unforeseen mishaps. The central notion in actuarial mathematics is the notion of risk. A risk can be described as an event that may or may not take place (thus, a random event), and that brings about some adverse financial consequences. It always contains an element of uncertainty: either the moment of its occurrence (as in life insurance), or the occurrence itself, or the nature and severity of its consequences (as in automobile insurance).

The actuary models an insurance risk by an rv which represents the random amount of money the insurance company will have to pay out to indemnify the policyholder and/or the third party for the consequences of the occurrence of the insured peril. From the remarks above, the rvs modelling the insurance risks may generally be assumed to be non-negative. This leads to the following formal definition.

Definition 1.4.3. A risk X is a non-negative rv representing the random amount of money paid by an insurance company to indemnify a policyholder, a beneficiary and/or a third-party in execution of an insurance contract. ∇

In return for providing coverage, the insurer will receive premiums. The insurer will often be interested in the total cash flow associated with a policy. The loss (over a certain reference period) is defined as the (discounted value of the) payments to be made by the insurer minus the (discounted value of the) premiums to be paid by the insured.

Definition 1.4.4. Given a risk X covered by an insurance company in return of a premium payment p (p is the discounted value of premiums to be paid), the associated loss L is defined as $L = X - p$. ∇

Remark 1.4.5. In many actuarial textbooks, the premium p is assumed to be a known amount of money, fixed by the policy conditions. The insurance business thus consists of replacing the random consequences of the insured peril by a deterministic premium amount. For one-year policies with a single premium payment (at policy issue), the premium reduces to a fixed amount p. There are, however, many situations where the premium p itself is an rv. In life insurance, for instance, p will often be a non-trivial rv depending on the remaining lifetime of the insured. Also, in automobile insurance, the implementation of merit-rating systems (such as bonus–malus mechanisms) makes the premium paid by the policyholder contingent on the claims reported in the past. ∇

1.5 DISTRIBUTION FUNCTIONS

1.5.1 Univariate distribution functions

1.5.1.1 Definition

In many cases, neither the universe Ω nor the function X need be given explicitly. The practitioner only has to know the probability law governing X or, in other words, its distribution. This means that he is interested in the probabilities that X takes values in appropriate subsets of the real line.

To each rv X is associated a function F_X called the distribution function of X, describing the stochastic behaviour of X. Of course, F_X does not indicate the actual outcome of X, but how the possible values of X are distributed (hence its name).

Definition 1.5.1. The distribution function (df) of the rv X, denoted by F_X, is defined as

$$F_X(x) = \Pr[X^{-1}((-\infty, x])] \equiv \Pr[X \leq x], \quad x \in \mathbb{R}.$$

In words, $F_X(x)$ represents the probability that the rv X assumes a value that is less than or equal to x. ∇

If X is the total monetary amount of claims generated by some policyholder, $F_X(x)$ is the probability that this policyholder produces a total claim amount of at most x. The df F_X corresponds to an estimated physical probability distribution or a well-chosen subjective probability distribution.

Remark 1.5.2. Each rv X induces a probability measure $\mathbb{P}_X$ on $(\Omega, \mathcal{F})$, defined for $A \in \mathcal{F}$ as

$$\mathbb{P}_X[A] = \Pr[X^{-1}(A)] \equiv \Pr[X \in A].$$

In order to describe an rv X, one would need to know $\mathbb{P}_X[B]$ for all possible $B \in \mathcal{F}$. However, it turns out that it suffices to know the value of $\Pr[X \in B]$ for sets B of the form $(-\infty, x]$, $x \in \mathbb{R}$. The probability distribution of an rv X is then uniquely determined by its df F_X. ∇

1.5.1.2 Characterization

Let us now examine the set of properties satisfied by all dfs. This allows us to characterize the set of all possible dfs.

Property 1.5.3
Any df F_X maps the real line $\mathbb{R}$ to the unit interval $[0, 1]$ and possesses the following properties:

P1 F_X is non-decreasing.

P2 F_X is right-continuous, that is,

$$\lim_{\Delta x \to 0+} F_X(x+\Delta x) = F_X(x)$$

holds for any $x \in \mathbb{R}$; the limit

$$F_X(x-) \equiv \lim_{\Delta x \to 0+} F_X(x-\Delta x) = \Pr[X < x]$$

is thus well defined.

P3 F_X satisfies $\lim_{x\to-\infty} F_X(x) = 0$ and $\lim_{x\to+\infty} F_X(x) = 1$.

P1–P3 are direct consequences of Definition 1.5.1.

Example 1.5.4. The knowledge of F_X provides the actuary with the complete description of the stochastic behaviour of the rv X. For instance, let us consider the graph of F_X depicted in Figure 1.2. Since $F_X(0) = 0$, X cannot assume negative values. Considering x_1, $F_X(x_1)$ gives the probability of X being smaller than x_1. Since F_X is continuous at x_1,

$$F_X(x_1) = F_X(x_1-) \Leftrightarrow \Pr[X \leq x_1] = \Pr[X < x_1].$$

Flat parts of the graph of F_X indicate forbidden values for X; for instance, X cannot assume a value between x_2 and x_3 since

$$\Pr[x_2 < X \leq x_3] = F_X(x_3) - F_X(x_2) = 0.$$

Discontinuity jumps in F_X indicate atoms (i.e., points receiving a positive probability mass); for instance,

$$\Pr[X = x_4] = F_X(x_4) - F_X(x_4-).$$

∇

In general, we have

$$\Pr[a < X \leq b] = F_X(b) - F_X(a),$$
$$\Pr[a \leq X \leq b] = F_X(b) - F_X(a-),$$
$$\Pr[a < X < b] = F_X(b-) - F_X(a),$$
$$\Pr[a \leq X < b] = F_X(b-) - F_X(a-).$$

In these relations we may have $a = -\infty$ or $b = +\infty$.

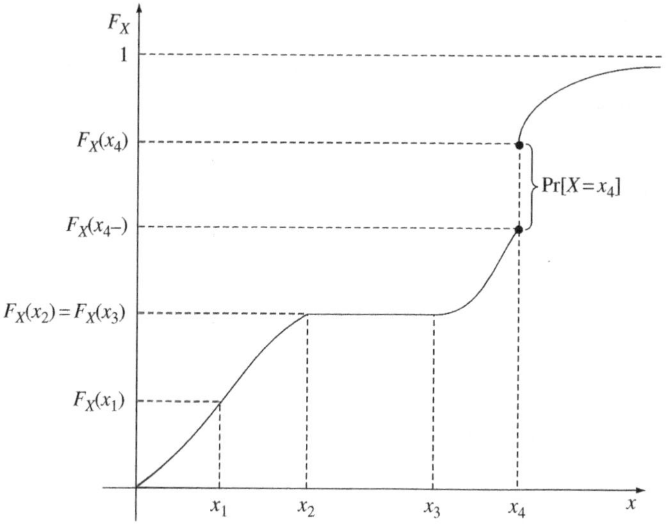

Figure 1.2 Graph of a df F_X

Remark 1.5.5. Actuaries are often more interested in the df of an rv than in the rv itself. For two rvs X and Y which are equal in distribution, that is, $F_X \equiv F_Y$, we will write $X =_d Y$. ∇

1.5.2 Multivariate distribution functions

1.5.2.1 Definition

Suppose that $X_1, X_2, \ldots, X_n$ are n rvs defined on the same probability space $(\Omega, \mathcal{F}, \Pr)$. Their marginal dfs $F_1, F_2, \ldots, F_n$ contain all the information about their associated probabilities. But how can the actuary encapsulate information about their properties relative to each other? As explained above, the key idea is to think of $X_1, X_2, \ldots, X_n$ as being components of a random vector $\boldsymbol{X} = (X_1, X_2, \ldots, X_n)^t$ taking values in $\mathbb{R}^n$ rather than being unrelated rvs each taking values in $\mathbb{R}$.

As was the case for rvs, each random vector $\boldsymbol{X}$ possesses a df $F_{\boldsymbol{X}}$ that describes its stochastic behaviour.

Definition 1.5.6. The df of the random vector $\boldsymbol{X}$, denoted by $F_{\boldsymbol{X}}$, is defined as

$$\begin{aligned} F_{\boldsymbol{X}}(x_1, x_2, \ldots, x_n) &= \Pr\left[\boldsymbol{X}^{-1}((-\infty, x_1] \times (-\infty, x_2] \times \cdots \times (-\infty, x_n])\right] \\ &= \Pr[X_1 \leq x_1, X_2 \leq x_2, \ldots, X_n \leq x_n], \end{aligned}$$

$x_1, x_2, \ldots, x_n \in \mathbb{R}$. ∇

The value $F_{\boldsymbol{X}}(x_1, x_2, \ldots, x_n)$ represents the probability that simultaneously X_1 assumes a value that is less than or equal to x_1, X_2 assumes a value that is less than or equal to

$x_2, \ldots, X_n$ assumes a value that is less than or equal to x_n; a more compact way to express this is

$$F_X(x) = \Pr[\boldsymbol{X} \le \boldsymbol{x}], \quad \boldsymbol{x} \in \mathbb{R}^n.$$

Even if the df F_X does not tell us what is the actual value of $\boldsymbol{X}$, it thoroughly describes the range of possible values for $\boldsymbol{X}$ and the probabilities assigned to each of them.

1.5.2.2 Characterization

The next result establishes the properties that any multivariate df has to fulfil.

Property 1.5.7
A multivariate df F_X is a function mapping $\mathbb{R}^n$ to $[0, 1]$ such that:

P1 F_X is non-decreasing on $\mathbb{R}^n$;

P2 F_X is right-continuous on $\mathbb{R}^n$;

P3 F_X satisfies

(i) $\lim_{x_j \to -\infty} F_X(x_1, x_2, \ldots, x_n) = 0$ for $j = 1, 2, \ldots, n$;

(ii) $\lim_{x_1, x_2, \ldots, x_n \to +\infty} F_X(x_1, x_2, \ldots, x_n) = 1$;

(iii) for all $(\alpha_1, \alpha_2, \ldots, \alpha_n), (\beta_1, \beta_2, \ldots, \beta_n) \in \mathbb{R}^n$, with $\alpha_i \le \beta_i$ for $i = 1, 2, \ldots, n$, defining

$$\begin{aligned}\Delta_{\alpha_i, \beta_i} F_X(x) = F_X(x_1, \ldots, x_{i-1}, \beta_i, x_{i+1}, \ldots, x_n) \\ - F_X(x_1, \ldots, x_{i-1}, \alpha_i, x_{i+1}, \ldots, x_n),\end{aligned}$$

then

$$\Delta_{\alpha_1, \beta_1} \Delta_{\alpha_2, \beta_2} \ldots \Delta_{\alpha_n, \beta_n} F_X(x) \ge 0.$$

Remark 1.5.8. Note that condition P3 (iii) ensures that

$$\Pr[\boldsymbol{\alpha} \le \boldsymbol{X} \le \boldsymbol{\beta}] \ge 0 \text{ for any } \boldsymbol{\alpha} \le \boldsymbol{\beta} \in \mathbb{R}^n.$$

We observe that when F_X is differentiable, condition P3(iii) is equivalent to

$$\frac{\partial^n}{\partial x_1 \partial x_2 \ldots \partial x_n} F_X \ge 0 \text{ on } \mathbb{R}^n.$$

∇

1.5.3 Tail functions

In addition to the df, we also introduce a tail function (tf), often called a survival function in biostatistics, and defined as follows:

$$\overline{F}_X(x) = 1 - F_X(x) = \Pr[X > x], \quad x \in \mathbb{R}.$$

In words, $\overline{F}_X(x)$ represents the probability that X assumes a value larger than x. If X is the random future lifetime of a policyholder, then $\overline{F}_X(x)$ is the probability that the policyholder survives up to age x. If X is the total amount of claims produced by a given policyholder then $\overline{F}_X(x)$ is the probability that the corresponding policy generates a loss larger than x.

From Definition 1.5.1, we immediately deduce that $\overline{F}_X$ is non-increasing, right-continuous and such that

$$\lim_{x\to-\infty}\overline{F}_X(x)=1 \text{ and } \lim_{x\to+\infty}\overline{F}_X(x)=0.$$

We also define

$$\overline{F}_X(x-)=1-F_X(x-)=\Pr[X\geq x], \quad x\in\mathbb{R}.$$

Note that this function is non-increasing and left-continuous.

In addition to the multivariate df, we also introduce a multivariate tf $\overline{F}_{\boldsymbol{X}}$ defined as

$$\overline{F}_{\boldsymbol{X}}(\boldsymbol{x})=\Pr[\boldsymbol{X}>\boldsymbol{x}], \quad \boldsymbol{x}\in\mathbb{R}^n.$$

Of course, the simple identity $F_{\boldsymbol{X}}\equiv 1-\overline{F}_{\boldsymbol{X}}$ does not hold in general.

1.5.4 Support

As we can see from the graph of Figure 1.2, the points corresponding to jump discontinuities in the df (such as x_4) receive positive probability masses; this yields the following definition.

Definition 1.5.9. The point a is an atom of X if it is a discontinuity point of the df F_X, that is, $F_X(a-)\neq F_X(a)$. Then $\Pr[X=a]>0$ and the mass at the point a equals the jump of F_X at a. ∇

The set of all the possible outcomes for an rv X is called its support and is precisely defined next.

Definition 1.5.10. The support $\mathcal{S}_X$ of an rv X with df F_X is defined as the set of all the points $x\in\mathbb{R}$ where F_X is strictly increasing. Similarly, the support $\mathcal{S}_{\boldsymbol{X}}$ of a random vector $\boldsymbol{X}$ is defined as the subset of $\mathbb{R}^n$ consisting of all the points $\boldsymbol{x}$ such that $F_{\boldsymbol{X}}$ is strictly increasing at $\boldsymbol{x}$. ∇

1.5.5 Discrete random variables

According to the structure of their support, rvs can be classified in different categories. A discrete rv X assumes only a finite (or countable) number of values, $x_1, x_2, x_3, \ldots$, say. The support $\mathcal{S}_X$ of X thus contains a finite or countable number of elements; $\mathcal{S}_X=\{x_1,x_2,x_3,\ldots\}$. The df of a discrete rv has jump discontinuities at the values $x_1,x_2,x_3,\ldots$ and is constant in between. The (discrete) probability density function (pdf) is defined as

$$f_X(x_i)=\Pr[X=x_i], \quad i=1,2,3\ldots,$$

and $f_X(x)=0$ for $x \neq x_1, x_2, x_3, \ldots$. Of course, any discrete pdf f_X has to satisfy $\sum_i f_X(x_i)=1$.

The most important subclass of non-negative discrete rvs is the integer case, in which $x_i = i$ for $i \in \mathcal{J} \subseteq \mathbb{N} = \{0, 1, 2, \ldots\}$. The number of claims produced by a given policyholder during a certain reference period is of this type. The discrete probability models used in this book are summarized in Table 1.1.

1.5.6 Continuous random variables

An rv X is called continuous if its support is an interval, a union of intervals or the real (half-) line and the associated df F_X may be represented as

$$F_X(x) = \int_{-\infty}^{x} f_X(y)dy, \quad x \in \mathbb{R}, \tag{1.4}$$

for some integrable function $f_X : \mathbb{R} \to \mathbb{R}^+$; f_X is called the continuous probability density function (pdf) of X.

Remark 1.5.11. It is worth mentioning that rvs with df of the form (1.4) are called absolutely continuous in probability theory. Continuous rvs refer to rvs with a continuous df (i.e., without atoms). In this book, we will use the term continuous rvs for rvs with a df of the form (1.4). ∇

The function f_X involved in (1.4) has a physical intepretation: if we plot f_X in the two-dimensional cartesian coordinates (x, y) as in Figure 1.3, the area bounded by the plot of f_X, the horizontal axis and two vertical lines crossing the horizontal axis at a and b $(a < b)$ determines the value of the probability that X assumes values in $(a, b]$.

We obviously deduce from Definition 1.5.1 together with (1.4) that the pdf f_X satisfies

$$\int_{-\infty}^{+\infty} f_X(y)dy = 1.$$

Note that the df F_X of a continuous rv has derivative f_X. In other words, the continuous pdf f_X involved in (1.4) satisfies

$$f_X(x) = \lim_{\Delta x \to 0} \frac{F_X(x+\Delta x) - F_X(x)}{\Delta x} = \lim_{\Delta x \to 0} \frac{\Pr[x < X \leq x + \Delta x]}{\Delta x}$$

Table 1.1 Standard discrete probability models

Probability distribution	Notation	Parametric space	Support	Pdf
Bernoulli	$\mathcal{B}er(q)$	[0,1]	0,1	$q^k(1-q)^{1-k}$
Binomial	$\mathcal{B}in(m, q)$	$\{1, 2, \ldots\} \times [0, 1]$	$\{0, 1, \ldots, m\}$	$\binom{m}{k} q^k(1-q)^{m-k}$
Geometric	$\mathcal{G}eo(q)$	$[0, 1]$	$\mathbb{N}$	$q(1-q)^k$
Negative binomial	$\mathcal{NB}in(\alpha, q)$	$(0, +\infty) \times (0, 1)$	$\mathbb{N}$	$\binom{\alpha+k-1}{k} q^\alpha(1-q)^k$
Poisson	$\mathcal{P}oi(\lambda)$	$\mathbb{R}^+$	$\mathbb{N}$	$\exp(-\lambda)\frac{\lambda^k}{k!}$

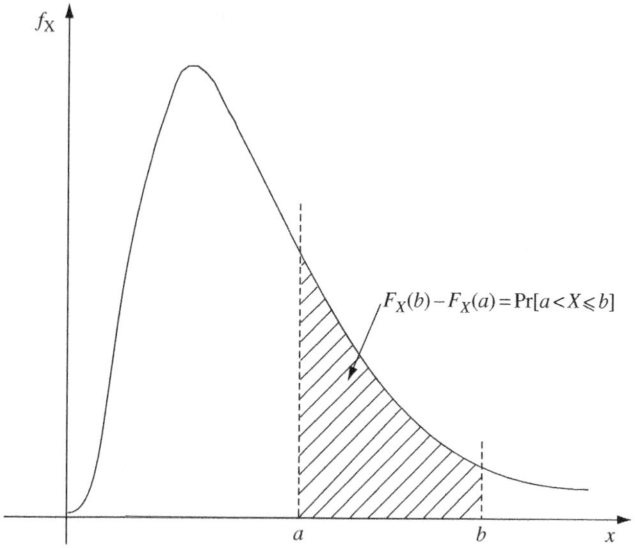

Figure 1.3 Graph of the pdf f_X corresponding to a continuous rv X

so that the approximation

$$\Pr[x < X \leq x + \Delta x] \approx f_X(x)\Delta x$$

is valid for small Δx. This yields the physical interpretation of the pdf: $f_X(x)$ can be regarded as the likelihood that $X \approx x$ (i.e., that X assumes a value in the neighbourhood of x).

Continuous models used in this book are summarized in Table 1.2.

1.5.7 General random variables

A more general type of df is a combination of the discrete and (absolutely) continuous cases, being continuous apart from a countable set of exception points $x_1, x_2, x_3, \ldots$ with positive

Table 1.2 Standard continuous probability models

Probability distribution	Notation	Parametric space	Support	Probability density function
Normal	$\mathcal{N}or(\mu, \sigma^2)$	$\mathbb{R} \times \mathbb{R}^+$	$\mathbb{R}$	$\frac{1}{\sigma\sqrt{2\pi}} \exp\left(-\frac{1}{2\sigma^2}(x-\mu)^2\right)$
Lognormal	$\mathcal{LN}or(\mu, \sigma^2)$	$\mathbb{R} \times \mathbb{R}^+$	$\mathbb{R}^+$	$\frac{1}{x\sigma\sqrt{2\pi}} \exp\left(-\frac{1}{2\sigma^2}(\ln(x)-\mu)^2\right)$
Exponential	$\mathcal{E}xp(\theta)$	$\mathbb{R}^+$	$\mathbb{R}^+$	$\theta \exp(-\theta x)$
Gamma	$\mathcal{G}am(\alpha, \tau)$	$\mathbb{R}^+ \times \mathbb{R}^+$	$\mathbb{R}^+$	$\frac{x^{\alpha-1}\tau^\alpha \exp(-x\tau)}{\Gamma(\alpha)}$
Pareto	$\mathcal{P}ar(\alpha, \theta)$	$\mathbb{R}^+ \times \mathbb{R}^+$	$\mathbb{R}^+$	$\frac{\alpha\theta^\alpha}{(x+\theta)^{\alpha+1}}$
Beta	$\mathcal{B}et(\alpha, \beta)$	$\mathbb{R}^+ \times \mathbb{R}^+$	$[0, 1]$	$\frac{\Gamma(\alpha+\beta)}{\Gamma(\alpha)\Gamma(\beta)} x^{\alpha-1}(1-x)^{\beta-1}$
Uniform	$\mathcal{U}ni(a, b)$	$\mathbb{R} \times \mathbb{R}$	(a, b)	$\frac{1}{b-a}$

probabilities of occurrence, causing jumps in the df at these points. Such a df F_X can be represented as

$$F_X(x) = (1-p)F_X^{(c)}(x) + pF_X^{(d)}(x), \quad x \in \mathbb{R}, \tag{1.5}$$

for some $p \in [0, 1]$, where $F_X^{(c)}$ is a continuous df and $F_X^{(d)}$ is a discrete df.

Example 1.5.12. A mixed type rv frequently encountered in actuarial science is an insurance risk for which there is a probability mass in zero (the probability of non-occurrence of claims), while the claim amount given that a claim occurs is a continuous rv. For instance, we could assume that the claim amount X relating to some policy of the portfolio during a given reference period has a df F_X of the form

$$F_X(x) = \begin{cases} 0, & \text{if } x < 0, \\ 1-(1-p)\exp(-\lambda x), & \text{if } x \geq 0. \end{cases}$$

Such an rv takes the value 0 (i.e., no claim reported by the policyholder) with the probability p. Given that $X > 0$ (i.e., at least one claim has occurred), the claim amount is $\mathcal{E}xp(\lambda)$ distributed. Hence,

$$F_X^{(d)}(x) = \begin{cases} 0, & \text{if } x < 0, \\ 1, & \text{if } x \geq 0, \end{cases}$$

$$F_X^{(c)}(x) = 1 - \exp(-\lambda x), \quad x \geq 0.$$

∇

Remark 1.5.13. Note that, in general, it can be proven that every df F_X may be represented as a mixture of three different kinds of df. Specifically, the identity

$$F_X(x) = p_1 F_X^{(d)}(x) + p_2 F_X^{(c)}(x) + p_3 F_X^{(s)}(x),$$

holds for any $x \in \mathbb{R}$ where $p_i \geq 0$ for $i = 1, 2, 3$ and $p_1 + p_2 + p_3 = 1$, $F_X^{(d)}$ is a discrete df, $F_X^{(c)}$ is an absolutely continuous df and $F_X^{(s)}$ is a singular continuous df (which is defined as a df that is a continuous function of x but $\frac{d}{dx}F_X^{(s)}(x) = 0$ almost everywhere, that is, $F_X^{(s)}$ is continuous but has its points of increase on a set of zero Lebesgue measure). In the remainder of this text, we will only consider dfs with $p_3 = 0$; this particular case covers all the situations encountered by actuaries in practice. ∇

1.5.8 Quantile functions

1.5.8.1 Definition

There are basically two ways to define a generalized inverse for a df; they are both given in the next definition.

Definition 1.5.14. Given a df F_X, we define the inverse functions F_X^{-1} and F_X^{-1+} of F_X as

$$F_X^{-1}(p) = \inf\{x \in \mathbb{R} \mid F_X(x) \geq p\} = \sup\{x \in \mathbb{R} \mid F_X(x) < p\},$$

and

$$F_X^{-1+}(p) = \inf\{x \in \mathbb{R} \mid F_X(x) > p\} = \sup\{x \in \mathbb{R} \mid F_X(x) \le p\},$$

for $p \in [0, 1]$, where, by convention, $\inf \emptyset = +\infty$ and $\sup \emptyset = -\infty$. ∇

Given some probability level p, $F_X^{-1}(p)$ is the pth quantile of X (it is sometimes denoted by q_p). To be specific, $F_X^{-1}(p)$ is a threshold exceeded by X with probability at most $1-p$. More generally, we adopt the same definitions for the inverses t^{-1} and t^{-1+} of any non-decreasing and right-continuous function t.

1.5.8.2 Properties

One can verify that F_X^{-1} and F_X^{-1+} are both non-decreasing, and that F_X^{-1} is left-continuous while F_X^{-1+} is right-continuous. We have that $F_X^{-1}(p) = F_X^{-1+}(p)$ if, and only if, p does not correspond to a 'flat part' of F_X (i.e., a segment (x_2, x_3) on Figure 1.2 or a probability level p_2 in Figure 1.4), or equivalently, if, and only if, F_X^{-1} is continuous at p. As F_X^{-1} is non-decreasing, it is continuous everywhere, except on an at most countable set of points.

Let us consider Figure 1.4 to illustrate the definition of F_X^{-1}. When F_X is one-to-one, as is the case for p_1, $F_X^{-1}(p_1)$ is the standard inverse for F_X evaluated at p_1 (i.e., the unique x-value mapped to p_1 by F_X) and $F_X^{-1}(p_1) = F_X^{-1+}(p_1)$. Two other situations may be encountered, corresponding to p_2 and p_3. Firstly, p_2 corresponds to a flat part of the graph of F_X. In this case, $F_X^{-1}(p_2)$ is the leftmost point of the interval and $F_X^{-1+}(p_2)$ is the rightmost point of the interval. Note that in this case $F_X^{-1}(p_2) \neq F_X^{-1+}(p_2)$. Secondly, p_3 is not a possible value for F_X (i.e., there is no x-value such that $F_X(x) = p_3$). In this case, $F_X^{-1}(p_3)$ is the smallest x-value mapped to a quantity at least equal to p_3, and $F_X^{-1}(p_3) = F_X^{-1+}(p_3)$.

The following lemma will be frequently used in this book.

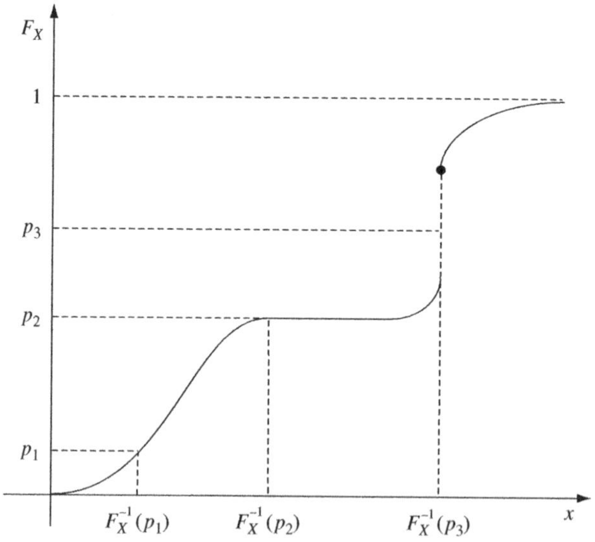

Figure 1.4 Inverse F_X^{-1} of the df F_X for different probability levels

Lemma 1.5.15
For any real number x and probability level p, the following equivalences hold:

(i) $F_X^{-1}(p) \leq x \Leftrightarrow p \leq F_X(x)$;

(ii) $x \leq F_X^{-1+}(p) \Leftrightarrow \Pr[X < x] = F_X(x-) \leq p$.

Proof. We only prove (i); (ii) can be proven in a similar way. The $\Rightarrow$ part of (i) is proven if we can show that

$$p > F_X(x) \Rightarrow x < F_X^{-1}(p).$$

Assume that $p > F_X(x)$. Then there exists an $\epsilon > 0$ such that $p > F_X(x+\epsilon)$. From the sup-definition of $F_X^{-1}(p)$ in Definition 1.5.14, we find that $x + \epsilon \leq F_X^{-1}(p)$, which implies that $x < F_X^{-1}(p)$.

We now prove the $\Leftarrow$ part of (i). If $p \leq F_X(x)$ then we find that $p \leq F_X(x+\epsilon)$ for all $\epsilon > 0$. From the inf-definition of $F_X^{-1}(p)$ we can conclude that $F_X^{-1}(p) \leq x + \epsilon$ for all $\epsilon > 0$. Taking the limit for $\epsilon \downarrow 0$, we obtain $F_X^{-1}(p) \leq x$. □

The following property relates the inverse dfs of the rvs X and $t(X)$, for a continuous non-decreasing function t.

Property 1.5.16
Let X be an rv. For any $0 < p < 1$, the following equalities hold:

(i) If t is non-decreasing and continuous then $F_{t(X)}^{-1}(p) = t\left(F_X^{-1}(p)\right)$.

(ii) If t is non-decreasing and continuous then $F_{t(X)}^{-1+}(p) = t\left(F_X^{-1+}(p)\right)$.

Proof. We only prove (i); (ii) can be proven in a similar way. By application of Lemma 1.5.15, we find that the following equivalences hold for all real x:

$$\begin{aligned} F_{t(X)}^{-1}(p) \leq x &\Leftrightarrow p \leq F_{t(X)}(x) \\ &\Leftrightarrow p \leq F_X\left(t^{-1+}(x)\right) \\ &\Leftrightarrow F_X^{-1}(p) \leq t^{-1+}(x) \\ &\Leftrightarrow t\left(F_X^{-1}(p)\right) \leq x. \end{aligned}$$

Note that the above proof only holds if t^{-1+} is finite. But one can verify that the equivalences also hold if $t^{-1+}(x) = \pm\infty$. □

Remark 1.5.17. Property 1.5.16 allows us to define an inverse for the tf. The inverses of the df F_X and of the tf $\overline{F}_X$ are related by

$$F_X^{-1}(p) = \overline{F}_X^{-1}(1-p) \text{ and } F_X^{-1+}(p) = \overline{F}_X^{-1+}(1-p),$$

for any probability level p. ∇

Remark 1.5.18. The continuity assumption put on the function t in Property 1.5.16 can be relaxed as follows: in (i) it is enough for t to be left-continuous, whereas in (ii) it is enough for t to be right-continuous. ∇

1.5.8.3 Probability integral transform theorem

The classical probability integral transform theorem emphasizes the central role of the law $\mathcal{U}ni(0, 1)$ among continuous dfs. It is stated next.

Property 1.5.19
If an rv X has a continuous df F_X, then $F_X(X) \sim \mathcal{U}ni(0, 1)$.

Proof. This follows from Lemma 1.5.15(i) which ensures that for all $0 < u < 1$,

$$\Pr[F_X(X) \geq u] = \Pr[X \geq F_X^{-1}(u)] = \overline{F}_X(F_X^{-1}(u)) = 1 - u,$$

from which we conclude that $F_X(X) \sim \mathcal{U}ni(0, 1)$. □

The probability integral transform theorem has an important 'inverse' which is sometimes referred to as the quantile transformation theorem and which is stated next.

Property 1.5.20
Let X be an rv with df F_X, not necessarily continuous. If $U \sim \mathcal{U}ni(0, 1)$ then

$$\begin{aligned} X &=_d F_X^{-1}(U) =_d \overline{F}_X^{-1}(U) \\ &=_d F_X^{-1+}(U) =_d \overline{F}_X^{-1+}(U). \end{aligned} \tag{1.6}$$

Proof. We see from Lemma 1.5.15(i) that

$$\Pr[F_X^{-1}(U) \leq x] = \Pr[U \leq F_X(x)] = F_X(x);$$

the other statements have similar proofs. □

1.5.9 *Independence for random variables*

A fundamental concept in probability theory is the notion of independence. Roughly speaking, the rvs $X_1, X_2, \ldots, X_n$ are mutually independent when the behaviour of one of these rvs does not influence the others. Formally, the rvs $X_1, X_2, \ldots, X_n$ are mutually independent if, and only if, all the random events constructed with these rvs are independent. This results from the following definition.

Definition 1.5.21. The rvs $X_1, X_2, \ldots, X_n$ are independent if, and only if,

$$F_{\boldsymbol{X}}(\boldsymbol{x}) = \prod_{i=1}^{n} F_{X_i}(x_i) \text{ holds for all } \boldsymbol{x} \in \mathbb{R}^n,$$

or equivalently, if, and only if,

$$\overline{F}_X(x) = \prod_{i=1}^{n} \overline{F}_{X_i}(x_i) \text{ holds for all } x \in \mathbb{R}^n.$$

∇

In words, the joint df (or tf) of a random vector $\boldsymbol{X}$ with independent components is thus the product of the marginal dfs (or tfs). Similarly, the joint (discrete or continuous) pdfs of independent random vectors factor into the product of the univariate pdfs.

Example 1.5.22. The random couple $\boldsymbol{X} = (X_1, X_2)$ with joint tf

$$\overline{F}_{\boldsymbol{X}}(x_1, x_2) = \exp(-\lambda_1 x_1 - \lambda_2 x_2), \quad x_1, x_2 \geq 0, \quad \lambda_1, \lambda_2 > 0,$$

has independent components since $\overline{F}_{\boldsymbol{X}}(\boldsymbol{x}) = \overline{F}_{X_1}(x_1)\overline{F}_{X_2}(x_2)$, where $\overline{F}_{X_i}$ is the tf associated with $\mathcal{E}xp(\lambda_i)$, $i = 1, 2$. ∇

Remark 1.5.23. It is worth mentioning that the mutual independence of Definition 1.5.21 is not equivalent to pairwise independence. In order to check this assertion, consider the random vector $\boldsymbol{X} = (X_1, X_2, X_3)$ with the distribution defined by $\Pr[\boldsymbol{X} = (1, 0, 0)] = \Pr[\boldsymbol{X} = (0, 1, 0)] = \Pr[\boldsymbol{X} = (0, 0, 1)] = \Pr[\boldsymbol{X} = (1, 1, 1)] = \frac{1}{4}$. Then, it is easy to see that X_1, X_2 and X_3 are pairwise independent. However,

$$\Pr[\boldsymbol{X} = (1, 1, 1)] = \frac{1}{4} \neq \frac{1}{8} = \Pr[X_1 = 1]\Pr[X_2 = 1]\Pr[X_3 = 1],$$

and hence X_1, X_2 and X_3 are not mutually independent. ∇

1.6 MATHEMATICAL EXPECTATION

1.6.1 Construction

Given an rv X, we can define an important characteristic which is called the mean, or the expected value, and is denoted by $\mathbb{E}[X]$. The construction of the operator $\mathbb{E}[\cdot]$ is briefly recalled next.

If $X > 0$ and $\Pr[X = +\infty] > 0$ (i.e., X is defective) we put $\mathbb{E}[X] = +\infty$, while if $\Pr[X < +\infty] = 1$ we define

$$\begin{aligned} \mathbb{E}[X] &= \lim_{n \to +\infty} \sum_{k=1}^{+\infty} \frac{k}{2^n} \Pr\left[\frac{k}{2^n} < X \leq \frac{k+1}{2^n}\right] \\ &= \lim_{n \to +\infty} \sum_{k=1}^{+\infty} \frac{k}{2^n} \left(F_X\left(\frac{k+1}{2^n}\right) - F_X\left(\frac{k}{2^n}\right)\right). \end{aligned} \tag{1.7}$$

For an arbitrary rv X, let us define $X_+ = \max\{X, 0\}$ and $X_- = \max\{-X, 0\}$. Since X_+ and X_- are non-negative, their expectations can be obtained by (1.7), and if either $\mathbb{E}[X_+] < +\infty$ or $\mathbb{E}[X_-] < +\infty$ then

$$\mathbb{E}[X] = \mathbb{E}[X_+] - \mathbb{E}[X_-].$$

We say that the expectation of X is finite if both $\mathbb{E}[X_+]$ and $\mathbb{E}[X_-]$ are finite. Since $|X|=X_+ + X_-$, the finiteness of $\mathbb{E}[X]$ is equivalent to $\mathbb{E}[|X|]<+\infty$.

Example 1.6.1. If X has a df of the form (1.4) then X has a finite expectation if, and only if,

$$\int_{-\infty}^{+\infty}|x|f_X(x)dx<+\infty$$

and it is easy to see from (1.7) that

$$\mathbb{E}[X]=\int_{-\infty}^{+\infty}xf_X(x)dx.$$

∇

Remark 1.6.2. The expectation $\mathbb{E}[X]$ of any non-negative rv X is thus defined but may be infinite. For instance, if $X\sim\mathcal{P}ar(\alpha,\theta)$ with $\alpha\leq 1$ then $\mathbb{E}[X]=+\infty$. ∇

Example 1.6.3. If X is discrete with support $\{x_1,x_2,x_3,\ldots\}$ and discrete pdf f_X then X has a finite expectation if, and only if

$$\sum_{j\geq 1}|x_j|f_X(x_j)<+\infty,$$

and (1.7) yields

$$\mathbb{E}[X]=\sum_{j\geq 1}x_jf_X(x_j).$$

∇

The representations of the mathematical expectation derived in Examples 1.6.1 and 1.6.3 can be used to compute the expectations associated with the standard probability models presented in Tables 1.1 and 1.2; Table 1.3 summarizes the results.

1.6.2 Riemann-Stieltjes integral

Let us assume that F_X is of the form (1.5) with

$$pF_X^{(d)}(t)=\sum_{d_n\leq t}\Big(F_X(d_n)-F_X(d_n-)\Big)=\sum_{d_n\leq t}\Pr[X=d_n],$$

Table 1.3 Expectations associated with classical parametric models

Probability law	Expectation	Probability law	Expectation
$\mathcal{P}oi(\lambda)$	λ	$\mathcal{N}or(\mu,\sigma^2)$	μ
$\mathcal{B}er(q)$	q	$\mathcal{LN}or(\mu,\sigma^2)$	$\exp(\mu+\frac{\sigma^2}{2})$
$\mathcal{B}in(m,q)$	mq	$\mathcal{E}xp(\theta)$	$1/\theta$
$\mathcal{G}eo(q)$	$\frac{1-q}{q}$	$\mathcal{G}am(\alpha,\tau)$	$\frac{\alpha}{\tau}$
$\mathcal{NB}in(\alpha,q)$	$\frac{\alpha(1-q)}{q}$	$\mathcal{P}ar(\alpha,\theta)$	$\frac{\theta}{\alpha-1}$ if $\alpha>1$
		$\mathcal{B}et(\alpha,\beta)$	$\frac{\alpha}{\alpha+\beta}$
		$\mathcal{U}ni(a,b)$	$\frac{a+b}{2}$

where $\{d_1, d_2, \ldots\}$ denotes the set of discontinuity points and

$$(1-p)F_X^{(c)}(t) = F_X(t) - pF_X^{(d)}(t) = \int_{-\infty}^{t} f_X^{(c)}(x)dx.$$

Then

$$\mathbb{E}[X] = \sum_{n\geq 1} d_n\Big(F_X(d_n) - F_X(d_n-)\Big) + \int_{-\infty}^{+\infty} x f_X^{(c)}(x)dx. \tag{1.8}$$

If we define the differential of F_X, denoted by dF_X, as

$$dF_X(x) = \begin{cases} F_X(d_n) - F_X(d_n-), & \text{if } x = d_n, \\ f_X^{(c)}(x), & \text{otherwise,} \end{cases}$$

we then have

$$\mathbb{E}[X] = \int_{-\infty}^{+\infty} x dF_X(x).$$

This unified notation allows us to avoid tedious repetitions of statements like 'the proof is given for continuous rvs; the discrete case is similar'. A very readable introduction to differentials and Riemann–Stieltjes integrals can be found in Carter and Van Brunt (2000).

Example 1.6.4. The rv X defined in Example 1.5.12 can be represented as

$$X = \begin{cases} 0, & \text{with probability } p, \\ Y, & \text{with probability } 1-p, \end{cases}$$

with $Y \sim \mathcal{E}xp(\lambda)$. In such a case, actuaries often write X as the product IY where I and Y are independent, and $I \sim \mathcal{B}er(1-p)$. Then,

$$pF_X^{(d)}(s) = \begin{cases} 0, & \text{if } s < 0, \\ p, & \text{if } s \geq 0, \end{cases}$$

and

$$\mathbb{E}[X] = 0 \times p + (1-p) \times \frac{1}{\lambda} = \frac{1-p}{\lambda}.$$

∇

Remark 1.6.5. Let $\boldsymbol{X}$ be an n-dimensional random vector and let $g : \mathbb{R}^n \to \mathbb{R}$ be a (measurable) function. Then, $g(\boldsymbol{X})$ is a univariate rv so that we can consider its mathematical expectation as

$$\mathbb{E}[g(\boldsymbol{X})] = \int_{-\infty}^{+\infty}\int_{-\infty}^{+\infty}\cdots\int_{-\infty}^{+\infty} g(\boldsymbol{x})dF_{\boldsymbol{X}}(\boldsymbol{x}),$$

with the notation of the Stieltjes integral. ∇

1.6.3 Law of large numbers

The importance of the mathematical expectation originates in the famous law of large numbers, relating this theoretical concept to the intuitive idea of averages in the long run. Specifically, given a sequence $\{X_1, X_2, \ldots\}$ of independent and identically distributed rvs with common expectation μ, the sequence of arithmetic averages of the X_i, that is,

$$\left\{\overline{X}^{(n)},\quad n=1,2,\ldots\right\} \text{ with } \overline{X}^{(n)}=\frac{1}{n}\sum_{i=1}^{n}X_i,$$

converges to μ in the following sense:

$$\Pr\left[\lim_{n\to+\infty}\overline{X}^{(n)}=\mu\right]=1. \tag{1.9}$$

This remarkable result plays a central role in risk management and explains the importance of expected values in actuarial science.

1.6.4 Alternative representations for the mathematical expectation in the continuous case

Let us prove that the mathematical expectation can be seen as an integrated right tail.

Property 1.6.6
Let X be a non-negative rv. Then

$$\mathbb{E}[X]=\int_0^{+\infty}\overline{F}_X(x)dx.$$

Proof. It suffices to invoke Fubini's theorem and to write

$$\begin{aligned}\mathbb{E}[X]&=\int_0^{+\infty}tdF_X(t)=\int_{t=0}^{+\infty}\int_{x=0}^{t}dxdF_X(t)\\&=\int_{x=0}^{+\infty}\int_{t=x}^{+\infty}dF_X(t)dx=\int_0^{+\infty}\overline{F}_X(x)dx.\end{aligned}$$

□

Remark 1.6.7. It is worth mentioning that Property 1.6.6 can be generalized to higher dimensions as follows. Let us show that the product moment of the components of an n-dimensional non-negative random vector $\boldsymbol{X}$ can be written as

$$\mathbb{E}\left[\prod_{i=1}^{n}X_i\right]=\int_{x_1=0}^{+\infty}\int_{x_2=0}^{+\infty}\cdots\int_{x_n=0}^{+\infty}\overline{F}_{\boldsymbol{X}}(\boldsymbol{x})dx_1dx_2\ldots dx_n. \tag{1.10}$$

To see this, first write

$$\begin{aligned}&\int_{x_1=0}^{+\infty}\int_{x_2=0}^{+\infty}\cdots\int_{x_n=0}^{+\infty}\overline{F}_{\boldsymbol{X}}(\boldsymbol{x})dx_1dx_2\ldots dx_n\\&=\int_{x_1=0}^{+\infty}\int_{x_2=0}^{+\infty}\cdots\int_{x_n=0}^{+\infty}\int_{y_1=x_1}^{+\infty}\int_{y_2=x_2}^{+\infty}\cdots\int_{y_n=x_n}^{+\infty}dF_{\boldsymbol{X}}(\boldsymbol{y})dx_1dx_2\ldots dx_n.\end{aligned}$$

Then invoke Fubini's theorem to get

$$\int_{y_1=0}^{+\infty}\int_{y_2=0}^{+\infty}\cdots\int_{y_n=0}^{+\infty}\int_{x_1=0}^{y_1}\int_{x_2=0}^{y_2}\cdots\int_{x_n=0}^{y_n} dx_1 dx_2 \ldots dx_n dF_{\boldsymbol{X}}(\boldsymbol{y})$$
$$=\int_{y_1=0}^{+\infty}\int_{y_2=0}^{+\infty}\cdots\int_{y_n=0}^{+\infty}\left(\prod_{i=1}^{n} y_i\right) dF_{\boldsymbol{X}}(\boldsymbol{y}) = \mathbb{E}\left[\prod_{i=1}^{n} X_i\right],$$

as required. ∇

1.6.5 Alternative representations for the mathematical expectation in the discrete case

Let us now establish a discrete analogue to Property 1.6.6.

Property 1.6.8
Let N be an integer-valued rv. Then

$$\mathbb{E}[N] = \sum_{k=0}^{+\infty} \Pr[N > k].$$

Proof. We argue as follows:

$$\begin{aligned}
\mathbb{E}[N] &= \Pr[N=1] + 2\Pr[N=2] + 3\Pr[N=3] + \ldots \\
&= \Pr[N=1] + \Pr[N=2] + \Pr[N=3] + \ldots + \\
&\quad \Pr[N=2] + \Pr[N=3] + \ldots + \\
&\quad \Pr[N=3] + \ldots \\
&= \Pr[N \geq 1] + \Pr[N \geq 2] + \Pr[N \geq 3] + \ldots \\
&= \sum_{k=1}^{+\infty} \Pr[N \geq k] = \sum_{k=0}^{+\infty} \Pr[N > k].
\end{aligned}$$

□

1.6.6 Stochastic Taylor expansion

1.6.6.1 Univariate case

Suppose we are interested in $\mathbb{E}[g(X)]$ for some fixed non-linear function g and some rv X whose first few moments $\mu_1, \mu_2, \ldots, \mu_n$ are known. A convenient approximation of $\mathbb{E}[g(X)]$ is based on a naive Taylor expansion of g around the origin yielding

$$\mathbb{E}[g(X)] \approx \sum_{k=0}^{n} \frac{g^{(k)}(0)}{k!} \mu_k. \tag{1.11}$$

However, there is no indication about the accuracy of (1.11). Massey and Whitt (1993), derived a probabilistic generalization of Taylor's theorem, suitably modified by Lin (1994).

They give the error when the actuary resorts to the approximation (1.11). In this book we will use some particular cases of their results that we recall now.

Property 1.6.9
Given a risk X, assume that the inequalities $0 < \mathbb{E}[X^s] < +\infty$ hold for some positive integer s. Let g be a real-valued function having an sth derivative $g^{(s)} \geq 0$. Then

$$\mathbb{E}[g(X)] = \sum_{k=0}^{s-1} \frac{g^{(k)}(0)}{k!} \mathbb{E}[X^k] + \int_0^{+\infty} \frac{\mathbb{E}[(X-t)_+^{s-1}]}{(s-1)!} g^{(s)}(t)dt. \tag{1.12}$$

Proof. Let us start from the Taylor expansion of g around the origin,

$$g(x) = \sum_{k=0}^{s-1} \frac{g^{(k)}(0)}{k!} x^k + \int_0^{+\infty} \frac{(x-t)_+^{s-1}}{(s-1)!} g^{(s)}(t)dt.$$

It suffices then to invoke Fubini's theorem to get the result. □

Corollary 1.6.10
It is interesting to note that for $s = 1$ and 2 we respectively get from (1.12) that

$$\mathbb{E}[g(X)] = g(0) + \int_0^{+\infty} \overline{F}_X(t) g'(t)dt, \tag{1.13}$$

$$\mathbb{E}[g(X)] = g(0) + g'(0)\mu_1 + \int_0^{+\infty} \mathbb{E}[(X-t)_+] g''(t)dt. \tag{1.14}$$

Note that (1.13) reduces to Property 1.6.6 when $g(x) = x$.

1.6.6.2 Bivariate case

Let us now extend the result of Property 1.6.9 to the bivariate case. The following property is taken from Denuit, Lefèvre and Mesfioui (1999) and will turn out to be useful in the next chapters.

Property 1.6.11
Let $\boldsymbol{X} = (X_1, X_2)$ be a pair of risks such that $0 < \mathbb{E}[X_1^{s_1}] < +\infty$ and $0 < \mathbb{E}[X_2^{s_2}] < +\infty$ for some positive integers s_1 and s_2. Let $g : \mathbb{R}^2 \to \mathbb{R}$ with derivatives $\frac{\partial^{k_1+k_2}}{\partial x_1^{k_1} \partial x_2^{k_2}} g \geq 0$ for $0 \leq k_1 \leq s_1$, $0 \leq k_2 \leq s_2$. Then

$$\begin{aligned}
\mathbb{E}[g(\boldsymbol{X})] &= \sum_{i_1=0}^{s_1-1} \sum_{i_2=0}^{s_2-1} \frac{\partial^{i_1+i_2} g(0,0)}{\partial x_1^{i_1} \partial x_2^{i_2}} \frac{\mathbb{E}\left[X_1^{i_1} X_2^{i_2}\right]}{i_1!\, i_2!} \\
&+ \sum_{i_1=0}^{s_1-1} \int_0^{+\infty} \frac{\mathbb{E}\left[(X_2 - t_2)_+^{s_2-1} X_1^{i_1}\right]}{(s_2-1)!\, i_1!} \frac{\partial^{i_1+s_2} g(0, t_2)}{\partial x_1^{i_1} \partial x_2^{s_2}} dt_2 \\
&+ \sum_{i_2=0}^{s_2-1} \int_0^{+\infty} \frac{\mathbb{E}\left[(X_1 - t_1)_+^{s_1-1} X_2^{i_2}\right]}{(s_1-1)!\, i_2!} \frac{\partial^{s_1+i_2} g(t_1, 0)}{\partial x_1^{s_1} \partial x_2^{i_2}} dt_1 \\
&+ \int_0^{+\infty} \int_0^{+\infty} \frac{\mathbb{E}\left[(X_1 - t_1)_+^{s_1-1} (X_2 - t_2)_+^{s_2-1}\right]}{(s_1-1)!\, (s_2-1)!} \frac{\partial^{s_1+s_2} g(t_1, t_2)}{\partial x_1^{s_1} \partial x_2^{s_2}} dt_2 dt_1.
\end{aligned}$$

Proof. By Taylor's expansion of g viewed as a function of x_1 around 0 (for fixed x_2), we get

$$g(x_1, x_2) = \sum_{i_1=0}^{s_1-1} \frac{\partial^{i_1} g(0, x_2)}{\partial x_1^{i_1}} \frac{x_1^{i_1}}{i_1!} + \int_0^{x_1} \frac{(x_1 - t_1)^{s_1-1}}{(s_1 - 1)!} \frac{\partial^{s_1} g(t_1, x_2)}{\partial x_1^{s_1}} dt_1. \qquad (1.15)$$

Then inserting

$$\frac{\partial^{i_1} g(0, x_2)}{\partial x_1^{i_1}} = \sum_{i_2=0}^{s_2-1} \frac{\partial^{i_1+i_2} g(0, 0)}{\partial x_1^{i_1} \partial x_2^{i_2}} \frac{x_2^{i_2}}{i_2!} + \int_0^{x_2} \frac{(x_2 - t_2)^{s_2-1}}{(s_2 - 1)!} \frac{\partial^{i_1+s_2} g(0, t_2)}{\partial x_1^{i_1} \partial x_2^{s_2}} dt_2,$$

and

$$\frac{\partial^{s_1} g(t_1, x_2)}{\partial x_1^{s_1}} = \sum_{i_2=0}^{s_2-1} \frac{\partial^{s_1+i_2} g(t_1, 0)}{\partial x_1^{s_1} \partial x_2^{i_2}} \frac{x_2^{i_2}}{i_2!} + \int_0^{x_2} \frac{(x_2 - t_2)^{s_2-1}}{(s_2 - 1)!} \frac{\partial^{s_1+s_2} g(t_1, t_2)}{\partial x_1^{s_1} \partial x_2^{s_2}} dt_2,$$

in (1.15) and using Fubini's theorem yields the result. □

Corollary 1.6.12
It is interesting to note that for $s_1 = s_2 = 1$ we get

$$\begin{aligned}\mathbb{E}[g(\boldsymbol{X})] = g(0, 0) &+ \int_0^{+\infty} \Pr[X_2 > t_2] \frac{\partial g(0, t_2)}{\partial x_2} dt_2 \\ &+ \int_0^{+\infty} \Pr[X_1 > t_1] \frac{\partial g(t_1, 0)}{\partial x_1} dt_1 \\ &+ \int_0^{+\infty} \int_0^{+\infty} \Pr[X_1 > t_1, X_2 > t_2] \frac{\partial^2 g(t_1, t_2)}{\partial x_1 \partial x_2} dt_2 dt_1.\end{aligned}$$

Note that Corollary 1.6.12 reduces to (1.10) with $n = 2$ when $g(\boldsymbol{x}) = x_1 x_2$ is considered.

1.6.7 Variance and covariance

The variance is the expected squared difference between an rv X and its mathematical expectation μ. Specifically, the variance of X, denoted by $\mathbb{V}[X]$, is given by

$$\mathbb{V}[X] = \mathbb{E}[(X - \mu)^2] = \mathbb{E}[X^2] - \mu^2$$

since the expectation acts as a linear operator.
The variances associated with the standard probability distributions are gathered in Table 1.4.
Given two rvs X and Y, the covariance between these rvs is defined as

$$\mathbb{C}[X, Y] = \mathbb{E}[XY] - \mathbb{E}[X]\mathbb{E}[Y].$$

The value of the covariance indicates the extent to which X and Y 'move together' (hence the name). Nevertheless, we will see in Chapter 5 that the value of the covariance may not be a solid indicator of the strength of dependence existing between two rvs.

Table 1.4 Variances associated with standard probability distributions

Law	Variance	Law	Variance
$\mathcal{B}er(q)$	$q(1-q)$	$\mathcal{LN}or(\mu,\sigma^2)$	$\exp(2\mu+\sigma^2)(\exp(\sigma^2)-1)$
$\mathcal{B}in(m,q)$	$mq(1-q)$	$\mathcal{E}xp(\theta)$	$\frac{1}{\theta^2}$
$\mathcal{G}eo(q)$	$\frac{1-q}{q^2}$	$\mathcal{G}am(\alpha,\tau)$	$\frac{\alpha}{\tau^2}$
$in(\alpha,q)$	$\frac{\alpha(1-q)}{q^2}$	$\mathcal{P}ar(\alpha,\theta)$	$\frac{\alpha\theta^2}{(\alpha-2)(\alpha-1)^2}$ if $\alpha>2$
$\mathcal{P}oi(\lambda)$	λ	$\mathcal{B}et(\alpha,\beta)$	$\frac{\alpha\beta}{(\alpha+\beta+1)(\alpha+\beta)^2}$
		$\mathcal{U}ni(a,b)$	$\frac{(b-a)^2}{12}$

When non-negative rvs are involved, the following result readily follows from Property 1.6.6 together with (1.10). But it remains valid for arbitrary rvs. The proof given here is taken from Drouet-Mari and Kotz (2001).

Property 1.6.13
Given two rvs X and Y, their covariance can be represented as

$$\mathbb{C}[X,Y]=\int_{-\infty}^{+\infty}\int_{-\infty}^{+\infty}\Big(\Pr[X>x,Y>y]-\overline{F}_X(x)\overline{F}_Y(y)\Big)dxdy$$
$$=\int_{-\infty}^{+\infty}\int_{-\infty}^{+\infty}\Big(\Pr[X\leq x,Y\leq y]-F_X(x)F_Y(y)\Big)dxdy.$$

Proof. Let (X_1,Y_1) and (X_2,Y_2) be two independent copies of (X,Y). Then,

$$2\mathbb{C}[X,Y]=2\mathbb{E}\big[X_1Y_1-\mathbb{E}[X_1]\mathbb{E}[Y_1]\big]$$
$$=\mathbb{E}\big[(X_1-X_2)(Y_1-Y_2)\big]$$
$$=\mathbb{E}\left[\int_{-\infty}^{+\infty}\int_{-\infty}^{+\infty}(\mathbb{I}[u\leq X_1]-\mathbb{I}[u\leq X_2])(\mathbb{I}[v\leq Y_1]-\mathbb{I}[v\leq Y_2])dudv\right].$$

Assuming the finiteness of $|\mathbb{E}[XY]|$, $\mathbb{E}|X|$ and $\mathbb{E}|Y|$, we are allowed to exchange the expectations and integral signs, which gives

$$2\mathbb{C}[X,Y]=\int_{-\infty}^{+\infty}\int_{-\infty}^{+\infty}\mathbb{E}\Big[(\mathbb{I}[u\leq X_1]-\mathbb{I}[u\leq X_2])(\mathbb{I}[v\leq Y_1]-\mathbb{I}[v\leq Y_2])\Big]dudv$$
$$=2\int_{-\infty}^{+\infty}\int_{-\infty}^{+\infty}\Big(\Pr[X\leq u,Y\leq v]-F_X(u)F_Y(v)\Big)dudv.$$

The proof of the other equality is similar. □

Property 1.6.13 is sometimes referred to as Höffding's lemma, and can be traced back to Höffding (1940). It will be useful in the next chapters.

1.7 TRANSFORMS

1.7.1 Stop-loss transform

1.7.1.1 Definition

Given an rv X, the rv $(X-t)_+$, where $\xi_+ = \max\{\xi, 0\}$, represents the amount by which X exceeds the threshold t. In an actuarial context, t is often called the deductible or priority (think of stop-loss reinsurance agreements, for instance).

Definition 1.7.1. The function $\pi_X(t) = \mathbb{E}[(X-t)_+]$ is called the stop-loss transform of X. ∇

See Kaas (1993) for details on the use and computation of stop-loss premiums.

1.7.1.2 Properties

It is useful to gather together some properties of the stop-loss transform π_X.

Property 1.7.2
Assume that $\mathbb{E}[|X|] < +\infty$. The stop-loss transform π_X has the following properties:

(i) it is decreasing and convex;

(ii) $\lim_{t\to+\infty} \pi_X(t) = 0$ and $\lim_{t\to-\infty}\{\pi_X(t) + t\} = \mathbb{E}[X]$.

Proof. (i) follows immediately from the representation

$$\pi_X(t) = \int_t^{+\infty} \overline{F}_X(\xi) d\xi. \tag{1.16}$$

This is a direct consequence of Property 1.6.6 since the tf of the rv $(X-t)_+$ is $\overline{F}_X(x+t)$, $x \geq 0$, and 0 otherwise.

Concerning (ii), the first limit is obvious from (1.16), while the second comes from

$$\lim_{t\to-\infty} \{\pi_X(t) + t\} = \lim_{t\to-\infty} \mathbb{E}[\max\{X, t\}] = \mathbb{E}[X].$$

□

1.7.1.3 Characterization

The following property basically states that given a function fulfilling (i)–(ii) of Property 1.7.2, there exists an rv X for which the function gives the stop-loss premium.

Property 1.7.3
For every function g which satisfies (i)–(ii) of Property 1.7.2, there exists an rv X such that $g = \pi_X$. The df of X is given by

$$F_X(t) = 1 + g'_+(t),$$

where g'_+ denotes the right-derivative of g.

Proof. If g is convex, then its right-derivative g'_+ exists and is right-continuous and non-decreasing. Now

$$\lim_{t\to+\infty} g(t)=0 \Rightarrow \lim_{t\to+\infty} g'_+(t)=0,$$

and $\lim_{t\to-\infty}\{g(t)+t\}$ can only exist if $\lim_{t\to-\infty} g'_+(t)=-1$. Hence, Property 1.5.3 ensures that $1+g'_+$ is a df, F_X say. Given $U\sim\mathcal{U}ni(0,1)$, it suffices to take $X=F_X^{-1}(U)$ according to Property 1.5.20. □

1.7.2 *Hazard rate*

1.7.2.1 Definition

The tf assesses the likelihood of a large loss: $\overline{F}_X(x)$ gives the probability of the loss X exceeding the value x. Large values of $\overline{F}_X(x)$ for given x indicate heavy-tailed behaviour. As pointed out in Klugman, Panjer and Willmot (1998), a quantity that can help the actuary in evaluating tail weight is the hazard rate, whose definition is recalled next.

Definition 1.7.4. Given a non-negative rv X with df (1.4), the associated hazard rate function r_X is defined as

$$r_X(x)=\frac{f_X(x)}{\overline{F}_X(x)}, \quad x\geq 0.$$

∇

The hazard rate is referred to as the failure rate in reliability theory. It corresponds to the well-known force of mortality in life insurance.

1.7.2.2 Equivalent expression

It is easy to see that

$$r_X(x)=\lim_{\Delta x\to 0}\frac{\Pr[x<X\leq x+\Delta x|X>x]}{\Delta x}.$$

To check this formula, it suffices to write

$$\begin{aligned}\Pr[x<X\leq x+\Delta x|X>x]&=\frac{\Pr[x<X\leq x+\Delta x]}{\overline{F}_X(x)}\\&=\frac{\overline{F}_X(x)-\overline{F}_X(x+\Delta x)}{\overline{F}_X(x)},\end{aligned}$$

whence it follows that

$$\begin{aligned}\lim_{\Delta x\to 0}\frac{\Pr[x<X\leq x+\Delta x|X>x]}{\Delta x}&=\frac{1}{\overline{F}_X(x)}\lim_{\Delta x\to 0}\frac{\overline{F}_X(x)-\overline{F}_X(x+\Delta x)}{\Delta x}\\&=-\frac{1}{\overline{F}_X(x)}\frac{d}{dx}\overline{F}_X(x).\end{aligned}$$

Thus, $r_X(x)$ may be intepreted as the probability of 'failure' at x given 'survival' to x. Intuitively speaking, if r_X becomes small then the distribution is heavy-tailed. Conversely, if r_X becomes large then the distribution is light-tailed.

Note that

$$r_X(x) = -\frac{d}{dx}\ln \overline{F}_X(x), \tag{1.17}$$

and that integrating both sides over x from 0 to t, taking $\overline{F}_X(0)=1$ into account, gives

$$\overline{F}_X(x)=\exp\left(-\int_0^x r_X(\xi)d\xi\right), \quad x\geq 0. \tag{1.18}$$

Equation (1.18) shows that r_X uniquely characterizes the distribution.

Example 1.7.5. The hazard rate for the $\mathcal{P}ar(\alpha,\theta)$ distribution is

$$r_X(x)=\frac{\alpha}{\theta+x}.$$

We see that r_X is strictly decreasing from $r_X(0)=\alpha/\theta$ to $r_X(+\infty)=0$. ∇

1.7.2.3 IFR and DFR distributions

If, as in the above example, r_X is decreasing then we say that X has a decreasing failure rate (DFR) distribution. On the other hand, if r_X is increasing then X is said to have an increasing failure rate (IFR) distribution. A DFR distribution has an heavier tail than an IFR one.

It is often difficult to examine r_X when $\overline{F}_X$ is complicated. Let us now establish the following results, relating the IFR/DFR concepts to log-convexity and log-concavity (precisely defined in Definition 2.8.6).

Property 1.7.6
If f_X is log-convex (log-concave) then X has a DFR (IFR) distribution.

Proof. Starting from

$$\frac{1}{r_X(x)}=\frac{\overline{F}_X(x)}{f_X(x)}=\int_0^{+\infty}\frac{f_X(x+y)}{f_X(x)}dy,$$

we see that if $f_X(x+y)/f_X(x)$ is an increasing function of x for any fixed $y\geq 0$ (i.e., f_X is log-convex) then $1/r_X(x)$ is increasing in x and X has a DFR distribution. Similarly, if f_X is log-concave (i.e., has a Pólya frequency of order 2) then X has an IFR distribution. □

The sufficient conditions of Property 1.7.6 are often easy to check. Let us now give an equivalent condition for DFR/IFR in terms of the log-convexity/log-concavity of the tfs. This result immediately follows from (1.17).

Property 1.7.7
The rv X has a DFR (IFR) distribution if, and only if, $\overline{F}_X$ is log-convex (log-concave).

1.7.3 Mean-excess function

1.7.3.1 Definition

Another function that is useful in analysing the thickness of tails is the mean-excess loss, whose definition is recalled next.

Definition 1.7.8. Given a non-negative rv X, the associated mean-excess function (mef) e_X is defined as

$$e_X(x) = \mathbb{E}[X - x | X > x], \quad x > 0.$$

∇

The mef corresponds to the well-known expected remaining lifetime in life insurance. In reliability theory, when X is a non-negative rv, X can be thought of as the lifetime of a device and $e_X(x)$ then expresses the conditional expected residual life of the device at time x given that the device is still alive at time x.

1.7.3.2 Equivalent expressions

Intuitively, if $e_X(x)$ is large for large x, then the distribution has a heavy tail since the expected loss $X - x$ is large. Conversely, if $e_X(x)$ is small for large x, then the distribution has a light tail. Clearly, if $F_X(0) = 0$ then $e_X(0) = \mathbb{E}[X]$.

Now Property 1.6.6 allows us to write

$$e_X(x) = \int_0^{+\infty} \Pr[X - x > t | X > x] dt = \frac{1}{\overline{F}_X(x)} \int_0^{+\infty} \overline{F}_X(x + t) dt$$

so that (1.16) yields the following useful relationship between the mef and the stop-loss transform

$$e_X(x) = \frac{\pi_X(x)}{\overline{F}_X(x)} = \frac{1}{\frac{d}{dx} \ln \pi_X(x)}, \quad x \geq 0. \tag{1.19}$$

1.7.3.3 Characterization

Clearly, $e_X(t) \geq 0$, but not every nonnegative function is an mef corresponding to some rv. The following property gives the characteristics of mefs.

Property 1.7.9
A function e_X is the mef of some continuous non-negative rv if, and only if, e_X satisfies the following properties:

(i) $0 \leq e_X(t) < \infty$ for all t ≥ 0.

(ii) $e_X(0) > 0$.

(iii) e_X is continuous.

(iv) $e_X(t)+t$ is non-decreasing on $\mathbb{R}^+$.

(v) When there exists a t_0 such that $e_X(t_0)=0$, then $e_X(t)=0$ for all $t\geq t_0$. Otherwise, when there does not exist such a t_0 with $e_X(t_0)=0$, then

$$\int_0^{+\infty}\frac{1}{e_X(t)}dt=+\infty.$$

1.7.3.4 Relationship between the mef and hazard rate

There is a close relationship between e_X and r_X. Provided the indicated limits exist, we can write

$$\lim_{x\to+\infty}e_X(x)=\lim_{x\to+\infty}\frac{\int_x^{+\infty}\overline{F}_X(t)dt}{\overline{F}_X(x)}=\lim_{x\to+\infty}\frac{\overline{F}_X(x)}{f_X(x)}=\lim_{x\to+\infty}\frac{1}{r_X(x)}.$$

This shows that the asymptotic behaviour of e_X is easily established from that of r_X, and vice versa.

1.7.3.5 IMRL and DMRL distributions

If e_X is non-decreasing then X is said to have an increasing mean residual lifetime (IMRL) distribution. Similarly, if e_X is non-increasing then X is said to have an decreasing mean residual lifetime (DMRL) distribution.

The following result shows that DFR implies IMRL and IFR implies DMRL.

Proposition 1.7.10
The following impications hold:

(i) F_X IFR $\Rightarrow F_X$ DMRL;

(ii) F_XDFR $\Rightarrow F_X$IMRL.

Proof. We only prove (i); the reasoning for (ii) is similar. Since F_X is IFR, we know from Property 1.7.7 that $\overline{F}_X$ is log-concave, that is, $x\mapsto\overline{F}_X(x+y)/\overline{F}_X(x)$ is non-increasing for each fixed $y\geq 0$. Hence, for all $t_1\leq t_2$, the inequality

$$\Pr[X-t_1>y|X>t_1]\geq\Pr[X-t_2>y|X>t_2]$$

is valid whatever the value of y. This allows us to write

$$\begin{aligned}e_X(t_1)&=\int_0^{+\infty}\Pr[X-t_1>y|X>t_1]dy\\&\geq\int_0^{+\infty}\Pr[X-t_2>y|X>t_2]dy=e_X(t_2),\end{aligned}$$

which concludes the proof. □

1.7.4 *Stationary renewal distribution*

1.7.4.1 Definition

The stationary renewal distribution plays an important role in ruin theory (see Kaas *et al.* 2001, Section 4.7). Let us recall the definition of this concept.

Definition 1.7.11. For a non-negative rv X with finite mean, let $X_{\{1\}}$ denote an rv with df

$$F_{X_{\{1\}}}(x) = \frac{1}{\mathbb{E}[X]} \int_0^x \overline{F}_X(y)\,dy = 1 - \frac{\pi_X(x)}{\mathbb{E}[X]}, \quad x \geq 0. \tag{1.20}$$

The df $F_{X_{\{1\}}}$ is known as the stationary renewal distribution associated with X. ∇

1.7.4.2 Hazard rate associated with stationary renewal distribution

The failure rate $r_{X_{\{1\}}}$ of $X_{\{1\}}$ can be written as

$$r_{X_{\{1\}}}(x) = \frac{f_{X_{\{1\}}}(x)}{\overline{F}_{X_{\{1\}}}(x)} = \frac{\overline{F}_X(x)}{\pi_X(x)} = \frac{1}{e_X(x)}$$

by virtue of (1.19). We get from this relationship that

$$\begin{aligned}
\overline{F}_X(x) &= e_X(0) f_{X_{\{1\}}}(x) \\
&= e_X(0) r_{X_{\{1\}}}(x) \overline{F}_{X_{\{1\}}}(x) \\
&= \frac{e_X(0)}{e_X(x)} \exp\left(- \int_0^x \frac{1}{e_X(t)} dt \right),
\end{aligned}$$

which demonstrates that e_X uniquely characterizes the distribution.

1.7.5 *Laplace transform*

1.7.5.1 Definition

Laplace transforms are useful when positive rvs are being studied. Their definition is recalled next.

Definition 1.7.12. The Laplace transform L_X associated with a risk X, is given by

$$L_X(t) = \mathbb{E}[\exp(-tX)], \quad t > 0.$$

∇

The expressions for L_X for the classical continuous parametric models are given in Table 1.5.

Table 1.5 Laplace transforms associated with standard parametric models

Probability law	$L_X(t)$
$\mathcal{U}ni(a,b)$	$\frac{\exp(-at)-\exp(-bt)}{(b-a)t}$
$\mathcal{B}et(\alpha,\beta)$	No closed form available
$\mathcal{N}or(\mu,\sigma^2)$	$\exp(-\mu t+\frac{1}{2}\sigma^2t^2)$
$\mathcal{E}xp(\theta)$	$\left(1+\frac{t}{\theta}\right)^{-1}$
$\mathcal{G}am(\alpha,\tau)$	$\left(1+\frac{t}{\tau}\right)^{-\alpha}$
$\mathcal{LN}or(\mu,\sigma^2)$	No closed form available
$\mathcal{P}ar(\alpha,\theta)$	No closed form available

1.7.5.2 Completely monotone functions and Bernstein's theorem

The theory of Laplace transforms makes extensive use of complete monotonicity. A function $g:(0,+\infty)\to\mathbb{R}^+$ is said to be completely monotone if it satisfies $(-1)^k g^{(k)}\geq 0$ for all $k\geq 1$, where $g^{(k)}$ denotes the kth derivative of g. As $x\to 0$, the derivatives of any completely monotone function g approach finite or infinite limits denoted by $g^{(k)}(0)$. Typical examples of completely monotone functions are $x\mapsto 1/x$ and $x\mapsto\exp(-x)$. It is easy to see that the Laplace transform of any non-negative rv X is completely monotone. A classical result from real analysis, known as Bernstein's theorem, states that conversely every completely monotone function g such that $g(0)=1$ is the Laplace transform of some non-negative rv.

Property 1.7.13
Given a completely monotone function g, there exists a measure μ on $\mathbb{R}^+$, not necessarily finite, such that

$$g(x)=\int_0^{+\infty}\exp(-tx)d\mu(t),\quad x\in\mathbb{R}^+. \tag{1.21}$$

For a proof of this result, see Theorem 1a of Feller (1966, p. 416).

1.7.5.3 Discrete Laplace transform: Probability generating function

Probability generating functions characterize integer-valued rvs. Their definition is recalled next.

Definition 1.7.14. The probability generating function (pgf) of the integer-valued rv N is defined as

$$\varphi_N(t)=\mathbb{E}[t^N]=L_N(-\ln t),\quad 0<t<1.$$

∇

Table 1.6 Probability generating functions associated with standard discrete probability models

Probability law	$\varphi_N(t)$
$\mathcal{B}er(q)$	$(1-q+qt)$
$\mathcal{B}in(m,q)$	$(1-q+qt)^m$
$\mathcal{G}eo(q)$	$\frac{q}{1-(1-q)t}$
$\mathcal{NB}in(\alpha,q)$	$\left(\frac{q}{1-(1-q)t}\right)^{\alpha}$
$\mathcal{P}oi(\lambda)$	$\exp(\lambda(t-1))$

The pgfs associated with the classical integer-valued parametric models are given in Table 1.6.

1.7.6 Moment generating function

1.7.6.1 Definition

The moment generating function (mgf) is a widely used tool in many statistics texts, as it is in Kaas *et al.* (2001). These functions serve to prove statements about convolutions of distributions, and also about limits. Unlike Laplace transforms or risks, mgfs do not always exist. If the mgf of an rv exists in some neighbourhood of 0, it is called light-tailed.

Definition 1.7.15. The mgf of the risk X, denoted by M_X, is given by

$$M_X(t) = \mathbb{E}[\exp(tX)], \quad t > 0.$$

∇

It is interesting to mention that M_X characterizes the probability distribution of X, that is, the information contained in F_X and M_X is equivalent.

The mgfs associated with the classical continuous parametric models are given in Table 1.7.

Table 1.7 Moment generating functions associated with standard parametric models

Probability laws	$M_X(t)$
$\mathcal{U}ni(a,b)$	$\frac{\exp(bt)-\exp(at)}{(b-a)t}$
$\mathcal{B}et(\alpha,\beta)$	No closed form available
$\mathcal{N}or(\mu,\sigma^2)$	$\exp(\mu t + \frac{1}{2}\sigma^2 t^2)$
$\mathcal{E}xp(\theta)$	$\left(1-\frac{t}{\theta}\right)^{-1}$ if $t<\theta$
$\mathcal{G}am(\alpha,\tau)$	$\left(1-\frac{t}{\tau}\right)^{-\alpha}$ if $t<\tau$

1.7.6.2 The mgf and thickness of tails

If $h > 0$ exists such that $M_X(t)$ exists and is finite for $0 < t < h$, then the Taylor expansion of the exponential function yields

$$M_X(t) = 1 + \sum_{n=1}^{+\infty} \frac{t^n}{n!} \mathbb{E}[X^n] \text{ for } 0 < t < h. \tag{1.22}$$

It is well known that if any moment of a distribution is infinite, the mgf does not exist. However, it is conceivable that there might exist distributions with moments of all orders and, yet, the mgf does not exist in any neighbourhood around 0. In fact, the $\mathcal{LN}or\ (\mu, \sigma^2)$ distribution is one such example.

The set $\mathcal{E} = \{t > 0 | M_X(t) < +\infty\}$ can be the positive real half-line, a finite interval or even the empty set. Let $t_{\max} = \sup \mathcal{E}$. If $\mathcal{E} \neq \emptyset$, we see that $t \mapsto M_X(t)$ is a well-defined continuous and strictly increasing function of $t \in [0, t_{\max})$, with value 1 at the origin. If the mgf of X is finite for a value $t_0 > 0$ then there exists a constant $b > 0$ such that for all $x \geq 0$,

$$\overline{F}_X(x) \leq b \exp(-t_0 x).$$

In other words, X has an exponentially bounded tail.

1.8 CONDITIONAL DISTRIBUTIONS

1.8.1 Conditional densities

Let $\boldsymbol{X} = (X_1, X_2, \ldots, X_n)^t$ and $\boldsymbol{Y} = (Y_1, Y_2, \ldots, Y_m)^t$ be two random vectors, possibly of different dimensions, and let $g(\boldsymbol{x}, \boldsymbol{y})$ be the value of their joint pdf at any points $\boldsymbol{x} \in \mathbb{R}^n$ and $\boldsymbol{y} \in \mathbb{R}^m$. Let $f_{\boldsymbol{Y}}$ be the pdf of $\boldsymbol{Y}$ and consider any point $\boldsymbol{y} \in \mathbb{R}^m$ such that $f_{\boldsymbol{Y}}(\boldsymbol{y}) > 0$. Then, the conditional pdf of $\boldsymbol{X}$ given $\boldsymbol{Y} = \boldsymbol{y}$, denoted by $f_{\boldsymbol{X}|\boldsymbol{Y}}(\boldsymbol{x}|\boldsymbol{y})$, is defined at any point $\boldsymbol{x} \in \mathbb{R}^n$ as

$$f_{\boldsymbol{X}|\boldsymbol{Y}}(\boldsymbol{x}|\boldsymbol{y}) = \frac{g(\boldsymbol{x}, \boldsymbol{y})}{f_{\boldsymbol{Y}(\boldsymbol{y})}}. \tag{1.23}$$

The definition of the conditional pdf $f_{\boldsymbol{X}|\boldsymbol{Y}}(\cdot|\boldsymbol{y})$ is irrelevant for any point $\boldsymbol{y} \in \mathbb{R}^m$ such that $f_{\boldsymbol{Y}}(\boldsymbol{y}) = 0$ since these points form a set having zero probability.

The next result is an extension of Bayes' theorem.

Proposition 1.8.1
Let $\boldsymbol{X} = (X_1, X_2, \ldots, X_n)^t$ and $\boldsymbol{Y} = (Y_1, Y_2, \ldots, Y_m)^t$ be two random vectors with respective pdfs $f_{\boldsymbol{X}}$ and $f_{\boldsymbol{Y}}$ and conditional pdfs $f_{\boldsymbol{X}|\boldsymbol{Y}}(\boldsymbol{x}|\boldsymbol{y})$ and $f_{\boldsymbol{Y}|\boldsymbol{X}}(\boldsymbol{y}|\boldsymbol{x})$ defined according to (1.23). Then, for any point $\boldsymbol{x} \in \mathbb{R}^n$ such that $f_{\boldsymbol{X}}(\boldsymbol{x}) > 0$,

$$f_{\boldsymbol{Y}|\boldsymbol{X}}(\boldsymbol{y}|\boldsymbol{x}) = \frac{f_{\boldsymbol{X}|\boldsymbol{Y}}(\boldsymbol{x}|\boldsymbol{y}) f_{\boldsymbol{Y}}(\boldsymbol{y})}{\int_{\boldsymbol{t} \in \mathbb{R}^n} f_{\boldsymbol{X}|\boldsymbol{Y}}(\boldsymbol{x}|\boldsymbol{t}) f_{\boldsymbol{Y}}(\boldsymbol{t}) d\boldsymbol{t}}.$$

As above, given a measurable function $\Psi: \mathbb{R}^{n+m} \to \mathbb{R}$, the conditional expectation of $\Psi(\boldsymbol{X}, \boldsymbol{Y})$ given $\boldsymbol{Y}$, denoted by $\mathbb{E}[\Psi(\boldsymbol{X}, \boldsymbol{Y}) | \boldsymbol{Y}]$, is defined as a function of the random vector $\boldsymbol{Y}$ whose value $\mathbb{E}[\Psi(\boldsymbol{X}, \boldsymbol{Y}) | \boldsymbol{Y} = \boldsymbol{y}]$ when $\boldsymbol{Y} = \boldsymbol{y}$ is given by

$$\mathbb{E}[\Psi(\boldsymbol{X}, \boldsymbol{Y}) | \boldsymbol{Y} = \boldsymbol{y}] = \int_{\boldsymbol{x} \in \mathbb{R}^n} \Psi(\boldsymbol{x}, \boldsymbol{y}) f_{\boldsymbol{X}|\boldsymbol{Y}}(\boldsymbol{x}|\boldsymbol{y}) d\boldsymbol{x}.$$

1.8.2 Conditional independence

Let $\boldsymbol{Y}$ be an m-dimensional random vector. The risks $X_1, X_2, \ldots, X_n$ are conditionally independent given $\boldsymbol{Y}$ if the identity

$$f_{\boldsymbol{X}|\boldsymbol{Y}}(\boldsymbol{x}|\boldsymbol{y}) = \prod_{i=1}^{n} f_{X_i|\boldsymbol{Y}}(x_i|\boldsymbol{y})$$

holds for every $\boldsymbol{x} \in \mathbb{R}^n$ and $\boldsymbol{y} \in \mathbb{R}^m$. In particular, if the risks $X_1, X_2, \ldots, X_n$ are conditionally independent given $\boldsymbol{Y}$, then

$$\mathbb{E}[X_i|X_j, j \neq i, \boldsymbol{Y}] = \mathbb{E}[X_i|\boldsymbol{Y}].$$

1.8.3 Conditional variance and covariance

Let $\boldsymbol{Y}$ be an m-dimensional random vector. The conditional covariance of the risks X_1 and X_2 given $\boldsymbol{Y}$ is the rv

$$\mathbb{C}[X_1, X_2|\boldsymbol{Y}] = \mathbb{E}\Big[(X_1 - \mathbb{E}[X_1|\boldsymbol{Y}])(X_2 - \mathbb{E}[X_2|\boldsymbol{Y}])\Big|\boldsymbol{Y}\Big].$$

The conditional variance of X_1 given $\boldsymbol{Y}$ is the rv

$$\mathbb{V}[X_1|\boldsymbol{Y}] = \mathbb{C}[X_1, X_1|\boldsymbol{Y}].$$

The conditional variances and covariances have the following properties.

Property 1.8.2

(i) $\mathbb{C}[X_1, X_2] = \mathbb{E}\Big[\mathbb{C}[X_1, X_2|\boldsymbol{Y}]\Big] + \mathbb{C}\Big[\mathbb{E}[X_1|\boldsymbol{Y}], \mathbb{E}[X_2|\boldsymbol{Y}]\Big]$.

(ii) $\mathbb{V}[X_1] = \mathbb{E}\Big[\mathbb{V}[X_1|\boldsymbol{Y}]\Big] + \mathbb{V}\Big[\mathbb{E}[X_1|\boldsymbol{Y}]\Big]$.

(iii) If X_1 and X_2 are conditionally independent given $\boldsymbol{Y}$, $\mathbb{C}[X_1, X_2|\boldsymbol{Y}] = 0$.

(iv) If $t: \mathbb{R}^n \to \mathbb{R}$ is square-integrable then $\mathbb{C}[t(\boldsymbol{Y}), X|\boldsymbol{Y}] = 0$.

1.8.4 The multivariate normal distribution

In the univariate case, an rv X is said to have a normal distribution with mean μ and variance σ^2 if its pdf is of the form

$$f_X(x) = \frac{1}{\sigma\sqrt{2\pi}} \exp\left(-\frac{1}{2} Q_1(x; \mu, \sigma^2)\right), \quad x \in \mathbb{R},$$

with

$$Q_1(x; \mu, \sigma^2) = \frac{1}{\sigma^2}(x-\mu)^2 = (x-\mu)(\sigma^2)^{-1}(x-\mu)$$

where $\mu \in \mathbb{R}$ and $\sigma^2 > 0$. The bivariate normal distribution introduced below is a natural extension of the univariate normal pdf.

Definition 1.8.3. (i) A random couple $\boldsymbol{X}=(X_1, X_2)'$ is said to have a non-singular bivariate normal distribution if its pdf is of the form

$$f_{\boldsymbol{X}}(\boldsymbol{x})=\frac{1}{2\pi|\boldsymbol{\Sigma}|^{1/2}}\exp\left(-\frac{1}{2}Q_2(\boldsymbol{x};\boldsymbol{\mu},\boldsymbol{\Sigma})\right), \quad \boldsymbol{x}\in\mathbb{R}^2,$$

where

$$Q_2(\boldsymbol{x};\boldsymbol{\mu},\boldsymbol{\Sigma})=(\boldsymbol{x}-\boldsymbol{\mu})'\boldsymbol{\Sigma}^{-1}(\boldsymbol{x}-\boldsymbol{\mu})$$

with

$$\boldsymbol{\mu}=\begin{pmatrix}\mu_1\\ \mu_2\end{pmatrix} \quad \text{and} \quad \boldsymbol{\Sigma}=\begin{pmatrix}\sigma_1^2 & \sigma_{12}\\ \sigma_{12} & \sigma_2^2\end{pmatrix},$$

$\sigma_i^2>0$, $i=1, 2$, $|\sigma_{12}|<\sigma_1\sigma_2$.
(ii) $\boldsymbol{X}$ is said to have a singular normal distribution function if there exist real numbers σ_1, σ_2, μ_1 and μ_2 such that $\boldsymbol{X}=_d(\sigma_1 Z+\mu_1, \sigma_2 Z+\mu_2)$, where Z is $\mathcal{N}or(0, 1)$ distributed and $\sigma_i>0, i=1,2$. ∇

The extension of Definition 1.8.3 to higher dimensions is straightforward. Given an $n\times n$ positive definite matrix $\boldsymbol{\Sigma}$ and a real vector $\boldsymbol{\mu}$, define $Q_n(\boldsymbol{x},\boldsymbol{\mu},\boldsymbol{\Sigma})=(\boldsymbol{x}-\boldsymbol{\mu})'\boldsymbol{\Sigma}^{-1}(\boldsymbol{x}-\boldsymbol{\mu})$. The random vector $\boldsymbol{X}=(X_1, X_2, \ldots, X_n)'$ is said to have a multivariate normal distribution if its pdf is of the form

$$f_{\boldsymbol{X}}(\boldsymbol{x})=\frac{1}{\sqrt{(2\pi)^n|\boldsymbol{\Sigma}|}}\exp\left(-\frac{1}{2}Q_n(\boldsymbol{x};\boldsymbol{\mu},\boldsymbol{\Sigma})\right), \quad \boldsymbol{x}\in\mathbb{R}^n. \tag{1.24}$$

Henceforth, we denote the fact that the random vector $\boldsymbol{X}$ has multivariate normal distribution with pdf (1.24) by $\boldsymbol{X}\sim\mathcal{N}or_n(\boldsymbol{\mu},\boldsymbol{\Sigma})$. A good reference for the multivariate normal distribution is Tong (1990).

A convenient characterization of the multivariate normal distribution is as follows: $\boldsymbol{X}\sim\mathcal{N}or_n(\boldsymbol{\mu},\boldsymbol{\Sigma})$ if, and only if, any rv of the form $\sum_{i=1}^n \alpha_i X_i$ with $\alpha\in\mathbb{R}^n$, has the univariate normal distribution.

Let us now compute the conditional distribution associated with the multivariate normal distribution.

Property 1.8.4
Let $\boldsymbol{X}=(X_1, X_2)$ have the bivariate normal distribution with parameters $\boldsymbol{\mu}$ and $\boldsymbol{\Sigma}$. Let $r=\sigma_{12}/\sigma_1\sigma_2$. Then:

(i) the marginal distribution of X_i is normal with parameters μ_i and σ_i^2, $i=1,2$;

(ii) for $|r|<1$, the conditional distribution of X_1 given $X_2=x_2$ is normal with mean

$$\mu_1+r\frac{\sigma_1}{\sigma_2}(x_2-\mu_2)$$

and variance $\sigma_1^2(1-r^2)$;

(iii) X_1 and X_2 are independent if, and only if, $r=0$.

Proof. Since $|\boldsymbol{\Sigma}| = \sigma_1^2\sigma_2^2(1-r^2)$, the inverse of $\boldsymbol{\Sigma}$ exists if, and only if, $|r|<1$. Straightforward calculation shows that

$$\boldsymbol{\Sigma}^{-1} = \frac{1}{\sigma_1^2\sigma_2^2(1-r^2)}\begin{pmatrix} \sigma_2^2 & -r\sigma_1\sigma_2 \\ -r\sigma_1\sigma_2 & \sigma_1^2 \end{pmatrix}.$$

For $|r|<1$, we can write

$$f_{\boldsymbol{X}}(\boldsymbol{x}) = \frac{1}{2\pi\sigma_1\sigma_2\sqrt{1-r^2}}\exp\left(-\frac{1}{2(1-r^2)}\right.$$
$$\left.\times\left(\left(\frac{x_1-\mu_1}{\sigma_1}\right)^2 - 2r\left(\frac{x_1-\mu_1}{\sigma_1}\right)\left(\frac{x_2-\mu_2}{\sigma_2}\right)+\left(\frac{x_2-\mu_2}{\sigma_2}\right)^2\right)\right).$$

From the identity

$$\left(\frac{x_1-\mu_1}{\sigma_1}\right)^2 - 2r\left(\frac{x_1-\mu_1}{\sigma_1}\right)\left(\frac{x_2-\mu_2}{\sigma_2}\right)+\left(\frac{x_2-\mu_2}{\sigma_2}\right)^2$$
$$=(1-r^2)\left(\frac{x_2-\mu_2}{\sigma_2}\right)^2+\left(\frac{x_1-\mu_1}{\sigma_1}-r\frac{x_2-\mu_2}{\sigma_2}\right)^2$$

we get

$$f_{\boldsymbol{X}}(\boldsymbol{x}) = f_2(x_2)f_{1|2}(x_1|x_2)$$

with

$$f_2(x_2) = \frac{1}{\sigma_2\sqrt{2\pi}}\exp\left(-\frac{1}{2\sigma^2}(x_2-\mu_2)^2\right)$$

and

$$f_{1|2}(x_1|x_2) = \frac{1}{\sqrt{2\pi}\sigma_1\sqrt{1-r^2}}\exp\left(-\frac{1}{2\sigma_1^2(1-r^2)}\times\left(x_1-\left(\mu_1+r\frac{\sigma_1}{\sigma_2}(x_2-\mu_2)\right)\right)^2\right).$$

Combining these expressions yields the required results. □

From the above results, it now becomes clear that μ and Σ satisfy

$$\mathbb{E}[\boldsymbol{X}] = \begin{pmatrix}\mathbb{E}[X_1]\\ \mathbb{E}[X_2]\end{pmatrix} = \boldsymbol{\mu}$$

and

$$\mathbb{C}[\boldsymbol{X}] = \mathbb{E}[(\boldsymbol{X}-\boldsymbol{\mu})(\boldsymbol{X}-\boldsymbol{\mu})^t] = \begin{pmatrix}\mathbb{V}[X_1] & \mathbb{C}[X_1,X_2]\\ \mathbb{C}[X_1,X_2] & \mathbb{V}[X_2]\end{pmatrix} = \boldsymbol{\Sigma}.$$

Thus, $\boldsymbol{\mu}$ and $\boldsymbol{\Sigma}$ are the mean vector and the covariance matrix of the multivariate normal distribution. The multivariate normal distribution also has the following useful invariance property.

Property 1.8.5
Let $\boldsymbol{C}$ be a given $n \times n$ matrix with real entries and let $\boldsymbol{b}$ be an n-dimensional real vector. If $\boldsymbol{X} \sim \mathcal{N}or_n(\boldsymbol{\mu}, \boldsymbol{\Sigma})$ then $\boldsymbol{Y} = \boldsymbol{C}\boldsymbol{X} + \boldsymbol{b}$ is $\mathcal{N}or_n(\boldsymbol{C}\boldsymbol{\mu} + \boldsymbol{b},\ \boldsymbol{C}\boldsymbol{\Sigma}\boldsymbol{C}^t)$.

Property 1.8.5 enables us to obtain a bivariate normal vector $\boldsymbol{X}$ with any mean vector μ and covariance matrix Σ through a transformation of two independent $\mathcal{N}or(0, 1)$ rvs Z_1 and Z_2. It suffices, indeed, to resort to the transformation $\boldsymbol{X} = \boldsymbol{C}\boldsymbol{Z} + \mu$ with

$$\boldsymbol{C} = \begin{pmatrix} \sigma_1 & 0 \\ \dfrac{\sigma_{12}}{\sigma_1} & \sigma_2\sqrt{1 - r^2} \end{pmatrix}$$

which is non-singular if, and only if, $|r| < 1$. Furthermore, $\boldsymbol{C}$ satisfies $\boldsymbol{C}\boldsymbol{C}^t = \Sigma$.

Note that any other 'square root' of Σ does the job as well. Quite convenient is the lower triangular matrix that can be constructed using the Cholesky decomposition; it also works for dimensions higher than 2.

1.8.5 The family of the elliptical distributions

This section is devoted to elliptical distributions that can be seen as convenient extensions of multivariate normal distributions. A standard reference on the topic is Fang, Kotz and Ng (1990). The reading of Gupta and Varga (1993) is also instructive. This section is based on Valdez and Dhaene (2004). We refer the reader to Frahm, Junker and Szimayer (2003) for a discussion about the applicability of the elliptical distributions.

The characteristic function plays an important role in the theory of elliptical distributions. The characteristic function of $\boldsymbol{X} \sim \mathcal{N}or_n(\boldsymbol{\mu}, \boldsymbol{\Sigma})$ is given by

$$\mathbb{E}[\exp(i\boldsymbol{\xi}^t\boldsymbol{X})] = \exp(i\boldsymbol{\xi}^t\boldsymbol{\mu}) \exp\left(-\frac{1}{2}\boldsymbol{\xi}^t\boldsymbol{\Sigma}\boldsymbol{\xi}\right), \qquad \boldsymbol{\xi} \in \mathbb{R}^n. \tag{1.25}$$

The class of multivariate elliptical distributions is a natural extension of the class of multivariate normal distributions, as can be seen from the next definition.

Definition 1.8.6. The random vector $\boldsymbol{X}$ is said to have an elliptical distribution with parameters μ and Σ if its characteristic function can be expressed as

$$\mathbb{E}[\exp(i\boldsymbol{\xi}^t\boldsymbol{X})] = \exp(i\boldsymbol{\xi}^t\mu)\ \phi(\boldsymbol{\xi}^t\Sigma\boldsymbol{\xi}), \tag{1.26}$$

for some function $\phi: \mathbb{R} \to \mathbb{R}$ and where $\boldsymbol{\Sigma}$ is given by

$$\boldsymbol{\Sigma} = \boldsymbol{A}\boldsymbol{A}^t \tag{1.27}$$

for some $n \times m$ matrix $\boldsymbol{A}$. We denote the fact that $\boldsymbol{X}$ has characteristic function (1.26) by $\boldsymbol{X} \sim \mathcal{E}ll_n(\boldsymbol{\mu}, \Sigma, \phi)$. ∇

In (1.25), the generator of the multivariate normal distribution is given by $\phi(u) = \exp(-u/2)$.

It is well known that the characteristic function of a random vector always exists and that there is a one-to-one correspondence between probability distributions and characteristic functions. Note, however, that not every function ϕ can be used to construct a characteristic function of an elliptical distribution. Obviously, this function ϕ should already fulfil the requirement $\phi(0)=1$. Moreover, a necessary and sufficient condition for the function ϕ to be a characteristic generator of an n -dimensional elliptical distribution is given in Theorem 2.2 of Fang, Kotz and Ng (1990).

Note that (1.27) guarantees that the matrix Σ is symmetric, positive definite and has positive elements on the main diagonal. Hence, denoting by σ_{kl} the elements of Σ for any k and l, one has that $\sigma_{kl}=\sigma_{lk}$, whereas $\sigma_{kk}>0$ (which is denoted by σ_k^2).

It is interesting to note that in the one-dimensional case, the class of elliptical distributions consists mainly of the class of symmetric distributions which include the well-known normal and Student distributions.

We have seen above that an n-dimensional random vector $\boldsymbol{X}$ is $\mathcal{N}or_n(\mu, \Sigma)$ distributed if, and only if, any linear combination $\alpha'\boldsymbol{X}$ of the X_k has a univariate normal distribution with mean $\boldsymbol{\alpha}'\boldsymbol{\mu}$ and variance $\boldsymbol{\alpha}'\Sigma\boldsymbol{\alpha}$. It is straightforward to generalize this result to the case of multivariate elliptical distributions.

Property 1.8.7

An n-dimensional random vector $\boldsymbol{X}$ has the $\mathcal{E}ll_n(\mu, \Sigma, \phi)$ distribution if, and only if, for any vector $\alpha\in\mathbb{R}^n$, one has

$$\boldsymbol{\alpha}'\boldsymbol{X}\sim\mathcal{E}ll_1\left(\boldsymbol{\alpha}'\mu, \boldsymbol{\alpha}'\Sigma\boldsymbol{\alpha}, \phi\right).$$

From Property 1.8.7, we find in particular that for $k=1,2,\ldots,n$,

$$X_k\sim\mathcal{E}ll_1\left(\mu_k,\sigma_k^2, \phi\right). \tag{1.28}$$

Hence, the marginal components of a multivariate elliptical distribution have an elliptical distribution with the same characteristic generator.

Defining

$$S=\sum_{k=1}^n X_k=\boldsymbol{e}'\boldsymbol{X}$$

where $\boldsymbol{e}=(1,1,\ldots,1)'$, it follows that

$$\boldsymbol{X}\sim\mathcal{E}ll_n(\boldsymbol{\mu}, \Sigma, \boldsymbol{\phi})\Rightarrow S\sim\mathcal{E}ll_1\left(\boldsymbol{e}'\boldsymbol{\mu}, \boldsymbol{e}'\Sigma\boldsymbol{e}, \phi\right) \tag{1.29}$$

where $\boldsymbol{e}'\mu=\sum_{k=1}^n\mu_k$ and $\boldsymbol{e}'\Sigma\boldsymbol{e}=\sum_{k=1}^n\sum_{l=1}^n\sigma_{kl}$.

In the following result, it is stated that any random vector with components that are linear combinations of the components of an elliptical distribution is again an elliptical distribution with the same characteristic generator.

Property 1.8.8
For any $m \times n$ matrix $\boldsymbol{B}$, any vector $\boldsymbol{c} \in \mathbb{R}^m$ and any random vector $\boldsymbol{X} \sim \mathcal{E}ll_n(\boldsymbol{\mu}, \boldsymbol{\Sigma}, \phi)$, we have that

$$\boldsymbol{BX} + \boldsymbol{c} \sim \mathcal{E}ll_m(\boldsymbol{B\mu} + \boldsymbol{c}, \boldsymbol{B\Sigma B}^t, \phi). \tag{1.30}$$

It is easy to see that Property 1.8.8 is a generalization of Property 1.8.7.

Suppose that for a random vector $\boldsymbol{X}$, the expectation $\mathbb{E}\left[\prod_{k=1}^n Y_k^{r_k}\right]$ exists for some set of non-negative integers $r_1, r_2, \ldots, r_n$. Then this expectation can be found from the relation

$$\mathbb{E}\left[\prod_{k=1}^{n} Y_k^{r_k}\right] = \frac{1}{i^{r_1+r_2+\cdots+r_n}}\left(\frac{\partial^{r_1+r_2+\cdots+r_n}}{\partial_{t_1}^{r_1}\partial_{t_2}^{r_2}\ldots\partial_{t_n}^{r_n}}\mathbb{E}\left[\exp\left(i\boldsymbol{\xi}^t\boldsymbol{X}\right)\right]\right)\Bigg|_{\boldsymbol{\xi}=\boldsymbol{0}} \tag{1.31}$$

where $\boldsymbol{0} = (0, 0, \ldots, 0)^t$.

The moments of $\boldsymbol{X} \sim \mathcal{E}ll_n(\boldsymbol{\mu}, \boldsymbol{\Sigma}, \phi)$ do not necessarily exist. However, from (1.26) and (1.31) we deduce that if $\mathbb{E}[X_k]$ exists, then it will be given by

$$\mathbb{E}[X_k] = \mu_k \tag{1.32}$$

so that $\mathbb{E}[\boldsymbol{X}] = \boldsymbol{\mu}$, if the mean vector exists. Moreover, if $\mathbb{C}[X_k, X_l]$ and/or $\mathbb{V}[X_k]$ exist, then they will be given by

$$\mathbb{C}[X_k, X_l] = -2\phi'(0)\,\sigma_{kl} \tag{1.33}$$

and/or

$$\mathbb{V}[X_k] = -2\phi'(0)\,\sigma_k^2, \tag{1.34}$$

where ϕ' denotes the first derivative of the characteristic generator. In short, if the covariance matrix of $\boldsymbol{X}$ exists, then it is given by $-2\phi'(0)\,\boldsymbol{\Sigma}$. A necessary condition for this covariance matrix to exist is

$$|\phi'(0)| < \infty,$$

see Cambanis, Huang and Simons (1981).

The following result, due to Kelker (1970), shows that any multivariate elliptical distribution with mutually independent components must necessarily be multivariate normal.

Property 1.8.9
Let $\boldsymbol{X} \sim \mathcal{E}ll_n(\boldsymbol{\mu}, \boldsymbol{\Sigma}, \phi)$ with mutually independent components. Assume that the expectations and variances of the X_k exist and that $\mathbb{V}[X_k] > 0$. Then it follows that $\boldsymbol{X}$ is multivariate normal.

Proof. Independence of the rvs and existence of their expectations imply that the covariances exist and are equal to 0. Hence, we find that $\boldsymbol{\Sigma}$ is a diagonal matrix, and that

$$\phi(\boldsymbol{\xi}^t\boldsymbol{\xi}) = \prod_{k=1}^{n} \phi(\xi_k^2)$$

holds for all n-dimensional vectors $\boldsymbol{\xi}$. This equation is known as Hamel's equation, and its solution has the form

$$\phi(x) = \exp(-\alpha x),$$

for some positive constant α satisfying $\alpha = -\phi'(0)$. To prove this, first note that

$$\phi(\boldsymbol{\xi}^t\boldsymbol{\xi}) = \phi\left(\sum_{k=1}^{n} \xi_k^2\right) = \prod_{k=1}^{n} \phi(\xi_k^2)$$

or equivalently,

$$\phi(u_1 + \cdots + u_n) = \phi(u_1)\ldots\phi(u_n).$$

Let us now make the (unnecessary) assumption of differentiability of ϕ.
Consider the partial derivative with respect to u_k, for some $k = 1, 2, \ldots, n$. We have

$$\begin{aligned}
\frac{\partial\phi}{\partial u_k} &= \lim_{h\to 0} \frac{\phi(u_1 + \ldots + (u_k + h) + \ldots + u_n) - \phi(u_1 + \ldots + u_n)}{h} \\
&= \lim_{h\to 0} \frac{\phi(u_1 + \ldots + u_n)\phi(h) - \phi(u_1 + \ldots + u_n)}{h} \\
&= \lim_{h\to 0} \frac{\phi(u_1 + \ldots + u_n)[\phi(h) - \phi(0)]}{h} \\
&= \phi(u_1)\ldots\phi(u_n)\phi'(0).
\end{aligned}$$

But the left-hand side is

$$\frac{\partial\phi}{\partial u_k} = \phi(u_1)\cdots\phi'(u_k)\cdots\phi(u_n) = \phi(u_1)\cdots\phi(u_n)\frac{\phi'(u_k)}{\phi(u_k)}.$$

Thus, equating the two, we get

$$\frac{\phi'(u_k)}{\phi(u_k)} = \phi'(0)$$

which gives the desired solution $\phi(x) = \exp(-\alpha x)$ with $\alpha = -\phi'(0)$. This leads to the characteristic generator of a multivariate normal. □

An elliptically distributed random vector $\boldsymbol{X} \sim \mathcal{E}ll_n(\boldsymbol{\mu}, \boldsymbol{\Sigma}, \phi)$ does not necessarily have a multivariate density function $f_{\boldsymbol{X}}$. A necessary condition for $\boldsymbol{X}$ to have a density is that $\text{rank}(\Sigma) = n$. If $\boldsymbol{X} \sim \mathcal{E}ll_n(\boldsymbol{\mu}, \boldsymbol{\Sigma}, \phi)$ has a density, then it will be of the form

$$f_{\boldsymbol{X}}(\boldsymbol{x}) = \frac{c}{\sqrt{|\Sigma|}} g\left((\boldsymbol{x} - \mu)^t \Sigma^{-1} (\boldsymbol{x} - \mu)\right) \tag{1.35}$$

for some non-negative function $g(\cdot)$ satisfying the condition

$$0 < \int_0^{\infty} z^{n/2-1} g(z) dz < \infty \tag{1.36}$$

and a normalizing constant c given by

$$c = \frac{\Gamma(n/2)}{\pi^{n/2}} \left(\int_0^\infty z^{n/2-1} g(z) dz \right)^{-1}. \tag{1.37}$$

Also, the converse statement holds. Any non-negative function $g(\cdot)$ satisfying (1.36) can be used to define an n-dimensional density of the form (1.35) for an elliptical distribution, with c given by (1.37). The function $g(\cdot)$ is called the *density generator*. One sometimes writes $\boldsymbol{X} \sim \mathcal{E}ll_n(\boldsymbol{\mu}, \boldsymbol{\Sigma}, g)$ for the n-dimensional elliptical distributions generated from the function $g(\cdot)$. A detailed proof of these results, using spherical transformations of rectangular coordinates, can be found in Landsman and Valdez (2002).

Note that for a given characteristic generator ϕ, the density generator g and/or the normalizing constant c may depend on the dimension of the random vector $\boldsymbol{X}$. Often one considers the class of elliptical distributions of dimensions $1, 2, 3, \ldots$, all derived from the same characteristic generator ϕ. If these distributions have a density, we will denote their respective density generators by g_n, where the subscript n denotes the dimension of the random vector $\boldsymbol{X}$.

Example 1.8.10. One immediately finds that the density generators and the corresponding normalizing constants of the multivariate normal random vectors $\boldsymbol{X} \sim \mathcal{N}or_n(\boldsymbol{\mu}, \boldsymbol{\Sigma})$ for $n = 1, 2, \ldots$ are given by

$$g_n(u) = \exp(-u/2) \tag{1.38}$$

and

$$c_n = (2\pi)^{-n/2}, \tag{1.39}$$

respectively. ∇

Example 1.8.11. As an example, let us consider the elliptical Student distribution $\boldsymbol{X} \sim \mathcal{E}ll_n(\boldsymbol{\mu}, \boldsymbol{\Sigma}, g_n)$, with

$$g_n(u) = \left(1 + \frac{u}{m}\right)^{-(n+m)/2}.$$

We will denote this multivariate distribution (with m degrees of freedom) by $t_n^{(m)}(\boldsymbol{\mu}, \boldsymbol{\Sigma})$. Its multivariate density is given by

$$f_{\boldsymbol{X}}(\boldsymbol{x}) = \frac{c_n}{\sqrt{|\boldsymbol{\Sigma}|}} \left(1 + \frac{(\boldsymbol{x}-\boldsymbol{\mu})^t \boldsymbol{\Sigma}^{-1} (\boldsymbol{x}-\boldsymbol{\mu})}{m}\right)^{-(n+m)/2}. \tag{1.40}$$

In order to determine the normalizing constant, first note from (1.37) that

$$\begin{aligned} c_n &= \frac{\Gamma(n/2)}{\pi^{n/2}} \left(\int_0^\infty z^{n/2-1} g(z) dz \right)^{-1} \\ &= \frac{\Gamma(n/2)}{\pi^{n/2}} \left(\int_0^\infty z^{n/2-1} \left(1 + \frac{z}{m}\right)^{-(n+m)/2} dz \right)^{-1}. \end{aligned}$$

Performing the substitution $u = 1 + (z/m)$, we find that

$$\int_0^\infty z^{n/2-1}\left(1+\frac{z}{m}\right)^{-(n+m)/2} dz = m^{n/2}\int_1^\infty \left(1-u^{-1}\right)^{n/2-1} u^{-m/2-1} du.$$

Making one more substitution $v = 1 - u^{-1}$, we get

$$\int_0^\infty z^{n/2-1}\left(1+\frac{z}{m}\right)^{-(n+m)/2} dz = m^{n/2}\frac{\Gamma(n/2)\Gamma(m/2)}{\Gamma((n+m)/2)},$$

from which we find that

$$c_n = \frac{\Gamma((n+m)/2)}{(m\pi)^{n/2}\Gamma(m/2)}. \tag{1.41}$$

From Property 1.8.7 and (1.28), we have that the marginals of the multivariate elliptical Student distribution are again Student distributions hence $X_k \sim t_1^{(m)}\left(\mu_k, \sigma_k^2\right)$. The results above lead to

$$f_{X_k}(x) = \frac{\Gamma\left(\frac{m+1}{2}\right)}{(m\pi)^{1/2}\Gamma\left(\frac{m}{2}\right)}\frac{1}{\sigma_k}\left(1+\frac{1}{m}\left(\frac{x-\mu_k}{\sigma_k}\right)^2\right)^{-(m+1)/2}, \quad k = 1, 2, \ldots, n, \tag{1.42}$$

which is indeed the well-known density of a univariate Student rv with m degrees of freedom. Its mean is

$$\mathbb{E}[Y_k] = \mu_k, \tag{1.43}$$

and it can be verified that its variance is given by

$$\mathbb{V}[X_k] = \frac{m}{m-2}\sigma_k^2, \tag{1.44}$$

provided the degrees of freedom $m > 2$. Note that $\frac{m}{m-2} = -2\phi'(0)$, where ϕ is the characteristic generator of the family of Student distributions with m degrees of freedom. ∇

In Table 1.8, we consider some well-known families of the class of multivariate elliptical distributions. Each family consists of all elliptical distributions constructed from one particular characteristic generator $\phi(u)$. For more details about these families of elliptical distributions, see Landsman and Valdez (2003) and the references therein.

An n-dimensional random vector $\boldsymbol{Z}$ is said to have a multivariate standard normal distribution if all the Z_i are mutually independent $\mathcal{N}or(0, 1)$ distributed. We will write this as $\boldsymbol{Z} \sim \mathcal{N}or_n(\boldsymbol{0}_n, \boldsymbol{I}_n)$, where $\boldsymbol{I}_n$ denotes the $n \times n$ identity matrix. The characteristic function of $\boldsymbol{Z}$ is given by

$$\mathbb{E}[\exp(i\boldsymbol{\xi}'\boldsymbol{Z})] = \exp\left(-\frac{1}{2}\boldsymbol{\xi}'\boldsymbol{\xi}\right). \tag{1.45}$$

Hence, from (1.45), we find that the characteristic generator of $N_n(\boldsymbol{0}_n, \boldsymbol{I}_n)$ is given by $\phi(u) = \exp(-u/2)$. The class of multivariate spherical distributions is an extension of the class of standard multivariate normal distributions.

Table 1.8 Some families of elliptical distributions with their characteristic generator and/or density generator

Family	Density $g_n(\cdot)$ or characteristic $\phi(\cdot)$ generator
Cauchy	$g_n(u)=(1+u)^{-(n+1)/2}$
Exponential power	$g_n(u)=\exp(-r(u)^s)$, $r,s>0$
Laplace	$g_n(u)=\exp(-\lvert u\rvert)$
Logistic	$g_n(u)=\frac{\exp(-u)}{(1+\exp(-u))^2}$
Normal	$g_n(u)=\exp(-u/2)$; $\phi(u)=\exp(-u/2)$
Stable laws	$\phi(u)=\exp\left(-r(u)^{s/2}\right)$, $0<s\leq 2, r>0$
Student	$g_n(u)=\left(1+\frac{u}{m}\right)^{-(n+m)/2}$, $m>0$ an integer

Definition 1.8.12. A random vector $\boldsymbol{Z}$ is said to have an n-dimensional spherical distribution with characteristic generator ϕ if $\boldsymbol{Z}\sim\mathcal{E}ll_n(\boldsymbol{0}_n,\boldsymbol{I}_n,\phi)$. ∇

We will often use the notation $\mathcal{S}ph_n(\phi)$ for $\mathcal{E}ll_n(\boldsymbol{0}_n,\boldsymbol{I}_n,\phi)$ in the case of spherical distributions. From the definition above, we find that the random vector $\boldsymbol{Z}\sim\mathcal{S}ph_n(\phi)$ if, and only if,

$$\mathbb{E}[\exp(i\boldsymbol{\xi}'\boldsymbol{Z})]=\phi(\boldsymbol{\xi}'\boldsymbol{\xi}). \tag{1.46}$$

Consider an m-dimensional random vector $\boldsymbol{X}$ such that

$$\boldsymbol{X}=_d\boldsymbol{\mu}+\boldsymbol{A}\boldsymbol{Z} \tag{1.47}$$

for some vector $\boldsymbol{\mu}$, some $n\times m$ matrix $\boldsymbol{A}$ and some m-dimensional random vector $\boldsymbol{Z}\sim\mathcal{S}ph_n(\phi)$. Then it is straightforward to prove that $\boldsymbol{X}\sim\mathcal{E}ll_n(\boldsymbol{\mu},\boldsymbol{\Sigma},\phi)$, where $\boldsymbol{\Sigma}=\boldsymbol{A}\boldsymbol{A}'$.

Observe that from the characteristic functions of $\boldsymbol{Z}$ and $\boldsymbol{\alpha}'\boldsymbol{Z}$, one immediately finds the following result.

Property 1.8.13
$\boldsymbol{Z}\sim\mathcal{S}ph_n(\phi)$ if, and only if, for any n-dimensional vector $\boldsymbol{\alpha}$, one has

$$\frac{\boldsymbol{\alpha}'\boldsymbol{Z}}{\sqrt{\boldsymbol{\alpha}'\boldsymbol{\alpha}}}\sim\mathcal{S}ph_1(\phi). \tag{1.48}$$

As a special case of this result, we find that any component Z_i of $\boldsymbol{Z}$ has a $\mathcal{S}ph_1(\phi)$ distribution.

From the results concerning elliptical distributions, we find that if a spherical random vector $\mathcal{S}ph_n(\phi)$ possesses a density $f_{\boldsymbol{Z}}$, then it has to be a pdf of the form

$$f_{\boldsymbol{Z}}(\boldsymbol{z})=cg(\boldsymbol{z}'\boldsymbol{z}), \tag{1.49}$$

where the density generator g satisfies (1.36) and the normalizing constant c satisfies (1.37). Furthermore, the converse also holds: any non-negative function $g(\cdot)$ satisfying (1.36) can be used to define an n -dimensional pdf $cg(z^t z)$ of a spherical distribution with the normalizing constant c satisfying (1.37). One often writes $\mathcal{S}ph_n(g)$ for the n -dimensional spherical distribution generated from the density generator $g(\cdot)$.

The following result explores the conditional distributions in the case of elliptical random vectors. It extends Property 1.8.4 to the class of elliptical laws. For a proof, see Valdez and Dhaene (2004).

Property 1.8.14

Let the random vector $\boldsymbol{Y}$ be $\mathcal{E}ll_n(\boldsymbol{\mu}, \boldsymbol{\Sigma}, \phi)$ distributed with density generator $g_n(\cdot)$. Define Λ_α and Λ_β to be linear combinations of the components of $\boldsymbol{X}$, that is, $\Lambda_\alpha = \boldsymbol{\alpha}^t\boldsymbol{X}$ and $\Lambda_\beta = \boldsymbol{\beta}^t\boldsymbol{X}$, for some $\boldsymbol{\alpha}$ and $\boldsymbol{\beta} \in \mathbb{R}^n$. Then, we have that

$$(\Lambda_\alpha, \Lambda_\beta) \sim \mathcal{E}ll_2(\boldsymbol{\mu}_{\alpha\beta}, \boldsymbol{\Sigma}_{\alpha\beta}, \phi), \tag{1.50}$$

where

$$\boldsymbol{\mu}_{\alpha\beta} = \begin{pmatrix} \mu_\alpha \\ \mu_\beta \end{pmatrix} = \begin{pmatrix} \boldsymbol{\alpha}^t\boldsymbol{\mu} \\ \boldsymbol{\beta}^t\boldsymbol{\mu} \end{pmatrix}, \tag{1.51}$$

$$\begin{aligned} \boldsymbol{\Sigma}_{\alpha\beta} &= \begin{pmatrix} \sigma_\alpha^2 & r_{\alpha\beta}\sigma_\alpha\sigma_\beta \\ r_{\alpha\beta}\sigma_\alpha\sigma_\beta & \sigma_\beta^2 \end{pmatrix} \\ &= \begin{pmatrix} \boldsymbol{\alpha}^t\boldsymbol{\Sigma}\boldsymbol{\alpha} & \boldsymbol{\alpha}^t\boldsymbol{\Sigma}\boldsymbol{\beta} \\ \boldsymbol{\alpha}^t\boldsymbol{\Sigma}\boldsymbol{\beta} & \boldsymbol{\beta}^t\boldsymbol{\Sigma}\boldsymbol{\beta} \end{pmatrix}. \end{aligned} \tag{1.52}$$

Furthermore , given $\Lambda_\beta = \lambda$, the rv Λ_α has the univariate elliptical distribution

$$\mathcal{E}ll_1\left(\mu_\alpha + r_{\alpha\beta}\frac{\sigma_\alpha}{\sigma_\beta}(\lambda - \mu_\beta), (1 - r_{\alpha\beta}^2)\sigma_\alpha^2, \phi_a\right), \tag{1.53}$$

for some characteristic generator $\phi_a(\cdot)$ depending on $a = (\lambda - \mu_\beta)^2/\sigma_\beta^2$.

From this result, it follows that the characteristic function of $\Lambda_\alpha | \Lambda_\beta = \lambda$ is given by

$$\mathbb{E}\left[\exp(it\Lambda_\alpha) | \Lambda_\beta = \lambda\right] = \exp\left(i\,\mu_{\Lambda_\alpha|\Lambda_\beta=\lambda}\, t\right)\phi_a\left(\sigma^2_{\Lambda_\alpha|\Lambda_\beta=\lambda}\, t^2\right),$$

where

$$\mu_{\Lambda_\alpha|\Lambda_\beta=\lambda} = \mu_\alpha + r_{\alpha\beta}\frac{\sigma_\alpha}{\sigma_\beta}(\lambda - \mu_\beta)$$

and

$$\sigma^2_{\Lambda_\alpha|\Lambda_\beta=\lambda} = (1 - r_{\alpha\beta}^2)\sigma_\alpha^2.$$

1.9 COMONOTONICITY

1.9.1 Definition

A standard way of modelling situations where individual rvs $X_1, \ldots, X_n$ are subject to the same external mechanism is to use a secondary mixing distribution. The uncertainty about the external mechanism is then described by a structure variable z, which is a realization of an rv Z and acts as a (random) parameter of the distribution of $\boldsymbol{X}$. The aggregate claims can then be seen as a two-stage process: first, the external parameter $Z=z$ is drawn from the df F_Z of Z. The claim amount of each individual risk X_i is then obtained as a realization from the conditional df of X_i given $Z=z$. This construction is known as a common mixture model and will be studied in detail in Chapter 7.

A special type of mixing model is the case where given $Z=z$, the claim amounts X_i are degenerate on x_i, where the $x_i = x_i(z)$ are non-decreasing in z. Such a model is in a sense an extreme form of a mixing model, as in this case the external parameter $Z=z$ completely determines the aggregate claims. In such a case, the risks $X_1, \ldots, X_n$ are said to be comonotonic. Comonotonicity is discussed in Kaas *et al.* (2001, Section 10.6). The definition of this concept is recalled next.

Definition 1.9.1. A random vector $\boldsymbol{X}$ is comonotonic if and only if there exist an rv Z and non-decreasing functions $t_1, t_2, \ldots, t_n$, such that

$$\boldsymbol{X} =_d \big(t_1(Z), t_2(Z), \ldots, t_n(Z)\big)^t.$$

∇

In this book, the notation $(X_1^c, \ldots, X_n^c)$ will be used to indicate a comonotonic random vector. The support of $\boldsymbol{X}^c$ is

$$\mathcal{S}_{\boldsymbol{X}^c} = \left\{\big(F_{X_1}^{-1}(p), F_{X_2}^{-1}(p), \ldots, F_{X_n}^{-1}(p)\big) \,|\, 0 < p < 1\right\}.$$

Note that this support is an ordered set, since $\boldsymbol{s}, \boldsymbol{t} \in \mathcal{S}_{\boldsymbol{X}^c}$ entails either $\boldsymbol{s} \leq \boldsymbol{t}$ or $\boldsymbol{s} \geq \boldsymbol{t}$ componentwise.

1.9.2 Comonotonicity and Fréchet upper bound

Fréchet spaces offer the natural framework for studying dependence. These spaces gather together all the probability distributions with fixed univariate marginals. Elements in a given Fréchet space only differ in their dependence structures, and not in their marginal behaviours.

Definition 1.9.2. Let $F_1, F_2, \ldots, F_n$ be univariate dfs. The Fréchet space $\mathcal{R}_n(F_1, F_2, \ldots, F_n)$ consists of all the n-dimensional (dfs $F_{\boldsymbol{X}}$ of) random vectors $\boldsymbol{X}$ possessing $F_1, F_2, \ldots, F_n$ as marginal dfs, that is,

$$F_i(x) = \Pr[X_i \leq x], \quad x \in \mathbb{R}, \quad i = 1, 2, \ldots, n.$$

∇

The elements of $\mathcal{R}_n(F_1, F_2, \ldots, F_n)$ are bounded above by a special multivariate df, called the Fréchet upper bound, as shown in the next result.

Property 1.9.3
Define the Fréchet upper bound as

$$W_n(\boldsymbol{x}) = \min\{F_1(x_1), F_2(x_2), \ldots, F_n(x_n)\}, \quad \boldsymbol{x} \in \mathbb{R}^n.$$

Then the inequality

$$F_{\boldsymbol{X}}(\boldsymbol{x}) \leq W_n(\boldsymbol{x}) \tag{1.54}$$

holds for all $\boldsymbol{x} \in \mathbb{R}^n$ and $\boldsymbol{X} \in \mathcal{R}_n(F_1, F_2, \ldots, F_n)$.

Proof. This is obvious since $\cap_{i=1}^n [X_i \leq x_i] \subseteq [X_j \leq x_j]$ for any $j \in \{1, \ldots, n\}$. □

Note that W_n is an element of $\mathcal{R}_n(F_1, F_2, \cdots, F_n)$. Indeed, given an rv $U \sim \mathcal{U}ni(0, 1)$, W_n is the df of

$$(F_1^{-1}(U), F_2^{-1}(U), \ldots, F_n^{-1}(U)) \in \mathcal{R}_n(F_1, F_2, \ldots, F_n),$$

since

$$\begin{aligned} &\Pr\left[F_1^{-1}(U) \leq x_1, F_2^{-1}(U) \leq x_2, \ldots, F_n^{-1}(U) \leq x_n\right] \\ &= \Pr\left[U \leq \min\{F_1(x_1), F_2(x_2), \ldots, F_n(x_n)\}\right] = W_n(\boldsymbol{x}). \end{aligned}$$

We have thus proven the next result, which relates comonotonicity to the Fréchet upper bound.

Proposition 1.9.4
A random vector $\boldsymbol{X} \in \mathcal{R}_n(F_1, F_2, \ldots, F_n)$ is comonotonic if, and only if, its multivariate df is W_n.

Remark 1.9.5. Early results about dependence are due to Höffding (1940) and Fréchet (1951). Until recently, the work of Höffding did not receive the attention it deserved, due primarily to the fact that his papers were published in relatively obscure German journals at the outbreak of World War II. Unaware of Höffding's work, Fréchet independently rediscovered many of the same results, which has led to terms such as 'Fréchet spaces' and 'Fréchet bounds'.

Fréchet bounds have attracted a lot of interest in different fields of application. They have been extended in a number of ways during the last few decades. See Nelsen *et al.* (2004) for an illustration. ∇

1.10 MUTUAL EXCLUSIVITY

1.10.1 Definition

In this section we introduce, following Dhaene and Denuit (1999), a kind of opposite of comonotonicity, namely mutual exclusivity. Note that we restrict ourselves to risks, that is, to non-negative rvs in this section. We will work in Fréchet spaces $\mathcal{R}_n^+(F_1, F_2, \ldots, F_n)$, where the F_i are such that $F_1(0-) = F_2(0-) = \ldots = F_n(0-) = 0$.

Roughly speaking, the risks $X_1, X_2, \ldots, X_n$ are said to be mutually exclusive when at most one of them can be different from zero. This can be considered as a sort of dual notion of comonotonicity. Indeed, the knowledge that one risk assumes a positive value directly implies that all the others vanish.

Definition 1.10.1. The multivariate risk $\boldsymbol{X}$ in $\mathcal{R}_n^+(F_1, F_2, \ldots, F_n)$ is said to be mutually exclusive when

$$\Pr\left[X_i > 0, X_j > 0\right] = 0 \text{ for all } i \neq j.$$

∇

We observe that mutual exclusivity of $\boldsymbol{X}$ means that its multivariate pdf $f_{\boldsymbol{X}}$ is concentrated on the axes.

Remark 1.10.2. In the bivariate case, the concept of countermonotonicity has attracted a lot of interest. Let us recall that the bivariate risk is said to be countermonotonic if it is distributed as $(t_1(Z), t_2(Z))$ for some rv Z, an increasing function t_1 and a decreasing function t_2. Therefore, increasing the value of one component tends to decrease the value of the other. Countermonotonicity does not extend to higher dimensions. This is why mutual exclusivity has been used instead for dimensions higher than 2. ∇

1.10.2 Fréchet lower bound

The elements of $\mathcal{R}_n(F_1, F_2, \ldots, F_n)$ are bounded below by a special function, called the Fréchet lower bound, as shown in the next result.

Property 1.10.3
Let us define the Fréchet lower bound as

$$M_n(\boldsymbol{x}) = \max\left\{\sum_{i=1}^{n} F_i(x_i) - (n-1), 0\right\}, \quad \boldsymbol{x} \in \mathbb{R}^n.$$

Then the inequality

$$M_n(\boldsymbol{x}) \leq F_{\boldsymbol{X}}(\boldsymbol{x}) \tag{1.55}$$

holds for all $\boldsymbol{x} \in \mathbb{R}^n$ and $\boldsymbol{X} \in \mathcal{R}_n(F_1, F_2, \ldots, F_n)$.

Proof. Obviously, $\Pr[\cup_{i=1}^{n}\overline{A}_i] \leq \sum_{i=1}^{n}\Pr[\overline{A}_i]$ for any choice of events $A_1, A_2, \ldots, A_n$. Therefore, $\Pr[\cap_{i=1}^{n}A_i] \geq \sum_{i=1}^{n}\Pr[A_i] - n + 1$. Now take $A_i = [X_i \leq x_i]$, $i = 1, 2, \ldots, n$. □

Remark 1.10.4. In the bivariate case, the Fréchet lower bound M_2 is an element of $\mathcal{R}_2(F_1, F_2)$. Specifically, M_2 is the df of $(F_1^{-1}(U), F_2^{-1}(1-U))$, where $U \sim \mathcal{U}ni(0, 1)$. This is easily deduced from

$$\begin{aligned}\Pr[F_1^{-1}(U) \leq x_1, F_2^{-1}(1-U) \leq x_2] &= \Pr[U \leq F_1(x_1), 1 - U \leq F_2(x_2)] \\ &= M_2(x_1, x_2).\end{aligned}$$

When $n \geq 3$, however, M_n is no longer always a df (it is just a signed measure), as shown by the following counterexample proposed by Tchen (1980): for $n = 3$, take X_1, X_2 and $X_3 \sim \mathcal{U}ni(0, 1)$; then the 'probability' that $\boldsymbol{X}$ lies in $[0.5, 1] \times [0.5, 1] \times [0.5, 1]$ is equal to

$$\begin{aligned}&1 - \Pr[X_1 < 0.5 \text{ or } X_2 < 0.5 \text{ or } X_3 < 0.5] \\ &= 1 - F_1(0.5) - F_2(0.5) - F_3(0.5) + F_{(X_1,X_2)}(0.5, 0.5) + F_{(X_1,X_3)}(0.5, 0.5) \\ &+ F_{(X_2,X_3)}(0.5, 0.5) - F_{(X_1,X_2,X_3)}(0.5, 0.5, 0.5) = -0.5\end{aligned}$$

when the dependence structure is described by M_3. Hence, M_3 cannot be a proper df. ∇

From inequalities (1.54) and (1.55) we can derive many useful results, such as the following. They provide bounds on probabilities involving the minimum and the maximum of a set of correlated risks.

Corollary 1.10.5
For any $\boldsymbol{X} \in \mathcal{R}_n(F_1, F_2, \ldots, F_n)$,

$$\begin{aligned}&1 - \min\{F_1(x), F_2(x), \ldots, F_n(x)\} \\ &\leq \Pr[\max\{X_1, X_2, \ldots, X_n\} > x] \leq \min\left\{1, \sum_{i=1}^{n}(1 - F_i(x))\right\}, \text{ for all } x \in \mathbb{R},\end{aligned}$$

and

$$\begin{aligned}&\max\{F_1(x), F_2(x), \ldots, F_n(x)\} \\ &\leq \Pr[\min\{X_1, X_2, \ldots, X_n\} \leq x] \leq \min\left\{1, \sum_{i=1}^{n}F_i(x)\right\}, \text{ for all } x \in \mathbb{R}.\end{aligned}$$

These inequalities also provide useful bounds on the distribution of the largest and smallest claims in an insurance portfolio consisting of dependent risks. Therefore, they can be used to get bounds on the premium of an $LCR(1)$ treaty. By the latter we mean a reinsurance agreement covering the largest claim occuring during a given reference period (one year, say). Of course, when the X_i are thought of as being time-until-death random variables, these inequalities also yield bounds on life insurance policies or annuities based on either a joint-life status or a last-survivor status. These bounds have been used by Dhaene, Vanneste and Wolthuis (2000) in order to find extremal joint-life and last-survivor statuses.

1.10.3 Existence of Fréchet lower bounds in Fréchet spaces

As shown in Remark 1.10.4, Fréchet lower bounds are not necessarily dfs. The following result provides us with necessary and sufficient conditions for M_n to be a df in $\mathcal{R}_n(F_1, F_2, \ldots, F_n)$.

Proposition 1.10.6
A necessary and sufficient condition for M_n to be a proper df in $\mathcal{R}_n(F_1, F_2, \ldots, F_n)$ is that, for each $\boldsymbol{x}$ with $0 < F_j(x_j) < 1$ for $j = 1, 2, \ldots, n$, either

$$\sum_{j=1}^{n} F_j(x_j) \leq 1 \tag{1.56}$$

or

$$\sum_{j=1}^{n} \overline{F}_j(x_j) \leq 1 \tag{1.57}$$

holds true.

For a proof of this result, we refer the reader to Joe (1997, Theorem 3.7).

1.10.4 Fréchet lower bounds and maxima

Despite the fact that M_n is not always a proper df, Tchen (1980, Theorem 4) proved that there exists $\boldsymbol{X} \in \mathcal{R}_n(F_1, F_2, \ldots, F_n)$ achieving the lower bound M_n when all the x_i are equal. This is formally stated in the next result.

Proposition 1.10.7
There exists $\boldsymbol{X} \in \mathcal{R}_n(F_1, F_2, \ldots, F_n)$ such that

$$\Pr[\max\{X_1, X_2, \ldots, X_n\} \leq x] = M_n(x, x, \ldots, x)$$

for any $x \in \mathbb{R}$.

1.10.5 Mutual exclusivity and Fréchet lower bound

A Fréchet space does not always contain mutually exclusive risks. A necessary and sufficient condition is provided in the following result.

Proposition 1.10.8
A Fréchet space $\mathcal{R}_n^+(F_1, F_2, \ldots, F_n)$ contains mutually exclusive risks if, and only if, it satisfies

$$\sum_{i=1}^{n} q_i \leq 1 \text{ where } q_i = 1 - F_i(0), \qquad i = 1, 2, \ldots, n. \tag{1.58}$$

Proof. First, assume that $\boldsymbol{X}$ is mutually exclusive and belongs to $\mathcal{R}_n^+(F_1, F_2, \ldots, F_n)$. Define the indicator variables $I_1, I_2, \ldots, I_n$ as

$$I_i = \begin{cases} 1, & \text{if } X_i > 0, \\ 0, & \text{if } X_i = 0, \end{cases}$$

so that $I_i \sim \mathcal{B}er(q_i)$, $i = 1, 2, \ldots, n$. Note that since $\boldsymbol{X}$ is mutually exclusive,

$$\begin{aligned} \Pr[I_1 = I_2 = \ldots = I_n = 0] &= 1 - \Pr[I_1 = 1 \text{or } I_2 = 1 \text{or} \ldots \text{or} I_n = 1] \\ &= 1 - \sum_{i=1}^{n} q_i, \end{aligned}$$

so that (1.58) has to be fulfilled.

Conversely, assume that $\mathcal{R}_n^+(F_1, F_2, \ldots, F_n)$ satisfies (1.58). From Proposition 1.10.6, we know that M_n is a df in $\mathcal{R}_n^+(F_1, F_2, \ldots, F_n)$. Consider $\boldsymbol{X} \in \mathcal{R}_n^+(F_1, F_2, \ldots, F_n)$ with df M_n. Then we find that

$$\Pr[X_i = 0, X_j = 0] = 1 - q_i - q_j \text{ for all } i \neq j,$$

whence it follows that

$$\Pr[X_i > 0, X_j > 0] = 0 \text{ for all } i \neq j,$$

which, in turn, means that $\boldsymbol{X}$ is mutually exclusive. □

Let us prove the following characterization of mutual exclusivity, which relates this notion to the Fréchet lower bound (just as comonotonicity corresponds to the Fréchet upper bound). More precisely, we prove that when (1.58) is fulfilled, the multivariate df of the mutually exclusive risks in the Fréchet space $\mathcal{R}_n^+(F_1, F_2, \ldots, F_n)$ is given by the Fréchet lower bound M_n.

Proposition 1.10.9
Consider a Fréchet space $\mathcal{R}_n^+(F_1, F_2, \ldots, F_n)$ satisfying (1.58) and let $\boldsymbol{X} \in \mathcal{R}_n^+(F_1, F_2, \ldots, F_n)$. Then, $\boldsymbol{X}$ is mutually exclusive if, and only if,

$$F_{\boldsymbol{X}}(\boldsymbol{x}) = M_n(\boldsymbol{x}), \quad \boldsymbol{x} \in \mathbb{R}^n.$$

Proof. Assume that $\boldsymbol{X}$ is mutually exclusive. Defining the indicator variables I_i as in the proof of Proposition 1.10.8, we have for $\boldsymbol{x} \geq \boldsymbol{0}$ that

$$\begin{aligned} F_{\boldsymbol{X}}(\boldsymbol{x}) &= \sum_{i=1}^{n} \Pr[X_1 \leq x_1, X_2 \leq x_2, \ldots, X_n \leq x_n | I_i = 1] \Pr[I_i = 1] \\ &\quad + \Pr[I_1 = I_2 = \ldots = I_n = 0] \\ &= \sum_{i=1}^{n} \Pr[X_i \leq x_i | I_i = 1] q_i + 1 - \sum_{i=1}^{n} q_i \\ &= \sum_{i=1}^{n} (F_i(x_i) - F_i(0)) + 1 - \sum_{i=1}^{n} q_i \\ &= \sum_{i=1}^{n} F_i(x_i) + 1 - n = M_n(\boldsymbol{x}), \end{aligned}$$

which proves that the condition is necessary. That it is also sufficient follows from the second part of the proof of Proposition 1.10.8. □

Combining Propositions 1.10.8 and 1.10.9, we find that a Fréchet space $\mathcal{R}_n^+(F_1, F_2, \ldots, F_n)$ has the property that the Fréchet lower bound is the unique df of $\mathcal{R}_n^+(F_1, F_2, \ldots, F_n)$ with pdf concentrated on the axes if, and only if, it satisfies (1.58).

Remark 1.10.10. In view of Remarks 1.10.2 and 1.10.4 we have that the bivariate risk (X_1, X_2) is countermonotonic if, and only if, it has M_2 as joint df. For instance, with unit uniform marginals, $(U, 1-U)$ with $U \sim \mathcal{U}ni(0,1)$ is countermonotonic but not mutually exclusive. Note that in this case, (1.58) is not satisfied. ∇

1.11 EXERCISES

Exercise 1.11.1. Show that

$$F_X(x) = F_1(x_1)F_2(x_2)\left\{1 + \epsilon\overline{F}_1(x_1)\overline{F}_2(x_2)\right\}, \quad x \in \mathbb{R}^2,$$

is a two-dimensional df whose marginals are F_1 and F_2 for $0 < \epsilon < 1$.

Exercise 1.11.2. Prove that the following chain of equivalences holds true for any $x \in \mathbb{R}^2$: for any $X \in \mathcal{R}_2(F_1, F_2)$,

(i) $F_X(x_1, x_2) = \min\{F_1(x_1), F_2(x_2)\} \Leftrightarrow \overline{F}_X(x_1, x_2) = \min\{\overline{F}_1(x_1), \overline{F}_2(x_2)\} \Leftrightarrow \Pr[X_1 \leq x_1, X_2 > x_2] = \max\{F_1(x_1) + \overline{F}_2(x_2) - 1, 0\}$;

(ii) $F_X(x_1, x_2) = \max\{F_1(x_1) + F_2(x_2) - 1, 0\} \Leftrightarrow \overline{F}_X(x_1, x_2) = \max\{\overline{F}_1(x_1) + \overline{F}_2(x_2) - 1, 0\} \Leftrightarrow \Pr[X_1 \leq x_1, X_2 > x_2] = \min\{F_1(x_1), \overline{F}_2(x_2)\}$.

Exercise 1.11.3. Let $(X_1, X_2) \in \mathcal{R}_2(F_1, F_2)$ be a random pair with continuous marginals. Prove that:

(i) the random pair (X_1, X_2) has df W_2 if, and only if,

$$(X_1, X_2) =_d (X_1, F_2^{-1}(F_1(X_1)));$$

(ii) the random pair (X_1, X_2) has df M_2 if, and only if,

$$(X_1, X_2) =_d (X_1, F_2^{-1}(\overline{F}_1(X_1))).$$

Exercise 1.11.4. Let X be the value of a share at a future time t, $t \geq 0$. Consider European options with expiration date t, exercise price d and the share as underlying asset. Let $Y^{(c)}$ be the payoff of the call option at time t, that is,

$$Y^{(c)} = \max\{0, X - d\}.$$

Similarly, let $Y^{(p)}$ be the payoff of the put option at time t, that is,

$$Y^{(p)} = \max\{0, d - X\}.$$

Show that $(X, Y^{(c)})$ are comonotonic, while both $(X, Y^{(p)})$ and $(Y^{(p)}, Y^{(c)})$ have M_2 as df.

Exercise 1.11.5. Let $X=(X_1, X_2, X_3) \in \mathcal{R}_3(F_1, F_2, F_3)$, for some continuous univariate dfs F_1, F_2 and F_3. Prove the following assertions:

(i) If (X_1, X_2) and (X_2, X_3) are both comonotonic then so is (X_1, X_3) and $F_X \equiv W_3$.

(ii) If (X_1, X_2) is comonotonic and (X_2, X_3) is countermonotonic then (X_1, X_3) is countermonotonic and

$$F_X(x) = \max\Big\{0, \min\{F_1(x_1), F_2(x_2)\} + F_3(x_3) - 1\Big\}.$$

(iii) If (X_1, X_2) and (X_2, X_3) are both countermonotonic then (X_1, X_3) is comonotonic and

$$F_X(x) = \max\Big\{0, \min\{F_1(x_1), F_3(x_3)\} + F_2(x_2) - 1\Big\}.$$

Exercise 1.11.6. Show that the inverse df $F_{S^c}^{-1}$ of a sum S^c of comonotonic rvs $X_1^c, X_2^c, \ldots, X_n^c$ is given by

$$F_{S^c}^{-1}(p) = \sum_{i=1}^{n} F_{X_i}^{-1}(p), \qquad 0 < p < 1. \tag{1.59}$$

Exercise 1.11.7. Assume in Exercise 1.11.6 that $X_i^c \sim \mathcal{E}xp(1/b_i)$, $i=1, 2, \ldots, n$. Show that

$$F_{S^c}^{-1}(p) = -b_\bullet \ln(1-p),$$

where $b_\bullet = \sum_{i=1}^n b_i$, so that $S^c \sim \mathcal{E}xp(1/b_\bullet)$. In words, the comonotonic sum of exponentially distributed rvs still has an exponential distribution.

Exercise 1.11.8. Let $F_{i_1 i_2 \ldots i_k}$ denote the marginal df of $(X_{i_1}, X_{i_2}, \ldots, X_{i_k})$, $1 \le i_1 < i_2 < \ldots < i_k \le n$, $k=1, 2, \ldots, n$, that is,

$$F_{i_1 i_2 \ldots i_k}(x_{i_1}, x_{i_2}, \ldots, x_{i_k}) = \Pr[X_{i_1} \le x_{i_1}, X_{i_2} \le x_{i_2}, \ldots, X_{i_k} \le x_{i_k}],$$

$x_{i_1}, x_{i_2}, \ldots, x_{i_k} \in \mathbb{R}$. Assume that all the marginals $F_{i_1 i_2 \ldots i_k}$ are compatible (i.e., that there exists at least one proper multivariate cdf F_X with these marginals). For any $\boldsymbol{x} \in \mathbb{R}^3$, show that the inequalities

$$\begin{aligned} F_X(x) \le F_U(x) \equiv \min\Big\{&F_{12}(x_1, x_2), F_{13}(x_1, x_3), F_{23}(x_2, x_3),\\ &1 - F_1(x_1) - F_2(x_2) - F_3(x_3) + F_{12}(x_1, x_2) + F_{13}(x_1, x_3) + F_{23}(x_2, x_3)\Big\} \end{aligned}$$

and

$$\begin{aligned} F_X(x) \ge F_L(x) \equiv \max\Big\{&0, F_{12}(x_1, x_2) + F_{13}(x_1, x_3) - F_1(x_1),\\ &F_{12}(x_1, x_2) + F_{23}(x_2, x_3) - F_2(x_2), F_{13}(x_1, x_3) + F_{23}(x_2, x_3) - F_3(x_3)\Big\} \end{aligned}$$

hold for any $\boldsymbol{X} \in \mathcal{R}_3(F_1, F_2, F_3)$.

Exercise 1.11.9. Suppose all the bivariate marginals of $\boldsymbol{X} \in \mathcal{R}_n(F_1, F_2, \ldots, F_n)$ are Fréchet upper bounds, that is,

$$F_{i_1 i_2}(x_{i_1}, x_{i_2}) = \min\left\{F_{i_1}(x_{i_1}), F_{i_2}(x_{i_2})\right\} \text{ for all} 1 \leq i_1 < i_2 \leq n.$$

Show that $F_{\boldsymbol{X}} \equiv W_n$, that is, $\boldsymbol{X}$ is comonotonic.

Exercise 1.11.10. Show that

$$F_{S_n}(x) = M_n(x, x, \ldots, x) \tag{1.60}$$

if $\boldsymbol{X}$ is mutually exclusive.

Exercise 1.11.11. A franchise deductible divides the risk X in two parts $X = X_1 + X_2$, with the retained part given by

$$X_1 = \begin{cases} X, & \text{if } X < d, \\ 0, & \text{if } X \geq d, \end{cases}$$

and the insured part by

$$X_2 = \begin{cases} 0, & \text{if } X < d, \\ X, & \text{if } X \geq d. \end{cases}$$

Show that X_1 and X_2 are mutually exclusive.

2
Measuring Risk

Developed economies offer instruments to buy and sell risks as if they were goods. Insurance companies and banks are willing to buy risks at specific prices, reflecting their respective dangerousness. This chapter reviews different methods for measuring risk. Some scalar risk measures are presented: value-at-risk (commonly abbreviated VaR), tail VaR, conditional tail expectation, conditional VaR, expected shortfalls, zero-utility premiums, Esscher risk measures, and (Yaari–)Wang risk measures. Also, their respective properties are discussed: non-negative loading, non-excessive loading (or no ripoff), translativity, constancy (or no unjustified loading), subadditivity, comonotonic additivity, positive homogeneity, monotonicity, continuity with respect to convergence in distribution, and objectivity. Some of these risk measures are based on expected utility theory, others on distorted expectation theory.

2.1 INTRODUCTION

For centuries, the function of insurers and reinsurers has been to sell risk coverage. In the last few decades, they have been joined in this activity by banks and financial institutions. Today, both groups face the same challenge: to collect and manage risks by looking for markets where these risks may be hedged or unbundled.

When hedges do not exist, for instance due to the structural incompleteness of the corresponding market, a careful measure of risk needs to be established and, if necessary, prudent reserves built up. Companies nowadays take an interest in the recently developed techniques for measuring the risk and assessing profitable areas of business. Their management is faced continually with the difficult task of reconciling the conflicting interests of clients and policyholders on the one hand, and shareholders on the other. The former are interested in strong financial wealth, while the latter require a return on equity that is in line with the risk inherent in their investment.

Numerous risk measures have been proposed in insurance and finance, ranging from the most elementary to the most elaborate. As long as risk measurement is based on an axiomatic approach, it is senseless to look for the 'right' risk measure (since appropriate risk measures are those complying with the axioms). Different classes of risk measures represent different schools of thought. Nevertheless, in practice, the appropriate measure to use to quantify risk for insurance portfolios continues to be a subject for debate. Recent years have witnessed the emergence in the financial literature of a sophisticated theory of risk measures, as a

Actuarial Theory for Dependent Risks M. Denuit, J. Dhaene, M. Goovaerts and R. Kaas

means of determining capital requirements for the holders of risky portfolios. A landmark in this development was the axiomatic approach to risk measures. The functional forms and fundamental properties or risk measures have been extensively studied in the actuarial literature since 1970, in the guise of premium calculation principles (see Kaas *et al.* 2001, Chapter 5). The present chapter outlines a range of specific risk measures and studies their respective properties.

Some risk measures are derived using methods for choice under risk. In this chapter, we present two different approaches to decision-making under risk. These approaches have in common that the preference relations of a decision-maker, which are qualitative in nature, follow from simple comparisons of numerical quantities to be associated with the alternative choices under consideration. The first approach is the classical expected utility theory that originated in the St Petersburg paradox and was axiomatized by von Neumann and Morgenstern (1947). Expected utility theory is extensively reviewed in Kaas *et al.* (2001, Chapter 1). In the framework of expected utility theory, a utility function assigns a value to any monetary amount. Utility functions are of a subjective nature, they reflect the preferences of individuals or insurance companies. Moreover, different individuals usually have different utility functions, even if all the reasonable utility functions have to share some common properties, such as non-decreasingness (which expresses the fact that every decision-maker prefers more wealth to less wealth). Expected utility theory has greatly contributed to our understanding of the economics of risk and uncertainty over the past several decades. Risk measures originating in the expected utility theory framework are obtained via economic indifference arguments: a prominent example is the zero-utility premium principle.

The second approach we will present is Yaari's (1987) dual theory for choice under risk. Yaari developed a parallel theory by modifying the independence axiom of von Neumann and Morgenstern (1947): instead of requiring independence with respect to probability mixtures of risky prospects, he required independence with respect to direct mixing of payments of risky prospects. In Yaari's framework, the concept of the distortion function emerges, which can be considered as the parallel to the concept of the utility function in the classical expected utility theory. In Yaari's dual theory, attitudes towards risks are characterized by a distortion applied to probability distribution functions, in contrast to expected utility theory in which attitudes towards risks are characterized by a utility function of wealth: risky prospects are evaluated in this theory by a cardinal numerical scale which resembles an expected utility, except that the roles of the payments and probabilities are reversed. Our purpose is to describe and compare these two theories of decision-making under risk, as well as to illustrate their applicability to actuarial problems.

Note that Goovaerts *et al.* (2003) have proposed a unified approach to generating risk measures. More precisely, they showed that many risk measures and premium principles can be derived by minimizing a Markov bound for the tail probability. We refer the reader to this paper for more details.

2.2 RISK MEASURES

2.2.1 Definition

Since risks are modelled as non-negative rvs (see Definition 1.4.3), measuring risk is equivalent to establishing a correspondence ϱ between the space of rvs and non-negative real numbers $\mathbb{R}^+$. The real number denoting a general risk measure associated with the risk

X will henceforth be denoted as $\varrho[X]$. Thus, a risk measure is nothing but a functional that assigns a non-negative real number to a risk. See Szegö (2004) for an overview.

It is essential to understand which aspect of the riskiness associated with the uncertain outcome the risk measure attempts to quantify. No risk measure can grasp the whole picture of the danger inherent in some real-life situation, but each of them will focus on a particular aspect of the risk. There is a parallel with mathematical statistics, where characteristics of distributions may have quite different meanings and uses – for example, the mean to measure central tendency, the variance to measure spread, the skewness to reflect asymmetry and the peakedness to measure the thickness of the tails.

In this chapter, we will focus on risk measures that can be used for determining provisions and capital requirements in order to avoid insolvency. In that respect, we will concentrate on risk measures that measure upper tails of distribution functions. For simplicity, we consider market models without interest rates; it is straightforward, however, to extend all definitions and results to the 'real' case, by appropriate discounting.

We are now ready to state the definition of a risk measure.

Definition 2.2.1. A risk measure is a functional ϱ mapping a risk X to a non-negative real number $\varrho[X]$, possibly infinite, representing the extra cash which has to be added to X to make it acceptable. ∇

The idea is that ϱ quantifies the riskiness of X: large values of $\varrho[X]$ tell us that X is 'dangerous'. Specifically, if X is a possible loss of some financial portfolio over a time horizon, we interpret $\varrho[X]$ as the amount of capital that should be added as a buffer to this portfolio so that it becomes acceptable to an internal or external risk controller. In such a case, $\varrho[X]$ is the risk capital of the portfolio. Such risk measures are used for determining provisions and capital requirements in order to avoid insolvency; see Panjer (1998).

2.2.2 *Premium calculation principles*

Risk measures are in many respects akin to actuarial premium calculation principles. For an insurance company exposed to a liability X, a premium calculation principle Π gives the minimum amount $\Pi[X]$ that the insurer must raise from the insured in order that it is in the insurer's interest to proceed with the contract. Premium principles are thus prominent examples of possible risk measures. Their characteristic is that the number resulting from their application to some insurance risk X is a candidate for the premium associated with the contract providing coverage against X. The foundations of premium principles were laid by Bühlmann (1970), Gerber (1979); for a more comprehensive discussion, see Goovaerts, De Vijlder and Haezendonck (1984). See also Kaas *et al.* (2001, Chapter 5) for an overview.

Premium principles are the most common risk measures in actuarial science. Although there is a consensus (at least if everyone agrees on the risk distribution) about the net premium (which is the expected claim amount), there are many ways to add a loading to it to get the gross premium. The safety loading added to the expected claim cost by the company reflects the danger associated to the risk borne by the insurer. Premium calculation principles are thus closely related to risk measures. Indeed, those principles have to express the insurer's feelings about the risk he bears. The premium for a less attractive risk should exceed the premium for a more attractive risk. Therefore, a premium calculation principle is a particular case of a risk measure.

Goovaerts, De Vijlder and Hazendonck (1984) studied a set of premium calculation principles, most of which relate to utility theory, namely, the net premium principle, expected value principle, maximum loss principle, variance principle, standard deviation principle, exponential principle, mean value principle, zero-utility principle, Swiss principle, Orlicz principle and Esscher principle. We will discuss some of these concepts further in this chapter.

2.2.3 Desirable properties

Even if Definition 2.2.1 is very general, risk measures have to satisfy certain axioms, such as those discussed in this section. Among the enormous group of statistical characteristics which can be associated to the risks expectation, median, variance, mean absolute deviation, coefficient of variation, Gini measure, etc. – only some qualify as acceptable risk measures. An axiomatic approach to the study of risk measures in economics can be found in Fishburn (1982). In actuarial science, Goovaerts, De Vijlder and Hazendonck (1984) pioneered the systematic study of the properties that any premium principle should possess. Subsequently, numerous authors suggested various requirements that any risk measure should satisfy. We provide hereafter a list of reasonable (non-independent) requirements that a risk measure should fulfil and discuss their interpretation.

2.2.3.1 Non-excessive loading (or no-ripoff)

$\varrho[X] \leq \max[X] = F_X^{-1}(1)$ for all rvs X. Clearly, it is useless to keep more capital than the maximal loss value.

2.2.3.2 Non-negative loading

$\varrho[X] \geq \mathbb{E}[X]$ for all rvs X. The minimal capital must exceed the expected loss, otherwise ruin becomes certain (under the conditions of the law of large numbers).

2.2.3.3 Translativity

$\varrho[X+c] = \varrho[X] + c$ for all rvs X and each constant c. Recall that a risk measure has been defined as a functional giving the amount of safely invested capital that the holder of a risky position has to add to this position to make it acceptable. Then it is obvious than any increase in the liability by a deterministic amount c should result in the same increase in the capital. Translativity implies the natural property

$$\varrho\big[X - \varrho[X]\big] = 0,$$

that is, when we add $\varrho[X]$ to the initial position $-X$, we obtain a 'neutral' position.

2.2.3.4 Constancy (or no unjustified loading)

Whatever the constant c, we should have $\varrho[c]=c$. In order to deal with a loss of c, it is clear that the insurer only needs to have a capital of the same amount at its disposal. In particular, $\varrho[0]=0$, and the quantity $\varrho[X]$ can be interpreted as a margin requirement, that is, the minimal amount of capital which, if added to X at the beginning of the period and invested in a risk-free asset, makes X 'acceptable'.

2.2.3.5 Subadditivity

$\varrho[X+Y]\leq\varrho[X]+\varrho[Y]$ for all rvs X and Y. The rationale behind subadditivity can be summarized as 'a merger does not create extra risk'. Subadditivity reflects the idea that risk can be reduced by diversification. When equality holds, we speak about additivity. In this case, the dependence structure between X and Y is often specified: we speak about additivity for independent risks or additivity for comonotonic risks (see below).

The diversification effect is then defined as the difference between the sum of the risk measures of stand-alone risks and the risk measure of all risks taken together, that is,

$$\sum_{i=1}^{n}\varrho[X_i]-\varrho\left[\sum_{i=1}^{n}X_i\right].$$

The diversification effect is always positive for subadditive risk measures. The risk allocation problem consists of apportioning the non-negative diversification effect of a portfolio of risks in a fair manner to its components.

Subadditivity is a very convenient mathematical property. In portfolio optimization, subadditivity and positive homogeneity ensure that the risk surface to be minimized in the space of portfolios is convex. Only if the surfaces are convex will they always be endowed with a unique absolute minimum, and only then will the risk minimization process always find a unique, well-diversified, optimal solution.

2.2.3.6 Comonotonic additivity

$\varrho[X+Y]=\varrho[X]+\varrho[Y]$ for all comonotonic rvs X and Y. This requirement is justified by the fact that putting comonotonic risks together never decreases the riskiness of the situation: comonotonic risks are bets on the same event and cannot act as a hedge against each other. Because of the no-hedge condition, insurers are not willing to give a reduction in the risk-load for a combined policy, resulting in comonotonic additivity.

2.2.3.7 Positive homogeneity

$\varrho[cX]=c\varrho[X]$ for all rvs X and any positive constant c. Positive homogeneity is often associated with independence with respect to the monetary unit used.

Positive homogeneity is closely related to comonotonic additivity. Indeed, assume that c is an integer; then comonotonic additivity ensures that

$$\varrho[cX]=\varrho[\underbrace{X+X+\ldots+X}_{c\text{ terms}}]=\varrho[X]+\varrho[X]+\ldots+\varrho[X]=c\varrho[X].$$

2.2.3.8 Monotonicity

$\Pr[X \leq Y] = 1 \Rightarrow \varrho[X] \leq \varrho[Y]$ for all rvs X and Y. Monotonicity says that the amount of capital required as a cushion against the loss X is always smaller than the corresponding amount for Y when Y always exceeds X. Seen from this perspective, monotonicity appears as a very natural property.

2.2.3.9 Continuity with respect to convergence in distribution

Let $\{X_n,\ n = 1, 2, \ldots\}$ be a sequence of risks such that $X_n \to_d X$ as $n \to +\infty$, that is,

$$\lim_{n\to+\infty} F_{X_n}(x) = F_X(x)$$

for every continuity point x of F_X. Then,

$$\lim_{n\to+\infty} \varrho[X_n] = \varrho[X].$$

2.2.3.10 Objectivity

$\varrho[X]$ depends on X only through the df F_X of X. This condition ensures that F_X contains all the information needed to measure the riskiness of X. This property is sometimes called 'law invariance', and phrased as $X =_d Y \Rightarrow \varrho[X] = \varrho[Y]$. It is of crucial importance for applications since it is a necessary condition for a risk measure to be estimable from empirical data. The lack of objectivity therefore seriously jeopardizes any concrete applicability of these risk measures in the financial industry.

Note that some risk measures depend on the actual rv X (and not only on its df F_X). This is the case, for instance, when a risk measure is defined as the supremum of the expectation of X computed over a set of different probability measures (called scenarios). This is essentially what is understood under the notion of coherent risk measures, as shown below; see (2.1).

Remark 2.2.2. The conditions listed above are not independent. For instance, if ϱ is monotone there is no unjustified loading since $X \leq \max[X]$ always holds. ∇

Remark 2.2.3. It should be stressed that even premium calculation principles generally fail to comply with all the requirements listed above: except for the net premium principle, none of the principles considered by Goovaerts, De Vijlder and Hazendonck (1984) satisfies both positive homogeneity and translativity. The Dutch premium principle introduced by Van Heerwaarden and Kaas (1992) is a remarkable exception since it does satisfy these two properties. ∇

Remark 2.2.4. Subadditivity and positive homogeneity are subject to debate. Whether subadditivity describes reality is debatable because it neglects the notion of residual risk completely. Föllmer and Schied (2002) observed that the positive homogeneity and subadditivity properties make risk measures insensitive to liquidity risk. According to Rootzén and Klüppelberg (1999), subadditivity is a convenient mathematical property that does not hold in reality. Similarly, subadditive risk measures turn out to be incompatible with expected utility theory. The behaviour of a risk measure with respect to the aggregation of risks, manifested by the award of diversification discounts and the imposition of penalties, is crucial in that respect. The question can be posed as follows: given two portfolios X and Y and their joint probability distribution, how does the risk of the aggregate $\varrho[X+Y]$ relate to the risks of the individual positions $\varrho[X]$ and $\varrho[Y]$? The answer to this question might be related to the way in which X and Y stochastically depend on each other. Comonotonic additivity is in line with this approach: if X and Y are perfectly dependent, then no diversification discount can be granted. Apart from this extreme case, some diversification effect occurs and subadditivity prevails.

Another school of thought holds that aggregating 'positively dependent' risks (this concept will be made precise in Part II) actually increases the riskiness of the portfolio and that this should induce higher capital requirements. This leads to superadditivity for positively dependent risks and additivity for independent risks. ∇

2.2.4 *Coherent risk measures*

Several authors have selected some of these conditions to form a set of requirements that any risk measure should satisfy. The following definition is taken from Artzner *et al.* (1999).

Definition 2.2.5. A risk measure that is translative, positive homogeneous, subadditive and monotone is called coherent. ∇

It is worth mentioning that coherence is defined with respect to a set of axioms, and no set is universally accepted. Modifying the set of axioms regarded as desirable leads to other 'coherent' risk measures.

2.2.5 *Coherent and scenario-based risk measures*

Scenario-based risk measures are defined as

$$\varrho[X]=\sup\left\{\mathbb{E}^{Q}[X]\mid Q\in\mathcal{P}\right\}, \tag{2.1}$$

where the superscript 'Q' in to $\mathbb{E}^{Q}$ indicates that the expectation is computed under the probability distribution Q, and $\mathcal{P}$ is a non-empty set of probability measures. Such risk measures have been considered for a long time in actuarial science, especially when $\mathcal{P}$ is a moment space (or, more generally, when $\mathcal{P}$ is defined by a set of integral constraints). See Section 5.3 of Goovaerts, De Vijlder and Hazendonck (1984) for a detailed account.

Artzner *et al.* (1999) call the elements of $\mathcal{P}$ *generalized scenarios*. Notice that any risk measure as defined in (2.1) can be interpreted as an expectation with respect to a *worst-case* scenario (since we take the supremum over a set $\mathcal{P}$ of scenarios corresponding to the different Qs).

It is straightforward to prove that any scenario-based risk measure defined in (2.1) satisfies the properties of monotonicity, positive homogeneity, translativity and subadditivity (however, they fail to be objective). Furthermore, Artzner *et al.* (1999) show that each coherent risk measure (on a finite set of states of nature Ω) is of the form (2.1).

In this chapter, we will not consider scenario-based risk measures of the form (2.1). Instead, we confine ourselves to model-dependent risk measures, constructed from a single explicit probability measure on the set of states of nature Ω.

2.2.6 Economic capital

Insurance companies as well as banks should hold some form of capital cushion against unexpected losses. The most common way to quantify risk capital is the concept of economic capital (EC) defined as follows.

Definition 2.2.6. The economic capital is defined with respect to some risk measure ϱ as

$$\mathrm{EC}[S] = \varrho[S] - \mathbb{E}[S],$$

where S is the total loss of the company (related to some line of business). ∇

The reason for reducing the risk measure $\varrho[S]$ by the expected loss $\mathbb{E}[S]$ is due to the 'best practice' of decomposing the total risk capital $\varrho[S]$ into a first part $\mathbb{E}[S]$ covering expected losses and a second part $\mathrm{EC}[S]$ meant as a cushion against unexpected losses.

Remark 2.2.7. It is worth mentioning that expected losses do not depend upon the dependence structure of the portfolio. This is because $\mathbb{E}[S] = \sum_i \mathbb{E}[S_i]$, where S_i denotes the total loss generated by policy i in the portfolio. But the economic capital very strongly depends on the current composition of the portfolio in which the new policy is included. For instance, if the portfolio is already well diversified and homogeneous then the economic capital does not have to be as large as it would be in the case of a portfolio in which the new policy would be correlated to existing ones. This makes the computation of the economic capital more complicated. ∇

2.2.7 Expected risk-adjusted capital

Portfolios are most often analysed by means of a risk-adjusted performance measurement. A good profit measure evaluates financial performance with due consideration to risk exposure: a euro earned or expected to be earned when there is substantial risk is not worth as much as when there is little risk. This means that the corresponding return is computed via the return on risk-adjusted capital (RORAC) method. Specifically, let R denote the profit of the company, that is, the difference between the premium p and the total claim amount S. Provided $\varrho[S] \neq 0$, we define the expected risk-adjusted return (ERAR) for the portfolio as

$$\mathrm{ERAR}[R, \varrho] = \frac{\mathbb{E}[R]}{\varrho[S]}.$$

In practice, the company aims to maximize the ERAR.

2.3 VALUE-AT-RISK

2.3.1 Definition

The last decade has seen a growing interest in quantiles of probability distributions on the part of practitioners. Since quantiles have a simple interpretation in terms of over- or undershoot probabilities they have found their way into current risk management practice in the form of the concept of value-at-risk (VaR). This concept was introduced to answer the following question: how much can we expect to lose in one day, week, year, ... with a given probability? In today's financial world, VaR has become the benchmark risk measure: its importance is unquestion since regulators accept this model as the basis for setting capital requirements for market risk exposure. A textbook treatment of VaR is given in Jorion (2000).

VaR is defined as follows.

Definition 2.3.1. Given a risk X and a probability level $p \in (0, 1)$, the corresponding VaR, denoted by $\text{VaR}[X; p]$, is defined as

$$\text{VaR}[X; p] = F_X^{-1}(p).$$

∇

Note that the VaR risk measure reduces to the percentile principle of Goovaerts, De Vijlder and Hazendonck (1984).

Remark 2.3.2. Alternatively, we could define the VaR at level p as $F_X^{-1+}(p)$. This definition of VaR is sometimes encountered in the literature (and referred to as VaR^+). In fact, any convex combination of $F_X^{-1}(p)$ and $F_X^{-1+}(p)$ is eligible as VaR. In this chapter, we will adhere to the definition of VaR in terms of F_X^{-1}. ∇

It is worth mentioning that VaRs always exist and are expressed in the proper unit of measure, namely in lost money. Since VaR is defined with the help of the quantile function F_X^{-1}, all the properties derived in Chapter 1 immediately apply to VaR. We will often resort to the following equivalence relation, which holds for all $x \in \mathbb{R}$ and $p \in (0, 1)$:

$$\text{VaR}[X; p] \leq x \Leftrightarrow p \leq F_X(x). \tag{2.2}$$

This is a direct consequence of Lemma 1.5.15.

2.3.2 Properties

2.3.2.1 VaR is no-ripoff

Since $X \leq \max[X]$ we have that $\text{VaR}[X; p] \leq \max[X]$ whatever p, so that VaR is indeed no-ripoff.

2.3.2.2 VaR does not necessarily entail non-negative loading

Let us define $p^* = F_X(\mathbb{E}[X])$. It is clear that VaR does not exceed the expected loss $\mathbb{E}[X]$ for probability levels less than p^*.

2.3.2.3 VaR is translative and positively homogeneous

VaR possesses a very convenient stability property: the VaR of a non-decreasing function t of some rv X is obtained by applying the same function to the initial VaR. This is easily deduced from Property 1.5.16(i). In particular, VaR has the translativity and positive homogeneity properties.

2.3.2.4 VaR does not induce unjustified loading

It is easy to see that for any probability level $p > 0$, $\text{VaR}[c\,;p] = c$.

2.3.2.5 VaR is comonotonic additive

We know from Exercise 1.11.6 that the inverse df of a sum of comonotonic rvs is simply the sum of the inverse dfs of each summand. Exercise 1.11.6 thus easily yields the following result, which states that VaR is comonotonic additive.

Property 2.3.3
Given comonotonic risks $X_1^c, X_2^c, \ldots, X_n^c$, the VaR of their sum S^c can be written as

$$\text{VaR}[S^c; p] = \sum_{i=1}^{n} \text{VaR}[X_i\,; p], \qquad 0 < p < 1. \tag{2.3}$$

2.3.2.6 VaR is not subadditive

VaR fails to be subadditive (except in some very special cases, such as when the X_i are multivariate normal). Thus, in general, VaR has the surprising property that the VaR of a sum may be higher than the sum of the VaRs. In such a case, diversification will lead to more risk being reported. Exercises 2.7.5 and 2.7.6 illustrate why VaR is not subadditive.

A possible harmful aspect of the lack of subadditivity is that a decentralized risk management system may fail because VaRs calculated for individual portfolios may not be summed to produce an upper bound for the VaR of the combined portfolio.

2.3.2.7 VaR is monotone

Clearly, if $\Pr[X \le Y] = 1$ holds then $F_X(x) \ge F_Y(x)$ is true for any x. Therefore, $\text{VaR}[X\,; p] \le \text{VaR}[Y\,; p]$ holds in such a case for any probability level p.

2.3.2.8 VaR is continuous with respect to convergence in distribution

It is well known that the weak convergence of the dfs ensures the same type of convergence for the quantile functions.

2.3.2.9 VaR is objective

This is a direct consequence of the definition of VaR, since it only depends on the df of X.

2.3.2.10 VaR is an optimal capital requirement for insurance companies

In an insurance business, the production cycle is inverted, meaning that premiums are paid by the policyholder before claims are paid by the insurer. A portfolio may get into trouble if its loss X is positive (or equivalently, its gain $-X$ is negative), because the liabilities to the insureds cannot be fulfilled completely in this case. Solvency reflects the financial capacity of a particular risky business to meet its contractual obligations. In order to protect the policyholders, the regulatory authority imposes a *solvency capital requirement* $\varrho[X]$. This means that the regulator requires that the available capital in the company, the surplus of assets over liabilities (reserves), has to be at least equal to $\varrho[X]$. This capital is used as a buffer against the risk that the premiums and reserves combined with the investment income will turn out to be insufficient to cover future policyholder claims. In principle, $\varrho[X]$ will be chosen such that one can be 'fairly sure' that the event $\left[X > \varrho[X]\right]$ will not occur.

Consider a portfolio with loss X. The regulator wants the solvency capital requirement related to the loss X to be large enough to ensure that the shortfall is sufficiently small. In order to reach this goal, the regulator measures the shortfall risk as $\mathbb{E}\left[(X-\varrho[X])_+\right]$. The process of setting capital requirements requires two different risk measures: the risk measure to determine the solvency capital, and $\mathbb{E}\left[(X-\varrho[X])_+\right]$ to measure the shortfall.

Clearly, the regulator wants $\mathbb{E}\left[(X-\varrho[X])_+\right]$ to be sufficiently small. Obviously, the larger the capital, the better, from the viewpoint of minimizing $\mathbb{E}\left[(X-\varrho[X])_+\right]$. On the other hand, holding capital has a cost. The regulator can avoid requiring an excessive solvency capital by taking this cost of capital into account. The capital requirement ϱ could be determined as the solution to the following minimization problem:

$$\min_{\varrho[X]}\left\{\mathbb{E}\left[(X-\varrho[X])_+\right]+\varrho[X]\,\varepsilon\right\}, \qquad 0<\varepsilon<1, \tag{2.4}$$

which balances the two conflicting criteria of low residual risk and low cost of capital. Here, ε can be interpreted as a measure of the extent to which the cost of capital is taken into account. The regulatory authority can decide to let ε be company-specific or risk-specific. If $\varepsilon=0$, the cost of capital is not taken into account at all and a solvency capital $\varrho[X]=\max[X]$ results. Increasing the value of ε means that the regulator increases the relative importance of the cost of capital and hence will decrease the optimal solution of the problem.

The following result is taken from Dhaene, Goovaerts and Kaas (2003).

Property 2.3.4

The smallest capital $\varrho[X]$ that is a solution of (2.4) is the VaR, that is,

$$\varrho[X]=\text{VaR}[X;1-\varepsilon].$$

Proof. Let us introduce the cost function

$$C[X, d] = \mathbb{E}\left[(X - d)_+\right] + d\varepsilon, \tag{2.5}$$

and assume first that $\mathrm{VaR}[X; 1-\varepsilon] > 0$. When $d > 0$, we know from (1.16) that the function $C[X, d]$ corresponds to the surface between the df of X and the horizontal line $y = 1$, from d on, together with the surface $d\varepsilon$. A similar interpretation of $C[X, d]$ as a surface holds when $d < 0$. One can easily verify that $C[X, d]$ is decreasing in d if $d \leq \mathrm{VaR}[X; 1-\varepsilon]$, while $C[X, d]$ is increasing in d if $d \geq \mathrm{VaR}[X; 1-\varepsilon]$. We can conclude that the cost function $C[X, d]$ is minimized by choosing $d = \mathrm{VaR}[X; 1-\varepsilon]$.

Let us now assume that $\mathrm{VaR}[X; 1-\varepsilon] < 0$. A similar geometric reasoning leads to the conclusion that in this case, too, the cost function is minimized by $\mathrm{VaR}[X; 1-\varepsilon]$.

Note that the minimum of (2.4) is uniquely determined, except when $1-\varepsilon$ corresponds to a flat part of the df. In the latter case, the minimum is obtained for any x for which $F_X(x) = 1 - \varepsilon$. Determining the capital requirement as the smallest amount for which the cost function in (2.4) is minimized leads to the VaR. □

Property 2.3.4 provides a theoretical justification for the use of VaR to set solvency capital requirements. Hence, to some extent the theorem supports the current regulatory regime established by the Basel II capital accord, which has put forward a VaR-based capital requirement approach. However, it is important to emphasize that the VaR is not used to 'measure risk' here; it (merely) appears as an optimal capital requirement.

The risk that we measure and want to keep under control is the shortfall $(X - \varrho[X])_+$. This shortfall risk is measured by $\mathbb{E}\left[(X - \varrho[X])_+\right]$. This approach corresponds to the classical actuarial approach of measuring or comparing risks by determining or comparing their respective stop-loss premiums.

2.3.3 VaR-based economic capital

As underlined in the preceding section, the most common way to quantify risk capital is certainly based on VaR. If S denotes the aggregate claims of an insurance portfolio over a given reference period and P denotes the aggregate premium (or the provision) for this portfolio, then $\mathrm{VaR}[X; p] - P$ is the smallest 'additional capital' required such that the insurer becomes technically insolvent with a (small) probability of at most $1 - p$.

Specifically, for a prescribed level of confidence p, the VaR-based economic capital is defined as

$$\mathrm{EC}[S; p] = \mathrm{VaR}[S; p] - \mathbb{E}[S].$$

For instance, if the level of confidence is set to $p = 99.98\,\%$, the risk capital $\mathrm{EC}[S; p]$ will on average be sufficient to cover unexpected losses in 9998 out of 10,000 years.

Remark 2.3.5. Using the VaR for determining a solvency capital is meaningful in situations where the default event should be avoided, but the size of the shortfall is not important. For shareholders or management, for example, the quantile risk measure gives useful information since avoiding default is the primary concern, whereas the size of the shortfall is only secondary (because of limited liability). ∇

2.3.4 VaR and the capital asset pricing model

An important feature of the multivariate normal (and more generally of the elliptical) distributions is that these distributions are amenable to the standard approaches of risk management. They support both the use of VaR as a measure of risk and the mean–variance (Markowitz) approach to risk management and portfolio optimization.

Suppose that $\boldsymbol{X}$ represents an n-dimensional random vector with a multivariate normal distribution and that we consider linear portfolios of such risks, that is, portfolios in the class

$$\mathcal{P}=\left\{P|P=\sum_{i=1}^{n}\alpha_i X_i,\ \alpha_i\in\mathbb{R}\right\}. \tag{2.6}$$

In such a case, the use of any positive homogeneous, translative measure of risk to determine optimal risk-minimizing portfolio weights $\alpha_1, \alpha_2, \ldots, \alpha_n$ under the condition that a certain return is attained, is equivalent to the Markowitz approach where the variance is used as a risk measure. Alternative risk measures give different numerical values, but have no effect on the management of risks. We make these assertions more precise in the following result taken from Embrechts, McNeil and Straumann (2002).

Proposition 2.3.6
Consider $\boldsymbol{X}\sim\mathcal{N}or_n(\boldsymbol{\mu},\boldsymbol{\Sigma})$ and let $\mathcal{P}$ be the set of all linear portfolios defined according to (2.6). Then the following statements are true:

(i) Subadditivity of VaR: for any two portfolios $P_1, P_2\in\mathcal{P}$ and $0.5\leq p<1$,

$$\text{VaR}[P_1+P_2;\,p]\leq\text{VaR}[P_1;\,p]+\text{VaR}[P_2;\,p].$$

(ii) Equivalence of variance to any positive homogeneous risk measure ϱ: for $P_1, P_2\in\mathcal{P}$,

$$\varrho[P_1-\mathbb{E}[P_1]]\leq\varrho[P_2-\mathbb{E}[P_2]]\Leftrightarrow\mathbb{V}[P_1]\leq\mathbb{V}[P_2].$$

Proof. (i) The main observation is that (P_1, P_2) has a bivariate normal distribution so that P_1, P_2 and P_1+P_2 all have univariate normal distributions. Let z_p be the pth quantile of the $\mathcal{N}or(0, 1)$ distribution. Then,

$$\begin{aligned}\text{VaR}[P_1;p]&=\mathbb{E}[P_1]+z_p\sqrt{\mathbb{V}[P_1]},\\ \text{VaR}[P_2;p]&=\mathbb{E}[P_2]+z_p\sqrt{\mathbb{V}[P_2]},\\ \text{VaR}[P_1+P_2;p]&=\mathbb{E}[P_1+P_2]+z_p\sqrt{\mathbb{V}[P_1+P_2]}.\end{aligned}$$

The result then follows since $\sqrt{\mathbb{V}[P_1+P_2]}\leq\sqrt{\mathbb{V}[P_1]}+\sqrt{\mathbb{V}[P_2]}$ always holds and $z_p\geq 0$ (because we assumed that $p\geq 0.5$).

(ii) Since P_1 and P_2 are both normally distributed, there exists an $a>0$ such that

$$P_1-\mathbb{E}[P_1]=_d a(P_2-\mathbb{E}[P_2]).$$

It follows that

$$\varrho[P_1 - \mathbb{E}[P_1]] \leq \varrho[P_2 - \mathbb{E}[P_2]] \Leftrightarrow a \leq 1 \Leftrightarrow \mathbb{V}[P_1] \leq \mathbb{V}[P_2],$$

which concludes the proof. □

2.4 TAIL VALUE-AT-RISK

2.4.1 Definition

A single VaR at a predetermined level p does not give any information about the thickness of the upper tail of the distribution function. This is a considerable shortcoming since in practice a regulator is not only concerned with the frequency of default, but also with the severity of default. Also shareholders and management should be concerned with the question 'how bad is bad?' when they want to evaluate the risks at hand in a consistent way. Therefore, one often uses another risk measure, which is called the tail value-at-risk (TVaR) and defined next.

Definition 2.4.1. Given a risk X and a probability level p, the corresponding TVaR, denoted by $\mathrm{TVaR}[X\,;p]$, is defined as

$$\mathrm{TVaR}[X\,;p] = \frac{1}{1-p}\int_p^1 \mathrm{VaR}[X\,;\xi]\,d\xi, \qquad 0 < p < 1.$$

We thus see that $\mathrm{TVaR}[X\,;p]$ can be viewed as the 'arithmetic average' of the VaRs of X, from p on. ∇

2.4.2 Some related risk measures

2.4.2.1 Conditional tail expectation

The conditional tail expectation (CTE) represents the conditional expected loss given that the loss exceeds its VaR:

$$\mathrm{CTE}[X\,;p] = \mathbb{E}\Big[X\Big|X > \mathrm{VaR}[X\,;p]\Big].$$

Thus the CTE is nothing but the mathematical transcription of the concept of 'average loss in the worst $100(1-p)\%$ cases'. Defining by $c = \mathrm{VaR}[X;p]$ a critical loss threshold corresponding to some confidence level p, $\mathrm{CTE}[X;p]$ provides a cushion against the mean value of losses exceeding the critical treshold c.

2.4.2.2 Conditional VaR

An alternative to CTE is the conditional VaR (or CVaR). The CVaR is the expected value of the losses exceeding VaR:

$$\begin{aligned}\mathrm{CVaR}[X\,;p] &= \mathbb{E}\Big[X - \mathrm{VaR}[X;p]\Big|X > \mathrm{VaR}[X;p]\Big]\\ &= \mathrm{CTE}[X;p] - \mathrm{VaR}[X;p].\end{aligned}$$

It is easy to see from Definition 1.7.8 that CVaR is related to the mean-excess function through

$$\text{CVaR}[X;p] = e_X\Big(\text{VaR}[X;p]\Big).$$

Therefore, evaluating the mef at quantiles yields CVaR.

2.4.2.3 Expected shortfall

As the VaR at a fixed level only gives local information about the underlying distribution, a promising way to escape from this shortcoming is to consider the so-called expected shortfall over some quantile. Expected shortfall at probability level p is the stop-loss premium with retention VaR$[X; p]$. Specifically,

$$\text{ES}[X;p] = \mathbb{E}\big[(X - \text{VaR}[X;p])_+\big] = \pi_X(\text{VaR}[X;p]).$$

2.4.2.4 Relationships between risk measures

The following relation holds between the three risk measures defined above.

Property 2.4.2
For any $p \in (0, 1)$, the following identities are valid:

$$\text{TVaR}[X;p] = \text{VaR}[X;p] + \frac{1}{1-p}\text{ES}[X;p], \tag{2.7}$$

$$\text{CTE}[X;p] = \text{VaR}[X;p] + \frac{1}{\overline{F}_X(\text{VaR}[X;p])}\text{ES}[X;p], \tag{2.8}$$

$$\text{CVaR}[X;p] = \frac{\text{ES}[X;p]}{\overline{F}_X(\text{VaR}[X;p])}. \tag{2.9}$$

Proof. Expression (2.7) follows from

$$\begin{aligned}\text{ES}[X;p] &= \int_0^1 \Big(\text{VaR}[X;\xi] - \text{VaR}[X;p]\Big)_+ d\xi \\ &= \int_p^1 \text{VaR}[X;\xi]\, d\xi - \text{VaR}[X;p](1-p).\end{aligned}$$

Expression (2.8) follows from

$$\begin{aligned}\text{ES}[X;p] &= e_X\big(\text{VaR}[X;p]\big)\overline{F}_X\big(\text{VaR}[X;p]\big) \\ &= \mathbb{E}\Big[X - \text{VaR}[X;p]\Big| X > \text{VaR}[X;p]\Big]\overline{F}_X\big(\text{VaR}[X;p]\big),\end{aligned}$$

where the first equality comes from (1.19). Finally, (2.9) immediately follows from (2.8) or from (1.19). □

Corollary 2.4.3
Note that if F_X is continuous then by combining (2.7) and (2.8) we find

$$\text{CTE}[X;p]=\text{TVaR}[X;p], \qquad p\in(0,1), \tag{2.10}$$

so that CTE and TVaR coincide for all p in this special case. In general, however, we only have

$$\text{TVaR}[X;p]=\text{CTE}[X;p]+\left(\frac{1}{1-p}-\frac{1}{\overline{F}_X(\text{VaR}[X;p])}\right)\text{ES}[X;p].$$

Since the quantity between the brackets can be different from 0 for some values of p, TVaR and CTE are not always equal. Looking back at Figure 1.4, we see that the values of p for which the quantity between the brackets does not vanish correspond to jumps in the df (e.g., for p_3, $F_X\big(F_x^{-1}(p_3)\big)>p_3$). See also Acerbi and Tasche (2002).

Remark 2.4.4. From (2.7) in Property 2.4.2 it follows that the minimal value of the cost function in (2.4) can be expressed as

$$\begin{aligned} C[X,\text{VaR}[X;1-\varepsilon]] &= \mathbb{E}\big[(X-\text{VaR}[X;1-\varepsilon])_+\big]+\text{VaR}[X;1-\varepsilon]\varepsilon \\ &= \varepsilon\text{TVaR}[X;1-\varepsilon]. \end{aligned} \tag{2.11}$$

A more general version of the minimization problem (2.4), involving a *distortion risk measure*, is considered in Dhaene, Goovaerts and Kaas (2003), Laeven and Goovaerts (2004) and Goovaerts, Van den Borre and Laeven (2004). ∇

2.4.3 Properties

2.4.3.1 TVaR is no-ripoff

This comes from the fact that VaR is known to be no-ripoff, so that

$$\text{TVaR}[X;p]\leq\frac{1}{1-p}\int_p^1 \max[X]d\xi=\max[X].$$

2.4.3.2 TVaR does not induce unjustified loading

This is again an immediate consequence of the corresponding properties for VaRs, since

$$\text{TVaR}[c;p]=\frac{1}{1-p}\int_p^1 c\,d\xi=c.$$

2.4.3.3 TVaR induces a non-negative loading

Since for $U\sim\mathcal{U}ni(0,1)$,

$$\mathbb{E}[X]=\mathbb{E}[F_X^{-1}(U)]=\int_0^1 F_X^{-1}(p)dp=\text{TVaR}[X;0], \tag{2.12}$$

the claimed property holds if we are able to show that TVaR is non-decreasing in the probability level. This is precisely the content of the next result.

Property 2.4.5
The function $p \mapsto \text{TVaR}[X; p]$ is non-decreasing in p.

Proof. We clearly have from (2.12) that

$$\text{TVaR}[X; p] = \frac{1}{1-p}\left(\mathbb{E}[X] - \int_0^p \text{VaR}[X; \xi]\, d\xi\right). \tag{2.13}$$

Therefore, using (2.13) we can write

$$\frac{d}{dp}\text{TVaR}[X; p] = \frac{\text{TVaR}[X; p]}{1-p} - \frac{\text{VaR}[X; p]}{1-p}.$$

Since $p \mapsto \text{VaR}[X; p]$ is non-decreasing,

$$\text{TVaR}[X; p] = \frac{1}{1-p}\int_p^1 \underbrace{\text{VaR}[X; \xi]}_{\geq \text{VaR}[X; p]}\, d\xi \geq \text{VaR}[X; p],$$

which gives $\frac{d}{dp}\text{TVaR}[X; p] \geq 0$. □

Property 2.4.5 gives

$$\text{TVaR}[X; p] \geq \text{TVaR}[X; 0] = \mathbb{E}[X],$$

so that TVaR induces a non-negative loading whatever the probability level p.

2.4.3.4 TVaR is translative, positively homogeneous, comonotonic additive and monotone

This is immediate from the corresponding properties of the VaRs. For instance, the translativity of VaR allows us to write, for any constant c,

$$\begin{aligned}\text{TVaR}[X + c; p] &= \frac{1}{1-p}\int_p^1 \text{VaR}[X + c; \xi]\, d\xi \\ &= \frac{1}{1-p}\int_p^1 \left(\text{VaR}[X; \xi] + c\right) d\xi \\ &= \text{TVaR}[X; p] + c.\end{aligned}$$

2.4.3.5 TVaR is subadditive

Unlike VaR, TVaR is subadditive. In order to check this assertion, first note that Remark 2.4.4 allows us to write the following representation of TVaR:

$$\text{TVaR}[X; p] = \inf_{a \in \mathbb{R}}\left\{a + \frac{1}{1-p}\pi_X(a)\right\}. \tag{2.14}$$

We thus have for any $0<\lambda<1$ that

$$\begin{aligned}
&\mathrm{TVaR}[\lambda X+(1-\lambda)Y;p]\\
&\leq \lambda\mathrm{VaR}[X;p]+(1-\lambda)\mathrm{VaR}[Y;p]\\
&\quad+\frac{1}{1-p}\mathbb{E}\Big[\big(\lambda X+(1-\lambda)Y-\lambda\mathrm{VaR}[X;p]-(1-\lambda)\mathrm{VaR}[Y;p]\big)_+\Big]\\
&\leq \lambda\mathrm{VaR}[X;p]+(1-\lambda)\mathrm{VaR}[Y;p]\\
&\quad+\frac{\lambda}{1-p}\mathbb{E}\Big[\big(X-\mathrm{VaR}[X;p]\big)_+\Big]+\frac{1-\lambda}{1-p}\mathbb{E}\Big[\big(Y-\mathrm{VaR}[Y;p]\big)_+\Big]\\
&=\lambda\mathrm{TVaR}[X;p]+(1-\lambda)\mathrm{TVaR}[Y;p],
\end{aligned}$$

where the second inequality comes from the convexity of $y\mapsto y_+$. Taking $\lambda=\frac{1}{2}$ gives

$$\tfrac{1}{2}\mathrm{TVaR}[X+Y;p]\leq\tfrac{1}{2}\Big(\mathrm{TVaR}[X;p]+\mathrm{TVaR}[Y;p]\Big)$$

by the positive homogeneity of TVaR, so that we have established the validity of the result.

Remark 2.4.6. The subadditivity of TVaR will also be obtained as a particular case of Property 2.6.6, when Wang risk measures are studied. ∇

It is also easy to check that TVaR is objective and continuous with respect to convergence in distribution. Let us now briefly discuss the subadditivity of CTE.

2.4.3.6 CTE is subadditive for continuous risks

When X is assumed to be continuous, TVaR and CTE coincide (see (2.10)) and thus generate a coherent risk measure. In particular, CTE is subadditive in this case. It is possible to establish the subadditivity of the CTE directly using the following useful property.

Property 2.4.7
Let X and x be such that $\overline{F}_X(x)>0$. For any event A such that $\Pr[A]=\overline{F}_X(x)$,

$$\mathbb{E}[X|A]\leq\mathbb{E}[X|X>x].$$

Proof. It suffices to write

$$\begin{aligned}
\mathbb{E}[X|X>x]&=x+\mathbb{E}[X-x|X>x,A]\Pr[A|X>x]\\
&\quad+\mathbb{E}[X-x|X>x,\overline{A}]\Pr[\overline{A}|X>x]\\
&\geq x+\mathbb{E}[X-x|X>x,A]\Pr[A|X>x]\\
&=x+\mathbb{E}[X-x|X>x,A]\Pr[X>x|A]\\
&\geq x+\mathbb{E}[X-x|X>x,A]\Pr[X>x|A]\\
&\quad+\mathbb{E}[X-x|X\leq x,A]\Pr[X\leq x|A]\\
&=\mathbb{E}[X|A],
\end{aligned}$$

which completes the proof. □

Invoking Property 2.4.7, it is then easy to see that CTE is subadditive when the dfs are continuous. In this case, we indeed have that

$$\Pr\Big[X > \text{VaR}[X; p]\Big] = 1 - p,$$

so that

$$\begin{aligned}\text{CTE}[X+Y; p] &= \mathbb{E}\big[X \big| X+Y > \text{VaR}[X+Y; p]\big] \\ &\quad + \mathbb{E}\big[Y \big| X+Y > \text{VaR}[X+Y; p]\big] \\ &\leq \mathbb{E}\big[X \big| X > \text{VaR}[X; p]\big] + \mathbb{E}\big[Y \big| Y > \text{VaR}[Y; p]\big] \\ &= \text{CTE}[X; p] + \text{CTE}[Y; p].\end{aligned}$$

Remark 2.4.8. Property 2.4.7 sheds a new light on CTE, which can be represented as a worst-case conditional expectation. More precisely,

$$\text{CTE}[X; p] = \sup\Big\{\mathbb{E}[X|A] \Big| \Pr[A] \geq \overline{F}_X\big(\text{VaR}[X; p]\big)\Big\},$$

which reduces to

$$\text{CTE}[X; p] = \sup\Big\{\mathbb{E}[X|A] \Big| \Pr[A] \geq 1 - p\Big\}$$

when F_X is continuous. This result is closely related to the notion of scenario or stress testing: the CTE appears as the largest possible expected value of X under the set of all plausible scenarios (that is, those whose probabilities exceed $1 - p$). ∇

2.4.4 TVaR-based economic capital

Let S again denote the aggregate claims of an insurance portfolio over a given reference period and P the aggregate premium (or the provision) for this portfolio. Setting the amount of 'additional capital' equal to $\text{TVaR}[S; p] - P$, we could define 'bad times' as those where S takes a value in the interval $\big[\text{VaR}[S; p], \text{TVaR}[S; p]\big]$. Hence, 'bad times' are those where the aggregate claims exceed the threshold $\text{VaR}[S; p]$, but do not use up all available capital. The width of the interval is a 'cushion' that is used in 'bad times'. For more details, see Overbeck (2000). For a prescribed level p, the TVaR-based economic capital is thus defined as

$$\text{EC}[S; p] = \text{TVaR}[S; p] - \mathbb{E}[S].$$

2.5 RISK MEASURES BASED ON EXPECTED UTILITY THEORY

2.5.1 Brief introduction to expected utility theory

Expected utility theory is extensively discuss in Kaas *et al.* (2001, Chapter 1). We only briefly recall the basic features of this approach to decision-making, mainly to contrast it with the distorted expectation approach. We examine zero-utility premiums and Esscher risk measures.

2.5.1.1 Genesis

Consider a decision-maker who has to choose between two uncertain future incomes modelled by the rvs X and Y. One possible methodology for making a choice between these two alternatives involves computing their respective expectations and then selecting the income with the highest expected value. This simple valuation method was challenged by Bernoulli (1738) with the paradox known in the literature as the St Petersburg paradox. He posed the following problem: 'A fair coin is tossed repeatedly until it lands heads. The income you receive is equal to 2^n if the first head appears on the nth toss. How much are you willing to pay to enter this game?' Assuming that the coin is fair, it is easy to verify that the expected income of the gamble is equal to infinity. It has been noticed, however, that although the expected income is infinite, the maximum amount almost all decision-makers would pay to take part in the game is finite and even moderate.

2.5.1.2 Expected utility hypothesis

A way to solve this paradox consists in stating that decision-makers do not base their decisions on simply comparing the expectations of the incomes under consideration. For many decision-makers, the value of different potential levels of wealth is apparently not equal to the wealth level itself. The concept of 'utility' thus emerged: each decision-maker possesses a utility function u such that the utility (or 'moral value') of having a fortune x is given by $u(x)$.

A decision-maker is said to base his preferences on the 'expected utility hypothesis' if he acts in order to maximize his expected utility. This means that there exists a real-valued function u which represents the decision-maker's utility-of-wealth for each fortune. The decision-maker will prefer Y over X if, and only if, $\mathbb{E}[u(X)] \leq \mathbb{E}[u(Y)]$, provided that the expectations exist. In words, he will prefer fortune Y over X if the expected utility of Y exceeds the expected utility of X.

Returning to the St Petersburg paradox, if the decision-maker's initial fortune is w, then the decision-maker is willing to play the coin tossing game for a price P if, and only if, the following inequality is satisfied:

$$u(w) \leq \sum_{n=1}^{+\infty} u\left(w - P + 2^n\right) \frac{1}{2^n}.$$

This inequality says that the decision-maker will enter the game only if the expected utility of playing the game is greater than the utility of not playing. Cramer proposed that the utility $u(x)$ of a fortune x is given by the square root $\sqrt{x}$ of this fortune. Bernoulli, on the other hand, suggested a logarithmic utility function $u(x) = \log x$.

We refer the reader to Kaas *et al.* (2001, Section 1.3) for relevant examples of utility functions (including linear, quadratic, logarithmic, exponential and power utility functions).

Remark 2.5.1. Note that a decision-maker's utility function need only be determined up to positive linear transformations. This follows from the fact that the utility function u^* defined by

$$u^*(x) = au(x) + b, \quad x \in \mathbb{R}, \tag{2.15}$$

for real constants $a > 0$ and b leads to the same preference structure as the utility function u (in such a case, u^* is said to be equivalent to u). Hence, it is always possible to standardize a utility function u, for example by requiring that

$$u(x_0) = 0 \text{ and } u'(x_0) = 1, \tag{2.16}$$

for a particular point $x_0 \in \mathbb{R}$. ∇

2.5.1.3 Axioms of expected utility theory

The pioneering work in the modern application of utility theory was done by John von Neumann and Oskar Morgenstern who, in the mid-1940s, developed a theory building on Daniel Bernoulli's idea. They showed that if a preference ordering for a set of risky situations follows certain consistency requirements, then there is a utility function that will give the same preference ordering in these situations.

The first statement of axioms supporting expected utility theory was given by von Neumann and Morgenstern (1947) in their famous book *Theory of Games and Economic Behavior*. However, this axiomatization was not complete (see Fishburn 1964, 1982). Numerous axiomatizations have been formulated, partly to deal with objections raised against the initial statements and partly to render them more parsimonious. It appears that the most succinct statement of axioms is that of Yaari (1987).

(i) **Axiom EU1** If X and Y are identically distributed then the decision-maker considers X and Y as equivalent. This axiom enables us to assume that decision-makers only take into account the probability distribution of the random income and are not influenced by other details of the income or by other aspects of the state of the world.

(ii) **Axiom EU2** The preferences of the decision-maker generate a complete weak order, that is to say, it is reflexive, transitive and connected. Reflexivity is in the spirit of Axiom EU1 and does not beg any question. Transitivity is generally regarded as the most innocuous axiom in expected utility theory. In fact, it may be argued that decision-makers who exhibit intransitive preferences may be deprived of their wealth for no advantage.

(iii) **Axiom EU3** The preferences of the decision-maker are continuous with respect to the Wasserstein distance d_W, defined as

$$d_W(X, Y) = \int_{t=-\infty}^{+\infty} |F_X(t) - F_Y(t)| dt.$$

This distance (as well as others) will be studied in detail in Chapter 9. More precisely, Axiom EU3 requires that given any X, $\widetilde{X}$, Y and $\widetilde{Y}$, there exists $\epsilon > 0$ such that the fact that Y is preferred over X together with

$$\max\left\{d_W(X, \widetilde{X}), d_W(Y, \widetilde{Y})\right\} < \epsilon$$

imply that $\widetilde{Y}$ is preferred over $\widetilde{X}$. Roughly speaking, Axiom EU3 means that if Y is preferred over X, the same ordering holds for pairs $\widetilde{X}$ and $\widetilde{Y}$ of risky prospects sufficiently close to X and Y.

(iv) **Axiom EU4** If $F_X \geq F_Y$ then Y is preferred over X. This means that, in a choice between hypothetical incomes, the decision-maker prefers the prospect that gives the greater probability of receiving the better outcome and the lesser probability of receiving the worse outcome.

(v) **Axiom EU5** If the fortune Y is preferred to the fortune X and if we define the rvs $\tilde{X}_p$ and $\tilde{Y}_p$ as

$$\tilde{X}_p = \begin{cases} X, & \text{with probability } p, \\ Z, & \text{with probability } 1-p, \end{cases}$$

and

$$\tilde{Y}_p = \begin{cases} Y, & \text{with probability } p, \\ Z, & \text{with probability } 1-p, \end{cases}$$

for an arbitrary rv Z independent of both X and Y, then the mixed fortune $\tilde{Y}_p$ is preferred over $\tilde{X}_p$ for any $p \in [0, 1]$.

It is not our intention to discuss these axioms in detail. We only examine the fifth axiom (since the modification of this axiom gives rise to the distorted expectation theory examined later in this chapter). Axiom EU5 is generally referred to as the independence axiom. In itself it appears reasonable: it seems that the decision-maker's preference between X and Y will not be affected by the introduction in each case of a third alternative Z with a specified probability. Thus there is independence with respect to mixtures of uncertain outcomes.

2.5.1.4 Expected utility and insurance

The considerations above indicate that a general theory of insurance must, or at least could, be based on the utility concept. This has in fact been recognized for a long time. Barrois (1834) constructed a very complete theory of fire insurance, based on the particular utility function $u(x) = \log(x)$, originally used by Bernoulli. It must, however, be admitted that the modern use of the utility concept in insurance literature is due to the results provided by von Neumann and Morgenstern. The expected utility theory became popular after these authors developed their axiomatic approach to it in 1947. Borch (1974, 1990) explains the relevance of the expected utility theory in order to solve problems in insurance. As Trowbridge (1989) pointed out, utility theory can be seen as the philosophical basis of actuarial science. For more details concerning expected utility, we refer the interested reader to Huang and Litzenberger (1988), Schmidt (1998) and Panjer (1998), as well as the references therein.

2.5.1.5 Risk aversion in expected utility theory

A crucial concept in the economics of insurance is risk aversion. Risk aversion is the attitude that induces people to avoid uncertainty, to be protected from unpredictable events, to buy insurance. Decision-makers are said to be risk-averse if they always prefer a certain yield $\mathbb{E}[X]$ to the risky prospect X, whatever the distribution of X. Their utility function then satisfies $\mathbb{E}[u(X)] \leq u(\mathbb{E}[X])$ for all X. It is a simple consequence of Jensen's inequality that this holds if u is concave. Considering $x < y \in \mathbb{R}$ and $0 < \lambda < 1$, and taking for X the two-point rv

$$X = \begin{cases} x, & \text{with probability } \lambda, \\ y, & \text{with probability } 1-\lambda, \end{cases}$$

we see that risk aversion implies

$$\mathbb{E}[u(X)] = \lambda u(x) + (1-\lambda)u(y) \leq u(\mathbb{E}[X]) = u\big(\lambda x + (1-\lambda)y\big),$$

which shows that u is concave. Therefore, a decision-maker is said to be risk-averse if his utility function is concave. Since concavity and convexity play a crucial role in this book, we have gathered the important results about these concepts in an appendix to this chapter (Section 2.8).

If u is twice differentiable, concavity reduces to $u'' \leq 0$. Note that risk aversion induces some smoothness property on u, since a function which is concave on an interval I is necessarily continuous on I, except possibly at its endpoints.

Another way to justify the concavity assumption is to note that it implies that the marginal utility u' is a decreasing function of wealth, or equivalently, that the increase of utility resulting from a gain of Δ, $u(x+\Delta) - u(x)$, is a decreasing function of the wealth x. Roughly speaking, risk aversion, that is, the concavity of a utility function u, means that as more wealth is accumulated less value is placed on an additional euro.

Remark 2.5.2. Note that in the framework of expected utility, the agent's attitude towards risk and the agent's attitude towards wealth are forever tied together (since they are both derived from the characteristics of u): risk aversion and diminishing marginal utility of wealth are synonymous. Nevertheless, risk aversion expresses an attitude towards wealth. In the dual theory of choice under risk proposed by Yaari (1987), we will see that these two notions are kept separate from each other. ∇

2.5.2 *Zero-Utility Premiums*

2.5.2.1 Definition

Consider an insurance company with initial wealth w and with a utility function u. The company covers a risk X and sets its price for coverage $\Pi[X]$ as the solution of the following indifference equation:

$$\mathbb{E}[u(w + \Pi[X] - X)] = u(w). \tag{2.17}$$

Condition (2.17) expresses the fact that the premium $\Pi[X]$ is fair in terms of utility: the right-hand side represents the utility of not issuing the contract; the left-hand side represents the expected utility of the insurer assuming the random financial loss X. Therefore (2.17) means that the expected utility of wealth with the contract is equal to the utility without the contract.

Putting $w = 0$, we get the so-called zero-utility principle proposed by Bühlmann (1970): the premium $\Pi[X]$ calculated according to this principle is the root of the equation

$$\mathbb{E}[u(\Pi[X] - X)] = u(0) \tag{2.18}$$

which can be interpreted as an equality between the expected utility of the income $\Pi[X]-X$ and the utility of not accepting the risk.

2.5.2.2 Properties of zero-utility premiums

The zero-utility premium $\Pi[X]$ is defined as the solution of the implicit equation (2.18); no explicit solution is available in general.

Henceforth, we assume without loss of generality that u has been standardized in such a way that $u(0)=0$ and $u'(0)=1$ (see Remark 2.5.1). Because u is non-decreasing, we have

$$0=\mathbb{E}[u(\Pi[X]-X)]\geq u(\Pi[X]-\max[X])$$

so that $\Pi[X]\leq\max[X]$ holds, and the zero-utility premiums satisfy the no-ripoff condition. Further, if u is concave then Jensen's inequality ensures that

$$0=\mathbb{E}[u(\Pi[X]-X)]\leq u(\Pi[X]-\mathbb{E}[X])$$

so that $\Pi[X]\geq\mathbb{E}[X]$ and the zero-utility premiums contain a non-negative loading. The zero-utility premiums clearly satisfy translativity. Nevertheless, they are not positively homogeneous in general; Goovaerts, De Vijlder and Hazendonck (1984, Theorem 4, p. 135) give the utility functions for which this property holds.

2.5.3 Esscher risk measure

2.5.3.1 Definition

The Esscher principle was introduced by Bühlmann (1980) as a special case of an economic premium principle: he derived the Esscher premium as a Pareto-optimal solution to a market situation with risk exchanges, where all risks are stochastically independent and all agents use an exponential utility function. Here, we follow the approach of Goovaerts, De Vijlder and Hazendonck (1984), who described the Esscher premium as the expected value of the risk after multiplying its pdf by an increasing exponential weight function (which of course makes the risk less attractive to the insurer).

Given that it has to cover a risk X, an insurance company could want to determine the premium p by maximizing the utility of the contract, $\mathbb{E}[u(p-X)]$. Of course, this leads to $p=+\infty$ because u is increasing. Assume now that the company agrees to restrict its choice to a premium of the form

$$p=\mathbb{E}[Xw(X)] \tag{2.19}$$

for some function w and that its utility function is of the form

$$u(x)=\frac{1-\exp(-cx)}{c}. \tag{2.20}$$

The constant $c>0$ involved in (2.20) is equal to $-\frac{d}{dx}\ln u$ and measures the risk aversion of the insurance company; the exponential utility function (2.20) yields a constant risk aversion. The following result is taken from Goovaerts, De Vijlder and Hazendonck (1984, Section 2.12); see also Kaas *et al.* (2001, Theorem 5.5.3).

Property 2.5.3
The maximization of $\mathbb{E}[u(p-X)]$ with p of the form (2.19) and u of the form (2.20) over all continuous increasing functions w such that $\mathbb{E}[w(X)]=1$ yields

$$w(x)=\frac{\exp(cx)}{M_X(c)}. \tag{2.21}$$

Note that (2.21) gives a premium (2.19) equal to

$$\mathbb{E}[Xw(X)]=\mathbb{E}\left[X\frac{\exp(cX)}{M_X(c)}\right]=\int_0^{+\infty} x\frac{\exp(cx)f_X(x)}{M_X(c)}dx.$$

We have thus operated a reweighting of the original pdf f_X by transforming it into $w(x)f_X(x)$. The weight function w puts more mass on large values of X, and so entails a safety loading.

This yields the following definition.

Definition 2.5.4. The Esscher premium $\text{Es}[X;c]$ is given by (2.19) with the weight function w given in (2.21). More precisely, the Esscher premium for risk X is

$$\text{Es}[X;c]=\frac{\mathbb{E}[X\exp(cX)]}{M_X(c)}=\frac{d}{dc}\ln M_X(c). \qquad \nabla$$

Appealing characteristics of the Esscher principle were given in Bühlmann (1980) and Gerber (1980). Critical comments can be found in Zehnwirth (1981), Gerber (1981a) and Van Heerwaarden, Kaas and Goovaerts (1989).

2.5.3.2 Link with Esscher transform

The Esscher transform was developed to approximate the aggregate claim amount distribution around a point of interest x_0, by applying Edgeworth series to the transformed distribution with the parameter h chosen such that that the new mean is equal to x_0. In this section, we show that Esscher transforms are implicitly used when computing the Esscher risk measure.

In fact, to compute $\text{Es}[X;c]$, the df F_X is first replaced with its Esscher transform, denoted by $F_{X,c}$ and given by

$$dF_{X,c}(x)=\frac{\exp(cx)dF_X(x)}{M_X(c)}, \quad c>0.$$

Then the Esscher premium of X, with parameter c, can be calculated as the expectation of the rv X_c with df $F_{X,c}$:

$$\text{Es}[X;c]=\mathbb{E}[X_c]=\int_0^{+\infty} x dF_{X,c}(\xi).$$

The Esscher parameter c reflects the degree of risk aversion of the insurer, as shown in the following result.

Property 2.5.5
The function $c\mapsto \text{Es}[X;c]=\mathbb{E}[X_c]$ is increasing for every risk X.

Proof. This follows directly from

$$\frac{d}{dc}\mathbb{E}[X_c] = \int_0^{+\infty} x^2 dF_{X,c}(\xi) - \left(\int_0^{+\infty} x dF_{X,c}(\xi)\right)^2 = \mathbb{V}[X_c] \geq 0. \tag{2.22}$$

□

This result ensures that, for $c > 0$,

$$\text{Es}[X; c] \geq \text{Es}[X; 0] = \mathbb{E}[X]$$

so that the Esscher risk measure contains a non-negative loading. Further,

$$\text{Es}[X; c] \leq \lim_{c \to +\infty} \text{Es}[X; c] = \max[X]$$

so that the Esscher risk measure is no-ripoff. The Esscher risk measure is not positively homogeneous (except in the trivial case $c = 0$). It is translative, and it violates the monotonicity condition, as shown in Exercise 2.7.22.

Remark 2.5.6. Let us explain why using Esscher risk measures resembles the risk-neutral valuation method in option pricing theory. If no arbitrage opportunities exist, then premiums are given by mathematical expectations, not with respect to the original probability distribution but with respect to a new probability distribution, called the risk-neutral distribution. The risk-neutral distribution changes the original probability distribution involved in order to give more weight to unfavourable events in a risk-free environment. With the Esscher risk measure, the risk-neutral probability distribution is associated with the df $F_{X,c}$.

Originally brought into insurance to approximate the total claim amount in a fixed period of time in risk theory, the Esscher transform now plays a fundamental role as an actuarial pricing mechanism in finance. Of course, when it comes down to the pricing of derivatives in insurance and finance, the Esscher transform has to be defined on stochastic processes (see Gerber and Shiu 1994). Under a specific Esscher transformed probability measure, discounted price processes are martingales, hence no-arbitrage prices can be calculated. ∇

2.6 RISK MEASURES BASED ON DISTORTED EXPECTATION THEORY

2.6.1 Brief introduction to distorted expectation theory

2.6.1.1 Genesis

Since the axiomatization of expected utility theory by von Neumann and Morgenstern (1947), numerous objections have been levelled against it. Many of these relate to the descriptive value of the theory, that is, to empirical evidence of the extent to which agents conform to expected utility theory. Such arguments generally take the form of experiments or field tests to establish whether the behaviour of individual decision-makers agrees with the axioms or their implications.

Motivated by the empirical evidence that individuals often tend to violate the expected utility hypothesis, several researchers have developed alternative theories of choice under risk that are able to explain the observed patterns of behaviour. A review of such models, usually termed 'non-expected utility' or 'generalizations of expected utility', is given in Sugden (1997) and Schmidt (1998). The ideas that will be developed hereafter originate from Yaari (1987); see also Roëll (1987) and Schmeidler (1989). It turns out that Yaari's 'dual theory of choice under risk' is a special case of Quiggin's (1982) 'anticipated utility theory'.

2.6.1.2 Distorted expectation hypothesis

Consider a decision-maker with a future random fortune equal to X. Using integration by parts, the expectation of X can be written as

$$\mathbb{E}[X]=-\int_{-\infty}^{0}\left(1-\overline{F}_X(x)\right)dx+\int_{0}^{+\infty}\overline{F}_X(x)dx.$$

Under the 'distorted expectations hypothesis' it is assumed that each decision-maker has a non-decreasing function $g:[0,1]\to[0,1]$ with $g(0)=0$ and $g(1)=1$ (called a distortion function) and that he values a fortune X at its 'distorted expectation' $\mathbb{H}_g[X]$ defined as

$$\mathbb{H}_g[X]=-\int_{-\infty}^{0}\left(1-g\big(\overline{F}_X(x)\big)\right)dx+\int_{0}^{+\infty}g\big(\overline{F}_X(x)\big)dx. \tag{2.23}$$

The function g is called a distortion because it distorts the probabilities $\overline{F}_X(x)$ before calculating a generalized expected value. As $g(\overline{F}_X(x))$ is a non-decreasing function of $\overline{F}_X(x)$, where $\overline{F}_X(x)$ is a non-increasing function of x, $g(\overline{F}_X(x))$ is also a non-increasing function of x, and can be thought of as the risk-adjusted tail function. Note that $g\big(\overline{F}_X(x)\big)$ is not necessarily a tf (indeed the right-continuity condition involved in Property 1.5.3 is not always fulfilled). Hence $\mathbb{H}_g[X]$ is not necessarily the expectation of some transformed rv. We will see that under additional assumptions on g, this will be the case. If X is non-negative, then we find from (2.23) that

$$\mathbb{H}_g[X]=\int_{0}^{+\infty}g\left(\overline{F}_X(x)\right)dx.$$

Note that $g(0)=0$ implies $\mathbb{H}_g[0]=0$ and that $g(1)=1$ implies $\mathbb{H}_g[1]=1$.

A decision-maker is said to base his preferences on the 'distorted expectations hypothesis' if he acts in order to maximize the distorted expectation of his wealth. This means that there exists a distortion function g such that the decision-maker prefers Y to a fortune X if, and only if, $\mathbb{H}_g[X]\leq\mathbb{H}_g[Y]$.

2.6.1.3 Axioms for distorted expectation theory

Distorted expectation theory can be considered as a dual theory of choice under risk in the sense that it uses the concept of the 'distortion function' as opposed to the 'utility function' used in utility theory. Starting from an axiomatic setting slightly different from that of utility theory, Yaari (1987) showed that there must exist a distortion function g such that the decision-maker will prefer fortune Y to X (or be indifferent between them) if, and only if,

$\mathbb{H}_g[X] \leq \mathbb{H}_g[Y]$ holds. Yaari's axiomatic setting differs from von Neumann and Morgenstern's by the independence axiom EU5. An important implication of the independence axiom EU5 underlying expected utility theory is that the preference function is linear in the probabilities. Experimental evidence has suggested that decision-making behaviour does not agree with the independence axiom. A famous experiment in this context is known as the Allais paradox; see Kaas *et al.* (2001, Remark 1.3.4). This is a particular example of what is referred to as the 'common consequence effect'. Numerous authors have addressed the Allais problem either empirically or from a normative point of view. Empirical studies have tested various modifications of the Allais paradox. In all cases, a significant number of subjects violated the independence axiom EU5. It is precisely the modification of EU5 which gives rise to the dual theory of choice under risk considered by Yaari (1987): instead of requiring independence with respect to probability mixtures of risky prospects, Yaari (1987) required independence with respect to direct mixing of payments of risky prospects.

(i) **Axiom DU5** Given two rvs X and Y such that Y is preferred to X, then $\tilde{Y}_p$ is preferred to $\tilde{X}_p$ for any $p \in [0, 1]$, if the inverse tfs of $\tilde{X}_p$ and $\tilde{Y}_p$ are respectively given by

$$\overline{F}_{\tilde{X}_p}^{-1}(q) = p\overline{F}_X^{-1}(q) + (1-p)\overline{F}_Z^{-1}(q)$$

and

$$\overline{F}_{\tilde{Y}_p}^{-1}(q) = p\overline{F}_Y^{-1}(q) + (1-p)\overline{F}_Z^{-1}(q)$$

for an arbitrary tf $\overline{F}_Z$.

In order to better understand the relation between EU5 and DU5, let us restate EU5 as follows: if Y is preferred over X and if the dfs of $\tilde{X}_p$ and $\tilde{Y}_p$ are given by

$$F_{\tilde{X}_p}(x) = pF_X(x) + (1-p)F_Z(x), \quad x \in \mathbb{R},$$

and

$$F_{\tilde{Y}_p}(x) = pF_Y(x) + (1-p)F_Z(x), \quad x \in \mathbb{R},$$

for an arbitrary distribution function F_Z, then $\tilde{Y}_p$ is preferred over $\tilde{X}_p$ for any $p \in [0, 1]$.

Instead of independence being postulated for convex combinations which are formed along the probability axis, independence is postulated in Yaari's theory for convex combinations which are formed along the payment axis. In DU4, an rv $pX + (1-p)Z$ is compared with $pY + (1-p)Z$; in EU5, the comparison is between $IX + (1-I)Z$ and $IY + (1-I)Z$, for some $I \sim \mathcal{B}er(p)$ independent of X, Y and Z.

2.6.1.4 Risk aversion in distorted expectation theory

Risk aversion plays a crucial role in the economics of insurance. We now describe how this notion can be translated into the framework of distorted expectations.

Under the distorted expectations hypothesis, a decision-maker is said to be risk-averse if his distortion function is convex. This is due to the fact that a convex distortion function satisfies

$$g(p) \leq p \text{ for all } p \Rightarrow g(\overline{F}_X(x)) \leq \overline{F}_X(x), \quad x \in \mathbb{R}.$$

This means that a risk-averse decision-maker systematically underestimates his tail probabilities related to levels of fortune, which is of course a prudent attitude. As we immediately find for convex g that

$$\mathbb{H}_g[X] \leq \mathbb{E}[X] = \mathbb{H}_g\Big[\mathbb{E}[X]\Big], \tag{2.24}$$

we see that a risk-averse decision-maker will always prefer a certain fortune to a random fortune with the same expected value. Therefore, the philosophy of risk aversion is similar in the two theories.

A decision-maker is said to be risk-neutral if $g(p) = p$. In this case, the distorted expectation hypothesis coincides with comparing expected values. The notion of risk neutrality is therefore also very similar in the two approaches.

2.6.1.5 Comparison with expected utility theory

In expected utility theory, the attractiveness of a risk X is evaluated with the help of

$$\mathbb{E}[u(X)] = \int_0^1 u(\text{VaR}[X; p])dp, \tag{2.25}$$

whereas in distorted expectation theory, (2.25) is replaced by

$$\begin{aligned}\mathbb{H}_g[X] &= \int_{x=0}^{+\infty} \int_{p=0}^{\overline{F}_X(x)} dg(p)dx \\ &= \int_0^1 \text{VaR}[X; 1-p]dg(p) \\ &= \int_0^1 \text{VaR}[X; p]dg(1-p). \end{aligned} \tag{2.26}$$

Expressions (2.25) and (2.26) highlight the difference between the two approaches: under the expected utility hypothesis, the possible amounts of fortune $\text{VaR}[X; p]$ are adjusted by a utility function, while under the distorted expectation hypothesis, the tail probabilities are adjusted. In other words, distortion functions modify the probability, and keep the wealth function unchanged, whereas utility functions modify the wealth and keep the probability unchanged.

Remark 2.6.1. Consider the case where g is differentiable, an assumption that is made throughout many papers. Then integration by parts yields the following rewriting:

$$\begin{aligned}\mathbb{H}_g[X] &= \int_0^{+\infty} g(\overline{F}_X(x))dx \\ &= \int_0^{+\infty} xg'(\overline{F}_X(x))dF_X(x) \\ &= \mathbb{E}\Big[Xg'\big(\overline{F}_X(X)\big)\Big].\end{aligned}$$

The factor $g'\big(\overline{F}_X(X)\big)$ in the expectation effects a reweighting of the probability distribution of X, placing a higher weight on adverse outcomes of X (adverse in the sense of having a high rank in the set of possible outcomes).

Alternatively, we may formally interpret the distortion in terms of utility, since for a fortune X, $\mathbb{H}_g[X]=\mathbb{E}[u(X)]$, where the 'utility function' is defined as

$$u(x)=xg'(\overline{F}_X(x)),\quad x\geq 0. \tag{2.27}$$

However, this is fundamentally different from the expected utility approach, as the function u in (2.27) changes according to the probability distribution under consideration. ∇

Remark 2.6.2. From (2.26), we see that $\mathbb{H}_g$ is a mixture of VaRs, the distortion function g giving the weights granted to each VaR. Mixtures of VaRs are called spectral measures of risk by Acerbi (2002). ∇

2.6.1.6 The rank-dependent expected utility hypothesis

To conclude, we briefly present a theory which combines the expected utility and the distorted expected utility assumptions to a certain extent. For more details, we refer the interested reader to Chateauneuf, Cohen and Meilijson (1997).

Under the rank-dependent expected utility model, a decision-maker is characterized by a non-negative utility function u in conjunction with a distortion function g. Such a decision-maker prefers the fortune Y to the fortune X if, and only if,

$$\mathbb{H}_g^u[X]\leq \mathbb{H}_g^u[Y], \tag{2.28}$$

where $\mathbb{H}_g^u[X]$ is defined as

$$\begin{aligned}\mathbb{H}_g^u[X] &= -\int_{-\infty}^{+\infty} u(x)dg(\overline{F}_X(x))\\ &= \int_0^{+\infty} g\left(\Pr[u(X)>t]\right)dt.\end{aligned}$$

It is easy to see that if $g(p)=p$, we get the expected utility model while if $u(x)=x$, we get Yaari's dual theory. For more details, see Landsberger and Meilijson (1990, 1994a, b).

Recently, Tsanakas and Desli (2003) developed a class of convex risk measures in the rank-dependent framework. Using an exponential utility function, they derived a distortion-exponential principle having attractive properties. This risk measure behaves approximately as a coherent risk measure for small portfolios of risks, while for larger portfolios the risk aversion induced by the utility function becomes prevalent, and the sensitivity to liquidity risk and risk aggregation issues generally increases. We will not consider the rank-dependent expected utility paradigm further in this book and we refer the interested reader to the aforementioned literature for details.

2.6.2 Wang risk measures

2.6.2.1 Definition

The analogue of the zero-utility principle in the distorted expectation theory is as follows: the premium $\Pi[X]$ is the solution of the indifference equation

$$w=\mathbb{H}_g[w]=\mathbb{H}_g[w+\Pi[X]-X]. \tag{2.29}$$

Note the similarity to (2.17). The assumption that g is convex reflects the risk aversion in this situation.

The right-hand side of (2.29) is equal to

$$\mathbb{H}_g[w+\Pi[X]-X]=w+\Pi[X]+\mathbb{H}_g[-X]=w+\Pi[X]-\mathbb{H}_{\overline{g}}[X],$$

where $\overline{g}(p)=1-g(1-p)$ is a dual distortion function. The solution of (2.29) is then given by

$$\Pi[X]=\mathbb{H}_{\overline{g}}(X).$$

When the distortion function g is convex (expressing risk aversion) the dual $\overline{g}$ is concave and we obtain the Wang distortion principle. This leads to the following definition.

Definition 2.6.3. The Wang risk measure ρ_g of risk X is defined as

$$\rho_g[X]=\int_0^{+\infty} g(\overline{F}_X(x))dx$$

for some non-decreasing distortion function g satisfying $g(0)=0$ and $g(1)=1$. ∇

Note that Wang risk measures ρ_g are the distorted expectation equivalent of the zero-utility risk measures in the classical expected utility theory.

2.6.2.2 Properties

Wang risk measures have many convenient properties, as stated next.

Property 2.6.4
Wang risk measures ρ_g are no-ripoff, positively homogeneous, translative and monotone.

Proof. Since VaR possesses these properties and any ρ_g can be represented as a mixture of VaRs by virtue of (2.26), it also has these properties. For instance, since VaR is no-ripoff,

$$\begin{aligned}\rho_g[X] &\leq \int_0^1 \max[X]dg(p)\\ &=\max[X]\big(g(1)-g(0)\big)=\max[X].\end{aligned}$$

Similarly, the positive homogeneity of ρ_g comes from

$$\begin{aligned}\rho_g[cX] &=\int_0^1 \mathrm{VaR}[cX;1-p]dg(p)\\ &=c\int_0^1 \mathrm{VaR}[X;1-p]dg(p)=c\rho_g[X].\end{aligned}$$

The other properties are deduced from a similar reasoning. □

Wang risk measures contain a non-negative loading provided g lies above the first diagonal, that is,

$$g(t) \geq t \text{ for all } t \in [0, 1] \Rightarrow \rho_g[X] \geq \mathbb{E}[X].$$

This is the case for any concave g. Wang risk measures do not induce unjustified loading, since

$$\rho_g[c] = \int_0^c g(1)dx = c.$$

Property 2.6.5
Wang risk measures ρ_g are comonotonic additive.

Proof. Let X and Y be comonotonic risks. Since the VaRs are comonotonic additive, we have

$$\begin{aligned}
\rho_g[X+Y] &= \int_0^1 \text{VaR}[X+Y; 1-p]dg(p) \\
&= \int_0^1 \Big(\text{VaR}[X; 1-p] + \text{VaR}[Y; 1-p]\Big)dg(p) \\
&= \rho_g[X] + \rho_g[Y],
\end{aligned}$$

which concludes the proof. □

Property 2.6.6
Wang risk measures ρ_g are subadditive if, and only if, g is concave.

Proof. Let us assume that g admits a continuous second derivative g''. The concavity of g ensures that $g'' \leq 0$. Remember that any Wang risk measure can be written as a mixture of VaRs according to (2.26). Now

$$\begin{aligned}
\rho_g[X] &= \int_0^1 \text{VaR}[X; 1-p]dg(p) \\
&= -\int_0^1 \left(\int_0^\xi \text{VaR}[X; 1-p]dp\right) g''(\xi)d\xi + g'(1)\mathbb{E}[X] \\
&= -\int_0^1 \text{TVaR}[X; 1-\xi](1-\xi)g''(\xi)d\xi + g'(1)\mathbb{E}[X].
\end{aligned}$$

This shows that any Wang risk measure associated with a concave distortion function can be written as a mixture of TVaRs. Now

$$\begin{aligned}
\rho_g[X+Y] &= -\int_0^1 \text{TVaR}[X+Y; 1-\xi](1-\xi)g''(\xi)d\xi + g'(1)\mathbb{E}[X+Y] \\
&\leq -\int_0^1 \Big(\text{TVaR}[X; 1-\xi] + \text{TVaR}[Y; 1-\xi]\Big)(1-\xi)g''(\xi)d\xi \\
&\quad + g'(1)\mathbb{E}[X+Y] \\
&= \rho_g[X] + \rho_g[Y],
\end{aligned}$$

where the inequality follows from the subadditivity of TVaR.

Let us now establish the necessity of the concavity condition imposed to the distortion function g for ρ_g to be subadditive. The negation of concavity of g leads to the conclusion that g has to have a strictly convex section if g is twice differentiable. Therefore, we prove that if g has a strictly convex section then ρ_g cannot be subadditive (i.e., it is possible to find two risks X and Y such that $\rho_g[X+Y] > \rho_g[X]+\rho_g[Y]$); the example is taken from Wirch and Hardy (1999). Specifically, suppose that g is strictly convex in $[a, b] \subseteq [0, 1]$, and let $c=\frac{a+b}{2}$. Convexity over (a, b) implies from (2.35) that for any $z<\frac{b-a}{2}$,

$$g(c+z)-g(c)>g(c)-g(c-z).$$

Consider the rvs X and Y with discrete joint distribution given by

X \ Y	0	$w+\frac{z}{2}$	$w+z$
0	$1-c-z$	z	0
$w+z$	z	0	$c-z$

where $w>0$ and $z<\frac{b-a}{2}$. For these rvs, we have

$$\begin{aligned}
\rho_g[X] &= (w+z)g(c),\\
\rho_g[Y] &= \left(w+\frac{z}{2}\right)g(c)+\frac{z}{2}g(c-z),\\
\rho_g[X+Y] &= \left(w+\frac{z}{2}\right)g(c+z)+\frac{z}{2}g(c)+(w+z)g(c-z),
\end{aligned}$$

so that

$$\rho_g[X+Y]-\rho_g[X]-\rho_g[Y]=\left(w+\frac{z}{2}\right)\big(g(c+z)-2g(c)+g(c-z)\big)>0.$$

Hence, ρ_g cannot be subadditive. □

Thus, when the distortion function is concave, Wang risk measures are coherent. Note that in this case, the measuring process proceeds in two steps: first, the original risk X is transformed into a new risk X_g with tf

$$\Pr[X_g>t]=g(\overline{F}_X(t)), \quad t\in\mathbb{R};$$

second, the expectation $\mathbb{E}[X_g]$ is computed; and finally, $\rho_g[X]=\mathbb{E}[X_g]$.

Remark 2.6.7. It can also be shown that every risk measure that satisfies the five key properties of monotonicity, translativity, positive homogeneity, subadditivity and comonotonic additivity can be represented as a distorted expectation (subject to a technical condition). For more details, see Kusuoka (2001). ∇

2.6.2.3 Extra loading for parameter uncertainty

In practice, actuaries face parameter uncertainty in the models they use: the true values of the parameters are unknown and only estimated values are available. A common method to deal with parameter uncertainty is to use a secondary mixing distribution, that is, to describe the loss distribution by the conditional df $F_X(\cdot|\theta)$ where the parameter itself is given a distribution. It is a desirable property for a risk measure to yield extra risk-load for parameter uncertainty. Wang risk measures possess this desirable property when the distortion function is concave.

Property 2.6.8
Assume that the distortion function g is concave. For any risk X with conditional df $F_X(\cdot|\theta)$ and conditional Wang risk measure $\rho_g[X|\theta]$,

$$\rho_g[X] \geq \mathbb{E}\Big[\rho_g[X|\Theta]\Big].$$

Proof. Applying Jensen's inequality to the concave distortion function g yields

$$\begin{aligned}
\rho_g[X] &= \int_0^{+\infty} g\Big(\overline{F}_X(t)\Big)dt \\
&= \int_0^{+\infty} g\left(\int_{-\infty}^{+\infty} \overline{F}_X(t|\theta)dF_\Theta(\theta)\right)dt \\
&\geq \int_{-\infty}^{+\infty} \underbrace{\int_0^{+\infty} g\Big(\overline{F}_X(t|\theta)\Big)dt}_{=\rho_g[X|\theta]}\, dF_\Theta(\theta) = \mathbb{E}[\rho_g[X|\Theta]],
\end{aligned}$$

which concludes the proof. □

Remark 2.6.9. Property 2.6.8 is related to the concept of iterativity discussed, for example, in Goovaerts, De Vijlder and Hazendonck (1984). ∇

2.6.3 *Some particular cases of Wang risk measures*

2.6.3.1 Distorted expectations and VaRs

Let the distortion function g be defined by $g(x) = \mathbb{I}[x \leq 1-p]$, $0 \leq x \leq 1$, for an arbitrary, but fixed, $p \in [0, 1)$. Then it is easy to see from (2.26) that for any risk X,

$$\rho_g[X] = \text{VaR}[X; p].$$

The distortion function giving rise to the VaR is not concave, so that VaRs are not coherent (as previously established).

2.6.3.2 Distorted expectations and TVaRs

Let the distortion function g be defined by

$$g(x) = \min\left\{\frac{x}{1-p}, 1\right\},$$

$0 \leq x \leq 1$, for an arbitrary, but fixed, $p \in [0, 1]$. In this case we find from (2.26) that

$$\begin{aligned}\rho_g[X] &= \frac{1}{1-p}\int_0^{1-p} \text{VaR}[X; 1-\xi]d\xi \\ &= \frac{1}{1-p}\int_p^1 \text{VaR}[X; \xi]d\xi = \text{TVaR}[X; p].\end{aligned}$$

The distortion function giving rise to the TVaR is concave, so that TVaRs are coherent (as previously established). Furthermore, this gives a new interpretation of the measure of risk with TVaR. First, the original risk X is transformed into a new risk X_p^* with tail function

$$\begin{aligned}\overline{F}_p^*(t) &= \min\left\{\frac{\overline{F}_X(t)}{1-p}, 1\right\} \\ &= \begin{cases} \frac{\overline{F}_X(t)}{1-p}, & \text{if } \overline{F}_X(t) \leq 1-p \Leftrightarrow t \geq \overline{F}_X^{-1}(1-p) = \text{VaR}[X; p], \\ 1, & \text{otherwise.}\end{cases}\end{aligned}$$

Then the mathematical expectation $\mathbb{E}[X_p^*]$ is computed. Again, the risk measuring process proceeds in two steps: first, a reweighting is operated and then an expected value under the new measure is computed.

2.6.3.3 Some risk measures that are not distorted expectations

Not all commonly encountered risk measures are Wang risk measures, as is shown next.

Property 2.6.10
Expected shortfall is not a distortion risk measure.

Proof. Assume that the risk measure ES$[X; p]$ can be expressed as a distorted expectation for some distortion function g. Let us first consider $X \sim \mathcal{U}ni(0, 1)$. Hence, for the given $p \in (0, 1)$, we have

$$\begin{aligned}\text{ES}[X; p] &= \int_p^1 s ds = \tfrac{1}{2}(1-p)^2 \\ &= \rho_g[X] = \int_0^1 g(s)ds. \end{aligned} \tag{2.30}$$

Let us now consider $X \sim \mathcal{B}er(r)$ for an arbitrarily fixed r in $(0, 1-p]$. We easily obtain

$$\text{ES}[X; p] = \mathbb{E}[X] = r = \rho_g[X] = \int_0^1 g(r)ds,$$

so that $g(r) = r$ for $0 < r \leq 1-p$. Then substituting this into (2.30) yields

$$\tfrac{1}{2}(1-p)^2 = \int_0^{1-p} s ds + \int_{1-p}^1 g(s)ds \geq \tfrac{1}{2}(1-p)^2 + p(1-p),$$

which is obviously a self-contradiction since $0 < p < 1$. This proves the result. □

Property 2.6.11
Conditional tail expectation is not a distortion risk measure.

Proof. Using the same approach as above, we assume that the risk measure CTE$[X; p]$ can be expressed as a distorted expectation for some distortion function g. We first consider $X \sim \mathcal{U}ni(0, 1)$. Hence, for the given $p \in (0, 1)$, recalling (2.8), we have

$$p + \frac{1}{2}(1-p) = \int_0^1 g(1-x)\,dx.$$

Simplifying the above equation gives that

$$\int_0^1 g(x)\,dx = \tfrac{1}{2}(1+p). \tag{2.31}$$

Let us now consider $Y \sim \mathcal{B}er(r)$, for an arbitrarily fixed r in $(0, 1-p]$. Again applying (2.8), we obtain CTE$[Y; p]$. Hence, we should have that $g(r) = 1$. By virtue of the monotonicity of the distortion function g and the arbitrariness of $0 < r \leq 1 - p$ we conclude that $g(\cdot) \equiv 1$ on $(0, 1]$, which contradicts (2.31). This proves that CTE$[X; p]$ is not a distortion risk measure. □

2.6.3.4 Dual-power risk measure

Considering $g(p) = 1 - (1-p)^{\xi}$, $\xi \geq 1$, we get

$$\rho_g[X] = \int_0^{+\infty} \left(1 - (F_X(x))^{\xi}\right) dx.$$

When ξ is an integer, $\rho_g[X]$ can be interpreted as the expected value of the maximum $\max\{X_1, \ldots, X_\xi\}$ of a set of ξ independent rvs distributed as X.

The dual-power approach for measuring risk is therefore a two-step approach. First, the original risk X is transformed into

$$X_\xi^* = \max\{X_1, \ldots, X_\xi\}$$

which is obviously less favourable than X, and then the mathematical expectation $\mathbb{E}[X_\xi^*]$ is computed.

2.6.3.5 Proportional hazard risk measure

The proportional hazard (PH) transform approach to measuring risk was proposed by Wang (1995). Taking $g(p) = p^{1/\xi}$, $\xi \geq 1$, gives the PH risk measure

$$\mathrm{PH}_\xi[X] = \rho_g[X] = \int_0^{+\infty} \left(\overline{F}_X(x)\right)^{1/\xi} dx$$

which can be interpreted as the risk-adjusted risk measure, where ξ is the index of risk aversion. Clearly, the function $\overline{F}_\xi^*$ defined as

$$\overline{F}_\xi^*(x) = \left(\overline{F}_X(x)\right)^{1/\xi}$$

is a tail function. Hence,

$$\text{PH}_\xi[X] = \mathbb{E}[X_\xi^*],$$

where X_ξ^* has tail function $\overline{F}_\xi^*$. The PH risk measure proceeds in two steps: first the original risk X is replaced with its transform X_ξ^*, and then an expected value is computed. Note that for $\xi = 1$, $\text{PH}_1[X] = \mathbb{E}[X]$.

Example 2.6.12. If $X \sim \mathcal{P}ar(\alpha, \theta)$, the tail function $\left(\overline{F}_X(x)\right)^{1/\xi}$ corresponds to $\mathcal{P}ar(\alpha/\xi, \theta)$ so that

$$\text{PH}_\xi[X] = \begin{cases} \frac{\theta}{\alpha/\xi - 1} & \text{if } \xi < \alpha, \\ +\infty & \text{if } \xi \geq \alpha. \end{cases}$$

∇

2.6.3.6 Normal transform risk measure

The normal transform risk measure was introduced by Wang (2000). For any $0 < p < 1$, define the distortion function

$$g_p(q) = \Phi\Big(\Phi^{-1}(q) + \Phi^{-1}(p)\Big), \qquad 0 < q < 1, \ 0 < p < 1, \tag{2.32}$$

where Φ is the df of the $\mathcal{N}or(0, 1)$ distribution. The distortion function defined in (2.32) is called the 'normal transform at level p'. The corresponding distortion risk measure is called the normal transform risk measure and denoted by $\text{NT}_p(X)$.

If $X \sim \mathcal{N}or(\mu, \sigma^2)$ then the normal transform risk measure is identical to VaR at the same level, that is,

$$\text{NT}_p(X) = \text{VaR}[X\,; p]. \tag{2.33}$$

Examples illustrating the fact that the NT risk measure uses the whole distribution and that it accounts for extreme low-frequency and high severity losses can be found in Wang (2002).

2.7 EXERCISES

Exercise 2.7.1. (Quota-share insurance). Show that any comonotonic additive risk measure ϱ is additive for quota share insurance, that is,

$$\varrho[X] = \varrho[\alpha X] + \varrho[(1-\alpha)X] \text{ for any } 0 \leq \alpha \leq 1.$$

Exercise 2.7.2. (Convex risk measures). Some authors, including Deprez and Gerber (1985), replaced translativity and positive homogeneity with the condition that ϱ be convex, that is, that the inequality

$$\varrho\big[\lambda X + (1-\lambda)Y\big] \leq \lambda\varrho[X] + (1-\lambda)\varrho[Y]$$

holds for all rvs X and Y, and constant $\lambda \in [0, 1]$. Convexity encourages diversification, that is, the risk of a diversified position $\lambda X + (1 - \lambda)Y$ is less than or equal to the weighted average of the individual risks. Prove the following:

(i) A positively homogeneous risk measure ϱ is convex if, and only if, it is subadditive.

(ii) If a convex risk measure does not entail excessive loading nor unjustified loading then it is also monotone.

(iii) Any convex risk measure ensures a non-negative loading provided it does not entail unjustified loading and is continuous with respect to convergence in distribution.

Exercise 2.7.3. (Convexity and marginal risk measures). Given two rvs X and Y, consider the real function

$$\vartheta(\alpha) = \varrho[X + \alpha Y]$$

which describes the variation of risk associated with the addition of a fraction α of a new rv Y to the existing portfolio X.

Prove that a translative risk measure ϱ is convex if, and only if, the function ϑ is convex for all couples (X, Y).

Exercise 2.7.4. (Sum of comonotonic Paretos). Prove that the sum of $\mathcal{P}ar(\alpha, \theta_i)$ comonotonic random variables is $\mathcal{P}ar(\alpha, \theta_\bullet)$, where $\theta_\bullet = \sum_{i=1}^n \theta_i$.

Exercise 2.7.5. (VaR fails to be subadditive for continuous risks). Consider two independent $\mathcal{P}ar(1, 1)$ risks X and Y. Show that the inequality

$$\text{VaR}[X; p] + \text{VaR}[Y; p] < \text{VaR}[X + Y; p]$$

holds for any p, so that VaR cannot be subadditive in this simple case.

Exercise 2.7.6. (VaR fails to be subadditive for discrete risks). Let X_i, $i = 1, \ldots, 100$, be 100 independent defaultable bonds with 1 % default probability, 2 % coupon when they do not default and €100 face value:

$$X_i = \begin{cases} -€100, & \text{with probability } 0.01, \\ +€2, & \text{with probability } 0.99. \end{cases}$$

Consider two portfolios

$$P_1 = \sum_{i=1}^{100} X_i (\text{diversified}) \text{ and } P_2 = 100X_1 (\text{non-diversified}).$$

Show that for some probability level p it may happen that

$$\text{VaR}[P_1; p] > \text{VaR}[P_2; p] = 100\text{VaR}[X_1; p].$$

The non-diversified portfolio, which intuitively is more risky, is nevertheless chosen by VaR as the less risky portfolio. This demonstrates how over-reliance on VaR (as on other risk measures) can lead to perverse conclusions.

Exercise 2.7.7. (A basic moment inequality for VaR). Show that the inequality

$$\text{VaR}[X;p] \leq \frac{\mathbb{E}[X]}{1-p}$$

is valid for any p.

Hint: use the Markov inequality that states that for any positive rv X, $\Pr[X > t] \leq \mathbb{E}[X]/t$ holds for any positive t.

Exercise 2.7.8. (VaR for normal rvs). Consider $X \sim \mathcal{N}or(\mu, \sigma^2)$. Show that

$$\text{VaR}[X;p] = \mu + \sigma\,\Phi^{-1}(p), \qquad p \in (0,1),$$

where Φ denotes the standard normal df. Deduce that VaR is subadditive as far as Gaussian rvs are considered.

Exercise 2.7.9. (VaR for lognormal rvs). Consider $X \sim \mathcal{LN}or(\mu, \sigma^2)$. Show that

$$\text{VaR}[X;p] = \exp(\mu + \sigma\,\Phi^{-1}(P)), \qquad p \in (0,1).$$

Exercise 2.7.10. (Marginal VaR). The analytically tractable expression for the derivatives of VaR can be used to perform local risk analysis, as shown in Gouriéroux, Laurent and Scaillet (2000). Show that for any continuous rvs X and Y with joint pdf $f(\cdot,\cdot)$,

$$\frac{\partial}{\partial\alpha}\text{VaR}[X+\alpha Y;p] = \mathbb{E}\big[Y\big|X+\alpha Y = \text{VaR}[X+\alpha Y;p]\big].$$

Exercise 2.7.11. (Non-convexity of VaR). Show that the second derivative of VaR with respect to α for any continuous rvs X and Y is given by

$$\frac{\partial^2}{\partial\alpha^2}\text{VaR}[X+\alpha Y;p] = \left[\frac{\partial}{\partial s}\mathbb{V}[Y|X+\alpha Y = s] + \mathbb{V}[Y|X+\alpha Y = s]\frac{\partial}{\partial s}\ln f_{X+\alpha Y}(s)\right]_{s=\text{VaR}[X;p]}.$$

Hint: use the fact that

$$\text{VaR}[X+\alpha Y;p] = -\frac{d}{dp}\Big((1-p)\text{TVaR}[X+\alpha Y;p]\Big).$$

Exercise 2.7.12. (Stop-loss premium for normal rvs). Consider $X \sim \mathcal{N}or(\mu, \sigma^2)$. Show that the stop-loss premiums of X are given by

$$\pi_X(d) = \sigma\,\Phi'\left(\frac{d-\mu}{\sigma}\right) - (d-\mu)\left(1 - \Phi\left(\frac{d-\mu}{\sigma}\right)\right).$$

Exercise 2.7.13. (Stop-loss premium for lognormal rvs). Consider $X \sim \mathcal{LN}or(\mu, \sigma^2)$. Show that the stop-loss premiums of X are given by

$$\pi_X(d) = \exp(\mu + \sigma^2/2)\Phi(d_1) - d\,\Phi(d_2), \qquad d > 0, \tag{2.34}$$

where d_1 and d_2 are given by

$$d_1 = \frac{\mu - \ln d}{\sigma} + \sigma \text{ and } d_2 = d_1 - \sigma,$$

respectively. Note the close connection with the option pricing formula derived by Black and Scholes (1973).

Exercise 2.7.14. (Mixtures of TVaRs). Show that any mixure of TVaRs of the form

$$\varrho[X] = \int_0^1 \text{TVaR}[X;\, p]dH(p),$$

where H is any monotonic, right-continuous function on (0,1), can be represented as

$$\varrho[X] = \int_0^1 \text{VaR}[X;\, p]h(p)dp, \quad \text{where } h(p) = \int_0^1 \frac{1}{\xi}dH(\xi).$$

Exercise 2.7.15. (A basic moment inequality for TVaR). Let us consider an rv X with mean μ and variance σ^2. Show that the inequality

$$\text{TVaR}[X;\, p] \leq \mu + \sigma\sqrt{p(1-p)}$$

holds for any p.

Exercise 2.7.16. (TVaR for normal rvs). Consider $X \sim \mathcal{N}or\ (\mu,\, \sigma^2)$. Show that

$$\text{TVaR}[X;\, p] = \mu + \sigma\frac{\Phi'\left(\Phi^{-1}(p)\right)}{1-p}, \qquad p \in (0,\, 1)\,.$$

Exercise 2.7.17. (TVaR for lognormal rvs). Consider $X \sim \mathcal{LN}or\ (\mu,\, \sigma^2)$. Show that

$$\text{TVaR}[X;\, p] = \exp(\mu + \sigma^2/2)\frac{\Phi\left(\sigma - \Phi^{-1}(p)\right)}{1-p}, \qquad p \in (0,\, 1)\,.$$

Exercise 2.7.18. (Marginal TVaR). Scaillet (2004) (see also Tasche 2000) proved that the first derivative of TVaR with respect to the proportion of extra risk is its conditional mean given the VaR has been exceeded. Specifically, show that for any continuous rvs X and Y,

$$\frac{\partial}{\partial\alpha}\text{TVaR}[X+\alpha Y\,;\, p] = \mathbb{E}\big[Y\big|X+\alpha Y \geq \text{VaR}[X+\alpha Y\,;\, p]\big].$$

Exercise 2.7.19. (Convexity of TVaR for continuous risks). Show that for any continuous rvs X and Y,

$$\begin{aligned}\frac{\partial^2}{\partial\alpha^2}\text{TVaR}[X+\alpha Y;\, p] = {} & \frac{1}{1-p}\mathbb{V}\big[Y\big|X+\alpha Y = \text{VaR}[X+\alpha Y;\, p]\big] \\ & \times f_{X+\alpha Y}(\text{VaR}[X+\alpha Y;\, p]).\end{aligned}$$

Argue from Exercise 2.7.3 that TVaR is a convex risk measure.

Exercise 2.7.20. (ES for normal rvs). Consider $X \sim \mathcal{N}or\,(\mu, \sigma^2)$. Show that

$$\mathrm{ES}[X;\, p] = \sigma\, \Phi'\left(\Phi^{-1}(p)\right) - \sigma\, \Phi^{-1}(p)\,(1-p), \quad p \in (0,1).$$

Exercise 2.7.21. (ES for lognormal rvs). Consider $X \sim \mathcal{LN}or\,(\mu, \sigma^2)$. Show that

$$\mathrm{ES}[X;\, p] = \exp\left(\mu + \sigma^2/2\right)\Phi\left(\sigma - \Phi^{-1}(p)\right) - \exp\left(\mu + \sigma\, \Phi^{-1}(p)\right)(1-p), \quad p \in (0,1).$$

Exercise 2.7.22. Van Heerwaarden, Kaas and Goovaerts (1989) take X and Y such that

$$\Pr[X=0, Y=0] = \frac{1}{3},$$
$$\Pr[X=0, Y=3] = \frac{1}{3},$$
$$\Pr[X=6, Y=6] = \frac{1}{3}.$$

Show that $\Pr[X \le Y] = 1$ but that the Esscher premium $\mathrm{Es}[X\,;\,1/2] > \mathrm{Es}[Y\,;\,1/2]$.

Exercise 2.7.23. (PH risk measure for exponential risks). If $X \sim \mathcal{E}xp\,(1/b)$ then show that $\mathrm{PH}_\xi[X] = \xi b$.

Exercise 2.7.24. When a risk X is divided into layers $(x_i, x_{i+1}]$, $i = 0, 1, \ldots$, show that

$$\mathrm{PH}_\xi[X] = \sum_{i \ge 0} \mathrm{PH}_\xi[X_{(x_i, x_{i+1}]}],$$

where

$$X_{(x_i, x_{i+1}]} = \left(\min\{X, x_{i+1}\} - x_i\right)\mathbb{I}[X > x_i].$$

For more results in the same vein, see Wang (1996).

Exercise 2.7.25. Consider

$$U = \begin{cases} 0, & \text{with probability } 0.75, \\ 4, & \text{with probability } 0.25, \end{cases}$$

and $V \sim \mathcal{P}ar\,(3, 2)$. Clearly, $\mathbb{E}[U] = \mathbb{E}[V] = 1$ and $\mathbb{V}[U] = \mathbb{V}[V] = 3$. Show that for any $\xi > 1$, $\mathrm{PH}_\xi[U] < \mathrm{PH}_\xi[V]$ so that the safety loading is always larger for the Pareto risk than for the two-point risk with the same first two moments.

Exercise 2.7.26. If $X \sim \mathcal{U}ni(0, a)$ show that $\mathrm{PH}_\xi[X] = \frac{a\xi}{\xi+1}$.

Exercise 2.7.27. Show that if

$$X = \begin{cases} U, & \text{with probability } p, \\ V, & \text{with probability } 1-p, \end{cases}$$

or $X = IU + (1-I)V$ with $I \sim \mathcal{B}er\,(p)$ independent of U and V, then for $\xi > 1$,

$$\mathrm{PH}_\xi[X] > p\mathrm{PH}_\xi[U] + (1-p)\mathrm{PH}_\xi[V].$$

Exercise 2.7.28. (Normal transform risk measure for lognormal rvs). For any $Y \sim \mathcal{LN}or\,(\mu, \sigma^2)$, show that

$$\mathrm{NT}_p(Y) = \mathrm{VaR}\Big[Y\,;\,\Phi\Big(\Phi^{-1}(p) + \frac{\sigma}{2}\Big)\Big] > \mathrm{VaR}[Y\,;\,p].$$

2.8 APPENDIX: CONVEXITY AND CONCAVITY

2.8.1 Definition

Convexity has received full treatment in several readily available sources and in this section we merely gather together results useful for our work. For further details and proofs, the reader is referred, for example, to Roberts and Varberg (1973).

Let us start with the standard definition of convexity.

Definition 2.8.1. Let I be an interval in $\mathbb{R}$. Then the function $f: I \to \mathbb{R}$ is said to be convex if for all $x, y \in I$ and all $\alpha \in [0, 1]$, the inequality

$$f(\alpha x + (1-\alpha)y) \le \alpha f(x) + (1-\alpha) f(y)$$

holds. If this inequality is strict for all $x \neq y$ and $\alpha \in (0, 1)$ then f is said to be strictly convex. ∇

A closely related concept is that of concavity: f is said to be (strictly) concave if, and only if, $-f$ is (strictly) convex. In modern mathematics texts, 'convex' and 'concave' are sometimes replaced by 'concave upwards' and 'concave downwards', respectively.

2.8.2 Equivalent conditions

Of course the inequality of Definition 2.8.1 can be restated in a number of equivalent forms. Let us mention some of them in the following property.

Property 2.8.2

(i) For $x, y \in I$, $p, q \ge 0$ such that $p + q > 0$,

$$f\left(\frac{px + qy}{p+q}\right) \ge \frac{pf(x) + qf(y)}{p+q}.$$

(ii) For $x_1 < x_2 < x_3 \in I$,

$$f(x_2) \le \frac{x_2 - x_3}{x_1 - x_3} f(x_1) + \frac{x_1 - x_2}{x_1 - x_3} f(x_3).$$

(iii) For $x_1, x_2, x_3 \in I$ such that $x_1 < x_3$ and $x_1, x_3 \neq x_2$,

$$\frac{f(x_1) - f(x_2)}{x_1 - x_2} \le \frac{f(x_2) - f(x_3)}{x_2 - x_3}$$

so that a function f is convex on I if, and only if, for every point $c \in I$ the function $\dfrac{f(x) - f(c)}{x - c}$ is non-decreasing on $I \setminus \{c\}$.

The simple geometric interpretation of convexity is that the graph of a convex function f lies below its chords. Now, invoking Property 2.8.2(iii), we get the following result: if f is a convex function on I and if $x_1 \leq y_1$, $x_2 \leq y_2$, $x_1 \neq x_2$, $y_1 \neq y_2$, then the following inequality is valid:

$$\frac{f(x_2) - f(x_1)}{x_2 - x_1} \leq \frac{f(y_2) - f(y_1)}{y_2 - y_1}.$$

By letting $x_1 = x$, $x_2 = x + z$, $y_1 = y$, $y_2 = y + z$ ($x \leq y$ and $z \geq 0$), we then have

$$f(x+z) - f(x) \leq f(y+z) - f(y), \tag{2.35}$$

which is just

$$f(x+z) + f(y) \leq f(x) + f(y+z).$$

Of course the only functions that are simultaneously convex and concave are the linear functions: f is both convex and concave if, and only if, $f(x) = ax + b$ for some $a, b \in \mathbb{R}$.

2.8.3 Properties

The following result concerns derivatives of some convex functions.

Proposition 2.8.3

(i) $f: [a, b] \to \mathbb{R}$ is convex if, and only if, there exist a non-decreasing function $g: [a, b] \to \mathbb{R}$ and a real number c ($a < c < b$) such that for all x ($a < x < b$),

$$f(x) = f(c) + \int_{t=c}^{x} g(t)dt.$$

(ii) If f is strictly convex then g in (i) is strictly increasing.

(iii) If f is differentiable then f is convex (strictly convex) if, and only if, f' is non-decreasing (increasing).

(iv) If f'' exists on (a, b) then f is convex if, and only if, $f'' \geq 0$. If $f'' > 0$ then f is strictly convex.

The next result concerns closure properties of convex functions.

Proposition 2.8.4

(i) If $\{f_n, n = 1, 2, 3, \ldots\}$ is a sequence of convex functions $f_n : I \to \mathbb{R}$ converging to a finite limit function f on I, then f is convex. Moreover, the convergence is uniform on any closed subinterval of I.

(ii) Every continuous function f convex on $[a, b]$ is the uniform limit of the sequence

$$f_n(x) = \alpha_1^{(n)} + \alpha_2^{(n)} x + \sum_{j=0}^{n} \beta_j^{(n)} (x - t_j^{(n)})_+,$$

with $\beta_j^{(n)} \geq 0$, knots $t_j^{(n)} \in [a, b]$ for $k = 0, 1, \ldots, n$ and real constants α_1, α_2.

2.8.4 Convex sequences

Sometimes we are interested in functions defined on arithmetic grids (typically, subsets of $\mathbb{N}$) and we need an appropriate definition of convexity. Functions defined on $\mathbb{N}$ are also called sequences of real numbers. The following definition makes the convexity concept clear in that case.

Definition 2.8.5. A finite sequence $\{a_k, k=0, 1, \ldots, n\}$ of real numbers is said to be a convex sequence if

$$2a_k \leq a_{k-1} + a_{k+1} \quad \text{for all } k=1, \ldots, n-1.$$

∇

Let us define the forward operator Δ as $\Delta a_k = a_{k+1} - a_k$. Informally, Δ can be considered as a discrete counterpart of the usual derivative. Obviously, the sequence $\{a_k, k=0, 1, \ldots, n\}$ is non-decreasing if

$$\Delta a_k \geq 0 \quad \text{for all } k=0, 1, \ldots, n-1.$$

Now, the second-order difference operator Δ^2 is given by

$$\begin{aligned}\Delta^2 a_k &= \Delta(\Delta a_k) = \Delta(a_{k+1} - a_k)\\ &= a_{k+2} - 2a_{k+1} + a_k.\end{aligned}$$

We immediately see that the sequence $\{a_k, k=0, 1, \ldots, n\}$ is convex if, and only if,

$$\Delta^2 a_k \geq 0 \quad \text{for all } k=0, 1, \ldots, n-2. \tag{2.36}$$

The infinite sequence $\{a_k, k \in \mathbb{N}\}$ is convex if, and only if,

$$\Delta^2 a_k \geq 0 \quad \text{for all } k \in \mathbb{N}.$$

Note that if the sequence $\{a_k, k \in \mathbb{N}\}$ is convex then the function f whose graph is the polygonal line with corner points (k, a_k), $k \in \mathbb{N}$, is also convex on $\mathbb{R}^+$.

2.8.5 Log-convex functions

Another important concept is log-convexity (note that we have already encountered this notion in Properties 1.7.6 and 1.7.7, and it will often be used again in the remainder of the book).

Definition 2.8.6. Let I be an interval in $\mathbb{R}$. A function $f: I \to \mathbb{R}$ is said to be log-convex, or multiplicatively convex, if $\ln f$ is convex, or equivalently if for all $x, y \in I$ and all $\alpha \in [0, 1]$,

$$f(\alpha x + (1-\alpha)y) \leq \big(f(x)\big)^{\alpha}\big(f(y)\big)^{1-\alpha}.$$

It is said to be log-concave if this inequality is reversed.

∇

If f and g are convex and g is increasing then $g \circ f$ is convex. Since $f = \exp(\ln f)$, it follows that every log-convex function is convex (but the converse is not true).

3

Comparing Risks

Now that we are able to measure the riskiness associated with various random prospects, our aim is to formalize the intuitive idea that one rv is more dangerous than another. Of course, we could base our comparisons on a single risk measure, and totally order the rvs. The result of this strategy is, however, too crude and we prefer to base our comparison on a wide range of risk measures. This leads to partial orders among rvs, called stochastic orderings. This chapter expands on Kaas *et al.* (2001, Chapter 10).

3.1 INTRODUCTION

Roughly speaking, a stochastic ordering is an order relation that allows probability measures to be compared. As noted by Mosler and Scarsini (1993), questions related to this concept are as old as probability itself. Let us consider, for instance, the problem of comparing two gambles in order to decide which one is more profitable from the player's point of view. Sometimes, the choice is easy. For example, suppose that, for a stake of €1, you have to opt for one of the following two die-tossing games:

1. You win €2 if you throw a '6'.
2. You win €5 if you throw a '7'.

You will certainly choose the second, at least if you desire to grow rich. Nevertheless, the choice is seldom so simple. Indeed, consider now the two following two die-tossing games, which again require a stake of €1:

3. You win €1 if you throw a '1' and €3 if you throw a '6'.
4. You win €2 if you throw a '1' or a '6'.

Which of these two would you choose? If you are risk-averse, it can be shown that you should choose game 4. This is because the expected utility of wealth associated with game 4 is larger than that associated with game 3, for any concave utility function. Since many practical situations can be represented as a choice among different 'games', there is thus a need for sophisticated comparison methods between random outcomes.

The easiest way to rank risky situations is to compute some risk measure and to order the random prospects accordingly. In many situations, however, even if a risk measure is

Actuarial Theory for Dependent Risks M. Denuit, J. Dhaene, M. Goovaerts and R. Kaas

reasonable in the context at hand, the values of the associated parameters (probability levels for VaR and TVaR, risk-aversion coefficient for exponential utility functions, distortion functions for Wang risk measures, and so on) are not fixed by the problem. Therefore, actuaries may require much more than a simple comparison on one particular risk measure: they could ask for a risk to be more favorable than another for all given risk measures. This generates a partial order (and not a total one, that is, the actuary can no longer order all pairs of risks) called a stochastic ordering. General comments on partial orderings of distributions can be found in Oja (1985).

Let us briefly give the historical background to the theory of stochastic orderings in probability. The first work in which a concept of stochastic ordering is central is probably the book of Hardy, Littlewood and Pólya (1934) on inequalities (as well as several earlier papers by the same authors). Their notion of majorization is not formulated as a stochastic ordering. In fact, majorization is a way of comparing two non-negative vectors (of the same dimension) in terms of the dispersion of their components (see Section 3.4.11). However, its translation to a stochastic ordering is immediate by associating to each vector in $\mathbb{R}^n$ the discrete probability measure that puts mass $\frac{1}{n}$ on each component of the vector. For a discussion of majorization theory, see also Marshall and Olkin (1979) and Tong (1994). Marshall and Olkin's book deals with majorization inequalities. It contains a comprehensive treatment of majorization and its applications in linear algebra, geometry, probability and statistics (and a few other fields).

The theory of dilation extended majorization to general probability measures; see Karamata (1932), Choquet (1963) and Strassen (1965). In this respect, it can be seen as the first authentic development of a theory of stochastic ordering *per se* (namely, an order relation in a space of probability measures).

Quite surprisingly, the so-called stochastic dominance (which is unquestionably the best-known and most intuitive stochastic ordering) was not studied until later – it was introduced by Lehmann (1955) and thoroughly analyzed by Kamae, Krengel and O'Brien (1977). Stochastic dominance and the dilation order (as well as their variations) are the orderings that have attracted the most attention. Nevertheless, a large number of other orderings have been introduced in recent decades, mostly motivated by different areas of applications (statistics, queueing theory, reliability theory, economics, biomathematics, actuarial science, physics, etc.). They have given rise to a huge amount of literature, culminating in the classified bibliography by Mosler and Scarsini (1993) and the books by Shaked and Shanthikumar (1994), Szekli (1995) and Müller and Stoyan (2002).

The interest of the actuarial community in stochastic orderings originated in the seminal papers by Borch (1961), Bühlmann *et al.* (1977) and Goovaerts, De Vijlder and Haezendonck (1982). In recent decades, this interest has been growing to the point that they have become one of the most important tools for comparing the riskiness of different random situations. The reader interested in actuarial applications of stochastic orderings is referred to the comprehensive books by Goovaerts *et al.* (1990) and Kaas, Van Heerwaarden and Goovaerts (1994).

In this chapter, we compare risks with the help of various transforms associated with these rvs that were introduced in Chapter 1: comparing dfs yields stochastic dominance $\preceq_{\text{ST}}$, comparing stop-loss transforms yields convex order $\preceq_{\text{SL},=}$ and stop-loss order $\preceq_{\text{SL}}$, comparing hazard rate functions yields hazard rate order $\preceq_{\text{HR}}$, comparing mean-excess functions yields mean-excess order $\preceq_{\text{MEF}}$, comparing Laplace transforms yields Laplace transform order $\preceq_{\rm LT}$, comparing moment generating functions yields moment generating function order $\preceq_{\rm MGF}$, and so on.

Remark 3.1.1. Stochastic orderings have been used successfully to solve various problems in applied probability and risk management. Once the validity of such a relation is established, it can be exploited to derive a host of inequalities among various quantities. Now that the probabilistic theory of stochastic orderings is well developed, there is a need for formal statistical tests to decide on the basis of empirical data that some stochastic ranking does indeed hold.

Despite the importance of this problem for practical applications, we will not discuss these issues in this book. We merely mention several references: the papers by Xu, Fisher and Willson (1996), Schmid and Trede (1998), Davidson and Duclos (2000) and Barrett and Donald (2003) on stochastic dominance, and Dardanoni and Forcina (1999) on Lorenz ordering.

Recently, Denuit, Goderniaux and Scaillet (2004) proposed a Kolmogorov-type test for excess-wealth and right-spread orders. As pointed out in the conclusion, this approach is generally applicable for many stochastic orderings, defined by the pointwise comparison of some transform associated with the underlying distribution functions. Since many notions of ageing can be defined on the basis of a stochastic comparison with respect to the exponential distribution, these tests can also be applied to check for the validity of these assumptions. ∇

3.2 STOCHASTIC ORDER RELATIONS

3.2.1 Partial orders among distribution functions

Most of the order relations we consider in this work are partial orders on a set of dfs. Let us make this notion precise.

Definition 3.2.1. Let $\mathcal{Y}$ be a set of univariate dfs. The binary relation $\preceq$ is a partial order on $\mathcal{Y}$ if for any elements F_X, F_Y and F_Z in $\mathcal{Y}$, the following properties hold:

(i) If $F_X \preceq F_Y$ and $F_Y \preceq F_Z$ then $F_X \preceq F_Z$ (transitivity).

(ii) $F_X \preceq F_X$ (reflexivity).

(iii) If $F_X \preceq F_Y$ and $F_Y \preceq F_X$ then $F_X \equiv F_Y$ (antisymmetry).

If, in addition, for any given pair F_X and F_Y of elements of $\mathcal{Y}$ either $F_X \preceq F_Y$ or $F_Y \preceq F_X$ holds, then $\preceq$ is said to be a total order. ∇

Although the order relations we use are often defined on sets of dfs, it is often convenient not to distinguish between an order relation for dfs and the corresponding relation for rvs. Extending the notation, we write $X \preceq Y$ but we actually mean $F_X \preceq F_Y$. In other words, when we say that a risk X is smaller than a risk Y for the stochastic order relation $\preceq$, we in fact assert that this ordering holds for the respective dfs of these risks. Therefore, the joint distribution of X and Y is irrelevant; only their marginal distributions are important. If $X \preceq Y$ then $X \preceq \widetilde{Y}$ also holds for any rv $\widetilde{Y}$ with the same marginal distribution as Y.

In such situations, we do not have to assume that the rvs being compared are defined on the same probability space. However, the question whether we can construct versions of the rvs that satisfy some additional properties on the same probability space is of interest. Such constructions utilize rvs that are dependent.

3.2.2 *Desirable properties for stochastic orderings*

As we did for risk measures, we will now enumerate a set of desirable properties for a stochastic order relation. These properties are of interest for their applications in actuarial science.

3.2.2.1 Stability under mixture

The idea is as follows: if the stochastic inequality $X \preceq Y$ holds conditionally upon $\Lambda = \theta$ for each θ, then we expect $X \preceq Y$ to hold also unconditionally. If this is indeed the case then $\preceq$ is said to be stable under mixture.

3.2.2.2 Stability under convolution

Consider two sequences $\{X_1, X_2, X_3, \ldots\}$ and $\{Y_1, Y_2, Y_3, \ldots\}$ of independent rvs such that $X_i \preceq Y_i$ holds for every i. The stochastic order $\preceq$ is said to be stable under convolution if $\sum_{i=1}^{n} X_i \preceq \sum_{i=1}^{n} Y_i$ holds for any integer n.

3.2.2.3 Stability under compounding

Let $\{X_1, X_2, X_3, \ldots\}$ and $\{Y_1, Y_2, Y_3, \ldots\}$ be two sequences of independent rvs such that $X_i \preceq Y_i$ holds for every i. If N is an integer-valued variable independent of the X_i and the Y_i, and if $\preceq$ is stable under mixture and under convolution, we obviously have $\sum_{i=1}^{N} X_i \preceq \sum_{i=1}^{N} Y_i$. The stochastic order $\preceq$ is said to be stable under compounding if, moreover, given two integer-valued rvs N and M such that $N \preceq M$, $\sum_{i=1}^{N} X_i \preceq \sum_{i=1}^{M} X_i$ holds.

3.2.2.4 Stability under limit (with respect to the convergence in distribution)

Consider two sequences of rvs $\{X_1, X_2, \ldots\}$ and $\{Y_1, Y_2, \ldots\}$ such that $X_i \preceq Y_i$ for all i and $X_i \to_d X$ and $Y_i \to_d Y$. Then $\preceq$ is said to be stable under taking limits when $X \preceq Y$ holds.

3.2.3 *Integral stochastic orderings*

3.2.3.1 Definition

Whitt (1986) introduced the notion of *integral stochastic orderings* for partial orders among dfs obtained by comparing the values of expectations for functions in a given class (often called the generator of the stochastic ordering). These stochastic order relations have been thoroughly studied by Marshall (1991) and Müller (1997a).

Definition 3.2.2. For two rvs X and Y, the integral stochastic ordering $\preceq_*$ generated by the class $\mathcal{U}_*$ of functions is defined by

$$X \preceq_* Y \Leftrightarrow \mathbb{E}[t(X)] \leq \mathbb{E}[t(Y)] \text{ for all } t \in \mathcal{U}_*, \tag{3.1}$$

provided that the expectations exist. ∇

The defining property (3.1) of integral stochastic orderings is closely related to expected utility theory, relating the test function t to some utility function u. We will return to this particular feature later on in this chapter.

A noteworthy feature of the integral stochastic ordering $\preceq_*$ is that many of its properties can be obtained directly from conditions satisfied by the underlying class of functions $\mathcal{U}_*$. This approach offers an opportunity for a unified study of the various orderings, and provides some insight into why some of the properties do not hold for all stochastic orderings. We will return to this approach in Chapter 9.

3.2.3.2 Analysis of mixtures

Given a family $\{X_\theta, \ \theta \in \Theta\}$, and a function t in $\mathcal{U}_*$, we define a new function t^*, with domain the parametric space Θ, as

$$t^*(\theta) = \mathbb{E}[t(X_\theta)]. \tag{3.2}$$

A natural question is then whether t^* also belongs to $\mathcal{U}_*$. For instance, if $\mathcal{U}_*$ is the class of non-decreasing functions, we wonder whether t^* is non-decreasing whenever t possesses this property. If this is the case, then the X_θ are said to be stochastically increasing; see Section 3.3.6. We will also explore this question when t is convex, non-decreasing and convex, as well as completely monotone.

If the implication $t \in \mathcal{U}_* \Rightarrow t^* \in \mathcal{U}_*$ holds, then for two rvs Λ_1 and Λ_2 taking values in the parametric space Θ we clearly have

$$\Lambda_1 \preceq_* \Lambda_2 \Rightarrow X_{\Lambda_1} \preceq_* X_{\Lambda_2}, \tag{3.3}$$

where for $i = 1, 2$,

$$\Pr[X_{\Lambda_i} \leq x] = \int_{-\infty}^{+\infty} \Pr[X_\theta \leq x] dF_{\Lambda_i}(\theta), \quad x \in \mathbb{R}. \tag{3.4}$$

Indeed, for any $t \in \mathcal{U}_*$, we have

$$\begin{aligned} \mathbb{E}[t(X_{\Lambda_1})] &= \mathbb{E}[t^*(\Lambda_1)] \\ &\leq \mathbb{E}[t^*(\Lambda_2)] \text{ since } \Lambda_1 \preceq_* \Lambda_2 \text{ and } t^* \in \mathcal{U}_* \\ &= \mathbb{E}[t(X_{\Lambda_2})]. \end{aligned}$$

The reasoning above is valid for each $t \in \mathcal{U}_*$, so that $X_{\Lambda_1} \preceq_* X_{\Lambda_2}$ does indeed hold.

As a particular case, we find stability under compounding when $X_\theta = \sum_{i=1}^{\theta} X_i$, $\Lambda_1 = N$ and $\Lambda_2 = M$.

3.3 STOCHASTIC DOMINANCE

3.3.1 Stochastic dominance and risk measures

3.3.1.1 Stochastic dominance and VaRs

In order to compare a pair of risks X and Y, it seems natural to resort to the concept of VaR, discussed in Chapter 2, and to consider X as less dangerous than Y if $\text{VaR}[X; \alpha_0] \leq \text{VaR}[Y; \alpha_0]$ for some prescribed probability level α_0. However, it is sometimes difficult to select such an α_0, and it is conceivable that $\text{VaR}[X; \alpha_0] < \text{VaR}[Y; \alpha_0]$ and $\text{VaR}[X; \alpha_1] > \text{VaR}[Y; \alpha_1]$ simultaneously for two probability levels α_0 and α_1. In this case, what can we conclude? It seems reasonable to adopt the following criterion: we place X before Y if the VaRs for X are smaller than the corresponding VaRs for Y, for *any* probability level.

Definition 3.3.1. Let X and Y be two rvs. Then X is said to be smaller than Y in stochastic dominance, denoted as $X \preceq_{\text{ST}} Y$, if the inequality $\text{VaR}[X; p] \leq \text{VaR}[Y; p]$ is satisfied for all $p \in [0, 1]$. ∇

Standard references for $\preceq_{\text{ST}}$ are the books of Lehmann (1959), Marshall and Olkin (1979), Ross (1983) and Stoyan (1983). The books mentioned in Section 3.1 all cover stochastic dominance.

Stochastic dominance can also be characterized by the relative inverse distribution function, defined as

$$x \mapsto \text{VaR}\big[X; F_Y(x)\big]. \tag{3.5}$$

It is nothing more than the VaR of X at probability level $p = F_Y(x)$.

Proposition 3.3.2
For two rvs X and Y, $X \preceq_{\text{ST}} Y$ holds if, and only if,

$$\text{VaR}\big[X; F_Y(x)\big] \leq x \text{ for all } x.$$

Proof. From the definition of $\preceq_{\text{ST}}$, we see that

$$\text{VaR}\big[X; F_Y(x)\big] \leq \text{VaR}\big[Y; F_Y(x)\big] = F_Y^{-1}\big(F_Y(x)\big).$$

Now, we see from the inf definition of F_Y^{-1} in Definition 1.5.14 that $F_Y^{-1}(F_Y(x)) \leq x$ obviously holds, which concludes the proof of the necessity part. To obtain sufficiency, it suffices to note that

$$\begin{aligned}
\text{VaR}\big[X; F_Y(x)\big] \leq x \text{ for all } x &\Leftrightarrow F_Y^{-1}\big(F_Y(x)\big) \leq x \text{ for all } x \\
&\Leftrightarrow F_Y(x) \leq F_X(x) \text{ for all } x \\
&\Leftrightarrow \text{VaR}[X; p] \leq \text{VaR}[Y; p] \text{ for all } p,
\end{aligned}$$

where the second equivalence comes from Lemma 1.5.15(i). □

For continuous dfs, we have also the following result that complements Proposition 3.3.2.

Proposition 3.3.3
Let X and Y be rvs with continuous dfs. Then $X \preceq_{\text{ST}} Y$ if, and only if,

$$F_X(\text{VaR}[Y; p]) \geq p \text{ for all } 0 < p < 1.$$

Proof. Invoking Proposition 3.3.2, we have that

$$\begin{aligned} X \preceq_{\text{ST}} Y &\Leftrightarrow F_X^{-1}\big(F_Y(x)\big) \leq x \text{ for all } x \\ &\Leftrightarrow F_Y(x) \leq F_X(x) \text{ for all } x \\ &\qquad\qquad\qquad\text{by Lemma 1.5.15(i)} \\ &\Leftrightarrow p \leq F_X\big(\text{VaR}[Y; p]\big) \text{ for all } p, \end{aligned}$$

where the last equivalence follows from the substitution $p = F_Y(x)$. This concludes the proof. □

The results derived above are related to the quantile–quantile and probability–probability plots associated with X and Y.

3.3.1.2 Stochastic dominance and monotonicity

An important characterization of $\preceq_{\text{ST}}$ is given in the next result. It essentially states that if $X \preceq_{\text{ST}} Y$ holds then there exist rvs $\widetilde{X}$ and $\widetilde{Y}$, distributed as X and Y for which $\Pr[\widetilde{X} \leq \widetilde{Y}] = 1$. In such a case, $\widetilde{Y}$ is larger than $\widetilde{X}$ according to Kaas *et al.* (2001, Definition 10.2.1). Proposition 3.3.4 shows that $\preceq_{\text{ST}}$ is closely related to pointwise comparison of rvs.

Proposition 3.3.4
Two rvs X and Y satisfy $X \preceq_{\text{ST}} Y$ if, and only if, there exist two rvs $\widetilde{X}$ and $\widetilde{Y}$ such that $X =_d \widetilde{X}$, $Y =_d \widetilde{Y}$ and $\Pr[\widetilde{X} \leq \widetilde{Y}] = 1$.

For a proof, see Kaas *et al.* (2001, Theorem 10.2.3). The construction of $\widetilde{X}$ and $\widetilde{Y}$ involved in Proposition 3.3.4 is known as a coupling technique (see Lindvall 1992). Proposition 3.3.4 can be rewritten as follows.

Proposition 3.3.5
Two rvs X and Y satisfy $X \preceq_{\text{ST}} Y$ if, and only if, there exists a comonotonic random couple (X^c, Y^c) such that $\Pr[X^c \leq Y^c] = 1$, $X =_d X^c$ and $Y =_d Y^c$.

Remark 3.3.6. In some applications, when the random variables X and Y are such that $X \preceq_{\text{ST}} Y$, one may wish to construct a $\widetilde{Y}$ on the probability space on which X is defined, such that $\widetilde{Y} =_d Y$ and $\Pr[X \leq \widetilde{Y}] = 1$. This is always possible if F_X is continuous since when this is the case, we know from Property 1.5.19 that $F_X(X) \sim \mathcal{U}ni(0, 1)$, and therefore $\widetilde{Y} = F_Y^{-1}(F_X(X))$ is the desired rv. By the same reasoning, it is also possible to construct $\widetilde{X}$ on the probability space on which Y is defined such that $\widetilde{X} =_d X$ and $\Pr[\widetilde{X} \leq Y] = 1$, provided F_Y is continuous (it suffices to take $\widetilde{X} = F_X^{-1}(F_Y(Y))$). ∇

As a consequence, monotone objective risk measures agree with a ranking in the $\preceq_{\text{ST}}$ sense, as stated in the following result.

Property 3.3.7
Let ϱ be a monotone objective risk measure. Then $X \preceq_{\text{ST}} Y \Rightarrow \varrho[X] \leq \varrho[Y]$.

Proof. This directly follows from Proposition 3.3.4 since

$$\varrho[X] = \varrho[\widetilde{X}] \leq \varrho[\widetilde{Y}] = \varrho[Y],$$

where the inequality follows from the monotonicity of ϱ. □

Remark 3.3.8. Some technical problems may arise on finite probability spaces. See, Bäuerle and Müller (2004). ∇

3.3.1.3 Stochastic dominance and stop-loss premiums

The following result relates $\preceq_{\text{ST}}$ to stop-loss transforms.

Proposition 3.3.9
Given two rvs X and Y, $X \preceq_{\text{ST}} Y$ if, and only if, $\pi_Y - \pi_X$ is non-increasing on $\mathbb{R}$.

Proof. Clearly, if $X \preceq_{\text{ST}} Y$, $\overline{F}_Y - \overline{F}_X$ is non-negative so that the result follows from (1.16). Now assume the non-increasingness of the difference $\pi_Y - \pi_X$. Differentiating this expression with respect to t yields $\overline{F}_X(t) - \overline{F}_Y(t) \leq 0$, whence $X \preceq_{\text{ST}} Y$ follows. □

It is interesting to give an actuarial interpretation for Proposition 3.3.9. It basically states that when $X \preceq_{\text{ST}} Y$ holds, the difference between their respective stop-loss premiums decreases with the level t of retention. Since

$$\lim_{t \to +\infty} \Big(\mathbb{E}[(Y - t)_+] - \mathbb{E}[(X - t)_+] \Big) = 0$$

we thus have that the largest difference occurs for $t = 0$ (and equals $\mathbb{E}[Y] - \mathbb{E}[X]$) and that this difference decreases with the level of retention. The pricing of stop-loss treaties will thus lead to very different premiums for small retentions, but this difference will decrease as the retention increases.

3.3.2 Stochastic dominance and choice under risk

3.3.2.1 Stochastic dominance and expected utility theory

Common preferences of satisficers

Let us consider decision-makers whose utility is a step function, equal to zero before some threshold t and to 1 afterwards:

$$u(x) = \begin{cases} 0, & \text{if } x \leq t, \\ 1, & \text{otherwise.} \end{cases} \tag{3.6}$$

Such agents prefer fortunes exceeding t over those below this threshold, but consider as equivalent two fortunes both above (or below) t. What matters for these decision-makers is to get more than t: once their wealth reaches this target, they are satisfied and do not care about increasing their fortune. Such people in fact base their decision on the value of the survival function at t, that is, for u in (3.6), they prefer Y over X if

$$\mathbb{E}[u(X)] = \overline{F}_X(t) \leq \overline{F}_Y(t) = \mathbb{E}[u(Y)].$$

Such decision-makers are known in the economic literature as *satisficers*, after Simon (1957).

Proposition 3.3.10
If all decision-makers with a utility of the form (3.6) agree about the ranking of two random prospects X and Y, then $X \preceq_{\text{ST}} Y$.

Proof. If all the satisficers prefer X over Y, then

$$\begin{aligned} &\overline{F}_X(t) \leq \overline{F}_Y(t) \text{ for all } t \in \mathbb{R} \\ &\Leftrightarrow F_X(t) \geq F_Y(t) \text{ for all } t \in \mathbb{R} \\ &\Leftrightarrow \text{VaR}[X; p] \leq \text{VaR}[Y; p] \text{ for all } p, \end{aligned}$$

which concludes the proof. □

Note that

$$X \preceq_{\text{ST}} Y \Leftrightarrow F_X(t) \geq F_Y(t) \text{ for all } t \in \mathbb{R}. \tag{3.7}$$

Thus, $X \preceq_{\text{ST}} Y$ means that the probability that X assumes small values (i.e., less than x) is always greater than the corresponding probability for Y. Intuitively, X is thus 'smaller' than Y. Stochastic dominance is usually termed first-degree stochastic dominance in economics and denoted by $\preceq_{\text{FSD}}$ or $\preceq_1$ (see Levy 1992).

Remark 3.3.11. The characterization (3.7) of $\preceq_{\text{ST}}$ also shows that $\preceq_{\text{ST}}$ is stable under taking limits (with respect to convergence in distribution). ∇

Remark 3.3.12. Note that $\preceq_{\text{ST}}$ can be considered as a generalization of the usual order $\leq$ for real numbers. Indeed, given $a \leq b \in \mathbb{R}$ we have $a \preceq_{\text{ST}} b$ (where in this stochastic inequality a and b are viewed as degenerate rvs). ∇

Example 3.3.13. The shifted exponential family with parameters $\lambda > 0$ and $\alpha \in \mathbb{R}$ is defined as

$$F_X(x) = \begin{cases} 1 - \exp(-\lambda(x - \alpha)), & \text{if } x \geq \alpha, \\ 0, & \text{otherwise.} \end{cases}$$

The special case $\alpha = 0$ corresponds to the $\mathcal{E}xp(\lambda)$ distribution. Let X and Y be two shifted exponential random variables with respective parameters (λ, α) and (θ, β). We have that

$$X \preceq_{\text{ST}} Y \Leftrightarrow \lambda \geq \theta \text{ and } \alpha \leq \beta.$$

∇

Common preferences shared by profit-seeking decision-makers

A ranking in the $\preceq_{\rm ST}$ sense reflects the common preferences of all the satisficers. Let us now prove that all the profit-seeking decision-makers in fact agree with satisficers. Satisficers can thus be regarded as the leaders of this group of economic agents.

Proposition 3.3.14
Given any rvs X and Y, the following equivalences hold:

$$
\begin{aligned}
X \preceq_{\rm ST} Y \Leftrightarrow\ & \mathbb{E}[v(X)] \leq \mathbb{E}[v(Y)] \text{ for all non-decreasing} && (3.8)\\
& \text{functions } v, \text{ such that the expectations exist}\\
\Leftrightarrow\ & \mathbb{E}[v(X)] \leq \mathbb{E}[v(Y)] \text{ for all functions } v \text{ with } v' \geq 0, && (3.9)\\
& \text{such that the expectations exist.}
\end{aligned}
$$

Proof. Let us first establish the (3.8). The $\Leftarrow$ part is obvious since $\overline{F}_X(z)$ can be cast into the form $\mathbb{E}\big[\mathbb{I}[X > z]\big]$ and the function $x \mapsto \mathbb{I}[x > z]$ is non-decreasing for any z. To get the converse implication, it suffices to invoke Proposition 3.3.4 to write

$$
\begin{aligned}
\mathbb{E}[v(X)] &= \mathbb{E}[v(\widetilde{X})]\\
&\leq \mathbb{E}[v(\widetilde{Y})] \text{since} \Pr[\widetilde{X} \leq \widetilde{Y}] = 1\\
&= \mathbb{E}[v(Y)].
\end{aligned}
$$

Let us now prove (3.9). The $\Rightarrow$ part is obviously true. The converse directly follows from (1.13). □

Let us now comment on the meaning of $\preceq_{\rm ST}$ in economics and in actuarial science. In economics, the rvs represent fortunes, incomes, etc., so that $X \preceq_{\rm ST} Y$ means that all the profit-seeking decision-makers prefer Y over X, since Y is 'larger' than X. In actuarial science, however, the risks to be compared represent future random financial losses, so that $X \preceq_{\rm ST} Y$ means that all the profit-seeking actuaries prefer X over Y, since the loss X is 'smaller' than Y. Another way to bridge these two disciplines is based on the following equivalence:

$$X \preceq_{\rm ST} Y \Leftrightarrow -Y \preceq_{\rm ST} -X.$$

3.3.2.2 Stochastic dominance and distorted expectation theory

Since VaRs correspond to distorted expectations with a step function as distortion function, we see from the very definition of $\preceq_{\rm ST}$ that it expresses the common preferences of all the decision-makers whose distortion function is a non-decreasing step function. These individuals form the dual class to the satisficers. As in the case of the expected utility framework, it can be shown that $\preceq_{\rm ST}$ expresses the common preferences of a much broader class of decision-makers. Specifically, we have seen above that, within the framework of expected utility theory, stochastic dominance between two risks is equivalent to saying that one risk is preferred over another by all the profit-seeking decision-makers. A similar interpretation exists within the framework of Yaari's theory of choice under risk, as shown in the next result.

Proposition 3.3.15
Given any rvs X and Y, $X \preceq_{\text{ST}} Y$ if, and only if, $\rho_g[X] \leq \rho_g[Y]$ for all non-decreasing distortion functions g.

Proof. We obviously have that

$$\begin{aligned} X \preceq_{\text{ST}} Y &\Rightarrow \overline{F}_X(t) \leq \overline{F}_Y(t) \text{ for all } t \in \mathbb{R} \\ &\Rightarrow g(\overline{F}_X(t)) \leq g(\overline{F}_Y(t)) \text{ for all } t \in \mathbb{R} \\ &\Rightarrow \rho_g[X] \leq \rho_g[Y] \end{aligned}$$

which ends the proof of the $\Rightarrow$ part. The $\Leftarrow$ part is obviously true since VaRs correspond to non-decreasing step distortion functions. □

In other words, an rv X is smaller than an rv Y in the stochastic dominance sense if, and only if, X is preferred over Y by all the decision-makers with non-decreasing distortion function.

3.3.3 Comparing claim frequencies

This section investigates the comparison of integer-valued rvs by means of $\preceq_{\text{ST}}$. The following result exploits the particular form of the support, namely the set $\mathbb{N}$ of the non-negative integers.

Proposition 3.3.16
If N and M are integer-valued rvs, then $N \preceq_{\text{ST}} M$ if, and only if, one of the following equivalent conditions holds:

(i) for all $i \in \mathbb{N}$,

$$\sum_{j=0}^{i} \Pr[N=j] \geq \sum_{j=0}^{i} \Pr[M=j];$$

(ii) for all $i \in \mathbb{N}$,

$$\sum_{j=i}^{+\infty} \Pr[N=j] \leq \sum_{j=i}^{+\infty} \Pr[M=j];$$

(iii) $\mathbb{E}[v(N)] \leq \mathbb{E}[v(M)]$ for every function $v: \mathbb{N} \to \mathbb{R}$ such that $\Delta v(i) \geq 0$ for all integers i, provided the expectations exist.

Stochastic order relations tailor-made for comparing discrete distributions have been proposed by Denuit, Lefèvre and Utev (1999b).

3.3.4 Some properties of stochastic dominance

We summarize the main properties of $\preceq_{\text{ST}}$ in the next result.

Proposition 3.3.17

(i) $X \preceq_{\text{ST}} Y \Rightarrow t(X) \preceq_{\text{ST}} t(Y)$ for every non-decreasing function t.

(ii) Let $X_1, X_2, \ldots, X_n$ and $Y_1, Y_2, \ldots, Y_n$ be independent rvs. If $X_i \preceq_{\text{ST}} Y_i$ for $i=1,2,\ldots,n$, then, for any increasing function $\Psi: \mathbb{R}^n \to \mathbb{R}$,

$$\Psi(X_1, X_2, \ldots, X_n) \preceq_{\text{ST}} \Psi(Y_1, Y_2, \ldots, Y_n).$$

In particular, $\preceq_{\text{ST}}$ is stable under convolution.

(iii) If $X \preceq_{\text{ST}} Y$ and $\mathbb{E}[X]=\mathbb{E}[Y]$ then $X =_d Y$.

Proof. Part (i) directly follows from the fact that for any non-decreasing function v, the composition $x \mapsto v(t(x))$ is non-decreasing so that $X \preceq_{\text{ST}} Y$ ensures

$$\mathbb{E}[v(t(X))] \leq \mathbb{E}[v(t(Y))].$$

To prove (ii), we use an induction argument. The result in (ii) is true for $n=1$ by (i). Now assume that (ii) is valid for n; we will prove it also holds for $n+1$. Without loss of generality, assume that the X_i and the Y_i are mutually independent. Consider a non-decreasing function v. Then,

$$\begin{aligned}
\mathbb{E}[v(\Psi(X_1, \ldots, X_n, X_{n+1}))] &= \int_{-\infty}^{+\infty} \mathbb{E}[v(\Psi(X_1, \ldots, X_n, x_{n+1}))] dF_{X_{n+1}}(x_{n+1}) \\
&\leq \int_{-\infty}^{+\infty} \mathbb{E}[v(\Psi(Y_1, \ldots, Y_n, x_{n+1}))] dF_{X_{n+1}}(x_{n+1}) \\
&= \mathbb{E}[v(\Psi(Y_1, \ldots, Y_n, X_{n+1}))],
\end{aligned}$$

where the inequality follows from the induction hypothesis and the fact that X_{n+1} is independent of both $X_1, X_2, \ldots, X_n$ and $Y_1, Y_2, \ldots, Y_n$. Now

$$\begin{aligned}
\mathbb{E}[v(\Psi(Y_1, \ldots, Y_n, X_{n+1}))] &= \int_{-\infty}^{+\infty} \cdots \int_{-\infty}^{+\infty} \mathbb{E}[v(\Psi(y_1, \ldots, y_n, X_{n+1}))] dF_{Y_1}(y_1) \ldots dF_{Y_n}(y_n) \\
&\leq \int_{-\infty}^{+\infty} \cdots \int_{-\infty}^{+\infty} \mathbb{E}[v(\Psi(y_1, \ldots, y_n, Y_{n+1}))] dF_{Y_1}(y_1) \ldots dF_{Y_n}(y_n) \\
&= \mathbb{E}[v(\Psi(Y_1, \ldots, Y_n, Y_{n+1}))],
\end{aligned}$$

where the inequality follows from (i) and the fact that $Y_1, Y_2, \ldots, Y_n$ are independent of both X_{n+1} and Y_{n+1}.

Finally, (iii) follows from the representation of the mean derived in Property 1.6.6, yielding

$$\mathbb{E}[Y] - \mathbb{E}[X] = \int_0^{+\infty} \underbrace{\left(\overline{F}_Y(x) - \overline{F}_X(x)\right)}_{\geq 0 \text{ for all } x \text{ when } X \preceq_{\text{ST}} Y} dx = 0,$$

so that the equality $\overline{F}_X(x) = \overline{F}_Y(x)$ has to hold for all x. □

Let us provide interpretations for the results of Proposition 3.3.17. Part (i) means that the introduction of deductibles or the limitation of the insurer's payments does not modify the preferences, that is,

$$\begin{aligned} X \preceq_{\text{ST}} Y &\Rightarrow (X-d)_+ \preceq_{\text{ST}} (Y-d)_+ \text{ for any deductible } d \\ &\Rightarrow \min\{X, \omega\} \preceq_{\text{ST}} \min\{Y, \omega\} \text{ for any policy limit } \omega. \end{aligned}$$

From Proposition 3.3.17(iii), $\preceq_{\text{ST}}$ cannot be used to compare rvs with identical means. This situation is not purely theoretical, but often occurs in practice, for instance when the parameters of some distribution are estimated using the method of moments. This means that there is a need for a stochastic order relation able to compare rvs with identical means such as the convex order described in the next section.

Note that the conclusion of Proposition 3.3.17(iii) is still valid if $\mathbb{E}[t(X)] = \mathbb{E}[t(Y)]$, for some strictly increasing function t, is substituted for $\mathbb{E}[X] = \mathbb{E}[Y]$. Indeed, combining (i) and (iii), we find that $X \preceq_{\text{ST}} Y$, together with $\mathbb{E}[t(X)] = \mathbb{E}[t(Y)]$, implies $t(X) =_d t(Y)$ which in turn yields $X =_d Y$ when t is strictly increasing.

Let $X_1, X_2, \ldots, X_n$ be independent rvs with common df F_X. Let $X_{(1)} \leq X_{(2)} \leq \ldots \leq X_{(n)}$ be the associated order statistics (i.e., the ordered X_i). We obviously have

$$X_{(1)} \preceq_{\text{ST}} X_{(2)} \preceq_{\text{ST}} \cdots \preceq_{\text{ST}} X_{(n)}. \tag{3.10}$$

Let us now investigate the impact of the sample size n on the order statistics. This is quite natural since the stochastic inequalities

$$\min\left\{X_1, \ldots, X_n, X_{n+1}\right\} \preceq_{\text{ST}} \min\left\{X_1, \ldots, X_n\right\}$$

and

$$\max\left\{X_1, \ldots, X_n\right\} \preceq_{\text{ST}} \max\left\{X_1, \ldots, X_n, X_{n+1}\right\}$$

obviously hold. We emphasize the dependence on n by denoting the order statistics as $X_{(1:n)} \leq X_{(2:n)} \leq \ldots \leq X_{(n:n)}$. We then have the following result.

Property 3.3.18
We have $X_{(k-1:n-1)} \preceq_{\text{ST}} X_{(k:n)}$ for $k = 2, \ldots, n-1$, and $X_{(k:n)} \preceq_{\text{ST}} X_{(k:n-1)}$ for $k = 1, \ldots, n-1$.

Let us now compare the order statistics associated with random samples whose underlying distributions are ordered with respect to $\preceq_{\text{ST}}$. A direct application of Property 3.3.17(ii) yields the following result.

Property 3.3.19
Let $X_1, X_2, \ldots, X_n$ be independent and identically distributed rvs. Similarly, let $Y_1, Y_2, \ldots, Y_n$ be another set of independent and identically distributed rvs. If $X_1 \preceq_{\text{ST}} Y_1$ then $X_{(i)} \preceq_{\text{ST}} Y_{(i)}$ for all $i = 1, \ldots, n$.

The marginal distributions of the order statistics $X_{(1)}, X_{(2)}, \ldots, X_{(n)}$ are constrained, as shown by Rychlik (1992, 1994). Specifically, the df of the mth order statistic $X_{(m)}$ has to satisfy the following conditions.

Proposition 3.3.20
A df G is a possible df for $X_{(m)}$ if, and only if, the following conditions are fulfilled:

(i) $L(t) \leq G(t) \leq R(t)$ for all t, where

$$\begin{aligned} T(t) &= \min\{\max\{0, t\}, 1\}, \\ L(t) &= T\left(\frac{nF_X(t) - m + 1}{n - m + 1}\right), \\ R(t) &= T\left(\frac{n}{m}F_X(t)\right); \end{aligned}$$

(ii) $0 \leq G(t) - G(s) \leq n(F_X(t) - F_X(s))$ for all $s < t$.

Proof. Let us prove the necessity of conditions (i)–(ii). We obviously have that

$$\sum_{i=1}^{n} \Pr[X_{(i)} \leq t] = nF_X(t).$$

After some elementary algebra, we can obtain

$$\begin{aligned} \Pr[X_{(m)} \leq t] &= \frac{1}{n - m + 1}\left(nF_X(t) - m + 1 + \sum_{i=1}^{m-1} \Pr[X_{(i)} > t]\right. \\ &\quad \left. + \sum_{i=m+1}^{n} \Pr[X_{(m)} \leq t < X_{(i)}]\right) \\ &= \frac{1}{m}\left(nF_X(t) - \sum_{i=1}^{m-1} \Pr[X_{(i)} \leq t < X_{(m)}] - \sum_{i=m+1}^{n} \Pr[X_{(i)} \leq t]\right). \end{aligned}$$

This directly yields (i). To get (ii), note that

$$\begin{aligned} G(t) - G(s) &= \Pr[t < X_{(m)} \leq s] \\ &\leq \sum_{i=1}^{n} \Pr[t < X_i = X_{(m)} \leq s] \\ &\leq n\big(F_X(t) - F_X(s)\big). \end{aligned}$$

Let us now establish the sufficiency of (i)–(ii). The proof is constructive. Suppose that G satisfies (i)–(ii) and define

$$G_1(t) = T\left(\frac{nF_X(t) - G(t) - m + 1}{n-m}\right) \text{ for } m = 1, \ldots, n-1,$$

$$G_2(t) = T\left(\frac{nF_X(t) - G(t)}{m-1}\right) \text{ for } m = 2, \ldots, n.$$

By (ii), the function $nF_X - G$ is non-decreasing and right-continuous and consequently the same applies to G_1 and G_2. Since, moreover,

$$\lim_{t\to-\infty} G_i(t) = 0 \text{ and } \lim_{t\to+\infty} G_i(t) = 1, \quad i = 1, 2,$$

we see that G_1 and G_2 are proper dfs. Applying (i), it can be verified that $G_1(t) \le G(t) \le G_2(t)$ for every t. For the quantile functions, we obtain the reversed inequalities $G_1^{-1}(p) \ge G^{-1}(p) \ge G_2^{-1}(p)$ for every $p \in [0, 1]$. Now define

$$Q_i(p) = \begin{cases} G_2^{-1}(p), & \text{for } i = 1, \ldots, m-1, \\ G^{-1}(p), & \text{for } i = m, \\ G_1^{-1}(p), & \text{for } i = m+1, \ldots, n. \end{cases}$$

Let $U \sim \mathcal{U}ni(0, 1)$ and J be uniformly distributed on $\{1, 2, \ldots, n\}$. Now the random vector

$$\mathbf{Z} = \left(Q_J(U), Q_{J+1}(U), \ldots, Q_n(U), Q_1(U), \ldots, Q_{J-1}(U)\right)$$

has identically distributed components with common marginal dfs F_X. Furthermore, $Z_{(m)}$ has df G, because

$$(X_{(1)}, \ldots, X_{(n)}) =_d (Q_1(U), Q_2(U), \ldots, Q_n(U))$$

and $X_{(m)} =_d G^{-1}(U)$ has df G. To conclude the proof, we note that for all $i = 1, 2, \ldots, n$,

$$\begin{aligned} \Pr[X_i \le t] &= \frac{1}{n}\Big((m-1)\Pr[X_i = G_2^{-1}(U) \le t] \\ &\quad + \Pr[X_i = G^{-1}(U) \le t] \\ &\quad + (n-m)\Pr[X_i = G_1^{-1}(U) \le t]\Big) \\ &= F_X(t). \end{aligned}$$

□

Note that L and R are admissible dfs for $X_{(m)}$ and are extremal with respect to $\preceq_{\mathrm{ST}}$. This yields the following result.

Property 3.3.21
For any $m = 1, \ldots, n$, the stochastic inequalities

$$X_{(m)}^- \preceq_{\mathrm{ST}} X_{(m)} \preceq_{\mathrm{ST}} X_{(m)}^+$$

hold, where $X_{(m)}^-$ has df $R(\cdot)$ and $X_{(m)}^+$ has df $L(\cdot)$ given in Proposition 3.3.20.

Let us now derive conditions for the (discrete or continuous) pdf g to be admissible for $X_{(m)}$.

Proposition 3.3.22
The pdf g is admissible for $X_{(m)}$ if, and only if, the inequalities $0 \leq g(x) \leq nf_X(x)$ hold for all $x \in \mathbb{R}$, where f_X is the pdf corresponding to F_X and

$$G(t) = \begin{cases} \int_{-\infty}^{t} g(x)dx \\ \sum_{x=0}^{t} g(x) \end{cases}$$

fulfils condition (i) of Proposition 3.3.20.

Our objective is now to find an upper bound for $\mathbb{E}[t(X_{(m)})]$, where g is non-decreasing. Of course, from Proposition 3.3.22, we directly get

$$\begin{aligned} \mathbb{E}[t(X_{(m)})] &= \int_{-\infty}^{+\infty} t(x)g(x)dx \\ &\leq n\int_{-\infty}^{+\infty} t(x)f_X(x)dx \\ &= n\mathbb{E}[t(X_1)] \text{ for every } m \text{ and } n. \end{aligned}$$

Rychlik (1994) provided an effective method for calculating accurate bounds on $\mathbb{E}[t(X_{(m)})]$. In the following proposition we summarize some of his results; the proof directly follows from the fact that R and L are extremal in the $\preceq_{\text{ST}}$ sense.

Proposition 3.3.23
Let us consider a non-decreasing function t. Define

$$a = F_X^{-1}\left(\frac{m-1}{n}\right) \quad \text{and} \quad b = F_X^{-1}\left(\frac{m}{n}\right).$$

Then

$$\mathbb{E}[t(X_{(m)})] \geq \mathbb{E}[t(X_{(m)}^{-})] = \frac{n}{m}\int_{-\infty}^{b} t(x)dF_X(x),$$

$$\mathbb{E}[t(X_{(m)})] \leq \mathbb{E}[t(X_{(m)}^{+})] = \frac{n}{n-m+1}\int_{a}^{+\infty} t(x)dF_X(x).$$

3.3.5 *Stochastic dominance and notions of ageing*

3.3.5.1 Remaining lifetimes and IFR/DFR

The next result characterizes IFR and DFR notions of ageing by means of a $\preceq_{\text{ST}}$ comparison between remaining lifetimes.

Proposition 3.3.24

(i) X is IFR $\Leftrightarrow [X-t|X>t] \preceq_{\text{ST}} [X-t'|X>t']$ whenever $t \leq t'$.

(ii) X is DFR $\Leftrightarrow [X-t'|X>t'] \preceq_{\text{ST}} [X-t|X>t]$ whenever $t \leq t'$.

Proof. The result follows from the following representation of the conditional tail function:

$$\Pr[X - t > x | X > t] = \exp\left(-\int_t^{x+t} r_X(\xi)d\xi\right)$$

which easily follows from (1.18). Hence,

$$\frac{d}{dt}\Pr[X - t > x | X > t] = -\exp\left(-\int_t^{x+t} r_X(\xi)d\xi\right)\left(r_X(x+t) - r_X(t)\right),$$

for every x. It is then clear that $\Pr[X - t > x | X > t]$ is decreasing (increasing) in t if, and only if, r_X is increasing (decreasing). □

3.3.5.2 Remaining lifetimes and NBU/NWU

The non-negative rv X (or its df) is said to be NBU (for 'new better than used') if

$$\overline{F}_X(s)\overline{F}_X(t) \geq \overline{F}_X(s+t)$$

for all $s \geq 0$ and $t \geq 0$. It is said to be NWU (for 'new worse than used') if

$$\overline{F}_X(s)\overline{F}_X(t) \leq \overline{F}_X(s+t)$$

for all $s \geq 0$ and $t \geq 0$.

Proposition 3.3.25

(i) The non-negative rv X is NBU if, and only if, $[X - t|X > t] \preceq_{\text{ST}} X$ for all $t > 0$.

(ii) The non-negative rv X is NWU if, and only if, $X \preceq_{\text{ST}} [X - t|X > t]$ for all $t > 0$.

Proof. To get (i) it suffices to note that X is NBU if, and only if,

$$\begin{aligned}\frac{\overline{F}_X(s+t)}{\overline{F}_X(t)} &= \Pr[X > s + t | X > t] \\ &= \Pr[X - t > s | X > t] \leq \overline{F}_X(s)\end{aligned}$$

whence the result follows. Similar reasoning leads to (ii). □

3.3.5.3 Stationary renewal distributions and NBUE/NWUE

The non-negative rv X (or its distribution) is said to be NBUE (for 'new better than used in expectation') if $e_X(t) \leq \mathbb{E}[X]$ for all $t \geq 0$. It is said to be NWUE (for 'new worse than used in expectation') if $e_X(t) \geq \mathbb{E}[X]$ for all $t \geq 0$.

The following result connects NBUE/NWUE with the stationary renewal distribution defined in (1.20).

Proposition 3.3.26
The non-negative rv X with finite mean is NBUE if, and only if, $X_{\{1\}} \preceq_{ST} X$, while X is NWUE if, $X \preceq_{ST} X_{\{1\}}$.

Proof. The tf of $X_{\{1\}}$ is given by

$$\overline{F}_{X_{\{1\}}}(x) = \frac{\pi_X(x)}{\mathbb{E}[X]} = \frac{e_X(x)\overline{F}_X(x)}{\mathbb{E}[X]},$$

so that $\overline{F}_{X_{\{1\}}}(x) \leq \overline{F}_X(x)$ if X is NBUE, whereas $\overline{F}_{X_{\{1\}}}(x) \geq \overline{F}_X(x)$ if X is NWUE. □

3.3.6 *Stochastic increasingness*

3.3.6.1 Definition

Let $\{X_\theta, \ \theta \in \Theta\}$ be a family of rvs indexed by a single parameter $\theta \in \Theta \subseteq \mathbb{R}$. Given any function $t: \mathbb{R} \to \mathbb{R}$, let us define the function $t^*(\theta) = \mathbb{E}[t(X_\theta)]$ as in (3.2). In the present section, our main purpose is to investigate whether the non-decreasingness of the function t can be transmitted to the function t^*. This yields the following definition.

Definition 3.3.27. If

$$t \text{ non-decreasing} \Rightarrow t^* \text{ non-decreasing}, \tag{3.11}$$

then the X_θ are said to be stochastically increasing. ∇

It is clear from the definition that the X_θ are stochastically increasing if, and only if, they increase in θ with respect to $\preceq_{ST}$, that is,

$$X_\theta \preceq_{ST} X_{\theta'} \text{ whenever } \theta \leq \theta'. \tag{3.12}$$

3.3.6.2 Properties

Let us point out several situations of interest; we omit their proofs, which are straightforward from Proposition 3.3.4.

Property 3.3.28
The following families are stochastically increasing:

(i) Let Y be a non-negative rv, and define X_θ as $X_\theta = \theta Y$ with $\theta \in \mathbb{R}$.

(ii) Let Y be any rv, and define X_θ as $X_\theta = Y + \theta$ with $\theta \in \mathbb{R}$.

(iii) Let $\{Y_1, Y_2, Y_3, \ldots\}$ be a sequence of non-negative independent rvs and define

$$X_\theta = \sum_{n=1}^{\theta} Y_n \text{ with } \theta \in \mathbb{N}.$$

The following result shows that one is allowed to compose stochastically increasing families to form new families possessing this property.

Property 3.3.29

(i) Let $\{X_\theta,\ \theta \in \mathbb{R}\}$ be a stochastically increasing family of rvs. Then, for any non-decreasing function g, the family of rvs $\{g(X_\theta),\ \theta \in \mathbb{R}\}$ is also stochastically increasing.

(ii) Let $\{Y_1, Y_2, Y_3, \ldots\}$ be a sequence of non-negative independent rvs. Let $\{N_\theta,\ \theta \in \Theta\}$ be a family of integer-valued rvs, independent of the Y_n, and define

$$X_\theta = \sum_{n=1}^{N_\theta} Y_n \quad \text{with } \theta \in \Theta.$$

If the N_θ are stochastically increasing, then so are the X_θ.

3.3.7 Ordering mixtures

The property of stochastic increasingness provides a natural way for comparing mixed distributions through their mixing kernel, in stochastic dominance.

Property 3.3.30
If the X_θ are stochastically increasing then

$$\Lambda_1 \preceq_{\text{ST}} \Lambda_2 \Rightarrow X_{\Lambda_1} \preceq_{\text{ST}} X_{\Lambda_2},$$

where X_{Λ_1} and X_{Λ_2} have df (3.4).

The proof of the implication in Poperty 3.3.30 follows in exactly the same way as (3.3).

3.3.8 Ordering compound sums

Using Property 3.3.30, we are able to compare random sums, through their number of terms, in stochastic dominance. The following result shows that $\preceq_{\text{ST}}$ is stable under compounding.

Property 3.3.31
Let $\{X_1, X_2, X_3, \ldots\}$ and $\{Y_1, Y_2, Y_3, \ldots\}$ be two sequences of non-negative independent rvs, and let N and M be two integer-valued random variables, independent of those sequences. Then,

$$\left.\begin{array}{l} X_n \preceq_{\text{ST}} Y_n \text{ for all } n \\ M \preceq_{\text{ST}} N \end{array}\right\} \Rightarrow \sum_{n=1}^{M} X_n \preceq_{\text{ST}} \sum_{n=1}^{N} Y_n.$$

Proof. From Property 3.3.28(iii), we know that

$$t^*(n) = \Pr[X_1 + X_2 + \ldots + X_n > x]$$

is a non-decreasing function. Considering $M \preceq_{\mathrm{ST}} N$, we then get

$$\mathbb{E}[t^*(M)] = \Pr\left[\sum_{i=1}^{M} X_i > x\right] \leq \mathbb{E}[t^*(N)] = \Pr\left[\sum_{i=1}^{N} X_i > x\right],$$

for any x, giving

$$\sum_{i=1}^{M} X_i \preceq_{\mathrm{ST}} \sum_{i=1}^{N} X_i. \tag{3.13}$$

Since $\preceq_{\mathrm{ST}}$ is stable under mixing and under convolution, we are allowed to write, for any real t,

$$\begin{aligned}
\Pr\left[\sum_{i=1}^{N} X_i > t\right] &= \sum_{n=0}^{+\infty} \Pr\left[\sum_{i=1}^{n} X_i > t\right] \Pr[N = n] \\
&\leq \sum_{n=0}^{+\infty} \Pr\left[\sum_{i=1}^{n} Y_i > t\right] \Pr[N = n] \\
&= \Pr\left[\sum_{i=1}^{N} Y_i > t\right],
\end{aligned}$$

so that

$$\sum_{i=1}^{N} X_i \preceq_{\mathrm{ST}} \sum_{i=1}^{N} Y_i. \tag{3.14}$$

It now suffices to combine (3.14) and (3.13) to get the desired result by the transitivity of $\preceq_{\mathrm{ST}}$. □

Note that this result can also be established using the coupling theorem stated in Proposition 3.3.4.

3.3.9 *Sufficient conditions*

A sufficient condition of crossing type for $\preceq_{\mathrm{ST}}$ is given next. It states that if the difference of the differentials of the dfs of the rvs X and Y to be compared exhibits exactly one sign change, then X and Y are ordered in the $\preceq_{\mathrm{ST}}$ sense.

Property 3.3.32
Let X and Y be two rvs. If there exists a real number c for which $dF_X(x) \geq dF_Y(x)$ for all $x < c$ and $dF_X(x) \leq dF_Y(x)$ for all $x > c$, then, $X \preceq_{\mathrm{ST}} Y$.

Proof. For $x < c$, we get

$$F_X(x) = \int_{-\infty}^{x} dF_X(y) \geq \int_{-\infty}^{x} dF_Y(y) = F_Y(x).$$

For $x > c$, we get

$$\begin{aligned} F_X(x) &= 1 - \int_{x}^{+\infty} dF_X(y) \\ &\geq 1 - \int_{x}^{+\infty} dF_Y(y) = F_Y(x), \end{aligned}$$

and this concludes the proof. □

Example 3.3.33. Let us consider $X \sim \mathcal{P}oi(\lambda)$ and $Y \sim \mathcal{P}oi(\theta)$, with $0 < \lambda < \theta$. For any integer n, we then have that

$$\frac{dF_X(n)}{dF_Y(n)} = \exp(\theta - \lambda)\left(\frac{\lambda}{\theta}\right)^n;$$

this ratio clearly decreases as n grows, starting from $\exp(\theta - \lambda) > 1$ for $n = 0$. Property 3.3.32 then ensures that $X \preceq_{\mathrm{ST}} Y$ holds. ∇

Hesselager (1995) derived another sufficient condition for $\preceq_{\mathrm{ST}}$.

Proposition 3.3.34

(i) For a non-negative continuous rv X, define $h_X(x) = \frac{d}{dx}\log(f_X(x))$. Given two continuous rvs X and Y,

$$h_X(x) \leq h_Y(x) \text{ for all } x \Rightarrow X \preceq_{\mathrm{ST}} Y.$$

(ii) Similarly, for an integer-valued rv N, define $h_N(n) = f_N(n)/f_N(n-1)$. Then, given two integer-valued rvs N and M,

$$h_N(n) \leq h_M(n) \text{ for all } n \geq 1 \Rightarrow N \preceq_{\mathrm{ST}} M.$$

Remark 3.3.35. Given two integer-valued rvs N and M, if $h_N \leq h_M$ we will see that N precedes M in the likelihood ratio order. ∇

3.3.10 Conditional stochastic dominance I: Hazard rate order

3.3.10.1 Definition

Starting with $\preceq_{\mathrm{ST}}$, it is possible to define many related stochastic order relations by conditioning with respect to a class of random events. The idea is as follows: instead of comparing X and Y, we compare their respective conditional distributions given that some events did occur. If we think of X and Y as being two lifetimes, we could be interested in having $X \preceq_{ST} Y$ but also in the remaining lifetimes beyond any attained age remaining ordered, that is, $[X-t|X>t] \preceq_{ST} [Y-t|Y>t]$ for every $t>0$.

If one requires that for X and Y the excesses over t $[X-t|X>t]$ and $[Y-t|Y>t]$, given that this threshold has been reached, are comparable with respect to $\preceq_{ST}$ for all t then one is naturally led to the *hazard rate order*. This ordering has a nice interpretation in reinsurance. In this context, $[X-t|X>t]$ represents the amount paid by the reinsurer in a stop-loss agreement, given that the retention t is reached: the reinsurer is not at all interested in the loss below t, for which he often has no information at his disposal, only in the loss above t.

Note that since $\preceq_{ST}$ is shift invariant, comparing $[X-t|X>t]$ and $[Y-t|Y>t]$ is equivalent to comparing $[X|X>t]$ and $[Y|Y>t]$. Now, since

$$
\begin{aligned}
&[X|X>t] \preceq_{ST} [Y|Y>t] \text{ for all } t \in \mathbb{R} \\
&\Leftrightarrow \Pr[X>t+s|X>t] \leq \Pr[Y>t+s|Y>t] \text{ for all } t \text{ and } s \geq 0 \\
&\Leftrightarrow \frac{\overline{F}_X(t+s)}{\overline{F}_X(t)} \leq \frac{\overline{F}_Y(s+t)}{\overline{F}_Y(t)} \text{ for all } t \text{ and } s \geq 0 \\
&\Leftrightarrow \frac{\overline{F}_Y(t)}{\overline{F}_X(t)} \leq \frac{\overline{F}_Y(s+t)}{\overline{F}_X(s+t)} \text{ for all } t \text{ and } s \geq 0,
\end{aligned}
$$

we get the following definition.

Definition 3.3.36. Given two rvs X and Y, X is said to precede Y in the hazard rate order, denoted as $X \preceq_{HR} Y$, if one of the following equivalent conditions holds:

(i) $[X|X>t] \preceq_{ST} [Y|Y>t]$ for all $t \in \mathbb{R}$;

(ii) $t \mapsto \frac{\overline{F}_Y(t)}{\overline{F}_X(t)}$ non-decreasing;

(iii) $\overline{F}_X(u)\overline{F}_Y(v) \geq \overline{F}_X(v)\overline{F}_Y(u)$ for all $u \leq v$. ∇

It is easy to see from the definition of $\preceq_{HR}$ that this stochastic order is stable under taking weak limits.

Remark 3.3.37. Many natural properties established for $\preceq_{ST}$ no longer hold for $\preceq_{HR}$. For instance, if $X_1 \preceq_{HR} Y_1$ and $X_2 \preceq_{HR} Y_2$, where X_1 and X_2 are independent rvs and Y_1 and Y_2 are also independent rvs, then it is not necessarily true that $X_1+X_2 \preceq_{HR} Y_1+Y_2$. However, if these rvs are IFR then it is true. For a review of the properties of $\preceq_{HR}$, we refer the interested reader to Shaked and Shanthikumar (1994). ∇

3.3.10.2 Hazard rate order and hazard rate function

The term 'hazard rate order' derives from the following result, which shows that when the dfs possess densities, a comparison in the $\preceq_{HR}$ sense boils down to comparing the hazard rate functions.

Property 3.3.38
If X and Y have continuous densities then $X \preceq_{HR} Y$ if, and only if, $r_X(t) \geq r_Y(t)$ for all t.

Proof. The ratio $\overline{F}_Y/\overline{F}_X$ is non-decreasing if, and only if, $\ln \overline{F}_Y/\overline{F}_X$ is non-decreasing. This is also equivalent to $\ln \overline{F}_Y - \ln \overline{F}_X$ being non-decreasing, which amounts to $r_X - r_Y > 0$ since

$$\frac{d}{dt}\Big(\ln \overline{F}_Y(t) - \ln \overline{F}_X(t)\Big) = r_X(t) - r_Y(t).$$

□

The hazard rate order has many applications in life insurance (since it originates in reliability theory for comparing remaining lifetimes). Given two rvs X and Y representing times until death, $X \preceq_{\text{HR}} Y$ means that insureds with remaining lifetime Y will tend to live longer than those with remaining lifetime X.

3.3.10.3 Hazard rate order and order statistics

We know from (3.10) that the $X_{(k)}$ increase in the index k with respect to $\preceq_{\text{ST}}$. This result remains true for $\preceq_{\text{HR}}$. Specifically, if the X_i are non-negative, independent and identically distributed rvs, the stochastic inequalities

$$X_{(1)} \preceq_{\text{HR}} X_{(2)} \preceq_{\text{HR}} \cdots \preceq_{\text{HR}} X_{(n)} \tag{3.15}$$

hold true. The following result, taken from Shaked and Shanthikumar (1994), deals with the comparison of order statistics from two $\preceq_{\text{HR}}$-ordered populations.

Property 3.3.39
Let $X_1, X_2, \ldots, X_n$ and $Y_1, Y_2, \ldots, Y_n$ be two sets of independent and identically distributed rvs such that $X_i \preceq_{\text{HR}} Y_i i = 1, 2, \ldots, n$. Then $X_{(k)} \preceq_{\text{HR}} Y_{(k)}, k = 1, 2, \ldots, n$.

Proof. Define $N_x(\boldsymbol{X}) \equiv \sum_{i=1}^{n} \mathbb{I}[X_i \geq x]$ as the number of X_i exceeding x. The hazard rate of $X_{(k)}$ is given by

$$\begin{aligned} r_{X_{(k)}}(x) &= (n-k+1) r_X(x) \Pr[N_x(\boldsymbol{X}) = n-k+1 \,|\, N_x(\boldsymbol{X}) \geq n-k+1] \\ &= (n-k+1) r_X(x) \left(\sum_{i=n-k+1}^{n} \binom{n}{i} \left(\frac{\overline{F}_X(x)}{F_X(x)} \right)^{i-n+k-1} \right)^{-1}. \end{aligned}$$

Similarly, the hazard rate of $Y_{(k)}$ at x is

$$r_{Y_{(k)}}(x) = (n-k+1) r_Y(x) \left(\sum_{i=n-k+1}^{n} \binom{n}{i} \left(\frac{\overline{F}_Y(x)}{F_Y(x)} \right)^{i-n+k-1} \right)^{-1}.$$

By assumption, $r_X(x) \geq r_Y(x)$, from which it follows that $\overline{F}_X(x) \leq \overline{F}_Y(x)$ and therefore $r_{X_{(k)}}(x) \geq r_{Y_{(k)}}(x)$. □

3.3.10.4 Hazard rate order and PH transforms

If we assume a proportional change to the hazard rate function, that is, we switch from r_X to $r_{X_\xi^*}$ defined as

$$r_{X_\xi^*}(t) = \frac{r_X(t)}{\xi} \leq r_X(t), \text{ for some } \xi \geq 1,$$

we get

$$\overline{F}_{X_\xi^*}(t) = \exp\left(-\int_0^t \frac{r_X(s)}{\xi} ds\right) = \left(\overline{F}_X(t)\right)^{1/\xi}.$$

Hence, $\text{PH}[X; \xi] = \mathbb{E}[X_\xi^*]$. The PH risk measure thus comes down to computing the expected value of the transform X_ξ^* such that $X \preceq_{\text{HR}} X_\xi^*$. All profit-seeking decision-makers consider this to be a prudent strategy.

3.3.10.5 Comparing claim frequencies

Let N and M be two integer-valued rvs. Definition 3.3.36(iii) shows that $N \preceq_{\text{HR}} M$ if, and only if,

$$\Pr[N \geq n_1]\Pr[M \geq n_2] \geq \Pr[N \geq n_2]\Pr[M \geq n_1] \text{ for all } n_1 \leq n_2. \tag{3.16}$$

Writing (3.16) with $n_1 = n_2 = n$ and with $n_1 = n + 1$ and $n_2 = n$, and substracting the two expressions, shows that (3.16) is equivalent to

$$\frac{\Pr[N = n]}{\Pr[N \geq n]} \geq \frac{\Pr[M = n]}{\Pr[M \geq n]}, \text{ for all } n \in \mathbb{N}. \tag{3.17}$$

The ratios involved in (3.7) can be seen as discrete versions of the hazard rate function.

3.3.10.6 Hazard rate order and notions of ageing

The next results relate $\preceq_{\text{HR}}$ to the notions of IFR and DFR. See also Proposition 3.3.24.

Property 3.3.40
The rv X is DFR if, and only if,

$$[X - t | X > t] \preceq_{\text{HR}} [X - t' | X > t'] \text{ for all } t \leq t'.$$

Similarly, X is IFR if, and only if,

$$[X - t' | X > t'] \preceq_{\text{HR}} [X - t | X > t] \text{ for all } t \leq t'.$$

Proof. This result follows from Property 3.3.38 since the hazard rate associated with $[X - t|X > t]$ is

$$\frac{d}{dx} \ln \Pr[X - t > x | X > t] = \frac{d}{dx}\left(\ln \overline{F}_X(x + t) - \ln \overline{F}_X(t)\right) = r_X(x + t).$$

□

Using the stationary renewal distribution (1.20) together with $\preceq_{\mathrm{HR}}$, it is possible to characterize the notions of IMRL and DMRL.

Proposition 3.3.41
The non-negative rv X with finite mean is IMRL if, and only if, $X \preceq_{\mathrm{HR}} X_{\{1\}}$. Similarly, X is DMRL if, and only if, $X_{\{1\}} \preceq_{\mathrm{HR}} X$.

Proof. To get the result, let us use Definition 3.3.36(iii), which gives

$$\begin{aligned} X \preceq_{\mathrm{HR}} X_{\{1\}} &\Leftrightarrow \overline{F}_X(u)\overline{F}_{X_{\{1\}}}(v) \geq \overline{F}_X(v)\overline{F}_{X_{\{1\}}}(u) \text{ for all } u \leq v \\ &\Leftrightarrow \overline{F}_X(u)\pi_X(v) \geq \overline{F}_X(v)\pi_X(u) \text{ for all } u \leq v \\ &\Leftrightarrow e_X(v) \geq e_X(u) \text{ for all } u \leq v, \end{aligned}$$

which amounts to X being IMRL. □

3.3.11 *Conditional stochastic dominance II: Likelihood ratio order*

3.3.11.1 Definition

If $[X|a \leq X \leq a+h] \preceq_{\mathrm{ST}} [Y|a \leq Y \leq a+h]$ is also required for any $a \in \mathbb{R}$ and $h > 0$ then the *likelihood ratio order* is obtained. This can be applied in the situation where the claim amount is known to hit some reinsurance layer. Specifically, a layer $(a, a+h]$ of risk X is defined as an excess-of-loss cover

$$X_{(a,a+h]} = \begin{cases} 0, & \text{if } X < a, \\ X - a, & \text{if } a \leq X < a+h, \\ h, & \text{if } a+h \leq X, \end{cases}$$

where a is the deductible (or retention) and h is the limit. Likelihood ratio order compares payments, given that the layer is hit. In that respect, the likelihood ratio order defined next is particularly useful.

Definition 3.3.42. Let X and Y be two rvs. Then $X \preceq_{\mathrm{LR}} Y$ if $[X|a \leq X \leq b] \preceq_{\mathrm{ST}} [Y|a \leq Y \leq b]$ for all $a < b \in \mathbb{R}$. ∇

Likelihood ratio order is a powerful tool in parametric models. It is clear from Definition 3.3.42 that $\preceq_{\mathrm{LR}}$ is stronger than $\preceq_{\mathrm{ST}}$ and $\preceq_{\mathrm{HR}}$:

$$X \preceq_{\mathrm{LR}} Y \Rightarrow X \preceq_{\mathrm{HR}} Y \Rightarrow X \preceq_{\mathrm{ST}} Y.$$

3.3.11.2 Likelihood ratio order and ratio of pdfs

As indicated by its name, the likelihood ratio order is closely related to the behaviour of the ratio of the pdfs associated with the rvs: namely, given two rvs X and Y, $X \preceq_{LR} Y$ if, and only if,

$$\frac{f_X(t)}{f_Y(t)} \quad \text{decreases over the union of the supports of } X \text{ and } Y \tag{3.18}$$

(here $a/0$ is taken to be equal to $+\infty$ whenever $a > 0$). This comes from the following result.

Proposition 3.3.43
Let X and Y be continuous or discrete rvs with pdfs f_X and f_Y. Then

$$X \preceq_{LR} Y \Leftrightarrow f_X(u)f_Y(v) \geq f_X(v)f_Y(u) \quad \text{for all } u \leq v. \tag{3.19}$$

Proof. Select $a < b$. Then $X \preceq_{LR} Y$ ensures that

$$\frac{\Pr[u \leq X \leq b]}{\Pr[a \leq X \leq b]} \leq \frac{\Pr[u \leq Y \leq b]}{\Pr[a \leq Y \leq b]} \quad \text{for every } u \in [a, b].$$

It follows then that

$$\frac{\Pr[a \leq X < u]}{\Pr[u \leq X \leq b]} \geq \frac{\Pr[a \leq Y < u]}{\Pr[u \leq Y \leq b]} \quad \text{for every } u \in [a, b];$$

that is,

$$\frac{\Pr[a \leq X < u]}{\Pr[a \leq Y < u]} \geq \frac{\Pr[u \leq X \leq b]}{\Pr[u \leq Y \leq b]} \quad \text{for every } u \in [a, b].$$

In particular, for $u < b \leq v$,

$$\frac{\Pr[u \leq X < b]}{\Pr[u \leq Y < b]} \geq \frac{\Pr[b \leq X \leq v]}{\Pr[b \leq Y \leq v]}.$$

Therefore, when X and Y are continuous rvs,

$$\frac{\Pr[a \leq X < u]}{\Pr[a \leq Y < u]} \geq \frac{\Pr[b \leq X \leq v]}{\Pr[b \leq Y \leq v]} \quad \text{for every } a < u \leq b \leq v.$$

Now let $a \to u$ and $b \to v$ to obtain (3.19). The proof for discrete rvs is similar. □

Remark 3.3.44. Note that the structures of $\preceq_{HR}$ and $\preceq_{LR}$ are relatively similar. Comparing (3.19) to Definition 3.3.36(iii), we see that the inequalities are similar, the former involving pdfs and the latter tfs. ∇

At first glance, (3.18) and (3.19) seem to be unintuitive technical conditions. However, it turns out that in many situations they are very easy to verify, and this is one of the major reasons for the usefulness and importance of the order $\preceq_{LR}$.

3.3.11.3 Equivalent conditions

The following result offers a very general definition of a ranking in the $\preceq_{\text{LR}}$ sense. Before formally stating the result, let us introduce the following notation: given two subsets A and B of the real line, we write $A \leq B$ if the inequality $x \leq y$ holds for every $x \in A$ and $y \in B$.

Property 3.3.45
Given two rvs X and Y, $X \preceq_{\text{LR}} Y$ holds if, and only if,

$$\Pr[X \in A]\Pr[Y \in B] \geq \Pr[X \in B]\Pr[Y \in A] \text{ whenever } A \leq B \subseteq \mathbb{R}.$$

Proof. Assuming the existence of pdfs f_X and f_Y, it suffices to write

$$\begin{aligned} X \preceq_{\text{LR}} Y &\Leftrightarrow f_X(u)f_Y(v) \geq f_X(v)f_Y(u) \text{ for all } u \leq v \\ &\Rightarrow \int_{u \in A} f_X(u)du \int_{v \in B} f_Y(v)dv \geq \int_{v \in B} f_X(v)dv \int_{u \in A} f_Y(u)du \\ &\Leftrightarrow \Pr[X \in A]\Pr[Y \in B] \geq \Pr[X \in B]\Pr[Y \in A]. \end{aligned}$$

To prove the $\Leftarrow$ part, it suffices to proceed as in the proof of (3.19). □

Remark 3.3.46. The likelihood ratio order is obviously stronger than stochastic dominance (it suffices to let a tend to $-\infty$ and b to $+\infty$ in the definition to obtain this result). We can also establish the implication $X \preceq_{\text{LR}} Y \Rightarrow X \preceq_{\text{ST}} Y$ directly from (3.18) as follows. Consider two rvs X and Y such that $X \preceq_{\text{LR}} Y$. Inserting $B=(t,+\infty)$ and $A=(-\infty,t]$ in Property 3.3.45 yields

$$\begin{aligned} &\Pr[X \leq t]\Pr[Y > t] \geq \Pr[X > t]\Pr[Y \leq t] \\ &\Leftrightarrow \big(1-\Pr[X>t]\big)\Pr[Y>t] \geq \Pr[X>t]\big(1-\Pr[Y>t]\big) \\ &\Leftrightarrow \Pr[Y>t] \geq \Pr[X>t]. \end{aligned}$$

Since the reasoning is valid for any $t \in \mathbb{R}$, we conclude that the implication holds. ∇

3.3.11.4 Comparing claim frequencies

Given a claim frequency N, the ratio

$$h_N(n) = \frac{\Pr[N=n]}{\Pr[N=n-1]}, \quad n=1,2,\ldots,$$

introduced in Proposition 3.3.34(ii) is particularly appealing in actuarial science. Indeed, for the members of the Panjer family, $h_N(n)=a+\frac{b}{n}$ for some constants a and b (this is true for the Poisson, binomial and negative binomial distributions).

Proposition 3.3.47
Given two integer-valued rvs N and M,

$$N \preceq_{\text{LR}} M \Leftrightarrow h_N(n) \leq h_M(n) \text{ for all } n \in \mathbb{N}.$$

Example 3.3.48. For the $\mathcal{P}oi(\theta)$ distribution, $h_N(n) = \frac{\theta}{n}$ so that $\mathcal{P}oi(\theta) \preceq_{\text{LR}} \mathcal{P}oi(\theta')$ whenever $\theta \leq \theta'$. ∇

3.3.11.5 Stability of the likelihood ratio order under convolution

If $X_1 \preceq_{\text{LR}} Y_1$ and $X_2 \preceq_{\text{LR}} Y_2$, where X_1 and X_2 are independent rvs and Y_1 and Y_2 are also independent rvs, then it is not necessarily true that $X_1 + X_2 \preceq_{\text{LR}} Y_1 + Y_2$. However, if these rvs have log-concave densities then it is true. This is precisely stated in the following result, which can be found, for example, in Shanthikumar and Yao (1991).

Proposition 3.3.49
Let $X_1, X_2, \ldots, X_n$ and $Y_1, Y_2, \ldots, Y_n$ be two sets of independent and identically distributed rvs with log-concave pdfs such that $X_i \preceq_{\text{LR}} Y_i$, $i = 1, 2, \ldots, n$. Then $\preceq_{\text{LR}}$ is stable under convolution, that is,

$$\sum_{i=1}^{n} X_i \preceq_{\text{LR}} \sum_{i=1}^{n} Y_i.$$

3.3.11.6 Likelihood ratio order and VaRs

The order $\preceq_{\text{LR}}$ can be characterized as follows.

Proposition 3.3.50
Given two rvs X and Y,

$$X \preceq_{\text{LR}} Y \Leftrightarrow p \mapsto F_Y(\text{VaR}[X; p]) \text{ is convex.} \tag{3.20}$$

Proof. We only give the proof for the continuous case. It is clear that $p \mapsto F_Y(\text{VaR}[X; p])$ is convex if, and ony if, its first derivative is non-decreasing, that is,

$$\frac{f_Y(\text{VaR}[X; p])}{f_X(\text{VaR}[X; p])} \text{ is non-decreasing,}$$

which is equivalent to $t \mapsto \frac{f_Y(t)}{f_X(t)}$ being non-decreasing, which concludes the proof. □

3.3.11.7 Likelihood ratio order and Esscher transform

Writing down the ratio of the pdfs of X and of its associated Esscher transform X_c, it is easy to see that it is proportional to $\exp(-cx)$, which clearly decreases in x for $c > 0$. This indicates that $X \preceq_{\text{LR}} X_c$ holds. The Esscher risk measure comes down to replacing X with X_c, dominating the initial risk in the $\preceq_{\text{LR}}$ sense, before computing an expected value.

Further, increasing c is indeed a prudent strategy since the ratio of the pdfs of X_c and $X_{c'}$, $c < c'$, is proportional to $\exp((c - c')x)$ which decreases in x. Hence $X_{c'} \preceq_{\text{LR}} X_c$.

We have seen in Exercise 2.7.22 that the Esscher risk measure does not necessarily agree with $\preceq_{\text{ST}}$ because it does not satisfy the monotonicity condition. Let us now prove that it is in accordance with $\preceq_{\text{LR}}$.

Property 3.3.51
$X \preceq_{\text{LR}} Y \Rightarrow \text{Es}[X; c] \leq \text{Es}[Y; c]$ for any $c > 0$.

Proof. Since $X \preceq_{\text{LR}} Y$, we know that $f_X(u)f_Y(v) \geq f_X(v)f_Y(u)$ for any $u \leq v$. Multiplying both sides of this inequality by

$$\frac{\exp(cu)}{\int_0^{+\infty}\exp(c\xi)dF_X(\xi)}\frac{\exp(cv)}{\int_0^{+\infty}\exp(c\xi)dF_Y(\xi)}$$

yields the same inequality for the pdfs of X_c and Y_c, whence it follows that $X_c \preceq_{\text{LR}} Y_c$, concluding the proof. □

3.3.11.8 Total positivity of order 2 or likelihood ratio increasingness

Stochastic increasingness for a family $\{X_\theta, \quad \theta \in \Theta\}$ of rvs indexed by a univariate parameter θ amounts to requiring that $X_\theta \preceq_{\text{ST}} X_{\theta'}$ whenever $\theta \leq \theta'$. We can similarly define likelihood ratio increasingness as

$$X_\theta \preceq_{\text{LR}} X_{\theta'} \text{ whenever } \theta \leq \theta'.$$

This requirement is equivalent to the notion of total positivity of order 2, defined as follows.

Definition 3.3.52. Let f_θ denote the pdf of X_θ. The X_θ are said to be totally positive of order 2 (TP_2) when

$$f_{\theta_1}(x_1)f_{\theta_2}(x_2) \geq f_{\theta_1}(x_2)f_{\theta_2}(x_1)$$

whenever $x_1 \leq x_2$, $\theta_1 \leq \theta_2$, which is equivalent to $X_{\theta_1} \preceq_{\text{LR}} X_{\theta_2}$. ∇

Examples of TP_2 families include the binomial, Poisson, negative binomial and gamma distributions. Similarly, a function $g : \mathbb{R}^2 \to \mathbb{R}$ is said to be TP_2 if the inequality

$$g(s_1, t_1)g(s_2, t_2) \geq g(s_1, t_2)g(s_2, t_1) \tag{3.21}$$

holds for any $s_1 \leq s_2$ and $t_1 \leq t_2$. We will see that the TP_2 property for g is equivalent to requiring that $\ln g$ is supermodular (or 2-additive).

The following fundamental property of total positivity of order 2, known as the *basic composition formula*, will play a central role in the proofs of the results stated in the next chapters.

Property 3.3.53
Given some functions $h_1 : \mathcal{S} \times \mathcal{T} \to \mathbb{R}$ and $h_2 : \mathcal{T} \times \mathcal{U} \to \mathbb{R}$, let us define the function h_3 as

$$h_3(s, u) = \int_{t \in \mathcal{T}} h_1(s, t)h_2(t, u)d\sigma(t).$$

If h_1 is TP_2 on $\mathcal{S} \times \mathcal{T}$ and h_2 is TP_2 on $\mathcal{T} \times \mathcal{U}$, then h_3 is TP_2 on $\mathcal{S} \times \mathcal{U}$.

3.3.11.9 Ordering mixtures with the likelihood ratio order

Just as was the case for $\preceq_{\text{ST}}$, the TP_2 characteristic allows us to order mixtures by ordering the corresponding mixing distributions. This is formally stated in the next result.

Proposition 3.3.54
If the X_θ are TP_2 then

$$\Lambda_1 \preceq_{\text{LR}} \Lambda_2 \Rightarrow X_{\Lambda_1} \preceq_{\text{LR}} X_{\Lambda_2}, \tag{3.22}$$

where X_{Λ_1} and X_{Λ_2} have df (3.4).

Proof. We give the proof under the assumption that Λ_1 and Λ_2 are continuous with pdfs f_{Λ_1} and f_{Λ_2}, respectively. The proof for the discrete case is similar. The TP_2 assumption for the X_θ means that $f_\theta(y)$, as a function of θ and y, is TP_2. Assumption (3.22) means that $f_{\Lambda_i}(\theta)$, as a function of $i \in \{1, 2\}$ and θ, is TP_2. Therefore, the basic composition formula stated in Property 3.3.53 ensures that $f_{X_{\Lambda_i}}(y)$ is TP_2 in $i \in \{1, 2\}$ and y. □

3.3.11.10 Likelihood ratio increasingness of each term in the sum

Another connection between log-concavity and the likelihood ratio order is illustrated in the next result, taken from Shaked and Shanthikumar (1994).

Proposition 3.3.55
Let $X_1, X_2, \ldots, X_m$ be independent rvs having log-concave pdfs. Then

$$\left[X_i \left| \sum_{j=1}^m X_j = s_1 \right.\right] \preceq_{\text{LR}} \left[X_i \left| \sum_{j=1}^m X_j = s_2 \right.\right] \text{ whenever } s_1 \le s_2,\ i = 1, 2, \ldots, m.$$

Proof. Since the convolution of log-concave pdfs is log-concave, it is sufficient to prove the result for $m = 2$ and $i = 1$. The conditional pdf of X_1, given $X_1 + X_2 = s_1$, is

$$f_{X_1 | X_1+X_2=s_1}(x_1) = \frac{f_{X_1}(x_1) f_{X_2}(s_1 - x_1)}{\int f_{X_1}(u) f_{X_2}(s_1 - u)\, du}.$$

Thus,

$$\frac{f_{X_1 | X_1+X_2=s_2}(x_1)}{f_{X_1 | X_1+X_2=s_1}(x_1)} = \frac{f_{X_2}(s_2 - x_1) \int f_{X_1}(u) f_{X_2}(s_1 - u)\, du}{f_{X_2}(s_1 - x_1) \int f_{X_1}(u) f_{X_2}(s_2 - u)\, du}. \tag{3.23}$$

The log-concavity of f_{X_2} implies that the expression in (3.23) increases in x_1, whenever $s_1 \le s_2$. By (3.18) the proof is complete. □

3.3.11.11 Likelihood ratio order and order statistics

The results involving order statistics derived for $\preceq_{\text{ST}}$ and $\preceq_{\text{HR}}$ partly carry over to $\preceq_{\text{LR}}$. Let $X_1, X_2, \ldots$ be independent and identically distributed rvs. Unlike $\preceq_{\text{ST}}$ and $\preceq_{\text{HR}}$ (see formulas (3.10) and (3.15), respectively), it is in general not true that the $X_{(k)}$ increase in k with respect to $\preceq_{\text{LR}}$ (additional conditions are needed to reach this conclusion; see Shaked and Shanthikumar 1994 and the references therein).

The following result illustrates the influence of the sample size on order statistics.

Property 3.3.56
Let $X_1, X_2, \ldots, X_n$ be independent and identically distributed continuous rvs.

(i) $X_{(k-1:n-1)} \preceq_{\text{LR}} X_{(k:n)}$ for $k = 2, 3, \ldots, n-1$.

(ii) $X_{(k:n)} \preceq_{\text{LR}} X_{(k:n-1)}$ for $k = 1, 2, \ldots, n-1$.

Proof. Let us prove (i). The pdf of $X_{(k:n)}$ is given by

$$f_{X_{(k:n)}}(x) = n \binom{n-1}{k-1} F_X^{k-1}(x) f_X(x) \overline{F}_X^{n-k}(x).$$

The pdf of $X_{(k-1:n-1)}$ is given by

$$f_{X_{(k-1:n-1)}}(x) = (n-1) \binom{n-2}{k-2} F_X^{k-2}(x) f_X(x) \overline{F}_X^{n-k}(x),$$

so that $f_{X_{(k:n)}}(x)/f_{X_{(k-1:n-1)}}(x)$ is increasing. The proof of (ii) is similar. □

3.3.11.12 Likelihood ratio order and notions of ageing

The next result shows that a lifetime distribution with a log-concave density exhibits a particular ageing structure. We know from Property 1.7.6 that the log-concavity of f_X implies that X has an IFR distribution. The following result relates the log-concavity of f_X to the $\preceq_{\text{LR}}$-decreasingness of the remaining lifetimes. For a proof, see Shaked and Shanthikumar (1994) and the references therein.

Proposition 3.3.57
The random variable X has a log-concave density if, and only if,

$$[X - t_2 | X > t_2] \preceq_{\text{LR}} [X - t_1 | X > t_1] \text{ whenever } t_1 \leq t_2.$$

3.3.12 Comparing shortfalls with stochastic dominance: Dispersive order

3.3.12.1 Definition

Instead of conditioning with respect to some class of events, we can also generate stochastic order relations with the help of $\preceq_{\text{ST}}$ by requiring that the $\preceq_{\text{ST}}$-ranking remains unaltered whatever the transformation chosen in a suitable class. We have seen above that the hazard rate order and the likelihood ratio order can both be obtained as conditional stochastic dominance. We follow a different route here and compare shortfalls instead of the risks X and Y. This leads to the following definition.

Definition 3.3.58. Given two risks X and Y, X is said to be smaller than Y in the dispersive order, denoted as $X \preceq_{\text{DISP}} Y$, if, and only if,

$$\left(X - \text{VaR}X; p]\right)_+ \preceq_{\text{ST}} \left(Y - \text{VaR}[Y; p]\right)_+$$

for all $0 < p < 1$. ∇

Early references on $\preceq_{\text{DISP}}$ include Doksum (1969), Deshpande and Kochar (1983) and Shaked (1982). See also Bartoszewicz (1986, 1995), Muñoz-Perez (1990) and Landsberger and Meilijson (1994a,b).

Remark 3.3.59. The relation $\preceq_{\text{DISP}}$ is reflexive and transitive, but not antisymmetric on the set of dfs. Indeed, if $X \preceq_{\text{DISP}} Y$ and $Y \preceq_{\text{DISP}} X$ simultaneously hold, this means that $Y =_d X + c$ for some real constant c. This is easily seen from the fact that $X' - \text{VaR}[X'; p] =_d X - \text{VaR}[X; p]$ if $X' =_d X + c$. ∇

3.3.12.2 Dispersive order and VaR spreads

Several stochastic orderings are based on distances between the respective VaRs of the underlying rvs. For instance, two positive rvs X and Y are said to be star-ordered if the ratio $\text{VaR}[Y; p]/\text{VaR}[X; p]$ of their VaRs is increasing in p. The dispersive order possesses a similar property, dealing with difference between VaRs.

Property 3.3.60
Given two rvs X and Y, $X \preceq_{\text{DISP}} Y$ holds if, and only if,

$$\text{VaR}[X; p_2] - \text{VaR}[X; p_1] \leq \text{VaR}[Y; p_2] - \text{VaR}[Y; p_1] \tag{3.24}$$

whenever $0 < p_1 \leq p_2 < 1$, or equivalently if, and only if,

$$\text{VaR}[Y; p] - \text{VaR}[X; p] \text{ increases in } p \in (0, 1). \tag{3.25}$$

Proof. If $X_p = \left(X - \text{VaR}[X; p]\right)_+$ then

$$\text{VaR}[X_p; q] = \begin{cases} 0, & \text{if } q \leq p, \\ \text{VaR}[X; q] - \text{VaR}[X; p], & \text{if } q > p, \end{cases}$$

so that

$$\begin{aligned} X_p \preceq_{\text{ST}} Y_p &\Leftrightarrow \text{VaR}[X_p; q] \leq \text{VaR}[Y_p; q] \text{ for all } 0 < q < 1 \\ &\Leftrightarrow \text{VaR}[X; q] - \text{VaR}[X; p] \leq \text{VaR}[Y; q] - \text{VaR}[Y; p] \text{ for all } 0 < p < q < 1, \end{aligned}$$

which concludes the proof. □

The characterization (3.24) was taken as the definition of $\preceq_{\text{DISP}}$ by Bickel and Lehmann (1979). It shows that $\preceq_{\text{DISP}}$ is indeed an ordering of dispersion, since it implies that any pair of quantiles of X are at most as widely separated as the corresponding quantiles of Y.

Example 3.3.61. Let us consider $X \sim \mathcal{E}xp(\lambda_X)$ and $Y \sim \mathcal{E}xp(\lambda_Y)$. Since

$$\text{VaR}[Y; p] - \text{VaR}[X; p] = \ln(1-p)\left(\frac{1}{\lambda_X} - \frac{1}{\lambda_Y}\right)$$

is clearly non-decreasing for $p \in [0, 1]$ when $\lambda_Y \leq \lambda_X$, we have that

$$\lambda_Y \leq \lambda_X \Rightarrow X \preceq_{\text{DISP}} Y.$$

∇

3.3.12.3 Dispersive order and hazard rate

The following property relates $\preceq_{\text{DISP}}$ to hazard rates evaluated at VaRs.

Property 3.3.62
Given two rvs X and Y, $X \preceq_{\text{DISP}} Y$ holds if, and only if,

$$r_Y\left(\text{VaR}[Y; p]\right) \leq r_X\left(\text{VaR}[X; p]\right)$$

for all $0 < p < 1$.

Proof. Formula (3.25) ensures that

$$0 \leq \frac{d}{dp}\left(\text{VaR}[Y; p] - \text{VaR}[X; p]\right) = \frac{1}{f_Y\left(\text{VaR}[Y; p]\right)} - \frac{1}{f_X\left(\text{VaR}[X; p]\right)}$$

from which it follows that

$$\begin{aligned}
& f_Y\left(\text{VaR}[Y; p]\right) \leq f_X\left(\text{VaR}[X; p]\right) \text{ for all } p \\
\Leftrightarrow & \frac{f_Y\left(\text{VaR}[Y; p]\right)}{1-p} \leq \frac{f_X\left(\text{VaR}[X; p]\right)}{1-p} \text{ for all } p \\
\Leftrightarrow & \frac{f_Y\left(\text{VaR}[Y; p]\right)}{\overline{F}_Y\left(\text{VaR}[Y; p]\right)} \leq \frac{f_X\left(\text{VaR}[X; p]\right)}{\overline{F}_X\left(\text{VaR}[X; p]\right)} \text{ for all } p \\
\Leftrightarrow & r_Y\left(\text{VaR}[Y; p]\right) \leq r_X\left(\text{VaR}[X; p]\right) \text{for all } p,
\end{aligned}$$

which concludes the proof. □

3.3.12.4 Dispersive order and comonotonicity

The dispersive order is related to comonotonicity as follows: $X \preceq_{\text{DISP}} Y$ if, and only if, there exists a comonotonic pair $(t(Y), Y)$ such that $X =_d t(Y)$ for some increasing function t with slope at most one. This is a consequence of the next result.

Proposition 3.3.63
Let X and Y be continuous rvs. Then:

(i) $X \preceq_{\text{DISP}} Y$ if, and only if, $X =_d t(Y)$ for some non-decreasing function t such that $t(y) - t(x) \leq y - x$ for all $x < y$;

(ii) $X \preceq_{\text{DISP}} Y$ if, and only if, $Y =_d t(X)$ for some non-decreasing function t such that $t(y) - t(x) \geq y - x$ for all $x < y$.

Proof. Clearly $X =_d F_X^{-1}(F_Y(Y))$, and from (3.24) we have

$$F_X^{-1}(p_2) - F_X^{-1}(p_1) \leq F_Y^{-1}(p_2) - F_Y^{-1}(p_1) \text{ for all } 0 < p_1 \leq p_2 < 1$$
$$\Leftrightarrow F_X^{-1}(F_Y(x_2)) - F_X^{-1}(F_Y(x_1)) \leq x_2 - x_1 \text{ for all } x_1 \leq x_2.$$

It suffices to consider $t(x) = F_X^{-1}(F_Y(x))$ to prove (i). The reasoning for (ii) is similar. □

Following Muñoz-Perez (1990), we say that Y is the VaR-addition of the rvs X and Z if

$$\text{VaR}[Y; p] = \text{VaR}[X; p] + \text{VaR}[Z; p] \text{ for all } 0 < p < 1.$$

Hence, if $U \sim \mathcal{U}ni(0, 1)$ then

$$Y = \text{VaR}[X; U] + \text{VaR}[Z; U] = F_X^{-1}(U) + F_Z^{-1}(U),$$

which shows that Y is the sum of the elements of the comonotonic pair $\left(F_X^{-1}(U), F_Z^{-1}(U)\right)$.

Property 3.3.64
$X \preceq_{\text{DISP}} Y$ if, and only if, there exists an rv Z such that Y is the VaR-addition of the rvs X and Z, that is, $Y =_d X + Z$ with X and Z comonotonic.

Proof. If $X \preceq_{\text{DISP}} Y$ we know that $p \mapsto \text{VaR}[Y; p] - \text{VaR}[X; p]$ is non-decreasing and left-continuous on $(0, 1)$. This function is thus the VaR of some rv, Z say.

Conversely, if there exists an rv Z such that

$$\text{VaR}[Y; p] = \text{VaR}[X; p] + \text{VaR}[Z; p] \text{ for all } 0 < p < 1$$

we get that the difference between the VaRs associated with Y and the corresponding ones for X,

$$\text{VaR}[Y; p] - \text{VaR}[X; p] = \text{VaR}[Z; p],$$

is a non-decreasing function. The result then follows from (3.25). □

Remark 3.3.65. Similar properties hold for the orders $\preceq_{\text{ST}}$ and $\preceq_{\text{HR}}$: $X \preceq_{\text{ST}} Y$ if $Y =_d X' + Z'$ with $\Pr[Z' \geq 0] = 1$, and $X \preceq_{\text{HR}} Y$ if $X =_d \min\{Y, Z\}$. ∇

3.3.12.5 Dispersive order and stochastic dominance

Ordering of risks through $\preceq_{\text{DISP}}$ is rather strong. Indeed, it is easy to see that

$$X \preceq_{\text{DISP}} Y \Rightarrow X \preceq_{\text{ST}} Y$$

if the left endpoints of the supports of X and Y are equal (and assumed here to be 0), since we then have that

$$\text{VaR}[Y; p] - \text{VaR}[X; p] \geq \text{VaR}[Y; 0] - \text{VaR}[X; 0] = 0 \text{ for any } p \in (0, 1).$$

The next result gives another link between $\preceq_{\text{DISP}}$ and $\preceq_{\text{ST}}$.

Proposition 3.3.66
Let X and X' be two independent and identically distributed rvs and let Y and Y' be two other independent and identically distributed rvs. If $X \preceq_{\text{DISP}} Y$ then $|X - X'| \preceq_{\text{ST}} |Y - Y'|$, that is,

$$\Pr\Big[|X - X'| > z\Big] \leq \Pr\Big[|Y - Y'| > z\Big] \text{ for all } z \geq 0. \tag{3.26}$$

Proposition 3.3.66 provides an intuitive meaning for the dispersive order. If Y is more dispersed than X then the absolute distance between two independent realizations of Y, $|Y - Y'|$, is larger in the $\preceq_{\text{ST}}$ sense than the corresponding distance for X.

3.3.13 *Mixed stochastic dominance: Laplace transform order*

3.3.13.1 Definition

The idea behind mixed stochastic dominance is quite natural: instead of requiring that $\Pr[X > t]$ be smaller than $\Pr[Y > t]$ for all t, we consider a family $\mathcal{P}$ of dfs and require that

$$\int_{-\infty}^{+\infty} \Pr[X > t] dF(t) \leq \int_{-\infty}^{+\infty} \Pr[Y > t] dF(t) \text{ for all } F \in \mathcal{P}. \tag{3.27}$$

If we take $\mathcal{P}$ to be the family of negative exponential distributions, we get the Laplace transform order, as formally stated next.

Definition 3.3.67. Let X and Y be two risks. Then X is said to be smaller than Y in the Laplace transform order, written as $X \preceq_{\text{LT}} Y$, if inequality (3.27) holds with $\mathcal{P}$ as the family of the $\mathcal{E}xp(\lambda)$ distributions, $\lambda > 0$, that is, if the inequality

$$\int_{0}^{+\infty} \Pr[X > t] \lambda \exp(-\lambda t) dt \leq \int_{0}^{+\infty} \Pr[X > t] \lambda \exp(-\lambda t) dt$$

holds for all $\lambda > 0$. ∇

Note that the fixed threshold t to be exceeded by X and Y in the definition of $\preceq_{\text{ST}}$ is thus replaced with a random threshold distributed according to $\mathcal{E}xp(\lambda)$ to get $\preceq_{\text{LT}}$. Specifically,

$$X \preceq_{\text{LT}} Y \Leftrightarrow \Pr[X > E_t] \geq \Pr[Y > E_t] \text{ for all } t > 0, \tag{3.28}$$

where $E_t \sim \mathcal{E}xp(t)$, independent of both X and Y. Formula (3.28) provides an intuitive explanation of a $\preceq_{\text{LT}}$-ranking for claim amounts, by reference to exponentially distributed risks. Note that broad classes of stochastic orderings can be obtained by substituting another parametric family for $\{E_t,\ t>0\}$ in (3.28). By considering non-negative constants in (3.28), one simply gets $\preceq_{\text{ST}}$.

The Laplace transform order has been studied by Stoyan (1983, Section 1.8) and Alzaid, Kim and Proschan (1991). The order $\preceq_{\text{LT}}$ is an useful tool in reliability theory. It is worth mentioning that many concepts of reliability theory have found interesting applications in actuarial science, following the works of Straub (1971) and Heilmann (1983). The Laplace transform order has been comprehensively reviewed by Denuit (2001). It has also been widely used in economics; see Thistle (1993) and the references therein.

3.3.13.2 Laplace transform order and Laplace transforms

Let us show that the Laplace transform order boils down to requiring that the Laplace transforms of two non-negative random variables are uniformly ordered. This is formally stated next.

Property 3.3.68
Given two risks X and Y,

$$X \preceq_{\text{LT}} Y \Leftrightarrow L_X(t) \leq L_Y(t) \text{ holds for all } t \geq 0. \tag{3.29}$$

Proof. Using integration by parts, one finds for $t \geq 0$ that

$$\begin{aligned} L_X(t) &= F_X(0) + \int_{0+}^{+\infty} \exp(-tx) dF_X(x) \\ &= F_X(0) + \Big[\exp(-tx)F_X(x)\Big]_{x=0+}^{+\infty} - \int_0^{+\infty} F_X(x) d\big(\exp(-tx)\big) \\ &= t\int_0^{+\infty} \exp(-tx)F_X(x)dx. \end{aligned} \tag{3.30}$$

This yields

$$\frac{1-L_X(t)}{t} = \int_0^{+\infty} \exp(-tx)\overline{F}_X(x)dx, \quad t>0. \tag{3.31}$$

□

Remark 3.3.69. Note that (3.31) can be considered as the expected value of $\min\{X, E_t\}$, where $E_t \sim \mathcal{E}xp(t)$ and independent of X. Therefore,

$$X \preceq_{\text{LT}} Y \Leftrightarrow \mathbb{E}[\min\{X, E_t\}] \geq \mathbb{E}[\min\{Y, E_t\}] \text{ for all } t > 0, \tag{3.32}$$

where E_t is independent of both X and Y. ∇

Example 3.3.70. Several classes of probability distributions have been defined as $\min\{X_\theta, E_t\}$, where $E_t \sim \mathcal{E}xp(t)$, for some parametric family $\{X_\theta,\ \theta \in \Theta\}$, $\Theta \subseteq \mathbb{R}^n$. For instance, Davis and Feldstein (1979) considered the family of probability distributions with hazard rate function of the form

$$r(x) = \beta + \frac{\alpha}{x+\lambda}, \quad \alpha, \beta, \lambda > 0;$$

each member of this family can be represented as $\min\{X_{(\alpha,\lambda)}, E_\beta\}$, where $X_{(\alpha,\lambda)} \sim \mathcal{P}ar(\alpha, \lambda)$. ∇

Note that the Laplace transforms involved in (3.29) always exist (since X and Y are non-negative).

3.3.13.3 Moment generating function order

Laplace transforms and moment generating functions are closely related: formally, they differ only in the sign of the argument inside the exponential. The moment generating function order is thus a close companion to the Laplace transform order.

From a probabilistic point of view, the moment generating function order boils down to requiring that the moment generating functions of the non-negative rvs X and Y are uniformly ordered. This is formally stated next.

Definition 3.3.71. Given two risks X and Y, X is smaller than Y in the moment generating function order, written as $X \preceq_{\mathrm{MGF}} Y$, when the inequality

$$M_X(t) \leq M_Y(t) \text{ holds for all } t \geq 0. \tag{3.33}$$

∇

Note that the relation $\preceq_{\mathrm{MGF}}$ is useless for comparing pairs of rvs with heavy tails (such as Pareto distributions), for which $M_X(t) = +\infty$ for all $t > 0$. The order $\preceq_{\mathrm{MGF}}$ is also incapable of comparing two lognormally distributed rvs.

3.3.13.4 Moment generating function order and exponential premiums

In an actuarial framework, $\preceq_{\mathrm{MGF}}$ also possesses a nice interpretation. Consider an insurance company quoting premiums according to the exponential premium calculation principle. In such a case, the amount of premium $\pi_t[X]$ relating to the risk X is given by

$$\pi_t[X] = \frac{1}{t} \ln M_X(t), \quad t > 0. \tag{3.34}$$

From (3.33) and (3.34), we obviously have that

$$X \preceq_{\mathrm{MGF}} Y \Leftrightarrow \pi_t[X] \leq \pi_t[Y] \text{ for all } t > 0.$$

Therefore, $X \preceq_{\mathrm{MGF}} Y$ is equivalent to X needing smaller premiums than Y when the exponential premium calculation principle is used, whatever the risk-aversion coefficient t is. We thus see that the exponential order is closely related to the classical exponential premium calculation principle.

3.3.13.5 Laplace transform order and expected utility theory

The relation $\preceq_{LT}$ expresses the common preferences of all decision-makers with a utility function u of the form

$$u(x) = 1 - \exp(-tx), \quad t > 0. \tag{3.35}$$

In other words, $X \preceq_{LT} Y$ means that the income X is preferred to the income Y by all decision-makers with a utility function of the form (3.35), that is, those people with a constant risk aversion.

3.3.13.6 Relations with other stochastic orderings

It is easy to see that, given two non-negative rvs X and Y, the implications

$$X \preceq_{ST} Y \Rightarrow \begin{cases} X \preceq_{MGF} Y \\ Y \preceq_{LT} X \end{cases} \tag{3.36}$$

are valid.

3.3.13.7 Some properties

Let us now examine the invariance and closure properties of $\preceq_{LT}$. We omit the proof since it is similar to the reasoning applied in the proof of Proposition (3.3.17) for $\preceq_{ST}$.

Property 3.3.72

(i) Let X and Y be two non-negative rvs, and let $t: \mathbb{R}^+ \to \mathbb{R}^+$ be a continuous function such that t' is completely monotone. Then

$$X \preceq_{LT} Y \Rightarrow t(X) \preceq_{LT} t(Y).$$

(ii) Let $X_1, X_2, \ldots, X_n$ (and also $Y_1, Y_2, \ldots, Y_n$) be independent non-negative rvs and let $\Psi: (\mathbb{R}^+)^n \to \mathbb{R}$ be such that $x_i \mapsto \partial\Psi/\partial x_i$ is completely monotone for $i = 1, 2, \ldots, n$; then

$$X_i \preceq_{LT} Y_i \text{ for } i = 1, 2, \ldots, n \Rightarrow \Psi(X_1, X_2, \ldots, X_n) \preceq_{LT} \Psi(Y_1, Y_2, \ldots, Y_n).$$

In particular, $\preceq_{LT}$ is closed under convolution.

(iii) Closure under compounding: let $\{X_1, X_2, X_3, \ldots\}$ and $\{Y_1, Y_2, Y_3, \ldots\}$ be two sequences of non-negative independent and identically distributed rvs and let N and M be positive integer-valued rvs, independent of the X_i and of the Y_j. Then

$$\left.\begin{array}{l} X_i \preceq_{LT} Y_i \text{ for all } i \\ N \preceq_{LT} M \end{array}\right\} \Rightarrow \sum_{i=1}^{N} X_i \preceq_{LT} \sum_{i=1}^{M} Y_i.$$

3.3.13.8 Stochastic complete monotonicity

Let us consider a family of non-negative rvs $\{X_\theta,\quad \theta\in\Theta\}$, indexed by a single parameter $\theta\in\Theta\subseteq\mathbb{R}^+$. We study in this section the validity of the implication

$$t \text{ completely monotone} \Rightarrow t^*\text{completely monotone}, \tag{3.37}$$

where $t^*(\theta)=\mathbb{E}[t(X_\theta)]$ is defined as in (3.2). At first sight, this sounds very theoretical. However, if (3.37) holds, we immediately find that

$$\Lambda_1\preceq_{\rm LT}\Lambda_2\Rightarrow X_{\Lambda_1}\preceq_{\rm LT}X_{\Lambda_2} \tag{3.38}$$

where the X_{Λ_i} have df (3.4).

Property 3.3.73

(i) Given a non-negative random variable Y, the family $\{X_\theta,\quad \theta\in\mathbb{R}^+\}$ defined as either $X_\theta=\theta Y$ or $X_\theta=Y+\theta$ satisfies (3.37). In other words, families with a location or a scale parameter fulfill (3.37).

(ii) Given a sequence $\{Y_1, Y_2, Y_3, \ldots\}$ of non-negative independent and identically distributed rvs, the family $\{X_\theta,\quad \theta\in\mathbb{N}\}$ defined as $X_\theta=\sum_{k=1}^{\theta}Y_k$ satisfies (3.37).

3.3.13.9 Comparing claim frequencies

When N is a non-negative integer-valued rv then it is customary and convenient to analyse it using its probability generating function φ_N, rather than its Laplace transform. Comparing the respective pgf's turns out to be equivalent to $\preceq_{\rm LT}$, as formally stated next.

Property 3.3.74
Let N and M be two non-negative integer-valued rvs. Then

$$\varphi_N(t)\leq\varphi_M(t)\text{ for all }t\in(0,1)\Leftrightarrow N\preceq_{\rm LT}M. \tag{3.39}$$

3.3.13.10 Laplace transform order and notions of ageing

Exponential distributions have been widely used in actuarial sciences. Many concepts of super- and subexponentiality have been discussed in the literature. This section expands on this issue by considering the $\mathcal{L}$-class of life distributions, defined by Klefsjö (1983).

Definition 3.3.75. Let X be a non-negative rv with a finite mean $\mathbb{E}[X]$; X is said to belong to the $\mathcal{L}$-class if, and only if, $X\preceq_{\rm LT}\mathcal{E}xp(1/\mathbb{E}[X])$, that is, if, and only if, its Laplace transform satisfies

$$L_X(t)\leq\frac{1}{1+t\mathbb{E}[X]}\text{ for all }t\in\mathbb{R}^+.$$

∇

From (3.31), X belongs to the $\mathcal{L}$-class if, and only if,

$$\int_0^{+\infty} \exp(-tx)\overline{F}_X(x)dx \geq \frac{\mathbb{E}[X]}{1+t\mathbb{E}[X]} \text{ for } t>0. \tag{3.40}$$

The $\mathcal{L}$-class contains the smaller NBUE, NBU and IFR classes of distributions.

If the reverse inequality holds in (3.40), then X is said to belong to the $\overline{\mathcal{L}}$-class; that is, $X \in \overline{\mathcal{L}}$ if, and only if, $\mathcal{E}xp(1/\mathbb{E}[X]) \preceq_{\text{LT}} X$. The $\overline{\mathcal{L}}$-class contains the smaller NWUE, NWU and DFR classes of distributions.

We summarize below some interesting properties of the $\mathcal{L}$- and $\overline{\mathcal{L}}$-classes.

Property 3.3.76

(i) $X, Y \in \mathcal{L} \Rightarrow X+Y \in \mathcal{L}$; this is not true for the $\overline{\mathcal{L}}$-class.

(ii) The coefficient of variation of a distribution belonging to the $\mathcal{L}$-class (resp. ($\overline{\mathcal{L}}$-class) is ≤ 1 (≥ 1).

(iii) $X \in \mathcal{L} \Leftrightarrow X \preceq_{\text{LT}} X_{\{1\}}$.

The next result relates $\preceq_{\text{LT}}$ to the stationary renewal distribution.

Property 3.3.77
Let X and Y be two non-negative random variables such that $\mathbb{E}[X]=\mathbb{E}[Y]$. Then

$$X \preceq_{\text{LT}} Y \Leftrightarrow Y_{\{1\}} \preceq_{\text{LT}} X_{\{1\}}.$$

Proof. Using (3.30), we have for $t \geq 0$ that

$$\begin{aligned}
L_{X_{\{1\}}}(t) &= t\int_0^{+\infty} \exp(-tx)\left(\int_0^x \frac{\overline{F}_X(y)}{\mathbb{E}[X]}dy\right)dx \\
&= \frac{t}{\mathbb{E}[X]}\int_0^{+\infty}\left(\int_{x=y}^{+\infty} \exp(-tx)dx\right)\overline{F}_X(y)dy \\
&= \frac{1}{\mathbb{E}[X]}\int_0^{+\infty} \exp(-ty)\overline{F}_X(y)dy \\
&= \frac{1-L_X(t)}{t\mathbb{E}[X]},
\end{aligned}$$

by (3.31). This concludes the proof. □

Remark 3.3.78. Note that $X \preceq_{\text{MGF}} Y \Leftrightarrow X_{\{1\}} \preceq_{\text{MGF}} Y_{\{1\}}$. ∇

3.3.14 *Multivariate extensions*

3.3.14.1 Definition

It turns out that the equivalent conditions for the univariate $\preceq_{\text{ST}}$ lead to different multivariate extensions. Let us start with the ordering known in the literature as multivariate stochastic dominance.

Definition 3.3.79. Given two random vectors $\boldsymbol{X}$ and $\boldsymbol{Y}, \boldsymbol{X}$ is said to be smaller than $\boldsymbol{Y}$ in stochastic dominance, written as $\boldsymbol{X} \preceq_{\text{ST}} \boldsymbol{Y}$, if $\mathbb{E}[t(\boldsymbol{X})] \leq \mathbb{E}[t(\boldsymbol{Y})]$ for every non-decreasing function $t: \mathbb{R}^n \to \mathbb{R}$, provided the expectations exist. ∇

An early reference on multivariate stochastic dominance is Marshall and Olkin (1979); a nice description of this stochastic order relation and of its properties can be found in Section 4.B of Shaked and Shanthikumar (1994). A comparison in the $\preceq_{\text{ST}}$ sense is rather strong and sometimes difficult to establish. Of course, if a $\preceq_{\text{ST}}$-ranking holds, the actuary is in a position to resort to a host of stochastic inequalities.

Let us also examine another multivariate generalization of the univariate $\preceq_{\text{ST}}$, based on the no-crossing condition between the respective dfs or tfs. The resulting multivariate stochastic orderings are referred to as orthant orders. Whereas we had equivalence in the univariate case, the generalizations based on dfs and tfs become distinct in a multivariate setting. Early references on orthant orders include Marshall and Olkin (1979). A self-contained presentation is given by Shaked and Shanthikumar (1994).

Definition 3.3.80. If

$$\overline{F}_{\boldsymbol{X}}(\boldsymbol{x}) \leq \overline{F}_{\boldsymbol{Y}}(\boldsymbol{x}) \quad \text{for all } \boldsymbol{x} \in \mathbb{R}^n \tag{3.41}$$

then $\boldsymbol{X}$ is said to be smaller than $\boldsymbol{Y}$ in the upper orthant order (denoted by $\boldsymbol{X} \preceq_{\text{UO}} \boldsymbol{Y}$). If

$$F_{\boldsymbol{X}}(\boldsymbol{x}) \geq F_{\boldsymbol{Y}}(\boldsymbol{x}) \quad \text{for all } \boldsymbol{x} \in \mathbb{R}^n \tag{3.42}$$

then $\boldsymbol{X}$ is said to be smaller than $\boldsymbol{Y}$ in the lower orthant order (denoted by $\boldsymbol{X} \preceq_{\text{LO}} \boldsymbol{Y}$). ∇

The reason for this terminology is that sets of the form $\{\boldsymbol{x} \in \mathbb{R}^n | \boldsymbol{x} > \boldsymbol{a}\}$, for some fixed $\boldsymbol{a}$, are called upper orthants and sets of the form $\{\boldsymbol{x} \in \mathbb{R}^n | \boldsymbol{x} \leq \boldsymbol{a}\}$, for some fixed $\boldsymbol{a}$, are called lower orthants.

Remark 3.3.81. When $\boldsymbol{Y} \preceq_{\text{LO}} \boldsymbol{X}$ and $\boldsymbol{X} \preceq_{\text{UO}} \boldsymbol{Y}$ simultaneously hold, $\boldsymbol{X}$ is said to be smaller than $\boldsymbol{Y}$ in the concordance order introduced by Joe (1990). For $n = 2$, and as far as random couples with identical marginals are concerned, there is a huge literature about the concordance order, which coincides with the correlation order of Dhaene and Goovaerts (1996, 1997); see Part II for more details. ∇

Let us now introduce a multivariate analogue of the univariate likelihood ratio order $\preceq_{\text{LR}}$, sometimes also called the TP_2 order. Standard references on the multivariate likelihood ratio order include Whitt (1982, 1985). Before stating the formal definition of the multivariate $\preceq_{\text{LR}}$, let us introduce the following notation: for $\boldsymbol{x}$ and $\boldsymbol{y}$ in $\mathbb{R}^n$, we denote by $\boldsymbol{x} \wedge \boldsymbol{y}$ and $\boldsymbol{x} \vee \boldsymbol{y}$ the componentwise minima and maxima, respectively, that is,

$$\boldsymbol{x} \wedge \boldsymbol{y} = \big(\min\{x_1, y_1\}, \ldots, \min\{x_n, y_n\}\big)$$

and

$$\boldsymbol{x} \vee \boldsymbol{y} = \big(\max\{x_1, y_1\}, \ldots, \max\{x_n, y_n\}\big).$$

Definition 3.3.82. Let $\boldsymbol{X}$ and $\boldsymbol{Y}$ be two n-dimensional random vectors with continuous (or discrete) pdfs $f_{\boldsymbol{X}}$ and $f_{\boldsymbol{Y}}$. If

$$f_{\boldsymbol{X}}(\boldsymbol{x})f_{\boldsymbol{Y}}(\boldsymbol{y}) \leq f_{\boldsymbol{X}}(\boldsymbol{x}\wedge\boldsymbol{y})f_{\boldsymbol{Y}}(\boldsymbol{x}\vee\boldsymbol{y}) \quad \text{for every } \boldsymbol{x} \text{ and } \boldsymbol{y} \text{ in } \mathbb{R}^n, \tag{3.43}$$

then $\boldsymbol{X}$ is said to be smaller than $\boldsymbol{Y}$ in the multivariate likelihood ratio order (written as $\boldsymbol{X}\preceq_{\text{LR}}\boldsymbol{Y}$). ∇

In the univariate case $n=1$, (3.43) reduces to (3.19).

Remark 3.3.83. Note that $\boldsymbol{X} \preceq_{\text{LR}} \boldsymbol{X}$ does not necessarily hold, which makes $\preceq_{\text{LR}}$ quite different from the other stochastic order relations studied so far ($\preceq_{\text{LR}}$ is not reflexive). We will see in Part II that $\boldsymbol{X} \preceq_{\text{LR}} \boldsymbol{X}$ expresses a very particular dependence structure called multivariate total positivity of order 2. ∇

3.3.14.2 Equivalent conditions

The following result offers a characterization of the multivariate $\preceq_{\text{ST}}$ by means of its univariate counterpart.

Proposition 3.3.84
Given two n-dimensional random vectors $\boldsymbol{X}$ and $\boldsymbol{Y}, \boldsymbol{X} \preceq_{\text{ST}} \boldsymbol{Y}$ if, and only if, the stochastic inequality $\Psi(\boldsymbol{X}) \preceq_{\text{ST}} \Psi(\boldsymbol{Y})$ holds true for any non-decreasing function $\Psi: \mathbb{R}^n \to \mathbb{R}$.

Proof. Since $\Psi(\boldsymbol{X}) \preceq_{\text{ST}} \Psi(\boldsymbol{Y}) \Rightarrow \mathbb{E}[\Psi(\boldsymbol{X})] \leq \mathbb{E}[\Psi(\boldsymbol{Y})]$, the condition is obviously sufficient. Now, given any non-decreasing function $t: \mathbb{R} \to \mathbb{R}$, the composition $t \circ \Psi$ is also non-decreasing so that

$$\begin{aligned} \boldsymbol{X} \preceq_{\text{ST}} \boldsymbol{Y} &\Rightarrow \mathbb{E}\left[t(\Psi(\boldsymbol{X}))\right] \leq \mathbb{E}\left[t(\Psi(\boldsymbol{Y}))\right] \quad \text{for every non-decreasing } t \\ &\Leftrightarrow \Psi(\boldsymbol{X}) \preceq_{\text{ST}} \Psi(\boldsymbol{Y}), \end{aligned}$$

which concludes the proof. □

When $\boldsymbol{X}$ and $\boldsymbol{Y}$ represent multivariate risks, $\boldsymbol{X} \preceq_{\text{ST}} \boldsymbol{Y}$ means that all profit-seeking decision-makers prefer a loss $\Psi(\boldsymbol{X})$ over a loss $\Psi(\boldsymbol{Y})$ for any non-decreasing function Ψ.

The following result was obtained by Scarsini and Shaked (1990). It essentially states that, as far as random couples are concerned, it is sufficient to check for the stochastic inequality $\Psi(\boldsymbol{X}) \preceq_{\text{ST}} \Psi(\boldsymbol{Y})$ involved in Proposition 3.3.84 for functions $\Psi: \mathbb{R}^2 \to \mathbb{R}$ that can be decomposed as a sum of two univariate functions t_1 and t_2, that is, $\Psi(\boldsymbol{x}) = t_1(x_1) + t_2(x_2)$.

Proposition 3.3.85
Let (X_1, X_2) and (Y_1, Y_2) be two random couples. Then $(X_1, X_2) \preceq_{\text{ST}} (Y_1, Y_2)$ if, and only if,

$$t_1(X_1) + t_2(X_2) \preceq_{\text{ST}} t_1(Y_1) + t_2(Y_2) \tag{3.44}$$

for all non-decreasing functions t_1 and t_2.

Broadly speaking, $\preceq_{\text{ST}}$ coincides with almost sure comparison as can be seen from the following result, which is an extension of Proposition 3.3.4.

Proposition 3.3.86
The random vectors $\boldsymbol{X}$ and $\boldsymbol{Y}$ satisfy $\boldsymbol{X} \preceq_{\text{ST}} \boldsymbol{Y}$ if, and only if, there exist two random vectors $\widetilde{\boldsymbol{X}}$ and $\widetilde{\boldsymbol{Y}}$, defined on the same probability space, such that $\widetilde{\boldsymbol{X}} =_d \boldsymbol{X}$, $\widetilde{\boldsymbol{Y}} =_d \boldsymbol{Y}$ and $\Pr[\widetilde{\boldsymbol{X}} \leq \widetilde{\boldsymbol{Y}}] = 1$.

The sufficiency of the coupling construction described in Proposition 3.3.86 is obvious. The proof of its necessity is more difficult and will not be given here. The interested reader may consult Kamae, Krengel and O'Brien (1977) for details.

Let us now examine some characterizations of the orthant orders.

Proposition 3.3.87
Let $\boldsymbol{X}$ and $\boldsymbol{Y}$ be two n-dimensional random vectors.

(i) $\boldsymbol{X} \preceq_{\text{UO}} \boldsymbol{Y}$ if, and only if,

$$\mathbb{E}\left[\prod_{i=1}^{n} g_i(X_i)\right] \leq \mathbb{E}\left[\prod_{i=1}^{n} g_i(Y_i)\right] \tag{3.45}$$

for every collection $\{g_1, g_2, \ldots, g_n\}$ of univariate non-negative non-decreasing functions.

(ii) $\boldsymbol{X} \preceq_{\text{LO}} \boldsymbol{Y}$ if, and only if,

$$\mathbb{E}\left[\prod_{i=1}^{n} h_i(X_i)\right] \geq \mathbb{E}\left[\prod_{i=1}^{n} h_i(Y_i)\right] \tag{3.46}$$

for every collection $\{h_1, h_2, \ldots, h_n\}$ of univariate non-negative non-increasing functions.

It is clear from Proposition 3.3.87, that

$$\boldsymbol{X} \preceq_{\text{ST}} \boldsymbol{Y} \Rightarrow \boldsymbol{X} \preceq_{\text{UO}} \boldsymbol{Y} \text{ and } \boldsymbol{X} \preceq_{\text{LO}} \boldsymbol{Y}. \tag{3.47}$$

Consider now non-negative random vectors $\boldsymbol{X}$ and $\boldsymbol{Y}$. The next result describes the orders $\preceq_{\text{UO}}$ and $\preceq_{\text{LO}}$ in a new fashion when the underlying random vectors are non-negative, using minima and maxima.

Proposition 3.3.88
Let $\boldsymbol{X}$ and $\boldsymbol{Y}$ be two nonnegative random vectors.

(i) $\boldsymbol{X} \preceq_{\text{UO}} \boldsymbol{Y}$ if, and only if, $\min\{a_1X_1, \ldots, a_nX_n\} \preceq_{\text{ST}} \min\{a_1Y_1, \ldots, a_nY_n\}$ whenever $a_i > 0$, $i = 1, 2, \ldots, n$.

(ii) $\boldsymbol{X} \preceq_{\text{LO}} \boldsymbol{Y}$ if, and only if, $\max\{a_1X_1, \ldots, a_nX_n\} \preceq_{\text{ST}} \max\{a_1Y_1, \ldots, a_nY_n\}$ whenever $a_i > 0$, $i = 1, 2, \ldots, n$.

Proof. The $\preceq_{\rm ST}$ inequality in (i) is the same as

$$\overline{F}_X\left(\frac{t}{a_1},\frac{t}{a_2},\ldots,\frac{t}{a_n}\right)\leq\overline{F}_Y\left(\frac{t}{a_1},\frac{t}{a_2},\ldots,\frac{t}{a_n}\right)$$

whenever $t\geq 0$, $a_i>0$, $i=1,2,\ldots,n$, which is the same as

$$\overline{F}_X(t_1,t_2,\ldots,t_n)\leq\overline{F}_Y(t_1,t_2,\ldots,t_n) \tag{3.48}$$

whenever $t_i>0$, $i=1,2,\ldots,n$. Using standard limiting arguments it can be seen that (3.48) is the same as $\boldsymbol{X}\preceq_{\rm UO}\boldsymbol{Y}$. This proves (i). The proof of (ii) is similar. □

3.3.14.3 Properties

As pointed out above, it is often difficult to establish that $\boldsymbol{X}\preceq_{\rm ST}\boldsymbol{Y}$ from Definition 3.3.79 or from the equivalent conditions detailed in the preceding section. Nevertheless, there are several standard constructions that naturally lead to a ranking in the multivariate stochastic dominance sense. Some of them are described in the present section.

The next result is due to Veinott (1965).

Proposition 3.3.89
Let $\boldsymbol{X}$ and $\boldsymbol{Y}$ be two n-dimensional random vectors. If

$$X_1\preceq_{\rm ST}Y_1, \tag{3.49}$$

$$[X_2|X_1=x_1]\preceq_{\rm ST}[Y_2|Y_1=y_1]\quad\text{whenever } x_1\leq y_1, \tag{3.50}$$

and, in general, for $i=2,3,\ldots,n$,

$$[X_i|X_1=x_1,\ldots,X_{i-1}=x_{i-1}]\preceq_{\rm ST}[Y_i|Y_1=y_1,\ldots,Y_{i-1}=y_{i-1}] \tag{3.51}$$

whenever $x_j\leq y_j$, $j=1,2,\ldots,i-1$, then $\boldsymbol{X}\preceq_{\rm ST}\boldsymbol{Y}$.

Let us consider n independent rvs $X_1,X_2,\ldots,X_n$, say. Given a non-decreasing function $\Psi:\mathbb{R}^n\to\mathbb{R}$, assume we are interested in the stochastic behaviour of $[\boldsymbol{X}|\Psi(\boldsymbol{X})=s]$ as a function of s. We intuitively expect non-decreasingness (in some sense to be made precise later) in s. The next result indicates that our intuition is true under some specific conditions. Let us first consider the case where $\Psi(\boldsymbol{x})=\sum_{i=1}^n x_i$. Efron (1965) obtained the following result; see also Daduna and Szekli (1996) for applications in queueing theory.

Property 3.3.90
Let $X_1,X_2,\ldots,X_n$ be independent rvs with log-concave densities. Then

$$\left[\boldsymbol{X}\middle|\sum_{i=1}^n X_i=s_1\right]\preceq_{\rm ST}\left[\boldsymbol{X}\middle|\sum_{i=1}^n X_i=s_2\right]$$

whenever $s_1\leq s_2$.

Joag–Dev (1990) proved the stochastic monotonicity of a random vector conditioned on some of its order statistics.

Property 3.3.91
Let $X_1, X_2, \ldots, X_n$ be independent and identically distributed continuous or discrete rvs. Let $X_{(1)} \leq X_{(2)} \leq \ldots \leq X_{(n)}$ denote the corresponding order statistics. Then for $1 \leq k_1 < k_2 < \ldots < k_r \leq n$, $1 \leq r \leq n$, one has

$$\left[\boldsymbol{X} \middle| X_{(k_1)} = s_1, X_{(k_2)} = s_2, \ldots, X_{(k_r)} = s_r\right] \preceq_{\mathrm{ST}} \left[\boldsymbol{X} \middle| X_{(k_1)} = s_1', X_{(k_2)} = s_2', \ldots, X_{(k_r)} = s_r'\right]$$

whenever $s_1 \leq s_2 \leq \ldots \leq s_r$, $s_1' \leq s_2' \leq \ldots \leq s_r'$ and $s_i \leq s_i'$ for $i = 1, 2, \ldots, n$.

Let us now examine stochastic comparison of partial sums of independent rvs. The following result is due to Boland, Proschan and Tong (1992). Extensions of it can be found in Shaked, Shanthikumar and Tong (1995).

Proposition 3.3.92
Let $X_1, X_2, \ldots, X_n$ be independent rvs such that $X_1 \preceq_{\mathrm{LR}} X_2 \preceq_{\mathrm{LR}} \cdots \preceq_{\mathrm{LR}} X_n$. Then

$$\left(X_1, X_1 + X_2, \ldots, \sum_{i=1}^n X_i\right) \preceq_{\mathrm{ST}} \left(X_{\pi_1}, X_{\pi_1} + X_{\pi_2}, \ldots, \sum_{i=1}^n X_{\pi_i}\right) \preceq_{\mathrm{ST}} \left(X_n, X_n + X_{n-1}, \ldots, \sum_{i=1}^n X_i\right),$$

for every permutation $(\pi_1, \pi_2, \ldots, \pi_n)$ of $(1, 2, \ldots, n)$.

Clearly, $\boldsymbol{X} \preceq_{\mathrm{ST}} \boldsymbol{Y} \Rightarrow \mathbb{E}[X_i] \leq \mathbb{E}[Y_i]$ for $i = 1, 2, \ldots, n$. However, similarly to the univariate case (see Proposition 3.3.17(iii)), if two random vectors are ordered in the $\preceq_{\mathrm{ST}}$ sense and have the same expected values then they must have the same distribution. This is shown in the following result, which is due to Baccelli and Makowski (1989).

Property 3.3.93
If $\boldsymbol{X} \preceq_{\mathrm{ST}} \boldsymbol{Y}$ and if $\mathbb{E}[h_i(X_i)] = \mathbb{E}[h_i(Y_i)]$ for some strictly increasing functions h_i, $i = 1, 2, \ldots, n$, then $\boldsymbol{X} =_d \boldsymbol{Y}$.

An ordering in the $\preceq_{\mathrm{LR}}$ sense is stronger than one in the $\preceq_{\mathrm{ST}}$ sense, as shown in the next result, which can be found in Holley (1974) or Preston (1974).

Proposition 3.3.94
If $\boldsymbol{X}$ and $\boldsymbol{Y}$ are two n-dimensional random vectors such that $\boldsymbol{X}\preceq_{\text{LR}}\boldsymbol{Y}$, then $\boldsymbol{X}\preceq_{\text{ST}}\boldsymbol{Y}$.

Let us now examine stochastic inequalities for vectors of spacings. Let $X_{(1:n)} \leq X_{(2:n)} \leq \ldots \leq X_{(n:n)}$ denote the order statistics corresponding to n independent and identically distributed rvs $X_1, X_2, \ldots, X_n$. Similarly, let $Y_{(1:n)} \leq Y_{(2:n)} \leq \cdots \leq Y_{(n:n)}$ denote the order statistics corresponding to another set of n independent and identically distributed rvs $Y_1, Y_2, \ldots, Y_n$. The corresponding spacings are defined by

$$U_{(i:n)} = X_{(i:n)} - X_{(i-1:n)}$$

and

$$V_{(i:n)} = Y_{(i:n)} - Y_{(i-1:n)},$$

$i = 2, 3, \ldots, n$. Denote by $\boldsymbol{U} = (U_{(2:n)}, \ldots, U_{(n:n)})$ and $\boldsymbol{V} = (V_{(2:n)}, \ldots, V_{(n:n)})$ the corresponding spacing vectors.

Bartoszewicz (1986) proved the following result.

Property 3.3.95
If $X_1 \preceq_{\text{DISP}} Y_1$ then $\boldsymbol{U}\preceq_{\text{ST}}\boldsymbol{V}$.

Proof. Define

$$\widetilde{Y}_{(i:n)} = F_Y^{-1}(F_X(X_{(i:n)})), \quad i=1,2,\ldots,n,$$

and

$$\widetilde{V}_{(i:n)} = \widetilde{Y}_{(i:n)} - \widetilde{Y}_{(i-1:n)}, \quad i=2,3,\ldots,n.$$

Clearly,

$$(V_{(2:n)}, V_{(3:n)}, \ldots, V_{(n:n)}) =_d (\widetilde{V}_{(2:n)}, \widetilde{V}_{(3:n)}, \ldots, \widetilde{V}_{(n:n)}).$$

Furthermore, as $X \preceq_{\text{DISP}} Y$, the inequality

$$x_2 - x_1 \leq F_Y^{-1}\big(F_X(x_2)\big) - F_Y^{-1}\big(F_X(x_1)\big)$$

holds for any $x_1 \leq x_2$ (to establish this, proceed as in the proof of Proposition 3.3.63(i)). Therefore,

$$\begin{aligned}\widetilde{V}_{(i:n)} &= F_Y^{-1}(F_X(X_{(i:n)})) - F_Y^{-1}(F_X(X_{(i-1:n)})) \\ &\geq X_{(i:n)} - X_{(i-1:n)} = U_{(i:n)}, \quad i=2,3,\ldots,n.\end{aligned}$$

The desired result follows from Proposition 3.3.86. □

3.4 CONVEX AND STOP-LOSS ORDERS

3.4.1 Convex and stop-loss orders and stop-loss premiums

3.4.1.1 Definition of the convex order

Where $\preceq_{\text{ST}}$ compares the sizes of the rvs, convex order focuses on their variability. Convex order allows one to compare pairs of rvs with identical means (throughout this section, we will adhere to the assumption that all the rvs have a finite mean). Recall from Property 3.3.17(iii) that $\preceq_{\text{ST}}$ cannot be used to compare such rvs.

Definition 3.4.1. Given two rvs X and Y such that $\mathbb{E}[X] = \mathbb{E}[Y]$, X is said to be smaller than Y in the convex order, written as $X \preceq_{\text{SL},=} Y$, if $\pi_X(t) \leq \pi_Y(t)$ for all $t \in \mathbb{R}$. ∇

Given two risks X and Y, $X \preceq_{\text{SL},=} Y$ thus means that the pure premium for X is identical to that of Y, but the stop-loss premiums for X are always smaller than (or equal to) the corresponding stop-loss premiums for Y, uniformly for all deductibles. The resulting theory has many applications in actuarial modelling. It enables us to construct models for the total claims of which it can be shown that the stop-loss premiums provide upper bounds for the actual stop-loss premiums.

Some standard references on the convex order are Ross (1983) and Stoyan (1983). Another monograph that studies the convex order (under the guise of the Lorenz order) is Arnold (1987).

An immediate consequence of Definition 3.4.1 is that $X \preceq_{\text{SL},=} Y \Rightarrow \min[Y] \leq \min[X]$ and $\max[Y] \geq \max[X]$ so that Y has a wider range than X. By way of proof, suppose that $\max[Y] < \max[X]$. Let t be such that $\max[Y] < t < \max[X]$. Then $\pi_Y(t) = 0 < \pi_X(t)$, in contradiction to $X \preceq_{\text{SL},=} Y$. Therefore we must have $\max[Y] \geq \max[X]$. Similarly, it can be shown that $\min[Y] \leq \min[X]$.

3.4.1.2 Definition of the stop-loss order

Where $\preceq_{\text{ST}}$ compares the size of the rvs and $\preceq_{SL,=}$ their variability, the stop-loss order $\preceq_{SL}$ combines these two aspects: being smaller in the stop-loss order means that the rv is simultaneously 'smaller' and 'less variable'. The stop-loss order can be defined with the help of stop-loss premiums (hence its name), as was the case for $\preceq_{\text{SL},=}$. Note, however, that the restriction to pairs of rvs with the same mean is dropped.

Definition 3.4.2. Given two rvs X and Y, X is said to precede Y in the stop-loss order, written as $X \preceq_{\text{SL}} Y$, if $\pi_X(t) \leq \pi_Y(t)$ for all $t \in \mathbb{R}$. ∇

So, X is smaller than Y in the stop-loss sense when the stop-loss premiums for X are smaller than the corresponding ones for Y, for any level t of the deductible. The stop-loss order is widely used by actuaries. It can be considered as dual to the well-known second-degree stochastic dominance of economists (see, Levy 1992), and is usually termed increasing convex order in the mathematical literature (see, Shaked and Shanthikumar 1994). The link between $\preceq_{\text{SL},=}$ and $\preceq_{\text{SL}}$ is apparent from the following equivalence:

$$\left.\begin{array}{r} X \preceq_{\text{SL}} Y \\ \mathbb{E}[X] = \mathbb{E}[Y] \end{array}\right\} \Leftrightarrow X \preceq_{\text{SL},=} Y.$$

3.4.2 Convex and stop-loss orders and choice under risk

3.4.2.1 Convex order and convex functions

Let us first establish the following result, which explains why $\preceq_{\mathrm{SL},=}$ is termed 'convex order'.

Proposition 3.4.3
Given two rvs X and Y, the following equivalences hold:

$$X \preceq_{\mathrm{SL},=} Y \Leftrightarrow \mathbb{E}[v(X)] \leq \mathbb{E}[v(Y)] \text{ for all convex functions} \quad (3.52)$$
$$\text{such that the expectations exist}$$
$$\Leftrightarrow \mathbb{E}[v(X)] \leq \mathbb{E}[v(Y)] \text{ for all functions } v \quad (3.53)$$
$$\text{with } v'' \geq 0, \text{ such that the expectations exist.}$$

Proof. Let us prove (3.52). The $\Leftarrow$ implication is obvious since the function $x \mapsto (x-t)_+$ is convex for all $t \in \mathbb{R}$. Note that since the functions $x \mapsto \pm x$ are both convex, one has $\mathbb{E}[X] = \mathbb{E}[Y]$, as required.

To get the converse, we use Proposition 2.8.4, which allows us to write

$$\mathbb{E}[v_n(X)] = \alpha_1 + \alpha_2\mathbb{E}[X] + \sum_{j=0}^{n} \beta_j^{(n)} \mathbb{E}[(X - t_j^{(n)})_+]$$
$$\leq \alpha_1 + \alpha_2\mathbb{E}[Y] + \sum_{j=0}^{n} \beta_j^{(n)} \mathbb{E}[(Y - t_j^{(n)})_+] = \mathbb{E}[v_n(Y)],$$

for every n. Taking the limit yields $\mathbb{E}[v(X)] \leq \mathbb{E}[v(Y)]$, as expected. Then (3.35) is immediate from (1.14). □

3.4.2.2 Convex order and variability

The function v, defined by $v(x) = x^2$, is convex, so that

$$X \preceq_{\mathrm{SL},=} Y \Rightarrow \mathbb{V}[X] \leq \mathbb{V}[Y]. \quad (3.54)$$

This explains why $\preceq_{\mathrm{SL},=}$ is a variability order: it only applies to rvs with the same expected value and compares the dispersion of these variables. It is a more sophisticated comparison than only focusing on the variances, yet (3.54) indicates that it agrees with this approach.

The order $\preceq_{\mathrm{SL},=}$ allows us to compare risks with identical expectations, but it cannot be used to compare risks with identical variances. This is a consequence of the following result.

Lemma 3.4.4
For any rv X we can write

$$\frac{1}{2}\mathbb{V}[X] = \int_{-\infty}^{\infty} \Big(\mathbb{E}[(X-t)_+] - (\mathbb{E}[X] - t)_+ \Big)\, dt. \quad (3.55)$$

Proof. To prove this relation, write

$$\int_{-\infty}^{\infty}\Big(\mathbb{E}[(X-t)_+]-(\mathbb{E}[X]-t)_+\Big)dt=\int_{-\infty}^{\mathbb{E}[X]}\mathbb{E}[(t-X)_+]\,dt+\int_{\mathbb{E}[X]}^{\infty}\mathbb{E}[(X-t)_+]\,dt.$$

Interchanging the order of the integrations and using partial integration leads to

$$\begin{aligned}\int_{-\infty}^{\mathbb{E}[X]}\mathbb{E}[(t-X)_+]\,dt &= \int_{-\infty}^{\mathbb{E}[X]}\int_{-\infty}^{t}F_X(x)\,dx\,dt\\ &=\frac{1}{2}\int_{-\infty}^{\mathbb{E}[X]}(x-\mathbb{E}[X])^2\,dF_X(x).\end{aligned}$$

Similarly,

$$\int_{\mathbb{E}[X]}^{\infty}\mathbb{E}[(X-t)_+]\,dt=\frac{1}{2}\int_{\mathbb{E}[X]}^{\infty}(x-\mathbb{E}[X])^2\,dF_X(x).$$

This proves (3.55). □

Property 3.4.5
If $X\preceq_{\mathrm{SL},=}Y$ and $\mathbb{V}[X]=\mathbb{V}[Y]$ simultaneously hold, then $X=_d Y$.

Proof. From (3.55) we deduce that if $X\preceq_{\mathrm{SL},=}Y$ then

$$\int_{-\infty}^{\infty}\Big(\mathbb{E}[(Y-t)_+]-\mathbb{E}[(X-t)_+]\Big)dt=\frac{1}{2}\big(\mathbb{V}[Y]-\mathbb{V}[X]\big).\tag{3.56}$$

The integrand above is non-negative, so if in addition to $X\preceq_{\mathrm{SL},=}Y$ we have $\mathbb{V}[X]=\mathbb{V}[Y]$, then X and Y must necessarily have equal stop-loss premiums. This in turn implies that they are equal in distribution. □

3.4.2.3 Convex order and expected utility theory

Let us now consider a risk-averse decision-maker with concave utility function u and initial wealth w. Given two risks X and Y, if $X\preceq_{\mathrm{SL},=}Y$ then $\mathbb{E}[u(w-X)]\geq\mathbb{E}[u(w-Y)]$ since the function $t\mapsto -u(w-t)$ is convex. Hence, every risk-averse decision-maker prefers $w-X$ over $w-Y$, and the risk X is preferred over Y.

3.4.2.4 Stop-loss order and increasing convex functions

Let us now move on to $\preceq_{\mathrm{SL}}$. The following result establishes analogues to (3.52) and (3.53) for $\preceq_{\mathrm{SL}}$. It explains why the stop-loss order is termed 'increasing convex order' in probability theory. The proof of (3.57) is similar to that of (3.52), while the proof of (3.58) is similar to that of (3.53).

Proposition 3.4.6
Given two rvs X and Y, the following equivalences hold:

$$X \preceq_{SL} Y \Leftrightarrow \mathbb{E}[v(X)] \leq \mathbb{E}[v(Y)] \text{ for all non-decreasing convex functions such that the expectations exist} \tag{3.57}$$

$$\Leftrightarrow \mathbb{E}[v(X)] \leq \mathbb{E}[v(Y)] \text{ for all functions } v \text{ with } v' \geq 0 \text{ and } v'' \geq 0 \text{ such that the expectations exist.} \tag{3.58}$$

3.4.2.5 Stop-loss order and expected utility theory

Let us consider a profit-seeking risk-averse decision-maker with concave non-decreasing utility function u. If $X \preceq_{SL} Y$ then $\mathbb{E}[u(w-X)] \geq \mathbb{E}[u(w-Y)]$ since the function $x \mapsto -u(w-x)$ is non-decreasing and convex. The risk X is therefore preferred over Y.

3.4.2.6 Convex and stop-loss orders and distorted expectation theory

Within the framework of expected utility theory, we have seen that the stop-loss ordering of two risks is equivalent to saying that one risk is preferred over another by all profit-seeking risk-averse decision-makers. Within the framework of Yaari's theory of choice under risk, $X \preceq_{SL} Y$ holds if, and only if, all decision-makers with a non-decreasing and concave distortion function prefer the risk X. This is precisely stated in the next result, which can be found in Ribas, Goovaerts and Dhaene (1998).

Proposition 3.4.7
Given two risks X and Y, one can show that $X \preceq_{SL} Y$ if, and only if, one of the two following equivalent conditions is fulfilled:

(i) $\mathbb{H}_g[w-Y] \leq \mathbb{H}_g[w-X]$ for all non-decreasing and convex distortion functions g;

(ii) $\rho_g[X] \leq \rho_g[Y]$ for all non-decreasing concave distortion functions g.

Proof. We know from Section 2.6.2.1 that (i) and (ii) are equivalent, so we only prove (ii). Let us prove that if $\rho_g[X] \leq \rho_g[Y]$ for every non-decreasing and concave distortion function g then the stochastic inequality $X \preceq_{SL} Y$ must hold. Taking the distortion function $g_1(p) = p$ yields

$$\rho_{g_1}[X] = \mathbb{E}[X] \leq \mathbb{E}[Y] = \rho_{g_1}[Y].$$

Now, let us consider $d \in \mathbb{R}^+$ and define $p = \overline{F}_X(d)$. Note that $\overline{F}_X^{-1}(p) \leq d$. Considering the distortion function $g(x) = \min\{x/p, 1\}$ yields

$$\int_0^p \overline{F}_X^{-1}(t)dt \leq \int_0^p \overline{F}_Y^{-1}(t)dt \text{ for all } p.$$

Integration by parts then yields

$$p\overline{F}_X^{-1}(p) - \int_0^p td\overline{F}_X^{-1}(t) \leq p\overline{F}_Y^{-1}(p) - \int_0^p td\overline{F}_Y^{-1}(t),$$

which is still equivalent to

$$p\overline{F}_X^{-1}(p) + \int_{\overline{F}_X^{-1}(p)}^{+\infty} \overline{F}_X(t)dt \leq p\overline{F}_Y^{-1}(p) + \int_{\overline{F}_Y^{-1}(p)}^{+\infty} \overline{F}_Y(t)dt.$$

Since $\overline{F}_X^{-1}$ is constantly equal to p between $\overline{F}_X^{-1}(p)$ and d (if $\overline{F}_X^{-1}(p) \neq d$), we have that

$$p\Big(d - \overline{F}_X^{-1}(p)\Big) = \int_{\overline{F}_X^{-1}(p)}^{d} \overline{F}_X(t)dt.$$

This inequality can then be cast into the form

$$\int_d^{+\infty} \overline{F}_X(t)dt + pd \leq \int_d^{+\infty} \overline{F}_Y(t)dt + p\overline{F}_Y^{-1}(p) + \int_{\overline{F}_Y^{-1}(p)}^{d} \overline{F}_Y(t)dt.$$

We finally get

$$\begin{aligned}
\pi_X(d) &= \int_d^{+\infty} \overline{F}_X(t)dt \\
&\leq \int_d^{+\infty} \overline{F}_Y(t)dt + \underbrace{\int_{\overline{F}_Y^{-1}(p)}^{d} (\overline{F}_Y(t) - p)dt}_{\leq 0} \\
&\leq \int_d^{+\infty} \overline{F}_Y(t)dt = \pi_Y(d).
\end{aligned}$$

This concludes the proof of the $\Leftarrow$ part.

The proof of the $\Rightarrow$ part is as follows. Let us prove that $X \preceq_{SL} Y \Rightarrow \rho_g[X] \leq \rho_g[Y]$ for any $g(x) = \min\{x/p, 1\}$. Equivalently, we need to prove that

$$X \preceq_{\text{SL}} Y \Rightarrow \text{TVaR}[X; p] \leq \text{TVaR}[Y; p] \text{ for all } p.$$

This is straightforward: invoking the representation (2.14) of TVaR, we have

$$\begin{aligned}
\text{TVaR}[X; p] &= \inf_{a\in\mathbb{R}} \left\{ a + \frac{1}{1-p}\mathbb{E}[(X-a)_+] \right\} \\
&\leq \text{VaR}[Y; p] + \frac{1}{1-p}\mathbb{E}[(X - \text{VaR}[Y; p])_+] \\
&\leq \text{VaR}[Y; p] + \frac{1}{1-p}\mathbb{E}[(Y - \text{VaR}[Y; p])_+] \\
&= \text{TVaR}[Y; p].
\end{aligned}$$

Now, by Proposition 2.8.4 any concave distortion function g can be approximated from below by concave piecewise linear distortion functions g_n such that for any $x \in [0, 1]$, we have that $g_1(x) \leq g_2(x) \leq \ldots \leq g_n(x) \leq \ldots \leq g(x)$ and $\lim_{n\to\infty} g_n(x) = g(x)$. Any g_n can be written as a positive linear combination of distortion functions of the form $\min\{x/p, 1\}$, so that $\rho_{g_n}[X] \leq \rho_{g_n}[Y] \leq \rho_g[Y] < \infty$ for all n. From the monotone convergence theorem we find that $\lim_{n\to\infty} \rho_{g_n}[X] = \rho_g[X]$, so that we can conclude that $\rho_g[X] \leq \rho_g[Y]$. □

Within the framework of expected utility theory, the stop-loss order of two risks is equivalent to saying that one risk is preferred over the other by all risk-averse decision-makers. From Proposition 3.4.7, we see that we have a similar interpretation for the stop-loss order within the framework of Yaari's theory of choice under risk: the stop-loss order of two risks is equivalent to saying that one risk is preferred over the other by all decision-makers who have non-decreasing concave distortion functions.

The next result identifies a subclass of distortion functions characterizing $\preceq_{\mathrm{SL}}$; its proof transpires from the reasoning used to establish Proposition 3.4.7.

Proposition 3.4.8
For any risks X and Y, $X \preceq_{\mathrm{SL}} Y$ if, and only if, $\rho_g[X] \leq \rho_g[Y]$ for all distortion functions g defined by $g(x) = \min\{x/p, 1\}$, $p \in (0, 1]$, that is,

$$X \preceq_{SL} Y \Leftrightarrow \mathrm{TVaR}[X; p] \leq \mathrm{TVaR}[Y; p] \text{ for all } 0 < p < 1.$$

3.4.3 Comparing claim frequencies

When comparing integer-valued variables, we can resort to the following characterization of $\preceq_{\mathrm{SL},=}$ and $\preceq_{\mathrm{SL}}$.

Proposition 3.4.9
Let N and M be two integer-value rvs.

(i) $N \preceq_{\mathrm{SL},=} M$ if one of the following equivalent conditions is fulfilled:

(a) $\mathbb{E}[N] = \mathbb{E}[M]$ and $\mathbb{E}[(N-k)_+] \leq \mathbb{E}[(M-k)_+]$ for all $k \in \mathbb{N}$;

(b) $\mathbb{E}[v(N)] \leq \mathbb{E}[v(M)]$ for all functions $v : \mathbb{N} \to \mathbb{R}$ such that $\Delta^2 v(k) \geq 0$ for all $k \in \mathbb{N}$, provided the expectations exist.

(ii) $N \preceq_{\mathrm{SL}} M$ if one of the following equivalent conditions is fulfilled:

(a) $\mathbb{E}[(N-k)_+] \leq \mathbb{E}[(M-k)_+]$ for all $k \in \mathbb{N}$;

(b) $\mathbb{E}[v(N)] \leq \mathbb{E}[v(M)]$ for all functions $v :\to \mathbb{R}$ such that $\Delta v(k) \geq 0$ and $\Delta^2 v(k) \geq 0$ for all $k \in \mathbb{N}$, provided the expectations exist.

There is also an efficient sufficient condition obtained by Hesselager (1995). The notation is that introduced in Proposition 3.3.47.

Proposition 3.4.10
Let N and M be two integer-valued rvs such that $\mathbb{E}[N] = \mathbb{E}[M]$. If there is a constant c such that $h_M(k) \leq h_N(k)$ for $k \leq c$ and $h_M(k) \geq h_N(k)$ for $k > c$, then $N \preceq_{\mathrm{SL},=} M$.

Example 3.4.11. This result is particularly appealing for the members of the Panjer family (satisfying $h_N(k) = a + \frac{b}{k}$). In this case, the mathematical expectation $\mu(a, b)$ is given by

$$\mu(a, b) = \sum_{k=1}^{+\infty} k\left(a + \frac{b}{k}\right) p_{k-1} = a\big(\mu(a, b) + 1\big) + b,$$

giving

$$\mu(a, b) = \frac{a+b}{1-a}.$$

Let us fix the expected value $\mu(a, b) = \mu$, so that $b = \mu - a(1+\mu)$; there thus remains a unique parameter a. Then,

$$h_N(k) = \frac{a(k-1-\mu)+\mu}{k}, \quad k = 1, 2, \ldots.$$

Given two integer-valued rvs N and M with the same mean μ, both in the Panjer family with respective parameters a_N and a_M, we clearly have

$$a_N \leq a_M \Rightarrow \begin{cases} h_M(k) \leq h_N(k), & \text{for } k \leq 1+\mu, \\ h_M(k) \geq h_N(k), & \text{for } k \geq 1+\mu, \end{cases}$$

so that $N \preceq_{\text{SL},=} M$. In particular,

$$\mathcal{B}in(m, q) \preceq_{\text{SL},=} \mathcal{P}oi(\mu) \preceq_{\text{SL},=} \mathcal{N}\mathcal{B}in(r, p)$$

with $\mu = mq = \frac{rp}{1-p}$. ∇

3.4.4 Some characterizations for convex and stop-loss orders

3.4.4.1 Convex order and dispersion function

The dispersion of X can be interpreted in terms of the distance of X from a, that is, in terms of $|X-a|$, for all $a \in \mathbb{R}$. The dispersion function of X is defined as

$$D_X(a) = \mathbb{E}\Big[|X-a|\Big] = \int_0^1 \Big|\text{VaR}[X; p] - a\Big| dp.$$

It is thus the absolute moment of order 1 with respect to $a \in \mathbb{R}$.

The following lemma states that D_X characterizes the probability distribution of X.

Property 3.4.12
We have that

$$F_X(t) = \frac{1}{2}\Big(D'_X(t) + 1\Big)$$

for all t where F_X is continuous.

Proof. Let us define q as $t=\mathrm{VaR}[X;q]$. Then it is easily deduced from

$$D_X'(t)=\int_0^q dp-\int_q^1 dp=q-(1-q)=2q-1$$

that $q=\frac{1}{2}\Big(D_X'(t)+1\Big)$ as claimed. □

We also have the following result that characterizes the set of dispersion functions. For a proof, see Muñoz–Perez and Sanchez–Gomez (1990).

Property 3.4.13
A function g is a dispersion function if, and only if, it has the following four properties:

(i) it is differentiable and its derivative has at most a countable set of discontinuity points;

(ii) it is convex;

(iii) $\lim_{x\to+\infty} g'(x)=1$ and $\lim_{x\to-\infty} g'(x)=-1$;

(iv) $\lim_{x\to+\infty}(g(x)-x)=-\mathbb{E}[X]$ and $\lim_{x\to-\infty}(g(x)+x)=\mathbb{E}[X]$.

The following property shows that the degree of approximation between D_X and the straight lines $y=\mathbb{E}[X]-u$ and $y=u-\mathbb{E}[X]$ gives us an indication of its dispersion. Note that $|\mathbb{E}[X]-a|\leq D_X(a)$ holds for any $a\in\mathbb{R}$. The proof of the following result is similar to that of Lemma 3.4.4.

Property 3.4.14
Let X be an rv with finite variance σ^2. Then,

$$\int_{-\infty}^{+\infty}\Big|D_X(t)-D_{\mathbb{E}[X]}(t)\Big|dt=\sigma^2$$

where $D_{\mathbb{E}[X]}(t)=|\mathbb{E}[X]-t|$ is the dispersion function of the degenerate rv at $\mathbb{E}[X]$.

As $\preceq_{\mathrm{SL},=}$ compares the variability of the underlying rvs, it seems intuitively acceptable that it can be characterized by means of the dispersion function. This is formally stated in the following result.

Proposition 3.4.15
Let X and Y be two random variables such that $\mathbb{E}[X]=\mathbb{E}[Y]$. Then $X\preceq_{\mathrm{SL},=}Y$ if, and only if,

$$D_X(a)\leq D_Y(a)\text{ for all }a\in\mathbb{R}.\tag{3.59}$$

Proof. Clearly, if $X\preceq_{\mathrm{SL},=}Y$ then (3.59) holds, the function $x\mapsto|x-a|$ being convex for all a. So suppose that (3.59) holds. Without loss of generality it can be assumed that $\mathbb{E}[X]=\mathbb{E}[Y]=0$. A straightforward computation gives

$$D_X(a)=a+2\int_a^\infty \overline{F}_X(u)\,du=a+2\pi_X(a).\tag{3.60}$$

The result now follows from the definition of $\preceq_{\mathrm{SL},=}$. □

3.4.4.2 Martingale construction

In the framework of expected utility theory, risk increases are often formalized as mean-preserving spreads, that is, increases of the risk variance with the payoff means remaining constant. Let us formalize this idea by the following martingale characterization of $\preceq_{\mathrm{SL},=}$.

Proposition 3.4.16
The risks X and Y satisfy $X \preceq_{\mathrm{SL},=} Y$ if, and only if, there exist two rvs $\widetilde{X}$ and $\widetilde{Y}$ (defined on the same probability space) such that $\widetilde{X} =_d X$, $\widetilde{Y} =_d Y$ and $\mathbb{E}[\widetilde{Y}|\widetilde{X}] = \widetilde{X}$.

Proof. The constructive part of this characterization is difficult to prove; we refer the interested reader to Müller and Stoyan (2002, Theorem 1.5.20), for a self-contained constructive proof. It is nevertheless easy to prove that if such rvs $\widetilde{X}$ and $\widetilde{Y}$ exist then $X \preceq_{\mathrm{SL},=} Y$. This follows from

$$\begin{aligned}\mathbb{E}[v(X)] &= \mathbb{E}[v(\widetilde{X})] = \mathbb{E}\Big[v\Big(\mathbb{E}[\widetilde{Y}|\widetilde{X}]\Big)\Big]\\ &\leq \mathbb{E}\Big[\mathbb{E}[v(\widetilde{Y})|\widetilde{X}]\Big] = \mathbb{E}[v(\widetilde{Y})] = \mathbb{E}[v(Y)]\end{aligned}$$

which holds for any convex function v by virtue of Jensen's inequality. □

The martingale characterization of $\preceq_{\mathrm{SL}}$ allows for numerous interesting applications in actuarial science. Let us now state the analogue of Proposition 3.4.16 for $\preceq_{\mathrm{SL}}$.

Proposition 3.4.17
The risks X and Y satisfy $X \preceq_{\mathrm{SL}} Y$ if, and only if, there exist two rvs $\widetilde{X}$ and $\widetilde{Y}$ (defined on the same probability space) such that $\widetilde{X} =_d X$, $\widetilde{Y} =_d Y$ and $\mathbb{E}[\widetilde{Y}|\widetilde{X}] \geq \widetilde{X}$.

3.4.4.3 Separation theorem

The separation theorem explains why $X \preceq_{\mathrm{SL}} Y$ means that X is both smaller and less variable than Y.

Proposition 3.4.18 (Separation theorem)
Assume that X and Y are two risks. Then, $X \preceq_{\mathrm{SL}} Y$ if, and only if, there exists an rv Z such that

$$X \preceq_{\mathrm{ST}} Z \preceq_{\mathrm{SL},=} Y.$$

Proof. Let us define

$$X_b = \max\{X, b\}.$$

Of course, $\Pr[X \leq X_b] = 1$ so that $X \preceq_{\mathrm{ST}} X_b$ holds. Let us choose b in such a way that $\mathbb{E}[X_b] = \mathbb{E}[Y]$. Now it can easily be shown that both for $t \geq b$ and for $t < b$, we have

$$\mathbb{E}[(X_b - t)_+] \leq \mathbb{E}[(Y - t)_+].$$

So provided $X \preceq_{\mathrm{SL}} Y$, we have constructed an rv $Z = X_b$ such that $X \preceq_{\mathrm{ST}} Z \preceq_{\mathrm{SL},=} Y$. □

3.4.4.4 Integrated lower tails

From the identity

$$\mathbb{E}[(X-d)_+]-\mathbb{E}\left[(d-X)_+\right]=\mathbb{E}\left[X\right]-d,$$

we find

$$X\preceq_{\mathrm{SL},=}Y\Leftrightarrow\begin{cases}\mathbb{E}[X]=\mathbb{E}[Y],\\ \mathbb{E}\left[(d-X)_+\right]\leq\mathbb{E}\left[(d-Y)_+\right], \text{ for all } d\in\mathbb{R}.\end{cases}$$

Note that partial integration leads to

$$\mathbb{E}[(d-X)_+]=\int_{-\infty}^{d}F_X(x)dx, \tag{3.61}$$

which means that $\mathbb{E}[(d-X)_+]$ can be interpreted as the weight of a lower tail of X: it is the surface from $-\infty$ to d between the constant function 0 and the df of X. We have seen that the stop-loss order entails uniformly heavier upper tails. The additional condition of equal means implies that convex order also leads to uniformly heavier lower tails.

If $d>0$, then from (3.61) we find that

$$d-\mathbb{E}[(d-X)_+]=-\int_{-\infty}^{0}F_X(x)dx+\int_{0}^{d}\overline{F}_X(x)dx,$$

and also

$$\lim_{d\to+\infty}(d-\mathbb{E}[(d-X)_+])=\mathbb{E}[X].$$

This implies that the convex order can also be characterized as follows:

$$X\preceq_{\mathrm{SL},=}Y\Leftrightarrow\begin{cases}\mathbb{E}[(X-d)_+]\leq\mathbb{E}[(Y-d)_+],\\ \mathbb{E}[(d-X)_+]\leq\mathbb{E}[(d-Y)_+],\end{cases}\text{for all } d\in\mathbb{R}.$$

Indeed, the $\Leftarrow$ implication follows from observing that the upper tail inequalities imply $\mathbb{E}[X]\leq\mathbb{E}[Y]$, while the lower tail inequalities imply $\mathbb{E}[X]\geq\mathbb{E}[Y]$, hence $\mathbb{E}[X]=\mathbb{E}[Y]$ must hold.

3.4.4.5 Stop-loss order and dangerousness order

According to Bühlmann's terminology, a df F_Y is said to be more dangerous than F_X when $\mathbb{E}[X]\leq\mathbb{E}[Y]<+\infty$ and there exists a constant c such that

$$F_X(x)\begin{cases}\leq F_Y(x), & \text{for all } x<c,\\ \geq F_Y(x), & \text{for all } x\geq c;\end{cases}$$

this is denoted by $X \preceq_{\mathrm{D}} Y$. We also define the relation $\preceq_{\mathrm{D},=}$ as

$$X \preceq_{\mathrm{D},=} Y \Leftrightarrow \begin{cases} X \preceq_{\mathrm{D}} Y \\ \mathbb{E}[X] = \mathbb{E}[Y]. \end{cases}$$

A very useful sufficient condition for $\preceq_{\mathrm{SL}}$ is given next in terms of $\preceq_{\mathrm{D}}$: $X \preceq_{\mathrm{D}} Y \Rightarrow X \preceq_{\mathrm{SL}} Y$ (see Kaas *et al.* 2001, Section 10.3). In the actuarial literature, this famous result is often referred to as Ohlin's lemma. Outside actuarial circles, it is known as the Karlin–Novikoff cut criterion following the work of Karlin and Novikoff (1963). We provide an elementary proof of these results.

Property 3.4.19
Given two risks X and Y, we have that

(i) $X \preceq_{\mathrm{D}} Y \Rightarrow X \preceq_{\mathrm{SL}} Y$.

(ii) $X \preceq_{\mathrm{D},=} Y \Rightarrow X \preceq_{\mathrm{SL},=} Y$.

Proof. In order to prove (i), let us consider the function

$$t \mapsto \Delta(t) = \mathbb{E}[(Y-t)_+] - \mathbb{E}[(X-t)_+].$$

Since $\mathbb{E}[X] \leq \mathbb{E}[Y]$, $\Delta(0) \geq 0$, and obviously $\lim_{t\to+\infty} \Delta(t) = 0$. Now observe that

$$\Delta(t) = \int_t^{+\infty} \Big(F_X(x) - F_Y(x)\Big) dx,$$

so that Δ first increases on $(0, c)$ and then decreases on $(c, +\infty)$ when $X \preceq_{\mathrm{D}} Y$. It thus remains non-negative and ensures that $X \preceq_{\mathrm{SL}} Y$. The proof of (ii) is similar. □

It is interesting to have another look at Property 3.6.19 when the condition on the means is dropped. To this end, we need the following lemma.

Lemma 3.4.20
Define

$$\Delta(x) = \int_{-\infty}^{x} F_Y(\xi) d\xi - \int_{-\infty}^{x} F_X(\xi) d\xi$$

and consider a function H of the form

$$H(x) = \int_{\xi \leq x} h(\xi) d\xi + H(-\infty).$$

If there is some z such that $\Delta(z) = 0$, then

$$\int H(x) d\Big(F_Y(x) - F_X(x)\Big) = \int_{x \leq z} \Delta(x) dh(x) - \int_{x \geq z} h(x) d\Delta(x).$$

Proof. Integrating the left-hand side of this expression by parts gives

$$\begin{aligned}\int H(x)d\Big(F_Y(x)-F_X(x)\Big) &= -\int \Big(F_Y(x)-F_X(x)\Big)dH(x)\\ &= -\int_{x\le z}\Big(F_Y(x)-F_X(x)\Big)h(x)dx\\ &\quad -\int_{x\ge z}\Big(F_Y(x)-F_X(x)\Big)h(x)dx\\ &= -\int_{x\le z} h(x)d\Delta(x)-\int_{x\ge z} h(x)d\Delta(x)\\ &= -\int_{x\le z} \Delta(x)dh(x)-\int_{x\ge z} h(x)d\Delta(x)\end{aligned}$$

which concludes the proof. □

The following result shows that if we drop the condition imposed on the means in Property 3.4.19, we have that if a risk-averse decision-maker considers the risk X more favourable than another risk Y, all more risk-averse decision-makers will agree with this conclusion. This is formally stated next.

Property 3.4.21

If there is a constant c such that $F_X(x)\le F_Y(x)$ for all $x<c$ and $F_X(x)\ge F_Y(x)$ for all $x\ge c$, then

$$\mathbb{E}[v(X)]\le\mathbb{E}[v(Y)]\Rightarrow\mathbb{E}[u(X)]\le\mathbb{E}[u(Y)]$$

for all non-decreasing and convex functions u and v such that

$$u(x)=g\big(v(x)\big)$$

with g non-decreasing and convex.

Proof. Let us fix some real number z and then define the function

$$h_z(x)=u'(x)-\frac{u'(z)}{v'(z)}v'(x).$$

Now, $u'(x)=g'(v(x))v'(x)$ so that $u'(x)/v'(x)=g'(v(x))$ is non-decreasing. This implies that

$$h_z(x)=v'(x)\left(\frac{u'(x)}{v'(x)}-\frac{u'(z)}{v'(z)}\right)$$

has a single sign change in z, from negative to positive. Moreover, it is a non-decreasing function (as the product of two non-decreasing functions).

Let H_z be such that $H_z'=h_z$, and let us consider for z the crossing point c of F_X and F_Y. Then,

$$\int H_c(x)d\Big(F_Y(x)-F_X(x)\Big)=\int\left(u(x)-\frac{u'(c)}{v'(c)}v(x)\right)d\Big(F_Y(x)-F_X(x)\Big).$$

We will now prove that this quantity is non-negative, which gives

$$\mathbb{E}[u(Y)]-\mathbb{E}[u(X)]\geq\frac{u'(c)}{v'(c)}\Big(\mathbb{E}[v(Y)]-\mathbb{E}[v(X)]\Big)$$

and concludes the proof. We use Lemma 3.4.20 with $h(x)=h_c(x)$. Then,

$$\int H_c(x)d\Big(F_Y(x)-F_X(x)\Big)=\int_{x\leq c}\Delta(x)dh_c(x)-\int_{x\geq c}h_c(x)d\Delta(x).$$

The first term is non-negative since $F_Y\geq F_X$ on $(-\infty,c)$ and h_c is non-decreasing. Similarly, the second term is non-negative since h_c is positive on $(c,+\infty)$ and Δ is a decreasing function on the same domain. □

3.4.4.6 Stop-loss order as transitive closure of dangerousness order

The following characterizations of $\preceq_{\text{SL}}$ and $\preceq_{\text{SL},=}$ which can be found in Müller (1996) are useful in the theoretical developments related to these orderings. They basically state that $\preceq_{\text{SL}}$ and $\preceq_{\text{SL},=}$ are the transitive closure of $\preceq_{\text{D}}$ and $\preceq_{\text{D},=}$, respectively.

Proposition 3.4.22

(i) Let X and Y be two rvs with equal means. Then $X\preceq_{\text{SL},=}Y$ if, and only if, there exist rvs $Z_1,Z_2,\ldots$, such that $Z_1=_dX$, $Z_j\to_dY$ as $j\to\infty$ and $Z_j\preceq_{\text{D},=}Z_{j+1}$, $j=1,2,\ldots$.

(ii) Let X and Y be two rvs. Then $X\preceq_{\text{SL}}Y$ if, and only if, there exist rvs $Z_1,Z_2,\ldots$, such that $Z_1=_dX$, $Z_j\to_dY$ as $j\to\infty$, $\mathbb{E}[Z_j]\to\mathbb{E}[Y]$ as $j\to\infty$, and $Z_j\preceq_{\text{D}}Z_{j+1}$, $j=1,2,\ldots$.

Proof. Let us prove (i). We know from Proposition 2.8.4(i) that the convex decreasing function π_Y is the supremum of a countable set of affine decreasing functions $h_1,h_2,\ldots$. Define $\pi_1=\pi_X$ and, recursively,

$$\pi_{n+1}=\max\{\pi_n,h_n\}.$$

All the π_n fulfil conditions (i) and (ii) of Property 1.7.2 and are thus proper stop-loss transforms by virtue of Property 1.7.3. Then let Z_n correspond to the stop-loss transform π_n, and the proof is complete if we can prove that $Z_n\preceq_{\text{D}}Z_{n+1}$. If $h_n\leq\pi_n$ then $Z_n\preceq_{\text{D}}Z_{n+1}$ obviously holds. Let us assume that there is an interval (a_n,b_n) such that

$$\pi_{n+1}(t)=\begin{cases}h_n(t), & \text{for } t\in(a_n,b_n),\\ \pi_n(t), & \text{otherwise.}\end{cases}$$

This means that π_{n+1} is linear on (a_n,b_n) and the corresponding df is constant on that interval. Outside (a_n,b_n), the stop-loss transforms π_n and π_{n+1} coincide, and so do the associated dfs. As $\mathbb{E}[Z_n]=\mathbb{E}[Z_{n+1}]$ this implies that $Z_n\preceq_{\text{D}}Z_{n+1}$, and concludes the proof of (i). The proof of (ii) is similar. □

For related results, we refer the interested reader to Machina and Pratt (1997).

3.4.5 Some properties of the convex and stop-loss orders

3.4.5.1 Properties inherited from the martingale construction

The martingale characterization of $\preceq_{SL,=}$, stated in Proposition 3.4.16 allows for numerous applications in risk theory. The next result illustrates this fact. Item (ii) is taken from Denuit and Vermandele (1998).

Proposition 3.4.23

(i) Given a sequence $X_1, X_2, X_3, \ldots$ of independent and identically distributed risks, we have that

$$\overline{X}^{(n+1)} = \frac{1}{n+1}\sum_{i=1}^{n+1} X_i \preceq_{SL,=} \frac{1}{n}\sum_{i=1}^{n} X_i = \overline{X}^{(n)}.$$

(ii) Let $X_1, X_2, \ldots, X_n$ be n independent and identically distributed risks, and let Ψ be a measurable function $(\mathbb{R}^+)^n \to \mathbb{R}$. Then there exists a symmetric function $\Psi^* : (\mathbb{R}^+)^n \to \mathbb{R}$ such that

$$\Psi^*(X_1, X_2, \ldots, X_n) \preceq_{SL,=} \Psi(X_1, X_2, \ldots, X_n);$$

Ψ^* is given by

$$\Psi^*(x_1, x_2, \ldots, x_n) = \frac{1}{n!}\sum_{1\leq i_1\neq i_2\neq\ldots\neq i_n\leq n} \Psi(x_{i_1}, x_{i_2}, \ldots, x_{i_n}).$$

In particular, given any measurable functions $\psi_1, \psi_2, \ldots, \psi_n$, we have that

$$\sum_{i=1}^{n}\overline{\psi}(X_i) \preceq_{SL,=} \sum_{i=1}^{n}\psi_i(X_i),$$

where the function $\overline{\psi}$ is defined as $\overline{\psi}(x) = \frac{1}{n}\sum_{i=1}^{n}\psi_i(x)$.

Proof. (i) First observe that for any $i \neq j$,

$$\mathbb{E}\left[X_i \middle| \overline{X}^{(n)}\right] = \mathbb{E}\left[X_j \middle| \overline{X}^{(n)}\right] = \frac{1}{n}\sum_{k=1}^{n}\mathbb{E}\left[X_k \middle| \overline{X}^{(n)}\right] = \overline{X}^{(n)}.$$

Therefore,

$$\mathbb{E}\left[\overline{X}^{(n-1)} \middle| \overline{X}^{(n)}\right] = \overline{X}^{(n)},$$

and the result follows from Proposition 3.4.16.

(ii) Denoting by $X_{(1)}, X_{(2)}, \ldots, X_{(n)}$ the order statistics associated with the independent and identically distributed risks $X_1, X_2, \ldots, X_n$,

$$\min_{i=1,\ldots,n} X_i = X_{(1)} \leq X_{(2)} \leq \ldots \leq X_{(n)} = \max_{i=1,\ldots,n} X_i,$$

we deduce directly from Proposition 3.4.16 above that

$$\mathbb{E}\big[\Psi(X_1, X_2, \ldots, X_n)\,\big|X_{(1)}, X_{(2)}, \ldots, X_{(n)}\big] \preceq_{\mathrm{SL},=} \Psi(X_1, X_2, \ldots, X_n).$$

Now

$$\begin{aligned}
&\mathbb{E}\big[\Psi(X_1, X_2, \ldots, X_n)\,\big|X_{(1)}, X_{(2)}, \ldots, X_{(n)}\big]\\
&= \frac{1}{n!} \sum_{1\leq i_1\neq i_2\neq \ldots \neq i_n\leq n} \Psi(X_{(i_1)}, X_{(i_2)}, \ldots, X_{(i_n)})\\
&= \frac{1}{n!} \sum_{1\leq i_1\neq i_2\neq \ldots \neq i_n\leq n} \Psi(X_{i_1}, X_{i_2}, \ldots, X_{i_n})\\
&= \Psi^*(X_1, X_2, \ldots, X_n),
\end{aligned}$$

and the proof is complete. □

Proposition 3.4.23(i) gives an interesting interpretation of the law of large numbers. We know from (1.9) that $\overline{X}^{(n)}$ converges to $\mathbb{E}[X_1]$ as $n \to +\infty$. The result in (i) indicates that this convergence is monotone with respect to $\preceq_{\mathrm{SL},=}$, and illustrates the risk reduction with the size of the insurance portfolio.

The next corollary to Proposition 3.4.23(ii) shows that when the risks are independent and identically distributed and when proportional coverages are offered, it is always optimal (in the $\preceq_{\mathrm{SL},=}$ sense) to treat them in a similar way.

Corollary 3.4.24

Let $X_1, X_2, \ldots, X_n$ be independent and identically distributed rvs. Let $a_1, a_2, \ldots, a_n$ be real constants. Write $\overline{a} = \frac{1}{n}\sum_{i=1}^{n} a_i$. Then

$$\overline{a}\sum_{i=1}^{n} X_i \preceq_{\mathrm{SL},=} \sum_{i=1}^{n} a_i X_i.$$

This result will be generalized in Proposition 3.4.47.

3.4.5.2 Functional stability of convex and stop-loss orders

Let us now summarize the most important properties of $\preceq_{\mathrm{SL}}$.

Proposition 3.4.25

(i) Given two risks X and Y,

$$X \preceq_{\mathrm{SL}} Y \Leftrightarrow t(X) \preceq_{\mathrm{SL}} t(Y)$$

for any non-decreasing and convex function t.

(ii) Given two sequences of independent risks $X_1, X_2, \ldots, X_n$ and $Y_1, Y_2, \ldots, Y_n$ such that $X_i \preceq_{\mathrm{SL}} Y_i$ holds for $i = 1, 2, \ldots, n$, we have that

$$\Psi(X_1, X_2, \ldots, X_n) \preceq_{\mathrm{SL}} \Psi(Y_1, Y_2, \ldots, Y_n)$$

for every non-decreasing and componentwise convex function Ψ; in particular, $\preceq_{\rm SL}$ is closed under convolution.

(iii) Given two sequences $\{X_1, X_2, X_3, \ldots\}$ and $\{Y_1, Y_2, Y_3, \ldots\}$ of rvs satisfying $X_j \preceq_{\rm SL} Y_j$ for all j, $X_j \to_d X$ and $Y_j \to_d Y$ as $j \to +\infty$. Provided $\mathbb{E}[(X_j)_+] \to \mathbb{E}[(X)_+]$ and $\mathbb{E}[(Y_j)_+] \to \mathbb{E}[(Y)_+]$ as $j \to +\infty$, we have that $X \preceq_{\rm SL} Y$.

Proof. Result (i) comes from the fact that the composition of two non-decreasing and convex functions is itself non-decreasing and convex.

The proof of (ii) is as follows. Without loss of generality we can assume that all the $2n$ random variables are independent because such an assumption does not affect the distributions of $\Psi(X_1, X_2, \ldots, X_n)$ and $\Psi(Y_1, Y_2, \ldots, Y_n)$. The proof is by induction on n. For $n=1$ the result is just (i). Assume that the result is true for vectors of size $n-1$. Let Ψ and v be increasing and componentwise convex functions. Then

$$\begin{aligned}\mathbb{E}[v(\Psi(X_1, X_2, \ldots, X_n))|X_1 = x] &= \mathbb{E}[v(\Psi(x, X_2, \ldots, X_n))]\\ &\leq \mathbb{E}[v(\Psi(x, Y_2, \ldots, Y_n))]\\ &= \mathbb{E}[v(\Psi(X_1, Y_2, \ldots, Y_n))|X_1 = x],\end{aligned}$$

where the equalities follow from the independence assumption and the inequality follows from the induction hypothesis. Taking expectations with respect to X_1, we obtain

$$\mathbb{E}[v(\Psi(X_1, X_2, \ldots, X_n))] \leq \mathbb{E}[v(\Psi(X_1, Y_2, \ldots, Y_n))].$$

Repeating the argument, but this time conditioning on $Y_2, \ldots, Y_n$ and using the induction hypothesis with $n=1$, we see that

$$\mathbb{E}[v(\Psi(X_1, Y_2, \ldots, Y_n))] \leq \mathbb{E}[v(\Psi(Y_1, Y_2, \ldots, Y_n))],$$

and this proves the result.

Finally, to obtain (iii), recall that $X_j \to_d X$ guarantees that $\mathbb{E}[g(X_j)] \to \mathbb{E}[g(X)]$ for any continuous bounded function g. It follows from $X_j \preceq_{\rm SL} Y_j$ that

$$\mathbb{E}[(X_j - t)_+] \leq \mathbb{E}[(Y_j - t)_+] \text{ for all } t.$$

Now

$$\mathbb{E}[(X_j - t)_+] = \mathbb{E}[(X_j)_+] - \mathbb{E}[\min\{(X_j)_+, t\}],$$

where the second expectation on the right-hand side involves a continuous bounded function. Hence,

$$\begin{aligned}\lim_{j\to+\infty} \mathbb{E}[(X_j - t)_+] &= \underbrace{\lim_{j\to+\infty} \mathbb{E}[(X_j)_+]}_{=\mathbb{E}[X_+] \text{ by assumption}} - \underbrace{\lim_{j\to+\infty} \mathbb{E}[\min\{(X_j)_+, t\}]}_{=\mathbb{E}[\min\{X_+, t\}] \text{ since } X_j \to_d X}\\ &= \mathbb{E}[(X - t)_+],\end{aligned}$$

whence the result follows. □

Remark 3.4.26. Proposition 3.4.25(iii) indicates that $\preceq_{\text{SL}}$ is not closed under taking limits. Additional conditions are needed for this to hold. The assumption about convergence of $\mathbb{E}[(X_j)_+]$ to $\mathbb{E}[X]$ and similarly for the Y_j is necessary for the result to be true, as shown in Müller (1996). ∇

Let us now turn to $\preceq_{\text{SL},=}$. This stochastic order does not have the functional invariance property contained in Proposition 3.4.25(i). The order $\preceq_{\text{SL},=}$ is nevertheless closed under convolution and the following result examines the stability of $\preceq_{\text{SL},=}$ under taking limits.

Proposition 3.4.27
Suppose two sequences $\{X_1, X_2, X_3, \ldots\}$ and $\{Y_1, Y_2, Y_3, \ldots\}$ of risks satisfy $X_j \preceq_{\text{SL},=} Y_j$ for all j, $X_j \to_d X$ and $Y_j \to_d Y$ as $j \to +\infty$. Provided $\mathbb{E}[(X_j)_+] \to \mathbb{E}[(X)_+]$ and $\mathbb{E}[(Y_j)_+] \to \mathbb{E}[(Y)_+]$ as $j \to +\infty$, we have that $X \preceq_{\text{SL},=} Y$.

Proof. Without loss of generality, it can be assumed that $\mathbb{E}[X] = \mathbb{E}[Y] = \mathbb{E}[X_j] = \mathbb{E}[Y_j] = 0$ for all j. Now

$$\begin{aligned}\mathbb{E}\Big[|X_j - t|\Big] &= -t + 2\int_{-\infty}^{t} F_{X_j}(x)dx \\ &= \mathbb{E}\Big[|X_j|\Big] - t + 2\int_{0}^{t} F_{X_j}(x)dx\end{aligned}$$

which implies

$$\mathbb{E}\Big[|X_j - t|\Big] \to \mathbb{E}\Big[|X|\Big] - t + 2\int_{0}^{t} F_X(x)dx = \mathbb{E}\Big[|X - t|\Big]$$

and, by invoking Proposition 3.4.15, concludes the proof. □

Remark 3.4.28. Without the condition on the convergence of the means, the conclusion of Proposition 3.4.27 need not be true. For example, let the X_j all be $\mathcal{U}ni(0.5, 1.5)$, and let the Y_j be such that $\Pr[Y_j = 0] = (j-1)/j$ and $\Pr[Y_j = j] = 1/j$, $j \geq 2$. Note that the distributions of the Y_j converge to a distribution that is degenerate at 0. Here $X_j \preceq_{\text{SL},=} Y_j$, $j = 2, 3, \ldots$, but it is not true that $X \preceq_{\text{SL},=} Y$. ∇

3.4.5.3 Convex and stop-loss orders and comonotonicity

We know from Proposition 3.4.25(ii) that the stop-loss order is preserved under convolution of mutually independent risks. In the following result we consider the case of mutually comonotonic risks.

Proposition 3.4.29
If $X_1, X_2, \ldots, X_n$ and $Y_1, Y_2, \ldots, Y_n$ are sequences of risks with $X_i \preceq_{\text{SL}} Y_i$ for $i = 1, \ldots, n$ and with $Y_1, Y_2, \ldots, Y_n$ mutually comonotonic, then

$$\sum_{i=1}^{n} X_i \preceq_{\text{SL}} \sum_{i=1}^{n} Y_i.$$

Proof. For any concave distortion function g, we know from Property 2.6.6 that ρ_g is subadditive, so that

$$\rho_g[X_1 + X_2 + \ldots + X_n] \le \sum_{i=1}^{n} \rho_g[X_i].$$

Now Property 2.6.5 ensures that any Wang risk measure ρ_g is comonotonic additive, so that

$$\sum_{i=1}^{n} \rho_g[Y_i] = \rho_g[Y_1 + Y_2 + \ldots + Y_n].$$

The result then follows from Proposition 3.4.7 together with the fact that $\rho_g[X_i] \le \rho_g[Y_i]$ as $X_i \preceq_{\mathrm{SL}} Y_i$. □

Note that in Proposition 3.4.29 we make no assumption concerning the dependence among the risks X_i. This means that the result is valid for any dependence among these risks.

The following result is a particular case of Proposition 3.4.29.

Corollary 3.4.30
For $U \sim \mathcal{U}ni[0, 1]$, and any risks $X_1, X_2, \ldots, X_n$, we have

$$\sum_{i=1}^{n} X_i \preceq_{\mathrm{SL},=} \sum_{i=1}^{n} F_{X_i}^{-1}(U).$$

3.4.6 *Convex ordering and notions of ageing*

3.4.6.1 Link with the IMRL/DMRL notions

We have seen in Proposition 3.3.24 that a non-negative rv is IFR/DFR if, and only if, $[X - t|X > t]$ and $[X - t'|X > t']$ are comparable in the $\preceq_{\mathrm{ST}}$ sense whenever $t \le t'$. A question of interest then is what one gets if in the above condition one replaces the order $\preceq_{\mathrm{ST}}$ by the order $\preceq_{\mathrm{SL}}$. It turns out that the order $\preceq_{\mathrm{SL}}$ can characterize familiar notions of ageing.

Property 3.4.31
The non-negative rv X is IMRL if, and only if, $[X - t|X > t] \preceq_{\mathrm{SL}} [X - t'|X > t']$ whenever $t \le t'$. It is DMRL if, and only if, $[X - t'|X > t'] \preceq_{\mathrm{SL}} [X - t|X > t]$ whenever $t \le t'$.

3.4.6.2 Characterization with stationary renewal distributions

In the case of non-negative rvs with the same expectation, it is possible to characterize $\preceq_{\mathrm{SL},=}$ by means of $\preceq_{\mathrm{ST}}$ using the stationary renewal distribution.

Proposition 3.4.32
Given two non-negative rvs X and Y such that $\mathbb{E}[X] = \mathbb{E}[Y]$,

$$X \preceq_{\mathrm{SL}=} Y \Leftrightarrow X_{\{1\}} \preceq_{\mathrm{ST}} Y_{\{1\}}.$$

Proof. The $\Rightarrow$ part of the result is obvious from (1.20). The reciprocal comes from the fact that

$$X_{\{1\}} \preceq_{\mathrm{ST}} Y_{\{1\}} \Leftrightarrow \frac{\pi_X(x)}{\mathbb{E}[X]} \leq \frac{\pi_Y(x)}{\mathbb{E}[Y]} \text{ for all } x,$$

which in turn yields $X \preceq_{\mathrm{SL},=} Y$ since $\mathbb{E}[X] = \mathbb{E}[Y]$. □

3.4.7 Stochastic (increasing) convexity

3.4.7.1 Definition

Let us consider for $\preceq_{\mathrm{SL},=}$ the problem investigated in Section 3.3.6 for $\preceq_{\mathrm{ST}}$. For $t^*(\theta) = \mathbb{E}[t(X_\theta)]$ as in (3.2), if the implication

$$t \text{ convex} \Rightarrow t^* \text{convex} \tag{3.62}$$

holds, the X_θ are said to be stochastically convex. Similarly, if the increasing convexity is transmitted from t to t^*, that is, if

$$t \text{ increasing convex} \Rightarrow t^* \text{ increasing convex},$$

then the X_θ are said to be stochastically increasing convex.

The notion of stochastic convexity, introduced by Shaked and Shanthikumar (1988), can be traced back to Schweder (1982) who described it by saying that the X_θ are 'convexly parametrized'. It is thoroughly reviewed (with several variants) in Shaked and Shanthikumar (1994).

3.4.7.2 Properties

Let us now gather some properties of stochastic convexity.

Property 3.4.33
The X_θ described in Property 3.3.28(i)–(ii) are stochastically convex. The X_θ described in Property 3.3.28(iii) are stochastically convex provided the Y_n are identically distributed.

Proof. For any function t such that $t'' \geq 0$, we get

$$\frac{d^2}{d\theta^2} t^*(\theta) = \frac{d^2}{d\theta^2} \mathbb{E}[t(\theta Y)] = \mathbb{E}\left[Y^2 t''(\theta Y)\right] \geq 0,$$

hence (i) follows. Item (ii) is obvious. For (iii), we have to show that, given a convex function t,

$$\Delta^2 t^*(\theta) = \mathbb{E}\left[t\left(\sum_{n=1}^{\theta+2} Y_n\right)\right] - 2\mathbb{E}\left[t\left(\sum_{n=1}^{\theta+1} Y_n\right)\right] + \mathbb{E}\left[t\left(\sum_{n=1}^{\theta} Y_n\right)\right] \geq 0.$$

Let us denote by F_Y the common df of the Y_n. Then

$$\begin{aligned}\Delta^2 t^*(\theta) &= \mathbb{E}\Big[t(X_\theta + Y_{\theta+1} + Y_{\theta+2}) - 2t(X_\theta + Y_{\theta+1}) + t(X_\theta)\Big]\\ &= \int_0^{+\infty}\int_0^{+\infty}\int_0^{+\infty}\Big(t(s+y_1+y_2) - 2t(s+y_1) + t(s)\Big)dF_{X_\theta}(s)dF_Y(y_1)dF_Y(y_2)\\ &= \frac{1}{2}\int_0^{+\infty}\int_0^{+\infty}\int_0^{+\infty}\Big(2t(s+y_1+y_2) - 2t(s+y_1) - 2t(s+y_2) + 2t(s)\Big)\\ &\quad \times dF_{X_\theta}(s)dF_Y(y_1)dF_Y(y_2).\end{aligned}$$

Since t is assumed to be convex, (2.35) ensures that

$$\begin{aligned}t(s+y_1+y_2) - t(s+y_1) &\geq t(s+y_2) - t(s),\\ t(s+y_1+y_2) - t(s+y_2) &\geq t(s+y_1) - t(s),\end{aligned}$$

so that the integrand is non-negative, whence the result follows. □

Remark 3.4.34. We mention that Property 3.3.29 does not hold for stochastic convexity. The reason is that the proof uses the fact that the composition of two increasing functions is itself an increasing function, and that this does not hold for convexity. ∇

Let us summarize the results about stochastic increasing convexity in the next property.

Property 3.4.35

(i) The family $\{X_\theta,\ \theta \in \mathbb{R}\}$ defined in Property 3.3.28(i)–(ii) is stochastically increasing convex. The family $\{X_\theta,\ \theta \in \mathbb{N}\}$ defined in Property 3.3.28(iii) is stochastically increasing convex provided the Y_n are identically distributed.

(ii) The families $\{g(X_\theta),\ \theta \in \mathbb{R}\}$ and $\{X_\theta,\ \theta \in \Theta\}$ defined in Property 3.3.29 are stochastically increasing convex.

3.4.7.3 A sufficient condition

Denuit, Lefèvre and Utev (1999a) have pointed out the special role played by the families of distributions that are totally positive.

Property 3.4.36
Let $\{X_\theta,\ \theta \in \Theta\}$ be a TP_2 family. If, in addition, $\mathbb{E}[X_\theta] = a + b\theta$, $\theta \in \Theta$, where b is a positive real constant, then the X_θ are stochastically convex.

Remark 3.4.37. Examples of parametric distributions that are not stochastically convex are rather frequent. It can be verified, for instance, that if $X_\theta \sim \mathcal{E}xp(1/\theta)$, then $\{\sqrt{X_\theta},\ \theta \in \Theta\}$ is not stochastically convex (although being TP_2). ∇

3.4.8 Ordering mixtures

Like stochastic increasingness, the property of stochastic convexity provides a natural way for comparing mixed distributions through their mixing kernel, in the convex order. The proof of the following result is similar to the proof of Property 3.3.30, and is thus omitted.

Property 3.4.38
In the notation of Property 3.3.30,

(i) if the X_θ's are stochastically convex, then $\Lambda_1 \preceq_{\text{SL},=} \Lambda_2 \Rightarrow X_{\Lambda_1} \preceq_{\text{SL},=} X_{\Lambda_2}$;

(ii) similarly, if the X_θ are stochastically increasing convex, then $\Lambda_1 \preceq_{\text{SL}} \Lambda_2 \Rightarrow X_{\Lambda_1} \preceq_{\text{SL}} X_{\Lambda_2}$.

3.4.9 Ordering compound sums

Using Property 3.4.38, we are able to compare compound sums, through their number of terms, in the convex sense.

Property 3.4.39
Let $\{X_1, X_2, X_3, \ldots\}$ and $\{Y_1, Y_2, Y_3, \ldots\}$ be two sequences of non-negative independent and identically distributed rvs, and let N and M be two integer-valued rvs, independent of that sequence. Then,

$$\left.\begin{array}{r} X_n \preceq_{\text{SL}=} Y_n \text{ for all } n \\ M \preceq_{\text{SL}=} N \end{array}\right\} \Rightarrow \sum_{n=1}^{M} X_n \preceq_{\text{SL}=} \sum_{n=1}^{N} Y_n;$$

$$\left.\begin{array}{r} X_n \preceq_{\text{SL}} Y_n \text{ for all } n \\ M \preceq_{\text{SL}} N \end{array}\right\} \Rightarrow \sum_{n=1}^{M} X_n \preceq_{\text{SL}} \sum_{n=1}^{N} Y_n.$$

3.4.10 Risk-reshaping contracts and Lorenz order

3.4.10.1 Lorenz curves

The Lorenz order is defined by means of pointwise comparison of the Lorenz curves. These are used in economics to measure the inequality of incomes. More precisely, let X be a non-negative rv with df F_X. The Lorenz curve LC_X associated with X is then defined by

$$LC_X(p) = \frac{1}{\mathbb{E}[X]} \int_{\xi=0}^{p} \text{VaR}[X; \xi] d\xi, \quad p \in [0, 1]. \tag{3.63}$$

In an economics framework, when X models the income of the individuals in some population, LC_X maps $p \in [0, 1]$ to the proportion of the total income of the population which accrues to the poorest $100p\,\%$ of the population. An interpretation of LC_X in insurance business is the following: $LC_X(p)$ can be thought of as being the fraction of the aggregate claims caused by the $100p\,\%$ of the treaties with the lowest claim size.

3.4.10.2 Lorenz order

We are now in a position to define the Lorenz order.

Definition 3.4.40. Consider two risks X and Y. Then, X is said to be smaller than Y in the Lorenz order, henceforth denoted by $X \preceq_{\text{Lorenz}} Y$, when $LC_X(p) \geq LC_Y(p)$ for all $p \in [0, 1]$. ∇

A standard reference on $\preceq_{\text{Lorenz}}$ is Arnold (1987). We mention that $<_3$ in Heilmann (1985) is in fact $\preceq_{\text{Lorenz}}$. We also mention that the Lorenz order is the k-order introduced by Heilmann (1986) (see also Heilmann and Schröter 1991, Remark 5).

3.4.10.3 Lorenz and convex orders

Clearly, convex and Lorenz orders are closely related.

Property 3.4.41
Given two risks X and Y,

$$X \preceq_{\text{Lorenz}} Y \Leftrightarrow \frac{X}{\mathbb{E}[X]} \preceq_{\text{SL},=} \frac{Y}{\mathbb{E}[Y]}. \tag{3.64}$$

Let us stress that, although only risks with the same means can be compared through $\preceq_{\text{SL},=}$, ordering risks through $\preceq_{\text{Lorenz}}$ does not require that X and Y have the same first moment. Obviously, when $\mathbb{E}[X] = \mathbb{E}[Y]$, we have from (3.64) that

$$X \preceq_{\text{Lorenz}} Y \Leftrightarrow X \preceq_{\text{SL},=} Y \tag{3.65}$$

since the convex order is scale-invariant. It is worth mentioning that other approaches to comparing rvs with unequal means via $\preceq_{\text{SL},=}$ have been proposed. The dilation order, for instance, compares $X - \mathbb{E}[X]$ to $Y - \mathbb{E}[Y]$.

3.4.10.4 Risk-reshaping contracts

Insurance and banks are ready to buy risk. Typically, the seller's risk is not fully taken by the buyer. Rather his risk distribution is reshaped. Formally, the individual will substitute a function $\vartheta(X)$ for the original risk X. This section examines which conditions have to be fulfilled in order that the deal is judged profitable by a risk-averse decision-maker. Of course, $\mathbb{E}[\vartheta(X)] \neq \mathbb{E}[X]$ so that the Lorenz order will be used to compare the situation X without insurance to the situation $\vartheta(X)$ with insurance.

An interesting result about the Lorenz order is stated next; it can be found in Shaked and Shanthikumar (1994, Theorem 2.A.10).

Proposition 3.4.42
Let $\vartheta : \mathbb{R}^+ \to \mathbb{R}^+$ be a measurable function and consider the risk X with $\mathbb{E}[X] > 0$. Then, $\vartheta(X) \preceq_{\text{Lorenz}} X$ if, and only if,

$$\begin{cases} \mathbb{E}[\vartheta(X)] > 0, \\ \vartheta \text{ is non-decreasing on } \mathbb{R}^+, \\ x \mapsto \vartheta(x)/x \text{ is non-increasing on } (0, +\infty). \end{cases}$$

Proposition 3.4.42 explains when an insurance contract reduces the risk. Indeed, insurers only offer partial coverage in reality (for many reasons, including avoiding moral hazard). Basically, policyholders will prefer $\vartheta(X)$ to X when ϑ increases more slowly than the identity function.

The next result is then easily deduced from Proposition 3.4.42. It is closely related to some properties obtained by Wilfling (1996).

Corollary 3.4.43
Let ϑ_1 and $\vartheta_2 : \mathbb{R}^+ \to \mathbb{R}^+$ be two non-decreasing continuous measurable functions and consider the risk X with $\mathbb{E}[X] > 0$. Then, $\vartheta_1(X) \preceq_{\text{Lorenz}} \vartheta_2(X)$ if, and only if, the function $x \mapsto \vartheta(x) = \vartheta_1 \circ \vartheta_2^{-1}(x)$ satisfies the conditions of Proposition 3.4.42.

The following result is also interesting for actuarial applications.

Proposition 3.4.44
Let X be a non-negative rv and let $\vartheta_1, \vartheta_2 : \mathbb{R}^+ \to \mathbb{R}^+$ be such that $\vartheta_1(x) > 0$ and $\vartheta_2(x) > 0$ for all $x > 0$. If $\frac{\vartheta_2(x)}{\vartheta_1(x)}$ is non-decreasing on $\mathbb{R}^+$ then $\vartheta_1(X) \preceq_{\text{Lorenz}} \vartheta_2(X)$.

Proof. By assumption,

$$\frac{\mathbb{E}[\vartheta_1(X)]}{\mathbb{E}[\vartheta_2(X)]} \cdot \frac{\vartheta_2(x)}{\vartheta_1(x)} \quad \text{is non-decreasing in } x.$$

Therefore, we have that

$$\frac{\mathbb{E}[\vartheta_1(X)]}{\mathbb{E}[\vartheta_2(X)]} \cdot \frac{\vartheta_2(\text{VaR}[X;p])}{\vartheta_1(\text{VaR}[X;p])} \quad \text{is non-decreasing in } p,$$

which in turn implies that

$$\frac{\text{VaR}\left[\frac{\vartheta_2(X)}{\mathbb{E}[\vartheta_2(X)]}; p\right]}{\text{VaR}\left[\frac{\vartheta_1(X)}{\mathbb{E}[\vartheta_1(X)]}; p\right]} \quad \text{is non-decreasing in } p.$$

Thus,

$$\frac{\vartheta_1(X)}{\mathbb{E}[\vartheta_1(X)]} \preceq_{\text{SL},=} \frac{\vartheta_2(X)}{\mathbb{E}[\vartheta_2(X)]}$$

and the required result comes from (3.64). □

3.4.11 Majorization

3.4.11.1 Definition

In this section, we describe the concept of majorization, which is closely related to convexity. The notion of majorization arose as a measure of diversity of the components of an

n-dimensional vector. It has been comprehensively treated by Marshall and Olkin (1979); a brief introduction is given by Arnold (1987).

We aim to formalize the idea that the components of a vector $\boldsymbol{x}$ are 'less spread out' or 'more nearly equal' than the components of $\boldsymbol{y}$. In many cases, the appropriate precise statement is '$\boldsymbol{y}$ majorizes $\boldsymbol{x}$'. Majorization is a partial order defined on the positive orthant $(\mathbb{R}^+)^n$. For a vector $\boldsymbol{x} \in (\mathbb{R}^+)^n$ we denote its elements ranked in ascending order as

$$x_{(1:n)} \leq x_{(2:n)} \leq \ldots \leq x_{(n:n)}.$$

Thus $x_{(1:n)}$ is the smallest of the x_i, while $x_{(n:n)}$ is the largest.

Definition 3.4.45. Let $\boldsymbol{x}, \boldsymbol{y} \in (\mathbb{R}^+)^n$. We say that $\boldsymbol{y}$ majorizes $\boldsymbol{x}$, and write $\boldsymbol{x} \preceq_{\text{MAJ}} \boldsymbol{y}$, if

$$\sum_{i=1}^{k} x_{(i:n)} \geq \sum_{i=1}^{k} y_{(i:n)} \text{ for } k = 1, 2, \ldots, n-1 \text{ and } \sum_{i=1}^{n} x_i = \sum_{i=1}^{n} y_i.$$

∇

It is easy to see that $\boldsymbol{x} \preceq_{\text{MAJ}} \boldsymbol{y}$ is also equivalent to

$$\sum_{i=k}^{n} x_{(i:n)} \leq \sum_{i=k}^{n} y_{(i:n)} \text{ for } k = 1, 2, \ldots, n \text{ and } \sum_{i=1}^{n} x_i = \sum_{i=1}^{n} y_i.$$

Definition 3.4.45 provides a partial ordering: $\boldsymbol{x} \preceq_{\text{MAJ}} \boldsymbol{y}$ implies that, for a fixed sum, the y_i are more diverse than the x_i. To illustrate this point, we see that $\overline{\boldsymbol{y}} \preceq_{\text{MAJ}} \boldsymbol{y}$ always holds, with

$$\overline{\boldsymbol{y}} = (\overline{y}, \overline{y}, \ldots, \overline{y}) \quad \text{where} \quad \overline{y} = \frac{1}{n} \sum_{i=1}^{n} y_i,$$

and that

$$\boldsymbol{x} \preceq_{\text{MAJ}} \left(\sum_{i=1}^{n} x_i, 0, \ldots, 0 \right).$$

The following are trivial though important examples of majorization.

Example 3.4.46. We always have

$$\begin{aligned} \left(\frac{1}{n}, \frac{1}{n}, \ldots, \frac{1}{n} \right) &\preceq_{\text{MAJ}} \left(\frac{1}{n-1}, \frac{1}{n-1}, \ldots, \frac{1}{n-1}, 0 \right) \\ &\preceq_{\text{MAJ}} \cdots \\ &\preceq_{\text{MAJ}} \left(\frac{1}{2}, \frac{1}{2}, 0, \ldots, 0 \right) \\ &\preceq_{\text{MAJ}} (1, 0, \ldots, 0). \end{aligned}$$

More generally, if $m \geq l$ and $lc = m\alpha c$ (i.e., $\alpha = \frac{l}{m} \leq 1$) then

$$(\underbrace{\alpha c, \ldots, \alpha c}_{m \text{ times}}, 0, \ldots, 0) \preceq_{\text{MAJ}} (\underbrace{c, \ldots, c}_{l \text{ times}}, 0, \ldots, 0).$$

∇

3.4.11.2 Majorization and convexity

The inequality

$$\sum_{i=1}^{n} g(\overline{y}) \leq \sum_{i=1}^{n} g(y_i)$$

holds for all convex functions $g:\mathbb{R}\to\mathbb{R}$. So, considering the fact that $\overline{\boldsymbol{y}} \preceq_{\text{MAJ}} \boldsymbol{y}$, it is natural to ask for conditions on $\boldsymbol{x}$ and $\boldsymbol{y}$ in order that

$$\sum_{i=1}^{n} g(x_i) \leq \sum_{i=1}^{n} g(y_i) \tag{3.66}$$

for all convex functions ϕ. This question was posed by Hardy, Littlewood and Pólya (1934) and they provided this answer: a necessary and sufficient condition for (3.66) to hold for all convex functions g is that $\boldsymbol{y}$ majorizes $\boldsymbol{x}$. This is formally stated in the next result.

Proposition 3.4.47
Let I be an interval in $\mathbb{R}$ and let $\boldsymbol{x}$, $\boldsymbol{y}$ be two n-dimensional vectors such that $x_i, y_i \in I$ for $i=1,\ldots,n$. Then (3.66) holds for every continuous convex function $g: I\to\mathbb{R}$ if, and only if, $\boldsymbol{x} \preceq_{\text{MAJ}} \boldsymbol{y}$ holds.

3.4.11.3 Majorization and convex order

The next result strengthens Corollary 3.4.24.

Property 3.4.48
Let $X_1, X_2, \ldots, X_n$ be independent and identically distributed rvs. Let $\boldsymbol{a}$ and $\boldsymbol{b}$ be two vectors of constants. If $\boldsymbol{a} \preceq_{\text{MAJ}} \boldsymbol{b}$ then

$$\sum_{i=1}^{n} a_i X_i \preceq_{\text{SL},=} \sum_{i=1}^{n} b_i X_i.$$

This is but one example of the numerous results linking majorization and convex order.

3.4.12 Conditional stop-loss order: Mean-excess order

3.4.12.1 Definition

Clearly, the smaller the mean-excess function, the smaller X should be in some stochastic sense. This is the motivation for the order discussed in this section.

Definition 3.4.49. Let X and Y be two random variables such that

$$[X-s \mid X>s] \preceq_{\text{SL}} [Y-s \mid Y>s] \quad \text{for all } s. \tag{3.67}$$

Then X is said to be smaller than Y in the mean-excess function order (denoted by $X \preceq_{\text{MEF}} Y$).
∇

As was the case for $\preceq_{\text{HR}}$ with respect to $\preceq_{\text{ST}}$, the order $\preceq_{\text{MEF}}$ can be seen as a conditional version of $\preceq_{\text{SL}}$.

3.4.12.2 Mean-excess order and mean-excess function

As indicated by its name, $\preceq_{\text{MEF}}$ is closely related to mefs. In fact, comparing rvs in the $\preceq_{\text{MEF}}$ sense is equivalent to pointwise comparison of the underlying mefs.

Property 3.4.50
Let X and Y be two random variables. Then $X \preceq_{\text{MEF}} Y$ if, and only if,

$$e_X(t) \leq e_Y(t) \quad \text{for all } t. \tag{3.68}$$

Proof. Condition (3.67) can be written as

$$\frac{\int_t^\infty \overline{F}_X(s+u)\,du}{\overline{F}_X(s)} \leq \frac{\int_t^\infty \overline{F}_Y(s+u)\,du}{\overline{F}_Y(s)} \quad \text{for all } s \text{ and all } t \geq 0,$$

which is equivalent to (3.68) by (1.19). □

An early reference on $\preceq_{\text{MEF}}$ is Alzaid (1988). Note that we obviously have

$$X \preceq_{\text{HR}} Y \Rightarrow X \preceq_{\text{MEF}} Y.$$

Analogously to (3.68), we also have that $X \preceq_{\text{MEF}} Y$ if, and only if,

$$\frac{\overline{F_X}(s)}{\pi_X(t)} \geq \frac{\overline{F}_Y(s)}{\pi_Y(t)} \tag{3.69}$$

for all $s \leq t$ such that the denominators are positive.

3.4.12.3 Comparing claim frequencies

For integer-valued rvs, the definition of the mef should be slightly modified. Let N be such an rv with a finite mean μ. The discrete mef of N at n is defined as

$$e_N(n) = \begin{cases} \mathbb{E}[N-n|N \geq n], & \text{for } n \leq n^*, \\ 0, & \text{otherwise,} \end{cases}$$

where $n^* = \max\{n \in \mathbb{N} | \Pr[N \geq n] > 0\}$. Note that for such rvs we have $e_N(0) = \mu$.

Property 3.4.51
Let N and M be two integer-valued rvs. We have $N \preceq_{\text{MEF}} M$ if, and only if,

$$e_N(n) \leq e_M(n) \quad \text{for all } n \geq 0. \tag{3.70}$$

3.4.12.4 Mean-excess order and notions of ageing

The order $\preceq_{\text{MEF}}$ can be used to characterize DMRL rvs.

Proposition 3.4.52
The rv X is DMRL if, and only if,

$$[X - t'|X > t'] \preceq_{\text{MEF}} [X - t|X > t] \text{ whenever } t \leq t'.$$

3.4.13 Comparing shortfall with the stop-loss order: Right-spread order

3.4.13.1 Definition

The dispersive order was defined by the comparison of $(X - \text{VaR}[X; p])_+$ and $(Y - \text{VaR}[Y; p])_+$ with the help of $\preceq_{\text{ST}}$. There is of course no reason to restrict this comparison to $\preceq_{\text{ST}}$ and this section is devoted to an analogue of $\preceq_{\text{DISP}}$ obtained by replacing $\preceq_{\text{ST}}$ with $\preceq_{\text{SL}}$ (note that replacing $\preceq_{\text{ST}}$ with $\preceq_{\text{SL}=}$ is not relevant because this would imply $\mathbb{E}[(X - \text{VaR}[X; p])_+] = \mathbb{E}[(Y - \text{VaR}[Y; p])_+]$ for all p, which is in turn equivalent to $X =_d Y + c$).

Definition 3.4.53. X is smaller than Y in the right-spread order, written as $X \preceq_{\text{RS}} Y$, if

$$(X - \text{VaR}[X; p])_+ \preceq_{\text{SL}} (Y - \text{VaR}[Y; p])_+$$

for all $0 < p < 1$. ∇

References on $\preceq_{\text{RS}}$ include Shaked and Shanthikumar (1998), Fagiuoli, Pellerey and Shaked (1999) and Fernandez-Ponce, Kochar and Muñoz–Perez (1998).

3.4.13.2 Right-spread order and expected shortfalls

The following result shows that a comparison in the $\preceq_{\text{RS}}$ sense boils down to comparing expected shortfalls.

Proposition 3.4.54
Given two risks X and Y, $X \preceq_{\text{RS}} Y$ if, and only if, $\text{ES}[X; p] \leq \text{ES}[Y; p]$ for all $0 < p < 1$, that is, if, and only if, $\pi_X(\text{VaR}[X; p]) \leq \pi_Y(\text{VaR}[Y; p])$ for all $0 < p < 1$.

Proof. The df of $X_p = (X - \text{VaR}[X; p])_+$ is given by

$$F_{X_p}(x) = \begin{cases} 0, & \text{if } x < 0 \\ F_X\big(x + \text{VaR}[X; p]\big), & \text{if } x \geq 0. \end{cases}$$

The $\Rightarrow$ part is obvious since a comparison in the $\preceq_{\text{SL}}$ sense implies the corresponding ordering of the means. Let us consider the $\Leftarrow$ part. Clearly, $X \preceq_{\text{RS}} Y$ is equivalent to

$$\begin{cases} \int_{t+\text{VaR}[X;p]}^{+\infty} \overline{F}_X(x)dx \leq \int_{t+\text{VaR}[Y;p]}^{+\infty} \overline{F}_Y(x)dx \text{ for all } t > 0, \\ \text{ES}[X; p] \leq \text{ES}[Y; p] \text{ for all } 0 < p < 1. \end{cases}$$

We have to establish that the function

$$H(t, p) = \int_{t+\text{VaR}[Y;p]}^{+\infty} \overline{F}_Y(x)dx - \int_{t+\text{VaR}[X;p]}^{+\infty} \overline{F}_X(x)dx$$

is non-negative for all $(t, p) \in \mathbb{R}^+ \times (0, 1)$. Note that for any $p \in (0, 1)$, $\lim_{t \to +\infty} H(t, p) = 0$. Let us now establish that for every fixed $p \in (0, 1)$, the function H attains a minimum at a point t^* such that $H(t^*, p) \geq 0$. Since H is continuous and differentiable, t^* satisfies

$$\frac{\partial}{\partial p} H(t, p)\Big|_{t=t^*} = 0$$

which gives the relation

$$F_X\Big(t^* + \mathrm{VaR}[X\,;p]\Big) = F_Y\Big(t^* + \mathrm{VaR}[Y\,;p]\Big).$$

Let us now assume that F_X and F_Y are strictly increasing in $t^* + \mathrm{VaR}[X\,;p]$ and $t^* + \mathrm{VaR}[Y\,;p]$, respectively (for a proof without this assumption, see Belzunce 1999). Then, denoting by q the common value $F_X(t^* + \mathrm{VaR}[X;p]) = F_Y(t^* + \mathrm{VaR}[Y;p])$, we have $\mathrm{VaR}[X;q] = t^* + \mathrm{VaR}[X;p]$ and $\mathrm{VaR}[Y;q] = t^* + \mathrm{VaR}[Y;p]$. Therefore

$$\begin{aligned} H(t^*, p) &= \int_{t^*+\mathrm{VaR}[Y;p]}^{+\infty} \overline{F}_Y(x)dx - \int_{t^*+\mathrm{VaR}[X;p]}^{+\infty} \overline{F}_X(x)dx \\ &= \int_{\mathrm{VaR}[Y;q]}^{+\infty} \overline{F}_Y(x)dx - \int_{\mathrm{VaR}[X;q]}^{+\infty} \overline{F}_X(x)dx \\ &= \mathrm{ES}[Y;q] - \mathrm{ES}[X;q] \geq 0 \end{aligned}$$

by assumption. □

3.4.13.3 Right-spread order and Excess-wealth tranforms

The right-spread order can also be defined by means of pointwise comparison of the excess-wealth transforms. More precisely, let X be a non-negative rv with df F_X. The excess-wealth tranform W_X associated with F_X is then defined by

$$W_X(p) = \int_{\mathrm{VaR}[X;p]}^{+\infty} \overline{F}_X(x)dx, \quad p \in [0, 1]. \tag{3.71}$$

In the context of economics, if F_X is thought of as the distribution of an income accross the population, then $W_X(p)$ can be viewed as the additional wealth (on top of the pth percentile) of the richest $100(1-p)\%$ individuals in the population. Another transform of interest associated with F_X is the so-called total-time-on-test transform, denoted by T_X. This transform is complementary to W_X and is defined by

$$T_X(p) = \int_0^{\mathrm{VaR}[X;p]} \overline{F}_X(x)dx, \quad p \in [0, 1]. \tag{3.72}$$

In the actuarial literature, T_X has already been encountered in Heilmann (1985). Of course, L_X, W_X and T_X are closely related; see Pham and Turkkan (1994) and Shaked and Shanthikumar (1998) for more details.

We then have the following result.

Property 3.4.55
Consider two risks X and Y. Then $X \preceq_{\mathrm{RS}} Y$, if, and only if,

$$W_X(p) \leq W_Y(p) \text{ for all } p \in [0, 1]. \tag{3.73}$$

Of course, as $T_X(p) + W_X(p) = \mathbb{E}[X]$ for all $p \in [0, 1]$, we easily get that

$$X \preceq_{\mathrm{RS}} Y \Leftrightarrow T_X(p) \geq T_Y(p) \text{ for all } p \in [0, 1]. \tag{3.74}$$

The order $\preceq_{\mathrm{RS}}$ (defined through (3.74)) has been implicitly considered by Heilmann (1985).

3.4.13.4 Shortfall order and expected utility theory

The absolute risk-aversion function is an excellent measure of the strength of risk aversion; it is defined as

$$RA(w) = \frac{-u''(w)}{u'(w)} = -\frac{d}{dw} \ln u'(w). \tag{3.75}$$

It is easy to see that $RA \geq 0$ for any profit-seeking risk-averse decision-maker. The coefficient of absolute risk aversion has often demonstrated its usefulness in a wide range of both theoretical and empirical studies of behaviour under uncertainty.

Moreover, (3.75) measures the local propensity to insure under the utility function u. Specifically, assume a decision-maker with a twice differentiable utility function u is ready to pay a premium Π in order to replace a random income Z with its expected value $\mathbb{E}[Z]$. The premium Π (not necessarily non-negative) depends on the initial wealth (assumed to be a deterministic sum w) and on the distribution of Z, that is, $\Pi = \Pi(w, F_Z)$. The premium Π can be formally defined as the unique value satisfying the equation

$$u(w + \mathbb{E}[Z] - \Pi) = \mathbb{E}[u(w + Z)].$$

It can be shown that

$$\Pi(w, F_Z) \approx \frac{1}{2}\sigma_Z^2 RA(w + \mathbb{E}[Z]).$$

The definition (3.75) of RA is local: it pertains to the decision-maker's behaviour when he has to insure against small (infinitesimal) risks. The following theorem, due to Pratt (1964) and Arrow (1974), shows that there is an analogy between the behaviour with respect to risk aversion in the small and in the large.

Proposition 3.4.56
Let u_1 and u_2 be two utility functions with respective absolute risk-aversion coefficients RA_1 and RA_2, and risk premiums Π_1 and Π_2. The following conditions are equivalent:

(i) $RA_1(w) \geq RA_2(w)$ for all w;

(ii) $\Pi_1(w, F_Z) \geq \Pi_2(w, F_Z)$ for all w and F_Z;

(iii) there exists a function f, increasing and concave, such that

$$u_1(w) = f(u_2(w)) \text{ for all } w.$$

If one condition of Proposition 3.4.56 is satisfied (hence if all of them are) then u_1 is said to be more risk-averse than u_2.

Property 3.4.57
Given two risks X and Y such that $\mathbb{E}[X] = \mathbb{E}[Y]$ and $X \preceq_{\text{RS}} Y$, then

$$\begin{gathered} \mathbb{E}[u_2(w - Y)] = \mathbb{E}[u_2(w - X - \Pi)] \\ \Downarrow \\ \mathbb{E}[u_1(w - X - \Pi)] \geq \mathbb{E}[u_1(w - Y)] \end{gathered} \tag{3.76}$$

whenever u_1 and u_2 are non-decreasing and concave utility functions with u_1 more risk-averse than u_2.

This result has a natural interpretation in actuarial science. Indeed, Π appears as the risk premium the decision-maker with utility function u_2 is willing to pay in order to replace the loss X with the loss Y. Then (3.76) expresses the fact that anybody who is more risk-averse than this decision-maker is ready to pay more than Π in order to replace X with Y. In other words, every decision-maker u_1 more risk-averse than u_2 will prefer $X+\Pi$ over Y. We mention that the above concepts are closely related to the location-free methods for comparing random assets introduced by Jewitt (1989) and further studied by Landsberger and Meilijson (1994a).

3.4.14 Multivariate extensions

3.4.14.1 Multivariate convex order

As was the case for multivariate stochastic dominance, the multivariate version of the convex order is obtained by substituting the cone of the convex functions on $\mathbb{R}^n$ for the corresponding cone of functions on $\mathbb{R}$. This yields the following definition.

Definition 3.4.58. Given two random vectors $\boldsymbol{X}$ and $\boldsymbol{Y}$, $\boldsymbol{X}$ is said to be smaller than $\boldsymbol{Y}$ in the multivariate convex order, written as $\boldsymbol{X} \preceq_{\text{SL},=} \boldsymbol{Y}$, if $\mathbb{E}[g(\boldsymbol{X})] \leq \mathbb{E}[g(\boldsymbol{Y})]$ for every convex function $g: \mathbb{R}^n \to \mathbb{R}$, provided the expectations exist. ∇

An excellent reference on the multivariate convex order is Scarsini (1998). It is worth mentioning that some orders weaker than the multivariate $\preceq_{\text{SL},=}$ are studied in Koshevoy and Mosler (1996, 1997, 1998); for example, they study the order between random vectors $\boldsymbol{X}$ and $\boldsymbol{Y}$ defined by $\mathbb{E}[g(a_1X_1+a_2X_2+\ldots+a_nX_n)] \leq \mathbb{E}[g(a_1Y_1+a_2Y_2+\ldots+a_nY_n)]$ for all univariate convex functions g and constants $a_1, a_2, \ldots, a_n$ for which the expectations exist.

3.4.14.2 Multivariate stop-loss order

The multivariate stop-loss order is obtained by substituting the cones of the non-decreasing convex functions on $\mathbb{R}^n$ for the corresponding cone of univariate functions. This yields the following definition.

Definition 3.4.59. Given two random vectors $\boldsymbol{X}$ and $\boldsymbol{Y}$, $\boldsymbol{X}$ is said to be smaller than $\boldsymbol{Y}$ in the multivariate stop-loss order, written as $\boldsymbol{X} \preceq_{\text{SL}} \boldsymbol{Y}$, if $\mathbb{E}[g(\boldsymbol{X})] \leq \mathbb{E}[g(\boldsymbol{Y})]$ for every non-decreasing convex function $g: \mathbb{R}^n \to \mathbb{R}$, provided the expectations exist. ∇

From Definitions 3.4.58 and 3.4.59, it is clear that given two n-dimensional random vectors $\boldsymbol{X}$, and $\boldsymbol{Y}$, $\boldsymbol{X} \preceq_{\text{SL}=} \boldsymbol{Y} \Rightarrow \boldsymbol{X} \preceq_{\text{SL}} \boldsymbol{Y}$. Moreover, examining Definition 3.3.79, we also get $\boldsymbol{X} \preceq_{\text{ST}} \boldsymbol{Y} \Rightarrow \boldsymbol{X} \preceq_{\text{SL}} \boldsymbol{Y}$.

3.4.14.3 Supermodular and directionally convex functions

Several extensions of convexity (and corresponding orders) from the univariate to the multivariate case have been proposed, yielding the symmetric convex order, the componentwise convex order, and many others. In particular, the so-called directional convexity has proved useful in several applications in applied probability; see Shaked and Shanthikumar (1990), Chang *et al.* (1991), Meester and Shanthikumar (1993) and Bäuerle and Rolski (1998).

The usual notion of convexity does not take into account a possible order structure of the space, whereas directional convexity does. Therefore, this notion seems to be particularly useful in economic models where concepts such as risk aversion and positivity of a price vector have to be taken into account simultaneously. A particular case of directional convexity was used by Finkelshtain, Kella and Scarsini (1999) in order to characterize risk aversion with one insurable and one uninsurable risk.

In order to define directional convexity, we need to introduce the notion of supermodularity.

Definition 3.4.60. A function $g:\mathbb{R}^n \to \mathbb{R}$ is said to be supermodular if for any $\boldsymbol{x}, \boldsymbol{y} \in \mathbb{R}^n$ it satisfies

$$g(\boldsymbol{x}) + g(\boldsymbol{y}) \leq g(\boldsymbol{x} \wedge \boldsymbol{y}) + g(\boldsymbol{x} \vee \boldsymbol{y}),$$

where the operators $\wedge$ and $\vee$ denote coordinatewise minimum and maximum, respectively. ∇

Saying that g is supermodular is equivalent to requiring that

$$g(x_1, \ldots, x_i + \epsilon, \ldots, x_j + \delta, \ldots, x_n) - g(x_1, \ldots, x_i + \epsilon, \ldots, x_j, \ldots, x_n)$$

$$\geq g(x_1, \ldots, x_i, \ldots, x_j + \delta, \ldots, x_n) - g(x_1, \ldots, x_i, \ldots, x_j, \ldots, x_n)$$

holds for all $\boldsymbol{x} \in \mathbb{R}^n$, $1 \leq i < j \leq n$ and all $\epsilon, \delta > 0$. Considering this inequality, an intuitive explanation of the notion of supermodularity can be given as follows. Let $x_1, x_2, \ldots, x_n$ be the individual claim amounts of n policyholders and let $g(x_1, x_2, \ldots, x_n)$ be the loss for the insurance company caused by these claims. Then supermodularity of g means that the consequences of an increase of a single claim are worse the higher the other claims are.

The following properties of the supermodular functions are well known.

Property 3.4.61

(i) If $g:\mathbb{R}^n \to \mathbb{R}$ is twice differentiable then it is supermodular if, and only if,

$$\frac{\partial^2}{\partial x_i \partial x_j} g \geq 0 \text{ for every } 1 \leq i < j \leq n. \tag{3.77}$$

(ii) If $g:\mathbb{R}^n \to \mathbb{R}$ is supermodular then the function Ψ, defined by $\Psi(x_1, x_2, \ldots, x_n) = g(t_1(x_1), t_2(x_2), \ldots, t_n(x_n))$, is also supermodular, whenever $t_i:\mathbb{R} \to \mathbb{R}$, $i = 1, 2, \ldots, n$, are all increasing or are all decreasing.

Many examples of supermodular functions can be found in Chapter 6 of Marshall and Olkin (1979).

The following definition relates directional convexity to supermodularity.

Definition 3.4.62. The function g is directionally convex if, and only if, one of the following equivalent conditions is fulfilled:

(i) The function g is supermodular and coordinatewise convex.

(ii) For any $\boldsymbol{x}_1, \boldsymbol{x}_2, \boldsymbol{y} \in \mathbb{R}^n$, such that $\boldsymbol{x}_1 \leq \boldsymbol{x}_2$ and $\boldsymbol{y} \geq \boldsymbol{0}$, one has

$$g(\boldsymbol{x}_1 + \boldsymbol{y}) - g(\boldsymbol{x}_1) \leq g(\boldsymbol{x}_2 + \boldsymbol{y}) - g(\boldsymbol{x}_2).$$

∇

If g is twice differentiable then it is directionally convex if, and only if, all its second derivatives are non-negative, that is,

$$\frac{\partial^2}{\partial x_i \partial x_j} g \geq 0 \text{ for all } i, j.$$

Directional convexity neither implies, nor is implied by, conventional convexity. However, a univariate function is directionally convex if, and only if, it is convex.

3.4.14.4 Directional and increasing directional convex orders

We are now in a position to define the directional convex order.

Definition 3.4.63. Let $\boldsymbol{X}$ and $\boldsymbol{Y}$ be two n-dimensional random vectors. Suppose that $\boldsymbol{X}$ and $\boldsymbol{Y}$ are such that

$$\mathbb{E}[g(\boldsymbol{X})] \leq \mathbb{E}[g(\boldsymbol{Y})] \text{for all directionally convex functions } g : \mathbb{R}^n \to \mathbb{R},$$

provided the expectations exist. Then $\boldsymbol{X}$ is said to be smaller than $\boldsymbol{Y}$ in the directionally convex order (written as $\boldsymbol{X} \preceq_{\text{DCX}} \boldsymbol{Y}$). ∇

Definition 3.4.64. Let $\boldsymbol{X}$ and $\boldsymbol{Y}$ be two n-dimensional random vectors. Suppose that $\boldsymbol{X}$ and $\boldsymbol{Y}$ are such that

$$\mathbb{E}[g(\boldsymbol{X})] \leq \mathbb{E}[g(\boldsymbol{Y})] \quad \text{for all non-decreasing functions } g : \mathbb{R}^n \to \mathbb{R} \text{ that are directionally convex,}$$

provided the expectations exist. Then $\boldsymbol{X}$ is said to be smaller than $\boldsymbol{Y}$ in the increasing directionally convex order (denoted by $\boldsymbol{X} \preceq_{\text{IDCX}} \boldsymbol{Y}$). ∇

The directional convex order was first introduced by Shaked and Shanthikumar (1990). It is closely related to the supermodular order (studied in Part II). The main difference between the directionally convex order and the supermodular order is that latter compares only dependence structures of random vectors with fixed marginals, whereas the former additionally takes into account the variability of the marginals, which may then be different.

3.4.14.5 Equivalent conditions

The following result offers a characterization of the multivariate $\preceq_{\rm SL}$ by means of its univariate counterpart.

Proposition 3.4.65
Given two n-dimensional random vectors $\boldsymbol{X}$ and $\boldsymbol{Y}$, $\boldsymbol{X} \preceq_{\rm SL} \boldsymbol{Y}$ if, and only if, the stochastic inequality $\Psi(\boldsymbol{X}) \preceq_{\rm SL} \Psi(\boldsymbol{Y})$ holds for any non-decreasing convex function $\Psi : \mathbb{R}^n \to \mathbb{R}$.

Proof. Since $\Psi(\boldsymbol{X}) \preceq_{\rm SL} \Psi(\boldsymbol{Y}) \Rightarrow \mathbb{E}[\Psi(\boldsymbol{X})] \leq \mathbb{E}[\Psi(\boldsymbol{Y})]$, the condition is obviously sufficient. Now, given any non-decreasing convex function $v : \mathbb{R} \to \mathbb{R}$, the composition $v \circ \Psi$ is also non-decreasing so that

$$\begin{aligned} \boldsymbol{X} \preceq_{\rm SL} \boldsymbol{Y} &\Rightarrow \mathbb{E}\big[v\big(\Psi(\boldsymbol{X})\big)\big] \leq \mathbb{E}\big[v\big(\Psi(\boldsymbol{Y})\big)\big] \text{ for every non-decreasing convex } v \\ &\Leftrightarrow \Psi(\boldsymbol{X}) \preceq_{\rm SL} \Psi(\boldsymbol{Y}), \end{aligned}$$

which concludes the proof. □

When $\boldsymbol{X}$ and $\boldsymbol{Y}$ represent multivariate risks, $\boldsymbol{X} \preceq_{\rm SL} \boldsymbol{Y}$ means that all profit-seeking risk-averse decision-makers prefer a loss $\Psi(\boldsymbol{X})$ over a loss $\Psi(\boldsymbol{Y})$ for any non-decreasing convex function Ψ. In particular, the implication

$$\boldsymbol{X} \preceq_{\rm SL} \boldsymbol{Y} \Rightarrow \sum_{i=1}^{n} \alpha_i X_i \preceq_{\rm SL} \sum_{i=1}^{n} \alpha_i Y_i$$

holds.

The multivariate convex and stop-loss orders can be characterized by construction on the same probability space as their univariate counterparts. This is stated next.

Proposition 3.4.66

(i) The random vectors $\boldsymbol{X}$ and $\boldsymbol{Y}$ satisfy $\boldsymbol{X} \preceq_{\rm SL,=} \boldsymbol{Y}$ if, and only if, there exist two random vectors $\widetilde{\boldsymbol{X}}$ and $\widetilde{\boldsymbol{Y}}$, defined on the same probability space, such that $\widetilde{\boldsymbol{X}} =_d \boldsymbol{X}$, $\widetilde{\boldsymbol{Y}} =_d \boldsymbol{Y}$ and $\mathbb{E}[\widetilde{\boldsymbol{Y}}|\widetilde{\boldsymbol{X}}] = \widetilde{\boldsymbol{X}}$.

(ii) Two random vectors $\boldsymbol{X}$ and $\boldsymbol{Y}$ satisfy $\boldsymbol{X} \preceq_{\rm SL} \boldsymbol{Y}$ if, and only if, there exist two random vectors $\widetilde{\boldsymbol{X}}$ and $\widetilde{\boldsymbol{Y}}$, defined on the same probability space, such that $\widetilde{\boldsymbol{X}} =_d \boldsymbol{X}$, $\widetilde{\boldsymbol{Y}} =_d \boldsymbol{Y}$ and $\mathbb{E}[\widetilde{\boldsymbol{Y}}|\widetilde{\boldsymbol{X}}] \geq \widetilde{\boldsymbol{X}}$.

3.4.14.6 Ordering for nonnegative linear combinations

The main interest of the multivariate stochastic orderings studied in this section is to be found in the following result.

Proposition 3.4.67
Let $\boldsymbol{X}$ and $\boldsymbol{Y}$ be two random vectors. If $\boldsymbol{X} \preceq_{\rm IDCX} \boldsymbol{Y}$ then $\Psi(\boldsymbol{X}) \preceq_{\rm SL} \Psi(\boldsymbol{Y})$ for any non-decreasing supermodular function $\Psi: \mathbb{R}^n \to \mathbb{R}$.

Proof. It suffices to note that the function g defined as $g(\boldsymbol{x})=t(\Psi(\boldsymbol{x}))$, with t non-decreasing and convex, is non-decreasing and directionally convex. Non-decreasingness is obvious, and the other properties come, for regular functions, from

$$\frac{\partial^2}{\partial x_i^2}g(\boldsymbol{x})=t''(\Psi(\boldsymbol{x}))\left(\frac{\partial}{\partial x_i}\Psi(\boldsymbol{x})\right)^2+t'(\Psi(\boldsymbol{x}))\frac{\partial^2}{\partial x_i^2}\Psi(\boldsymbol{x})\geq 0,$$

$$\frac{\partial^2}{\partial x_i\partial x_j}g(\boldsymbol{x})=t''(\Psi(\boldsymbol{x}))\frac{\partial}{\partial x_i}\Psi(\boldsymbol{x})\frac{\partial}{\partial x_j}\Psi(\boldsymbol{x})+t'(\Psi(\boldsymbol{x}))\frac{\partial^2}{\partial x_i\partial x_j}\Psi(\boldsymbol{x})\geq 0.$$

□

In particular, we have that

$$\boldsymbol{X}\preceq_{\text{IDCX}}\boldsymbol{Y}\Rightarrow\sum_{i=1}^{n}\alpha_iX_i\preceq_{\text{SL=}}\sum_{i=1}^{n}\alpha_iY_i$$

for all non-negative constants $\alpha_1,\alpha_2,\ldots,\alpha_n$.

3.5 EXERCISES

Exercise 3.5.1. (Stochastic majorant and minorant). Show that, given any pair (X,Y) of rvs, it is always possible to construct an rv Z_+ such that the stochastic inequalities $X\preceq_{\text{ST}}Z_+$ and $Y\preceq_{\text{ST}}Z_+$ both hold. Similarly, find Z_- such that the stochastic inequalities $Z_-\preceq_{\text{ST}}X$ and $Z_-\preceq_{\text{ST}}Y$ are both valid.

Exercise 3.5.2. Let X and Y be independent rvs. Show that $X\preceq_{\text{ST}}Y$ if, and only if, $g(X,Y)\preceq_{\text{ST}}g(Y,X)$ for all functions $g:\mathbb{R}^2\to\mathbb{R}$ such that $g(x,y)$ is non-decreasing in x and non-increasing in y.

Exercise 3.5.3. Let $X_{(1)}\leq X_{(2)}\leq\ldots\leq X_{(m)}$ be the order statistics corresponding to the rvs $X_1,X_2,\ldots,X_m$, and let $Y_{(1)}\leq Y_{(2)}\leq\ldots\leq Y_{(m)}$ be the order statistics corresponding to the rvs $Y_1,Y_2,\ldots,Y_m$. Prove the following statements:

(i) Let $X_1,X_2,\ldots,X_m$ be independent rvs with respective dfs $F_1,F_2,\ldots,F_m$. Let $Y_1,Y_2,\ldots,Y_m$ be independent rvs with a common df G. Then $X_{(i)}\preceq_{\text{ST}}Y_{(i)}$ for all $i=1,2,\ldots,m$ if, and only if,

$$\prod_{j=1}^{m}F_j(x)\geq G^m(x)\quad\text{for all } x,$$

that is, if, and only if, $X_{(m)}\preceq_{\text{ST}}Y_{(m)}$.

(ii) Let $X_1,X_2,\ldots,X_m$ be independent rvs with respective tfs $\overline{F}_1,\overline{F}_2,\ldots,\overline{F}_m$. Let $Y_1,Y_2,\ldots,Y_m$ be independent rvs with a common tf $\overline{G}$. Then $Y_{(i)}\preceq_{\text{ST}}Y_{(i)}$ for all $i=1,2,\ldots,m$ if, and only if,

$$\prod_{j=1}^{m}\overline{F}_j(x)\geq\overline{G}^m(x)\quad\text{for all } x,$$

that is, if, and only if, $Y_{(1)}\preceq_{\text{ST}}X_{(1)}$.

Exercise 3.5.4. (Stochastic increasingness). Check that the families $X_\theta =_d [X|X \leq \theta]$ and $X_\theta =_d [X|X > \theta]$ are both stochastically increasing.

Exercise 3.5.5. Let X and Y be two independent rvs. Show that the following conditions are equivalent:

(i) $X \preceq_{\text{HR}} Y$.

(ii) $\mathbb{E}[\alpha(X)]\mathbb{E}[\beta(Y)] \leq \mathbb{E}[\alpha(Y)]\mathbb{E}[\beta(X)]$ for all functions α and β for which the expectations exist and such that β is non-negative and α/β and β are non-decreasing.

(iii) For any two non-decreasing functions a and b such that b is non-negative, if $\mathbb{E}[a(X)b(X)] = 0$, then $\mathbb{E}[a(Y)b(Y)] \geq 0$.

Exercise 3.5.6. (Hazard Rate order and extrema). Let X and Y be two independent rvs. Show that $X \preceq_{\text{HR}} Y$ if,and only if,

$$\left[X\middle|\min\{X, Y\} = z\right] \preceq_{\text{ST}} \left[Y\middle|\min\{X, Y\} = z\right] \quad \text{for all } z.$$

Exercise 3.5.7. Let g be a non-decreasing and convex function such that $g(0) = 0$. Let X and Y be non-negative rvs such that $X \preceq_{\text{HR}} Y$. Show that

$$\frac{\mathbb{E}[g(X)]}{\mathbb{E}[X]} \leq \frac{\mathbb{E}[g(Y)]}{\mathbb{E}[Y]}.$$

Exercise 3.5.8. Show that if $X \preceq_{\text{HR}} Y$ and if $\dfrac{r_Y(t)}{r_X(t)}$ increases in t, then $X \preceq_{\text{LR}} Y$.

Exercise 3.5.9. Let X be a non-negative rv with a log-concave pdf, and let $a \leq 1$ be a positive constant. Show that $aX \preceq_{\text{LR}} X$.

Exercise 3.5.10. Let $\{X_j,\ j = 1, 2, \ldots\}$ and $\{Y_j,\ j = 1, 2, \ldots\}$ be two sequences of rvs such that $X_j \to_d X$ and $Y_j \to_d Y$ as $j \to +\infty$. If $X_j \preceq_{\text{LR}} Y_j$ for all $j = 1, 2, \ldots$, then show that $X \preceq_{\text{LR}} Y$.

Exercise 3.5.11. Let X be any rv. Show that $X_{(-\infty,a]}$ and $X_{(a,\infty)}$ are increasing in a in the sense of the likelihood ratio order.

Exercise 3.5.12. Let X and Y be two independent rvs such that both have continuous or both have discrete distributions.

(i) Show that if $X \preceq_{\text{LR}} Y$, then $X \preceq_{\text{LR}} \max\{X, Y\}$.

(ii) Show that if $X \preceq_{\text{LR}} Y$, then $\min\{X, Y\} \preceq_{\text{LR}} Y$.

Exercise 3.5.13. Let X, Y and Z be independent rvs. If $X \preceq_{\text{LR}} Y$ then show that

$$\left[X\middle|X + Y = v\right] \preceq_{\text{LR}} \left[Y\middle|X + Y = v\right] \quad \text{for all } v,$$

$$\left[X\middle|X + Z = v\right] \preceq_{\text{LR}} \left[Y\middle|Y + Z = v\right] \quad \text{for all } v,$$

$$\left[Z\middle|X + Z = v\right] \preceq_{\text{LR}} \left[Z\middle|Y + Z = v\right] \quad \text{for all } v.$$

Exercise 3.5.14. Let X, Y and Z be three independent rvs with continuous dfs.

(i) Show that if $X \preceq_{\rm LR} Y \preceq_{\rm LR} Z$, then $\max\{X, Y\} \preceq_{\rm LR} \max\{Y, Z\}$.

(ii) Show that if $X \preceq_{\rm LR} Y \preceq_{\rm LR} Z$, then $\min\{X, Y\} \preceq_{\rm LR} \min\{Y, Z\}$.

Exercise 3.5.15. Let X and Y be two non-negative rvs with finite means. Then show that $X \preceq_{\rm HR} Y$ if, and only if, $X_{\{1\}} \preceq_{\rm LR} Y_{\{1\}}$.

Exercise 3.5.16. Let X and Y be independent rvs. Show that $\mathbb{E}[Y]X \preceq_{\rm SL,=} YX$.

Exercise 3.5.17. For any positive X with mean μ and variance σ^2, show that $\overline{F}_X$ is dominated everywhere by

$$\overline{F}_{\max}(x) = \begin{cases} 1, & \text{if } x \leq \mu, \\ \frac{\mu}{x}, & \text{if } \mu < x < \mu + \frac{\sigma^2}{\mu}, \\ \frac{1}{1+\left(\frac{x-\mu}{\sigma}\right)^2}, & \text{if } x > \mu + \frac{\sigma^2}{\mu}. \end{cases}$$

Exercise 3.5.18. For any positive X with mean μ and variance σ^2, define $p_1 = F_X(\mu)$ and $p_2 = F_X(\mu + \frac{\sigma^2}{\mu})$. Show that

$$\mathrm{VaR}[X; p] \leq \begin{cases} \frac{\mu}{1-p}, & \text{if } p_1 < p < p_2, \\ \mu + \sigma\sqrt{\frac{p}{1-p}}, & \text{if } p > p_2. \end{cases}$$

Exercise 3.5.19. For any positive X with mean μ and variance σ^2 such that $\max[X] = b < +\infty$, show that $\overline{F}_X$ is dominated everywhere by

$$\overline{F}_{\max}(x) = \begin{cases} 1, & \text{if } x \leq \mu - \frac{\sigma^2}{b-\mu}, \\ \frac{\mu(b-x)-\sigma^2-\mu^2}{bx}, & \text{if } \mu - \frac{\sigma^2}{b-\mu} < x < \mu + \frac{\sigma^2}{\mu}, \\ \frac{1}{1+\left(\frac{x-\mu}{\sigma}\right)^2}, & \text{if } x > \mu + \frac{\sigma^2}{\mu}. \end{cases}$$

Exercise 3.5.20. For two rvs X and Y, show that $X \preceq_{\rm HR} Y$ if, and only if,

$$\frac{\overline{F}_X(\mathrm{VaR}[Y; 1-u])}{u} \leq \frac{\overline{F}_X(\mathrm{VaR}[Y; 1-v])}{v} \tag{3.78}$$

for all $0 < u \leq v < 1$.

Exercise 3.5.21. Let X have support in $[a, b]$ and mean μ. Consider the rvs $X_{\min}$ and $X_{\max}$ defined by $X_{\min} = \mu$ and

$$X_{\max} = \begin{cases} a, & \text{with probability } p_1 = \frac{b-\mu}{b-a}, \\ b, & \text{with probability } p_2 = \frac{\mu-a}{b-a}. \end{cases}$$

Show that $X_{\min} \preceq_{\rm SL,=} X \preceq_{\rm SL,=} X_{\max}$.

Exercise 3.5.22. Let X be a non-negative rv with mean μ.

(i) Suppose that X has a pdf that is decreasing on $[0, \infty)$ and $Y \sim \mathcal{U}ni(0, 2\mu)$. Then show that $Y \preceq_{\mathrm{SL},=} X$.

(ii) Suppose that X has a pdf that is decreasing and convex on $[0, \infty)$. Let Z have pdf

$$f_Z(x) = \begin{cases} \frac{2}{3\mu} - \frac{2}{9\mu^2}x, & \text{if } 0 \le x \le 3\mu, \\ 0, & \text{otherwise.} \end{cases}$$

Show that $Z \preceq_{\mathrm{SL},=} X$.

Exercise 3.5.23. Let X be an rv with a finite mean. Show that $X + \mathbb{E}[X] \preceq_{\mathrm{SL},=} 2X$.

Exercise 3.5.24. Let X and Y be independent random variables with finite means and suppose that $\mathbb{E}[Y] = 0$. Show that $X \preceq_{\mathrm{SL},=} X + Y$.

Exercise 3.5.25. Given two rvs X and Y, show that $X \preceq_{\mathrm{MEF}} Y$ if, and only if,

$$\frac{\mathbb{E}[(X-t)_+]}{\mathbb{E}[(Y-t)_+]} \quad \text{decreases in } t \text{ over} \{t : \mathbb{E}[(Y-t)_+] > 0\}. \tag{3.79}$$

Exercise 3.5.26. Let X and Y be two rvs and suppose that $\frac{e_X(t)}{e_Y(t)}$ increases in t. Show that $X \preceq_{\mathrm{MEF}} Y \Rightarrow X \preceq_{\mathrm{HR}} Y$.

Exercise 3.5.27. Let X and Y be two nonnegative rvs and

$$\frac{e_X(t)}{e_Y(t)} \ge \frac{e_X(0)}{e_Y(0)} = \frac{\mathbb{E}[X]}{\mathbb{E}[Y]}.$$

Show that $X \preceq_{\mathrm{MEF}} Y \Rightarrow X \preceq_{\mathrm{ST}} Y$.

Exercise 3.5.28. For non-negative rvs X and Y with finite means, show that $X \preceq_{\mathrm{MEF}} Y \Leftrightarrow X_{\{1\}} \preceq_{\mathrm{HR}} Y_{\{1\}}$.

Exercise 3.5.29. Let X_1 and X_2 be a pair of independent non-negative rvs, and let Y_1 and Y_2 be another pair of independent non-negative rvs. If $X_i \preceq_{\mathrm{SL},=} Y_i$, $i = 1, 2$, then show that $X_1 X_2 \preceq_{\mathrm{SL},=} Y_1 Y_2$.

Exercise 3.5.30. Let X and Y be two rvs with finite means. Show that

$$X \preceq_{\mathrm{DISP}} Y \Rightarrow X - \mathbb{E}[X] \preceq_{\mathrm{SL}=} Y - \mathbb{E}[Y].$$

Exercise 3.5.31. Let X be a continuous rv. Show that:

(i) If F_X is log-concave then $X_{(-\infty,a]}$ increases in a in the $\preceq_{\mathrm{DISP}}$ sense.

(ii) If $\overline{F}_X$ is log-concave (i,e., if X is IFR) then $X_{(a,\infty)}$ decreases in a in the $\preceq_{\mathrm{DISP}}$ sense.

(iii) If f_X is log-concave then $X_{(a,b)}$ decreases in $a < b$ and increases in $b > a$ in the $\preceq_{\mathrm{DISP}}$ sense.

Exercise 3.5.32. When X and Y have finite means, X is said to precede Y in the dilation order, written as $X \preceq_{\text{DIL}} Y$, if

$$X - \mathbb{E}[X] \preceq_{\text{SL}=} Y - \mathbb{E}[Y]. \tag{3.80}$$

Prove the following:

(i) $X \preceq_{\text{DIL}} Y$ holds if, and only if,

$$\frac{1}{1-p}\int_p^1 (\text{VaR}[X;u] - \text{VaR}[Y;u])\,du$$
$$\leq \int_0^1 (\text{VaR}[X;u] - \text{VaR}[Y;u])\,du \quad \text{for all } p \in [0,1). \tag{3.81}$$

(ii) $X \preceq_{\text{DIL}} Y$ holds if, and only if,

$$\int_0^1 (\text{VaR}[X;u] - \text{VaR}[Y;u])\,du$$
$$\leq \frac{1}{p}\int_0^p (\text{VaR}[X;u] - \text{VaR}[Y;u])\,du \quad \text{for all } p \in (0,1].$$

(iii) $X \preceq_{\text{DIL}} Y$ holds if, and only if,

$$\frac{1}{1-p}\int_p^1 (\text{VaR}[X;u] - \text{VaR}[Y;u])\,du$$
$$\leq \frac{1}{p}\int_0^p (\text{VaR}[X;u] - \text{VaR}[Y;u])\,du \quad \text{for all } p \in (0,1).$$

(iv) Each of the following three statements is a necessary and sufficient condition for $X \preceq_{\text{DIL}} Y$:

$$\mathbb{E}\big[X \big| X \geq \text{VaR}[X;p]\big] - \mathbb{E}\big[Y \big| Y \geq \text{VaR}[Y;p]\big] \leq \mathbb{E}[X] - \mathbb{E}[Y] \tag{3.82}$$

for all $p \in [0,1)$;

$$\mathbb{E}\big[X \big| X \leq \text{VaR}[X;p]\big] - \mathbb{E}\big[Y \big| Y \leq \text{VaR}[Y;p]\big] \geq \mathbb{E}[X] - \mathbb{E}[Y] \tag{3.83}$$

for all $p \in (0,1]$;

$$\mathbb{E}\big[X \big| X \geq \text{VaR}[X;p]\big] - \mathbb{E}\big[Y \big| Y \geq \text{VaR}[Y;p]\big]$$
$$\leq \mathbb{E}\big[X \big| X \leq \text{VaR}[X;p]\big] - \mathbb{E}\big[Y \big| Y \leq \text{VaR}[Y;p]\big]$$

for all $p \in (0,1)$.

(v) The non-negative rv X is IMRL if, and only if,

$$[X \big| X > t] \preceq_{\text{DIL}} [X \big| X > t'] \quad \text{whenever } t \leq t'.$$

(vi) $X \preceq_{\text{DIL}} kX$ whenever $k \geq 1$.

(vii) $X \preceq_{\text{DIL}} Y \Leftrightarrow -X \preceq_{\text{DIL}} -Y$.

(viii) Let X_1 and X_2 (Y_1 and Y_2) be two independent copies of X (of Y), where X and Y have finite means. If $X \preceq_{\text{DIL}} Y$ then $X_1 - X_2 \preceq_{\text{DIL}} Y_1 - Y_2$.

Exercise 3.5.33. Let $\boldsymbol{X}$ and $\boldsymbol{Y}$ be two n-dimensional random vectors. If $Y_1, Y_2, \ldots, Y_n$ are independent and if

$$X_1 \preceq_{\text{SL},=} Y_1, \tag{3.84}$$

$$[X_2|X_1] = x_1 \preceq_{\text{SL},=} Y_2 \quad \text{for all } x_1, \tag{3.85}$$

and, in general, for $i = 2, 3, \ldots, n$,

$$[X_i | X_1 = x_1, \ldots, X_{i-1} = x_{i-1}] \preceq_{\text{SL},=} Y_i \quad \text{for all } x_j,\ j = 1, 2, \ldots, i-1, \tag{3.86}$$

then show that $\boldsymbol{X} \preceq_{\text{SL},=} \boldsymbol{Y}$.

In particular,

(i) deduce that under (3.84)–(3.86) the stochastic inequality $\sum_{j=1}^n X_j \preceq_{\text{SL},=} \sum_{j=1}^n Y_j$ holds;

(ii) let $X_1, X_2, \ldots, X_n$ be a set of independent rvs and let $Y_1, Y_2, \ldots, Y_n$ be another set of independent rvs. If $X_i \preceq_{\text{SL},=} Y_i$ for $i = 1, 2, \ldots, n$, then show that $\boldsymbol{X} \preceq_{\text{SL},=} \boldsymbol{Y}$.

Exercise 3.5.34. Let $\boldsymbol{X}_1, \boldsymbol{X}_2, \ldots$ be independent and identically distributed m-dimensional random vectors. Denote by $\overline{\boldsymbol{X}}_n$ the sample mean of $\boldsymbol{X}_1, \boldsymbol{X}_2, \ldots, \boldsymbol{X}_n$, that is, $\overline{\boldsymbol{X}}_n = (\boldsymbol{X}_1 + \boldsymbol{X}_2 + \ldots$

Table 3.1 Stochastic order relations in parametric models

Probability dist.	Constraints on the parameters	Stochastic ineq.
Exponential	$\lambda_1 \leq \lambda_2$	$\mathcal{E}xp(\lambda_1) \preceq_{\text{LR}} \mathcal{E}xp(\lambda_2)$
Normal	$\sigma_1 \leq \sigma_2$	$\mathcal{N}or(\mu_1, \sigma_1) \preceq_{\text{DISP}} \mathcal{N}or(\mu_2, \sigma_2)$
	$\mu_1 \leq \mu_2,\ \sigma_1 = \sigma_2$	$\mathcal{N}or(\mu_1, \sigma_1) \preceq_{\text{LR}} \mathcal{N}or(\mu_2, \sigma_2)$
	$\mu_1 = \mu_2,\ \sigma_1 \leq \sigma_2$	$\mathcal{N}or(\mu_1, \sigma_1) \preceq_{\text{SL},=} \mathcal{N}or(\mu_2, \sigma_2)$
	$\mu_1 \leq \mu_2,\ \sigma_1 \leq \sigma_2$	$\mathcal{N}or(\mu_1, \sigma_1) \preceq_{\text{SL}} \mathcal{N}or(\mu_2, \sigma_2)$
Gamma	$\alpha_1 \leq \alpha_2,\ \tau_1 \geq \tau_2$	$\mathcal{G}am(\alpha_1, \tau_1) \preceq_{\text{LR}} \mathcal{G}am(\alpha_2, \tau_2)$
	$\alpha_1 \geq \alpha_2,\ \frac{\alpha_1}{\tau_1} \leq \frac{\alpha_2}{\tau_2}$	$\mathcal{G}am(\alpha_1, \tau_1) \preceq_{\text{SL}} \mathcal{G}am(\alpha_2, \tau_2)$
Lognormal	$\mu_1 \leq \mu_2,\ \sigma_1 = \sigma_2$	$\mathcal{LN}or(\mu_1, \sigma_1) \preceq_{\text{LR}} \mathcal{LN}or(\mu_2, \sigma_2)$
	$\exp(\mu_1 + \sigma_1^2/2) \leq \exp(\mu_2 + \sigma_2^2/2),\ \sigma_1 \leq \sigma_2$	$\mathcal{LN}or(\mu_1, \sigma_1) \preceq_{\text{SL}} \mathcal{LN}or(\mu_2, \sigma_2)$
Uniform	$a_1 \leq a_2,\ b_1 \leq b_2$	$\mathcal{U}ni(a_1, b_1) \preceq_{\text{ST}} \mathcal{U}ni(a_2, b_2)$
	$a_1 + b_1 \leq a_2 + b_2,\ b_1 \leq b_2$	$\mathcal{U}ni(a_1, b_1) \preceq_{\text{SL}} \mathcal{U}ni(a_2, b_2)$
	$b_1 - a_1 \leq b_2 - a_2$	$\mathcal{U}ni(a_1, b_1) \preceq_{\text{DISP}} \mathcal{U}ni(a_2, b_2)$
Poisson	$\lambda_1 \leq \lambda_2$	$\mathcal{P}oi(\lambda_1) \preceq_{\text{LR}} \mathcal{P}oi(\lambda_2)$
Binomial	$n_1 \leq n_2,\ p_1 \leq p_2$	$\mathcal{B}in(n_1, p_1) \preceq_{\text{LR}} \mathcal{B}in(n_2, p_2)$
Geometric	$q_{\leq} q_2$	$\mathcal{G}eo(q_1) \preceq_{\text{LR}} \mathcal{G}eo(q_2)$
		$\mathcal{G}eo(q_1) \preceq_{\text{DISP}} \mathcal{G}eo(q_2)$

$+X_n)/n$. If the expectation of X_1 exists, then for any choice of positive integers $n \leq n'$, show that one has

$$\overline{X}_{n'} \preceq_{\mathrm{SL},=} \overline{X}_n.$$

Exercise 3.5.35. Prove the stochastic inequalities shown in Table 3.1.

Exercise 3.5.36. Let $X_1, X_2, \ldots, X_n$ be a set of independent rvs and let $Y_1, Y_2, \ldots, Y_n$ be another set of independent rvs. If $X_i \preceq_{\mathrm{SL},=} Y_i$ for $i = 1, 2, \ldots, n$, then show that $\boldsymbol{X} \preceq_{\mathrm{SL},=} \boldsymbol{Y}$.

Exercise 3.5.37. (i) Let $\boldsymbol{X}$ and $\boldsymbol{Y}$ be two non-negative random vectors. If $\boldsymbol{X} \preceq_{\mathrm{SL}} \boldsymbol{Y}$, and if $\mathbb{E}[X_i X_j] = \mathbb{E}[Y_i Y_j]$ for all i and j, then show that $\boldsymbol{X} =_d \boldsymbol{Y}$.

(ii) Let $\boldsymbol{X}$ and $\boldsymbol{Y}$ be two random vectors. If $\boldsymbol{X} \preceq_{\mathrm{SL},=} \boldsymbol{Y}$, and if $\mathbb{V}[X_i] = \mathbb{V}[Y_i]$, $i = 1, 2, \ldots, n$, then show that $\boldsymbol{X} =_d \boldsymbol{Y}$.

PART II
Dependence Between Risks

The independence hypothesis is so commonly made that many authors forget to mention it.

Bühlmann (1960)

4

Modelling Dependence

Modern financial and insurance risk management is faced with a multitude of risk factors. Hence the need to model dependence beyond multivariate normality has become crucial in many applications. This chapter is concerned with the modelling of the dependence structure between several risks using the concept of copulas.

The essence of the copula approach is that a joint distribution of rvs can be expressed as a function of the marginal dfs. The basics of constructing a copula-based model are given in this chapter, showing how this approach can be implemented using standard parametric families of copulas.

4.1 INTRODUCTION

A central step in risk analysis is the construction of a statistical model that portrays the randomness inherent in the situation. For a long time, statistical modelling in actuarial science and finance basically relied on simplified assumptions. The normal distribution dominated the study of multivariate distributions: it was frequently assumed but seldom contested. Multivariate normal distributions are appealing because of their easy mathematical treatment and tractability. In this case, the association between two random outcomes can be fully described knowing only the marginal distributions and one additional parameter, the correlation coefficient. Over the years, statisticians have begun to recognize the need to examine alternatives to the normal distribution set-up. This is certainly true for actuarial applications where the normal distribution does not provide an adequate approximation to many data sets (think, for instance, of lifetime rvs or long-tailed claims variables). See Embrechts, McNeil and Straumann (2002) and Embrechts, Lindskog and McNeil (2003) for examples.

An extensive literature in statistics deals with non-normal multivariate distributions; see, for instance, Johnson and Kotz (1992) as well as Kotz, Balakrishnan and Johnson (2000). However, historically many multivariate distributions have been developed as immediate extensions of univariate distributions, examples being the bivariate Pareto, gamma, and so on. Possible drawbacks of these types of distributions are that (i) a different family is needed for each marginal distribution and (ii) measures of association often appear in the marginal distribution. The following two examples illustrate these facts.

Example 4.1.1. (The Marshall–Olkin bivariate exponential distribution). Suppose that we aim to model two remaining lifetimes that we suspect are subject to some common

Actuarial Theory for Dependent Risks M. Denuit, J. Dhaene, M. Goovaerts and R. Kaas

disaster, or 'shock', that may induce a dependence between the lives. Let us assume that Y_1 and Y_2 are two independent (underlying) lifetimes with dfs H_1 and H_2. We further assume that there exists an independent rv $Z \sim \mathcal{E}xp(\lambda)$ that represents the time until common disaster. Since both lives are subject to the same disaster, the age-at-death rvs X_1 and X_2 are given by

$$X_1 = \min\{Y_1, Z\} \text{ and } X_2 = \min\{Y_2, Z\}.$$

Let us now assume that $Y_1 \sim \mathcal{E}xp(\lambda_1)$ and $Y_2 \sim \mathcal{E}xp(\lambda_2)$. Denote by $\overline{F}_1$ and $\overline{F}_2$ the tfs for X_1 and X_2. Clearly,

$$\begin{aligned}\overline{F}_1(x_1) &= \Pr[Y_1 > x_1]\Pr[Z > x_1] = \exp\big(-(\lambda+\lambda_1)x_1\big),\\ \overline{F}_2(x_2) &= \Pr[Y_2 > x_2]\Pr[Z > x_2] = \exp\big(-(\lambda+\lambda_2)x_2\big),\end{aligned}$$

so that $X_1 \sim \mathcal{E}xp(\lambda+\lambda_1)$ and $X_2 \sim \mathcal{E}xp(\lambda+\lambda_2)$. Note that the joint tf of the couple $\boldsymbol{X} = (X_1, X_2)$ is given by

$$\begin{aligned}\overline{F}_{\boldsymbol{X}}(\boldsymbol{x}) &= \Pr[Y_1 > x_1, Y_2 > x_2, Z > \max\{x_1, x_2\}]\\ &= \exp(-\lambda_1 x_1)\exp(-\lambda_2 x_2)\exp(-\lambda \max\{x_1, x_2\})\\ &= \overline{F}_1(x_1)\overline{F}_2(x_2)\min\{\exp(\lambda x_1), \exp(\lambda x_2)\},\end{aligned}$$

so that the joint df of $\boldsymbol{X}$ is

$$\begin{aligned}F_{\boldsymbol{X}}(\boldsymbol{x}) &= F_1(x_1) + F_2(x_2) - 1\\ &\quad + \overline{F}_1(x_1)\overline{F}_2(x_2)\min\{\exp(\lambda x_1), \exp(\lambda x_2)\}.\end{aligned} \tag{4.1}$$

For actuarial applications of the bivariate exponential distribution, see Bowers *et al.* (1997, Section 9.6). ∇

Example 4.1.1 clearly illustrates the drawbacks mentioned above. To get a bivariate distribution with exponential marginals, we have had to opt for X_1, X_2 and Z exponentially distributed. This construction does not easily carry over to other distributions: lognormal marginals cannot be obtained in this way, for instance.

The dependence is induced by the common factor Z involved in both X_1 and X_2. The strength of dependence is driven by λ. This dependence parameter appears both in the marginal and in the joint distributions, which makes its interpretation more difficult.

Note that extension to the multivariate case is straightforward (simply using $X_i = \min\{Y_i, Z\}$, $i = 1, 2, \ldots, n$), but this is not always the case for such direct constructions.

Example 4.1.2. (Bivariate Pareto distribution). Consider a claims rv X that, given $\Theta = \theta$, is distributed according to the $\mathcal{E}xp(\theta)$ distribution. As is well known in credibility theory, if $\Theta \sim \mathcal{G}am(\alpha, \lambda)$ then $X \sim \mathcal{P}ar(\alpha, \lambda)$; this is because

$$\begin{aligned}F_X(x) &= 1 - \int_0^{+\infty} \exp(-\theta x)\frac{\alpha^\lambda}{\Gamma(\lambda)}\theta^{\alpha-1}\exp(-\lambda\theta)d\theta\\ &= 1 - \left(1 + \frac{x}{\lambda}\right)^{-\alpha}.\end{aligned}$$

Suppose that, conditionally on $\Theta=\theta$, $X_1 \sim \mathcal{E}xp(\theta)$ and $X_2 \sim \mathcal{E}xp(\theta)$ are independent rvs. If they share the same random effect, they become dependent and the joint df of $\boldsymbol{X}=(X_1, X_2)$ is obtained as follows:

$$\begin{aligned} F_{\boldsymbol{X}}(\boldsymbol{x}) &= 1-\overline{F}_{X_1}(x_1)-\overline{F}_{X_2}(x_2)+\overline{F}_{\boldsymbol{X}}(\boldsymbol{x}) \\ &= 1-\left(1+\frac{x_1}{\lambda}\right)^{-\alpha}-\left(1+\frac{x_2}{\lambda}\right)^{-\alpha}+\int_0^{+\infty}\exp(-\theta(x_1+x_2))\frac{\alpha^\lambda}{\Gamma(\lambda)}\theta^{\alpha-1}\exp(-\lambda\theta)d\theta \\ &= 1-\left(1+\frac{x_1}{\lambda}\right)^{-\alpha}-\left(1+\frac{x_2}{\lambda}\right)^{-\alpha}+\left(1+\frac{x_1+x_2}{\lambda}\right)^{-\alpha}, \end{aligned}$$

so that

$$F_{\boldsymbol{X}}(\boldsymbol{x})=F_{X_1}(x_1)+F_{X_2}(x_2)-1+\left(\left(\overline{F}_{X_1}(x_1)\right)^{-1/\alpha}+\left(\overline{F}_{X_2}(x_2)\right)^{-1/\alpha}-1\right)^{-\alpha}. \tag{4.2}$$

The dependence is induced here by a common mixture model. This construction is typically used in credibility theory to account for residual heterogeneity; this will be studied in Chapter 7. ∇

Again, Example 4.1.2 highlights some shortcomings of the direct construction of multivariate distributions. It is not clear whether we can generate bivariate distributions with any marginals in this way: for instance, exponential marginals cannot be obtained via common mixture. Multivariate extensions are straightforward. The dependence is induced by Θ and its strength is controlled by α, which appears both in the marginals and the joint distributions.

The construction of multivariate distributions based on copulas does not suffer from the drawbacks mentioned above. Using a copula as a basis for constructing a multivariate model is flexible because no restrictions are placed on the marginal distributions. With the copula construction offered by Sklar's theorem, we select different marginals for each outcome. For instance, if we are dealing with a bivariate outcome associated with the loss and the expenses associated with administering a property and casualty claim, we could use a lognormal distribution for expenses and a longer-tailed distribution, such as the Pareto, for losses associated with the claim. Then it suffices to plug these marginals into a suitable copula to get the bivariate distribution. So the copula construction does not constrain the choice of marginal distributions.

Although copulas are particularly useful for modelling dependencies between continuous rvs, their application to discrete distributions is rather disappointing. This is mainly due to the lack of a discrete analogue to the probability integral transform construction, recalled in Section 1.5.8.3. In this chapter, unless explicitly stated otherwise, all the rvs are assumed to be continuous.

Copulas were briefly presented in Kaas *et al.* (2001, Example 10.6.11). The present chapter offers a cursory introduction to copulas. Readers interested in a more advanced treatment of the topic are referred to Nelsen (1999) for a self-contained technical introduction. Applications of copulas to data modelling in an actuarial context have been proposed by Carrière and Chan (1986), Carrière (1994, 2000), Frees, Carrière and Valdez (1996), Frees and Valdez (1998), Klugman and Parsa (1999) and Valdez (2001). Readers interested in copulas who wish to continue their study of this statistical tool should consult Drouet-Mari and Kotz (2001), Hutchinson and Lai (1990) and Joe (1997). Let us also mention the book by Cherubini, Luciano and Vecchiato (2004) on copula methods in finance. Vaz de Melo Mendes and Martins de Souza (2004) point to potential applications of copulas in measuring financial risk. The annotated bibliography offered by Frees and Valdez (1998) is also very helpful.

4.2 SKLAR'S REPRESENTATION THEOREM

4.2.1 Copulas

Given a bivariate df F_X with univariate marginal dfs F_1 and F_2, we can associate three numbers with each pair of real numbers $\boldsymbol{x}=(x_1,x_2)$: $F_1(x_1)$, $F_2(x_2)$ and $F_X(\boldsymbol{x})$. Of course, each of these numbers lies in the unit interval $[0,1]$. In other words, each pair $\boldsymbol{x}$ of real numbers leads to a point $(F_1(x_1),F_2(x_2))$ in the unit square, and this pair in turn corresponds to a number $F_X(\boldsymbol{x})$ in $[0,1]$. We will see that this correspondence, which assigns the value of the joint df to each ordered pair of values of the individual dfs, is indeed a function; such functions are called copulas.

The word 'copula' was first employed in a statistical sense by Sklar (1959) in the theorem which now bears his name (see Theorem 4.2.2 below). His idea was to separate a joint df into a part that describes the dependence structure (the copula) and parts that describe the marginal behaviour only. As the term 'copula' is used to indicate a word or expression that links a subject to predicate, he felt that this would make an appropriate name for a function that links a multidimensional df to its one-dimensional marginals, and used it as such.

Let us define the notion of copula in the two-dimensional case. Essentially, a copula is a joint df for a bivariate random vector with $\mathcal{U}ni(0,1)$ marginals.

Definition 4.2.1. A bivariate copula C is a function mapping the unit square $[0,1]^2=[0,1]\times[0,1]$ to the unit interval $[0,1]$ that is non-decreasing and right-continuous, and satisfies the following conditions:

(i) $\lim_{u_i\to 0} C(u_1,u_2)=0$ for $i=1,2$;

(ii) $\lim_{u_1\to 1} C(u_1,u_2)=u_2$ and $\lim_{u_2\to 1} C(u_1,u_2)=u_1$;

(iii) C is supermodular, that is, the inequality

$$C(v_1,v_2)-C(u_1,v_2)-C(v_1,u_2)+C(u_1,u_2)\geq 0$$

is valid for any $u_1\leq v_1$, $u_2\leq v_2$.

∇

4.2.2 Sklar's theorem for continuous marginals

The theorem in the title of this section is central to the theory of copulas and is the foundation for most applications. Sklar's theorem elucidates the role that copulas play in the relationship between multivariate dfs and their univariate marginals.

Theorem 4.2.2. Let $F_X \in \mathcal{R}_2(F_1, F_2)$ have continuous marginal dfs F_1 and F_2. Then there exists a unique copula C such that for all $\boldsymbol{x} \in \mathbb{R}^2$,

$$F_X(x_1, x_2) = C\left(F_1(x_1), F_2(x_2)\right). \tag{4.3}$$

Conversely, if C is a copula and F_1 and F_2 are dfs then the function F_X defined by (4.3) is a bivariate df with margins F_1 and F_2.

Proof. Since the F_i are continuous, Property 1.5.19 guarantees that both $F_1(X_1)$ and $F_2(X_2)$ are $\mathcal{U}ni(0, 1)$. Let C be the joint df for the couple $\big(F_1(X_1), F_2(X_2)\big)$, that is,

$$\begin{aligned} C(u_1, u_2) &= \Pr\left[F_1(X_1) \leq u_1, F_2(X_2) \leq u_2\right] \\ &= \Pr\left[X_1 \leq F_1^{-1}(u_1), X_2 \leq F_2^{-1}(u_2)\right] \\ &= F_X\big(F_1^{-1}(u_1), F_2^{-1}(u_2)\big) \end{aligned}$$

where Lemma 1.5.15(i) has been used. Then the representation (4.3) holds since

$$\begin{aligned} F_X(x_1, x_2) &= \Pr[X_1 \leq x_1, X_2 \leq x_2] \\ &= \Pr\left[F_1(X_1) \leq F_1(x_1), F_2(X_2) \leq F_2(x_2)\right] \\ &= C\big(F_1(x_1), F_2(x_2)\big), \end{aligned}$$

as claimed. □

As can be seen from (4.3), C 'couples' the marginal dfs F_1 and F_2 to the joint distribution F_X of the pair $\boldsymbol{X}$. The dependence structure is entirely described by C and dissociated from the marginals F_1 and F_2. Thus, the manner in which X_1 and X_2 'move together' is captured by the copula, regardless of the scale in which the variable is measured.

As pointed out in the title of this section, we focus in this chapter on the mathematically tractable case where each F_i is continuous. In the discrete case, considered in Section 4.2.6, the copula is unique only on the Cartesian product of the ranges of F_1 and F_2 rather than on the whole unit cube. The proof of Sklar's decomposition in the general case is done in Theorem 4.2.19.

The rvs $F_1(X_1)$ and $F_2(X_2)$ are often called the ranks of X_1 and X_2. This makes the copula the joint df of the ranks.

Remark 4.2.3. Note that we have obtained in the proof of Theorem 4.2.2 an expression for the copula C involved in (4.3) when the marginals are continuous, that is,

$$C(\boldsymbol{u}) = F_X\big(F_1^{-1}(u_1), F_2^{-1}(u_2)\big), \quad \boldsymbol{u} \in [0, 1]^2. \tag{4.4}$$

∇

Let us now examine several elementary examples to illustrate the decomposition (4.3).

Example 4.2.4. (The independence copula C_I). Consider independent rvs X_1 and X_2, with respective dfs F_1 and F_2. Their joint df is given by $F_{\boldsymbol{X}}(\boldsymbol{x}) = F_1(x_1)F_2(x_2)$, so the underlying copula is

$$C_I(u_1, u_2) = u_1 u_2, \quad \boldsymbol{u} \in [0, 1]^2.$$

This is usually referred to as the independence copula.

The independence copula is shown in Figure 4.1 (middle panel). It corresponds to a pdf constantly equal to 1 over the unit square. If X_1 and X_2 possess the df (4.3) then they are independent if, and only if, $C \equiv C_I$. ∇

Example 4.2.5. (The Fréchet upper bound copula C_U). The Fréchet upper bound copula, denoted by C_U, is

$$C_U(u_1, u_2) = \min\{u_1, u_2\}, \quad \boldsymbol{u} \in [0, 1]^2.$$

It is shown in Figure 4.1 (top panel). It corresponds to a unit mass spread over the main diagonal $u_1 = u_2$ of the unit square. If X_1 and X_2 possess the df (4.3) then X_2 is a non-decreasing function of X_1 if, and only if, $C \equiv C_U$. So, (X_1, X_2) is comonotonic if, and only if, $C = C_U$. ∇

Example 4.2.6. (The Fréchet lower bound copula C_L). The Fréchet lower bound copula, denoted by C_L, is

$$C_L(u_1, u_2) = \max\{0, u_1 + u_2 - 1\}, \quad \boldsymbol{u} \in [0, 1]^2.$$

It is shown in Figure 4.1 (bottom panel). It corresponds to a unit mass spread over the secondary diagonal $u_1 = 1 - u_2$ of the unit square. If X_1 and X_2 possess the df (4.3) then X_2 is a non-increasing function of X_1 if, and only if, $C \equiv C_L$. So, (X_1, X_2) is countermonotonic if, and only if, $C = C_L$. ∇

Since copulas are bivariate dfs with unit uniform marginals, we know from (1.54) and (1.55) that the inequalities

$$C_L(u_1, u_2) \leq C(u_1, u_2) \leq C_U(u_1, u_2), \quad \text{for all } \boldsymbol{u} \in [0, 1]^2,$$

hold for every copula C. It follows that the graph of each copula is bounded from below by the two triangles that together make up the surface of C_L and from above by the two triangles that make up the surface C_U.

Example 4.2.7. (The bivariate Pareto copula). As an illustration, consider the bivariate Pareto distribution discussed in Example 4.1.2. Considering the expression (4.2) for the joint df, we see that the underlying copula function is

$$C(u_1, u_2) = u_1 + u_2 - 1 + \left((1 - u_1)^{-1/\alpha} + (1 - u_2)^{-1/\alpha} - 1\right)^{-\alpha},$$
$$\boldsymbol{u} \in [0, 1]^2.$$

∇

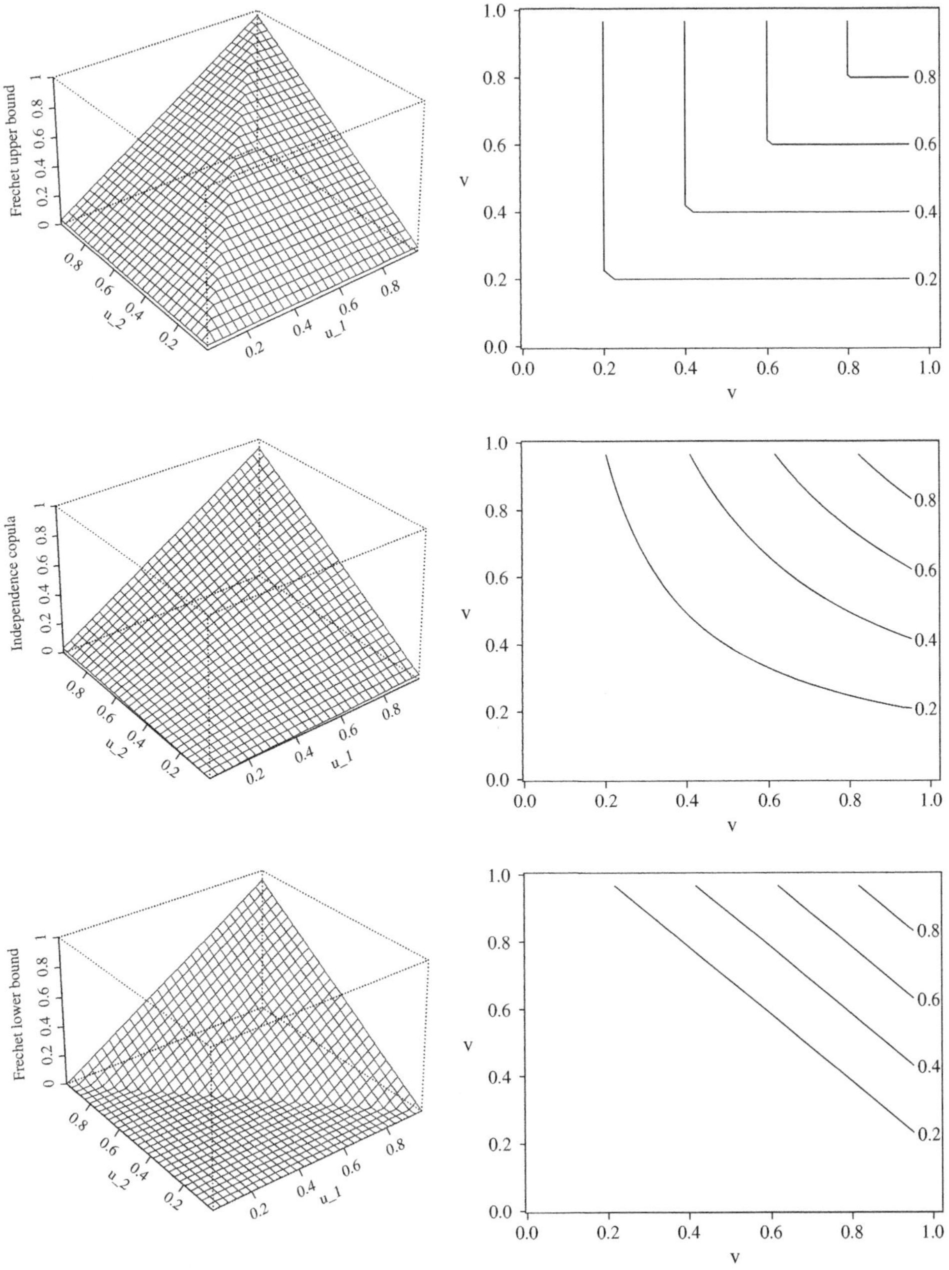

Figure 4.1 The Fréchet upper bound copula C_U (top), the independence copula C_I (middle) and the Fréchet lower bound copula C_L (bottom)

Example 4.2.8. (The Marshall–Olkin bivariate exponential copula). Return to the bivariate Marshall–Olkin distribution introduced in Example 4.1.1 and defined in (4.1), the underlying copula is not directly apparent. In order to find its actual expression, let us rewrite the joint tf as

$$\overline{F}_{\boldsymbol{X}}(\boldsymbol{x}) = \overline{F}_1(x_1)\overline{F}_2(x_2) \min\left\{\left(\overline{F}_1(x_1)\right)^{-\frac{\lambda}{\lambda_1+\lambda}}, \left(\overline{F}_2(x_2)\right)^{-\frac{\lambda}{\lambda_2+\lambda}}\right\}$$
$$= \min\left\{\overline{F}_2(x_2)\left(\overline{F}_1(x_1)\right)^{1-\frac{\lambda}{\lambda_1+\lambda}}, \overline{F}_1(x_1)\left(\overline{F}_2(x_2)\right)^{-\frac{\lambda}{\lambda_2+\lambda}}\right\}$$

so that Sklar's representation (4.3) for

$$F_{\boldsymbol{X}}(\boldsymbol{x}) = 1 - \overline{F}_1(x_1) - \overline{F}_2(x_2) + \overline{F}_{\boldsymbol{X}}(\boldsymbol{x}) = C\big(F_1(x_1), F_2(x_2)\big)$$

in (4.1) holds with

$$C(u_1, u_2) = 1 - (1-u_1) - (1-u_2)$$
$$+ \min\left\{(1-u_2)(1-u_1)^{1-\alpha_1}, (1-u_1)(1-u_2)^{1-\alpha_2}\right\},$$

$\boldsymbol{u} \in [0,1]^2$, where $\alpha_1 = \frac{\lambda}{\lambda_1+\lambda}$ and $\alpha_2 = \frac{\lambda}{\lambda_2+\lambda}$. ∇

4.2.3 Conditional distributions derived from copulas

Conditional distributions can be derived from the representation (4.3). To this end, we have to show that the partial derivatives $\frac{\partial}{\partial u_1}C$ and $\frac{\partial}{\partial u_2}C$ of the copula C exist. Let us first establish the following technical lemma.

Lemma 4.2.9
Let us consider $\boldsymbol{X} \in \mathcal{R}_2(F_1, F_2)$ with support $\mathcal{S}_1 \times \mathcal{S}_2$. Let x_1 and x_2 be in $\mathcal{S}_1$ with $x_1 \leq x_2$ and let y_1 and y_2 be in $\mathcal{S}_2$ with $y_1 \leq y_2$. Then, the function $t \mapsto F_{\boldsymbol{X}}(t, y_2) - F_{\boldsymbol{X}}(t, y_1)$ is non-decreasing on $\mathcal{S}_1$, and the function $t \mapsto F_{\boldsymbol{X}}(x_2, t) - F_{\boldsymbol{X}}(x_1, t)$ is non-decreasing on $\mathcal{S}_2$.

Proof. Consider $t_1 \leq t_2 \in \mathcal{S}_1$. Then

$$\Big(F_{\boldsymbol{X}}(t_2, y_2) - F_{\boldsymbol{X}}(t_2, y_1)\Big) - \Big(F_{\boldsymbol{X}}(t_1, y_2) - F_{\boldsymbol{X}}(t_1, y_1)\Big)$$
$$= \Pr\big[\boldsymbol{X} \in (t_1, t_2] \times (y_1, y_2]\big] \geq 0,$$

which concludes the proof. □

The following result establishes the continuity of copulas via a Lipschitz condition.

Proposition 4.2.10
Let $u_1, u_2, v_1, v_2 \in [0,1]$. Then

$$|C(u_1, u_2) - C(v_1, v_2)| \leq |u_1 - v_1| + |u_2 - v_2|.$$

Hence, C is uniformly continuous on $[0,1]^2$.

Proof. Let us show that given $\boldsymbol{X} \in \mathcal{R}_2(F_1, F_2)$ with support $\mathcal{S}_1 \times \mathcal{S}_2$, $\boldsymbol{x}$ and $\boldsymbol{y}$ any points in $\mathcal{S}_1 \times \mathcal{S}_2$, the inequality

$$|F_X(\boldsymbol{y}) - F_X(\boldsymbol{x})| \le |F_1(y_1) - F_1(x_1)| + |F_2(y_2) - F_2(x_2)|. \tag{4.5}$$

holds. From the triangle inequality, we have

$$|F_X(\boldsymbol{y}) - F_X(\boldsymbol{x})| \le |F_X(\boldsymbol{y}) - F_X(x_1, y_2)| + |F_X(x_1, y_2) - F_X(\boldsymbol{x})|.$$

Now assume that $x_1 \le y_1$. We get from Lemma 4.2.9 that

$$0 \le F_X(\boldsymbol{y}) - F_X(x_1, y_2) \le \lim_{y_2 \to +\infty} \Big(F_X(\boldsymbol{y}) - F_X(x_1, y_2) \Big) = F_1(y_1) - F_1(x_1).$$

An analogous inequality holds when $y_1 \le x_1$. Hence, it follows that for any $x_1, y_1 \in \mathcal{S}_1$,

$$|F_X(\boldsymbol{y}) - F_X(x_1, y_2)| \le |F_1(y_1) - F_1(x_1)|.$$

Similarly, for any x_2, y_2 in $\mathcal{S}_2$,

$$|F_X(x_1, y_2) - F_X(\boldsymbol{x})| \le |F_2(y_2) - F_2(x_2)|,$$

which completes the proof of (4.5), from which the required result directly follows. □

The following result is an immediate consequence of Lemma 4.2.9 and Proposition 4.2.10.

Corollary 4.2.11
Let C be a copula and let u_0 be any number in $[0, 1]$. The horizontal section of C at u_0 is the function from $[0, 1]$ to $[0, 1]$ given by $t \mapsto C(t, u_0)$. The vertical section of C at u_0 is the function from $[0, 1]$ to $[0, 1]$ given by $t \mapsto C(u_0, t)$. The diagonal section of C is the function from $[0, 1]$ to $[0, 1]$ defined by $t \mapsto C(t, t)$. The horizontal, vertical and diagonal sections of a copula C are all non-decreasing and uniformly continuous on $[0, 1]$.

Let us now state the following result concerning the partial derivatives of copulas (here, 'almost everywhere' means everywhere except perhaps on a countable set of points).

Proposition 4.2.12
Let C be a copula. For any $u_2 \in [0, 1]$ the partial derivative $\frac{\partial}{\partial u_1} C(u_1, u_2)$ exists almost everywhere, and for each (u_1, u_2) where it exists, we have

$$0 \le \frac{\partial}{\partial u_1} C(u_1, u_2) \le 1. \tag{4.6}$$

Similarly, for any $u_1 \in [0, 1]$ the partial derivative $\frac{\partial}{\partial u_2} C(u_1, u_2)$ exists almost everywhere and for each (u_1, u_2) where it exists, we have

$$0 \le \frac{\partial}{\partial u_2} C(u_1, u_2) \le 1. \tag{4.7}$$

Furthermore, the functions $u_1 \mapsto \frac{\partial}{\partial u_2} C(u_1, u_2)$ and $u_2 \mapsto \frac{\partial}{\partial u_1} C(u_1, u_2)$ are defined and non-decreasing almost everywhere on $[0, 1]$.

Proof. The existence of the partial derivatives $\frac{\partial}{\partial u_1} C(u_1, u_2)$ and $\frac{\partial}{\partial u_2} C(u_1, u_2)$ is immediate since monotone functions (here the horizontal and vertical sections of the copula) are differentiable almost everywhere. Inequalities (4.6) and (4.7) follow from Corollary 4.2.11. If $v_1 \leq v_2$ then from Lemma 4.2.9 the function $u \mapsto C(u, v_2) - C(u, v_1)$ is non-decreasing. Hence, $\frac{\partial}{\partial u}\big(C(u, v_2) - C(u, v_1)\big)$ is defined and non-negative almost everywhere on $[0, 1]$, from which it follows that $u_2 \mapsto \frac{\partial}{\partial u_1} C(u_1, u_2)$ is defined and non-decreasing almost everywhere on $[0, 1]$. A similar result holds for $u_1 \mapsto \frac{\partial}{\partial u_2} C(u_1, u_2)$. □

The technical results derived above essentially state that the partial derivatives of C exist and resemble dfs. Let us now formally relate these partial derivatives to conditional distributions.

Property 4.2.13
Let us define $C_{2|1}$ and $C_{1|2}$ as follows:

$$C_{2|1}(u_2|u_1) = \frac{\partial}{\partial u_1} C(u_1, u_2) \text{and} C_{1|2}(u_1|u_2) = \frac{\partial}{\partial u_2} C(u_1, u_2).$$

Then, given a random couple $\boldsymbol{X}$ with df of the form (4.3), the identities

$$\Pr[X_2 \leq x_2 | X_1 = x_1] = C_{2|1}(F_2(x_2)|F_1(x_1))$$

and

$$\Pr[X_1 \leq x_1 | X_2 = x_2] = C_{1|2}(F_1(x_1)|F_2(x_2))$$

hold for any $\boldsymbol{x} \in \mathbb{R}^2$.

Proof. Let (U_1, U_2) be a random couple with joint df C. The conditional df of U_2 given $U_1 = u_1$ is given by

$$\begin{aligned}
\Pr[U_2 \leq u_2 | U_1 = u_1] &= \lim_{\Delta u_1 \to 0} \frac{\Pr[u_1 \leq U_1 \leq u_1 + \Delta u_1, U_2 \leq u_2]}{\Pr[u_1 \leq U_1 \leq u_1 + \Delta u_1]} \\
&= \lim_{\Delta u_1 \to 0} \frac{C(u_1 + \Delta u_1, u_2) - C(u_1, u_2)}{\Delta u_1} \\
&= C_{2|1}(u_2|u_1).
\end{aligned}$$

The conditional df of X_2 given that $X_1 = x_1$ is then obtained by replacing u_i with $F_i(x_i)$, $i = 1, 2$, and the result follows. □

4.2.4 Probability density functions associated with copulas

The next result states that, under appropriate conditions, the joint pdf can be written as a product of the marginal pdfs and the copula density. It will become clear that the copula density encodes all the information about the dependence among the X_i (for this reason, the copula density is sometimes called the dependence function). Note that it follows from Proposition 4.2.12 that $\frac{\partial^2}{\partial u_1 \partial u_2} C(u_1, u_2)$ exists almost everywhere in $[0, 1]^2$ (i.e., everywhere except perhaps on a set with Lebesgue measure equal to zero).

Property 4.2.14
If the marginal dfs F_1 and F_2 are continuous with respective pdf f_1 and f_2, then the joint pdf of $\boldsymbol{X}$ can be written as

$$f_{\boldsymbol{X}}(\boldsymbol{x}) = f_1(x_1) f_2(x_2) c(F_1(x_1), F_2(x_2)), \quad \boldsymbol{x} \in \mathbb{R}^2,$$

where the copula density c is given by

$$c(u_1, u_2) = \frac{\partial^2}{\partial u_1 \partial u_2} C(u_1, u_2), \quad \boldsymbol{u} \in [0, 1]^2.$$

The second mixed derivative of the copula C (when it exists) can then be interpreted as a local dependence measure. Indeed, the pdf of $\boldsymbol{X}$ at the point $\boldsymbol{x}$ can be decomposed as follows:

$$f_{\boldsymbol{X}}(\boldsymbol{x}) = \underbrace{f_1(x_1) f_2(x_2)}_{\substack{\text{joint pdf corresponding} \\ \text{to independence}}} c(F_1(x_1), F_2(x_2)).$$

Hence, the joint pdf at $\boldsymbol{x}$ is equal to the pdf corresponding to independence evaluated at $\boldsymbol{x}$, multiplied by $c(F_1(x_1), F_2(x_2))$. This factor distorts independence to induce the actual dependence structure: the joint pdf $f_{\boldsymbol{X}}$ is obtained from the independence pdf $f_1(x_1) f_2(x_2)$ reweighted at $\boldsymbol{x}$ by $c(F_1(x_1), F_2(x_2))$. In particular, if the X_i are independent then $c \equiv 1$ and the joint pdf $f_{\boldsymbol{X}}$ factors into the product of the marginals f_1 and f_2.

4.2.5 Copulas with singular components

The copula density can be used to define the absolutely continuous component A_C and the singular component S_C of the copula C. This is formally stated next.

Definition 4.2.15. Any copula C can be decomposed into

$$C(\boldsymbol{u}) = A_C(\boldsymbol{u}) + S_C(\boldsymbol{u})$$

where A_C is called the absolutely continuous component of C given by

$$A_C(\boldsymbol{u}) = \int_0^{u_1} \int_0^{u_2} c(\xi_1, \xi_2) d\xi_1 d\xi_2$$

and S_C is called the singular part of C, given by

$$S_C(\boldsymbol{u}) = C(\boldsymbol{u}) - A_C(\boldsymbol{u}).$$

∇

Unlike bivariate distributions in general, the marginals of a copula are continuous; hence a copula has no atoms. If $C \equiv A_C$ on $[0, 1]^2$ then C is absolutely continuous, but if $C \equiv S_C$ on $[0, 1]^2$ (i.e., if $c = 0$ almost everywhere on $[0, 1]^2$) then C is singular. Otherwise, C has an absolutely continuous component A_C and a singular component S_C. In this case, neither A_C nor S_C is a copula (since neither has $\mathcal{U}ni(0, 1)$ marginals). When C is singular its support has Lebesgue measure 0.

Example 4.2.16. The support of C_U is the main diagonal of $[0, 1]^2$ (i.e., the graph of $u_1 = u_2$ in $[0, 1]^2$) so that C_U is singular. Note that

$$\frac{\partial^2}{\partial u_1 \partial u_2} C_U = 0$$

everywhere in $[0, 1]^2$ except on the main diagonal.

Similarly, the support of C_L is the secondary diagonal of $[0, 1]^2$ (i.e., the graph of $u_2 = 1 - u_1$ in $[0, 1]^2$), and thus C_L is singular as well. ∇

Example 4.2.17. The copula C_I is absolutely continuous since the second mixed derivative of C_I is uniformly equal to 1, and

$$A_{C_I}(\boldsymbol{u}) = \int_0^{u_1} \int_0^{u_2} d\xi_1 d\xi_2 = C_I(\boldsymbol{u})$$

and $S_{C_I} = 0$. ∇

Example 4.2.18. (The Marshall–Olkin copula). The Marshall–Olkin copula is related to the copula extracted from the Marshall–Olkin bivariate exponential distribution of Example 4.1.1. More specifically, this two-parameter copula is defined as

$$C(u_1, u_2) = \min\{u_1^{1-\alpha_1} u_2, u_1 u_2^{1-\alpha_2}\} = \begin{cases} u_1^{1-\alpha_1} u_2 & \text{if } u_1^{\alpha_1} \geq u_2^{\alpha_2}, \\ u_1 u_2^{1-\alpha_2} & \text{if } u_1^{\alpha_1} < u_2^{\alpha_2}. \end{cases}$$

The conditional copula is

$$C_{2|1}(u_2|u_1) = \begin{cases} (1-\alpha_1) u_1^{-\alpha_1} u_2 & \text{if } u_1^{\alpha_1} > u_2^{\alpha_2}, \\ u_2^{1-\alpha_2} & \text{if } u_1^{\alpha_1} < u_2^{\alpha_2}. \end{cases}$$

Then the copula density can be written as

$$c(u_1, u_2) = \begin{cases} (1-\alpha_1)u_1^{-\alpha_1} & \text{if} \quad u_1^{\alpha_1} \geq u_2^{\alpha_2}, \\ (1-\alpha_2)u_2^{-\alpha_2} & \text{if} \quad u_1^{\alpha_1} < u_2^{\alpha_2}, \end{cases}$$

so that

$$A_C(\boldsymbol{u}) = C(\boldsymbol{u}) - \frac{\alpha_1\alpha_2}{\alpha_1+\alpha_2-\alpha_1\alpha_2}\left(\min\{u_1^{\alpha_1}, u_2^{\alpha_2}\}\right)^{\frac{\alpha_1+\alpha_2-\alpha_1\alpha_2}{\alpha_1\alpha_2}}$$

and

$$S_C(\boldsymbol{u}) = C(\boldsymbol{u}) - A_C(\boldsymbol{u}) = \frac{\alpha_1\alpha_2}{\alpha_1+\alpha_2-\alpha_1\alpha_2}\left(\min\{u_1^{\alpha_1}, u_2^{\alpha_2}\}\right)^{\frac{\alpha_1+\alpha_2-\alpha_1\alpha_2}{\alpha_1\alpha_2}}.$$

The mass of the singular component is spread along the line $u_1^{\alpha_1} = u_2^{\alpha_2}$ in $[0, 1]^2$. ∇

4.2.6 *Sklar's representation in the general case*

The representation (4.3) suggests that we interpret a copula associated with $\boldsymbol{X}$ as being the dependence structure. This makes sense in particular when all the F_i are continuous and the copula is unique as in Theorem 4.2.2. In the discrete case there will be more than one way of writing the dependence structure. If F_1 and F_2 are not both continuous then Sklar's theorem ensures that the copula representation of $F_{\boldsymbol{X}}$ still holds, although in this case C is no longer unique and is referred to as a possible copula for $F_{\boldsymbol{X}}$ (and not as *the* copula for $F_{\boldsymbol{X}}$).

Let us give a proof of Sklar's theorem in this case. For the sake of completeness, we begin by reformulating Theorem 4.2.2 as follows.

Theorem 4.2.19. Let $F_{\boldsymbol{X}} \in \mathcal{R}_2(F_1, F_2)$ have arbitrary marginal dfs F_1 and F_2. Then there exists a copula C, not necessarily unique, on the unit square $[0, 1]^2$, such that the representation (4.3) is valid for each $\boldsymbol{x} \in \mathbb{R}^2$. Nevertheless, C is uniquely determined on $\text{Range}(F_1)\times\text{Range}(F_2)$.

Proof. The argument is divided into three different steps:

1. Let $F_{\boldsymbol{X}} \in \mathcal{R}_2(F_1, F_2)$. It is clear that the set of ordered pairs

$$\left\{\left((F_1(x_1), F_2(x_2)), F_{\boldsymbol{X}}(\boldsymbol{x})\right)\middle|\boldsymbol{x} \in \mathbb{R}^2\right\}$$

defines a real function D whose domain is $\text{Range}(F_1)\times\text{Range}(F_2)$. Note that if the F_i have discontinuities, then D is not defined on the whole unit square $[0, 1]^2$ but only on its subset $\text{Range}(F_1)\times\text{Range}(F_2)$. From the properties of $F_{\boldsymbol{X}}$, D satisfies the following conditions:

$$D(0, u_2) = D(u_1, 0) = 0, \text{ for any } u_1, u_2,$$

and

$$D(u_1, 1) = u_1, \quad D(1, u_2) = u_2, \text{ for any } u_1, u_2.$$

It is easy to see that

$$D(u_1, u_2) = F_X\left(F_1^{-1}(u_1), F_2^{-1}(u_2)\right),$$

for $u_1 \in \text{Range}(F_1)$ and $u_2 \in \text{Range}(F_2)$.

2. Any function D as used in step 1 can be extended from $\text{Range}(F_1)\times\text{Range}(F_2)$ to $[0, 1]^2$, that is, there exists a copula C such that $C(u_1, u_2) = D(u_1, u_2)$ for any $(u_1, u_2) \in \text{Range}(F_1)\times\text{Range}(F_2)$.

Let (u_1, u_2) be a point of the unit square. For $i = 1, 2$, let $\underline{u}_i$ and $\overline{u}_i$ be the greatest and least elements of $\text{Range}(F_i)$ that satisfy $\underline{u}_i \leq u_i \leq \overline{u}_i$. Note that if $u_i \in \text{Range}(F_i)$ then $\underline{u}_i = u_i = \overline{u}_i$. Now, let us introduce

$$\lambda_i(u_i) = \begin{cases} \frac{u_i - \underline{u}_i}{\overline{u}_i - \underline{u}_i}, & \text{if} \quad \underline{u}_i < \overline{u}_i, \\ 1, & \text{if} \quad \underline{u}_i = \overline{u}_i, \end{cases}$$

and let us define

$$\begin{aligned} C(u_1, u_2) = & \left(1 - \lambda_1(u_1)\right)\left(1 - \lambda_2(u_2)\right)D(\underline{u}_1, \underline{u}_2) \\ & + \left(1 - \lambda_1(u_1)\right)\lambda_2(u_2)D(\underline{u}_1, \overline{u}_2) \\ & + \lambda_1(u_1)\left(1 - \lambda_2(u_2)\right)D(\overline{u}_1, \underline{u}_2) \\ & + \lambda_1(u_1)\lambda_2(u_2)D(\overline{u}_1, \overline{u}_2). \end{aligned}$$

This formula is an interpolation of D to $[0, 1]^2$ that is linear in u_1 and u_2. To show that C defined in this way is indeed a copula, it suffices to check that the conditions of Definition 4.2.1 are satisfied. Conditions (i) and (ii) are obviously true, while some tedious direct reasoning shows that (iii) also holds.

3. The existence of a copula C such that (4.3) holds now follows from steps 1 and 2. □

Remark 4.2.20. In the remainder of this book, when we speak of the copula of a pair of rvs $\boldsymbol{X} = (X_1, X_2)$, we mean the copula whose existence is guaranteed by Sklar's theorem, using bilinear interpolation if one or both of the X_i have discontinuous dfs. Recall that when both dfs are continuous, the copula of $\boldsymbol{X}$ is uniquely determined without the need for an interpolation convention. ∇

4.3 FAMILIES OF BIVARIATE COPULAS

Many copulas and methods to construct them can be found in the literature. It is not our aim to present these aspects exhaustively; the interested reader is referred to Hutchinson and Lai (1990), Joe (1997) or Nelsen (1999) for more details. Rather, we give below the most common copulas, together with some of their characteristics.

4.3.1 Clayton's copula

The Clayton copula is usually attributed to Clayton (1978), but its origin can actually be traced back at least to Kimeldorf and Sampson (1975). It is defined for $\boldsymbol{u} \in [0,1]^2$ as

$$C_\alpha(u_1, u_2) = (u_1^{-\alpha} + u_2^{-\alpha} - 1)^{-1/\alpha}, \quad \alpha > 0. \tag{4.8}$$

The first systematic study of this class of distributions was published by Cook and Johnson (1981), who interpret the parameter α as a measure of the strength of the dependence between the u_i.

It can be verified that

$$\lim_{\alpha \to +\infty} C_\alpha(u_1, u_2) = \min\{u_1, u_2\} = C_U(\boldsymbol{u}),$$

so that the dependence structure approaches its maximum (i.e., comonotonicity) when α increases to $+\infty$. On the other hand,

$$\lim_{\alpha \to 0} C_\alpha(u_1, u_2) = u_1 u_2 = C_I(\boldsymbol{u});$$

hence independence is obtained when α tends to 0.

The conditional distributions are easily derived from the partial derivatives of the Clayton copula. More specifically, $C_{1|2}$ and $C_{2|1}$ involved in Property 4.2.13 are obtained as follows:

$$C_{2|1}(u_2|u_1) = \frac{\partial}{\partial u_1} C_\alpha(\boldsymbol{u}) = \left(1 + u_1^\alpha(u_2^{-\alpha} - 1)\right)^{-1-\frac{1}{\alpha}},$$

with a similar expression for $C_{1|2}$.

The pdf associated with Clayton's copula is given by

$$c_\alpha(\boldsymbol{u}) = \frac{1+\alpha}{(u_1 u_2)^{\alpha+1}} \left(u_1^{-\alpha} + u_2^{-\alpha} - 1\right)^{-2-\frac{1}{\alpha}}.$$

This pdf is displayed in Figure 4.2 for different values of α: it exhibits a peak around the origin. The higher the value of α, the higher the peak.

4.3.2 Frank's copula

Frank's copula first appeared in Frank (1979) as a solution to a functional equation problem. This family of copulas was studied by Genest (1987). Frank's copula is given for $\boldsymbol{u} \in [0,1]^2$ by

$$C_\alpha(u_1, u_2) = -\frac{1}{\alpha} \ln\left(1 + \frac{(\exp(-\alpha u_1) - 1)(\exp(-\alpha u_2) - 1)}{\exp(-\alpha) - 1}\right), \quad \alpha \neq 0.$$

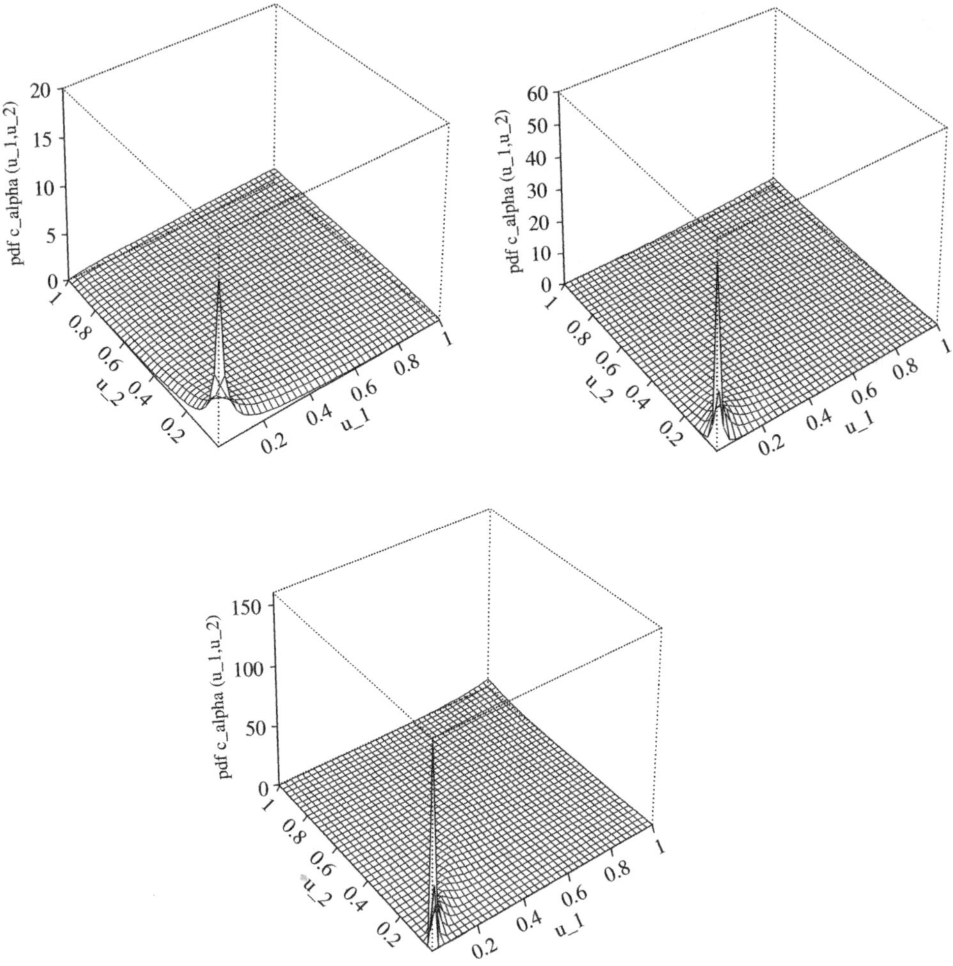

Figure 4.2 Graph of the pdf c_α associated with the Clayton copula for increasing positive values of α

It is easy to check that the limiting cases of C_α include C_L, C_U and C_I. Specifically,

$$\lim_{\alpha\to-\infty} C_\alpha = C_L, \quad \lim_{\alpha\to+\infty} C_\alpha = C_U \text{ and } \lim_{\alpha\to 0} C_\alpha = C_I.$$

The Frank family of copulas is thus said to be comprehensive.

The conditional distribution is obtained from

$$C_{2|1}(u_2|u_1) = \frac{\exp(-\alpha u_2) - \exp\big(-\alpha(u_1+u_2)\big)}{1-\exp(-\alpha)-\big(1-\exp\big(-\alpha u_1\big)\big)\big(1-\exp\big(-\alpha u_2\big)\big)}.$$

The pdf associated with Frank's copula can be written as

$$c_\alpha(\boldsymbol{u}) = \frac{\alpha\exp\big(-\alpha(u_1+u_2)\big)\big(1-\exp(-\alpha)\big)}{\Big(\exp\big(-\alpha(u_1+u_2)\big)-\exp(-\alpha u_1)-\exp(-\alpha u_2)+\exp(-\alpha)\Big)^2}.$$

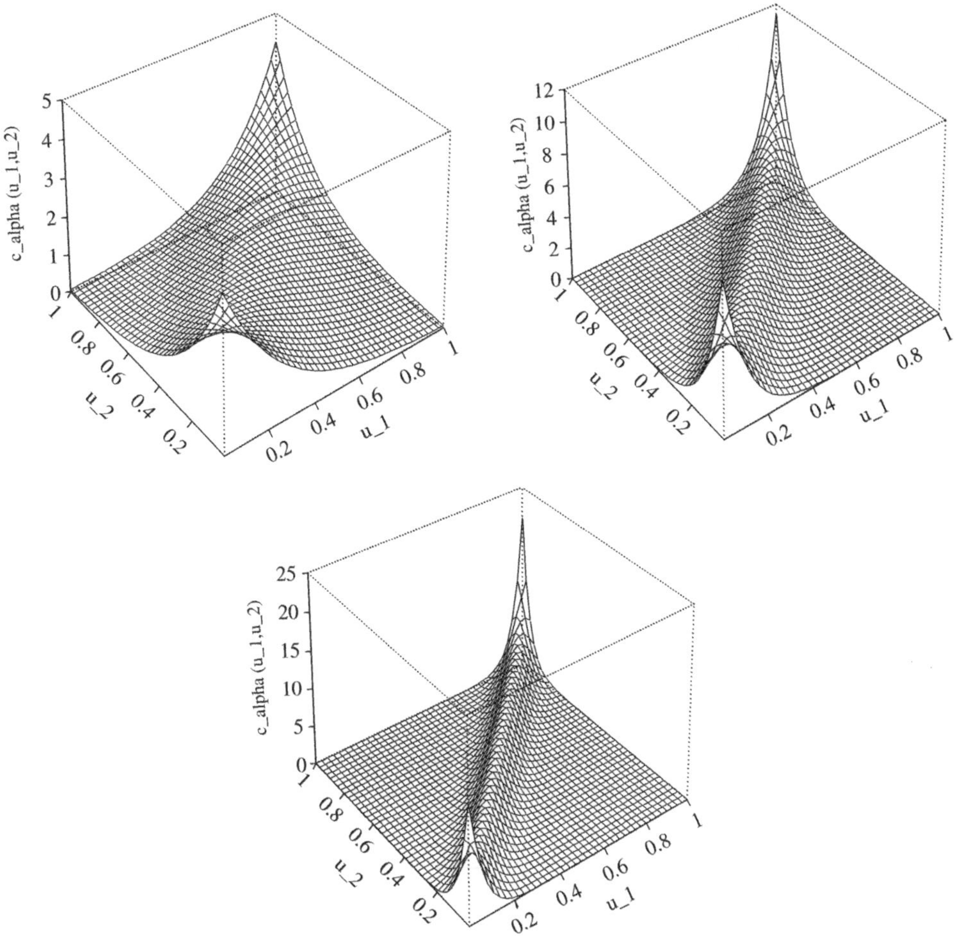

Figure 4.3 Graph of the pdf associated with the Frank copula for increasing positive values of α

It is shown in Figure 4.3 for increasing positive values of α. We will see in the next chapter how the parameter α determines the level of dependence between the underlying rvs.

4.3.3 The normal copula

The normal (or Gaussian) copula describes the dependence structure induced by the bivariate normal distribution. Without loss of generality, we can define it as the copula resulting from the Sklar's decomposition (4.3) applied to the joint df of a random couple (X_1, X_2) of $\mathcal{N}or\,(0, 1)$ rvs with covariance α. Invoking (4.4), we see that the normal copula is given by

$$C_\alpha(u_1, u_2) = H_\alpha\left(\Phi^{-1}(u_1), \Phi^{-1}(u_2)\right), \quad \alpha \in (-1, 1),$$

where Φ is the df of the univariate $\mathcal{N}or\,(0,1)$ distribution and H_α is the bivariate standard normal df with covariance α, so

$$C_\alpha(u_1,u_2)=\frac{1}{2\pi\sqrt{1-\alpha^2}}\int_{-\infty}^{\Phi^{-1}(u_1)}\int_{-\infty}^{\Phi^{-1}(u_2)}\exp\left(\frac{-(\xi_1^2-2\alpha\xi_1\xi_2+\xi_2^2)}{2(1-\alpha^2)}\right)d\xi_1 d\xi_2.$$

The corresponding pdf is obtained as follows. First, write

$$c_\alpha(u_1,u_2)=\frac{1}{2\pi\sqrt{1-\alpha^2}}\exp\left(\frac{-(\zeta_1^2-2\alpha\zeta_1\zeta_2+\zeta_2^2)}{2(1-\alpha^2)}\right)\frac{d}{du_1}\Phi^{-1}(u_1)\frac{d}{du_2}\Phi^{-1}(u_2),$$

where $\zeta_i=\Phi^{-1}(u_i)$, $i=1,2$. Now, denoting by $\varphi=\Phi'$ the pdf of the standard normal law, we have

$$\frac{d}{du_i}\Phi^{-1}(u_i)=\frac{1}{\varphi(\Phi^{-1}(u_i))}=\sqrt{2\pi}\exp(-\zeta_i^2/2),$$

so that the pdf of the Gaussian copula is given by

$$c_\alpha(u_1,u_2)=\frac{1}{\sqrt{1-\alpha^2}}\exp\left(\frac{-(\zeta_1^2-2\alpha\zeta_1\zeta_2+\zeta_2^2)}{2(1-\alpha^2)}\right)\exp\left(\frac{\zeta_1^2+\zeta_2^2}{2}\right).$$

This pdf is shown in Figure 4.4 for increasing positive values of α. It is clear that the strength of dependence increases with α.

The conditional distributions associated with Gaussian copulas are easily derived from Property 4.2.13. Indeed, the Gaussian copula can be represented as

$$C_\alpha(u_1,u_2)=\int_0^{u_1}\Phi\left(\frac{\Phi^{-1}(u_2)-\alpha\Phi^{-1}(t)}{\sqrt{1-\alpha^2}}\right)dt,$$

so that

$$C_{2|1}(u_2|u_1)=\Phi\left(\frac{\Phi^{-1}(u_2)-\alpha\Phi^{-1}(u_1)}{\sqrt{1-\alpha^2}}\right).$$

4.3.4 The Student copula

Just as the normal copula derived from the bivariate normal distribution, the Student copula is obtained from the bivariate Student distribution. Denote by

$$t_m(x)=\int_{-\infty}^{x}\frac{\Gamma\left(\frac{m+1}{2}\right)}{\sqrt{m\pi}\Gamma\left(\frac{m}{2}\right)}\left(1+\frac{\xi^2}{m}\right)^{-\frac{m+1}{2}}d\xi$$

the df of the univariate Student distribution with m degrees of freedom. Similarly, denote by

$$t_{m,\alpha}(\boldsymbol{x})=\int_{-\infty}^{x_1}\int_{-\infty}^{x_2}\frac{1}{2\pi\sqrt{1-\alpha^2}}\left(1+\frac{\xi_1^2+\xi_2^2-2\alpha\xi_1\xi_2}{m(1-\alpha^2)}\right)^{-\frac{m+2}{2}}d\xi_1 d\xi_2$$

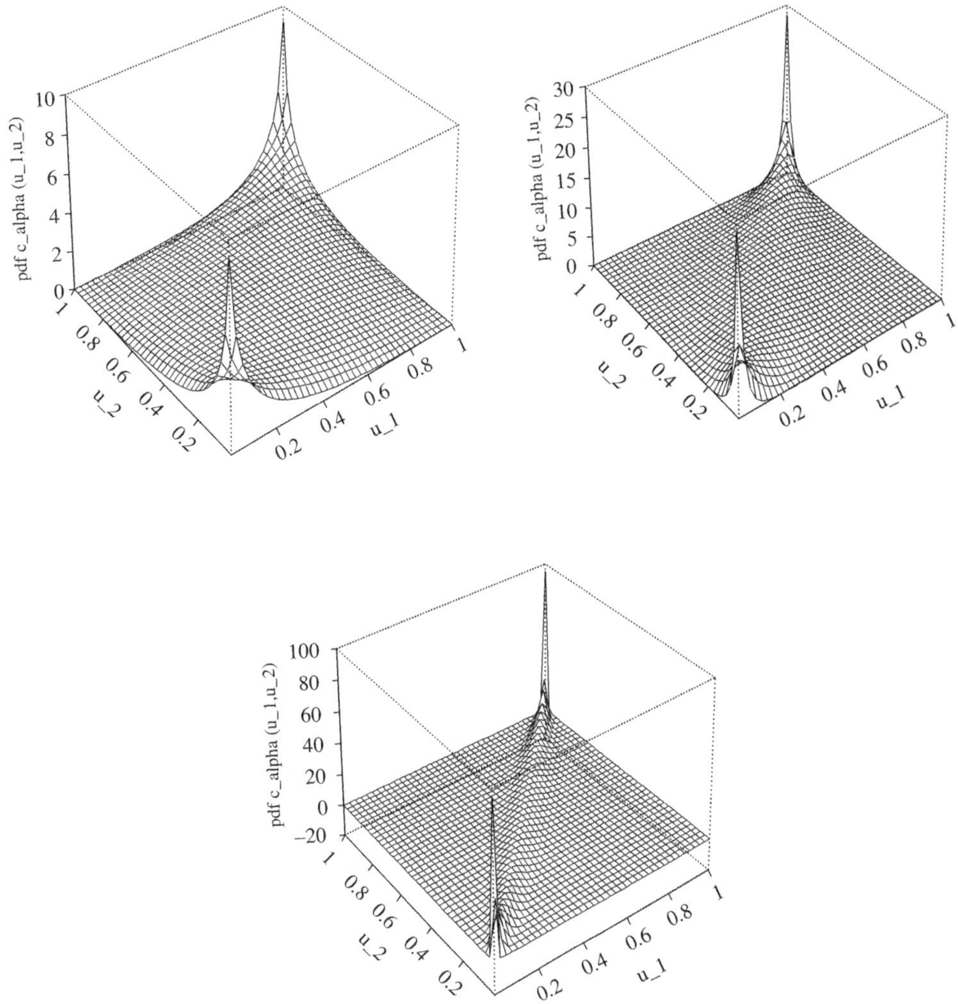

Figure 4.4 Graph of the normal copula for increasing positive values of the parameter α

the joint df of the bivariate Student distribution, with $0 < \alpha < 1$. The bivariate Student copula is then defined as

$$C_{m,\alpha}(u_1, u_2) = t_{m,\alpha}\left(t_m^{-1}(u_1), t_m^{-1}(u_2)\right)$$

$$= \int_{-\infty}^{t_m^{-1}(u_1)} \int_{-\infty}^{t_m^{-1}(u_2)} \frac{1}{2\pi\sqrt{1-\alpha^2}} \left(1 + \frac{\xi_1^2 + \xi_2^2 - 2\alpha\xi_1\xi_2}{m(1-\alpha^2)}\right)^{-\frac{m+2}{2}} d\xi_1 d\xi_2.$$

When the number m of degrees of freedom tends to $+\infty$ then the Student copula converges to the normal copula. For a limited number of degrees of freedom, however, the two copulas have quite different shapes.

The Student copula density is given by

$$c_{m,\alpha}(\boldsymbol{u}) = \alpha^{-1/2} \frac{\Gamma\left(\frac{m+2}{2}\right)\Gamma\left(\frac{m}{2}\right)}{\left(\Gamma\left(\frac{m+1}{2}\right)\right)^2} \left(1 + \frac{\zeta_1^2 + \zeta_2^2 - 2\alpha\zeta_1\zeta_2}{m(1-\alpha^2)}\right)^{-\frac{m+2}{2}}$$
$$\times \left(1 + \frac{\zeta_1}{m}\right)^{-\frac{m+2}{2}} \left(1 + \frac{\zeta_2}{m}\right)^{-\frac{m+2}{2}},$$

where $\zeta_1 = t_m^{-1}(u_1)$ and $\zeta_2 = t_m^{-1}(u_2)$.

Let us now derive the conditional Student copula. To this end, recall that for a random couple (X_1, X_2) with a bivariate Student distribution, the conditional distribution of $\sqrt{\frac{m+1}{m+x_1^2}} \frac{X_2 - \alpha x_1}{\sqrt{1-\alpha^2}}$ given $X_1 = x_1$ is univariate Student with m degrees of freedom. The conditional Student copula is then given by

$$C_{2|1}(u_2|u_1) = t_{m+1}\left(\sqrt{\frac{m+1}{m + \left(t_m^{-1}(u_1)\right)^2}} \frac{t_m^{-1}(u_2) - \alpha t_m^{-1}(u_1)}{\sqrt{1-\alpha^2}}\right).$$

Hence, the bivariate Student copula can be equivalently cast into the form

$$C_{m,\alpha}(\boldsymbol{u}) = \int_0^{u_1} t_{m+1}\left(\sqrt{\frac{m+1}{m + \left(t_m^{-1}(\xi)\right)^2}} \frac{t_m^{-1}(u_2) - \alpha t_m^{-1}(\xi)}{\sqrt{1-\alpha^2}}\right) d\xi.$$

The family of Student copulas is comprehensive in the sense that

$$\lim_{\alpha \to -1} C_{m,\alpha} = C_L \text{ and } \lim_{\alpha \to 1} C_{m,\alpha} = C_U,$$

whatever the value of m. However, $C_{m,0} \neq C_I$ for finite m.

Remark 4.3.1. Many other useful copulas can be derived from the elliptical family of multivariate distributions. We refer the interested reader to Frahm, Junker and Szimayer (2003) and Abdous, Genest and Rémillard (2004) for more details. ∇

Remark 4.3.2. All the bivariate copulas examined below satisfy the exchangeability condition $C(u_1, u_2) = C(u_2, u_1)$. In a situation where the appropriateness of this symmetry condition is doubtful, one may wish to have non-exchangeable models. Asymmetric copulas have been proposed in Genest, Ghoudi and Rivest (1998). ∇

4.3.5 Building multivariate distributions with given marginals from copulas

4.3.5.1 Multivariate distributions with normal marginals

The pdf of a random couple with $\mathcal{N}or(0, 1)$ marginals and Clayton copula is shown in Figure 4.5 for increasing values of α. The corresponding contour plots show how the ellipses characteristic of the bivariate normal distribution have become distorted.

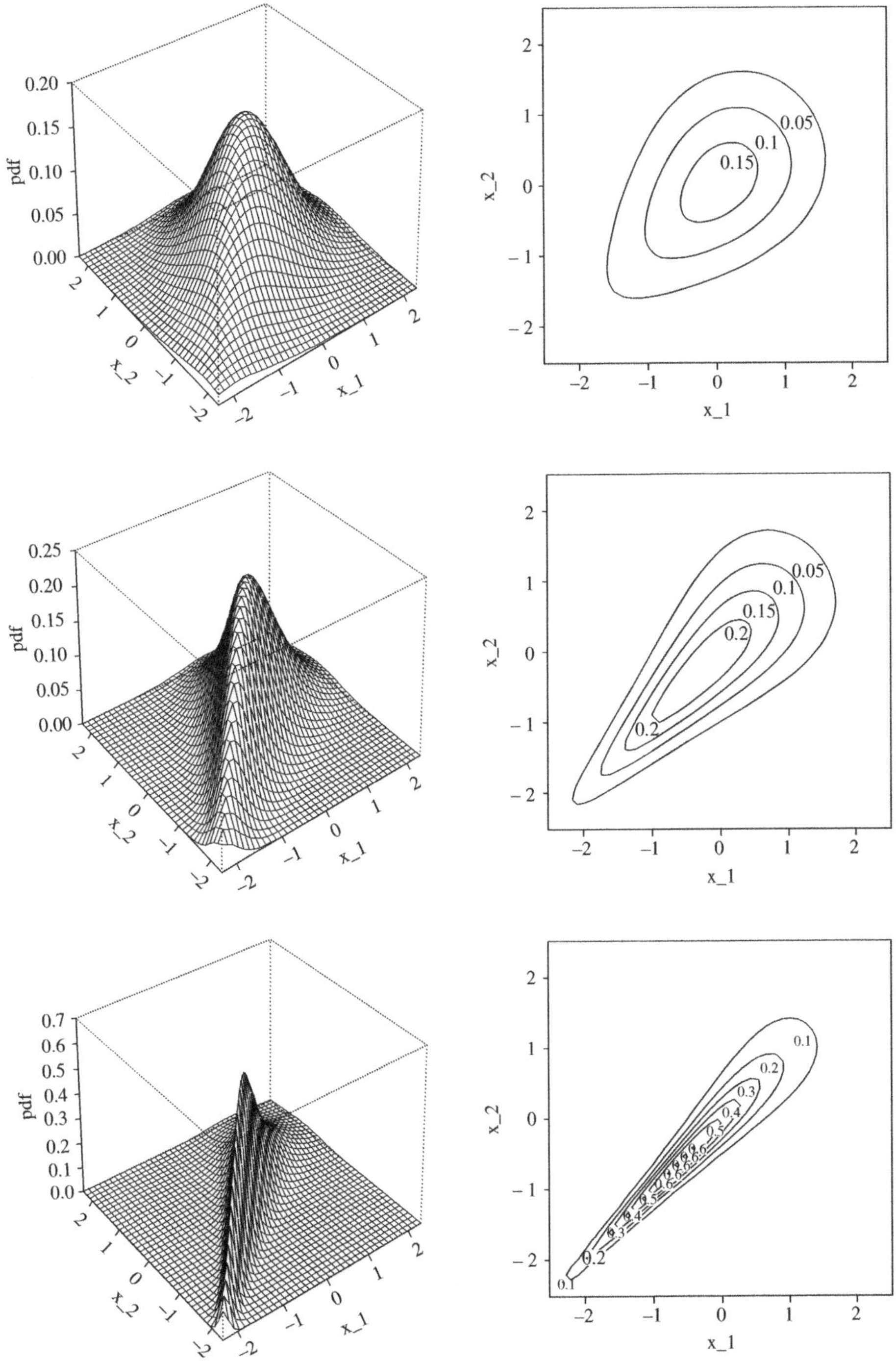

Figure 4.5 Graph of the pdf of a random couple with $\mathcal{N}or\,(0, 1)$ marginals and Clayton copula for positive increasing values of the dependence parameter α, and corresponding contour plots

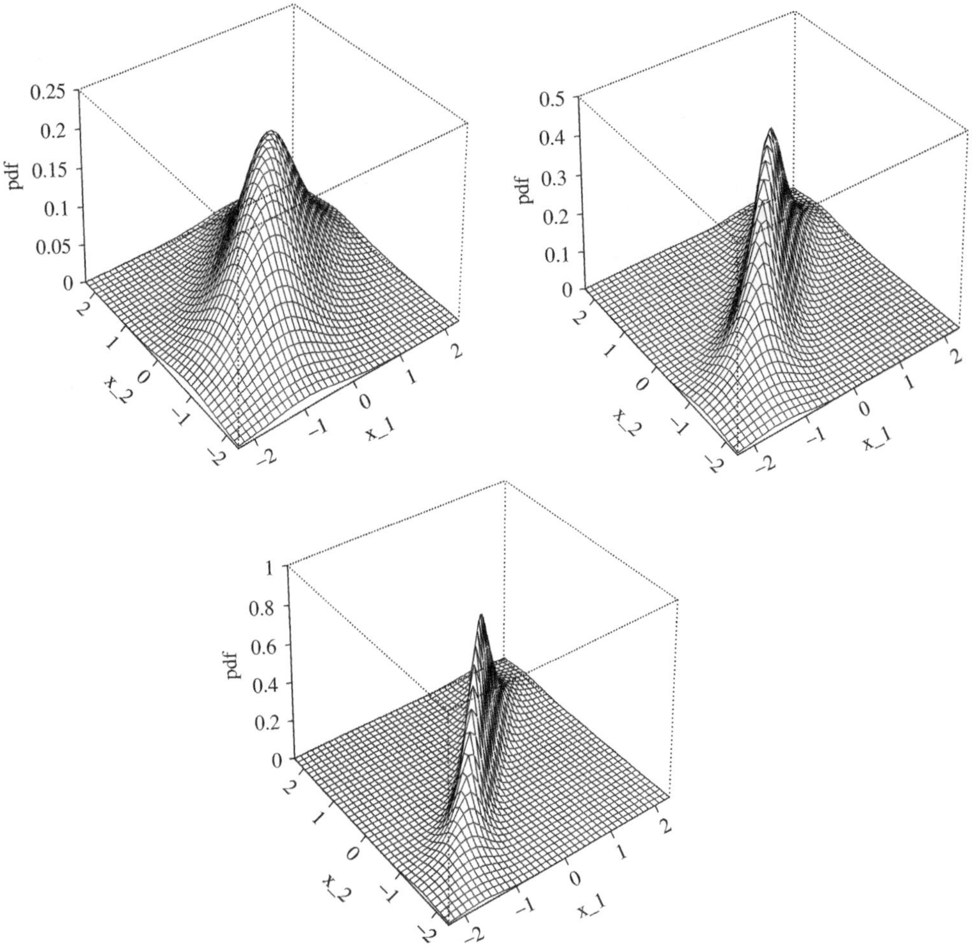

Figure 4.6 Graph of the pdf of a random couple with $\mathcal{N}or(0, 1)$ marginals and Frank copula for positive increasing values of the dependence parameter α

Plugging normal marginals into the Frank copula yields another multivariate distribution with normal marginals, but different from the multivariate normal law. This is shown in Figure 4.6.

4.3.5.2 Multivariate distributions with gamma marginals

The main advantage of the copula construction is that we are not limited in the choice of marginal distributions. To show this, we have displayed in Figure 4.7 for increasing values of α the pdf of a random couple with $\mathcal{G}am(3, 1)$ marginals and Clayton copula. In Figure 4.8 we have drawn for positive increasing values of the dependence parameter α the pdf of a random couple with $\mathcal{G}am(3, 1)$ marginals and normal copula.

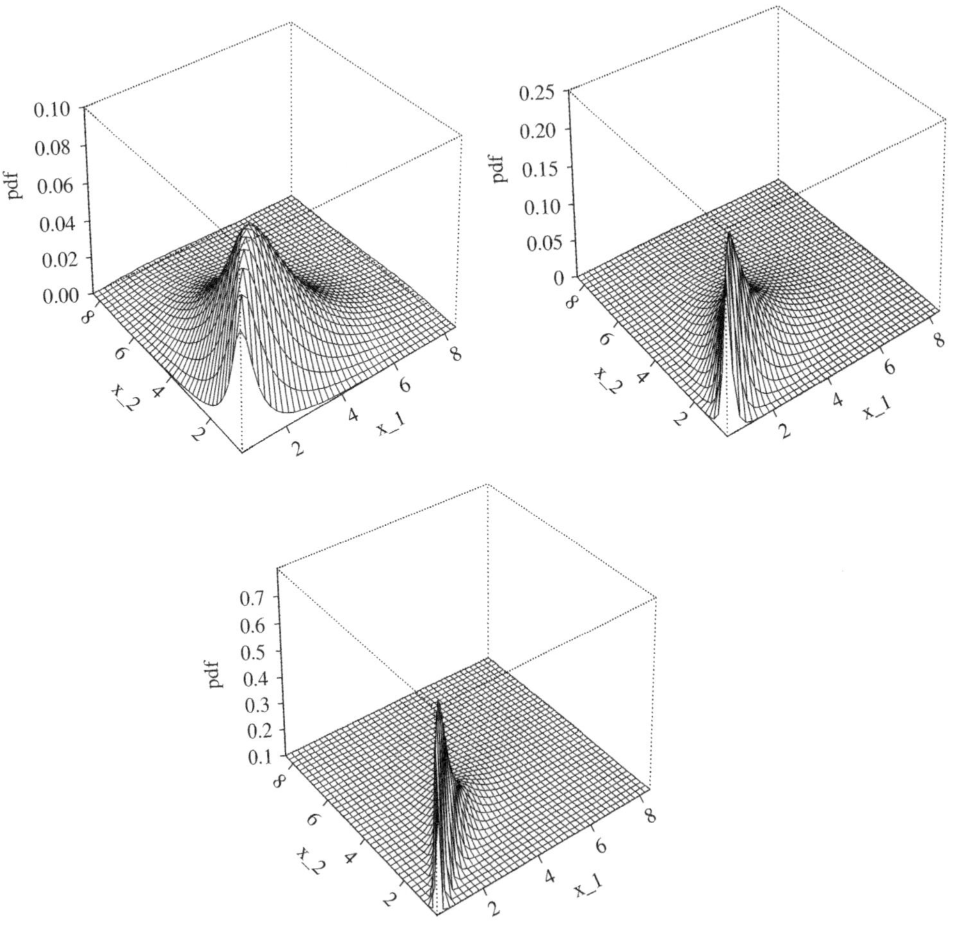

Figure 4.7 Graph of the pdf of a random couple with $\mathcal{G}am(3, 1)$ marginals and Clayton copula for positive increasing values of the dependence parameter α

4.4 PROPERTIES OF COPULAS

4.4.1 Survival copulas

This section introduces the notion of survival copulas and discusses the relationships between survival copulas and joint tfs. Let us start with the following definition.

Definition 4.4.1. If C is a copula then so is $\overline{C}$ defined for $\boldsymbol{u} \in [0, 1]^2$ as

$$\overline{C}(u_1, u_2) = C(1 - u_1, 1 - u_2) + u_1 + u_2 - 1.$$

The function $\overline{C}$ just defined is called the survival copula associated with C. ∇

It is easy to verify that $\overline{C}$ fulfils the conditions stated in Definition 4.2.1. Computed at $(1 - u_1, 1 - u_2)$, it represents the probability of two unit uniform rvs with copula C being

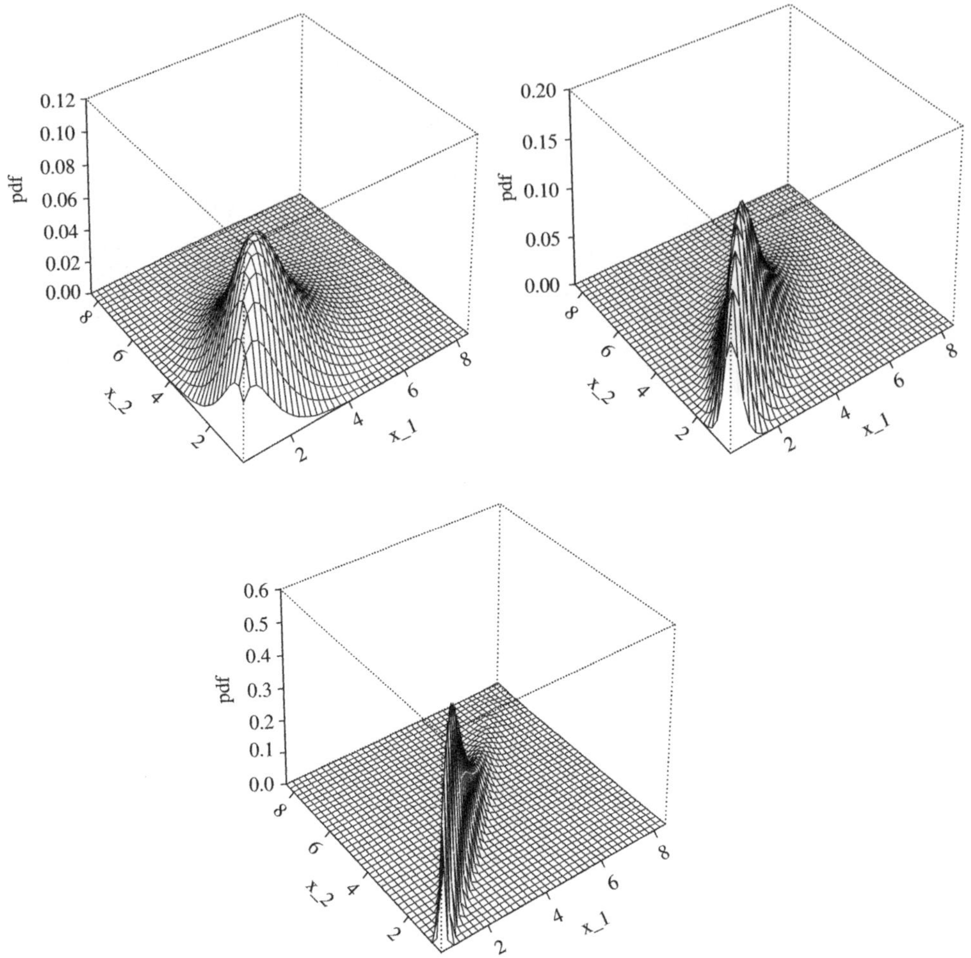

Figure 4.8 Graph of the pdf of a random couple with $\mathcal{G}am(3, 1)$ marginals and normal copula for positive increasing values of the dependence parameter α

larger than u_1 and u_2, respectively. Care should thus be taken not to confuse the survival copula $\overline{C}$ with the joint tf for two $\mathcal{U}ni(0, 1)$ rvs (U_1, U_2) whose joint df is C; indeed,

$$\Pr[U_1 > u_1, U_2 > u_2] = 1 - u_1 - u_2 + C(u_1, u_2) \neq \overline{C}(u_1, u_2)$$

but

$$\Pr[U_1 > u_1, U_2 > u_2] = \overline{C}(1 - u_1, 1 - u_2).$$

Since $\overline{C}$ is a copula, the inequalities

$$C_L(u_1, u_2) \leq \overline{C}(u_1, u_2) \leq C_U(u_1, u_2)$$

hold for all $\boldsymbol{u} \in [0,1]^2$. In addition, it can easily be verified that for the independence and Fréchet bound copulas, copulas and survival copulas coincide, that is,

$$\overline{C}_L = C_L, \quad \overline{C}_I = C_I \text{ and } \overline{C}_U = C_U.$$

Sklar's theorem can be restated in terms of survival copulas. Specifically, survival copulas can be used to express the joint tf $\overline{F}_{\boldsymbol{X}}$ of $\boldsymbol{X}$ in terms of the marginal tfs $\overline{F}_1$ and $\overline{F}_2$ as follows:

$$\overline{F}_{\boldsymbol{X}}(\boldsymbol{x}) = 1 - F_1(x_1) - F_2(x_2) + F_{\boldsymbol{X}}(\boldsymbol{x}) = \overline{C}(\overline{F}_1(x_1), \overline{F}_2(x_2));$$

$\overline{C}$ thus couples the joint tf to its univariate margins $\overline{F}_1$ and $\overline{F}_2$ in a manner completely analogous to the way in which a copula connects the joint df $F_{\boldsymbol{X}}$ to its margins F_1 and F_2.

Example 4.4.2. (Survival Pareto copula). Considering the bivariate Pareto distribution of Example 4.1.2, we see that

$$\overline{F}_{\boldsymbol{X}}(\boldsymbol{x}) = \overline{C}(\overline{F}_1(x_1), \overline{F}_2(x_2))$$

with

$$\overline{C}(\boldsymbol{u}) = \left(u_1^{-1/\alpha} + u_2^{-1/\alpha} - 1\right)^{-\alpha} - 1.$$

∇

4.4.2 *Dual and co-copulas*

In addition to the survival copula $\overline{C}$, we also associate with each copula C a dual $\widetilde{C}$ and a co-copula C^*, defined as follows.

Definition 4.4.3. The co-copula C^* associated with the copula C is given by

$$C^*(u_1, u_2) = 1 - C(1 - u_1, 1 - u_2), \quad \boldsymbol{u} \in [0,1]^2,$$

and the dual $\widetilde{C}$ of the copula C is given by

$$\widetilde{C}(u_1, u_2) = u_1 + u_2 - C(u_1, u_2), \quad \boldsymbol{u} \in [0,1]^2.$$

∇

Neither the co-copula nor the dual is a copula. However, they represent the probability that $X_1 > x_1$ or $X_2 > x_2$ and the probability that either $X_1 \le x_1$ or $X_2 \le x_2$. Specifically,

$$\Pr[X_1 > x_1 \text{ or } X_2 > x_2] = C^*\big(\overline{F}_1(x_1), \overline{F}_2(x_2)\big),$$

$$\Pr[X_1 \le x_1 \text{ or } X_2 \le x_2] = \widetilde{C}\big(F_1(x_1), F_2(x_2)\big).$$

Note also that the co-copula of the co-copula is the original copula, that is,

$$\left(C^*\right)^* = C.$$

Co-copulas associated with independent and Fréchet bound copulas are given for $\boldsymbol{u} \in [0, 1]^2$ by

$$\begin{aligned}C_L^*(u_1, u_2) &= \min\{u_1 + u_2, 1\},\\ C_I^*(u_1, u_2) &= u_1 + u_2 - u_1 u_2,\\ C_U^*(u_1, u_2) &= \max\{u_1, u_2\}.\end{aligned}$$

4.4.3 Functional invariance

Much of the usefulness of copulas follows from the fact that for strictly monotone transformations of rvs copulas are either invariant or change in predictable ways. This is shown in the following result, which is a direct consequence of the interpretation of the copula as the joint df of the ranks.

Proposition 4.4.4
Let X_1 and X_2 be continuous rvs with copula C. Let t_1 and t_2 be continuous monotone functions.

(i) If t_1 and t_2 are non-decreasing then $\big(t_1(X_1), t_2(X_2)\big)$ has copula C.

(ii) If t_1 is non-decreasing and t_2 is non-increasing then $\big(t_1(X_1), t_2(X_2)\big)$ has copula $u_1 - C(u_1, 1 - u_2)$.

(iii) If t_1 is non-increasing and t_2 is non-decreasing then $\big(t_1(X_1), t_2(X_2)\big)$ has copula $u_2 - C(1 - u_1, u_2)$.

(iv) If t_1 and t_2 are non-increasing then $\big(t_1(X_1), t_2(X_2)\big)$ has copula $\overline{C}$.

Note that in each case the form of the copula of $\big(t_1(X_1), t_2(X_2)\big)$ is independent of the particular choice of t_1 and t_2. When both t_1 and t_2 are non-decreasing, this is because the ranks for X_1 and X_2 coincide with the ranks for $t_1(X_1)$ and $t_2(X_2)$, so that the copula (which is the joint df of the ranks) is the same for the pairs (X_1, X_2) and $(t_1(X_1), t_2(X_2))$. In the other cases, the copula is modified according to the monotonicity of t_1 and t_2, but its actual expression does not depend on the particular expression for t_1 and t_2. This indicates that the copula accounts for all the dependence structure between two continuous rvs: the way in which X_1 and X_2 'move together' is captured by the copula, regardless of the scale in which each variable is measured.

Example 4.4.5. As a simple illustration of the relevance of the results given in Proposition 4.4.4, suppose that we have a probability model (multivariate distribution) for dependent insurance losses of various kinds. If we decide that our interest now lies in modelling the logarithm of these losses, the copula will not change. Similarly, if we change from a model of percentage returns on several financial assets to a model of logarithmic returns, the copula will not change, only the marginal distributions. ∇

From the behaviour of the copula with respect to monotone transformations established in Proposition 4.4.4, and in particular from the fact that the copula is invariant while the margins can be modified at will, a number of consequences follow. Basically, any functional or property of the joint df of two rvs that is invariant under strictly increasing transformation of the rvs is a functional or property of their copula.

4.4.4 *Tail dependence*

The deviation from normality in actuarial science is often caused by fat-tails. In a multivariate setting, the fat-tail problem can be referred both to the marginal univariate distributions or to the joint probability of large losses. This concept is called tail dependence and described in this section.

To represent tail dependence, let us consider the probability that an event with a small probability occurs in the first variable, given that an event with the same probability occurs in the second. Practically speaking, we are concerned with the probability of observing an unusually large loss for one policy given that an unusually large loss has occurred for another policy. More formally, the coefficient of (upper) tail dependence λ_U for a random couple (X_1, X_2) with copula C is defined as

$$\begin{aligned}\lambda_U &= \lim_{v\to 0} \Pr\left[X_1 > \overline{F}_1^{-1}(v) \middle| X_2 > \overline{F}_2^{-1}(v)\right] \\ &= \lim_{v\to 0} \frac{\Pr\left[X_1 > \overline{F}_1^{-1}(v), X_2 > \overline{F}_2^{-1}(v)\right]}{\Pr\left[X_2 > \overline{F}_2^{-1}(v)\right]}.\end{aligned}$$

The numerator can be rewritten as

$$\begin{aligned}\Pr\left[X_1 > \overline{F}_1^{-1}(v), X_2 > \overline{F}_2^{-1}(v)\right] = 1 &- \Pr\left[X_1 \le \overline{F}_1^{-1}(v)\right] - \Pr\left[X_2 \le \overline{F}_2^{-1}(v)\right] \\ &+ \Pr\left[X_1 \le \overline{F}_1^{-1}(v), X_2 \le \overline{F}_2^{-1}(v)\right].\end{aligned}$$

This allows us to cast λ_U into the form

$$\lambda_U = \lim_{v\to 0} \frac{1 - 2(1-v) + C(1-v, 1-v)}{v},$$

provided F_1 and F_2 are continuous. This yields the following definition, in line with Joe (1993).

Definition 4.4.6. The coefficient of tail dependence λ_U for the random couple (X_1, X_2) with copula C is defined as

$$\lambda_U = \lim_{v\to 1} \frac{1 - 2v + C(v, v)}{1 - v}.$$

If $\lambda_U > 0$, X_1 and X_2 are said to be asymptotically dependent in the upper tail; if $\lambda_U = 0$, they are said to be asymptotically independent. ∇

A coefficient for lower tail dependence can be similarly defined as the limit of $C(u, u)/u$ when u tends to 0. These concepts of tail dependence are useful in the study of dependence for extreme value distributions; see Tawn (1997).

Tail dependence is best understood as an asymptotic property of the copula. Calculation of λ_U for particular copulas is straightforward if the copula has a simple closed form. Let us examine the following examples.

Example 4.4.7. Consider the copula

$$C(\boldsymbol{u}) = pC_U(\boldsymbol{u}) + (1-p)C_I(\boldsymbol{u}), \quad \boldsymbol{u} \in [0,1]^2,$$

for some $0 < p < 1$. Then

$$\lambda_U = \lim_{v \to 1} \frac{1-(2-p)v+(1-p)v^2}{1-v} = p.$$

The coefficient of tail dependence coincides with the weight assigned to C_U. ∇

Example 4.4.8. Gaussian copulas do not exhibit tail dependence unless $\alpha = 1$. More specifically,

$$\lambda_U = \begin{cases} 0, & \text{if } \alpha < 1, \\ 1, & \text{if } \alpha = 1. \end{cases}$$

In the bivariate normal world, it is thus almost impossible to observe extreme losses for both components of a bivariate risk. This is sometimes viewed as a considerable shortcoming of the normal copula. ∇

Example 4.4.9. For Marshall – Olkin copulas introduced in Example 4.2.18, we have

$$\lambda_U = \min\{\alpha_1, \alpha_2\}.$$

∇

4.5 THE ARCHIMEDEAN FAMILY OF COPULAS

4.5.1 Definition

Genest and MacKay (1986a,b) described an important subclass of copulas, called the 'Archimedean' copulas. They discussed applications of this class in statistics. Most actuarial applications have focused on these copulas; see Frees and Valdez (1998), Klugman and Parsa (1999) or Denuit, Purcaru and Van Keilegom (2004).

Definition 4.5.1. Consider a function $\phi : [0,1] \to \mathbb{R}^+$, possibly infinite, having continuous first and second derivatives on (0,1) and satisfying

$$\phi(1) = 0, \quad \phi'(\tau) < 0 \text{ and } \phi''(\tau) > 0 \text{ for all } \tau \in (0,1). \tag{4.9}$$

Every function ϕ satisfying (4.9) generates a bivariate copula given by

$$C_\phi(u_1, u_2) = \begin{cases} \phi^{-1}(\phi(u_1) + \phi(u_2)) & \text{if } \phi(u_1) + \phi(u_2) \leq \phi(0), \\ 0 & \text{otherwise,} \end{cases} \tag{4.10}$$

for $0 \leq u_1, u_2 \leq 1$. Copulas C_ϕ of the form (4.10) with ϕ satisfying (4.9) are referred to as Archimedean copulas. The function ϕ is called the generator of the copula (note that ϕ and $c\phi$ generate the same copula C_ϕ for any positive constant c, so that ϕ is only defined up to a positive factor). ∇

Conditions (4.9) are enough to guarantee that ϕ has an inverse ϕ^{-1} also having two derivatives.

Now, a bivariate df F_X in $\mathcal{R}_2(F_1, F_2)$ is said to be generated by an Archimedean copula if, and only if, it can be expressed in the form (4.3) for some $C = C_\phi$ satisfying (4.9) and (4.10).

The Archimedean family provides a host of models that have been successfully used in a number of data modelling contexts; see the references provided in Section 2 of Genest, Ghoudi and Rivest (1998) as well as Hennessy and Lapan (2002). Moreover, this class of dependence functions is mathematically tractable and its elements have stochastic properties that make these functions attractive for the statistical treatment of data.

Example 4.5.2. The Clayton family of copulas is a subset of the Archimedean class, generated by

$$\phi(t) = \frac{t^{-\alpha} - 1}{\alpha}.$$

Similarly, the Frank family is also contained in the Archimedean class. It is generated by

$$\phi(t) = -\ln\left(\frac{\exp(-\alpha t) - 1}{\exp(-\alpha) - 1}\right).$$

∇

Note that not every symmetric copula is Archimedean, as is exemplified next.

Example 4.5.3. The Fréchet upper bound C_U is not Archimedean, since

$$C_\phi(u, u) = C_U(u, u) = u$$

would imply $2\phi(u) = \phi(u)$ for all $0 < u < 1$. ∇

4.5.2 *Frailty models*

This section presents a probabilistic construction yielding the Archimedean copulas. Random effects models are important in biological and epidemiological studies because they provide a method of modelling heterogeneity. A random effects model particularly suited for multivariate survival analysis is the frailty model.

Oakes (1989) showed how Archimedean copulas are related to frailty models. Specifically, suppose that X_1 and X_2 are conditionally independent given the value of a third, unobserved, rv Θ. Further, assume that conditionally on $\Theta = \theta$, the rvs X_1 and X_2 have dfs

$$\Pr[X_1 \le x_1 | \Theta = \theta] = \Big(H_1(x_1)\Big)^{\theta}$$

and

$$\Pr[X_2 \le x_2 | \Theta = \theta] = \Big(H_2(x_2)\Big)^{\theta}$$

for some baseline dfs H_1 and H_2. Then, the joint df of $\boldsymbol{X}$ can be expressed using the Laplace transform L_Θ of Θ as follows:

$$\begin{aligned} F_{\boldsymbol{X}}(\boldsymbol{x}) &= \mathbb{E}\Big[\Big(H_1(x_1)\Big)^{\Theta}\Big(H_2(x_2)\Big)^{\Theta}\Big] \\ &= L_\Theta\Big(-\ln H_1(x_1) - \ln H_2(x_2)\Big), \quad \boldsymbol{x} \in \mathbb{R}^2. \end{aligned}$$

This is an Archimedean copula model C_ϕ with $\phi^{-1} = L_\Theta$ and marginals

$$F_i(x_i) = L_\Theta(-\ln H_i(x_i)), \quad i = 1, 2.$$

Models of this form are natural in survival analysis, because of the close analogy with Cox's proportional hazard regression model.

4.5.3 Probability density function associated with Archimedean copulas

To find the pdf c_ϕ associated with C_ϕ, let us first differentiate C_ϕ with respect to u_1, yielding

$$\phi'\big(C_\phi(\boldsymbol{u})\big)\frac{\partial}{\partial u_1}C_\phi(\boldsymbol{u}) = \phi'(u_1). \tag{4.11}$$

Let us differentiate this expression with respect to u_2 to get

$$\phi''\big(C_\phi(\boldsymbol{u})\big)\frac{\partial}{\partial u_2}C_\phi(\boldsymbol{u})\frac{\partial}{\partial u_1}C_\phi(\boldsymbol{u}) + \phi'\big(C_\phi(\boldsymbol{u})\big)\frac{\partial^2}{\partial u_1^2}C_\phi(\boldsymbol{u}) = 0.$$

Substituting the expression obtained from (4.11) for $\frac{\partial}{\partial u_1}C_\phi(\boldsymbol{u})$ and $\frac{\partial}{\partial u_2}C_\phi(\boldsymbol{u})$ yields

$$c_\phi(\boldsymbol{u}) = \frac{\partial^2}{\partial u_1 \partial u_2}C_\phi(\boldsymbol{u}) = -\frac{\phi''\big(C_\phi(\boldsymbol{u})\big)\phi'(u_1)\phi'(u_2)}{\Big(\phi'\big(C_\phi(\boldsymbol{u})\big)\Big)^3}.$$

From the properties of ϕ given in (4.9) it is clear that $C_\phi(\boldsymbol{u}) > 0$ for all $\boldsymbol{u}$ such that $\phi(u_1) + \phi(u_2) < \phi(0)$. In general, the derivatives do not exist on the boundary $\phi(u_1) + \phi(u_2) = \phi(0)$.

Remark 4.5.4. The identity (4.11) provides a useful sufficient condition for a copula C to be Archimedean, known as the Abel criterion: a copula C is Archimedean if $\frac{\partial}{\partial u_1}C(\boldsymbol{u})$ and $\frac{\partial}{\partial u_2}C(\boldsymbol{u})$ both exist and if there is a function $g:(0, 1)\to(0, +\infty)$ such that

$$g(u_2)\frac{\partial}{\partial u_1}C(\boldsymbol{u})=g(u_1)\frac{\partial}{\partial u_2}C(\boldsymbol{u}) \text{ for all } \boldsymbol{u}\in[0, 1]^2.$$

The corresponding generator ϕ is then given by

$$\phi(t)=\int_t^1 g(\xi)d\xi, \quad t\in[0, 1].$$

∇

4.5.4 Properties of Archimedean copulas

4.5.4.1 Support

The support of the Archimedean copula C_ϕ is

$$\left\{\boldsymbol{u}\in[0, 1]^2\middle|\phi(u_1)+\phi(u_2)\leq\phi(0)\right\}$$

which is the complete unit square $[0, 1]^2$ if $\lim_{t\to 0+}\phi(t)=+\infty$.

4.5.4.2 Independence

The copula C_I is a member of the Archimedean class, as shown next.

Property 4.5.5
We have $C_\phi\equiv C_I$ if, and only if, $\phi(t)=-c\ln t$, where $c>0$ is arbitrary.

Proof. The equality $C_\phi=C_I$ yields

$$\phi(u_1)+\phi(u_2)=\phi(u_1u_2).$$

Let us now differentiate both sides of this equation with respect to u_1 and u_2. This yields the differential equation

$$0=\phi'(u_1u_2)+u_1u_2\phi''(u_1u_2).$$

Take $u_1u_2=t$ to see that

$$\phi'(t)=-t\phi''(t)$$

whose solution is $\phi(t)=c\ln t$ since $\phi(1)=0$. □

4.5.4.3 Singular components of Archimedean copulas

Recall that we assumed ϕ' continuous. If the Archimedean copula C_ϕ has a singular component then this component is concentrated on the set

$$\left\{\boldsymbol{u}\in[0,1]^2\middle|\phi(u_1)+\phi(u_2)=\phi(0)\right\},$$

since the derivatives $\frac{\partial}{\partial u_1}C_\phi$ and $\frac{\partial}{\partial u_2}C_\phi$ exist everywhere except on that curve. The following result makes this statement precise.

Proposition 4.5.6
The copula C_ϕ has a singular component if, and only if, $\phi(0)/\phi'(0)\neq 0$. In that case, $\phi(U_1)+\phi(U_2)=\phi(0)$ with probability $-\phi(0)/\phi'(0)$.

Proof. Let us integrate the density c_ϕ over its domain

$$\left\{\boldsymbol{u}\in[0,1]^2\middle|\phi(u_1)+\phi(u_2)<\phi(0)\right\}.$$

To perform this integration, let us make the following substitution

$$v_1=C_\phi(\boldsymbol{u})=\phi^{-1}\big(\phi(u_1+\phi(u_2)\big),\quad v_2=u_1,$$

so that $\boldsymbol{v}\in[0,1]^2$. For a given value of v_1, it is easy to see that $v_1\leq v_2\leq 1$. The Jacobian of the transformation is given by

$$\frac{\partial\boldsymbol{v}}{\partial\boldsymbol{u}}=-\frac{\phi'(u_2)}{\phi'\big(C_\phi(\boldsymbol{u})\big)}.$$

Therefore, the probability mass which is accounted for by the density is

$$\begin{aligned}\int\int_{\{\boldsymbol{u}\in[0,1]^2|\phi(u_1)+\phi(u_2)<\phi(0)\}}C_\phi(\boldsymbol{u})du_1du_2&=-\int\int_{0<v_1<v_2<1}\frac{\phi''(v_1)}{\big(\phi'(v_1)\big)^2}\phi'(v_2)dv_1dv_2\\&=\int_0^1\frac{\phi''(\xi)}{\big(\phi'(\xi)\big)^2}\phi(\xi)d\xi.\end{aligned}$$

Integrating by parts yields

$$p=-\left[\frac{\phi(\xi)}{\phi'(\xi)}\right]_0^1+1=\frac{\phi(0)}{\phi'(0)}+1.$$

This probability p is less than one if, and only if, $\phi(0)/\phi'(0)\neq 0$. In this case, the copula C_ϕ has a singular component on the curve $\phi(u_1)+\phi(u_2)=\phi(0)$ (i.e., with probability $-\phi(0)/\phi'(0)$, the pair (U_1, U_2) will be on the boundary curve). □

Example 4.5.7. If $\phi(t)=\frac{t^{-\alpha}-1}{\alpha}$ for some $\alpha>0$, we get the Clayton copula (4.8). In this case, we have

$$\lim_{t\to 0}\phi(t)=0 \text{ and } \frac{\phi(0)}{\phi'(0)}=0.$$

The Clayton copulas do not have any singular components and their support is $(0,1]^2$. ∇

Example 4.5.8. If $\phi(t) = (1-t)^\alpha$ where $\alpha \geq 1$, we get

$$C_\phi(\boldsymbol{u}) = \max\left\{0, 1 - \left((1-u_1)^\alpha + (1-u_2)^\alpha\right)^{1/\alpha}\right\}.$$

In this case, the boundary is

$$(1-u_1)^\alpha + (1-u_2)^\alpha = 1$$

and the probability that (U_1, U_2) falls on this curve is $-\phi(0)/\phi'(0) = 1/\alpha$. When $\alpha = 1$ we get C_L which is completely singular as $U_2 = 1 - U_1$ holds with probability one.

Note that C_L is generated by $\phi(t) = 1 - t$, a function which does not satisfy the conditions stated in (4.9). This shows that the aforementioned conditions are sufficient but not necessary to imply that C_ϕ is a copula. For necessary conditions, see Nelsen (1999). ∇

Remark 4.5.9. In general (i.e., when ϕ' exhibits discontinuity jumps), other singularities may arise along the curves $\phi(u_1) + \phi(u_2) = \phi(t)$ for the values of t where ϕ' jumps. For more details, see Theorem 4.3.3 in Nelsen (1999). ∇

4.6 SIMULATION FROM GIVEN MARGINALS AND COPULA

4.6.1 General method

Consider a random couple $\boldsymbol{X} = (X_1, X_2)$ and let F_1 and F_2 be the marginal dfs of $\boldsymbol{X}$. Now, denote by $F_{2|1}(\cdot|x_1)$ the conditional df of X_2 given that $X_1 = x_1$ as defined in Property 4.2.13. The corresponding quantile function is $F_{2|1}^{-1}(\cdot|x_1)$. Consider the transformation $\Psi_{\boldsymbol{X}} : \mathbb{R}^2 \to [0, 1]^2$ defined by

$$\Psi_{\boldsymbol{X}}(\boldsymbol{x}) = \left(F_1(x_1), F_{2|1}(x_2|x_1)\right).$$

It can be shown that when $F_{\boldsymbol{X}}$ is continuous, the random vector (U_1, U_2) defined as

$$(U_1, U_2) = \Psi_{\boldsymbol{X}}(\boldsymbol{X}) \tag{4.12}$$

consists of two independent $\mathcal{U}ni(0, 1)$ rvs.

By inverting $\Psi_{\boldsymbol{X}}$, we can express the X_i as functions of the independent $\mathcal{U}ni(0, 1)$ rvs U_1, U_2. Denote

$$x_1 = F_1^{-1}(u_1) \text{ and } x_2 = F_{2|1}^{-1}(u_2|x_1). \tag{4.13}$$

Consider the tranformation $\Psi_{\boldsymbol{X}}^{-1} : [0, 1]^2 \to \mathbb{R}^2$ defined by

$$\Psi_{\boldsymbol{X}}^{-1}(u_1, u_2) = (x_1, x_2),$$

where the x_i are functions of the u_i as given by (4.13). Then it can be shown that, given independent $\mathcal{U}ni(0, 1)$ rvs U_1 and U_2,

$$\Psi_{\boldsymbol{X}}^{-1}(U_1, U_2) =_d (X_1, X_2).$$

This construction is a well-known method of multivariate simulation.

4.6.2 Exploiting Sklar's decomposition

In the case where marginal dfs F_1 and F_2 and a copula C are specified, a unique multivariate distribution F_X can be found as in (4.3). The problem of simulating from this distribution can be tackled in a number of ways. Let (U_1, U_2) be a random couple with df C. Then, the random couple $(F_1^{-1}(U_1), F_2^{-1}(U_2))$ has joint df F_X. The technical difficulty now lies in simulating realizations from C. The general method involves recursive simulation using univariate conditional distributions.

Example 4.6.1. The conditional copula $C_{2|1}(\cdot|u_1)$ associated with the Clayton copula (4.8) can be inverted as

$$C_{2|1}^{-1}(q|u_1) = \left((q^{-\frac{\alpha}{1+\alpha}} - 1)u_1^{-\alpha} + 1\right)^{-\frac{1}{\alpha}}.$$

This provides a convenient method to simulate realizations of $X \in \mathcal{R}_2(F_1, F_2)$ with the Clayton copula:

1. Generate u_1 from the $\mathcal{U}ni(0, 1)$ distribution.
2. Generate q from the $\mathcal{U}ni(0, 1)$ distribution and derive $u_2 = C_{2|1}^{-1}(q|u_1)$.
3. The desired realization is then $(F_1^{-1}(u_1), F_2^{-1}(u_2))$.

∇

Of course, other constructions are possible, as exemplified in Exercise 4.9.7.

4.6.3 Simulation from Archimedean copulas

4.6.3.1 Simulation based on the frailty representation

The mixture representation of multivariate Archimedean copulas described in Section 4.5.2 suggests the following method for generating an observation from F_X satisfying (4.3) for some $C = C_\phi$:

1. Generate θ from F_Θ.
2. Generate two independent $\mathcal{U}ni(0, 1)$ random numbers u_1 and u_2.
3. Let $x_i = H_i^{-1}(u_i^{1/\theta})$, $i = 1, 2$.

4.6.3.2 Lee's simulation algorithm

Genest and MacKay (1986a) and Genest (1987) explored the idea of simulating the full distribution F_X by recursively simulating X_1 and then the conditional distribution of X_2 given X_1. This idea was subsequently developed by Lee (1993) and is described below.

The algorithm to generate outcomes from a bivariate df with copula C_ϕ is as follows:

1. Generate two independent $\mathcal{U}ni(0, 1)$ random numbers u_1 and u_2.
2. Set $x_1 = F_1^{-1}(u_1)$.

3. Calculate x_2 as the solution of

$$u_2 = F_{2|1}(x_2|x_1) = \frac{(\phi^{-1})'(\phi(F_2(x_2)))}{(\phi^{-1})'(0)}.$$

4.7 MULTIVARIATE COPULAS

4.7.1 Definition

In this section we extend some of the results of the preceding sections to the multivariate case. We start by defining the notion of multivariate copula. A multivariate copula can be seen as the joint df of an n-dimensional random vector with $\mathcal{U}ni(0, 1)$ marginals.

Definition 4.7.1. An n-dimensional copula C is a function mapping the unit hypercube $[0, 1]^n$ to the unit interval $[0, 1]$ which is non-decreasing and right-continuous, and satisfies:

(i) $C(u_1, \ldots, u_{i-1}, 0, u_{i+1}, \ldots, u_n) = 0$ for $i = 1, 2, \ldots, n$;

(ii) $C(1, \ldots, 1, u_i, 1, \ldots, 1) = u_i$ for $i = 1, 2, \ldots, n$;

(iii) for all $\boldsymbol{\alpha}, \boldsymbol{\beta} \in [0, 1]^n$ with $\alpha_i < \beta_i$ for $i = 1, 2, \ldots, n$,

$$\Delta_{\alpha_1,\beta_1}\Delta_{\alpha_2,\beta_2}\cdots\Delta_{\alpha_n,\beta_n}C(\boldsymbol{u}) \geq 0$$

for each $\boldsymbol{u} \in [0, 1]^n$, where the $\Delta_{\alpha_i,\beta_i}$ are as in Property 1.5.7(iii).

∇

4.7.2 Sklar's representation theorem

Every df $F_{\boldsymbol{X}}$ of a random vector $\boldsymbol{X} \in \mathcal{R}_n(F_1, F_2, \ldots, F_n)$ can be represented as

$$F_{\boldsymbol{X}}(\boldsymbol{x}) = C(F_1(x_1), F_2(x_2), \ldots, F_n(x_n)), \quad \boldsymbol{x} \in \mathbb{R}^n, \tag{4.14}$$

in terms of a copula C. If the marginals $F_1, F_2, \ldots, F_n$ are continuous then the copula C involved in (4.14) is unique and explicitly given by

$$C(\boldsymbol{u}) = F_{\boldsymbol{X}}\Big(F_1^{-1}(u_1), F_2^{-1}(u_2), \ldots, F_n^{-1}(u_n)\Big), \quad \boldsymbol{u} \in [0, 1]^n;$$

C is then the df of the random vector $(F_1(X_1), F_2(X_2), \ldots, F_n(X_n))$ which has $\mathcal{U}ni(0, 1)$ marginals by Property 1.5.19. If $F_1, F_2, \ldots, F_n$ are not all continuous, it can still be shown that the joint df $F_{\boldsymbol{X}}$ can always be expressed as in (4.14), although in this case C is no longer unique (it is usually referred to as a possible copula for $F_{\boldsymbol{X}}$).

Remark 4.7.2. It is worth mentioning that the formula

$$\overline{F}_{\boldsymbol{X}}(\boldsymbol{x}) = C(\overline{F}_1(x_1), \overline{F}_2(x_2), \ldots, \overline{F}_n(x_n)), \quad \boldsymbol{x} \in \mathbb{R}^n, \tag{4.15}$$

defines a joint tf with marginal tfs $\overline{F}_1, \overline{F}_2, \ldots, \overline{F}_n$. The multivariate distributions given by (4.14) and (4.15) are different in general. ∇

Remark 4.7.3. Note that if $\boldsymbol{X}$ has copula C and if $(U_1, U_2, \ldots, U_n)$ has df C, then

$$\boldsymbol{X} =_d \left(F_1^{-1}(U_1), F_2^{-1}(U_2), \ldots, F_n^{-1}(U_n)\right).$$

This result is a multivariate version of Property 1.5.20. ∇

The pdf associated with C exists almost everywhere on $[0, 1]^n$ (i.e., everywhere except perhaps on a set of Lebesgue measure 0) and is given by

$$c(\boldsymbol{u}) = \frac{\partial^n}{\partial u_1 \ldots \partial u_n} C(\boldsymbol{u}).$$

This density can be used to define the absolutely continuous and singular parts of C, just as in the bivariate case.

The pdf of $\boldsymbol{X}$ with copula C and marginal dfs $F_1, \ldots, F_n$ admits the representation

$$f_{\boldsymbol{X}}(\boldsymbol{x}) = \left(\prod_{i=1}^{n} f_i(x_i)\right) c\big(F_1(x_1), \ldots, F_n(x_n)\big), \quad \boldsymbol{x} \in \mathbb{R}^n.$$

As in the bivariate case, $f_{\boldsymbol{X}}$ is obtained by reweighting the pdf corresponding to independence using the copula density c.

4.7.3 Functional invariance

The following proposition shows an attractive feature of the copula representation of dependence, namely that the dependence structure as summarized by a copula is invariant under non-decreasing and continuous transformations of the marginals. It can be seen as a multivariate extension of Proposition 4.4.4(i).

Proposition 4.7.4
Let $\boldsymbol{X}$ be an n-dimensional random vector with copula C and $t_1, t_2, \ldots, t_n$ be non-decreasing and continuous functions. Then the random vector

$$\left(t_1(X_1), t_2(X_2), \ldots, t_n(X_n)\right)$$

also has copula C.

Proposition 4.7.4 shows that the copula accounts for all the dependence between the rvs $X_1, X_2, \ldots, X_n$, since the way in which the X_i 'move together' is captured by the copula, regardless of the scale in which each variable is measured. Non-decreasing transformations do not affect the rank of an rv.

4.7.4 Examples of multivariate copulas

Below, we give some of the most common multivariate copulas.

4.7.4.1 The Fréchet upper bound copula

The Fréchet upper bound copula, denoted by C_U, is defined by

$$C_U(\boldsymbol{u}) = \min\{u_1, u_2, \ldots, u_n\}, \quad \boldsymbol{u} \in [0, 1]^n.$$

We have that $\boldsymbol{X}$ is comonotonic if, and only if, $C = C_U$.

Remark 4.7.5. Every copula C satisfies the inequality

$$\max\left\{\sum_{i=1}^{n} u_i - (n-1), 0\right\} \leq C(\boldsymbol{u}) \leq C_U(\boldsymbol{u})$$

for every $\boldsymbol{u} \in [0, 1]^n$. The left-hand side is a multivariate extension of the bivariate Fréchet lower bound copula C_L. However, in general it does not satisfy the condition for being a copula, as is shown next.

Let us extend the reasoning in Remark 1.10.4 to an arbitrary dimension n. Consider the n-dimensional hypercube $[\frac{1}{2}, 1]^n$ and let us compute its mass. We get

$$\begin{aligned}
&\Delta_{\frac{1}{2},1}\Delta_{\frac{1}{2},1}\cdots\Delta_{\frac{1}{2},1} \max\left\{\sum_{i=1}^{n} u_i - (n-1), 0\right\} \\
&= \max\{1 + 1 + \ldots + 1 - (n-1), 0\} \\
&\quad -n \max\left\{\frac{1}{2} + 1 + \ldots + 1 - (n-1), 0\right\} \\
&\quad + \binom{n}{2} \max\left\{\frac{1}{2} + \frac{1}{2} + 1 + \ldots + 1 - (n-1), 0\right\} \\
&\quad + \ldots + \max\left\{\frac{1}{2} + \frac{1}{2} + \frac{1}{2} + \ldots + \frac{1}{2} - (n-1), 0\right\} \\
&= 1 - \frac{n}{2} < 0 \text{ for any } n \geq 3.
\end{aligned}$$

So, $\boldsymbol{u} \mapsto \max\{\sum_{i=1}^{n} u_i - (n-1), 0\}$ is not a copula for $n \geq 3$ since it violates condition (iii) in Definition 4.7.1. ∇

Nevertheless, the lower bound is reachable in the sense that for each $\boldsymbol{u} \in [0, 1]^n$, it is possible to find a copula C such that

$$C(\boldsymbol{u}) = \max\left\{\sum_{i=1}^{n} u_i - (n-1), 0\right\}$$

for the particular $\boldsymbol{u}$ chosen.

4.7.4.2 The independence copula

The independence copula, denoted by C_I, is defined by

$$C_I(\boldsymbol{u}) = \prod_{i=1}^{n} u_i, \quad \boldsymbol{u} \in [0, 1]^n.$$

If $\boldsymbol{X}$ possesses the copula C_I then the X_i are mutually independent.

4.7.4.3 The Clayton copula

The bivariate Clayton copula gives rise to a direct extension to dimension 3 or greater. Indeed, the multivariate Clayton copula is defined by

$$C_\alpha(\boldsymbol{u}) = \left(\sum_{i=1}^{n} u_i^{-\alpha} - n + 1 \right)^{-1/\alpha}, \quad \alpha > 0. \tag{4.16}$$

It can be shown that

$$\lim_{\alpha \to +\infty} C_\alpha(\boldsymbol{u}) = C_U(\boldsymbol{u}),$$

so that the dependence structure approaches its maximum (i.e., comonotonicity) when α increases to $+\infty$. On the other hand,

$$\lim_{\alpha \to 0} C_\alpha(\boldsymbol{u}) = C_I(\boldsymbol{u}),$$

hence independence is obtained when α tends to 0.

4.7.4.4 The multivariate normal copula

Let Σ be an $n \times n$ variance–covariance matrix with unit main diagonal (i.e., $\sigma_{kk} = 1$ for $k = 1, 2, \ldots, n$). Denoting by H_Σ the joint df of the $\mathcal{N}or\,(\boldsymbol{0}, \Sigma)$ distribution, the n-dimensional normal copula is given by

$$C_\Sigma(\boldsymbol{u}) = H_\Sigma\Big(\Phi^{-1}(u_1), \ldots, \Phi^{-1}(u_n)\Big).$$

The copula density can be obtained from the identity

$$\frac{1}{\sqrt{(2\pi)^n |\Sigma|}} \exp\left(-\frac{1}{2}\boldsymbol{x}^t\Sigma^{-1}\mathbf{x}\right) = c_\Sigma\Big(\Phi(x_1), \ldots, \Phi(x_n)\Big) \prod_{i=1}^{n} \frac{1}{\sqrt{2\pi}} \exp\left(-\frac{1}{2}x_i^2\right),$$

which gives

$$c_\Sigma\Big(\Phi(x_1), \ldots, \Phi(x_n)\Big) = |\Sigma|^{-1/2} \exp\left(-\frac{1}{2}\boldsymbol{x}^t\Sigma^{-1}\boldsymbol{x} + \frac{1}{2}\sum_{i=1}^{n} x_i^2\right).$$

If $u_i = \Phi(x_i) \Leftrightarrow x_i = \Phi^{-1}(u_i)$, then we get the copula density

$$c_\Sigma(\boldsymbol{u}) = |\Sigma|^{-1/2} \exp\left(-\frac{1}{2}\zeta^t\left(\Sigma^{-1} - \boldsymbol{I}\right)\zeta\right)$$

where $\zeta = (\Phi^{-1}(u_1), \ldots, \Phi^{-1}(u_n))^t$.

4.7.4.5 The multivariate Student copula

Let Σ be an $n \times n$ variance–covariance matrix with unit main diagonal. Denoting by $t_{m,\Sigma}$ the joint df corresponding to the multivariate Student distribution, given by

$$t_{m,\Sigma}(\boldsymbol{x}) = \int_{-\infty}^{x_1} \dots \int_{-\infty}^{x_n} \frac{\Gamma\left(\frac{m+n}{2}\right) |\Sigma|^{-1/2}}{\Gamma\left(\frac{m}{2}\right)(m\pi)^{n/2}} \left(1 + \frac{1}{m}\boldsymbol{x}'\Sigma^{-1}\boldsymbol{x}\right)^{-\frac{m+n}{2}} dx_1 \dots dx_n,$$

the multivariate Student copula is then given by

$$C_{m,\Sigma}(\boldsymbol{u}) = t_{m,\Sigma}\left(t_m^{-1}(u_1), \dots, t_m^{-1}(u_n)\right).$$

The copula density can be derived just as in the normal case. This gives

$$c_{m,\Sigma} = \frac{\Gamma\left(\frac{m+n}{2}\right)|\Sigma|^{-1/2}}{\Gamma\left(\frac{m}{2}\right)} \left(\frac{\Gamma\left(\frac{m}{2}\right)}{\Gamma\left(\frac{m+1}{2}\right)}\right)^n \left(1 + \frac{1}{m}\zeta'\Sigma^{-1}\zeta\right)^{-\frac{m+n}{2}} \prod_{i=1}^n \left(1 + \frac{\zeta_i}{m}\right)^{-\frac{m+1}{2}}$$

where $\zeta_i = t_m^{-1}(u_i)$, $i = 1, \dots, n$.

4.7.5 *Multivariate Archimedean copulas*

4.7.5.1 Definition

Let us start from the bivariate Archimedean copula with generator ϕ, given by

$$C^{[2]}(\boldsymbol{u}) = C_\phi(\boldsymbol{u}) = \phi^{-1}(\phi(u_1) + \phi(u_2)),$$

where the superscript [2] emphasizes the dimension. Then let us define iteratively, for $n \geq 3$,

$$C^{[n]}(\boldsymbol{u}) = C\left(C^{[n-1]}(u_1, u_2, \dots, u_{n-1}), u_n\right).$$

In general, $C^{[n]}$ is not a copula. Nevertheless, according to Kimberling (1974), $C^{[n]}$ is a copula if, and only if, ϕ^{-1} is completely monotonic on $\mathbb{R}^+$. The copulas obtained in this way are multivariate Archimedean copulas.

Definition 4.7.6. Given a completely monotone function $\phi: (0, 1] \to \mathbb{R}^+$ with $\phi(1) = 0$, the function $C_\phi: [0, 1]^n \to [0, 1]$ defined as

$$C_\phi(u_1, u_2, \dots, u_n) = \phi^{-1}\left(\phi(u_1) + \phi(u_2) + \dots + \phi(u_n)\right)$$

is called the Archimedean copula with generator ϕ. ∇

Example 4.7.7. The multivariate Clayton copula (4.16) is generated by $\phi(t) = t^{-\alpha} - 1$, with $\phi^{-1}(t) = (1 + t)^{-1/\alpha}$ completely monotonic provided $\alpha > 0$.

Similarly, Frank's copula is obtained with $\phi(t) = \ln\left(\frac{\exp(-\alpha t) - 1}{\exp(-\alpha) - 1}\right)$, completely monotonic if $\alpha > 0$, with $\phi^{-1}(t) = -\frac{1}{\alpha}\ln(1 + \exp(t)(\exp(-\alpha) - 1))$. Therefore, Frank's copula,

$$C_\alpha(\boldsymbol{u}) = \frac{1}{\alpha}\ln\left(1 + \frac{\prod_{i=1}^n \left(\exp(-\alpha u_i) - 1\right)}{\left(\exp(-\alpha) - 1\right)^{n-1}}\right),$$

is only defined with $\alpha>0$ when $n\geq 3$ (whereas in the bivariate case, negative values for the dependence parameter α are allowed). ∇

4.7.5.2 Frailty construction

A general method for constructing multivariate Archimedean copulas was proposed by Marshall and Olkin (1988). To describe this method, suppose that X_i is an rv whose conditional df, given a positive latent variable Θ, is specified by

$$\Pr[X_i\leq x|\Theta=\theta]=\big(H_i(x)\big)^{\theta}, \tag{4.17}$$

where H_i is some baseline df, for $i=1,2,\ldots,n$.

The df F_i of X_i is then given by

$$\begin{aligned} F_i(x) &= \int_0^{+\infty}\Pr[X_i\leq x|\Theta=\theta]dF_\Theta(\theta)\\ &= \int_0^{+\infty}\big(H_i(x)\big)^{\theta}dF_\Theta(\theta)\\ &= \int_0^{+\infty}\exp\big(\theta\ln H_i(x)\big)dF_\Theta(\theta)\\ &= L_\Theta\big(-\ln H_i(x)\big), \end{aligned}$$

where L_Θ is the Laplace transform of Θ. Laplace transforms have well-defined inverses, so that

$$H_i(x)=\exp\Big(-L_\Theta^{-1}(F_i(x))\Big),\quad i=1,2,\ldots,n, \tag{4.18}$$

also holds. A remarkable feature in this construction is that for any specified pair of dfs F_i and F_Θ there exists a df H_i for which the representation (4.17) holds; this df H_i is given by (4.18).

Now the cdf of $\boldsymbol{X}$ is given for $\boldsymbol{x}\in\mathbb{R}^n$ by

$$\begin{aligned} F_{\boldsymbol{X}}(\boldsymbol{x}) &= \int_{-\infty}^{+\infty}\left(\prod_{i=1}^{n}\big(H_i(x_i)\big)^{\theta}\right)dF_\Theta(\theta)\\ &= L_\Theta\left(\sum_{i=1}^{n}L_\Theta^{-1}(F_i(x_i))\right). \end{aligned} \tag{4.19}$$

We recognize in (4.19) a variant of the definition of Archimedean copulas, with generator $\phi^{-1}=L_\Theta$.

If the copula C_ϕ introduced in Definition 4.7.6 is used to define a multivariate df for all finite dimensions n, then according to a result of Schweizer and Sklar (1983), ϕ^{-1} must be proportional to a Laplace transform. The fact that ϕ is completely monotone implies that ϕ^{-1} is the Laplace transform of some distribution function F_Θ with $F_\Theta(0)=0$, in view of the classical Bernstein theorem (1.21).

4.8 LOSS–ALAE MODELLING WITH ARCHIMEDEAN COPULAS: A CASE STUDY

4.8.1 Losses and their associated ALAEs

Various processes in casualty insurance involve correlated pairs of rvs. The loss and allocated loss adjustment expenses (ALAEs) on a single claim are a prominent example. Here ALAEs are a type of insurance company expense specifically attributable to the settlement of individual claims such as lawyers' fees and claims investigation expenses.

Expensive claims generally need some time to be settled and induce considerable costs for the insurance company. Actuaries therefore expect some positive dependence between losses and their associated ALAEs, that is, large losses tend to be associated with large ALAEs. This positive dependence often has some practical implications in the pricing of reinsurance treaties. The reinsurer usually covers the largest losses (i.e., those exceeding some high threshold called the retention of the direct insurer) and pays that part exceeding this threshold. It also contributes to the associated settlement costs on a pro-rata basis. In many cases, neglecting the dependence exhibited by the data leads to serious underestimation of the reinsurer's expected payment. It is therefore crucial for the reinsurer to have an appropriate model for the random couple loss–ALAE available.

Typically, a given amount of loss is divided between the insurer and the reinsurer as follows. The insurance company pays the loss from zero up to a specified amount r called the insurer's retention. Then the reinsurer covers the claim from r, but with a maximum limit equal to ω. The excess over the limit ω remains with the direct insurer (but a policy limit, i.e., an upper bound to the amount paid by the insurer to the policyholder, may be specified in the contract). If we denote the loss by L and the associated ALAE by A, assuming a pro-rata sharing of expenses, the reinsurer's payment for a given realization (L, A) of loss and associated ALAE is described by the function:

$$g(L, A) = \begin{cases} 0, & \text{if } L < r, \\ L - r + \frac{L-r}{L} A, & \text{if } r \leq L < \omega, \\ \omega - r + \frac{\omega - r}{\omega} A, & \text{if } L \geq \omega. \end{cases}$$

The net premium of such a treaty involves the computation of $\mathbb{E}[g(L, A)]$, which in turn requires knowledge of the joint distribution for the pair (L, A). The possible dependence between losses and ALAEs therefore has to be accounted for when reinsurance treaties are priced.

4.8.2 Presentation of the ISO data set

We use the same data set as Frees and Valdez (1998) and Klugman and Parsa (1999). These data were collected by the US Insurance Services Office, and comprise general liability claims randomly chosen from late settlement lags. The data consist of $n = 1500$ observations, each accompanied by a policy limit ℓ (i.e., the maximal claim amount) specific to each contract. Therefore the loss variable will be censored when the amount of the claim exceeds the policy limit. More precisely, one observes a triple (M_i, A_i, Δ_i), where $M_i = \min\{L_i, \ell_i\}$, L_i is the ith loss and A_i the associated ALAE, $i = 1, \ldots, n$, and

$$\Delta_i = \mathbb{I}[M_i = \ell_i] = \begin{cases} 1, & \text{if} \quad L_i \leq \ell_i \text{ (uncensored claim)}, \\ 0, & \text{if} \quad L_i > \ell_i \text{ (censored claim)}. \end{cases} \tag{4.20}$$

Some summary statistics for the data are gathered in Table 4.1. It appears clearly that, even if the vast majority of losses are uncensored (1466 of the 1500 observations), the 34 censored data points have a much higher mean than the 1466 complete data (US$ 217,941 versus US$ 37,110). A scatterplot of (loss, ALAE) on log scales is depicted in Figure 4.9. Its shape suggests a positive relationship between loss and ALAE: large losses tend to be associated with large ALAEs, as expected. Moreover, censored data points (represented by triangles in Figure 4.9) clearly cluster to the right.

4.8.3 *Fitting parametric copula models to data*

4.8.3.1 Preliminary estimation of the dependence parameter: Omnibus approach

Oakes (1989) described in broad terms an omnibus semiparametric procedure for estimating the dependence parameter in a copula model when marginal distributions are treated as (infinite-dimensional) nuisance parameters. The resulting estimator was subsequently shown to be consistent and asymptotically normally distributed by Genest, Ghoudi and Rivest (1995) and Shih and Louis (1995).

In applications, actuaries face the problem of estimating the (univariate or multivariate) dependence parameter α of a copula model from a random sample $\{\boldsymbol{x}_i, i = 1, 2, \ldots, m\}$ where $\boldsymbol{x}_i = (x_{i1}, x_{i2}, \ldots, x_{in})$ is a realization from the n-dimensional vector $\boldsymbol{X}_i$ with df $F_{\boldsymbol{X}}$, copula C and marginal dfs F_j, $j = 1, 2, \ldots, n$. One simple approach involves first selecting specific forms for each of the F_j (lognormal or Pareto, for instance) and maximizing the joint likelihood. However, recognition that inappropriate choices for the marginals could appreciably affect the estimation of α has led many authors to treat the marginals as (infinite-dimensional) nuisance parameters and to seek semiparametric procedures for selecting the

Table 4.1 Summary statistics for losses and ALAEs

	Loss	ALAE	Loss (uncensored)	Loss (censored)
Total N	1,500	1,500	1,466	34
Min	10	15	10	5,000
1st Qu.	4,000	2,333	3,750	50,000
Mean	41,208	12,588	37,110	217,941
Median	12,000	5,471	11,049	100,000
3rd Qu.	35,000	12,577	32,000	300,000
Max	2,173,595	501,863	2,173,595	1,000,000
Std Dev.	102,748	28,146	92,513	258,205

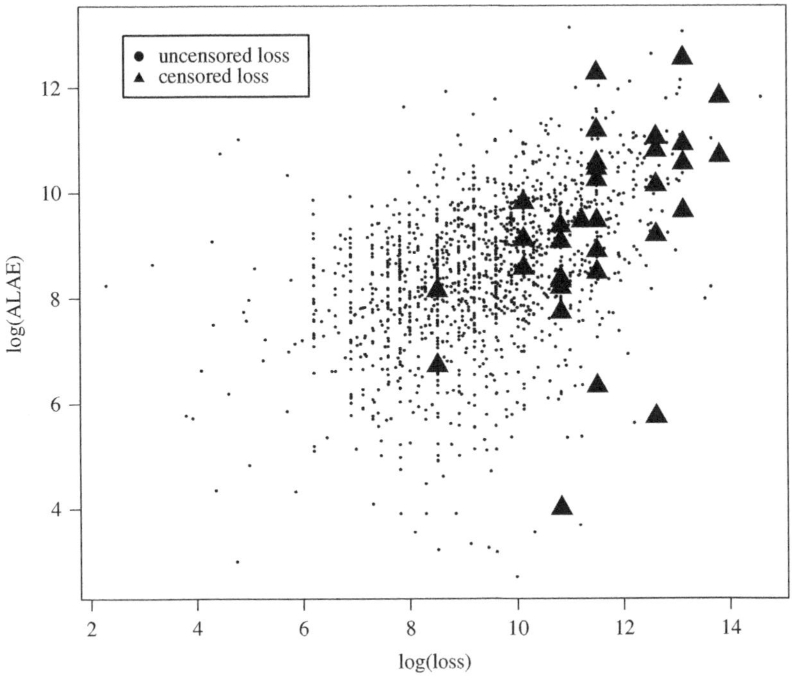

Figure 4.9 Scatterplot for loss and ALAE (on the log scale)

dependence parameter. *Ad hoc* proposals in specified contexts gradually led to the emergence of a global strategy for estimating θ semiparametrically.

This omnibus procedure, described in broad terms by Oakes (1989), is quite simple. For each $j = 1, 2, \ldots, n$, let

$$\widehat{F}_j^{(m)}(x) = \frac{1}{m+1} \sum_{i=1}^{m} \mathbb{I}[x_{ij} \leq x]$$

be the (rescaled) empirical df corresponding to the jth component of the vector of observations. Then, the estimate $\widehat{\alpha}$ of α is the value that maximizes the pseudo-log-likelihood

$$\sum_{i=1}^{m} \ln c_\alpha \left(\widehat{F}_1^{(m)}(x_{i1}), \ldots, \widehat{F}_n^{(m)}(x_{in}) \right)$$

where c_α is the pdf associated with C_α (assuming it is strictly positive on $[0, 1]^n$). Compared to a standard maximum likelihood approach, the semiparametric approach thus substitutes the empirical dfs $\widehat{F}_j^{(m)}$ for the population dfs F_j.

4.8.3.2 Maximum likelihood

The most appropriate theory for fitting parametric copula models seems to be maximum likelihood theory. Much of the classical statistical inference theory (exponential family results, sufficient statistics, minimum variance unbiased estimators, etc.) is difficult to apply. The following two-step procedure for copula-based models in which parameters for univariate marginals are separated from dependence parameters appears simple and robust. The basic idea is that, rather than maximizing the log-likelihood function in all of the parameters together, it is better to first estimate different marginal distributions and then perform a global optimization.

Consider the model

$$F_X(\boldsymbol{x}|\theta_1, \theta_2, \ldots, \theta_n, \alpha) = C_\alpha\Big(F_1(x_1|\theta_1), F_2(x_2|\theta_2), \ldots, F_n(x_n|\theta_n)\Big),$$

where $F_1, F_2, \ldots, F_n$ are univariate dfs with respective parameters $\theta_1, \theta_2, \ldots, \theta_n$ and C_α belongs to some family of copulas parameterized by α. For estimation of a parametric family of multivariate distributions of this form from a random sample of m independent and identically distributed n-dimensional random vectors $\boldsymbol{X}_1, \boldsymbol{X}_2, \ldots, \boldsymbol{X}_m$, the following procedure could be used:

1. Fit the n univariate marginal dfs $F_1, \ldots, F_n$ with the help of the observations $\{x_{11}, x_{21}, \ldots, x_{m1}\}, \ldots, \{x_{1m}, x_{2m}, \ldots, x_{mn}\}$, respectively; let $\widetilde{\theta}_1, \widetilde{\theta}_2, \ldots, \widetilde{\theta}_n$ be the corresponding maximum likelihood estimators of $\theta_1, \theta_2, \ldots, \theta_n$.
2. Estimate α using multivariate likelihood, with the parameters $\theta_1, \theta_2, \ldots, \theta_n$ fixed at the estimated values from step 1; let the result be $\widetilde{\alpha}$. A starting value is provided by the omnibus procedure.
3. Using $\widetilde{\theta}_1, \widetilde{\theta}_2, \ldots, \widetilde{\theta}_n$ and $\widetilde{\alpha}$ as starting values, determine the global maximum likelihood estimators $\widehat{\theta}_1, \widehat{\theta}_2, \ldots, \widehat{\theta}_n$ and $\widehat{\alpha}$ of the parameters $\theta_1, \theta_2, \ldots, \theta_n$ and α.

Several authors suggest comparing the values $\widetilde{\theta}_1, \ldots, \widetilde{\theta}_n, \widetilde{\alpha}$ to $\widehat{\theta}_1, \ldots, \widehat{\theta}_n, \widehat{\alpha}$ as an estimation consistency check to evaluate the adequacy of the copula. Note that for the multivariate normal distribution with parameters $\alpha = \boldsymbol{R}$ (the correlation matrix) and $\theta_j = (\mu_j, \sigma_j^2)$, $j = 1, \ldots, n$ (the marginal mean and variance), we have

$$\widetilde{\theta}_j = \widehat{\theta}_j \quad \text{and} \quad \widetilde{\alpha} = \widehat{\alpha}.$$

However, the equivalence of the estimators does not hold in general. We refer the reader to Joe (1997, Chapter 10) for a comparison of the asymptotic efficiencies of $\widetilde{\theta}_1, \ldots, \widetilde{\theta}_n, \widetilde{\alpha}$ and $\widehat{\theta}_1, \ldots, \widehat{\theta}_n, \widehat{\alpha}$.

4.8.4 Selecting the generator for Archimedean copula models

4.8.4.1 Semiparametric analysis of bivariate Archimedean copulas with complete data

Because copulas characterize the dependence structure of random vectors once the effect of the marginals has been eliminated, identifying and fitting a copula to data is not an easy task. In practice, it is often preferable to restrict the search for an appropriate copula to some reasonable family, such as the Archimedean. Then it is useful to have simple graphical procedures to select the best-fitting model from some competing alternatives for the data at hand.

Starting from the assumption that the Archimedean dependence structure is appropriate in a bivariate context, Genest and Rivest (1993) proposed a procedure for identifying a generator in empirical applications. Given observations from a random pair $\boldsymbol{X}=(X_1, X_2)$ with df $F_{\boldsymbol{X}}$, this procedure relies on the estimation of the univariate df associated with the probability integral transform $Z=F_{\boldsymbol{X}}(X_1, X_2)$.

The starting point of the method they proposed is furnished by the following result.

Proposition 4.8.1

Let $\boldsymbol{U}=(U_1, U_2)$ be a random couple with $\mathcal{U}ni(0, 1)$ marginals and joint df C_ϕ. Let us define the rvs

$$V=\frac{\phi(U_1)}{\phi(U_1)+\phi(U_2)} \text{ and } Z=C_\phi(U_1, U_2),$$

as well as the function

$$\lambda(\xi)=\frac{\phi(\xi)}{\phi'(\xi)}, \quad 0<\xi\leq 1.$$

Then,

(i) $V\sim\mathcal{U}ni(0, 1)$;

(ii) the df F_Z of Z is given by $K(z)=z-\lambda(z)$;

(iii) V and Z are independent rvs.

Proof. Consider the rvs $T_1=\phi(U_1)$ and $T_2=\phi(U_2)$ whose joint df is

$$\begin{aligned}\Pr[\boldsymbol{T}\leq \boldsymbol{t}]&=\Pr\left[U_1\geq\phi^{-1}(t_1), U_2\geq\phi^{-1}(t_2)\right]\\&=1-\Pr\left[U_1\leq\phi^{-1}(t_1)\right]-\Pr\left[U_2\leq\phi^{-1}(t_2)\right]+C_\phi\left(\phi^{-1}(t_1), \phi^{-1}(t_2)\right)\\&=1-\phi^{-1}(t_1)-\phi^{-1}(t_2)+\phi^{-1}(t_1+t_2).\end{aligned}$$

Then

$$\begin{aligned}\Pr[Z\leq z]&=\Pr[C_\phi(U_1, U_2)\leq z]\\&=\Pr[\phi(U_1)+\phi(U_2)\geq\phi(z)]\\&=\Pr\left[T_1\geq\phi(z)-T_2\right].\end{aligned}$$

The pdf of T_2 is $-1/\phi'\left(\phi^{-1}(t_2)\right)$, so that

$$\Pr[T_1\leq t_1|T_2=t_2]=1-\frac{\phi'\left(\phi^{-1}(t_2)\right)}{\phi'\left(\phi^{-1}(t_1+t_2)\right)}.$$

Conditioning on the value of T_2, we get

$$\begin{aligned}\Pr[Z \le z] &= -\int_0^{+\infty} \Pr\left[T_1 \ge \phi(z) - t_2 \middle| T_2 = t_2\right] \frac{1}{\phi'\big(\phi^{-1}(t_2)\big)} dt_2 \\ &= -\int_{\phi(z)}^{+\infty} \frac{1}{\phi'\big(\phi^{-1}(t_2)\big)} dt_2 - \int_0^{\phi(z)} \frac{1}{\phi'\big(\phi^{-1}(\phi(z))\big)} dt_2 \\ &= -\phi^{-1}(+\infty) + \phi^{-1}\big(\phi(z)\big) - \frac{\phi(z)}{\phi'(z)} \\ &= z - \lambda(z),\end{aligned}$$

as required.

Now,

$$\Pr[V \le v, Z \le z] = \Pr\left[T_1 \le \frac{vT_2}{1-v}, T_1 \ge \phi(z) - T_2\right]. \tag{4.21}$$

The pdf of T_2 is $1/\phi'\big(\phi^{-1}(t_2)\big)$, so that

$$\Pr[T_1 \le t_1 | T_2 = t_2] = 1 - \frac{\phi'\big(\phi^{-1}(t_2)\big)}{\phi'\big(\phi^{-1}(t_1 + t_2)\big)}.$$

Conditioning on the value of T_2, (4.21) can be expressed as

$$\begin{aligned}\Pr[V \le v, Z \le z] &= -\int_{(1-v)\phi(z)}^{\phi(z)} \frac{\Pr\left[\phi(z) - \xi \le T_1 \le \frac{v\xi}{1-v} \middle| T_2 = \xi\right]}{\phi'\big(\phi^{-1}(\xi)\big)} d\xi \\ &\quad - \int_{\phi(z)}^{\phi(0)} \frac{\Pr\left[T_1 \le \frac{v\xi}{1-v} \middle| T_2 = \xi\right]}{\phi'\big(\phi^{-1}(\xi)\big)} d\xi \\ &= vF_Z(z),\end{aligned}$$

which concludes the proof. □

Note that the existence of a function ϕ for which properties (i), (ii) and (iii) hold implies that the joint df of $\boldsymbol{U}$ is the Archimedean copula C_ϕ.

Given F_Z, it is possible to recover ϕ by solving the differential equation

$$\frac{\phi(z)}{\phi'(z)} = z - K(z)$$

which yields

$$\phi(z) = \exp\left(\int_{z_0}^{z} \frac{1}{\lambda(\xi)} d\xi\right), \tag{4.22}$$

where $0 < z_0 < 1$ is an arbitrary chosen constant. The function ϕ defined in (4.22) generates an Archimedean copula whenever $z - K(z)$ is negative and remains bounded away from

0 on the unit interval. Specifically, ϕ given in (4.22) is decreasing and convex and satisfies $\phi(1)=0$ if, and only if,

$$F_Z(z-) = \lim_{t\to z-} F_Z(z) > z \text{ for all } 0 < z < 1. \tag{4.23}$$

Let $\{(x_1^{(i)}, x_2^{(i)}),\ i=1,2,\ldots,n\}$ denote a sample of size n from a continuous bivariate distribution. The procedure proposed by Genest and Rivest (1993) assumes that the underlying distribution function F_X has an associated copula C_ϕ; the aim is thus to identify ϕ. The idea is to work with the intermediate rv $Z_i = F_X(X_1^{(i)}, X_2^{(i)})$ that has df K given in Proposition 4.8.1. To identify ϕ, the method proceeds in three steps:

1. Construct a nonparametric estimate of K as

$$\widehat{K}_n(z) = \frac{1}{n}\#\{i|z_i \le z\}$$

where

$$z_i = \frac{1}{n-1}\#\left\{(x_1^{(j)}, x_2^{(j)})\middle|x_1^{(j)} < x_1^{(i)}, x_2^{(j)} < x_2^{(i)}\right\}.$$

2. Construct a parametric estimate of K: for various choices of ϕ use the omnibus procedure to estimate α and the resulting $\widehat{\alpha}$ to estimate ϕ_α. Then, define

$$K_{\widehat{\alpha}}(z) = z - \frac{\phi_{\widehat{\alpha}}(z)}{\phi'_{\widehat{\alpha}}(z)}.$$

3. After having repeated step 2 for several choices of ϕ, it suffices to compare each parametric estimate with the nonparametric estimate constructed in Step 1. The idea is to select ϕ so that the parametric estimate resembles the nonparametric one. Measuring closeness can be done by minimizing a distance such as

$$S(\widehat{\alpha}) = \int \left(K_{\widehat{\alpha}}(z) - \widehat{K}_n(z)\right)^2 d\widehat{K}_n(z), \tag{4.24}$$

or graphically. The behaviour of the rv $S(\widehat{\alpha})$ depends on the behaviour of the $\widehat{K}_n(z)$, which has been characterized in Barbe *et al.* (1996). A detailed study can be found in Genest, Quessy and Rémillard (2004).

4.8.4.2 Semiparametric analysis of bivariate Archimedean copulas in the presence of censored data

The Genest–Rivest technique is no longer appropriate when the data have been censored. For such cases, Wang and Wells (2000) proposed a modified estimator of K. Since K can be written as

$$K(v) = \Pr[F_X(X_1, X_2) \le v] = \mathbb{E}\left[\mathbb{I}[F_X(X_1, X_2) \le v]\right],$$

the suggested estimator is given by

$$\widehat{K}_n(v) = \int_0^\infty \int_0^\infty \mathbb{I}[\widehat{F}_X(x_1, x_2) \le v] d\widehat{F}_X(x_1, x_2), \tag{4.25}$$

where $\widehat{F}_X$ stands for a nonparametric estimator of the joint df F_X taking censoring into account. As mentioned by the authors, this approach is sufficiently flexible to deal with various censorship mechanisms, as long as $\widehat{F}_X$ is an appropriate estimator for F_X. See Denuit, Purcaru and Van Keilegom (2004) for more details.

4.8.5 Application to loss-ALAE modelling

We consider four possible copula models in the Archimedean family: the Clayton and Frank families presented above, the Joe copula (see Exercise 4.9.2) and the Gumbel copula (see Exercise 5.4.17). The omnibus estimates of the dependence parameters are given next: 0.5174 for the Clayton copula, 3.0861 for the Frank copula, 1.4454 for the Gumbel copula and 1.6504 for the Joe copula.

Plotting in Figure 4.10 the nonparametric and the four parametric estimates $\lambda_{\widehat{\alpha}}$ (where the $\widehat{\alpha}$ are the omnibus estimates) of the function λ, as well as the nonparametric estimate $\widehat{\lambda}_n$, suggests that the closest parametric models are the Frank and Gumbel models.

In order to choose the best model from the parametric models considered, we compute the distance $S(\widehat{\alpha})$ for these four models, where the estimated values $\widehat{\alpha}$ of the dependence parameters are the omnibus estimates. It follows that the Gumbel model provides the best fit to the data, even though it is quite close to the Frank model. This confirms the choice made

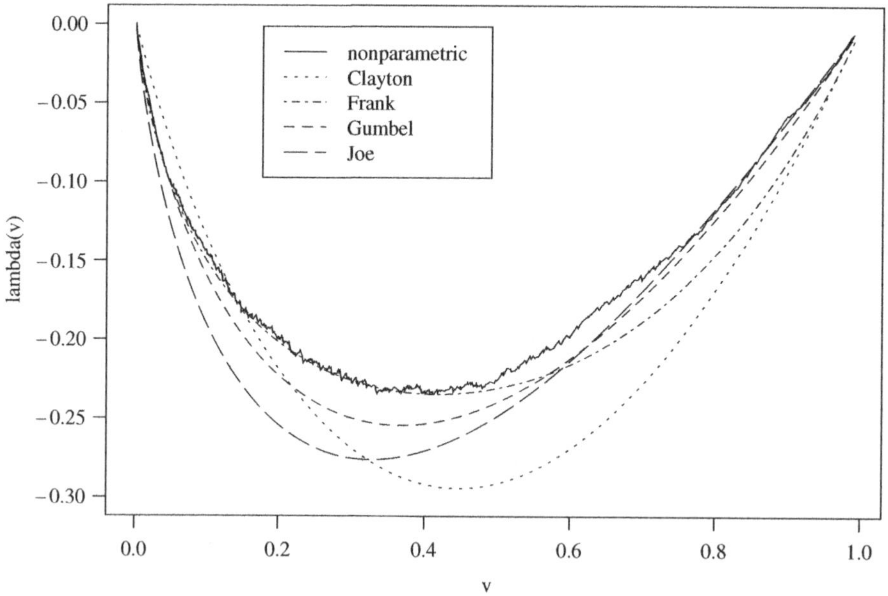

Figure 4.10 Nonparametric and parametric estimates of λ

in Frees and Valdez (1998), where the Gumbel copula was selected on the basis of the the Genest–Rivest procedure for complete data (thus, without taking censorship into account) as well as the choice in Klugman and Parsa (1999) who opted for the Frank copula.

4.8.5.1 Parametric modelling of loss-ALAE data

Now that the generator has been selected, we can proceed with a fully parametric analysis, as in Frees and Valdez (1998) and Klugman and Parsa (1999). In this section, we work with the Frank copula.

The marginal models are taken from the Pareto class. Specifically, $L \sim \mathcal{P}ar(\theta_1, \lambda_1)$ and $A \sim \mathcal{P}ar(\theta_2, \lambda_2)$. The parameters $\theta_1, \lambda_1, \theta_2$ and λ_2, as well as the dependence parameter α involved in the Frank copula, are estimated via maximum likelihood, taking censorship into account.

If the loss variable is not censored then the contribution of the observation (m_i, a_i) to the likelihood is

$$f_L(m_i)f_A(a_i)c_\alpha\big(F_L(m_i), F_A(a_i)\big).$$

If the loss variable is censored then the contribution of the observation (m_i, a_i) to the likelihood is

$$f_A(a_i)\Big(1 - C_{1|2}\big(F_L(m_i)\big|F_A(a_i)\big)\Big).$$

This gives a log-likelihood to be maximized of the form

$$\begin{aligned} L(\alpha, \theta_1, \lambda_1, \theta_2, \lambda_2) = & \sum_{i|\delta_i=1} \Big(\ln f_L(m_i) + \ln f_A(a_i) + \ln c_\alpha\big(F_L(m_i), F_A(a_i)\big)\Big) \\ & + \sum_{i|\delta_i=0} \Big(\ln f_A(a_i) + \ln\Big(1 - C_{1|2}\big(F_L(m_i)\big|F_A(a_i)\big)\Big)\Big). \end{aligned}$$

The three-step procedure to obtain the maximum likelihood estimates of the parameters that has been described in Section 4.8.3 gives the following results:

	Parameter	$\widetilde{\theta}_1, \widetilde{\lambda}_1, \widetilde{\theta}_2, \widetilde{\lambda}_2, \widetilde{\alpha}$	$\widehat{\theta}_1, \widehat{\lambda}_1, \widehat{\theta}_2, \widehat{\lambda}_2, \widehat{\alpha}$
Loss	λ_1	14,453	14,558
	θ_1	1.135	1.115
ALAE	λ_2	15,133	16,678
	θ_2	2.223	2.309
Dependence	α	3.086	3.158

The close agreement between $\widetilde{\theta}_1, \widetilde{\lambda}_1, \widetilde{\theta}_2, \widetilde{\lambda}_2, \widetilde{\alpha}$ and $\widehat{\theta}_1, \widehat{\lambda}_1, \widehat{\theta}_2, \widehat{\lambda}_2, \widehat{\alpha}$ suggests that the parametric fit is appropriate.

4.8.5.2 Some useful applications

Now that we have a fully specified model at our disposal, we can compute several interesting quantities. The calculation of $\mathbb{E}[g(L, A)]$ becomes a matter of numerical integration (a simulation procedure is described in Frees and Valdez 1998).

To give an idea of the behaviour of ALAE for some given loss level, Figure 4.11 displays the graph of $x \mapsto \Pr[A \leq x | L = l]$ for different values of l. We clearly see that the conditional dfs never cross for the levels considered. This comes from the fact that for any positive value of the dependence parameter α, the Frank copula expresses strong positive dependence (namely, total positivity of order 2, as will be seen in the next chapter). This ensures that ALAE increases in the $\preceq_{\text{LR}}$ sense given the value of the loss.

Another interesting graph is the ALAE quantile function for some given Loss level. The y-axis in Figure 4.12 shows the conditional VaR of ALAE given the value of loss (US$ 10,000, 100,000 or 1,000,000). Again, we see that for any probability level along the x-axis, the VaR for ALAE increases with the value of loss. This is in line with the $\preceq_{\text{LR}}$-increasingness mentioned above.

Figure 4.13 depicts the quantile regression curves (i.e., the qth quantiles of ALAE for some given loss level). For different probability levels, the loss (to be read along the x-axis) is mapped to the conditional quantile of ALAE (to be read along the y-axis). All these curves clearly increase, showing that ALAE tends to become larger as the loss increases.

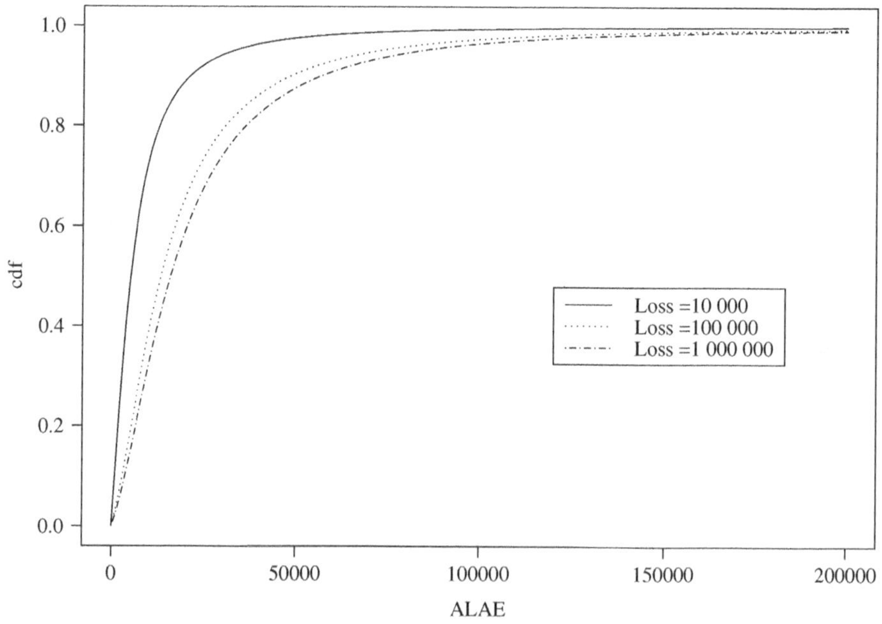

Figure 4.11 Conditional df for ALAE given some loss levels

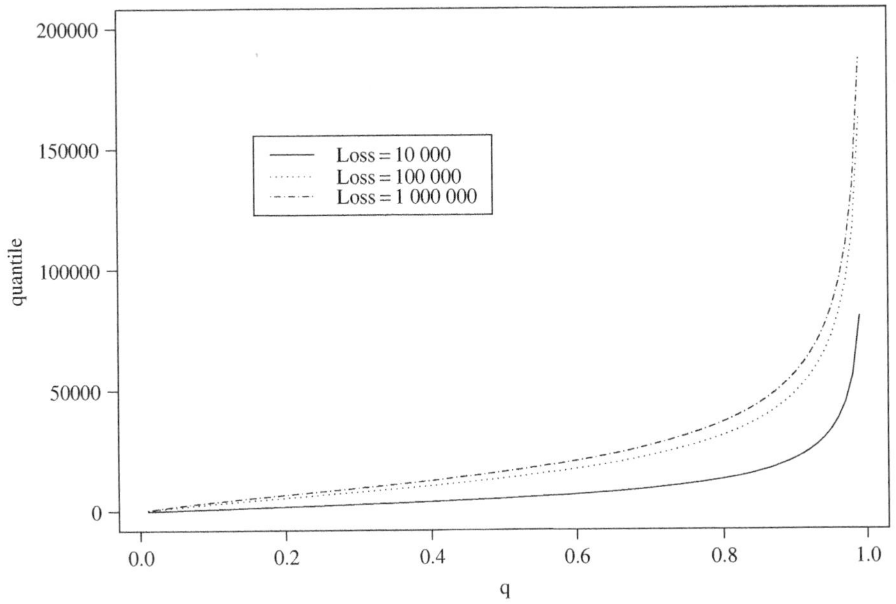

Figure 4.12 Conditional quantities for ALAE given some loss levels

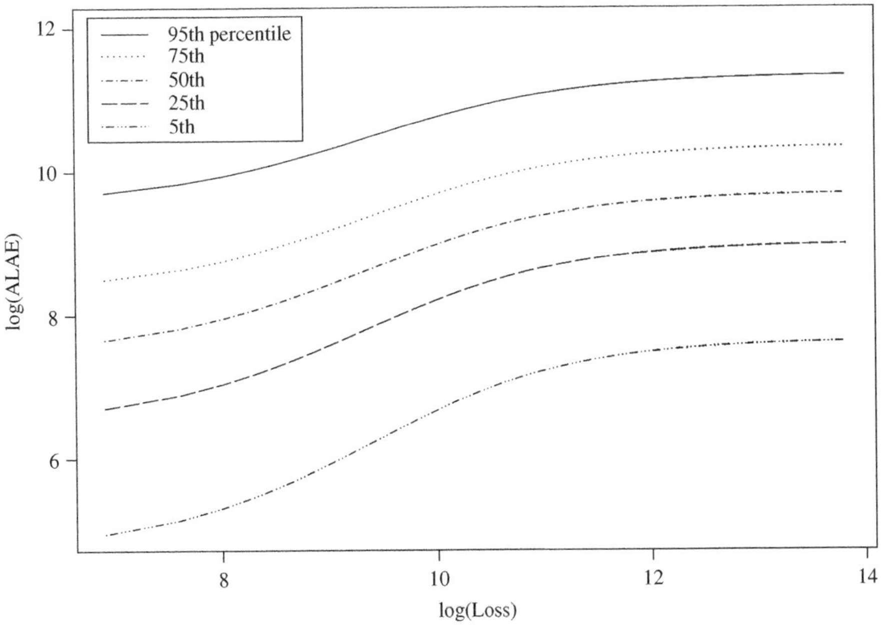

Figure 4.13 Quantile regression curves for ALAE given loss

4.9 EXERCISES

Exercise 4.9.1. (Bivariate probability integral transform). It is well known from Property 1.5.19 that, given any rv X with continuous df F_X, $F_X(X) \sim \mathcal{U}ni(0, 1)$. Now, following Genest and Rivest (2001), define the bivariate probability integral transform of (X_1, X_2) as

$$Z = F_X(X_1, X_2) = C(U_1, U_2),$$

where (U_1, U_2) has C as its joint df. Let K be the df of Z. Show that:

(i) for C_I, $K_I(z) = z - \ln z$, $0 \le z \le 1$.

(ii) for C_U, $K_U(z) = z$, $0 \le z \le 1$.

(iii) for C_L, $K_L(z) = 1$, $0 \le z \le 1$.

Exercise 4.9.2. Joe's copula is given by

$$C_\alpha(u, v) = 1 - \left(\bar{u}^\alpha + \bar{v}^\alpha - \bar{u}^\alpha \bar{v}^\alpha\right)^{1/\alpha}, \qquad \alpha \ge 1,$$

where $\bar{u} = 1 - u$ and $\bar{v} = 1 - u$.

(i) Show that it is the Archimedean copula generated by

$$\phi_\alpha(t) = -\ln\left(1 - (1 - t)^\alpha\right), \qquad \alpha \ge 1.$$

(ii) Show that the conditional copula is given by

$$(1 - \bar{u}^\alpha)(1 - \bar{u}^\alpha + \bar{u}^\alpha \bar{v}^{-\alpha})^{-1+1/\alpha}$$

Exercise 4.9.3. Let us consider

$$C(u_1, u_2) = \alpha C_U(u_1, u_2) + (1 - \alpha) C_I(u_1, u_2), \quad \boldsymbol{u} \in [0, 1]^2,$$

where $\alpha \in (0, 1)$. This copula was introduced by Konijn (1959). It was used in Li (2000) under the name of mixture copula.

(i) Check that C is indeed a copula.

(ii) If (U_1, U_2) has df C, compute the conditional df of (U_1, U_2) given that $U_1 \le v_1$ and $U_2 \le v_2$.

(iii) Compute the conditional df of U_1 given that $U_1 \le v$ and $U_2 \le v$.

(iv) Show that $\lambda_U = \alpha$.

Exercise 4.9.4. The two-parameter Fréchet copula is defined as

$$C(\boldsymbol{u}) = pC_L(\boldsymbol{u}) + (1 - p - q)C_I(\boldsymbol{u}) + qC_U(\boldsymbol{u}), \quad \boldsymbol{u} \in [0, 1]^2,$$

where $0 \leq p, q \leq 1$ and $p+q \leq 1$. This copula was introduced by Fréchet (1958). Show that the conditional copula $C_{2|1}$ is given by

$$C_{2|1}(u_2|u_1) = \begin{cases} p+(1-p-q)u_2+q, & \text{if} \quad u_1+u_2-1>0 \text{ and } u_1<u_2, \\ p+(1-p-q)u_2, & \text{if} \quad u_1+u_2-1>0 \text{ and } u_1>u_2, \\ (1-p-q)u_2, & \text{if} \quad u_1+u_2-1<0 \text{ and } u_1>u_2, \\ (1-p-q)u_2+q, & \text{if} \quad u_1+u_2-1<0 \text{ and } u_1<u_2. \end{cases}$$

Exercise 4.9.5. Show that for Archimedean copulas,

$$\lambda_U = 2 - 2 \lim_{t \to 0+} \frac{\phi'(t)}{\phi'(2t)}.$$

Exercise 4.9.6. Show that for Student copulas, we have that $\lambda_U > 0 \Leftrightarrow \alpha > -1$.

Exercise 4.9.7. (Simulating outcomes from Clayton's copula). Let Y_1 and Y_2 have $\mathcal{E}xp(1)$ distribution and Z a $\mathcal{G}am(\alpha^{-1}, 1)$ distribution. Show that the variables

$$U_1 = \left(1+\frac{Y_1}{Z}\right)^{-1/\alpha} \text{ and } U_2 = \left(1+\frac{Y_2}{Z}\right)^{-1/\alpha}$$

have Clayton's copula C_α as a joint df. This result can be exploited to generate outcomes from Clayton's copula.

5 Measuring Dependence

This chapter discusses the relationships between copulas and dependence measures for couples of rvs. Loosely speaking, these measures aim to capture the fact that the probability of having large (or small) values for both components is high, while the probability of having large values for the first component together with small values for the second component, or vice versa, is low. Pearson, Kendall and Spearman correlation coefficients are studied in detail. Several structures of dependence are presented too, including positive quadrant dependence and its multivariate extensions, conditional increasingness and total positivity.

5.1 INTRODUCTION

The study of concepts of positive dependence for rvs, which started in 1966 with the pioneering paper by E.L. Lehmann, yields numerous useful results in both statistical theory and applications. Applications of these concepts in actuarial science have recently received increased interest. The aim is to formalize the notion of 'positive dependence' existing between risks (i.e., the fact that large values of one risk tend to be associated with large values of the others). Early sources include Lehmann (1966), Esary, Proschan and Walkup (1967), Esary and Proschan (1972) and Kimeldorf and Sampson (1978). As pointed out by Drouet-Mari and Kotz (2001), the concept of correlation introduced by F. Galton in 1885 dominated statistics until the 1970s, serving as practically the only measure of dependence. This often resulted in somewhat misleading conclusions, for reasons that will become clear in this chapter.

It is obvious that the copula construction is closely related to dependence measures. Let us briefly expand on the links existing between these concepts. The marginals F_1 and F_2 can be inserted in any copula, so they carry no direct information about the coupling. At the same time any pair of marginals can be inserted into C, so C carries no direct information about the marginals. This being the case, it may seem reasonable to expect that the connections between the marginals of F_X are determined by C alone, and any question about the dependence structure can be answered with knowledge of C alone. However, as noted by Marshall (1996), things are not so simple. Problems stem from the fact that copulas are not unique when at least one marginal is discontinuous.

The following example indicates that there exist copulas which yield the Fréchet upper bound for some marginal pairs and the Fréchet lower bound for others.

Actuarial Theory for Dependent Risks M. Denuit, J. Dhaene, M. Goovaerts and R. Kaas

Example 5.1.1. Consider the copula C which has mass uniformly distributed on the line segments $u_2 = u_1$ for $0 \le u_1 \le 1/3$, $u_2 = u_1 + 1/3$ for $1/3 \le u_1 \le 2/3$ and $u_2 = u_1 - 1/3$ for $2/3 \le u_1 \le 1$. This copula coincides with the Fréchet upper bound in the region $0 \le u_1, u_2 < 1/3$ and with the Fréchet lower bound in the region $2/3 \le u_1, u_2 \le 1$. So, if the range of F_1 and F_2 is limited to the region $0 \le u_1, u_2 < 1/3$ then $F_X(x_1, x_2) = C(F_1(x_1), F_2(x_2))$ will be a Fréchet upper bound. On the other hand, if the range of F_1 and F_2 is limited to the region $2/3 \le u_1, u_2 \le 1$, F_X will be a Fréchet lower bound. Depending on the marginals, this copula can yield a Fréchet upper bound or a Fréchet lower bound.

This kind of extreme behaviour occurs only because discontinuous marginals are involved. The copula C has been constructed to show different characteristics over different parts of its domain. Because of this, the range of the marginals drastically affects the properties of the joint distribution. ∇

Let us now prove that there is no non-constant measure of dependence which depends only on the copula. The following result is taken from Marshall (1996). Its proof is omitted because it is rather technical.

Proposition 5.1.2
Let η be a dependence measure and let F_X be a bivariate df with copula C. Then,

$$\eta(F_X) = \eta(C_X) \text{ for every} F_X \Rightarrow \eta \text{ is constant.}$$

The problems come from the non-continuous nature of the rvs involved. We will see in this chapter that provided continuity is assumed, interesting results can be obtained.

The purpose of this chapter is twofold. First, we examine some classical scalar measures for the strength of dependence existing between a pair of risks. In that respect, this chapter aims to collect and clarify the essential ideas of dependence measures (linear correlation and rank correlation) that anyone wishing to model dependent phenomena should know. Second, different dependence structures for correlated risks are reviewed, namely positive quadrant dependence, conditional increasingness and total positivity. Numerous examples illustrate situations where these notions are encountered.

5.2 CONCORDANCE MEASURES

5.2.1 Definition

Scarsini (1984) defined certain desirable properties for a measure of association between two rvs (see also Definition 5.1.7 and Theorem 5.1.8 in Nelsen 1999) and coined the name 'concordance measures' for those satisfying these conditions. The intuitive idea that underlies the concept of concordance is this: two rvs X_1 and X_2 are concordant when large values of X_1 go together with large values of X_2.

Definition 5.2.1. The functional $r(\cdot, \cdot)$ assigning a real number to any (bivariate df F_X of a) pair of real-valued rvs X_1 and X_2 is a concordance measure if it fulfils the following properties:

P1 $r(X_1, X_2) = r(X_2, X_1)$ (symmetry);

P2 $-1 \le r(X_1, X_2) \le 1$ (normalization);

P3 $r(X_1, X_2) = 1$ if, and only if, X_1 and X_2 are comonotonic;

P4 $r(X_1, X_2) = -1$ if, and only if, X_1 and X_2 are countermonotonic;

P5 for $t: \mathbb{R} \to \mathbb{R}$ strictly monotonic,

$$r(t(X_1), X_2) = \begin{cases} r(X_1, X_2), & \text{if } t \text{ is increasing,} \\ -r(X_1, X_2), & \text{if } t \text{ is decreasing.} \end{cases}$$

∇

Remark 5.2.2. Of course, one might think of other desirable properties. These are nevertheless often incompatible with axioms P1–P5 listed in Definition 5.2.1. For instance, another interesting property could be

$$r(X_1, X_2) = 0 \text{ if, and only if, } X_1 \text{ and} X_2 \text{ are independent.} \tag{5.1}$$

Unfortunately, this contradicts P5: specifically, there is no non-trivial dependence measure satisfying P5 and (5.1). To prove this assertion, let (X_1, X_2) be uniformly distributed on the unit circle of $\mathbb{R}^2$, that is, $(X_1, X_2) = (\cos Z, \sin Z)$, with $Z \sim \mathcal{U}ni(0, 2\pi)$. Since $(-X_1, X_2) =_d (X_1, X_2)$, we have

$$r(-X_1, X_2) = r(X_1, X_2) = -r(X_1, X_2),$$

which implies that $r(X_1, X_2) = 0$ although X_1 and X_2 are clearly dependent. ∇

There are a variety of ways to discuss and to measure dependence. First and foremost is Pearson's correlation coefficient which captures the linear dependence between couples of rvs, but which is not invariant under monotone tranformations of the coordinate axes. In fact, in the next section it will be established that Pearson's correlation coefficient only fulfils P1 and P2 and is therefore not a concordance measure. As we shall see, other measures are scale-invariant, that is, they remain unchanged under strictly increasing transformations of the rvs; in this category, we find the population versions of Kendall's tau and Spearman's rho, both of which measure a form of dependence known as 'concordance'. In Sections 5.2.3 and 5.2.4, we will see that rank correlation coefficients fulfil P1–P5 provided X_1 and X_2 are continuous. The results presented here are taken for the most part from Denuit and Dhaene (2003) and Denuit and Lambert (2005).

5.2.2 *Pearson's correlation coefficient*

5.2.2.1 Definition

The Pearson correlation coefficient is a measure of association for two rvs that captures the degree of linear relationship. It is defined as follows.

Definition 5.2.3. For a random couple (X_1, X_2) having marginals with finite variances, Pearson's correlation coefficient r_P is defined by

$$r_P(X_1, X_2) = \frac{\mathbb{C}[X_1, X_2]}{\sqrt{\mathbb{V}[X_1]\mathbb{V}[X_2]}}.$$

∇

Remark 5.2.4. The variances of X_1 and X_2 have to be finite for Pearson's linear correlation coefficient to be defined. This is a drawback for dependence measures and causes problems when one works with heavy-tailed distributions. Non-life actuaries who model losses in different business lines with infinite variance distributions must be aware of this. ∇

5.2.2.2 Properties

Functional invariance

A serious drawback of Pearson's correlation coefficient is that r_P is not invariant under strictly increasing transformations t_1 and t_2, that is, for two rvs X_1 and X_2, we have in general

$$r_P(t_1(X_1), t_2(X_2)) \neq r_P(X_1, X_2). \tag{5.2}$$

However, r_P behaves in a predictable way when both t_1 and t_2 are linear. Specifically, r_P fulfils the linearity property

$$r_P(a_1X_1 + b_1, a_2X_2 + b_2) = \text{sign}(a_1a_2)r_P(X_1, X_2),$$

where $a_1, a_2 \neq 0$, $b_1, b_2 \in \mathbb{R}$ and $\text{sign}(x) = 1$ if $x > 0$, and -1 if $x < 0$. So, r_P is invariant under positive affine transformations (i.e., strictly increasing linear transformations).

Magnitude of Pearson's correlation coefficient and strength of dependence

It is known that the value of r_P may not be a solid indicator of the strength of dependence. For one thing, independence of two rvs implies they are uncorrelated (i.e., $r_P = 0$) but the converse does not hold in general, as shown in the next example (see also Exercise 5.4.1).

Example 5.2.5. (Two dependent variables with zero correlation). Let Y be an rv taking the values 0, $\pi/2$ and π with probability 1/3 each. Then, it is easy to see that $X_1 = \sin Y$ and $X_2 = \cos Y$ are uncorrelated (i.e., $r_P(X_1, X_2) = 0$). However, they are not independent since X_1 and X_2 are functionally connected (by the relation $X_1^2 + X_2^2 = 1$).

For a continuous counterexample, take $Z \sim \mathcal{U}ni(0, 2\pi)$ and $X_1 = \sin Z$, $X_2 = \cos Z$. Then,

$$\mathbb{E}[X_1] = \mathbb{E}[X_2] = \mathbb{E}[X_1X_2] = 0$$

so that X_1 and X_2 are uncorrelated but not independent since the relation $X_1^2 + X_2^2 = 1$ holds. ∇

There are thus situations in which correlations are zero but nevertheless strong nonlinear relationships do exist among rvs. Only in special cases, for instance multivariate normal or two-point distributions, does uncorrelatedness imply independence.

5.2.2.3 Copulas and r_P

As testified by (5.2), r_P is not invariant under increasing non-linear tranformations. This peculiarity is not surprising if r_P is cast into the form

$$r_P(X_1, X_2) = \frac{1}{\sqrt{\mathbb{V}[X_1]\mathbb{V}[X_2]}} \int_0^1 \int_0^1 \Big(C(u_1, u_2) - u_1 u_2\Big) dF_1^{-1}(u_1) dF_2^{-1}(u_1).$$

So r_P depends not only on the copula, but also on the marginals.

Example 5.2.6. In order to illustrate this phenomenon, let us consider the Farlie–Gumbel–Morgenstern copula given by

$$C_\alpha(\boldsymbol{u}) = u_1 u_2 \Big(1 + \alpha(1 - u_1)(1 - u_2)\Big), \quad \alpha \in [-1, 1].$$

It can be shown that the range of r_P for this family is $[-1/3, 1/3]$, and the maximum is obtained when both marginals are $\mathcal{U}ni(0, 1)$. All other marginals will result in a correlation smaller than $1/3$. For example, if we insert $\mathcal{E}xp(1)$ marginals in the Farlie–Gumbel–Morgenstern copula, the range for r_P is $[-1/4, 1/4]$. See also Exercise 5.4.16. ∇

5.2.2.4 Permissible range

Colinearity

By the Cauchy–Schwarz inequality, r_P always lies in $[-1, 1]$ so that P2 is satisfied. Pearson's correlation coefficient contains information on both the strength and direction of a linear relationship between two rvs:

$$r_P(X_1, X_2) = \text{sign}(a) \Leftrightarrow \Pr[X_2 = aX_1 + b] = 1,$$

for some constants a ($a > 0$ if $r_P(X_1, X_2) = 1$ and $a < 0$ if $r_P(X_1, X_2) = -1$) and $b \in \mathbb{R}$. If a linear relationship between X_1 and X_2 is not possible, the permissible range for $r_P(X_1, X_2)$ is further restricted.

A common fallacy concerning Pearson's correlation coefficient and dependence is as follows: given two arbitrary marginal dfs F_1 and F_2 for X_1 and X_2, all linear correlations between -1 and 1 can be attained through suitable specification of the joint distribution. This statement is false and it is simple to construct counterexamples, as shown by the following property.

Property 5.2.7
Let X_1 and X_2 be rvs with support $\mathbb{R}^+$, that is, such that $F_1(x) < 1$ and $F_2(x) < 1$ for all $x > 0$. Then, $r_P(X_1, X_2) > -1$.

Proof. Assume to the contrary that $r_P(X_1, X_2) = -1$, which implies that

$$X_2 = aX_1 + b \text{ with } a < 0, \quad b \in \mathbb{R}.$$

It follows that for all $x_2 < 0$,

$$F_2(x_2) = \Pr\left[X_1 \geq \frac{x_2 - b}{a}\right]$$
$$\geq \Pr\left[X_1 > \frac{x_2 - b}{a}\right]$$
$$= \overline{F}_1\left(\frac{x_2 - b}{a}\right) > 0$$

since the right endpoint of the support of the F_i is $+\infty$. This clearly contradicts the assumption $F_2(0) = 0$. □

Bounds on Pearson's correlation coefficient

Let us now examine which correlations are possible given marginal distributions. Shih and Huang (1992) and Schechtman and Yitzhaki (1999) noticed that unless the marginal distributions of two rvs differ only in location and/or scale parameters (see Section 5.2.2.5), the range of Pearson's r_P is narrower than $[-1, 1]$ and depends on the marginal dfs F_1 and F_2.

Proposition 5.2.8
For any $\boldsymbol{X}$ in $\mathcal{R}_2^+(F_1, F_2)$, $r_P(X_1, X_2)$ is constrained by

$$r_P^{\min}(F_1, F_2) \leq r_P(X_1, X_2) \leq r_P^{\max}(F_1, F_2), \tag{5.3}$$

where for some $U \sim \mathcal{U}ni(0, 1)$,

$$r_P^{\min}(F_1, F_2) = \frac{\mathbb{C}[F_1^{-1}(U), F_2^{-1}(1-U)]}{\sqrt{\mathbb{V}[X_1]\mathbb{V}[X_2]}}$$

and

$$r_P^{\max}(F_1, F_2) = \frac{\mathbb{C}[F_1^{-1}(U), F_2^{-1}(U)]}{\sqrt{\mathbb{V}[X_1]\mathbb{V}[X_2]}}.$$

Proof. It suffices to establish the inequalities

$$\mathbb{E}[F_1^{-1}(U)F_2^{-1}(1-U)] \leq \mathbb{E}[X_1X_2] \leq \mathbb{E}[F_1^{-1}(U)F_2^{-1}(U)]$$

for $U \sim \mathcal{U}ni(0, 1)$. By (1.10) we know that for any $\boldsymbol{Y}$ in $\mathcal{R}_2^+(F_1, F_2)$,

$$\mathbb{E}[Y_1Y_2] = \int_0^{+\infty}\int_0^{+\infty} \overline{F}_{\boldsymbol{Y}}(\boldsymbol{y})dy_1dy_2.$$

The required inequality then follows from $(F_1^{-1}(U), F_2^{-1}(1-U)) \sim M_2$, $(F_1^{-1}(U), F_2^{-1}(U)) \sim W_2$ and $M_2 \leq F_{\boldsymbol{X}} \leq W_2$ from (1.54) and (1.55). □

Proposition 5.2.8 indicates that a value ± 1 for r_P is in general not obtainable in $\mathcal{R}_2^+(F_1, F_2)$. The following example, taken from Embrechts, McNeil and Straumann (2002), shows that we can have correlation arbitrarily close to zero and perfect dependence.

Example 5.2.9. Consider the random couple $X \in \mathcal{R}_2^+(F_1, F_2)$ where $X_i \sim \mathcal{LN}or(\mu_i, \sigma_i)$, $i=1,2$. Using Proposition 5.2.8 and the fact that

$$F_i^{-1}(U)=\exp\left(\mu_i+\sigma_i\Phi^{-1}(U)\right)$$

and

$$F_i^{-1}(1-U)=\exp\left(\mu_i-\sigma_i\Phi^{-1}(U)\right),$$

we get the following results:

(i) If X_1 and X_2 are comonotonic then the correlation is maximal and equals

$$r_P^{\max}=\frac{\exp(\sigma_1\sigma_2)-1}{\sqrt{\exp(\sigma_1^2)-1}\sqrt{\exp(\sigma_2^2)-1}}.$$

(ii) If X_1 and X_2 are countermonotonic then the correlation is minimal and equals

$$r_P^{\min}=\frac{\exp(-\sigma_1\sigma_2)-1}{\sqrt{\exp(\sigma_1^2)-1}\sqrt{\exp(\sigma_2^2)-1}}.$$

In particular, if $(\mu_1, \sigma_1)=(0, 1)$ and $(\mu_2, \sigma_2)=(0, \sigma)$, the maximal correlation coefficient is attained for $X_2=X_1^\sigma$ and equals

$$r_P^{\max}(\sigma)=\frac{\exp(\sigma)-1}{\sqrt{\exp(\sigma^2)-1}\sqrt{e-1}}$$

and the maximal correlation coefficient is attained for $X_2=X_1^{-\sigma}$ and equals

$$r_P^{\min}(\sigma)=\frac{\exp(-\sigma)-1}{\sqrt{\exp(\sigma^2)-1}\sqrt{e-1}}.$$

These extremal correlations are shown graphically in Figure 5.1. We observe that

$$\lim_{\sigma\to+\infty} r_P^{\max}(\sigma)=\lim_{\sigma\to+\infty} r_P^{\min}(\sigma)=0.$$

As a consequence, it is possible to have a random couple where the correlation is almost zero even though the components are comonotonic or countermonotonic (and thus exhibit the strongest kind of dependence possible for this pair of marginals). This contradicts the intuition that small correlation implies weak dependence. ∇

Extremal values of r_P and perfect dependence

We show in the next result that when the bounds in (5.3) are attained, X_1 and X_2 must be comonotonic/counter-monotonic.

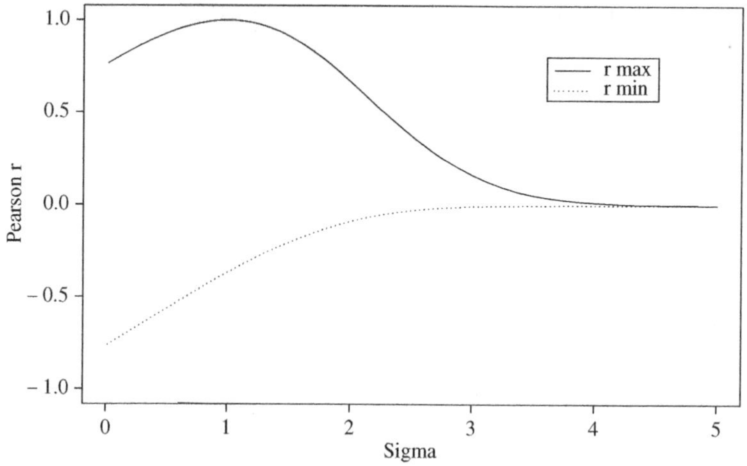

Figure 5.1 $r_P^{\max}(\sigma)$ and $r_P^{\min}(\sigma)$ as functions of σ in Example 5.2.9.

Proposition 5.2.10
Let $\boldsymbol{X} \in \mathcal{R}_2^+(F_1, F_2)$ and $U \sim \mathcal{U}ni(0, 1)$. Then, the following equivalences hold:

$$r_P(X_1, X_2) = r_P^{\max}(F_1, F_2) \Leftrightarrow \boldsymbol{X} =_d (F_1^{-1}(U), F_2^{-1}(U)), \tag{5.4}$$

and

$$r_P(X_1, X_2) = r_P^{\min}(F_1, F_2) \Leftrightarrow \boldsymbol{X} =_d (F_1^{-1}(U), F_2^{-1}(1-U)). \tag{5.5}$$

Proof. Let us begin with (5.4). The $\Leftarrow$ part is straightforward, so that we only consider the $\Rightarrow$ implication. It is easy to see that $r_P(X_1, X_2) = r_P^{\max}(F_1, F_2)$ yields

$$\mathbb{E}[X_1X_2] = \mathbb{E}[F_1^{-1}(U)F_2^{-1}(U)].$$

Formula (1.10) then gives

$$0 = \int_0^{+\infty}\int_0^{+\infty}\Big(F_{\boldsymbol{X}}(x_1, x_2) - W_2(x_1, x_2)\Big)dx_1dx_2.$$

By (1.54), the integrand is non-positive for all x_1 and x_2; we then conclude that the equality $F_{\boldsymbol{X}}(x_1, x_2) = W_2(x_1, x_2)$ holds everywhere, and this concludes the proof of (5.4). Similar reasoning is used to get (5.5). □

5.2.2.5 Pearson's correlation coefficient and location-scale families

In some circumstances, the non-negativity assumption involved in Proposition 5.2.10 can be dropped. This is the case, for example, if the marginals F_1 and F_2 belong to the same location–scale family of distributions, that is, if there exist a df G, real constants μ_1, μ_2 and positive real constants σ_1, σ_2 such that the relation

$$F_i(x) = G\left(\frac{x-\mu_i}{\sigma_i}\right) \text{ holds for any } x \in \mathbb{R} \text{ and } i = 1, 2.$$

In this case, one can derive that

$$F_i^{-1}(p) = \sigma_i G^{-1}(p) + \mu_i, \quad i = 1, 2, \quad p \in (0, 1),$$

so that we find

$$\boldsymbol{X} =_d (F_1^{-1}(U), F_2^{-1}(U)) \Leftrightarrow \boldsymbol{X} =_d (\sigma_1 G^{-1}(U) + \mu_1, \sigma_2 G^{-1}(U) + \mu_2).$$

Hence,

$$r_P(X_1, X_2) = 1 \Leftrightarrow \boldsymbol{X} =_d (\sigma_1 G^{-1}(U) + \mu_1, \sigma_2 G^{-1}(U) + \mu_2). \tag{5.6}$$

In such a case, the maximal value 1 is attained, whatever the marginals. Hence, $\boldsymbol{X}$ comonotonic implies that $r_P(X_1, X_2) = 1$. Also, the converse conclusion holds. Indeed, if $r_P(X_1, X_2) = 1$ then there exist some real constants $a > 0$ and b such that $(X_1, X_2) =_d (X_1, aX_1 + b)$ which in turn means that $\boldsymbol{X}$ is comonotonic. We can conclude that in a Fréchet space $\mathcal{R}_2(F_1, F_2)$ where F_1 and F_2 belong to the same location–scale family, the following equivalence holds:

$$\boldsymbol{X} \in \mathcal{R}_2(F_1, F_2) \text{ is comonotonic} \Leftrightarrow r_P(X_1, X_2) = 1.$$

Similarly, we can prove that in such a Fréchet space,

$$\boldsymbol{X} \in \mathcal{R}_2(F_1, F_2) \text{ is countermonotonic} \Leftrightarrow r_P(X_1, X_2) = -1.$$

Example 5.2.11. As a special case, we find that in a Fréchet space $\mathcal{R}_2(F_1, F_2)$ with normal marginals F_i, comonotonicity for $\boldsymbol{X} \in \mathcal{R}_2(F_1, F_2)$ is equivalent to $r_P(X_1, X_2) = 1$. We also find

$$F_i^{-1}(p) = \mu_i + \sigma_i \Phi^{-1}(p),$$

where μ_i and σ_i^2 are the expected value and variance of F_i, respectively, and Φ is the cdf associated with the standard normal distribution. ∇

5.2.3 *Kendall's rank correlation coefficient*

5.2.3.1 Definition

In general, the covariance will not reveal all the information on the dependence structure of a random couple. Hence, practitioners should also be aware of other dependence concepts such as rank correlations. Kendall's rank correlation coefficient (often called Kendall's tau) is a nonparametric measure of association based on the number of concordances and discordances in a sample of paired observations. Concordance occurs when pairs of observations vary together, and discordance occurs when pairs of observations vary differently.

More specifically, a pair of observations is concordant if the observation with the larger value of X_1 has also the larger value for X_2. The pair is discordant if the observation with the larger value of X_1 has the smaller value of X_2. If (X_1, X_2) and (X_1', X_2') are independent and identically distributed then they are said to be concordant if $(X_1 - X_1')(X_2 - X_2') > 0$, whereas they are said to be discordant when the reverse inequality is valid. Henceforth, we denote

$$\Pr[\text{concordance}] = \Pr[(X_1 - X_1')(X_2 - X_2') > 0]$$

and

$$\Pr[\text{discordance}] = \Pr[(X_1 - X_1')(X_2 - X_2') < 0].$$

The idea of using the concordance and discordance probabilities comes from the fact that probabilities of events involving only inequality relationships between two rvs are invariant with respect to increasing transformations of these variables. Hence, defining dependence measures from these probabilities ensures that they will only depend on the underlying copula.

Having defined the notion of concordance and discordance, we are now ready to introduce Kendall's rank correlation coefficient.

Definition 5.2.12. Kendall's rank correlation coefficient for a random couple (X_1, X_2) is defined as

$$r_K(X_1, X_2) = \Pr[\text{concordance}] - \Pr[\text{discordance}]$$

∇

If the marginals of X_1 and X_2 are continuous then r_K can be rewritten as

$$r_K(X_1, X_2) = 2\Pr\big[(X_1 - X_1')(X_2 - X_2') > 0\big] - 1,$$

where (X_1', X_2') is an independent copy of (X_1, X_2), that is, $(X_1, X_2) =_d (X_1', X_2')$ and the two random couples are mutually independent.

Kendall's rank correlation coefficient is encountered in Kaas *et al.* (2001, Exercise 10.6.17). We study the properties of this dependence measure in detail in this section.

5.2.3.2 Properties

The invariance of Kendall's rank correlation coefficient under strictly monotone transformations is obvious: if t_1 and t_2 are non-decreasing continuous functions on the support of X_1 and X_2, respectively, then

$$r_K(t_1(X_1), t_2(X_2)) = r_K(X_1, X_2). \tag{5.7}$$

This follows directly from the fact that $t_1(X_1) - t_1(X_1')$ and $X_1 - X_1'$ both have the same sign. The same applies to $t_2(X_2) - t_2(X_2')$ and $X_2 - X_2'$.

If X_1 and X_2 are mutually independent then $r_K(X_1, X_2) = 0$. This is easily seen from

$$\begin{aligned} r_K(X_1, X_2) &= 2\Pr[(X_1 - X_1')(X_2 - X_2') > 0] - 1 \\ &= 2\Big(\Pr[X_1 - X_1' > 0, X_2 - X_2' > 0] \\ &\quad + \Pr[X_1 - X_1' < 0, X_2 - X_2' < 0]\Big) - 1 \\ &= 2\left(\frac{1}{4} + \frac{1}{4}\right) - 1 = 0. \end{aligned}$$

5.2.3.3 Copulas and Kendall's rank correlation coefficient

In particular, (5.7) shows that when the X_i have continuous marginal dfs F_1 and F_2,

$$r_K(F_1(X_1), F_2(X_2)) = r_K(X_1, X_2)$$

so that the value of Kendall's rank correlation coefficient only depends on the ranks of X_1 and X_2, hence on the copula for (X_1, X_2).

Denoting by (X_1', X_2') an independent copy of (X_1, X_2), assumed to possess continuous marginals, Kendall's rank correlation coefficient can then be cast into the form

$$\begin{aligned} r_K(X_1, X_2) &= 2\Pr[(X_1 - X_1')(X_2 - X_2') > 0] - 1 \\ &= 4\Pr[X_1 \leq X_1', X_2 \leq X_2'] - 1. \end{aligned}$$

Therefore, r_K for a random couple (X_1, X_2) of continuous rvs with copula C can be expressed as

$$\begin{aligned} r_K(X_1, X_2) &= 4\int_0^1 \int_0^1 C(u_1, u_2) dC(u_1, u_2) - 1 \\ &= 4\mathbb{E}[C(U_1, U_2)] - 1, \end{aligned} \tag{5.8}$$

where (U_1, U_2) denotes a couple of $\mathcal{U}ni(0, 1)$ rvs with joint df C.

5.2.3.4 Permissible range

For all distributions, r_K exists and takes values in $[-1, 1]$. The maximal value 1 is attained when $X_2 = t(X_1)$ with t increasing. Indeed, Kendall's rank correlation coefficient is then given by

$$r_K\Big(X_1, t(X_1)\Big) = 2\Pr\Big[(X_1 - X_1')(t(X_1) - t(X_1')) > 0\Big] - 1 = 1,$$

since $X_1 - X_1'$ and $t(X_1) - t(X_1')$ obviously have the same sign. Similarly, the minimal value -1 for r_K is attained when $X_2 = t(X_1)$ for some decreasing function t.

Let us now prove that $r_K(X_1, X_2) = \pm 1$ if, and only if, the distribution of the random couple $\boldsymbol{X}$ coincides with one of the Fréchet bounds.

Proposition 5.2.13
Let $\boldsymbol{X} \in \mathcal{R}_2(F_1, F_2)$ with F_1 and F_2 continuous and strictly increasing, and let $U \sim \mathcal{U}ni(0, 1)$. Then the following equivalences hold:

$$r_K(X_1, X_2) = 1 \Leftrightarrow \boldsymbol{X} =_d (F_1^{-1}(U), F_2^{-1}(U)), \tag{5.9}$$

and

$$r_K(X_1, X_2) = -1 \Leftrightarrow \boldsymbol{X} =_d (F_1^{-1}(U), F_2^{-1}(1-U)). \tag{5.10}$$

Proof. The $\Leftarrow$ parts of (5.9) and (5.10) are straightforward, so that we only consider the $\Rightarrow$ parts of these formulas. Let C be the copula for $\boldsymbol{X}$, and let (U_1, U_2) be a random couple with joint df C. We have to prove that

$$r_K(U_1, U_2) = 1 \Rightarrow (U_1, U_2) =_d (U, U).$$

Clearly, $\mathbb{E}[C(U_1, U_2)] \leq \mathbb{E}[C_U(U_1, U_2)]$ holds since $C \leq C_U$. Furthermore, as $\min\{U_1, U_2\} \leq U_1$ obviously holds, we also have $\mathbb{E}[C_U(U_1, U_2)] \leq \mathbb{E}[C_U(U, U)]$. Combining these inequalities yields

$$\mathbb{E}[C(U_1, U_2)] \leq \mathbb{E}[C_U(U_1, U_2)] \leq \mathbb{E}[C_U(U, U)],$$

so that we deduce from (5.8) that

$$r_K(U_1, U_2) = r_K(U, U) \Leftrightarrow \mathbb{E}[C(U_1, U_2)] = \mathbb{E}[C_U(U, U)].$$

This in turn implies

$$\mathbb{E}\Big[C_U(U_1, U_2) - C(U_1, U_2)\Big] = \int_0^1 \int_0^1 \underbrace{\Big(C_U(u_1, u_2) - C(u_1, u_2)\Big)}_{\geq 0 \ \forall\ u_1, u_2 \in [0,1]} dC(u_1, u_2) = 0,$$

so that $C \equiv C_U$; this concludes the proof of (5.9).

To get (5.10), it suffices to note that $\mathbb{E}[C_L(U, 1-U)] \leq \mathbb{E}[C_L(U_1, U_2)]$ holds since $C_L \leq C$. Further, as $\max\{U_1 + U_2 - 1, 0\} \geq 0$, we also have $\mathbb{E}[C_L(U_1, U_2)] \leq \mathbb{E}[C(U_1, U_2)]$. Combining these inequalities gives

$$\mathbb{E}[C_L(U, 1-U)] \leq \mathbb{E}[C_L(U_1, U_2)] \leq \mathbb{E}[C(U_1, U_2)].$$

The proof then follows the same lines as (5.9). □

5.2.3.5 Kendall's rank correlation coefficient for Archimedean copulas

The Archimedean representation (4.10) allows us to reduce the study of a multivariate copula to a single univariate function: the generator ϕ. In general, evaluating r_K requires the evaluation of a double integral (as in (5.8), for instance). For an Archimedean copula, the situation is simpler in that r_K can be evaluated directly from the generator ϕ as follows.

Property 5.2.14
Kendall's rank correlation coefficient associated with C_ϕ, r_K^ϕ say, is given by

$$r_K^\phi = 4\int_0^1 \frac{\phi(t)}{\phi'(t)}dt + 1.$$

For a proof of this result, we refer the reader to Genest and MacKay (1986b). The following example illustrates the usefulness of Property 5.2.14.

Example 5.2.15. (Kendall's r_K for the Clayton copula). For Clayton's copula, $\phi(t) = \dfrac{t^{-\alpha}-1}{\alpha}$ and $\phi'(t) = -t^{-\alpha-1}$, for some $\alpha > 0$, so that

$$r_K^\phi = -4\int_0^1 \frac{t-t^{\alpha+1}}{\alpha}dt + 1 = \frac{\alpha}{\alpha+2}.$$

∇

5.2.4 *Spearman's rank correlation coefficient*

5.2.4.1 Definition

In statistics books, Spearman's rank correlation coefficient for a pair of continuous rvs X_1 and X_2 (generally called Spearman's rho) is usually defined as Pearson's r_P for the ranks $F_1(X_1)$ and $F_2(X_2)$. Spearman's rank correlation coefficient is defined in this way in Kaas *et al.* (2001, Example 10.6.10).

Definition 5.2.16. Spearman's rank correlation coefficient r_S for a pair of continuous rvs X_1 and X_2 is identical to Pearson's correlation coefficient for the ranks of F_1 and F_2:

$$r_S(X_1, X_2) = r_P(F_1(X_1), F_2(X_2)).$$

∇

Spearman's rank correlation coefficient can be rewritten as

$$\begin{aligned} r_S(X_1, X_2) = 3\Big(&\Pr[(X_1 - X_1^\perp)(X_2 - X_2^\perp) > 0] \\ &- \Pr[(X_1 - X_1^\perp)(X_2 - X_2^\perp) < 0]\Big), \end{aligned}$$

where $(X_1^{\perp}, X_2^{\perp})$ is an independent version of (X_1, X_2), that is, $(X_1^{\perp}, X_2^{\perp})$ is a random vector with independent components, such that $X_1 =_d X_1^{\perp}$, $X_2 =_d X_2^{\perp}$ and (X_1, X_2) and $(X_1^{\perp}, X_2^{\perp})$ mutually independent. This comes directly from

$$\begin{aligned} r_S(X_1, X_2) &= 3\Big(2\Pr[(X_1 - X_1^{\perp})(X_2 - X_2^{\perp}) > 0] - 1\Big) \\ &= 3\Big(4\Pr[X_1 < X_1^{\perp}, X_2 < X_2^{\perp}] - 1\Big) \\ &= 12F_X(X_1^{\perp}, X_2^{\perp}) - 3 \\ &= 12\int_0^1\int_0^1 C(u_1, u_2)du_1du_2 - 3 \\ &= 12\int_0^1\int_0^1 u_1u_2dC(u_1, u_2) - 3 \\ &= 12\mathbb{E}[U_1U_2] - 3, \end{aligned} \tag{5.11}$$

where (U_1, U_2), defined as above, has the same copula C as $\boldsymbol{X}$ and $\mathcal{U}ni(0, 1)$ marginals.

Spearman's rank correlation coefficient is thus proportional to the probability of concordance minus the probability of discordance for a pair of random vectors with the same marginals, where one of them has independent components.

5.2.4.2 Properties

Just like r_K, r_S is invariant under strictly monotone transformations, that is, if t_1 and t_2 are strictly increasing (or decreasing) functions on the supports of X_1 and X_2, respectively, then

$$r_S(t_1(X_1), t_2(X_2)) = r_S(X_1, X_2). \tag{5.12}$$

Also, if X_1 and X_2 are mutually independent then $r_S(X_1, X_2) = 0$.

As pointed out above, Spearman's rank correlation coefficient is simply Pearson's r_P for the ranks. Hence, assuming that the marginal dfs F_1 and F_2 are continuous and defining $U_1 = F_1(X_1)$ and $U_2 = F_2(X_2)$, $r_S(X_1, X_2)$ can be rewritten as

$$r_S(X_1, X_2) = r_P(U_1, U_2) = \frac{\mathbb{E}[U_1U_2] - 1/4}{1/12}. \tag{5.13}$$

5.2.4.3 Copulas and Spearman's rank correlation coefficient

Returning to the expression derived for Pearson's correlation coefficient, we find that

$$\begin{aligned} r_S(X_1, X_2) &= r_P\Big(F_1(X_1), F_2(X_2)\Big) \\ &= 12\int_0^1\int_0^1 (C(u_1, u_2) - u_1u_2)du_1du_2. \end{aligned}$$

5.2.4.4 Permissible range

Let us now prove the Spearman analogue to Proposition 5.2.13.

Proposition 5.2.17
Let $\boldsymbol{X} \in \mathcal{R}_2(F_1, F_2)$, with F_1 and F_2 continuous and strictly increasing, and $U \sim \mathcal{U}ni(0, 1)$. Then the following equivalences hold:

$$r_S(X_1, X_2) = 1 \Leftrightarrow \boldsymbol{X} =_d (F_1^{-1}(U), F_2^{-1}(U)), \tag{5.14}$$

and

$$r_S(X_1, X_2) = -1 \Leftrightarrow \boldsymbol{X} =_d (F_1^{-1}(U), F_2^{-1}(1-U)). \tag{5.15}$$

Proof. The $\Leftarrow$ parts of (5.14) and (5.15) are straightforward, so that we only consider the $\Rightarrow$ parts. It suffices to show that

$$r_S(U_1, U_2) = 1 \Rightarrow (U_1, U_2) =_d (U, U),$$

where (U_1, U_2) is a couple of $\mathcal{U}ni(0, 1)$ rvs with the same copula as (X_1, X_2). We have

$$r_P(U_1, U_2) = r_P(F_{U_1}(U_1), F_{U_2}(U_2)) = r_S(U_1, U_2) = 1$$

which implies by (5.6) that $\Pr[U_1 = U_2] = 1$. Hence, $(U_1, U_2) =_d (U, U)$ follows. Expression (5.15) is proven in the same way. □

5.2.5 Relationships between Kendall's and Spearman's rank correlation coefficients

The values of r_S and r_K are often quite different. Several works have been devoted since 1950 to the relationships existing between these dependance measures. The following result determines how different r_S and r_K can be. For a proof, see Joe (1997).

Proposition 5.2.18
The inequality

$$\frac{3r_K - 1}{2} \leq r_S \leq \frac{1 + 2r_K - r_K^2}{2} \text{ holds for } r_K \geq 0$$

and

$$\frac{r_K^2 + 2r_K - 1}{2} \leq r_S \leq \frac{1 + 3r_K}{2} \text{ holds for } r_K \leq 0.$$

Capéraá and Genest (1993) refined these inequalities under additional assumptions about the dependence structure of X_1 and X_2. They also give an extensive list of references on the topic.

5.2.6 Other dependence measures

5.2.6.1 Gini's correlation coefficient

Gini's coefficient is used in economics to measure the income differences between two populations. Technically, it is a kind of 'distance' between the dependence structure of the vector $\boldsymbol{X}$ and monotone dependence as represented by the Fréchet upper and lower bound copulas.

Definition 5.2.19. Given $\boldsymbol{X} \in \mathcal{R}_2(F_1, F_2)$, Gini's correlation coefficient is defined as

$$\begin{aligned} r_{\mathrm{G}}(X_1, X_2) &= r_{\mathrm{G}}(F_1(X_1), F_2(X_2)) \\ &= 2\int_0^1\int_0^1 (|u_1+u_2-1| - |u_1-u_2|)\, dC(u_1,u_2), \end{aligned}$$

where C is the copula of the couple (X_1, X_2). ∇

The following results hold for r_{G}.

Proposition 5.2.20
Let $\boldsymbol{X} \in \mathcal{R}_2(F_1, F_2)$ and $U \sim \mathcal{U}ni(0,1)$. Then, the following equivalences hold:

$$r_{\mathrm{G}}(X_1, X_2) = 1 \Leftrightarrow \boldsymbol{X} =_d (F_1^{-1}(U), F_2^{-1}(U)) \tag{5.16}$$

and

$$r_{\mathrm{G}}(X_1, X_2) = -1 \Leftrightarrow \boldsymbol{X} =_d (F_1^{-1}(U), F_2^{-1}(1-U)). \tag{5.17}$$

Proof. The $\Leftarrow$ parts of (5.16) and (5.17) are trivial. We have to show that

$$r_{\mathrm{G}}(U_1, U_2) = 1 \Rightarrow (U_1, U_2) =_d (U, U),$$

where (U_1, U_2) is a couple with $\mathcal{U}ni(0,1)$ marginals and copula C. Since

$$\begin{aligned} r_{\mathrm{G}}(U_1, U_2) &= 4\int_0^1\int_0^1 C(u_1,u_2)dC_U(u_1,u_2) \\ &\quad +4\int_0^1\int_0^1 C(u_1,u_2)dC_L(u_1,u_2) - 2, \end{aligned}$$

$r_{\mathrm{G}}(U_1, U_2) = r_{\mathrm{G}}(U, U)$ implies

$$\begin{aligned} &\int_0^1\int_0^1 \underbrace{\Big(C_U(u_1,u_2) - C(u_1,u_2)\Big)}_{\geq 0\ \forall\ u_1,u_2\in[0,1]} dC_U(u_1,u_2) \\ &+\int_0^1\int_0^1 \underbrace{\Big(C_U(u_1,u_2) - C(u_1,u_2)\Big)}_{\geq 0\ \forall\ u_1,u_2\in[0,1]} dC_L(u_1,u_2) = 0, \end{aligned}$$

which implies that $C \equiv C_U$ and concludes the proof of (5.16). The proof of (5.17) then follows the same lines. □

5.2.6.2 Blomqvist's correlation coefficient

Another measure of concordance is Blomqvist's correlation coefficient, also known as the medial correlation coefficient.

Definition 5.2.21. Given $X \in \mathcal{R}_2(F_1, F_2)$, Blomqvist's correlation coefficient is defined as

$$\begin{aligned} r_B(X_1, X_2) &= \Pr[(X_1 - F_1^{-1}(1/2))(X_2 - F_2^{-1}(1/2)) > 0] \\ &\quad - \Pr[(X_1 - F_1^{-1}(1/2))(X_2 - F_2^{-1}(1/2)) < 0] \\ &= 4F_X\left(F_1^{-1}(1/2), F_2^{-1}(1/2)\right) - 1, \end{aligned}$$

where $F_i^{-1}(1/2)$ is the median of X_i, $i = 1, 2$. ∇

The following results hold for r_B.

Proposition 5.2.22
Let $X \in \mathcal{R}_2(F_1, F_2)$ and $U \sim \mathcal{U}ni(0, 1)$. Then the following implications hold:

$$X =_d (F_1^{-1}(U), F_2^{-1}(U)) \Rightarrow r_B(X_1, X_2) = 1, \tag{5.18}$$

$$X =_d (F_1^{-1}(U), F_2^{-1}(1 - U)) \Rightarrow r_B(X_1, X_2) = -1 \tag{5.19}$$

and

$$X =_d (X_1^{\perp}, X_2^{\perp}) \Rightarrow r_B(X_1, X_2) = 0, \tag{5.20}$$

but the converses of (5.18), (5.19) and (5.20) are not, in general, true.

Proof. The properties (5.18)–(5.20) are obvious. They follow easily from the fact that

$$r_B(X_1, X_2) = r_B(U_1, U_2) = 4C(1/2, 1/2) - 1.$$

So, Blomqvist's correlation coefficient uses only one value of the copula. Hence, to give examples in which the converse implications fail to hold is easy. Consider, for example, the parametric family given in formula (3.2.2) in Nelsen (1999). For

$$C(u_1, u_2) = \begin{cases} \max\{0, u_1 + u_2 - \frac{1}{2}\}, & \text{for } 0 \le u_1, u_2 \le \frac{1}{2}, \\ \max\{\frac{1}{2}, u_1 + u_2 - 1\}, & \text{for } \frac{1}{2} < u_1, u_2 \le 1, \\ C_U(u_1, u_2), & \text{otherwise,} \end{cases}$$

we see that $r_B(U_1, U_2) = 1$ but C does not coincide with C_U, contradicting the reverse of (5.18). On the other hand, for

$$C(u_1, u_2) = \begin{cases} \max\{0, u_1 + u_2 - \frac{1}{4}\}, & \text{for } 0 \le u_1, u_2 \le \frac{1}{4}, \\ \max\{\frac{1}{4}, u_1 + u_2 - 1\}, & \text{for } \frac{1}{4} < u_1, u_2 \le 1, \\ C_U(u_1, u_2), & \text{otherwise,} \end{cases}$$

we have $r_B(U_1, U_2)=0$ but $C \neq C_I$, contradicting the reverse of (5.20). Finally, let us consider the member of the family in Exercise 3.9 of Nelsen (1999),

$$C(u_1, u_2) = \begin{cases} \min\{u_1, u_2 - \theta\}, & \text{for } (u_1, u_2) \in [0, 1-\theta] \times [\theta, 1], \\ \min\{u_1 + \theta - 1, u_2\}, & \text{for } (u_1, u_2) \in [1-\theta, 1] \times [0, \theta], \\ C_L(u_1, u_2), & \text{otherwise,} \end{cases}$$

coresponding to $\theta = 1/2$. We then have $r_B(U_1, U_2) = -1$ but $C \neq C_L$, contradicting the reverse of (5.19). □

5.2.7 *Constraints on concordance measures in bivariate discrete data*

This section aims to investigate the behaviour of dependence measures based on concordance, like Kendall's rank correlation coefficient, applied to discrete bivariate data. The main result will be that it becomes senseless to compare the actual value of the concordance measure to the classical bounds -1 and 1 inherited from the continuous case, since they cannot in general be attained with discrete margins. This section is based for the most part on Denuit and Lambert (2005).

5.2.7.1 The presence of ties

The main difference between the continuous and discrete cases is that in the latter situation many tied pairs (i.e., pairs of observations that have equal values of the first or second components) occur in practice. Specifically, if (X_1, X_2) and (X_1', X_2') are independent and identically distributed, those pairs are tied if $X_1 = X_1'$ or $X_2 = X_2'$. Henceforth,

$$\Pr[\text{tie}] = \Pr[X_1 = X_1' \text{ or } X_2 = X_2'].$$

When X_1 and X_2 are integer-valued,

$$\Pr[\text{concordance}] + \Pr[\text{discordance}] + \Pr[\text{tie}] = 1,$$

so that we have

$$\begin{aligned} r_K(X_1, X_2) &= 2\Pr[\text{concordance}] - 1 + \Pr[\text{tie}] \\ &= 4\Pr[X_1' < X_1, X_2' < X_2] - 1 \\ &\quad + \Pr[X_1 = X_1' \text{ or } X_2 = X_2'] \end{aligned} \qquad (5.21)$$

since

$$\begin{aligned} \Pr[X_1' < X_1, X_2' < X_2] &= \Pr[X_1' > X_1, X_2' > X_2] \\ &= \frac{\Pr[\text{concordance}]}{2}. \end{aligned}$$

As we will see below, Kendall's rank correlation coefficient cannot attain a very large value because a large proportion of the pairs are tied (especially when the number of possible values of X_1 and X_2 is small).

5.2.7.2 Bernoulli marginals

Consider $X_1 \sim \mathcal{B}er(q_1)$ and $X_2 \sim \mathcal{B}er(q_2)$. Let $h(i,j) = \Pr[X_1 = i, X_2 = j]$, $i, j \in \{0, 1\}$. Then,

$$r_K(X_1, X_2) = 2\Big(h(0,0)h(1,1) - h(1,0)h(0,1)\Big), \tag{5.22}$$

which is simply twice the odds ratio (under the models considered for the margins and for the copula).

Given the marginal probabilities of sucess p_1 and p_2, we can rewrite Kendall's rank correlation coefficient as

$$r_K(X_1, X_2) = 2\Big(h(1,1) - p_1 p_2\Big). \tag{5.23}$$

Once $h(1,1)$ is fixed, the whole bivariate distribution is specified. That probability of joint success is constrained by

$$\max\{0, p_1 + p_2 - 1\} \leq h(1,1) \leq \min\{p_1, p_2\},$$

which corresponds to the usual Fréchet bounds.

Considering (5.23), $r_K(X_1, X_2)$ attains its minimum when

$$h(1,1) = \max\{0, p_1 + p_2 - 1\},$$

in which case

$$r_K(X_1, X_2) = \begin{cases} -2p_1 p_2, & \text{when } p_1 + p_2 < 1, \\ -2(1-p_1)(1-p_2), & \text{when } p_1 + p_2 \geq 1. \end{cases} \tag{5.24}$$

Likewise, $r_K(X_1, X_2)$ is maximum when

$$h(1,1) = \min\{p_1, p_2\},$$

in which case

$$r_K(X_1, X_2) = \begin{cases} 2p_1(1-p_2), & \text{when } p_1 < p_2, \\ 2p_2(1-p_1), & \text{when } p_1 \geq p_2. \end{cases} \tag{5.25}$$

The largest possible value for $r_K(X_1, X_2)$ is obtained when $h(1,1) = h(0,0) = 0.5$ and $h(1,0) = h(0,1) = 0$ (zero probability of discordance) in which case $r_K(X_1, X_2)$ is equal to 0.50. Similarly, the smallest possible value for $r_K(X_1, X_2)$ is -0.50 when $h(0,0) = h(1,1) = 0$ (zero probability of concordance) and $h(1,0) = h(0,1) = 0.5$. Thus, even in the most favourable cases, we see that Kendall's rank correlation coefficient cannot reach 1 (-1).

5.2.7.3 Upper bound on Kendall's rank correlation coefficient for discrete variables

Obviously, $r_K(X_1, X_2)$ will be maximal when the probability of discordance is zero (which is not always possible). Hence, since

$$\Pr[\text{concordance}] + \Pr[\text{discordance}] + \Pr[\text{tie}] = 1,$$

we conclude, after combination with equation (5.21), that

$$r_K(X_1, X_2) \leq 1 - \Pr[\text{tie}],$$

with equality when the probability of discordance is zero.

Similarly, $r_K(X_1, X_2)$ will be minimal when the probability of concordance is zero (which is not always possible), yielding

$$r_K(X_1, X_2) \geq -1 + \Pr[\text{tie}]$$

with equality when the probability of concordance is zero.

Let (X_1', X_2') be an independent copy of (X_1, X_2). Combining these last results with

$$\Pr[\text{tie}] = \Pr[X_1 = X_1'] + \Pr[X_2 = X_2'] - \Pr[X_1 = X_1', X_2 = X_2'],$$

we conclude that

$$\begin{aligned} -1 &< -1 + \max\left\{\Pr[X_1 = X_1'], \Pr[X_2 = X_2']\right\} \\ &\leq -1 + \Pr[\text{tie}] \leq r_K(X, Y) \leq 1 - \Pr[\text{tie}] \\ &\leq 1 - \max\left\{\Pr[X_1 = X_1'], \Pr[X_2 = X_2']\right\} < 1, \end{aligned} \tag{5.26}$$

whatever the joint distribution of X_1 and X_2.

5.3 DEPENDENCE STRUCTURES

5.3.1 Positive dependence notions

Intuitively speaking, positive values of concordance measures indicate positive dependence between the outcomes X_1 and X_2. In this section, we aim to make the concept of positive dependence more precise. We will not only rely on a general scalar value but also examine the kind of dependence exhibited locally by random couples.

Kimeldorf and Sampson (1987, 1989) attempted to study dependence notions, orders and dependence measures in a unified framework in the bivariate case. They postulated some desirable properties that positive dependence notions should satisfy. This has been generalized to the multivariate case by Pellerey and Semeraro (2003). We will not explore these works in this book but rather refer the interested reader to Colangelo, Scarsini and Shaked (2004) for details.

5.3.2 *Positive quadrant dependence*

5.3.2.1 Definition

The concept of positive quadrant dependence introduced by Lehmann (1966) is defined as follows.

Definition 5.3.1. The random couple $\boldsymbol{X} = (X_1, X_2)$ is said to be positively quadrant dependent (PQD) if

$$X_1 \preceq_{\mathrm{ST}} [X_1|X_2 > x_2] \text{ for all } x_2 \text{ such that } \overline{F}_2(x_2) > 0$$

and

$$X_2 \preceq_{\mathrm{ST}} [X_2|X_1 > x_1] \text{ for all } x_1 \text{ such that } \overline{F}_1(x_1) > 0.$$

∇

This first positive dependence concept is defined by means of $\preceq_{\mathrm{ST}}$. It shows that each component of the random couple becomes larger (in the $\preceq_{\mathrm{ST}}$ sense) when the other component is known to exceed some threshold. This coincides with the intuitive content of 'positive dependence'.

5.3.2.2 Equivalent conditions

The definition of positive quadrant dependence can be restated in a number of equivalent ways, as shown next.

Property 5.3.2
Let $\boldsymbol{X} = (X_1, X_2)$ be a random couple in $\mathcal{R}_2(F_1, F_2)$. Then, $\boldsymbol{X}$ is PQD if, and only if, one of the following equivalent conditions is fulfilled:

(i) $\overline{F}_{\boldsymbol{X}}(x_1, x_2) \geq \overline{F}_1(x_1)\overline{F}_2(x_2)$ for all $x_1, x_2 \in \mathbb{R}$.

(ii) $F_{\boldsymbol{X}}(x_1, x_2) \geq F_1(x_1)F_2(x_2)$ for all $x_1, x_2 \in \mathbb{R}$.

(iii) $\Pr[X_2 > x_2|X_1 > x_1] \geq \overline{F}_2(x_2)$ for all $x_1, x_2 \in \mathbb{R}$ such that $\overline{F}_1(x_1) > 0$.

(iv) $\Pr[X_1 > x_1|X_2 > x_2] \geq \overline{F}_1(x_1)$ for all $x_1, x_2 \in \mathbb{R}$ such that $\overline{F}_2(x_2) > 0$.

We see from this definition that when $\boldsymbol{X}$ is PQD, its components X_1 and X_2 are more likely to be large together or to be small together compared with the theoretical situation in which X_1 and X_2 are independent. Conditions (iii) and (iv) possess an intuitive interpretation since they mean that the knowledge that X_1 is large (i.e., $X_1 > x_1$) increases the probability of X_2 being large.

5.3.2.3 Properties

Positive quadrant dependence possesses the following nice invariance property.

Property 5.3.3
(X_1, X_2) PQD $\Rightarrow (t_1(X_1), t_2(X_2))$ PQD for any non-decreasing continuous functions t_1 and t_2.

Proof. Indeed,

$$\begin{aligned}\Pr[t_1(X_1) \leq x_1, t_2(X_2) \leq x_2] &= \Pr[X_1 \leq t_1^{-1}(x_1), X_2 \leq t_2^{-1}(x_2)] \\ &\geq \Pr[X_1 \leq t_1^{-1}(x_1)] \Pr[X_2 \leq t_2^{-1}(x_2)] \\ &= \Pr[t_1(X_1) \leq x_1] \Pr[t_2(X_2) \leq x_2],\end{aligned}$$

which proves the result. □

Property 5.3.3 indicates that the notion of positive quadrant dependence is a characteristic of the underlying copula, as formally stated in the next result.

Corollary 5.3.4
Let $\boldsymbol{X}$ be a random couple with copula C. Then, $\boldsymbol{X}$ is PQD if, and only if,

$$C(\boldsymbol{u}) \geq C_I(\boldsymbol{u}) \text{ for all } \boldsymbol{u} \in [0, 1]^2.$$

5.3.2.4 Positive quadrant dependence and correlation coefficients

PQD risks are positively correlated, as follows immediately from Property 1.6.13.

Property 5.3.5
Consider $\boldsymbol{X} \in \mathcal{R}_2(F_1, F_2)$. If (X_1, X_2) is PQD then $r_P(X_1, X_2) \geq 0$. The converse is generally false, with the notable exception of the bivariate normal case.

Let us now examine rank correlation coefficients. Basically, the implication of Property 5.3.5 still holds for these dependence measures.

Property 5.3.6
If (X_1, X_2) is PQD then $r_K(X_1, X_2) \geq 0$ and $r_S(X_1, X_2) \geq 0$.

Proof. From Corollary 5.3.4, we know that positive quadrant dependence is a property of the underlying copula. On the other hand, Kendall's and Spearman's rank correlation coefficients are known to depend only on the copula. Let (U_1, U_2) be a random pair with $\mathcal{U}ni(0, 1)$ marginals and the same copula as (X_1, X_2). The result then follows from (5.8) for Kendall's rank correlation coefficient as

$$r_K(X_1, X_2) \geq 4\mathbb{E}[U_1 U_2] - 1 \geq 4\mathbb{E}[U_1]\mathbb{E}[U_2] - 1 = 0,$$

where the inequality comes from the fact that U_1 and U_2 are positively correlated from Property 5.3.5. The result for Spearman's rank correlation coefficient follows similarly from (5.13). □

We also have the following result, which relates independence to uncorrelatedness in the PQD case.

Property 5.3.7
Let $X \in \mathcal{R}_2(F_1, F_2)$ be PQD. Then, the following conditions are equivalent:

(i) X has independent components;

(ii) $r_P(X_1, X_2) = 0$;

(iii) $r_K(X_1, X_2) = 0$;

(iv) $r_S(X_1, X_2) = 0$.

Proof. Equivalence of (i) and (ii) is a direct consequence of Property 1.6.13. Turning to the equivalence of (i) and (iii), let us consider, without loss of generality, the case of $\mathcal{U}ni(0, 1)$ margins. To say that (U_1, U_2) is PQD means that its joint distribution function C satisfies $C \geq C_I$. Invoking Corollary 1.6.12 with $g = C_I$ then yields

$$\mathbb{E}[C(U_1, U_2)] \geq \mathbb{E}[C_I(U_1, U_2)] \geq \mathbb{E}[C_I(U_1^{\perp}, U_2^{\perp})],$$

whence it follows that $\mathbb{E}[C(U_1, U_2)] = \mathbb{E}[C_I(U_1, U_2)]$ since $\mathbb{E}[C(U_1, U_2)] = \mathbb{E}[C_I(U_1^{\perp}, U_2^{\perp})]$ holds by hypothesis. Therefore,

$$\mathbb{E}[C(U_1, U_2)] - \mathbb{E}[C_I(U_1, U_2)] = \int_0^1 \int_0^1 \underbrace{\Big(C(u_1, u_2) - C_I(u_1, u_2)\Big)}_{\geq 0 \ \forall\ u_1, u_2 \in [0,1]} dC(u_1, u_2) = 0$$

yields $C \equiv C_I$. The proof of the equivalence of (i) and (iv) is similar. □

The next result easily follows from Properties 5.3.3 and 5.3.5.

Proposition 5.3.8
The random couple X is PQD if, and only if,

$$\mathbb{C}[t_1(X_1), t_2(X_2)] \geq 0 \tag{5.27}$$

for any non-decreasing functions t_1 and t_2, provided the expectations exist.

5.3.2.5 Positive quadrant dependence and convex order

As is shown in the following result taken from Dhaene and Goovaerts (1996), the notion of positive quadrant dependence can be used to consider the effect of the independence assumption, when the risks are actually positively dependent.

Proposition 5.3.9
If the risks X_1 and X_2 are PQD then we have

$$X_1^{\perp} + X_2^{\perp} \preceq_{\text{SL},=} X_1 + X_2,$$

where $(X_1^{\perp}, X_2^{\perp})$ is an independent version of (X_1, X_2).

Proof. The stop-loss premiums with retention d can be written as

$$\mathbb{E}[(X_1+X_2-d)_+]=\mathbb{E}[X_1]+\mathbb{E}[X_2]+\mathbb{E}[(d-X_1-X_2)_+].$$

To prove the Proposition, we have to establish the validity of

$$\mathbb{E}[(X_1+X_2-d)_+]\geq\mathbb{E}[(X_1^{\perp}+X_2^{\perp}-d)_+]$$

whatever the retention d, which is equivalent to showing that

$$\mathbb{E}[(d-X_1-X_2)_+]\geq\mathbb{E}[(d-X_1^{\perp}-X_2^{\perp})_+].$$

Now, let us express $\mathbb{E}[(d-X_1-y)_+]$ in terms of the joint df of (X_1, X_2). For this purpose, note that

$$\begin{aligned}\int_0^d \mathbb{I}[x_1\leq t, x_2\leq d-t]dt &= \int_0^d \mathbb{I}[x_1\leq t\leq d-x_2]dt\\ &= \begin{cases}0, & \text{if } x_1>d-x_2,\\ d-x_2-x_1, & \text{if } x_1\leq d-x_2\end{cases}\\ &=(d-x_2-x_1)_+.\end{aligned}$$

It follows that

$$\begin{aligned}\mathbb{E}[(d-X_1-X_2)_+] &= \mathbb{E}\left[\int_0^d \mathbb{I}[X_1\leq t, X_2\leq d-t]dt\right]\\ &=\int_0^d F_X(t, d-t)dt.\end{aligned}$$

Finally,

$$\mathbb{E}[(d-X_1-X_2)_+]-\mathbb{E}[(d-X_1^{\perp}-X_2^{\perp})_+]=\int_0^d\Big(F_X(t,d-t)-F_1(t)F_2(d-t)\Big)dt\geq 0$$

provided X_1 and X_2 are PQD, which ends the proof. □

The Proposition indicates that if the marginal distributions are given, and if X_1 and X_2 are PQD, the independence assumption will always underestimate the actual stop-loss premiums.

Remark 5.3.10. Denuit and Scaillet (2004) proposed two types of procedure to test for positive quadrant dependence. The first procedure is based on the specification of the dependence concepts in terms of dfs, while the second exploits the copula representation. For each specification a distance test and an intersection–union test for inequality constraints are developed for time-dependent data. Empirical illustrations involving loss–ALAE data and HFR and CSFB/Tremont market-neutral hedge fund indices and the S & P 500 index are discussed.

A related notion, namely asymptotic dependence, is empirically analysed and tested in Poon, Rockinger and Tawn (2004). It corresponds exactly to positive quadrant dependence but for loss probabilities tending to zero. These authors discuss the use of asymptotic dependence concepts in a number of financial applications such as portfolio selection, risk management, Sharpe ratio targeting, hedging, option valuation and credit risk analysis. Most of their discussion remains valid in the PQD case but for less extreme risks. Note, however, that two asymptotically independent variables may still exhibit PQD behaviour (cf. the case of a Gaussian copula), and thus positive quadrant dependence should be the primary object of focus. Even risks that are far from extreme can lead to severe damages. ∇

5.3.2.6 Life insurance

From Property 5.3.2, it is easy to conclude that when $\boldsymbol{X}$ is PQD, the stochastic inequalities

$$\min\{X_1^{\perp}, X_2^{\perp}\} \preceq_{\mathrm{ST}} \min\{X_1, X_2\} \text{ and } \max\{X_1, X_2\} \preceq_{\mathrm{ST}} \max\{X_1^{\perp}, X_2^{\perp}\} \tag{5.28}$$

hold. Formula (5.28) explains the usefulness of positive quadrant dependence in a variety of situations, since it suggests a natural way of generating computable bounds for the maximum or the minimum of PQD risks.

Example 5.3.11. Consider the life statuses (x_1) and (x_2) with remaining lifetimes $T_{(x_1)}$ and $T_{(x_2)}$, respectively. The joint life status (x_1, x_2) exists as long as all individual statuses exist. This status has remaining lifetime

$$T_{(x_1,x_2)} = \min\left\{T_{(x_1)}, T_{(x_2)}\right\}.$$

The last survivor status $\overline{(x_1, x_2)}$ exists as long as at least one of the individual statuses is alive. Its remaining lifetime is given by

$$T_{\overline{(x_1,x_2)}} = \max\left\{T_{(x_1)}, T_{(x_2)}\right\}.$$

Let us now assume that $\boldsymbol{T} = (T_{(x_1)}, T_{(x_2)})$ is PQD. Let us also introduce the following notation:

$$T^{\perp}_{(x_1,x_2)} = \min\left\{T^{\perp}_{(x_1)}, T^{\perp}_{(x_2)}\right\}$$

and

$$T^{\perp}_{\overline{(x_1,x_2)}} = \max\left\{T^{\perp}_{(x_1)}, T^{\perp}_{(x_2)}\right\}.$$

From (5.28), it follows that

$$T^{\perp}_{(x_1,x_2)} \preceq_{\mathrm{ST}} T_{(x_1,x_2)} \text{ and } T_{\overline{(x_1,x_2)}} \preceq_{\mathrm{ST}} T^{\perp}_{\overline{(x_1,x_2)}},$$

which in turn implies the following inequalities for the life annuity pure premiums:

$$\ddot{a}^{\perp}_{(x_1,x_2)} \leq \ddot{a}_{(x_1,x_2)} \text{ and } \ddot{a}_{\overline{(x_1,x_2)}} \leq \ddot{a}^{\perp}_{\overline{(x_1,x_2)}},$$

where the superscript $\perp$ is used to indicate that the annuity is based on $T^{\perp}_{(x_1,x_2)}$ or $T^{\perp}_{\overline{(x_1,x_2)}}$. This means that for PQD remaining lifetimes, the independence assumption (while leaving the marginal dfs unchanged) leads to an underestimation of the net single premium (and reserves) of a joint life annuity. The opposite conclusion holds for the last survivor annuity. Similar conclusions can be drawn for endowment and whole life insurance. For more results in this vein, see Dhaene, Vanneste and Wolthuis (2000) or Denuit, Dhaene, Le Bailly de Tilleghem and Teghem (2001). ∇

5.3.2.7 Positive stop-loss dependence

Let us now introduce another positive dependence concept, called positive stop-loss dependence. The idea is to substitute $\preceq_{SL}$ for $\preceq_{ST}$ in the definition of positive quadrant dependence.

Definition 5.3.12. The risks X_1 and X_2 are said to be positively stop-loss dependent (PSLD,) if

$$X_1 \preceq_{SL} [X_1|X_2 > t_2] \text{ and} X_2 \preceq_{SL} [X_2|X_1 > t_1]$$

for all $t_1, t_2 \in \mathbb{R}^+$. ∇

Note that the risks X_1 and X_2 are PSLD if the inequalities

$$\mathbb{E}\Big[(X_1 - t_1)_+ \Big| X_2 > t_2\Big] \geq \mathbb{E}[(X_1 - t_1)_+]$$

and

$$\mathbb{E}\Big[(X_2 - t_2)_+ \Big| X_1 > t_1\Big] \geq \mathbb{E}[(X_2 - t_2)_+]$$

hold for all $t_1, t_2 \in \mathbb{R}^+$. An equivalent condition is provided by the next result.

Proposition 5.3.13
X_1 and X_2 are PSLD if, and only if, the inequalities

$$\mathbb{E}\Big[(X_1 - t_1)_+ \mathbb{I}[X_2 > t_2]\Big] \geq \mathbb{E}[(X_1 - t_1)_+] \Pr[X_2 > t_2]$$

and

$$\mathbb{E}\Big[\mathbb{I}[X_1 > t_1](X_2 - t_2)_+\Big] \geq \Pr[X_1 > t_1] \mathbb{E}[(X_2 - t_2)_+]$$

hold for all $t_1, t_2 \in \mathbb{R}^+$.

Proof. Apply the general equality $\mathbb{E}[Y] = \mathbb{E}[Y|A]\Pr[A] + \mathbb{E}[Y|\overline{A}]\Pr[\overline{A}]$ to the rv $Y = (X_1 - t_1)_+ \mathbb{I}[X_2 > t_2]$ and the event $A = [X_2 > t_2]$. Then use

$$\mathbb{E}[Y|A] = \mathbb{E}\Big[(X_1 - t_1)_+ | X_2 > t_2\Big]$$

to finish the proof. □

Let us now introduce a subset $\mathcal{R}_2(F_1, F_2; c)$ of $\mathcal{R}_2(F_1, F_2)$ consisting of all the elements of $\mathcal{R}_2(F_1, F_2)$ with prescribed covariances c (or Pearson's linear correlation coefficient r). Specifically, let

$$\mathcal{R}_2(F_1, F_2; c) = \Big\{\boldsymbol{X} \in \mathcal{R}_2(F_1, F_2) \Big| \mathbb{C}[X_1, X_2] = c\Big\},$$

where c is an admissible value for the covariance between members of $\mathcal{R}_2(F_1, F_2)$ (i.e., c satisfies the conditions of Proposition 5.2.8). We call $\mathcal{R}_2(F_1, F_2; c)$ a sub-Fréchet space.

Note that if $\boldsymbol{X}$ and $\boldsymbol{Y}$ both belong to $\mathcal{R}_2(F_1, F_2; c)$ then

$$\mathbb{V}[X_1 + X_2] = \mathbb{V}[X_1] + \mathbb{V}[X_2] + c = \mathbb{V}[Y_1 + Y_2].$$

This means that within $\mathcal{R}_2(F_1, F_2; c)$,

$$X_1 + X_2 \preceq_{\text{SL},=} Y_1 + Y_2 \Rightarrow X_1 + X_2 =_d Y_1 + Y_2.$$

Hence, neither the convex order nor the stop-loss order are suitable tools for comparing the riskiness of aggregate claims in a sub-Fréchet space.

Note that the fact that the stop-loss order is not suitable in $\mathcal{R}_2(F_1, F_2; c)$ is somewhat similar to the fact that stochastic dominance is not suited in $\mathcal{R}_2(F_1, F_2)$. Indeed, in $\mathcal{R}_2(F_1, F_2)$ we have that

$$X_1 + X_2 \preceq_{\text{ST}} Y_1 + Y_2 \Rightarrow X_1 + X_2 =_d Y_1 + Y_2$$

since $\mathbb{E}[X_1 + X_2] = \mathbb{E}[Y_1 + Y_2]$.

Nevertheless the sum of two components of a sub-Fréchet space can be compared with the aid of the prudence order $\preceq_{\text{PRUD}}$ (for which the two first moments of the rvs are equal, i.e., $X \preceq_{\text{PRUD}} Y$ if, and only if, $\mathbb{E}[g(X)] \leq \mathbb{E}[g(Y)]$ for all the functions g such that $g^{(3)} \geq 0$, provided the expectations exist).

The prudence order belongs to the class of s-convex orderings introduced by Denuit, Lefèvre and Shaked (1998) and further studied in Bassan, Denuit and Scarsini (1999), Denuit, De Vijlder and Lefèvre (1999), Denuit, Lefèvre and Shaked (2000a,b,c), Denuit, Lefèvre and Scarsini (2001) and Denuit (2002). For $s = 1$ we have $\preceq_{\text{ST}}$, for $s = 2$ we have $\preceq_{\text{SL},=}$, and $s = 3$ corresponds to the prudence order. The prudence order is useful for comparing probability distributions with equal means and variances (which cannot be ordered in the $\preceq_{\text{ST}}$ or $\preceq_{\text{SL},=}$ sense). Kaas and Hesselager (1995) proved that the gamma distribution precedes the lognormal with the same first two moments in the $\preceq_{\text{PRUD}}$ sense. Note that related orderings have been studied in economics; see Whitmore (1970).

Let us now prove the following result.

Proposition 5.3.14
If the risks X_1 and X_2 are PSLD then

$$X_1^{\perp} + X_2^{\perp} \preceq_{\text{PRUD}} X_1 + X_2.$$

Proof. Let us consider a function g such that $g^{(3)} \geq 0$. Then, Property 1.6.11 allows us to write

$$\begin{aligned}\mathbb{E}[g(X_1 + X_2)] &= g(0) + g'(0)\mathbb{E}[X_1] + \int_0^{+\infty} \Pr[X_2 > t_2] g'(t_2) dt_2 \\ &+ \int_0^{+\infty} \mathbb{E}\Big[\mathbb{I}[X_2 > t_2] X_1\Big] g''(t_2) dt_2 \\ &+ \int_0^{+\infty} \Pr[X_1 > t_1] g'(t_1) dt_1 \\ &+ \int_0^{+\infty} \int_0^{+\infty} \mathbb{E}\Big[(X_1 - t_1)_+ \mathbb{I}[X_2 > t_2]\Big] g^{(3)}(t_1 + t_2) dt_1 dt_2.\end{aligned}$$

The Proposition then follows easily from this expansion. □

5.3.2.8 Extension to n risks: Cumulative dependence and positive orthant dependence

The following multivariate extension was proposed by Denuit, Dhaene and Ribas (2001).

Definition 5.3.15. The rvs $X_1, X_2, \ldots, X_n$ are cumulative dependent (CD) if the random couples $(\sum_{i=1}^{j-1} X_i, X_j)$ are PQD for $j = 2, 3, \ldots, n$. ∇

The interest in cumulative dependence in actuarial sciences comes from the following result, which can also be found in Denuit, Dhaene and Ribas (2001).

Property 5.3.16
If $\boldsymbol{X}$ is CD, then the stochastic inequality

$$\sum_{i=1}^{n} X_i^{\perp} \preceq_{\mathrm{SL},=} \sum_{i=1}^{n} X_i$$

holds.

Proof. Without loss of generality, the random vectors $\boldsymbol{X}^{\perp}$ and $\boldsymbol{X}$ may be considered independent. We proceed by induction. First, $X_1^{\perp} \preceq_{\mathrm{SL},=} X_1$ trivially holds. Now assume that

$$X_1^{\perp} + X_2^{\perp} + \ldots + X_k^{\perp} \preceq_{\mathrm{SL},=} X_1 + X_2 + \ldots + X_k$$

holds for $k = 1, 2, \ldots, n-1$. Then, by the closure of $\preceq_{\mathrm{SL},=}$ under convolution, this stochastic inequality yields

$$X_1^{\perp} + X_2^{\perp} + \ldots + X_{n-1}^{\perp} + X_n^{\perp} \preceq_{\mathrm{SL},=} X_1 + X_2 + \ldots + X_{n-1} + X_n^{\perp}. \tag{5.29}$$

Now, since $\boldsymbol{X}$ is CD and X_n and $X_1 + X_2 + \ldots + X_{n-1}$ are PQD, we get from Proposition 5.3.9 that

$$X_1 + X_2 + \ldots + X_{n-1} + X_n^{\perp} \preceq_{\mathrm{SL},=} X_1 + X_2 + \ldots + X_{n-1} + X_n. \tag{5.30}$$

Combining (5.29) and (5.30) yields the claimed result by the transitivity property of $\preceq_{\mathrm{SL},=}$. □

It follows from Property 5.3.16 that making the assumption of mutual independence between the components of a CD risk $\boldsymbol{X}$ leads to an underestimation of the stop-loss premiums. This means that the insurer in fact does not base his decisions on the 'real' aggregate claims but on 'less risky' aggregate claims, which is of course a dangerous strategy.

Example 5.3.17. Let Y_n be the value of the premiums earned minus total incurred claims of an insurance company right after the occurrence of the nth claim, and κ the initial capital. Actuaries have been interested for centuries in the ruin event (i.e., the event that $Y_n < -\kappa$ for some $n \geq 1$). Let us write $Y_n = \sum_{i=1}^{n} X_i$ for identically distributed (but possibly dependent) X_i, where X_i is the net profit for the insurance company between the occurrence of claims number $i-1$ and i.

Müller and Pflug (2001) examined the way the marginal distributions of the X_i and their dependence structure affect the Lundberg coefficient R. The ordering of Lundberg coefficients yields an asymptotic ordering of ruin probabilities for some fixed initial capital κ. Specifically, Müller and Pflug (2001) proved that if $Y_n \preceq_{\mathrm{SL},=} \widetilde{Y}_n$ for all n then $R \geq \widetilde{R}$. Now assume that the X_i are CD. Then we know that $Y_n \preceq_{SL,=} \widetilde{Y}_n$, where the $\widetilde{X}_i$ are independent. Therefore, CD increases Lundberg's upper bound on the ruin probability. These results are in accordance with Gerber's (1981b, 1982) study of the ruin problem for annual gains forming a linear time series.

It is worth mentioning that for some particular models, the impact of dependence on ruin probabilities (and not only on Lundberg coefficients) has been studied; see Cossette and Marceau (2000), Yuen and Guo (2001) and Cossette, Landriault and Marceau (2003). Other papers devoted to ruin models with dependence between the waiting time for a claim and its actual size include Albrecher and Boxma (2003) and Albrecher and Teugels (2004). ∇

Of course, other multivariate extensions of bivariate positive quadrant dependence exist, such as the positive orthant dependence defined next.

Definition 5.3.18. A random vector $\boldsymbol{X}$ is said to be positively lower orthant dependent (PLOD) when the inequalities

$$\Pr[\boldsymbol{X} \leq x] \geq \Pr[\boldsymbol{X}^{\perp} \leq x] = \prod_{i=1}^{n} \Pr[X_i \leq x_i] \tag{5.31}$$

hold for any $\boldsymbol{x} \in \mathbb{R}^n$; it is said to be positively upper orthant dependent (PUOD) when the inequalities

$$\Pr[\boldsymbol{X} > x] \geq \Pr[\boldsymbol{X}^{\perp} > x] = \prod_{i=1}^{n} \Pr[X_i > x_i] \tag{5.32}$$

hold for any $\boldsymbol{x} \in \mathbb{R}^n$. ∇

Intuitively, (5.32) means that $X_1, X_2, \ldots, X_n$ are more likely simultaneously to have large values, compared with a vector of independent rvs with the same univariate marginals; (5.31) can be similarly interpreted. When (5.31) and (5.32) simultaneously hold, then $\boldsymbol{X}$ is said to be positively orthant dependent (POD). It is worth mentioning that (5.31) and (5.32) are usually referred to as the Šidák inequalities, or as the first-order product-type inequalities.

Remark 5.3.19. As with positive quadrant dependence, we can view the expression $\Pr[\boldsymbol{X} > \boldsymbol{x}] - \Pr[\boldsymbol{X}^{\perp} > \boldsymbol{x}]$ as a measure of the 'local' positive upper orthant dependence at each point $\boldsymbol{x}$ in $\mathbb{R}^n$. If we assume that the X_i are continuous and we set $U_i = F_i(X_i)$ for $i = 1, 2, \ldots, n$, then $\boldsymbol{X}$ is PUOD if, and only if, $\boldsymbol{U}$ is PUOD. The quantity $\Pr[\boldsymbol{U} > \boldsymbol{u}] - \Pr[\boldsymbol{U}^{\perp} > \boldsymbol{u}]$ also measures the local positive upper orthant dependence of $\boldsymbol{X}$. Nelsen (1996) proposed a measure of multivariate association r_n^+, derived from average positive upper orthant dependence, defined as

$$r_n^+ = \frac{n+1}{2^n - (n+1)} \left(2^n \int_0^1 \int_0^1 \ldots \int_0^1 u_1 u_2 \ldots u_n dC(\boldsymbol{u}) - 1 \right).$$

∇

From (5.31) and (5.32), it is easy to conclude that when $\boldsymbol{X}$ is POD, the stochastic inequalities

$$\min X_i^{\perp} \preceq_{ST} \min X_i \text{ and } \max X_i \preceq_{ST} \max X_i^{\perp} \tag{5.33}$$

hold. Formula (5.33) can be found in Baccelli and Makowski (1989) and explains the usefulness of positive orthant dependence in a variety of situations. Using (5.33), Example 5.3.11 can be generalized to n statuses.

Let us now examine a result in the same vein as Property 5.3.16 for POD risks. Unfortunately, $\preceq_{\text{SL},=}$ is replaced with the weaker $\preceq_{\text{MGF}}$.

Property 5.3.20
If $\boldsymbol{X}$ is POD, then the stochastic inequality

$$\sum_{i=1}^{n} X_i^{\perp} \preceq_{\text{MGF}} \sum_{i=1}^{n} X_i$$

holds.

Proof. The result follows directly from Proposition 3.3.87(i) together with the fact that $\boldsymbol{X}$ POD $\Rightarrow \boldsymbol{X}^{\perp} \preceq_{\text{UO}} \boldsymbol{X}$. □

Remark 5.3.21. Let us mention that in Property 5.3.20 the relation $\preceq_{\text{MGF}}$ can be replaced with the n-increasing convex order (or stop-loss order of degree $n-1$; see Kaas and Hesselager 1995). This ensures that under the assumptions of Property 5.3.20, the inequality

$$\mathbb{E}\left[g\left(\sum_{i=1}^{n} X_i^{\perp}\right)\right] \leq \mathbb{E}\left[g\left(\sum_{i=1}^{n} X_i\right)\right]$$

holds for all functions g with $g^{(k)} \geq 0$, $k=1,\ldots,n$, provided that the expectations exist. ∇

5.3.3 *Conditional increasingness in sequence*

5.3.3.1 Definition

The following dependence structure, called conditional increasingness in sequence, is obtained by requiring that the conditional distributions increase in the $\preceq_{\text{ST}}$ sense with the values of the conditioning variables. This is formally stated in the following definition.

Definition 5.3.22. A random vector $\boldsymbol{X}$ is said to be conditionally increasing in sequence (CIS) if, for all $i=2,3,\ldots,n$,

$$\begin{aligned}&[X_i|X_1=x_1, X_2=x_2, \ldots, X_{i-1}=x_{i-1}]\\ &\quad\preceq_{\text{ST}} [X_i|X_1=y_1, X_2=y_2, \ldots, X_{i-1}=y_{i-1}]\end{aligned}$$

for all $x_1 \leq y_1$, $x_2 \leq y_2$, $\ldots$, $x_{i-1} \leq y_{i-1}$ in the support of the X_i. ∇

5.3.3.2 Link with stochastic dominance

It is easy to see that the conditions of Proposition 3.3.89 are fulfilled if one of the random vectors is CIS; this yields the following result that can be found in Langberg (1988).

Proposition 5.3.23
If either $\boldsymbol{X}$ or $\boldsymbol{Y}$ is CIS, $X_1 \preceq_{\mathrm{ST}} Y_1$ and

$$[X_i | X_1 = x_1, \ldots, X_{i-1} = x_{i-1}] \preceq_{\mathrm{ST}} [Y_i | Y_1 = x_1, \ldots, Y_{i-1} = x_{i-1}]$$

for all x_j, $j = 1, 2, \ldots, i-1$, then $\boldsymbol{X} \preceq_{\mathrm{ST}} \boldsymbol{Y}$.

5.3.3.3 Conditional increasingness

In the remainder, we also need a stronger concept of dependence, closely related to conditional increasingness in sequence, introduced by Müller and Scarsini (2001).

Definition 5.3.24. An n-dimensional random vector $\boldsymbol{X}$ is said to be conditionally increasing (CI), if $(X_{\pi(1)}, X_{\pi(2)}, \ldots, X_{\pi(n)})$ is CIS for all permutations π of $\{1, 2, \ldots, n\}$, that is, if for any i,

$$[X_i | X_j = x_j, \quad j \in J] \preceq_{\mathrm{ST}} [X_i | X_j = x_j', \quad j \in J]$$

whenever $x_j \leq x_j'$, where $J \in \{1, 2, \ldots, n\}$ and $i \notin J$. ∇

Note that, as opposed to conditional increasingness in sequence, conditional increasingness is a symmetric dependence concept.

Remark 5.3.25. In order to see that the implication

$$\boldsymbol{X} \text{ is CI} \Rightarrow \boldsymbol{X} \text{ is CIS}$$

is strict, take $\boldsymbol{X} = (X_1, X_2)$ uniformly distributed over (1,1), (1,2), (2,1) and (2,3). Then $\boldsymbol{X}$ is CIS, but

$$\Pr[X_1 \geq 0 | X_2 = 1] = \frac{1}{2} > 0 = \Pr[X_1 \geq 2 | X_2 = 2],$$

so that $\boldsymbol{X}$ is not CI. ∇

5.3.3.4 Conditional increasingness and copulas

Checking conditional increasingness is easy in the bivariate case, where a complete characterization of CI copulas exists.

Property 5.3.26
A bivariate copula C is CI if, and only if, C is concave in each variable when the other is fixed.

For bivariate Archimedean copulas, we can use the following result.

Property 5.3.27
The Archimedean copula C_ϕ is CI if, and only if, the inequalities

$$-\frac{d}{du} \ln \phi'(u) \geq -\frac{\partial}{\partial u} \ln \frac{\partial}{\partial v} C(u, v)$$

and

$$-\frac{d}{dv}\ln\phi'(v) \geq -\frac{\partial}{\partial v}\ln\frac{\partial}{\partial u}C(u,v)$$

hold almost everywhere on $[0,1]^2$. Equivalently, C_ϕ is CI if, and only if, $\ln\left(-\frac{d}{du}\ln\phi^{-1}(u)\right)$ is convex on $(0,+\infty)$.

For more results along these lines, we refer the interested reader to Averous and Dortet–Bernadet (2004).

The multivariate Gaussian copula is CI when the inverse of the correlation matrix has non-negative elements outside the diagonal.

Property 5.3.28
The multivariate normal random vector $\boldsymbol{X}$ with variance–covariance matrix $\boldsymbol{\Sigma}$ is CI if, and only if, $\boldsymbol{\Sigma}^{-1}$ is an M-matrix, that is, its off-diagonal elements are non-negative.

5.3.4 Multivariate total positivity of order 2

5.3.4.1 Bivariate total positivity of order 2

Let us first define a useful dependence concept for random couples, known as total positivity of order 2. The aim is again to formalize the positive dependence existing between the two components of a random couple (i.e., the fact that large values of one component tend to be associated with large values for the other).

Definition 5.3.29. The random couple $\boldsymbol{X}=(X_1,X_2)$ is said to be totally positive of order 2 (TP_2) if $[X_2|X_1=x_1]\preceq_{\mathrm{LR}}[X_2|X_1=x_1']$ for all $x_1\leq x_1'$ and $[X_1|X_2=x_2]\preceq_{\mathrm{LR}}[X_1|X_2=x_2']$ for all $x_2\leq x_2'$ ∇

The TP_2 concept imposes $\preceq_{\mathrm{LR}}$-increasingness of one component of the random couple in the value assumed by the other component. This dependence notion is thus rather intuitive since the value assumed by one of the components increases in the value taken by the other, in the $\preceq_{\mathrm{LR}}$ sense.

Note that the couple $\boldsymbol{X}$ of continuous random variables is TP_2 if, and only if, its pdf $f_{\boldsymbol{X}}$ satisfies

$$f_{\boldsymbol{X}}(x_1,x_2)f_{\boldsymbol{X}}(x_1',x_2') \geq f_{\boldsymbol{X}}(x_1,x_2')f_{\boldsymbol{X}}(x_1',x_2) \text{ for any } x_1\leq x_1' \text{ and } x_2\leq x_2',$$

that is, according to (3.21), if $f_{\boldsymbol{X}}$ is TP_2. Note that this inequality possesses an intuitive interpretation in terms of likelihood. Assume that the values taken by the random couple $\boldsymbol{X}$ and its independent copy $\boldsymbol{X}'$ are x_1, x_2, x_1' and x_2'. Then it is more likely that one of the two random couples assumes the two largest values, and the other one assumes the two smallest values. This expresses the fact that it is more likely that both components of $\boldsymbol{X}$ are simultaneously large or small. Two integer-valued rvs M_1 and M_2 are TP_2 if, and only if, the inequality

$$\begin{aligned}&\Pr[M_1=k_1,M_2=k_2]\Pr[M_1=k_1',M_2=k_2']\\&\geq \Pr[M_1=k_1,M_2=k_2']\Pr[M_1=k_1',M_2=k_2]\end{aligned}$$

holds for any $k_1 \leq k_1'$ and $k_2 \leq k_2'$. Returning to (3.21), M_1 and M_2 are TP_2 if their discrete pdf is TP_2.

5.3.4.2 Multivariate extension

Karlin and Rinott (1980) defined a multivariate version of total positivity of order 2. This concept is precisely defined next, using the concept of supermodularity introduced in Definition 3.4.60.

Definition 5.3.30. Assume that the random vector $\boldsymbol{X}$ has a continuous or discrete density $f_{\boldsymbol{X}}$. Then $\boldsymbol{X}$ is said to be multivariate totally positive of order 2 (MTP_2) if $\ln f_{\boldsymbol{X}}$ is supermodular, that is, if the inequality

$$f_{\boldsymbol{X}}(\boldsymbol{x})f_{\boldsymbol{X}}(\boldsymbol{y}) \leq f_{\boldsymbol{X}}(\boldsymbol{x} \vee \boldsymbol{y})f_{\boldsymbol{X}}(\boldsymbol{x} \wedge \boldsymbol{y})$$

holds for any $\boldsymbol{x}$, $\boldsymbol{y}$ in $\mathbb{R}^n$. ∇

This definition assumes that the random vector $\boldsymbol{X}$ possesses a probability distribution that is absolutely continuous with respect to some sigma-finite product measure on $\mathbb{R}^n$. Milgrom and Weber (1982) extended the definition to arbitrary probability measures and called this concept affiliation. Their extension allows us to consider distributions that are not dominated by product measures, such as the Fréchet upper bound. Note that multivariate total positivity of order 2 naturally appears in a number of applied probability models. Let us mention the case of Archimedean copulas, extensively considered in Müller and Scarsini (2004).

5.3.4.3 Basic composition formula

The following fundamental property of multivariate total positivity of order 2, known as the *basic composition formula*, will play a central role in the proofs of many results stated in this book. It can be seen as a multivariate extension of Property 3.3.53, and can be found in Karlin (1968).

Property 5.3.31
Given functions $h_1 : \mathcal{S} \times \mathcal{T} \to \mathbb{R}$ and $h_2 : \mathcal{T} \times \mathcal{U} \to \mathbb{R}$, define the function h_3 as

$$h_3(\boldsymbol{s}, \boldsymbol{u}) = \int_{\boldsymbol{T} \in \mathcal{T}} h_1(\boldsymbol{s}, \boldsymbol{t})h_2(\boldsymbol{t}, \boldsymbol{u})d\sigma(\boldsymbol{t}).$$

If h_1 is MTP_2 on $\mathcal{S} \times \mathcal{T}$ and h_2 is MTP_2 on $\mathcal{T} \times \mathcal{U}$ then h_3 is MTP_2 on $\mathcal{S} \times \mathcal{U}$.

5.3.4.4 Link with the multivariate likelihood ratio order

It is easy to relate the multivariate version of $\preceq_{\mathrm{LR}}$ to multivariate total positivity of order 2.

Property 5.3.32
A random vector $\boldsymbol{X}$ is MTP_2 if, and only if, $\boldsymbol{X} \preceq_{\mathrm{LR}} \boldsymbol{X}$.

5.3.4.5 Equivalent conditions

The following result is due to Kemperman (1977). Recall that a subset $\mathcal{S}$ of $\mathbb{R}^n$ is called a lattice if, for all $\boldsymbol{x}$ and $\boldsymbol{y}$ in $\mathcal{S}$, $\boldsymbol{x} \vee \boldsymbol{y}$ and $\boldsymbol{x} \wedge \boldsymbol{y}$ are in $\mathcal{S}$ as well.

Proposition 5.3.33
Suppose the support of $\boldsymbol{X}$ is a lattice. Then $\boldsymbol{X}$ is MTP_2 if, and only if, its density function $f_{\boldsymbol{X}}$ is TP_2 in each pair of its variables when the other $n-2$ variables are held fixed, that is,

$$
\begin{aligned}
& f_{\boldsymbol{X}}(x_1, \ldots, x_i, \ldots, x_j, \ldots, x_n) f_{\boldsymbol{X}}(x_1, \ldots, y_i, \ldots, y_j, \ldots, x_n) \\
& \geq f_{\boldsymbol{X}}(x_1, \ldots, y_i, \ldots, x_j, \ldots, x_n) f_{\boldsymbol{X}}(x_1, \ldots, x_i, \ldots, y_j, \ldots, x_n)
\end{aligned}
$$

whenever $x_i \leq y_i$ and $x_j \leq y_j$.

Example 5.3.34. Tong (1990, Theorem 4.3.2) proved that if $\boldsymbol{X} \sim \mathcal{N}or(\boldsymbol{\mu}, \Sigma)$ then it is MTP_2 if all the off-diagonal components of $\boldsymbol{R} = \Sigma^{-1}$ are non-positive. This easily follows from Proposition 5.3.33 since

$$
\frac{\partial^2}{\partial x_i \partial x_j} \ln f_{\boldsymbol{X}}(\boldsymbol{x}) = \frac{\partial^2}{\partial x_i \partial x_j} \left(-\frac{1}{2}(\boldsymbol{x}-\boldsymbol{\mu})' \boldsymbol{\Sigma}^{-1} (\boldsymbol{x}-\boldsymbol{\mu}) \right) = -\frac{1}{2} r_{ij}
$$

for all $i \neq j$. Thus all the second mixed derivatives of $\ln f_{\boldsymbol{X}}(\boldsymbol{x})$ are non-negative provided $r_{ij} \leq 0$ for all $i \neq j$. ∇

Remark 5.3.35. It should be noted that in the literature on percolation theory and statistical mechanics, the term 'MTP_2' is usually not used but rather variables are said to satisfy the FKG inequalities (to commemorate the seminal paper by Fortuin, Kastelyn and Ginibre 1971). When the joint distribution of $\boldsymbol{X}$ is given by a smooth density function $f_{\boldsymbol{X}}$, which is strictly positive on $\mathbb{R}^n$, the FKG inequalities are fulfilled if, and only if,

$$
\frac{\partial^2}{\partial x_i \partial x_j} \ln f_{\boldsymbol{X}}(\boldsymbol{x}) \geq 0 \text{ for all } i \neq j \text{ and } \boldsymbol{x} \in \mathbb{R}^n,
$$

which is further equivalent to the MTP_2 property by Proposition 5.3.33. ∇

5.3.4.6 Properties

If $\boldsymbol{X}$ is MTP_2, then for $k = 1, 2, \ldots, n$,

$$
\mathbb{E}\left[g(X_1, X_2, \ldots, X_k) | X_{k+1} = x_{k+1}, X_{k+2} = x_{k+2}, \ldots, X_n = x_n\right]
$$

is non-decreasing in $x_{k+1}, x_{k+2}, \ldots, x_n$ for any non-decreasing function $g: \mathbb{R}^k \to \mathbb{R}$. A proof of this result can be found in Karlin and Rinott (1980). Moreover, the implication

$$
\boldsymbol{X} \ \text{MTP}_2 \Rightarrow \boldsymbol{X} \ \text{CI}
$$

holds.

If $\boldsymbol{X}$ is MTP_2, then any random vector of dimension $k \leq n$ formed with components of $\boldsymbol{X}$ is also MTP_2. Independent risks are obviously MTP_2.

5.4 EXERCISES

Exercise 5.4.1. Let $Z \sim \mathcal{N}or\ (0, 1)$ and define $X_1 = Z$ and $X_2 = Z^2$. Compute $r_P(X_1, X_2)$, $r_K(X_1, X_2)$ and $r_S(X_1, X_2)$.

Exercise 5.4.2. (i) Let r_- and r_+ be the extremal Pearson correlation coefficients in $\mathcal{R}_2(F_1, F_2)$. Let $r \in [r_-, r_+]$ and define the bivariate df

$$F_X(x_1, x_2) = \varrho M_2(x_1, x_2) + (1-\varrho) W_2(x_1, x_2), \qquad \varrho = \frac{r_+ - r}{r_+ - r_-},$$

with marginals F_1 and F_2. Show that the corresponding Pearson correlation coefficient $r_P = r$.

(ii) Consider now the bivariate df

$$F_X(x_1, x_2) = \varrho M_2(x_1, x_2) + (1-\varrho) W_2(x_1, x_2), \varrho = \frac{1-r}{2},$$

with marginal dfs F_1 and F_2. Show that;

(a) Kendall's rank correlation coefficient $r_K = r$;

(b) Spearman's rank correlation coefficient $r_S = r$.

Exercise 5.4.3. For the Marshall–Olkin copulas introduced in Example 4.2.18, show that

$$r_K = \frac{\alpha_1\alpha_2}{\alpha_1 - \alpha_1\alpha_2 + \alpha_2}$$

and

$$r_S = \frac{3\alpha_1\alpha_2}{2\alpha_1 - \alpha_1\alpha_2 + 2\alpha_2}.$$

Exercise 5.4.4. Show that the Kendall's rank correlation coefficients associated with (4.14) and (4.15) are identical.

Exercise 5.4.5. Assume that the dfs F_i, $i = 1, 2, \ldots, n$, are strictly increasing and continuous. Show that the n-dimensional risk $X \in \mathcal{R}_n(F_1, F_2, \ldots, F_n)$ is comonotonic if, and only if, $r_K(X_{i_1}, X_{i_2}) = 1$ (or $r_S(X_{i_1}, X_{i_2}) = 1$) holds for all $1 \le i_1 < i_2 \le n$.

Exercise 5.4.6. For Gaussian copulas, show that

$$r_K = \frac{2}{\pi} \arcsin \alpha \text{ and } r_S = \frac{6}{\pi} \arcsin \frac{\alpha}{2}.$$

Exercise 5.4.7. Let $X \in \mathcal{R}_3(F_1, F_2, F_3)$. Show that the inequalities

$$-1 + |r_K(X_{i_1}, X_{i_2}) + r_K(X_{i_2}, X_{i_3})| \le r_K(X_{i_1}, X_{i_3})$$

and

$$r_K(X_{i_1}, X_{i_3}) \le 1 - |r_K(X_{i_1}, X_{i_2}) - r_K(X_{i_2}, X_{i_3})|$$

hold for all permutations (i_1, i_2, i_3) of (1, 2, 3).

Exercise 5.4.8. (Two-point risks). Consider the special case in which F_i is a two-point distribution in 0 and $\alpha_i > 0$, $i = 1, 2$. Show that in this special case

$$X_1 \text{ and } X_2 \text{ are PQD } \Leftrightarrow \mathbb{C}[X_1, X_2] \geq 0.$$

Exercise 5.4.9. Let X_i represent a benefit K if person i, $i = 1, 2$, has died and the heir (person 3) has survived. The death probabilities in the insurance period are $q_1 > q_2 > q_3$. The life of person 3 is independent of that of persons 1 and 2. Show that X_1 and X_2 are PQD.

Exercise 5.4.10. Let us study a simplified example of a stochastic interest model. Take $S = \alpha_1 X_1 + \alpha_2 X_2$ with $X_1 = \exp(-Y_1)$ and $X_2 = \exp(-Y_1 - Y_2)$. This is the sum of the present values of a payment α_1 at time 1 and α_2 at time 2. Assume that Y_1 and Y_2 are both independent and $\mathcal{U}ni(0, 1)$ distributed. Show that X_1 and X_2 are PQD.

Exercise 5.4.11. An example of possible dependence among remaining lifetimes of insured persons occurs when a contract is issued to a married couple. A Markovian model with forces of mortality depending on marital status can be found in Norberg (1989). More precisely, assume that the husband's force of mortality at age $x + t$ is $\mu_{01}(t)$ if he is then still married and $\mu_{23}(t)$ if he is a widower. Likewise, the wife's force of mortality at age $y + t$ is $\mu_{02}(t)$ if she is then still married and $\mu_{13}(t)$ if she is a widow. The future development of the marital status for an x-year-old husband (with remaining lifetime T_x) and a y-year-old wife (with remaining lifetime T_y) may be regarded as a Markov process with state space and forces of transition as represented in Figure 5.2.

Show that, in this model,

$$\mu_{01} \equiv \mu_{23} \text{ and } \mu_{02} \equiv \mu_{13} \Leftrightarrow T_x \text{ and } T_y \text{ are independent,} \tag{5.34}$$

while

$$\mu_{01} \leq \mu_{23} \text{ and } \mu_{02} \leq \mu_{13} \Rightarrow T_x \text{ and } T_y \text{ are PQD.} \tag{5.35}$$

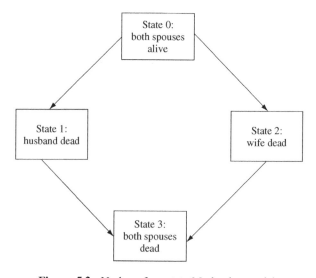

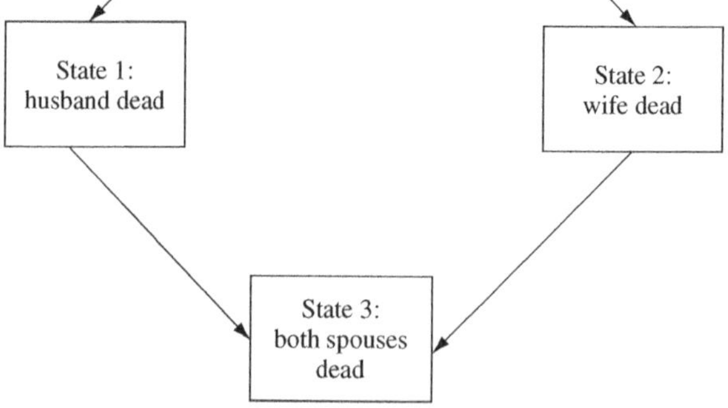

Figure 5.2 Norberg four-state Markovian model

Exercise 5.4.12. The widow's pension is a reversionary annuity with payments starting with the husband's death and terminating with the widow's death. The corresponding net single life premium for an x-year-old husband and his y-year-old wife, denoted by $a_{x|y}$, is given by

$$a_{x|y} = \sum_{k\geq 1} v^k \Pr[T_y > k] - \sum_{k\geq 1} v^k \Pr[T_x > k, T_y > k].$$

Let the superscript $\perp$ indicate that the corresponding amount of premium is calculated under the independence hypothesis; it is thus the premium from the tariff book. More precisely,

$$a^{\perp}_{x|y} = \sum_{k\geq 1} v^k \Pr[T_y > k] - \sum_{k\geq 1} v^k \Pr[T_x > k]\Pr[T_y > k].$$

When T_x and T_y are PQD, show that

$$a_{x|y} \leq a^{\perp}_{x|y}. \tag{5.36}$$

Exercise 5.4.13. Bivariate positive quadrant dependence has been generalized to higher dimensions in several ways; see Newman (1984). The random vector $\boldsymbol{X}$ is said to be pairwise PQD if X_i and X_j are PQD for all $i \neq j$. A second extension of bivariate positive quadrant dependence is as follows: $\boldsymbol{X}$ is said to be linearly PQD (LPQD) if for any non-negative reals $\alpha_1, \alpha_2, \ldots, \alpha_n$ and for any disjoint $A, B \subseteq \{1, 2, \ldots, n\}$,

$$\sum_{i\in A} \alpha_i X_i \text{ and } \sum_{i\in B} \alpha_i X_i \text{ are PQD.} \tag{5.37}$$

(i) Given a multivariate risk $\boldsymbol{X}$, show that $\boldsymbol{X}$ LPQD $\Rightarrow$ $\boldsymbol{X}$ pairwise PQD. Prove by providing a counterexample that the reverse implication is not necessarily true.

(ii) Let $X_1, X_2, \ldots, X_n$ be LPQD risks. Show that the following assertions hold:

(a) Any subset $X_{i_1}, X_{i_2}, \ldots, X_{i_k}$ of $X_1, X_2, \ldots, X_n$ is LPQD.

(b) Let $Y_1, Y_2, \ldots, Y_k$ be LPQD random variables independent of the X_i. Then $X_1, X_2, \ldots, X_n, Y_1, Y_2, \ldots, Y_k$ are LPQD.

(iii) Show that $\boldsymbol{X}^{\perp}$ is LPQD.

Exercise 5.4.14. According to Cohen and Sackrowitz (1995), a random vector $\boldsymbol{X}$ is said to be weakly conditionally increasing in sequence (WCIS) if, for $i = 2, 3, \ldots, n$,

$$\begin{aligned}&[(X_i, \ldots, X_n)|X_1 = x_1, \ldots, X_{i-2} = x_{i-2}, X_{i-1} = x_{i-1}]\\ &\qquad \preceq_{\mathrm{ST}} [(X_i, \ldots, X_n)|X_1 = x_1, \ldots, X_{i-2} = x_{i-2}, X_{i-1} = x'_{i-1}]\\ &\qquad\qquad \text{for all } x_j,\ j = 1, 2, \ldots, i-2, \text{ and } x_{i-1} \leq x'_{i-1}.\end{aligned}$$

A CIS random vector is obviously WCIS.

Now, let $\boldsymbol{X}$ and $\boldsymbol{Y}$ be two n-dimensional random vectors. If either $\boldsymbol{X}$ or $\boldsymbol{Y}$ is WCIS and

$$\begin{aligned}&[X_i|X_1 = x_1, \ldots, X_{i-1} = x_{i-1}] \preceq_{\mathrm{ST}} [Y_i|Y_1 = y_1, \ldots, Y_{i-1} = y_{i-1}]\\ &\qquad\qquad \text{whenever } x_j \leq y_j,\ j = 1, 2, \ldots, i-1,\end{aligned} \tag{5.38}$$

and

$$[X_i|X_1=x_1,\ldots,X_{i-1}=x_{i-1}]\preceq_{\mathrm{ST}}[Y_i|Y_1=x_1,\ldots,Y_{i-1}=x_{i-1}]$$
$$\text{for all } x_j,\ j=1,2,\ldots,i-1, \quad (5.39)$$

hold, then show that $\boldsymbol{X}\preceq_{\mathrm{ST}}\boldsymbol{Y}$.

Exercise 5.4.15. (Correlation ratio). Let X_1 and X_2 be rvs with first two moments finite. The quantity

$$K(X_2|X_1)=\frac{\mathbb{V}\big[\mathbb{E}[X_2|X_1]\big]}{\mathbb{V}[X_2]}$$

is called the correlation ratio of X_2 with respect to X_1. Show that:

(i) $0\leq K(X_2|X_1)\leq 1$;

(ii) if X_1 and X_2 are mutually independent, then $K(X_2|X_1)=0$;

(iii) $K(X_2|X_1)=0$ does not imply mutual independence of X_1 and X_2 (to see this, take (X_1,X_2) to be uniformly distributed on the unit disk $x^2+y^2<1$).

Exercise 5.4.16. (The FGM copula). Let us consider the Farlie–Gumbel–Morgenstern copula introduced in Example 5.2.6. Show the following:

(i) This family has

$$r_K=\frac{2}{9}\alpha\in\left[-\frac{2}{9},\frac{2}{9}\right]$$

and can thus be used only in situations where the dependence is not very strong.

(ii) $C_\alpha(\boldsymbol{u})\leq C_{\alpha'}(\boldsymbol{u})$ for all $\boldsymbol{u}\in[0,1]^2$ provided $\alpha\leq\alpha'$ (hence, C_α expresses positive quadrant dependence for $\alpha\geq 0$).

(iii) C_α is TP_2 when $\alpha\geq 0$.

Exercise 5.4.17. (Gumbel's copula). The copula introduced by Gumbel (1960) and studied by Hougaard (1986) has the form

$$C_\alpha(u_1,u_2)=\exp\Big(-\big((-\ln u_1)^\alpha+(-\ln u_2)^\alpha\big)^{1/\alpha}\Big),\quad \alpha\geq 1.$$

Show that:

(i) $r_K=1-\alpha^{-1}$;

(ii) $C_1=C_I$ and $\lim_{\alpha\to+\infty}C_\alpha=C_U$;

(iii) $C_\alpha(\boldsymbol{u})\leq C_{\alpha'}(\boldsymbol{u})$ for all $\boldsymbol{u}\in[0,1]^2$ provided $\alpha\leq\alpha'$;

(iv) C_α is PQD for all α;

(v) C_α is TP_2 for all α.

Exercise 5.4.18. (The normal copula). For the normal copula, show that:

(i) $C_\alpha(\boldsymbol{u}) \leq C_{\alpha'}(\boldsymbol{u})$ for all $\boldsymbol{u} \in [0, 1]^2$ whenever $\alpha \leq \alpha'$;

(ii) C_α is PQD for $\alpha \geq 0$;

(iii) C_α is TP_2 for $\alpha \geq 0$.

Exercise 5.4.19. Consider rvs X_1 and X_2 assuming the values $a_1 < a_2 < a_3$ with probabilities given in the following table:

	$X_1 = a_1$	$X_1 = a_2$	$X_1 = a_3$
$X_2 = a_1$	1/8	0	1/4
$X_2 = a_2$	0	1/4	0
$X_2 = a_3$	1/4	0	1/8

Show that these rvs are PQD.

6 Comparing Dependence

In this chapter, the strength of dependence is compared using the supermodular order. In the bivariate case, this ordering reduces to the so-called correlation order that has been successfully applied to solve actuarial problems involving pairs of correlated risks. Since we compare the dependence existing between the elements of a pair of random vectors, we naturally restrict ourselves to the elements of some Fréchet space (i.e., we fix the univariate marginals). This is the key difference from the multivariate orderings we encountered in Chapter 3, which can be used to compare random vectors differing in both the copula and the marginals (whereas in this chapter, only changes in the copula are allowed).

6.1 INTRODUCTION

Chapter 3 describes various stochastic order relations aiming to express mathematically such intuitive ideas as 'being larger than' and 'being less variable than' for rvs. We follow the same route here and present stochastic order relations for random vectors that translate the fact that the components of one of these vectors are more positively dependent than those of the other random vector. Such dependence orders have been reviewed by Scarsini and Shaked (1996).

Following Kimeldorf and Sampson (1987, 1989), Joe (1997) listed nine desirable properties that a stochastic ordering should have in order that higher in the ordering means greater positive dependence. In the bivariate case, this leads to the following definition.

Definition 6.1.1. Let $\preceq$ be a bivariate order in $\mathcal{R}_2(F_1, F_2)$. The relation $\preceq$ is a dependence order if it possesses the following properties:

A1 (concordance) $\boldsymbol{X} \preceq \boldsymbol{Y} \Rightarrow F_{\boldsymbol{X}}(\boldsymbol{x}) \leq F_{\boldsymbol{Y}}(\boldsymbol{x})$ for all $\boldsymbol{x} \in \mathbb{R}^n$;

A2 (transitivity) $\boldsymbol{X} \preceq \boldsymbol{Y}$ and $\boldsymbol{Y} \preceq \boldsymbol{Z} \Rightarrow \boldsymbol{X} \preceq \boldsymbol{Z}$;

A3 (reflexivity) $\boldsymbol{X} \preceq \boldsymbol{X}$;

A4 (antisymmetry) $\boldsymbol{X} \preceq \boldsymbol{Y}$ and $\boldsymbol{Y} \preceq \boldsymbol{X} \Rightarrow \boldsymbol{X} =_d \boldsymbol{Y}$;

A5 (Fréchet bounds) $(F_1^{-1}(U), F_2^{-1}(1-U)) \preceq \boldsymbol{X} \preceq (F_1^{-1}(U), F_2^{-1}(U))$ with $U \sim \mathcal{U}ni(0, 1)$;

A6 (weak convergence) if $\boldsymbol{X}_n \preceq \boldsymbol{Y}_n$ for every n and $\boldsymbol{X}_n \to_d \boldsymbol{X}$, $\boldsymbol{Y}_n \to_d \boldsymbol{Y}$ then $\boldsymbol{X} \preceq \boldsymbol{Y}$;

Actuarial Theory for Dependent Risks M. Denuit, J. Dhaene, M. Goovaerts and R. Kaas

A7 (invariance with respect to order of indices) $(X_1, X_2) \preceq (Y_1, Y_2) \Rightarrow (X_2, X_1) \preceq (Y_2, Y_1)$;

A8 (invariance with respect to increasing transforms) $(X_1, X_2) \preceq (Y_1, Y_2) \Rightarrow (t(X_1), X_2) \preceq (t(Y_1), Y_2)$ for all strictly increasing functions t;

A9 (invariance with respect to decreasing transforms) $(X_1, X_2) \preceq (Y_1, Y_2) \Rightarrow (t(Y_1), Y_2) \preceq (t(X_1), X_2)$ for all strictly decreasing functions t.

∇

Condition A5 implies that the Fréchet upper (lower) bound is the most (least) dependent one in the ordering $\preceq$. Conditions A6–A9 are quite natural invariance requirements.

Let us now generalize the notion of bivariate dependence order to the multivariate case. Several differences arise, particularly with respect to properties A5 and A9.

Definition 6.1.2. Let $\preceq$ be a multivariate order in $\mathcal{R}_n(F_1, \ldots, F_n)$ that is defined for all dimensions $n \geq 2$. The relation $\preceq$ is a multivariate dependence order if it possesses the following properties:

A1 (bivariate concordance) $\boldsymbol{X} \preceq \boldsymbol{Y}$ implies

$$\Pr[X_i \leq x_i, X_j \leq x_j] \leq \Pr[Y_i \leq y_i, Y_j \leq y_j]$$

for all $x_i, x_j \in \mathbb{R}$ and $1 \leq i < j \leq n$;

A2 (transitivity) $\boldsymbol{X} \preceq \boldsymbol{Y}$ and $\boldsymbol{Y} \preceq \boldsymbol{Z} \Rightarrow \boldsymbol{X} \preceq \boldsymbol{Z}$;

A3 (reflexivity) $\boldsymbol{X} \preceq \boldsymbol{X}$;

A4 (antisymmetry) $\boldsymbol{X} \preceq \boldsymbol{Y}$ and $\boldsymbol{Y} \preceq \boldsymbol{X} \Rightarrow \boldsymbol{X} =_d \boldsymbol{Y}$;

A5 (Fréchet upper bound) $\boldsymbol{X} \preceq (F_1^{-1}(U), F_2^{-1}(U), \ldots, F_n^{-1}(U))$ with $U \sim \mathcal{U}ni(0, 1)$;

A6 (weak convergence) if $\boldsymbol{X}_n \preceq \boldsymbol{Y}_n$ for every n and $\boldsymbol{X}_n \to_d \boldsymbol{X}$, $\boldsymbol{Y}_n \to_d \boldsymbol{Y}$ then $\boldsymbol{X} \preceq \boldsymbol{Y}$;

A7 (invariance with respect to order of indices) $\boldsymbol{X} \preceq \boldsymbol{Y}$ implies

$$(X_{\pi(1)}, X_{\pi(2)}, \ldots, X_{\pi(n)}) \preceq (Y_{\pi(1)}, Y_{\pi(2)}, \ldots, Y_{\pi(n)})$$

whatever the permutation π of $\{1, 2, \ldots, n\}$;

A8 (invariance with respect to increasing transforms) $\boldsymbol{X} \preceq \boldsymbol{Y}$ implies

$$(t(X_1), X_2, \ldots, X_n) \preceq (t(Y_1), Y_2, \ldots, Y_n)$$

for all strictly increasing functions t;

A9 (closure under marginalization) $\boldsymbol{X} \preceq \boldsymbol{Y}$ implies

$$(X_{i_1}, X_{i_2}, \ldots, X_{i_k}) \preceq (Y_{i_1}, Y_{i_2}, \ldots, Y_{i_k})$$

for all $1 \leq i_1 < i_2 < \ldots < i_k \leq n$, $2 \leq k < n$.

∇

Note that bivariate property A5 does not extend completely because there is no Fréchet lower bound in general for dimension $n \geq 3$ (see Remark 1.10.4). Similarly, the use of decreasing transformations to reverse the ordering of dependence does not extend to the multivariate case. So, bivariate property A9 is replaced by the natural property of closure under marginalization.

This chapter aims to present the supermodular order as a tool to compare the strength of dependence between rvs, as well as some of its variants, the symmetric supermodular and the increasing supermodular orders. These stochastic order relations have been successfully applied to various actuarial problems. We will see that the supermodular order is indeed a dependence order.

Several positive dependence notions introduced in the preceding chapter can be obtained by comparing the joint df of the random vector with the joint df that the random vector would have if the components were independent. The correlation order and positive quadrant dependence are linked in this way. Also, any dependence order determines a positive dependence notion by comparing a multivariate distribution with the distribution corresponding to the independence hypothesis.

6.2 COMPARING DEPENDENCE IN THE BIVARIATE CASE USING THE CORRELATION ORDER

6.2.1 Definition

Random variables are concordant if they tend to be all large together or small together. Concordance of rvs conveys the idea of clustering of large and small events. An ordering of concordance was initially considered for two rvs by Yanagimoto and Okamoto (1969), Cambanis, Simons, and Stout (1976) and Tchen (1980). This ordering corresponds to a natural notion of stochastic dominance between two distribution functions with fixed marginals. Large and small values will tend to be more often associated under the dominant distribution. Detection of concordant behaviour is especially important in risk management of large portfolios of insurance contracts or financial assets. In these portfolios the main risk is the occurrence of many joint default events or simultaneous downside evolution of prices. An accurate knowledge of concordance between claims or financial asset prices will help to assess this risk of loss clustering and thus, allow appropriate action to be taken to ensure that the risk incurred by the financial institution remains within its stated risk capacity. Clearly the presence of concordance affects risk measures and asset allocations resulting from optimal portfolio selection. Analysis of concordance cannot be neglected and reveals much of the danger associated with a given position.

The correlation order was introduced in the actuarial literature by Dhaene and Goovaerts (1996, 1997). The idea was to find an ordering between random couples $\boldsymbol{X} = (X_1, X_2)$ and $\boldsymbol{Y} = (Y_1, Y_2)$ such that the sums of their components are ordered in the stop-loss sense. They proved that the correlation order satisfies this condition. Let us start with the formal definition of the correlation order.

Definition 6.2.1. Consider two random couples $\boldsymbol{X} = (X_1, X_2)$ and $\boldsymbol{Y} = (Y_1, Y_2)$ in $\mathcal{R}_2(F_1, F_2)$. If

$$F_{\boldsymbol{X}}(x_1, x_2) \leq F_{\boldsymbol{Y}}(x_1, x_2), \text{ for all } \boldsymbol{x} \in \mathbb{R}^2, \tag{6.1}$$

or, equivalently, if

$$\overline{F}_X(x_1, x_2) \leq \overline{F}_Y(x_1, x_2), \text{ for all } \boldsymbol{x} \in \mathbb{R}^2, \tag{6.2}$$

then $\boldsymbol{X}$ is said to be smaller than $\boldsymbol{Y}$ in the correlation order (denoted by $\boldsymbol{X} \preceq_{\text{CORR}} \boldsymbol{Y}$). ∇

We will justify the name 'correlation order' in Proposition 6.2.7 below. We will see there that Pearson's correlation for any pair $(g_1(X_1), g_2(X_2))$ with g_1 and g_2 non-decreasing is smaller than Pearson's correlation for $(g_1(Y_1), g_2(Y_2))$ when $\boldsymbol{X} \preceq_{\text{CORR}} \boldsymbol{Y}$ holds.

Remark 6.2.2. The equivalence of (6.1) and (6.2) for fixed univariate marginal dfs F_1 and F_2 holds in the bivariate case only. It simply follows from the formula

$$F_X(x_1, x_2) = 1 - \overline{F}_1(x_1) - \overline{F}_2(x_2) + \overline{F}_X(x_1, x_2)$$

that holds for every $\boldsymbol{x} \in \mathbb{R}^2$. ∇

The intuitive meaning of a ranking with respect to $\preceq_{\text{CORR}}$ is clear from Definition 6.2.1. Indeed, $F_X(x_1, x_2)$ and $F_Y(x_1, x_2)$ read as 'X_1 and X_2 are both small' and 'Y_1 and Y_2 are both small', respectively (small meaning that X_1 (Y_1) is smaller than the threshold x_1, and X_2 (Y_2) is smaller than the threshold x_2). So (6.1) means that when $\boldsymbol{X} \preceq_{\text{CORR}} \boldsymbol{Y}$ holds, the probability that Y_1 and Y_2 are both small is larger than the corresponding probability for X_1 and X_2. Similarly from (6.2), $\boldsymbol{X} \preceq_{\text{CORR}} \boldsymbol{Y}$ also ensures that the probability that X_1 and X_2 are both large is smaller than the corresponding probability for Y_1 and Y_2. This corresponds to the intuitive content of '$\boldsymbol{Y}$ being more positively dependent than $\boldsymbol{X}$'.

Remark 6.2.3. Cebrian, Denuit and Scaillet (2004) proposed inference tools to analyse the $\preceq_{\text{CORR}}$ ordering of random couples. The analysis relies on tests for upper and lower quadrant dominance of the true distribution by a parametric or semiparametric model, that is, for a parametric or semiparametric model to give a probability that two rvs are simultaneously small or large is at least as large as if they were left unspecified. The parametric and semiparametric settings are based on the copula representation, which allows for disentangling behaviour of margins and dependence structure. A distance test and an intersection–union test for inequality constraints are developed depending on the definition of null and alternative hypotheses. An empirical illustration is given for loss–ALAE data. ∇

6.2.2 Relationship with orthant orders

Note that for random vectors $\boldsymbol{X}$ and $\boldsymbol{Y}$ in $\mathcal{R}_2(F_1, F_2)$, we have

$$\boldsymbol{X} \preceq_{\text{CORR}} \boldsymbol{Y} \Leftrightarrow \boldsymbol{X} \preceq_{\text{UO}} \boldsymbol{Y} \Leftrightarrow \boldsymbol{X} \preceq_{\text{LO}} \boldsymbol{Y};$$

see (3.41) and (3.42). The reader should notice, however, that in (3.41) and (3.42) $\boldsymbol{X}$ and $\boldsymbol{Y}$ are not required to have the same marginals. Therefore, whereas upper and lower orthant orders measure the size (or the location) of the underlying random vectors, the correlation order measures the amount of positive dependence of the underlying random vectors.

6.2.3 Relationship with positive quadrant dependence

Recalling Property 5.3.2(i)–(ii), the following result becomes obvious.

Property 6.2.4
The random couple $\boldsymbol{X}$ is PQD if, and only if, $\boldsymbol{X}^{\perp} \preceq_{\text{CORR}} \boldsymbol{X}$, where $\boldsymbol{X}^{\perp}$ is an independent version of $\boldsymbol{X}$ (i.e., the joint df of $\boldsymbol{X}^{\perp}$ is the product of the marginal dfs F_1 and F_2).

We see from this result that a positive dependence notion (here positive quadrant dependence) is closely related to a positive dependence order (here $\preceq_{\text{CORR}}$) in the sense that this dependence notion means dominating independence in terms of the dependence order.

6.2.4 Characterizations in terms of supermodular functions

As already pointed out several times, supermodular and log-supermodular functions play an important role in the theory of stochastic orderings and positive dependence. The following result is another illustration of this relationship: it shows that the $\preceq_{\text{CORR}}$ order is generated by the class of bivariate supermodular functions.

Proposition 6.2.5
For random couples $\boldsymbol{X}, \boldsymbol{Y} \in \mathcal{R}_2(F_1, F_2)$, we have

$$\boldsymbol{X} \preceq_{\text{CORR}} \boldsymbol{Y} \Leftrightarrow \mathbb{E}[g(\boldsymbol{X})] \leq \mathbb{E}[g(\boldsymbol{Y})] \text{ for all supermodular functions } g,$$

provided the expectations exist.

Proof. The $\Leftarrow$ part is obvious since dfs are expectations of supermodular functions. We give a proof of the $\Rightarrow$ part only for regular supermodular functions; in view of Denuit and Müller (2002), this is enough for the proposition to be true. Using Corollary 1.6.12, we get

$$\mathbb{E}[g(\boldsymbol{Y})] - \mathbb{E}[g(\boldsymbol{X})] = \int_0^{+\infty}\int_0^{+\infty}\Big(\overline{F}_{\boldsymbol{Y}}(t_1,t_2) - \overline{F}_{\boldsymbol{X}}(t_1,t_2)\Big)\frac{\partial^2}{\partial x_1 \partial x_2} g(t_1,t_2)\,dt_1 dt_2$$

whence the result obviously follows since $\frac{\partial^2}{\partial x_1 \partial x_2} g \geq 0$. □

It is in fact enough to reduce the set of test functions to the product of two non-decreasing functions, as stated next.

Proposition 6.2.6
For random couples $\boldsymbol{X}, \boldsymbol{Y} \in \mathcal{R}_2(F_1, F_2)$, we have

$$\boldsymbol{X} \preceq_{\text{CORR}} \boldsymbol{Y} \Leftrightarrow \mathbb{E}[g_1(X_1)g_2(X_2)] \leq \mathbb{E}[g_1(Y_1)g_2(Y_2)]$$

for all non-decreasing functions g_1 and g_2, provided the expectations exist.

As a consequence of Proposition 6.2.6, we have the following result in terms of covariances.

Proposition 6.2.7
For random couples $\boldsymbol{X}, \boldsymbol{Y} \in \mathcal{R}_2(F_1, F_2)$, we have

$$\boldsymbol{X} \preceq_{\text{CORR}} \boldsymbol{Y} \Leftrightarrow \mathbb{C}[g_1(X_1), g_2(X_2)] \leq \mathbb{C}[g_1(Y_1), g_2(Y_2)]$$

for all non-decreasing functions g_1 and g_2, provided the covariances exist.

Proposition 6.2.7 shows where $\preceq_{\text{CORR}}$ gets its name: the correlations between $g_1(X_1)$ and $g_2(X_2)$ are less than between $g_1(Y_1)$ and $g_2(Y_2)$ for all increasing functions g_1 and g_2.

6.2.5 Extremal elements

The next result identifies the extremal elements with respect to $\preceq_{\text{CORR}}$ in a given Fréchet space.

Property 6.2.8
Let $\boldsymbol{X} \in \mathcal{R}_2(F_1, F_2)$. Then, the inequalities

$$\left(F_1^{-1}(U), F_2^{-1}(1-U)\right) \preceq_{\text{CORR}} \boldsymbol{X} \preceq_{\text{CORR}} \left(F_1^{-1}(U), F_2^{-1}(U)\right)$$

hold when $U \sim \mathcal{U}ni(0, 1)$.

Proof. The result easily follows from (1.54), (1.55) and (6.1). □

6.2.6 Relationship with convex and stop-loss orders

The most important property of the $\preceq_{\text{CORR}}$ order is that it implies a ranking in the $\preceq_{\text{SL},=}$ sense for the respective sums. This is precisely stated next.

Property 6.2.9
Let $\boldsymbol{X}$ and $\boldsymbol{Y}$ in $\mathcal{R}_2(F_1, F_2)$ be such that $\boldsymbol{X} \preceq_{\text{CORR}} \boldsymbol{Y}$. Then, the stochastic inequality $X_1 + X_2 \preceq_{\text{SL},=} Y_1 + Y_2$ holds.

Proof. It suffices to adapt the reasoning used to prove Proposition 5.3.9 as follows. It is easy to reach the conclusion that

$$\mathbb{E}[(d - Y_1 - Y_2)_+] - \mathbb{E}[(d - X_1 - X_2)_+] = \int_0^d \Big(F_{\boldsymbol{Y}}(t, d-t) - F_{\boldsymbol{X}}(t, d-t)\Big) dt$$

holds, whence the result easily follows. □

Remark 6.2.10. As pointed out by Wang and Dhaene (1998), this shows that any $\preceq_{\text{SL}}$-monotone and comonotonic additive risk measure ϱ is necessarily subadditive. Indeed, combining Properties 6.2.8 and 6.2.9 yields the stochastic inequality

$$X_1 + X_2 \preceq_{\text{SL},=} F_1^{-1}(U) + F_2^{-1}(U)$$

which always holds with $U \sim \mathcal{U}ni(0,1)$, whatever $X \in \mathcal{R}_2(F_1, F_2)$. Therefore, we have

$$\begin{aligned} \varrho[X_1+X_2] &\leq \varrho\left[F_1^{-1}(U)+F_2^{-1}(U)\right] \\ &= \varrho\left[F_1^{-1}(U)\right]+\varrho\left[F_2^{-1}(U)\right] \\ &= \varrho[X_1]+\varrho[X_2]. \end{aligned}$$

This provides an alternative proof of the subadditivity of TVaR, for instance. ∇

In fact a stronger result than the one stated in Property 6.2.9 holds.

Property 6.2.11
Let X and Y in $\mathcal{R}_2(F_1, F_2)$ be such that $X \preceq_{\text{CORR}} Y$. Then, for every non-decreasing and supermodular function $\Psi: \mathbb{R}^2 \to \mathbb{R}$, the stochastic inequality $\Psi(X_1, X_2) \preceq_{\text{SL}} \Psi(Y_1, Y_2)$ holds.

Proof. We get that $g(x) = t(\Psi(x))$ is supermodular whenever t is non-decreasing and convex. For twice differentiable functions, this is easily seen from

$$\begin{aligned} \frac{\partial^2}{\partial x_1 \partial x_2} g(x) &= \frac{\partial}{\partial x_2}\left(t'(\Psi(x))\frac{\partial}{\partial x_1}\Psi(x)\right) \\ &= t''(\Psi(x))\frac{\partial}{\partial x_2}\Psi(x)\frac{\partial}{\partial x_1}\Psi(x) + t''(\Psi(x))\frac{\partial^2}{\partial x_1 \partial x_2}\Psi(x) \geq 0, \end{aligned}$$

which concludes the proof. □

The following result is due to Müller (2000).

Proposition 6.2.12
Let X and Y be two random couples. Then

$$X \preceq_{\text{CORR}} Y \Rightarrow Y_1 - Y_2 \preceq_{\text{SL},=} X_1 - X_2.$$

Proof. For any convex function g, we define the bivariate function Ψ as $\Psi(x) = -g(x_1 - x_2)$. Then

$$\begin{aligned} &\Psi(x_1+\epsilon, x_2+\delta) - \Psi(x_1+\epsilon, x_2) - \Psi(x_1, x_2+\delta) + \Psi(x_1, x_2) \\ &\quad = -g(x_1+\epsilon-x_2-\delta) + g(x_1+\epsilon-x_2) + g(x_1-x_2-\delta) - g(x_1-x_2) \\ &\quad = -g(x_1+\epsilon+z+\delta) - g(x_1+\epsilon+z) - g(x_1+z+\delta) + g(x_1+z) \end{aligned}$$

using the substitution $z = -x_2 - \delta$. Hence, Ψ is supermodular so that $X \preceq_{\text{CORR}} Y$ implies

$$\mathbb{E}[\Psi(X)] = -\mathbb{E}[g(X_1 - X_2)] \leq -\mathbb{E}[g(Y_1 - Y_2)] = \mathbb{E}[\Psi(Y)].$$

Since this holds for any convex function g, we have shown that $Y_1 - Y_2 \preceq_{\text{SL},=} X_1 - X_2$, as claimed. □

6.2.7 Correlation order and copulas

It is easy to see that a ranking in the $\preceq_{\text{CORR}}$ sense only depends on the copula, as pointed out in the next property.

Property 6.2.13
Let $\boldsymbol{X}$ and $\boldsymbol{Y}$ be in $\mathcal{R}_2(F_1, F_2)$, with respective copulas C_1 and C_2. Then,

$$\boldsymbol{X} \preceq_{\text{CORR}} \boldsymbol{Y} \Leftrightarrow C_1(u_1, u_2) \leq C_2(u_1, u_2) \text{ for all } \boldsymbol{u} \in [0, 1]^2.$$

6.2.8 Correlation order and correlation coefficients

The next result shows that Pearson's correlation coefficient as well as Kendall's and Spearman's rank correlation coefficients all agree with a ranking in the $\preceq_{\text{CORR}}$ sense. This reinforces the intuitive meaning of $\preceq_{\text{CORR}}$ as a tool to compare the strength of the dependence.

Property 6.2.14
Let $\boldsymbol{X}$ and $\boldsymbol{Y}$ in $\mathcal{R}_2(F_1, F_2)$ be such that $\boldsymbol{X} \preceq_{\text{CORR}} \boldsymbol{Y}$. Then

$$\begin{aligned} r_{\text{P}}(X_1, X_2) &\leq r_{\text{P}}(Y_1, Y_2), \\ r_{\text{K}}(X_1, X_2) &\leq r_{\text{K}}(Y_1, Y_2), \\ r_{\text{S}}(X_1, X_2) &\leq r_{\text{S}}(Y_1, Y_2). \end{aligned}$$

Proof. The inequality for Pearson's correlation coefficients follows directly from Proposition 6.2.7.

To get the inequality for Kendall's rank correlation coefficients, let us start from (5.8). Denote by C_1 the copula for $\boldsymbol{X}$ and by C_2 the copula for $\boldsymbol{Y}$. Then, if (U_1, U_2) has joint df C_1 and (V_1, V_2) joint df C_2,

$$\begin{aligned} r_{\text{K}}(X_1, X_2) &= 4\mathbb{E}[C_1(U_1, U_2)] - 1 \\ &\leq 4\mathbb{E}[C_2(U_1, U_2)] - 1 \\ &\leq 4\mathbb{E}[C_2(V_1, V_2)] - 1 = r_{\text{K}}(Y_1, Y_2), \end{aligned}$$

where the first inequality follows from $C_1 \leq C_2$ using Property 6.2.13 and the second from $(U_1, U_2) \preceq_{\text{CORR}} (V_1, V_2)$ together with the supermodularity of C_2 (using Proposition 6.2.5).

Finally, the result for Spearman's rank correlation coefficients follows at once from (5.11) together with $C_1 \leq C_2$. □

6.2.9 Ordering Archimedean copulas

The Archimedean copulas possess the following nice property, which provides the actuary with a practical condition for a ranking in the $\preceq_{\text{CORR}}$ sense to hold.

Proposition 6.2.15
Let C_1 and C_2 be Archimedean copulas generated by ϕ_1 and ϕ_2. Then $C_1(\boldsymbol{u}) \leq C_2(\boldsymbol{u})$ for all $\boldsymbol{u} \in [0, 1]^2$ if, and only if, $\phi_1 \circ \phi_2^{-1}$ is subadditive, that is, if the inequality

$$\phi_1 \circ \phi_2^{-1}(x+y) \leq \phi_1 \circ \phi_2^{-1}(x) + \phi_1 \circ \phi_2^{-1}(y)$$

holds for any x and y.

Proof. Let $f = \phi_1 \circ \phi_2^{-1}$. Note that f is continuous, non-decreasing and satisfies $f(0) = 0$. Clearly, $C_1(\boldsymbol{u}) \leq C_2(\boldsymbol{u})$ for all $\boldsymbol{u} \in [0, 1]^2$ if, and only if,

$$\phi_1^{-1}\big(\phi_1(u_1) + \phi_1(u_2)\big) \leq \phi_2^{-1}\big(\phi_2(u_1) + \phi_2(u_2)\big). \tag{6.3}$$

Let $x = \phi_2(u_1)$ and $y = \phi_2(u_2)$. Then (6.3) is equivalent to

$$\phi_1^{-1}\big(f(x) + f(y)\big) \leq \phi_2^{-1}(x+y) \tag{6.4}$$

for all x, y. Now, suppose that $C_1(\boldsymbol{u}) \leq C_2(\boldsymbol{u})$ for all $\boldsymbol{u} \in [0, 1]^2$. Applying ϕ_1 to both sides of (6.4) and noting that $\phi_1 \circ \phi_2^{-1}(u) \leq u$ for all $u \geq 0$ yields $f(x+y) \leq f(x) + f(y)$ for all $x, y \in \mathbb{R}^+$, hence f is subadditive. Conversely, if f is subadditive then applying ϕ_1^{-1} to both sides and noting that $\phi_1^{-1} \circ f = \phi_2^{-1}$ yields (6.3). □

The next result lists several sufficient conditions for the subadditivity of $\phi_1 \circ \phi_2^{-1}$.

Property 6.2.16

(i) Let f be defined on $\mathbb{R}^+$. If f is concave and $f(0) = 0$ then f is subadditive. Therefore, if $\phi_1 \circ \phi_2^{-1}$ is concave then $C_1(\boldsymbol{u}) \leq C_2(\boldsymbol{u})$ for all $\boldsymbol{u} \in [0, 1]^2$.

(ii) If ϕ_1/ϕ_2 is non-decreasing on $[0, 1]$ then $C_1(\boldsymbol{u}) \leq C_2(\boldsymbol{u})$ for all $\boldsymbol{u} \in [0, 1]^2$.

(iii) If ϕ_1'/ϕ_2' is non-decreasing on $[0, 1]$ then $C_1(\boldsymbol{u}) \leq C_2(\boldsymbol{u})$ for all $\boldsymbol{u} \in [0, 1]^2$.

6.2.10 Ordering compound sums

Let (M_1, M_2) and (M_1', M_2') be two pairs of integer-valued rvs, and let (S_{M_1}, S_{M_2}) and $(S'_{M_1'}, S'_{M_2'})$ be two pairs of random sums whose components are defined as

$$S_{M_i} = \sum_{k=1}^{M_i} X_{ik}, \quad S'_{M_i'} = \sum_{k=1}^{M_i'} X'_{ik}, \qquad i = 1, 2, \tag{6.5}$$

in terms of identically distributed sequences $\{X_{i1}, X_{i2}, \ldots\}$ and $\{X'_{i1}, X'_{i2}, \ldots\}$ of positive rvs, independent of $\boldsymbol{M}$ and $\boldsymbol{M}'$. Thc sequences $\{X_{11}, X_{12}, \ldots\}$ and $\{X_{21}, X_{22}, \ldots\}$ are also assumed to be independent. Then the following result, which can be found in Denuit, Genest and Marceau (2002), is valid.

Property 6.2.17
$(M_1, M_2) \preceq_{\text{CORR}} (M_1', M_2') \Rightarrow (S_{M_1}, S_{M_2}) \preceq_{\text{CORR}} (S'_{M_1'}, S'_{M_2'})$.

Proof. Given arbitrary positive increasing functions g_1 and g_2, one need only show that

$$\mathbb{E}[g_1(S_{M_1})g_2(S_{M_2})] \leq \mathbb{E}[g_1(S'_{M_1'})g_2(S'_{M_2'})]. \tag{6.6}$$

To this end, define

$$\Psi(m_1, m_2) \equiv \mathbb{E}\left[g_1(S_{m_1})g_2(S_{m_2})\right] = \mathbb{E}\left[g_1(S'_{m_1})g_2(S'_{m_2})\right]$$

and note that for arbitrary integers $m_i \leq m_i'$, one has $S_{m_i'} \geq S_{m_i}$ with probability one, because the X_{ij} are positive. Since the g_i are increasing by hypothesis, it follows that

$$\Psi(m_1, m_2) = \mathbb{E}\left[g_1(S_{m_1})\right]\mathbb{E}\left[g_2(S_{m_2})\right] \equiv t_1(m_1)t_2(m_2),$$

where t_1 and t_2 are positive increasing functions. Consequently, Proposition 6.2.6 ensures that

$$\mathbb{E}[\Psi(M_1, M_2)] \leq \mathbb{E}[\Psi(M_1', M_2')]$$

which is the same as (6.6). □

6.2.11 Correlation order and diversification benefit

Let us assume that two companies have aggregate losses X_1 and X_2. In order to be able to survive, the regulator requires a company with loss X to hold capital $\varrho[X]$.

Definition 6.2.18. Consider two losses X_1 and X_2, and a capital requirement ϱ. The random diversification benefit $D(X_1, X_2, \varrho)$ is given by

$$\begin{aligned} D(X_1, X_2, \varrho) = {} & (X_1 - \varrho[X_1])_+ + (X_2 - \varrho[X_2])_+ \\ & - (X_1 + X_2 - \varrho[X_1] - \varrho[X_2])_+. \end{aligned} \tag{6.7}$$

▽

Hence, the random diversification benefit is the decrease in shortfall caused by merging the two companies and putting their available capital together. It is important to note that the diversification benefit is to be understood from the regulator viewpoint (or the customer viewpoint).

The next result shows how the dependence structure between X_1 and X_2 influences the diversification benefit. It indicates that the more the components of a random couple with given marginals are dependent, the less is the expected diversification benefit.

Proposition 6.2.19
If $(X_1, X_2) \preceq_{\text{CORR}} (Y_1, Y_2)$ then $\mathbb{E}[D(X_1, X_2, \varrho)] \geq \mathbb{E}[D(Y_1, Y_2, \varrho)]$.

The proof follows immediately from Property 6.2.9 and the definition of the diversification benefit. Proposition 6.2.19 states a result which is intuitively clear. The more dependent the members of a random couple with given marginals, the less the expected diversification benefit.

We have from Property 6.2.8 that the comonotonic couple is always the largest in the correlation order sense, the countermonotonic couple the smallest. This implies that the expected diversification benefit for a random couple with given marginals will be minimal when the copula connecting the marginals is the Fréchet upper bound copula and maximal when it is the Fréchet lower bound copula:

$$\begin{aligned}\mathbb{E}[D(F_{X_1}^{-1}(U), F_{X_2}^{-1}(U), \varrho)] &\leq \mathbb{E}[D(X_1, X_2, \varrho)] \\ &\leq \mathbb{E}[D(F_{X_1}^{-1}(U), F_{X_2}^{-1}(1-U), \varrho)]. \qquad (6.8)\end{aligned}$$

Remark 6.2.20. It is often stated that merging comonotonic risks cannot lead to a diversification benefit. However, this is not true. Take as an example the comonotonic couple (X_1, X_2). We will assume that the marginal distributions are strictly increasing. Then we have that

$$\begin{aligned}(X_1 + X_2 - \varrho[X_1] - \varrho[X_2])_+ &= (X_1 - d_1)_+ + (X_2 - d_2)_+ \\ &\leq (X_1 - \varrho[X_1])_+ + (X_2 - \varrho[X_2])_+,\end{aligned}$$

where the d_j are given by

$$d_j = F_{X_j}^{-1}\left(F_{X_1+X_2}(\varrho[X_1] + \varrho[X_2])\right), \quad j = 1, 2.$$

For the random couple $\left(\frac{U}{2}, \frac{U}{2}\right)$, where $U \sim \mathcal{U}ni(0, 1)$, we find that

$$\begin{aligned}\left(\frac{U}{2} + \frac{U}{2} - \frac{1}{6} - \frac{1}{3}\right)_+ = \left(U - \frac{1}{2}\right)_+ &= \left(\frac{U}{2} - \frac{1}{4}\right)_+ + \left(\frac{U}{2} - \frac{1}{4}\right)_+ \\ &\leq \left(\frac{U}{2} - \frac{1}{6}\right)_+ + \left(\frac{U}{2} - \frac{1}{3}\right)_+.\end{aligned}$$

For an outcome of U equal to $\frac{1}{2}$ for instance, strict inequality holds.

Hence, we can conclude that merging of comonotonic risks can lead to a diversification benefit. Only when the capital allocation of the divided risks is comonotonic-optimal (in the sense that $d_j = \varrho[X_j]$) does diversification no longer make sense. ∇

6.3 COMPARING DEPENDENCE IN THE MULTIVARIATE CASE USING THE SUPERMODULAR ORDER

6.3.1 Definition

The supermodular and symmetric supermodular orders have been cursorily studied in the applied probability literature; standard references include Joe (1990), Meester and Shanthikumar (1993), Szekli, Disney and Hur (1994), Shaked and Shanthikumar (1997), Bäuerle (1997), Bäuerle and Müller (1998), Müller (1997b), and Müller and Scarsini (2000). Applications in actuarial science can be found in Goovaerts and Dhaene (1999).

The supermodular order can be seen as a multivariate extension of the correlation order to higher dimensions, based on the supermodular functions. It is precisely defined next (recall the concept of supermodularity from Definition 3.4.60).

Definition 6.3.1. Let $\boldsymbol{X}$ and $\boldsymbol{Y}$ be two n-dimensional random vectors such that $\mathbb{E}[g(\boldsymbol{X})] \leq \mathbb{E}[g(\boldsymbol{Y})]$ for all supermodular functions $g: \mathbb{R}^n \to \mathbb{R}$, provided the expectations exist. Then $\boldsymbol{X}$ is said to be smaller than $\boldsymbol{Y}$ in the supermodular order (denoted by $\boldsymbol{X} \preceq_{\text{SM}} \boldsymbol{Y}$). ∇

The supermodular order has been successfully applied to various problems in applied probability. Although the direct checking of $\preceq_{\text{SM}}$ using Definition 6.3.1 is generally hopeless, many interesting stochastic representations exist that are helpful for establishing a ranking in the $\preceq_{\text{SM}}$ sense.

6.3.2 Smooth supermodular functions

Unfortunately, no small generator is available for $\preceq_{\text{SM}}$. Nevertheless, it is permitted to assume that the generator consists only of differentiable functions. This is formally stated in the next result; for the proof of this technical result we refer the reader to Denuit and Müller (2002).

Proposition 6.3.2
Given two n-dimensional random vectors $\boldsymbol{X}$ and $\boldsymbol{Y}$, $\boldsymbol{X} \preceq_{\text{SM}} \boldsymbol{Y}$ if, and only if, $\mathbb{E}[g(\boldsymbol{X})] \leq \mathbb{E}[g(\boldsymbol{Y})]$ holds for all twice differentiable supermodular functions, that is, those functions $g: \mathbb{R}^n \to \mathbb{R}$ such that (3.77) holds.

6.3.3 Restriction to distributions with identical marginals

Since the functions $\boldsymbol{y} \mapsto \mathbb{I}[\boldsymbol{y} > \boldsymbol{x}]$ and $\boldsymbol{y} \mapsto \mathbb{I}[\boldsymbol{y} \leq \boldsymbol{x}]$ are supermodular for each fixed $\boldsymbol{x}$, we immediately have that

$$\boldsymbol{X} \preceq_{\text{SM}} \boldsymbol{Y} \Rightarrow \begin{cases} \Pr[\boldsymbol{X} > \boldsymbol{x}] \leq \Pr[\boldsymbol{Y} > \boldsymbol{x}] \text{ for all } \boldsymbol{x} \in \mathbb{R}^n, \\ \Pr[\boldsymbol{X} \leq \boldsymbol{x}] \leq \Pr[\boldsymbol{Y} \leq \boldsymbol{x}] \text{ for all } \boldsymbol{x} \in \mathbb{R}^n. \end{cases} \tag{6.9}$$

Note that from (6.9) it follows that if $\boldsymbol{X} \preceq_{\text{SM}} \boldsymbol{Y}$ then $X_i =_d Y_i$ for $i = 1, 2, \ldots, n$. Therefore, if $\boldsymbol{X} \preceq_{\text{SM}} \boldsymbol{Y}$ then $\boldsymbol{X}$ and $\boldsymbol{Y}$ necessarily belong to the same Fréchet space.

Remark 6.3.3. As opposed to Proposition 6.2.5, the implication (6.9) is strict for dimension $n \geq 3$, as shown next. For instance, for $n = 3$, let us consider the random vectors $\boldsymbol{X} = (X_1, X_2, X_3)$ and $\boldsymbol{Y} = (Y_1, Y_2, Y_3)$ such that $\boldsymbol{X}$ is uniformly distributed on the six points (2,2,1), (2,1,2), (1,2,2), (1,1,1), (0,0,2) and (2,0,0) and $\boldsymbol{Y}$ is uniformly distributed on the six points (2,2,2), (2,1,1), (1,2,1), (1,1,2), (2,0,2) and (0,0,0). Then it is easy to see that $\boldsymbol{X}$ and $\boldsymbol{Y}$ have the same marginal distributions, and a straightforward but tedious calculation shows that $\boldsymbol{X} \preceq_{\text{UO}} \boldsymbol{Y}$ and $\boldsymbol{Y} \preceq_{\text{LO}} \boldsymbol{X}$, but $\boldsymbol{X} \preceq_{\text{SM}} \boldsymbol{Y}$ does not hold. Indeed, as shown by Dyckerhoff and Mosler (1997), it is sufficient to check the 27 lattice points in $\{0, 1, 2\}^3$ and to observe that $F_{\boldsymbol{X}} \geq F_{\boldsymbol{Y}}$ and $\overline{F}_{\boldsymbol{X}} \geq \overline{F}_{\boldsymbol{Y}}$ at all these points. On the other hand, there are supermodular functions $g: \mathbb{R}^3 \to \mathbb{R}$ such that $\mathbb{E}[g(\boldsymbol{X})] > \mathbb{E}[g(\boldsymbol{Y})]$. Take, for example, $g(\boldsymbol{x}) = (x_1 + x_2 + x_3 - 4)_+$. This function is supermodular since it is a composition of an increasing convex real-valued function and an increasing supermodular function (see Property 3.4.61(ii)). For this function we get

$$\mathbb{E}[(X_1 + X_2 + X_3 - 4)_+] = \tfrac{1}{2} > \tfrac{1}{3} = \mathbb{E}[(Y_1 + Y_2 + Y_3 - 4)_+].$$

For dimensions $n \geq 4$, we refer the reader to Joe (1990) for an example which shows that the supermodular order is strictly stronger than the concordance order of Remark 3.3.81. ∇

6.3.4 A companion order: The symmetric supermodular order

In what follows, we will also use the symmetric supermodular order. As Shaked and Tong (1985) pointed out, restricting ourselves to symmetric supermodular functions also leads to useful stochastic order relations. Here, a function $g : \mathbb{R}^n \to \mathbb{R}$ is said to be symmetric if

$$g(x_1, x_2, \ldots, x_n) = g(x_{\pi(1)}, x_{\pi(2)}, \ldots, x_{\pi(n)})$$

holds for all the permutations π of $\{1, 2, \ldots, n\}$.

Definition 6.3.4. If the inequality in Definition 6.3.1 is required to hold only for symmetric supermodular functions $g : \mathbb{R}^n \to \mathbb{R}$ such that the expectations exist, then $\boldsymbol{X}$ is said to precede $\boldsymbol{Y}$ in the symmetric supermodular order, denoted as $\boldsymbol{X} \preceq_{\text{SYM-SM}} \boldsymbol{Y}$. ∇

Finally, we introduce the increasing supermodular order.

Definition 6.3.5. If the inequality in Definition 6.3.1 is required to hold only for non-decreasing supermodular functions $g : \mathbb{R}^n \to \mathbb{R}$, then $\boldsymbol{X}$ is said to be smaller than $\boldsymbol{Y}$ in the increasing supermodular order, denoted as $\boldsymbol{X} \preceq_{\text{ISM}} \boldsymbol{Y}$. ∇

6.3.5 Relationships between supermodular-type orders

The following result, due to Müller and Scarsini (2000), clarifies the relationship between $\preceq_{\text{ISM}}$ and $\preceq_{\text{SM}}$.

Property 6.3.6
Given two n-dimensional random vectors $\boldsymbol{X}$ and $\boldsymbol{Y}$, the following statements are equivalent:

(i) $\boldsymbol{X} \preceq_{\text{SM}} \boldsymbol{Y}$;

(ii) $\boldsymbol{X}$ and $\boldsymbol{Y}$ have the same marginals and $\boldsymbol{X} \preceq_{\text{ISM}} \boldsymbol{Y}$;

(iii) $\boldsymbol{X}$ and $\boldsymbol{Y}$ have the same expectation and $\boldsymbol{X} \preceq_{\text{ISM}} \boldsymbol{Y}$.

6.3.6 Supermodular order and dependence measures

Supermodular ordering is a useful tool for comparing dependence structures of random vectors. As pointed out above, only distributions with the same marginals can be compared in the supermodular sense. Moreover, the following implication holds for any $i \neq j$:

$$\boldsymbol{X} \preceq_{\text{SM}} \boldsymbol{Y} \Rightarrow \begin{cases} r_{\text{P}}(X_i, X_j) \leq r_{\text{P}}(Y_i, Y_j), \\ r_{\text{K}}(X_i, X_j) \leq r_{\text{K}}(Y_i, Y_j), \\ r_{\text{S}}(X_i, X_j) \leq r_{\text{S}}(Y_i, Y_j). \end{cases}$$

Müller and Scarsini (2000) proved that $\preceq_{\text{SM}}$ is a multivariate positive dependence order. Thus, it can be used to generate a positive dependence notion, as follows. A random vector $\boldsymbol{X}$ is said to be positively supermodularly dependent if $\boldsymbol{X}^{\perp} \preceq_{\text{SM}} \boldsymbol{X}$ holds true. This notion was considered in Shaked and Shanthikumar (1997).

6.3.7 Extremal dependence structures in the supermodular sense

The upper Fréchet bound provides the strongest dependence structure in the $\preceq_{\text{SM}}$ sense, as shown in the next result, which can be found in Heilmann (1986).

Proposition 6.3.7
For any $X \in \mathcal{R}_n(F_1, F_2, \ldots, F_n)$, we have

$$X \preceq_{\text{SM}} (F_1^{-1}(U), F_2^{-1}(U), \ldots, F_n^{-1}(U))$$

where $U \sim \mathcal{U}ni(0, 1)$.

In a Fréchet space $\mathcal{R}_n^+(F_1, F_2, \ldots, F_n)$ satisfying some suitable conditions, Dhaene and Denuit (1999) proved that the minimal element with respect to the supermodular order is precisely M_n, the Fréchet lower bound.

Proposition 6.3.8
Consider a Fréchet space $\mathcal{R}_n^+(F_1, F_2, \ldots, F_n)$ satisfying (1.58). Let X be a mutually exclusive risk in $\mathcal{R}_n^+(F_1, F_2, \ldots, F_n)$. Then, $X \preceq_{\text{SM}} Y$ holds for any $Y \in \mathcal{R}_n(F_1, F_2, \ldots, F_n)$.

Proof. Without loss of generality, the supermodular functions generating $\preceq_{\text{SM}}$ may be assumed to vanish on the axes. This is because it suffices to substitute for $g : (\mathbb{R}^+)^n \to \mathbb{R}$ the auxiliary function $g^* : (\mathbb{R}^+)^n \to \mathbb{R}$ defined as

$$g^*(x) = g(x) - \sum_{i=1}^{n} g(0, \ldots, 0, x_i, 0, \ldots, 0) + (n-1)g(0, 0, \ldots, 0),$$

and to notice that the inequality $\mathbb{E}[g(X)] \leq \mathbb{E}[g(Y)]$ holds if, and only if, $\mathbb{E}[g^*(X)] \leq \mathbb{E}[g^*(Y)]$, since X and Y both belong to $\mathcal{R}_n^+(F_1, F_2, \ldots, F_n)$. Now a supermodular function $g : (\mathbb{R}^+)^n \to \mathbb{R}$ that is zero on the axes is necessarily non-negative; this is easily seen from repeated use of the inequality in Definition 3.4.60, which gives

$$\begin{aligned} g(x_1, x_2, \ldots, x_n) &\geq g(x_1, x_2, \ldots, x_{n-1}, 0) \\ &\geq g(x_1, x_2, \ldots, x_{n-2}, 0, 0) \\ &\geq \cdots \\ &\geq g(0, 0, \ldots, 0) = 0, \end{aligned}$$

for all $x \in (\mathbb{R}^+)^n$. To conclude, it suffices to note that $\mathbb{E}[g(Y)] \geq 0$ for any $Y \in \mathcal{R}_n^+(F_1, F_2, \ldots, F_n)$, while $\mathbb{E}[g(X)] = 0$ since the df of X is concentrated on the axes. □

6.3.8 Supermodular, stop-loss and convex orders

Before stating the next result, it is worth mentioning that from Proposition 3.4.62 it follows that

$$X \preceq_{\text{SM}} Y \Longrightarrow X \preceq_{\text{DCX}} Y.$$

Hence, Proposition 3.4.67 holds a fortiori if $\boldsymbol{X} \preceq_{\text{SM}} \boldsymbol{Y}$. The following result should be compared to Proposition 3.4.67.

Proposition 6.3.9
Let $\boldsymbol{X}$ and $\boldsymbol{Y}$ be two random vectors. If $\boldsymbol{X} \preceq_{\text{SM}} \boldsymbol{Y}$ then $\Psi(\boldsymbol{X}) \preceq_{\text{SL}} \Psi(\boldsymbol{Y})$ for any non-decreasing supermodular function $\Psi: \mathbb{R}^n \to \mathbb{R}$.

Corollary 6.3.10
Let $\boldsymbol{X}$ and $\boldsymbol{Y}$ be n-dimensional random vectors with $\boldsymbol{X} \preceq_{\text{SM}} \boldsymbol{Y}$. Further, let $t_1, \ldots, t_n$ be non-decreasing non-negative functions. Then

$$t_1(X_1) + \ldots + t_n(X_n) \preceq_{\text{SL}} t_1(Y_1) + \ldots + t_n(Y_n).$$

Example 6.3.11. In the individual model of risk theory, the total claims amount in a policy period for a portfolio of n policies is given by

$$S_X = \sum_{i=1}^{n} X_i,$$

where X_i is the total claims amount generated by policy i, $i = 1, 2, \ldots, n$. Now, given two portfolios described by the individual total claims $\boldsymbol{X}$ and $\boldsymbol{Y}$, Proposition 6.3.9 indicates that

$$\boldsymbol{X} \preceq_{\text{SM}} \boldsymbol{Y} \Rightarrow S_X \preceq_{\text{SL},=} S_Y.$$

In general, the insurance company will not pay full compensation for the loss, but the compensation will be specified in the insurance contract as a function t_i which assigns to a loss x a compensation $t_i(x)$. A typical example is

$$t_i(x) = \min\{(x-d)_+, b\}$$

where b is the sum insured and d is the deductible. Now, if each policyholder has a compensation function t_i then the total claim to be paid by the insurance company for the portfolio $\boldsymbol{X}$ is $\sum_{i=1}^{n} t_i(X_i)$. Proposition 6.3.9 yields

$$\boldsymbol{X} \preceq_{\text{SM}} \boldsymbol{Y} \Rightarrow \sum_{i=1}^{n} t_i(X_i) \preceq_{\text{SL}} \sum_{i=1}^{n} t_i(Y_i)$$

for any non-decreasing $t_i : \mathbb{R}^+ \to \mathbb{R}$. ∇

6.3.9 Ordering compound sums

Let $\boldsymbol{M} = (M_1, \ldots, M_n)^t$, $\boldsymbol{M}' = (M_1', \ldots, M_n')^t$ be two vectors of integer-valued rvs, and let $\boldsymbol{S}_{\boldsymbol{M}} = (S_{M_1}, \ldots, S_{M_n})$ and $\boldsymbol{S}'_{\boldsymbol{M}'} = (S'_{M_1'}, \ldots, S'_{M_n'})$; their components are defined as in (6.5) in terms of identically distributed sequences $\{X_{i1}, X_{i2}, \ldots\}$ and $\{X_{i1}', X_{i2}', \ldots\}$ of positive rvs. Sequences $\{X_{i1}, X_{i2}, \ldots\}$ and $\{X_{i'1}, X_{i'2}, \ldots\}$ are also assumed to be independent for $i \neq i'$. The following result was obtained by Denuit, Genest and Marceau (2002).

Property 6.3.12
$M \preceq_{\text{SM}} M' \Rightarrow S_M \preceq_{\text{SM}} S'_{M'}$.

Proof. The argument hinges on the fact that the function

$$\Psi(m_1, \ldots, m_n) \equiv \mathbb{E}\left[g\left(S_{m_1}, \ldots, S_{m_n}\right)\right]$$

is supermodular whenever g is itself supermodular. To see this, consider $\Psi(m_1, \ldots, m_n)$ for fixed $m_1, \ldots, m_n$. Given $i < j$, $m_i < m'_i$ and $m_j < m'_j$, observe that

$$\Delta_{m_i, m'_i} \Delta_{m_j, m'_j} \Psi = \mathbb{E}\left[\Delta_{S_{m_i}, S_{m'_i}} \Delta_{S_{m_j}, S_{m'_j}} g\right],$$

and that the expression inside this expectation is positive for all possible values $S_{m_i} = s_{m_i}$ and $S_{m'_i} = s_{m'_i}$ because $S_{m_i} \leq S_{m'_i}$ with probability one and g is supermodular by hypothesis. Thus the argument is complete. □

6.3.10 Ordering random vectors with common values

Let $Z_1, Z_2, \ldots, Z_n$ be independent and identically distributed rvs. For any integer vector $\boldsymbol{k} = (k_1, k_2, \ldots, k_n) \in \mathbb{N}^n$ whose components sum to n (i.e., $k_1 + k_2 + \ldots + k_n = n$), define

$$X(\boldsymbol{k}) = (\underbrace{Z_1, Z_1, \ldots, Z_1}_{k_1 \text{times}}, \underbrace{Z_2, Z_2, \ldots, Z_2}_{k_2 \text{times}}, \ldots, \underbrace{Z_n, Z_n, \ldots, Z_n}_{k_n \text{times}}). \tag{6.10}$$

In this section, we study the amount of positive dependence (in the $\preceq_{\text{SM}}$ or $\preceq_{\text{SYM-SM}}$ sense) of the random vector $X(\boldsymbol{k})$ as a function of the level of multiplicity $\boldsymbol{k}$. The results of this section are taken from Shaked and Shanthikumar (1997).

Let $\Sigma(n, 2) \subset \mathbb{N}^2$ be the collection of all pairs (k_1, k_2) of non-negative integers that sum to n. First we study the random vectors

$$X(\boldsymbol{k}) = (\underbrace{Z_1, Z_1, \ldots, Z_1}_{k_1 \text{times}}, \underbrace{Z_2, Z_2, \ldots, Z_2}_{k_2 \text{times}})$$

as a function of $\boldsymbol{k} \in \Sigma(n, 2)$. We have the following result.

Proposition 6.3.13
For any $\boldsymbol{k}, \boldsymbol{k}' \in \Sigma(n, 2)$, we have that

$$\boldsymbol{k} \preceq_{\text{MAJ}} \boldsymbol{k}' \quad \Rightarrow \quad X(\boldsymbol{k}) \preceq_{\text{SYM-SM}} X(\boldsymbol{k}')$$

. That is, for all symmetric supermodular functions $g: \mathbb{R}^n \to \mathbb{R}$,

$$\boldsymbol{k} \preceq_{\text{MAJ}} \boldsymbol{k}' \quad \Rightarrow \quad \mathbb{E}[g(X(\boldsymbol{k}))] \leq \mathbb{E}[g(X(\boldsymbol{k}'))].$$

Proof. Without loss of generality, we may assume that $k_1 > k_2$. Then, for any symmetric supermodular function g, we have

$$
\begin{aligned}
&g(\underbrace{Z_1,\ldots,Z_1}_{k_1\text{times}},\underbrace{Z_2,\ldots,Z_2}_{k_2\text{times}})+g(\underbrace{Z_2,\ldots,Z_2}_{k_1\text{times}},\underbrace{Z_1,\ldots,Z_1}_{k_2\text{times}})\\
&=g(\underbrace{Z_1\vee Z_2,\ldots,Z_1\vee Z_2}_{k_1\text{times}},\underbrace{Z_1\wedge Z_2,\ldots,Z_1\wedge Z_2}_{k_2\text{times}})\\
&\quad+g(\underbrace{Z_1\wedge Z_2,\ldots,Z_1\wedge Z_2}_{k_1\text{times}},\underbrace{Z_1\vee Z_2,\ldots,Z_1\vee Z_2}_{k_2\text{times}})\\
&=g(\underbrace{Z_1\vee Z_2,\ldots,Z_1\vee Z_2}_{k_1-1\text{times}},\underbrace{Z_1\wedge Z_2,\ldots,Z_1\wedge Z_2}_{k_2\text{times}},Z_1\vee Z_2)\\
&\quad+g(\underbrace{Z_1\vee Z_2,\ldots,Z_1\vee Z_2}_{k_2\text{times}},\underbrace{Z_1\wedge Z_2,\ldots,Z_1\wedge Z_2}_{k_1-1\text{times}},Z_1\wedge Z_2)\\
&\geq g(\underbrace{Z_1\vee Z_2,\ldots,Z_1\vee Z_2}_{k_1-1\text{times}},\underbrace{Z_1\wedge Z_2,\ldots,Z_1\wedge Z_2}_{k_2\text{times}},Z_1\wedge Z_2)\\
&\quad+g(\underbrace{Z_1\vee Z_2,\ldots,Z_1\vee Z_2}_{k_2\text{times}},\underbrace{Z_1\wedge Z_2,\ldots,Z_1\wedge Z_2}_{k_1-1\text{times}},Z_1\vee Z_2)\\
&=g(\underbrace{Z_1\vee Z_2,\ldots,Z_1\vee Z_2}_{k_1-1\text{times}},\underbrace{Z_1\wedge Z_2,\ldots,Z_1\wedge Z_2}_{k_2+1\text{times}})\\
&\quad+g(\underbrace{Z_1\wedge Z_2,\ldots,Z_1\wedge Z_2}_{k_1-1\text{times}},\underbrace{Z_1\vee Z_2,\ldots,Z_1\vee Z_2}_{k_2+1\text{times}}),
\end{aligned}
$$

where the inequality follows from

$$
\begin{aligned}
&(\underbrace{Z_1\vee Z_2,\ldots,Z_1\vee Z_2}_{k_1-1\text{times}},\underbrace{Z_1\wedge Z_2,\ldots,Z_1\wedge Z_2}_{k_2\text{times}})\\
&\quad\geq(\underbrace{Z_1\vee Z_2,\ldots,Z_1\vee Z_2}_{k_2\text{times}},\underbrace{Z_1\wedge Z_2,\ldots,Z_1\wedge Z_2}_{k_1-1\text{times}})
\end{aligned}
$$

almost surely (since $k_1 - 1 \geq k_2$) and from the supermodularity of g. The in-between equalities follow from the symmetry of g. Since Z_1 and Z_2 are independent and identically distributed, we get that

$$
\mathbb{E}\big[g(\underbrace{Z_1,Z_1,\ldots,Z_1}_{k_1\text{times}},\underbrace{Z_2,Z_2,\ldots,Z_2}_{k_2\text{times}})\big]\geq\mathbb{E}\big[g(\underbrace{Z_1,Z_1,\ldots,Z_1}_{k_1-1\text{times}},\underbrace{Z_2,Z_2,\ldots,Z_2}_{k_2+1\text{times}})\big]
$$

whence the proposition follows. □

Let us now return to the general case. Denote by $\Sigma(n)$ the collection of all vectors $\boldsymbol{k} = (k_1, k_2, \ldots, k_n)$ of non-negative integers that sum to n. By using a conditioning argument and the property of majorization $\boldsymbol{k} \preceq_{\text{MAJ}} \boldsymbol{k}'$ with intermediate vectors that switch two components at a time, one can easily obtain from Proposition 6.3.13 the following result.

Proposition 6.3.14
Let $\boldsymbol{X}(\boldsymbol{k})$ be defined according to (6.10). For any $\boldsymbol{k}, \boldsymbol{k}' \in \Sigma(n)$, we have that

$$\boldsymbol{k} \preceq_{\text{MAJ}} \boldsymbol{k}' \quad \Rightarrow \quad \boldsymbol{X}(\boldsymbol{k}) \preceq_{\text{SYM-SM}} \boldsymbol{X}(\boldsymbol{k}').$$

That is, for all symmetric supermodular functions $g: \mathbb{R}^n \to \mathbb{R}$,

$$\boldsymbol{k} \preceq_{\text{MAJ}} \boldsymbol{k}' \quad \Rightarrow \quad \mathbb{E}[g(\boldsymbol{X}(\boldsymbol{k}))] \leq \mathbb{E}[g(\boldsymbol{X}(\boldsymbol{k}'))].$$

Let us now examine the properties of $\boldsymbol{X}(\boldsymbol{k})$ with respect to $\preceq_{\text{SM}}$. Counterexamples exist to show that, in general, the condition of symmetry is essential for the result in Proposition 6.3.14 to hold. However, we can establish the following bounds.

Proposition 6.3.15
Let $\boldsymbol{X}(\boldsymbol{k})$ be defined according to (6.10). Then

$$(Z_1, Z_2, \ldots, Z_n) \preceq_{\text{SM}} \boldsymbol{X}(\boldsymbol{k}) \preceq_{\text{SM}} (Z_1, Z_1, \ldots, Z_1)$$

for any $\boldsymbol{k} \in \Sigma(n)$.

6.3.11 Stochastic analysis of duplicates in life insurance portfolios

6.3.11.1 Context

Consider a portfolio of n life insurance policies, with each policy having a positive amount at risk during a certain reference period (one year, for example). In practice, it is common for individuals to hold more than one policy and hence to appear more than once in the count of people exposed to risk or death. In such a case, the portfolio is said to contain duplicates, that is, the portfolio contains several policies concerning the same life.

Our purpose here is to examine several possible consequences of the presence of duplicates in a portfolio. We utilize here the supermodular stochastic order to tackle the problems caused by the presence of duplicates. This section is based on Denuit (2000).

6.3.11.2 Life insurance portfolios with duplicates

Consider a portfolio with n policies. In the absence of duplicates, the portfolio consists of a vector $(T_1, T_2, \ldots, T_n)$ of insured lives, T_i representing the time-until-death rv for the ith policy. The T_i are assumed to be independent and identically distributed, that is, we focus on a (sub)portfolio with insured lives sharing some common risk characteristics (age, sex, smoking habits, and so on) and we neglect the effect of 'common shocks' such as epidemics or major natural disasters. Now, if there are duplicates, the portfolio depends in reality on $m < n$ insured lives, each one having k_i policies, $i = 1, 2, \ldots, m$. Mimicking (6.10), we represent such a portfolio as

$$\boldsymbol{T}(\boldsymbol{k}) = (\underbrace{T_1, T_1, \ldots, T_1}_{k_1 \text{times}}, \underbrace{T_2, T_2, \ldots, T_2}_{k_2 \text{times}}, \ldots, \underbrace{T_m, T_m, \ldots, T_m}_{k_m \text{times}}),$$

where the k_i are positive integers such that $k_1 + k_2 + \ldots + k_m = n$. A nice interpretation of the danger of duplicates in an insurance portfolio is provided by the notion of comonotonicity.

Mathematically speaking, introducing duplicates into an insurance portfolio comes down to replacing a block of independent components by its comonotonic version, and this leads thus to a more dangerous portfolio in the supermodular sense.

From Proposition 6.3.15, we know that

$$(T_1, T_2, \ldots, T_n) \preceq_{\mathrm{SM}} \boldsymbol{T}(\boldsymbol{k}) \preceq_{\mathrm{SM}} (T_1, T_1, \ldots, T_1). \tag{6.11}$$

This stochastic inequality gives the extremal portfolios. In view of (6.11), the most favourable situation for the insurer is thus to issue each policy on a different life, while the worst case is to sell all policies to the same individual.

Assume that the insurer faces two portolios with duplicates, each of them concerning m insured lives. Then, according to Proposition 6.3.14, it is possible to compare the structures of these portfolios as follows:

$$(k_1, k_2, \ldots, k_m) \preceq_{\mathrm{MAJ}} (k'_1, k'_2, \ldots, k'_m) \Rightarrow \boldsymbol{T}(\boldsymbol{k}) \preceq_{\mathrm{SYM\text{-}SM}} \boldsymbol{T}(\boldsymbol{k}'), \tag{6.12}$$

provided that the k_i (and thus also the k'_i) sum to n.

As a particular case of (6.12), we get (6.11) with $\preceq_{\mathrm{SYM\text{-}SM}}$ since for any positive integers $k_1, k_2, \ldots, k_m$ summing to n,

$$(1, 1, \ldots, 1) \preceq_{\mathrm{MAJ}} (k_1, k_2, \ldots, k_m, 0, 0, \ldots, 0) \preceq_{\mathrm{MAJ}} (n, 0, 0, \ldots, 0).$$

Therefore, the risk increases if the structure vector of the k_i is increased in the sense of majorization.

6.3.11.3 Aggregate claims in presence of duplicates

Now let $g_1, g_2, \ldots, g_n$ be measurable functions $\mathbb{R}^+ \to \mathbb{R}^+$, with $g_i(T_i)$ representing the discounted value of the insurer's payments for the ith policy, $i = 1, 2, \ldots, n$. It is natural to consider monotone g_i (decreasing g_i in the case of a whole life insurance portolio or increasing g_i in the case of an endowment or annuity portfolio, for instance). As a preliminary remark, note that policies with standardized conditions are more favourable for the insurance company; this comes from Proposition 3.4.23(ii) which ensures that there exists a standard policy represented by a measurable function g such that a homogeneous portfolio composed with this policy is better than the actual portfolio (in terms of the ordering of the aggregate losses in the $\preceq_{\mathrm{SL},=}$ sense):

$$\sum_{i=1}^{n} g(T_i) \preceq_{\mathrm{SL},=} \sum_{i=1}^{n} g_i(T_i).$$

Property 3.4.61(ii) combined with (6.11) gives

$$(g_1(T_1), g_2(T_2), \ldots, g_n(T_n)) \preceq_{\mathrm{SM}}$$

$$\begin{aligned}(g_1(T_1), g_2(T_1), \ldots, g_{k_1}(T_1), g_{k_1+1}(T_2), g_{k_1+2}(T_2), \ldots, g_{k_1+k_2}(T_2), \ldots,\\ g_{k_1+k_2+\ldots+k_{m-1}+1}(T_m), g_{k_1+k_2+\ldots+k_{m-1}+2}(T_m), \ldots, g_n(T_m)),\end{aligned} \tag{6.13}$$

As a consequence of this stochastic inequality, we get from Corollary 6.3.10 that the aggregate claims are ordered in the stop-loss sense, that is,

$$\sum_{i=1}^{n} g_i(T_i) \preceq_{\rm SL} \sum_{i=1}^{k_1} g_i(T_1) + \sum_{i=k_1+1}^{k_2} g_i(T_2) + \ldots + \sum_{i=k_1+k_2+\ldots+k_{m-1}+1}^{n} g_i(T_m).$$

6.4 POSITIVE ORTHANT DEPENDENCE ORDER

6.4.1 Definition

The following dependence orders (fulfilling all the requirements of Definition 6.1.2) can be seen as the restriction of the concordance order to the elements of some fixed Fréchet space.

Definition 6.4.1. Let $\boldsymbol{X} = (X_1, X_2, \ldots, X_n)$ and $\boldsymbol{Y} = (Y_1, Y_2, \ldots, Y_n)$ be random vectors. If

$$F_{\boldsymbol{X}}(\boldsymbol{x}) \leq F_{\boldsymbol{Y}}(\boldsymbol{x}) \qquad \text{for all } \boldsymbol{x}, \tag{6.14}$$

and

$$\overline{F}_{\boldsymbol{X}}(\boldsymbol{x}) \leq \overline{F}_{\boldsymbol{Y}}(\boldsymbol{x}) \qquad \text{for all } \boldsymbol{x}, \tag{6.15}$$

then $\boldsymbol{X}$ is said to be smaller than $\boldsymbol{Y}$ in the positive orthant dependence (POD) order, denoted by $\boldsymbol{X} \preceq_{\rm POD} \boldsymbol{Y}$). ∇

From (6.14) and (6.15) it follows that only random vectors with the same univariate marginals can be compared in the POD order. From (6.14) and (6.15) it follows that

$$\boldsymbol{X} \preceq_{\rm POD} \boldsymbol{Y} \Leftrightarrow \boldsymbol{X} \preceq_{\rm UO} \boldsymbol{Y} \text{ and } \boldsymbol{Y} \preceq_{\rm LO} \boldsymbol{X}. \tag{6.16}$$

6.4.2 Positive orthant dependence order and correlation coefficients

If $\boldsymbol{X} \preceq_{\rm POD} \boldsymbol{Y}$ then, for all $i_1 \neq i_2$, we have that

$$\mathbb{C}[X_{i_1}, X_{i_2}] \leq \mathbb{C}[Y_{i_1}, Y_{i_2}].$$

Since the univariate marginals of $\boldsymbol{X}$ and $\boldsymbol{Y}$ are equal, it also follows that

$$r_{\rm P}(X_{i_1}, X_{i_2}) \leq r_{\rm P}(Y_{i_1}, Y_{i_2}).$$

Similarly, under the same conditions,

$$r_{\rm K}(X_{i_1}, X_{i_2}) \leq r_{\rm K}(Y_{i_1}, Y_{i_2}) \text{ and } r_{\rm S}(X_{i_1}, X_{i_2}) \leq r_{\rm S}(Y_{i_1}, Y_{i_2})$$

also hold.

6.5 EXERCISES

Exercise 6.5.1. If $\boldsymbol{X} \preceq_{\text{CORR}} \boldsymbol{Y}$, show that

$$\Pr[X_2 > x_2 | X_1 > x_1] \leq \Pr[Y_2 > x_2 | Y_1 > x_1] \quad \text{for all } x_1 \text{ and } x_2,$$

and

$$\Pr[X_2 \leq x_2 | X_1 > x_1] \geq \Pr[Y_2 \leq x_2 | Y_1 > x_1] \quad \text{for all } x_1 \text{ and } x_2.$$

Exercise 6.5.2. If $\boldsymbol{X} \preceq_{\text{CORR}} \boldsymbol{Y}$, show that for all x_1 we have

$$\mathbb{E}[X_2 | X_1 > x_1] = \mathbb{E}[Y_2 | Y_1 > x_1].$$

Exercise 6.5.3. Given random pairs $\boldsymbol{X} = (X_1, X_2)$ and $\boldsymbol{Y} = (Y_1, Y_2)$ with distribution functions $F_{\boldsymbol{X}}$ and $F_{\boldsymbol{Y}}$ and bivariate probability integral tranform $Z_1 = F_{\boldsymbol{X}}(\boldsymbol{X})$ and $Z_2 = F_{\boldsymbol{Y}}(\boldsymbol{Y})$ distributed as K_1 and K_2 respectively, $\boldsymbol{X}$ is considered more positively dependent than $\boldsymbol{Y}$, written as $\boldsymbol{X} \preceq_{\text{PD}} \boldsymbol{Y}$, whenever

$$Z_2 \preceq_{\text{ST}} Z_1 \Leftrightarrow K_1(v) \leq K_2(v) \text{ for all } 0 \leq v \leq 1.$$

(i) Show that given two random couples (X_1, X_2) and (Y_1, Y_2), with respective Archimedean copulas C_{ϕ_1} and C_{ϕ_2}, $\boldsymbol{X} \preceq_{\text{PD}} \boldsymbol{Y} \Leftrightarrow \phi_1/\phi_2$ is non-decreasing.

(ii) Deduce from Property 6.2.16(ii) that for Archimedean copulas

$$\boldsymbol{X} \preceq_{\text{PD}} \boldsymbol{Y} \Rightarrow \boldsymbol{X} \preceq_{\text{CORR}} \boldsymbol{Y}.$$

Exercise 6.5.4. Prove the following closure properties of the supermodular order:

(i) Let $\boldsymbol{X}$ and $\boldsymbol{Y}$ be two n-dimensional random vectors. If $\boldsymbol{X} \preceq_{\text{SM}} \boldsymbol{Y}$, then

$$(g_1(X_1), g_2(X_2), \ldots, g_n(X_n)) \preceq_{\text{SM}} (g_1(Y_1), g_2(Y_2), \ldots, g_n(Y_n))$$

whenever $g_i : \mathbb{R} \to \mathbb{R}$, $i = 1, 2, \ldots, n$, are all increasing or are all decreasing.

(ii) Let $\boldsymbol{X}_1, \boldsymbol{X}_2, \ldots, \boldsymbol{X}_m$ be a set of independent random vectors where the dimension of $\boldsymbol{X}_i$ is k_i, $i = 1, 2, \ldots, m$. Let $\boldsymbol{Y}_1, \boldsymbol{Y}_2, \ldots, \boldsymbol{Y}_m$ be another set of independent random vectors where the dimension of $\boldsymbol{Y}_i$ is k_i, $i = 1, 2, \ldots, m$. If $\boldsymbol{X}_i \preceq_{\text{SM}} \boldsymbol{Y}_i$ for $i = 1, 2, \ldots, m$, then

$$(\boldsymbol{X}_1, \boldsymbol{X}_2, \ldots, \boldsymbol{X}_m) \preceq_{\text{SM}} (\boldsymbol{Y}_1, \boldsymbol{Y}_2, \ldots, \boldsymbol{Y}_m).$$

That is, the supermodular order is closed under conjunctions.

(iii) Let $\boldsymbol{X} = (X_1, X_2, \ldots, X_n)$ and $\boldsymbol{Y} = (Y_1, Y_2, \ldots, Y_n)$ be two n-dimensional random vectors. If $\boldsymbol{X} \preceq_{\text{SM}} \boldsymbol{Y}$ then $\boldsymbol{X}_I \preceq_{\text{SM}} \boldsymbol{Y}_I$ for each $I \subseteq \{1, 2, \ldots, n\}$. That is, the supermodular order is closed under marginalization.

Exercise 6.5.5. (i) Given two risks X and Y with arbitrary marginals, finite expected values μ_X and μ_Y and standard deviations σ_X and σ_Y, show that

$$\mathbb{E}[(X+Y-t)_+]\leq \tfrac{1}{2}\left(\sqrt{\sigma^2+(t-\mu)^2}-(t-\mu)\right),$$

with $\mu=\mu_X+\mu_Y$ and $\sigma=\sigma_X+\sigma_Y$.
(ii) Show that the upper bound is attained for the bivariate distribution with support $\{(x_1,y_1),(x_1,y_2),(x_2,y_1),(x_2,y_2)\}$, with

$$x_1=\mu_X-\sigma_X z_0,$$
$$x_2=\mu_X+\frac{\sigma_X}{z_0},$$
$$y_1=\mu_Y-\sigma_Y z_0,$$
$$y_2=\mu_Y+\frac{\sigma_Y}{z_0},$$
$$z_0=\frac{1}{\sigma}\left(\sqrt{\sigma^2+(t-\mu)^2}-(t-\mu)\right),$$

and joint probabilities

$$p_{ij}=\Pr[X=x_i, Y=y_j],\quad i,j=1,2,$$

given by

$$p_{11}=\frac{1}{1+z_0^2},\quad p_{22}=\frac{z_0^2}{1+z_0^2},\quad p_{12}=p_{21}=0.$$

See Hürlimann (1998) for related results.

Exercise 6.5.6. Colangelo, Scarsini and Shaked (2004) introduced the following dependence order. Given random vectors $\boldsymbol{X}$ and $\boldsymbol{Y}$ in $\mathcal{F}_n(F_1,\ldots,F_n)$, $\boldsymbol{X}$ is smaller than $\boldsymbol{Y}$ in the lower orthant decreasing ratio order, written as $\boldsymbol{X}\preceq_{\text{LODR}}\boldsymbol{Y}$, if $F_{\boldsymbol{Y}}(\boldsymbol{x})/F_{\boldsymbol{X}}(\boldsymbol{x})$ is non-increasing in $\boldsymbol{x}$ on $\{\boldsymbol{x}\in\mathbb{R}^n|F_{\boldsymbol{Y}}(\boldsymbol{x})>0\}$, with the convention that $a/0=+\infty$ whenever $a>0$. Similarly, $\boldsymbol{X}$ is smaller than $\boldsymbol{Y}$ in the upper orthant increasing ratio order, written as $\boldsymbol{X}\preceq_{\text{UOIR}}\boldsymbol{Y}$, if $\overline{F}_{\boldsymbol{Y}}(\boldsymbol{x})/\overline{F}_{\boldsymbol{X}}(\boldsymbol{x})$ is non-decreasing in $\boldsymbol{x}$ on $\{\boldsymbol{x}\in\mathbb{R}^n|\overline{F}_{\boldsymbol{Y}}(\boldsymbol{x})>0\}$, with the same convention as above.

(i) Show that $\preceq_{\text{LODR}}$ and $\preceq_{\text{UOIR}}$ satisfy all the conditions listed in Definition 6.1.2 except A5 (it is not true that any Fréchet upper bound is maximal for these orders).

(ii) Show that if $\boldsymbol{X}\preceq_{\text{LODR}}\boldsymbol{Y}$ then $(t_1(X_1),\ldots,t_n(X_n))\preceq_{\text{UOIR}}(t_1(Y_1),\ldots,t_n(Y_n))$ for all decreasing functions $t_1,\ldots,t_n$.

(iii) Show that if $\boldsymbol{X}\preceq_{\text{UOIR}}\boldsymbol{Y}$ then $(t_1(X_1),\ldots,t_n(X_n))\preceq_{\text{LODR}}(t_1(Y_1),\ldots,t_n(Y_n))$ for all decreasing functions $t_1,\ldots,t_n$.

(iv) Recall that $F^{\perp}$ and W_n are the independence df and the Fréchet upper bound in $\mathcal{R}_n(F_1,\ldots,F_n)$. Show that $F^{\perp}\preceq_{\text{LODR}}W_n$ and $F^{\perp}\preceq_{\text{UOIR}}W_n$ both hold.

Exercise 6.5.7. Colangelo, Scarsini and Shaked (2004) defined $\boldsymbol{X}$ to be positively lower orthant decreasing ratio dependent (PLODRD) if $\boldsymbol{X}^{\perp} \preceq_{\text{LODR}} \boldsymbol{X}$ holds, and to be positively upper orthant increasing ratio dependent (PUOIRD) if $\boldsymbol{X}^{\perp} \preceq_{\text{UOIR}} \boldsymbol{X}$ holds. Show that:

(i) if $\boldsymbol{X}$ is PLODRD then (X_i, X_j) is PQD for any $i < j \in \{1, \dots, n\}$;

(ii) if $\boldsymbol{X}$ is PUOIRD then (X_i, X_j) is PQD for any $i < j \in \{1, \dots, n\}$;

(iii) the Fréchet upper bound W_n is both PLODRD and PUOIRD;

(iv) the independence df $F^{\perp}$ is both PLODRD and PUOIRD;

(v) if $\boldsymbol{X}$ is PLODRD then so is $(t_1(X_1), \dots, t_n(X_n))$ for all increasing functions $t_1, \dots, t_n$;

(vi) if $\boldsymbol{X}$ is PUOIRD then so is $(t_1(X_1), \dots, t_n(X_n))$ for all increasing functions $t_1, \dots, t_n$.

PART III
Applications to Insurance Mathematics

7

Dependence in Credibility Models Based on Generalized Linear Models

In credibility theory, the serial dependence existing among annual claim characteristics (number of accidents, associated costs, etc.) is used to re-evaluate the amount of premium paid by policyholders according to their past claims history. To this end, credibility models induce time dependence via the sharing of common random effects. This chapter is devoted to an in-depth study of the kind of dependence arising from credibility models based on generalized linear models (GLMs).

7.1 INTRODUCTION

Credibility theory can be seen as the science that learns how to combine different collections of data to obtain an accurate overall estimate. In elementary cases, a compromise estimator is derived from a convex combination of a prior mean and the mean of the current observations. The weight given to the observed mean is called the credibility factor (since it fixes the extent to which the actuary may have confidence in the data). Credibility theory is presented in Kaas *et al.* (2001, Chapter 7), where appropriate references to the literature can be found.

In this chapter, we will consider credibility models superimposed on an a priori risk classification. One of the main tasks of the actuary is to design a tariff structure that will fairly distribute the burden of claims among policyholders. To this end, the portfolio is partitioned into homogeneous classes with all policyholders belonging to the same class paying the same premium. In motor third party liability insurance, the classification variables introduced to partition risks commonly include the age, gender and occupation of the policyholders, the type and use of their car, the place where they reside and sometimes even the number of cars in the household, marital status, smoking behaviour or the colour of the vehicle. Risk classification and a priori rate-making can be efficiently carried out using GLMs, as presented in Kaas *et al.* (2001, Chapter 8).

However, many important factors cannot be taken into account at this stage; think, for instance, of swiftness of reflexes or aggressiveness behind the wheel. Consequently, tariff cells are still quite heterogeneous despite of the use of many a priori variables. These

Actuarial Theory for Dependent Risks M. Denuit, J. Dhaene, M. Goovaerts and R. Kaas

hidden features are usually impossible to measure and to incorporate in a price list. But it is reasonable to believe that these characteristics are revealed by the number and/or the costs of the claims reported by policyholders over the successive insurance periods. Hence the adjustment of the premium based on the individual claims experience in order to restore fairness among policyholders.

The aim of this chapter is to study the kind of dependence arising from credibility models based on GLMs for the loss variable (frequency or severity). Before treating the problem in the general GLM framework, we present a detailed study of the Poisson credibility models for claim frequencies. Several results presented in this chapter are taken from Purcaru and Denuit (2002a,b, 2003) and Brouhns and Denuit (2003). They are closely related to fundamental results by Whitt (1979), Fahmy *et al.* (1982) and Shaked and Spizzichino (1998). For alternative treatments of credibility theory with dependent claims, see Frees (2003) and Pinquet (1997).

7.2 POISSON CREDIBILITY MODELS FOR CLAIM FREQUENCIES

7.2.1 Poisson static credibility model

7.2.1.1 Description of the model

In two seminal papers, Dionne and Vanasse (1989, 1992) proposed a credibility model which integrates a priori and a posteriori information on an individual basis. These authors introduced a regression component into the Poisson counting model in order to use all available information in the estimation of accident frequency. The unexplained heterogeneity was then modelled by the introduction of a latent variable representing the influence of hidden policy characteristics (the Θ_i in Definition 7.2.1 below). Assuming this random effect to be gamma-distributed yields the negative binomial model for the number of claims. Of course, there is no particular reason to restrict ourselves to gamma-distributed random effects (except perhaps mathematical convenience). In biostatistical circles, lognormally distributed random effects are widely used; see also Pinquet (1997) for an application in actuarial science. The use of the inverse Gaussian distribution was advocated by Willmot (1987) in conjunction with Poisson mixtures; see also Tremblay (1992). Another possible choice is Hoffman's distribution; see Kestemont and Paris (1985). Moreover, semiparametric approaches (retaining the Poisson assumption for the numbers of claims without specifying any distribution for the random effects) are conceivable in the spirit of the Bühlmann–Straub model. See Walhin and Paris (1999) as well as Denuit and Lambert (2001) for nonparametric maximum likelihood methods. Let us also mention other approaches with generalized Poisson distributions; see Denuit (1997).

Let us consider a portfolio with n policies, each one observed for T_i periods. Let N_{it} (with mean $\mathbb{E}[N_{it}] = \lambda_{it}$) be the number of claims reported by policyholder i in period t, $i = 1, 2, \ldots, n$, $t = 1, 2, \ldots, T_i$. We thus have a nested structure: each policyholder generates a sequence $\boldsymbol{N}_i = (N_{i1}, N_{i2}, \ldots, N_{iT_i})^t$ of claim numbers. It is reasonable to assume independence between the series $\boldsymbol{N}_1, \boldsymbol{N}_2, \ldots, \boldsymbol{N}_n$ (at least in motor third party liability insurance, for instance), but this assumption is highly questionable within each $\boldsymbol{N}_i$ (in fact, if the components of the $\boldsymbol{N}_i$ were independent, a posteriori rate-making would be senseless from the purely actuarial point of view, even if these systems remain commercially important because they counteract moral hazard).

Let

$$N_{i\bullet}=\sum_{t=1}^{T_i} N_{it} \text{ and } \lambda_{i\bullet}=\sum_{t=1}^{T_i}\lambda_{it}$$

be the total observed and expected numbers of claims for policyholder i during the T_i observation periods; the statistic $N_{i\bullet}$ is a convenient summary of past claims history. It is customary to assume that N_{it} is Poisson-distributed. Indeed, the Poisson distribution is the 'law of small numbers' and is well suited to rare events such as automobile accidents. This leads to the following model.

Definition 7.2.1. In the Poisson static credibility model, the ith policy of the portfolio, $i=1,2,\ldots,n$, is represented by a sequence $(\Theta_i, \boldsymbol{N}_i)$ where Θ_i is a positive rv with unit mean representing the unexplained heterogeneity. Moreover,

A1 given $\Theta_i=\theta$, the rvs N_{it}, $t=1,2,\ldots,$ are independent and have the $\mathcal{P}oi(\lambda_{it}\theta)$ distribution;

A2 at the portfolio level, the sequences $(\Theta_i, \boldsymbol{N}_i)$, $i=1,2,\ldots,n$, are assumed to be independent.

∇

Remark 7.2.2. To ensure the identifiability of the model, we have assumed that $\mathbb{E}[\Theta_i]=1$. This also guarantees that $\mathbb{E}[N_{it}]=\lambda_{it}\mathbb{E}[\Theta_i]=\lambda_{it}$. The a priori risk evaluation is thus correct on average. ∇

Remark 7.2.3. It is essential to understand the philosophy of this classical actuarial construction. In Definition 7.2.1, dependence between annual numbers of claims is a consequence of the heterogeneity of the portfolio (i.e., of Θ_i); the dependence is only apparent. If we had complete knowledge of policy characteristics then Θ_i would become deterministic and there would no longer be dependence between the N_{it} for fixed i. The unexplained heterogeneity (which has been modelled through the introduction of the risk parameter Θ_i for policyholder i) is then revealed by the claims and premiums histories in a Bayesian way. These histories modify the distribution of Θ_i and hence modify the premium. ∇

7.2.1.2 Exhaustive summary of past claims

Let us prove that in the credibility model of Definition 7.2.1, $N_{i\bullet}$ is an exhaustive summary of the past claims history.

Property 7.2.4
In the Poisson static credibility model of Definition 7.2.1, the predictive distribution of Θ_i only depends on $N_{i\bullet}$, that is to say, the distributional equality

$$[\Theta_i|N_{i1}, N_{i2}, \ldots, N_{iT_i}] =_d [\Theta_i|N_{i\bullet}]$$

holds.

Proof. Let $f_\Theta(\cdot|n_{i1}, n_{i2}, \ldots, n_{iT_i})$ be the conditional pdf of Θ_i given that $N_{i1} = n_{i1}, \ldots, N_{iT_i} = n_{iT_i}$. Using Proposition 1.8.1, we get

$$\begin{aligned} f_\Theta(\theta|n_{i1}, n_{i2}, \ldots, n_{iT_i}) &= \frac{\Pr[N_{i1} = n_{i1}, \ldots, N_{iT_i} = n_{iT_i}|\Theta_i = \theta] f_\Theta(\theta)}{\Pr[N_{i1} = n_{i1}, \ldots, N_{iT_i} = n_{iT_i}]} \\ &= \frac{\exp(-\theta\lambda_{i\bullet})\theta^{n_{i\bullet}} f_\Theta(\theta)}{\int_0^{+\infty} \exp(-\xi\lambda_{i\bullet})\xi^{n_{i\bullet}} f_\Theta(\xi) d\xi} \end{aligned}$$

which depends only on $n_{i\bullet}$. □

This result has an important practical consequence: the Poisson static credibility model disregards the age of the claims. The penalty induced by an old claim is strictly identical to that induced by a recent claim. This may of course sometimes be undesirable for commercial purposes or may not be in line with reality.

7.2.1.3 Expected results

When $\Theta_i \sim \mathcal{G}am(a, a)$ so that $\mathbb{E}[\Theta_i] = 1$, it is well known that the a posteriori distribution of Θ_i (i.e., the distribution of Θ_i given past claims history) remains gamma. More specifically, we have in this case that

$$[\Theta_i|N_{i\bullet}] =_d \mathcal{G}am\big(a + N_{i\bullet}, a + \lambda_{i\bullet}\big).$$

We refer the reader to Kaas *et al.* (2001, Section 7.5) for a detailed account of this model. Given the past expected claim frequencies $\lambda_{i1}, \lambda_{i2}, \ldots, \lambda_{iT_i}$, we know from Exercise 3.5.35 that the a posteriori distribution of Θ_i increases in the past claims in the $\preceq_{\mathrm{LR}}$ sense, that is, $[\Theta_i|N_{i\bullet} = n] \preceq_{\mathrm{LR}} [\Theta_i|N_{i\bullet} = n']$ whenever $n \leq n'$. This is clearly a very nice property since it expresses the increasing dangerousness inherent in policyholders making claims. We would like to investigate whether this important property still holds when other distributions are taken for Θ_i. Our main finding in that direction is that it remains valid in any Poisson mixture model.

Another nice feature of the Poisson-gamma model is that the theoretical bonus–malus coefficient is given by

$$\mathbb{E}[\Theta_i|N_{i1}, N_{i2}, \ldots, N_{iT_i}] = \frac{a + N_{i\bullet}}{a + \lambda_{i\bullet}}.$$

This exceeds unity if $N_{i\bullet} > \lambda_{i\bullet}$, that is, if policyholder i makes more claims than expected. On the other hand, it is less than unity if $N_{i\bullet} < \lambda_{i\bullet}$, that is, if fewer claims than expected have been filed. Note that the theoretical bonus–malus coefficient clearly increases in the past claims $N_{i\bullet}$. Again, we show that this holds whatever the mixture distribution selected by the actuary.

To sum up, in model A1–A2 of Definition 7.2.1, we intuitively feel that the following statements are true:

S1 Θ_i 'increases' in the past claims $N_{i\bullet}$.

S2 N_{i,T_i+1} 'increases' in the past claims $N_{i\bullet}$.

S3 N_{i,T_i+1} and $N_{i\bullet}$ are 'positively dependent'.

These statements will be made precise in Section 7.2.5.

7.2.2 Poisson dynamic credibility models

7.2.2.1 Description of the model

The vast majority of papers in the actuarial literature have considered time-independent (or static) heterogeneous models as introduced in Definition 7.2.1. Noticeable exceptions include the pioneering papers by Gerber and Jones (1975) and Sundt (1988), as well as Pinquet, Guillén and Bolancé (2001). The allowance for an unknown underlying random parameter that develops over time is justified since unobservable factors influencing the driving abilities are not constant. One might consider either shocks (induced by events such as divorce or nervous breakdown, for instance) or continuous modifications (e.g., due to learning effect).

Another reason to allow for time-varying random effects relates to moral hazard. Indeed, individual efforts to prevent accidents are unobserved and feature temporal dependence. Policyholders may adjust their efforts to prevent losses according to their experience with past claims, the amount of premium and awareness of future consequences of an accident (due to experience rating schemes).

The main technical reason for letting the random effects evolve over time is to take into account the date of claims. This reflects the fact that the predictive ability of a claim depends on its age: a recent claim is a worse sign to the insurer than a very old one. In contrast to the static case (see Property 7.2.4), the total number of claims $N_{i\bullet}$ reported in the past is no longer an exhaustive summary of policyholders' history. Rather, the sequence $\boldsymbol{N}_i$ of annual numbers of claims now has to be remembered to determine future premiums.

In this section, we will assume that the unknown characteristics relating to policyholder i in year t are represented by an rv Θ_{it}. The annual numbers of claims $N_{i1}, N_{i2}, N_{i3}, \ldots$ are assumed to be independent given the sequence $\boldsymbol{\Theta}_i = (\Theta_{i1}, \Theta_{i2}, \Theta_{i3}, \ldots)$ of random effects. The latent unobservable process $\boldsymbol{\Theta}_i$ characterizes the correlation structure of the N_{it}. Specifically, the dynamic credibility model is defined as follows.

Definition 7.2.5. In the Poisson dynamic frequency credibility model, the ith policy of the portfolio, $i = 1, 2, \ldots, n$, is represented by a sequence $(\boldsymbol{\Theta}_i, \boldsymbol{N}_i)$ where $\boldsymbol{\Theta}_i$ is a positive random vector representing unexplained heterogeneity. Moreover,

A1 given $\boldsymbol{\Theta}_i = \boldsymbol{\theta}_i$, the rvs N_{it}, $t = 1, 2, \ldots, T_i$, are independent and have the $\mathcal{P}oi(\lambda_{it}\theta_{it})$ distribution, that is,

$$\Pr[\boldsymbol{N}_i = \boldsymbol{k}_i | \boldsymbol{\Theta}_i = \boldsymbol{\theta}_i] = \prod_{t=1}^{T_i} \exp(-\lambda_{it}\theta_{it}) \frac{(\lambda_{it}\theta_{it})^{k_{it}}}{k_{it}!}, \quad \boldsymbol{k}_i \in \mathbb{N}^{T_i};$$

A2 at the portfolio level, the sequences $(\boldsymbol{\Theta}_i, \boldsymbol{N}_i)$, $i = 1, 2, \ldots, n$, are assumed to be independent. Moreover, the Θ_{it} are non-negative rvs with unit mean ($\mathbb{E}[\Theta_{it}] = 1$ for all i, t). Defining $T_{\max} = \max\{T_1, T_2, \ldots, T_n\}$, $\boldsymbol{\Theta}_i$ has the same distribution as the first T_i components of some stationary random vector, $(\Theta_1, \ldots, \Theta_{T_{\max}})$ say.

∇

Assuming that $\lambda_{it} = \lambda_{it+h}$, for some integer h, the stationarity of the random effects specified in condition A2 of Definition 7.2.5 implies that

$$\begin{aligned}\Pr[N_{i,t+h+1} = k_{t+1} | N_{i,h+1} = k_1, \ldots, N_{i,t+h} = k_t] \\ = \Pr[N_{i,t+1} = k_{t+1} | N_{i,1} = k_1, \ldots, N_{i,t} = k_t],\end{aligned}$$

whatever the integers $k_1, \ldots, k_{t+1}$. Therefore the predictive ability of claims will depend solely on the lag between the date of prediction and the date of occurrence, that is, the age of the claim.

7.2.2.2 Expected results

In model A1–A2 of Definition 7.2.5, we intuitively feel that the following statements should be valid: provided that the Θ_{it} are 'positively dependent',

S1 the N_{it} are 'positively dependent';

S2 $\boldsymbol{\Theta}_i$ 'increases' in the claims $\boldsymbol{N}_i$;

S3 Θ_{i,T_i+1} 'increases' in the past claims $\boldsymbol{N}_i$;

S4 N_{i,T_i+1} 'increases' in the past claims $\boldsymbol{N}_i$.

The purpose of the next sections will be to formalize these ideas and to make precise the concepts of positive dependence and increasingness involved in statements S1–S4. We will first study two dependence structures that play an important role in credibility theory, namely association and dependence by mixture.

7.2.3 Association

7.2.3.1 Definition

The concept of dependence called association was introduced by Esary, Proschan and Walkup (1967). It is defined as follows.

Definition 7.2.6. The rvs $X_1, X_2, \ldots, X_n$ are said to be associated, or equivalently the random vector $\boldsymbol{X}$ is said to possess this property, when the inequality

$$\mathbb{C}[\Psi_1(X_1, X_2, \ldots, X_n), \Psi_2(X_1, X_2, \ldots, X_n)] \geq 0 \tag{7.1}$$

is valid for all non-decreasing functions Ψ_1 and Ψ_2 for which the covariances exist. ∇

Association was first considered in actuarial science by Norberg (1989) who used it in order to investigate some alternatives to the independence assumption for multilife statuses in life insurance, as well as to quantify the consequences of a possible dependence on the amounts of premium relating to multilife insurance contracts. The intuitive meaning of association seems rather unclear. However, implicit in a conclusion that a set of rvs is associated is a wealth of inequalities, often of direct use in various problems.

7.2.3.2 Properties

It may appear impossible to check the condition (7.1) of association directly given a df $F_{\boldsymbol{X}}$ for $\boldsymbol{X}$. Where association of a random vector can be established, it is usually done by making use of a stochastic representation of $\boldsymbol{X}$ or of the following property that can be found in Esary, Proschan and Walkup (1967). It essentially states that association of rvs is preserved under (i) taking subsets, (ii) forming unions of independent sets and (iii) forming sets of non-decreasing functions.

Property 7.2.7

(i) If $\boldsymbol{X}$ is associated then any subset $(X_{i_1}, X_{i_2}, \ldots, X_{i_k})$ of $\boldsymbol{X}$ is associated.

(ii) If $\boldsymbol{X}$ and $\boldsymbol{Y}$ are associated and mutually independent then $(\boldsymbol{X}, \boldsymbol{Y})$ is associated.

(iii) If $\boldsymbol{X}$ is associated and $\psi_1, \psi_2, \ldots, \psi_k : \mathbb{R}^n \to \mathbb{R}$ are non-decreasing functions, then $\psi_1(\boldsymbol{X}), \psi_2(\boldsymbol{X}), \ldots, \psi_k(\boldsymbol{X})$ are associated.

(iv) Independent rvs $X_1, \ldots, X_n$ are associated.

Proof. (i) follows from Definition 7.2.6 by choosing non-decreasing functions Ψ_1 and Ψ_2 that depend only on the variables $x_{i_1}, x_{i_2}, \ldots, x_{i_k}$.

To prove (ii) we use Property 1.8.2 (i) to write

$$\begin{aligned}\mathbb{C}[\Psi_1(\boldsymbol{X}, \boldsymbol{Y}), \Psi_2(\boldsymbol{X}, \boldsymbol{Y})] = {} & \mathbb{E}\Big[\mathbb{C}[\Psi_1(\boldsymbol{X}, \boldsymbol{Y}), \Psi_2(\boldsymbol{X}, \boldsymbol{Y})|\boldsymbol{X}]\Big] \\ & + \mathbb{C}\Big[\mathbb{E}[\Psi_1(\boldsymbol{X}, \boldsymbol{Y})|\boldsymbol{X}], \mathbb{E}[\Psi_2(\boldsymbol{X}, \boldsymbol{Y})|\boldsymbol{X}]\Big].\end{aligned}$$

Since the association of $\boldsymbol{Y}$ ensures that $\mathbb{C}[\Psi_1(\boldsymbol{x}, \boldsymbol{Y}), \Psi_2(\boldsymbol{x}, \boldsymbol{Y})] \geq 0$ for each fixed $\boldsymbol{x}$, the first term is obviously non-negative. Moreover, since $\mathbb{E}[\Psi_1(\boldsymbol{x}, \boldsymbol{Y})]$ and $\mathbb{E}[\Psi_2(\boldsymbol{x}, \boldsymbol{Y})]$ are non-decreasing functions of $\boldsymbol{x}$, the second term is also non-negative, hence the result.

Next, (iii) is obvious since the function

$$\boldsymbol{x} \mapsto \Psi\big(\psi_1(\boldsymbol{x}), \psi_2(\boldsymbol{x}), \ldots, \psi_k(\boldsymbol{x})\big)$$

is non-decreasing whenever Ψ is non-decreasing.
Finally, (iv) follows from repeated use of (ii). □

Let us now examine a couple of examples where association naturally appears.

Example 7.2.8. (Marceau's risk model). Consider a portfolio consisting of n policies with individual risks $X_1, X_2, \ldots, X_n$ over a fixed time period. Let $S = \sum_{i=1}^n X_i$ be the aggregate claim amount for the insurance portfolio. Assume that the X_i are of the form

$$X_i = I_i V_i = \begin{cases} V_i, & \text{if } I_i = 1, \\ 0, & \text{if } I_i = 0, \end{cases}$$

where $I_i \sim \mathcal{B}er(q_i)$ and V_i is a positive rv modelling the claim amount provided at least one claim occurred. The random vectors $\boldsymbol{I} = (I_1, I_2, \ldots, I_n)$ and $\boldsymbol{V} = (V_1, V_2, \ldots, V_n)$ are assumed to be independent. Further, the V_i are assumed to be mutually independent.

Let us assume that the occurrence of a claim on policy i is a function of two independent rvs J_i and J_0 representing the possibility of a claim on policy i due respectively to an individual factor for the ith risk and a common risk factor for the entire portfolio. Specifically, we consider that

$$I_i = \min\{J_i + J_0, 1\}, \quad i = 1, \ldots, n,$$

where $J_i \sim \mathcal{B}er(q_i)$, $i = 1, 2, \ldots, n$, and $J_0 \sim \mathcal{B}er(q_0)$ are independent rvs. The random vector $\boldsymbol{I}$ has clearly dependent components. This construction was worked out in Cossette, Gaillardetz, Marceau and Rioux (2002).

The I_i are associated since, given any non-decreasing functions Ψ_1 and $\Psi_2 : \mathbb{R}^n \to \mathbb{R}$, there exist two non-decreasing functions $\widetilde{\Psi}_1$ and $\widetilde{\Psi}_2 : \mathbb{R}^{n+1} \to \mathbb{R}$ such that

$$\mathbb{C}[\Psi_1(I_1, I_2, \ldots, I_n), \Psi_2(I_1, I_2, \ldots, I_n)] = \mathbb{C}[\widetilde{\Psi}_1(J_0, J_1, \ldots, J_n), \widetilde{\Psi}_2(J_0, J_1, \ldots, J_n)],$$

which is non-negative since the J_i are independent, and thus associated by Property 7.2.7(iv). The X_i are then also associated. Indeed, from Property 7.2.7(ii) and the independence assumption it follows that $I_1, I_2, \ldots, I_n, B_1, B_2, \ldots, B_n$ are associated, and by Property 7.2.7(iii) we conclude that $\boldsymbol{X}$ is associated. ∇

Example 7.2.9. (Positively correlated normal rvs are associated). Let $\boldsymbol{X}$ be multivariate normal with mean vector 0 and covariance matrix $\boldsymbol{\Sigma} = \{\sigma_{ij}\}$. Pitt (1982) showed that $\sigma_{ij} \geq 0$ for all i, j implies that the X_i are associated. We do not repeat the proof here, since it is rather technical. ∇

Example 7.2.10. A single rv X is associated, that is, $\mathbb{C}[\Psi_1(X), \Psi_2(X)] \geq 0$ whatever the non-decreasing functions Ψ_1 and Ψ_2. This comes from the fact that (X, X) is PQD, since the inequality

$$\Pr[X > s, X > t] = \Pr[X > \max\{s, t\}] \geq \Pr[X > s]\Pr[X > t]$$

hold for all real s and t. We then invoke, Proposition 5.3.8 to get this result. ∇

7.2.3.3 CIS risks are associated

Let us show that conditional increasingness in sequence is a stronger dependence notion than association.

Property 7.2.11
Given an n-dimensional random vector $\boldsymbol{X}$, the implication $\boldsymbol{X}$ CIS $\Rightarrow \boldsymbol{X}$ associated holds.

Proof. To show that inequality (7.1) in Definition 7.2.6 holds for any CIS random vector $\boldsymbol{X}$, let us proceed iteratively. We will show that

$$\mathbb{C}[\Psi_1(X_1, X_2, \ldots, X_i), \Psi_2(X_1, X_2, \ldots, X_i)] \geq 0$$

is valid for every non-decreasing $\Psi_1, \Psi_2 : \mathbb{R}^i \to \mathbb{R}$ and for any $i = 1, 2, \ldots, n$. The result is obviously true for $i = 1$ since we know from Example 7.2.10 that a single rv is associated. Now, let us assume it holds for $i = 1, 2, \ldots, k$ and establish it for $i = k + 1$. To this end, we use Property 1.8.2(i) to write

$$\begin{aligned}
&\mathbb{C}[\Psi_1(X_1, X_2, \ldots, X_{k+1}), \Psi_2(X_1, X_2, \ldots, X_{k+1})] \\
&= \mathbb{E}\Big[\mathbb{C}[\Psi_1(X_1, X_2, \ldots, X_{k+1}), \Psi_2(X_1, X_2, \ldots, X_{k+1})|X_1, X_2, \ldots, X_k]\Big] \\
&+ \mathbb{C}\Big[\mathbb{E}[\Psi_1(X_1, X_2, \ldots, X_{k+1})|X_1, X_2, \ldots, X_k], \\
&\quad \mathbb{E}[\Psi_2(X_1, X_2, \ldots, X_{k+1})|X_1, X_2, \ldots, X_k]\Big].
\end{aligned}$$

Now, because $\boldsymbol{X}$ is CIS, the functions $\widetilde{\Psi}_1$ and $\widetilde{\Psi}_2$ defined by

$$\widetilde{\Psi}_\ell(x_1, \ldots, x_k) = \mathbb{E}[\Psi_\ell(X_1, \ldots, X_{k+1})|X_1 = x_1, \ldots, X_k = x_k], \quad \ell = 1, 2,$$

are non-decreasing. Therefore,

$$\begin{aligned}
&\mathbb{C}\Big[\mathbb{E}[\Psi_1(X_1, X_2, \ldots, X_{k+1})|X_1, X_2, \ldots, X_k], \mathbb{E}[\Psi_2(X_1, X_2, \ldots, X_{k+1})|X_1, X_2, \ldots, X_k]\Big] \\
&= \mathbb{C}\Big[\widetilde{\Psi}_1(X_1, X_2, \ldots, X_k), \widetilde{\Psi}_2(X_1, X_2, \ldots, X_k)\Big] \geq 0,
\end{aligned}$$

by virtue of the recurrence hypothesis. Furthermore, we clearly have that

$$\begin{aligned}
&\mathbb{C}[\Psi_1(x_1, \ldots, x_k, X_{k+1}), \Psi_2(x_1, \ldots, x_k, X_{k+1})|X_1 = x_1, \ldots, X_k = x_k] \geq 0 \\
&\Rightarrow \mathbb{E}\Big[\mathbb{C}[\Psi_1(X_1, X_2, \ldots, X_{k+1}), \Psi_2(X_1, X_2, \ldots, X_{k+1})|X_1, X_2, \ldots, X_k]\Big] \geq 0
\end{aligned}$$

which proves (7.1). □

Since association implies positive quadrant dependence in the bivariate case, and cumulative dependence/positive orthant dependence in the multivariate case, we have that association lies between conditional increasingness in sequence and these weaker positive dependence concepts.

7.2.4 Dependence by mixture and common mixture models

7.2.4.1 Definition

The purpose of this section is to further investigate what Wang (1998) called common mixture models. These models involve conditionally independent rvs and form the basis of credibility models (see assumption A1 in Definitions 7.2.1 and 7.2.5).

The intuition behind the common mixture construction is as follows: an external mechanism, described by the rv Θ, influences several risks. Given the environmental parameter Θ, the individual risks are independent. This is formally stated next.

Definition 7.2.12. A random vector $\boldsymbol{X}$ is dependent by mixture if its joint df can be written as

$$F_{\boldsymbol{X}}(\boldsymbol{x}) = \int_{-\infty}^{+\infty} \left(\prod_{i=1}^{n} F_i(x_i|\theta) \right) dF_{\Theta}(\theta), \quad \boldsymbol{x} \in \mathbb{R}^n, \tag{7.2}$$

for dfs $F_1(\cdot|\theta), \ldots, F_n(\cdot|\theta)$ and F_{Θ}. ∇

Note that $F_i(\cdot|\theta)$ is the df of $[X_i|\Theta=\theta]$, $i=1,2,\ldots,n$. Unconditionally, the df of X_i, $i=1,2,\ldots,n$, is

$$F_i(x_i) = \int_{-\infty}^{+\infty} F_i(x_i|\theta) dF_{\Theta}(\theta). \tag{7.3}$$

The following example illustrates this construction. It is related to Example 4.1.2.

Example 7.2.13. (Multivariate Pareto distribution). Let us consider the n-dimensional risk $\boldsymbol{X}$ such that $[X_j|\Theta=\theta] \sim \mathcal{E}xp(\lambda_j\theta)$. For any given $\theta > 0$, the rvs $[X_j|\Theta=\theta]$ are independent. Their conditional joint tf is given by

$$\Pr[X_1 > t_1, \ldots, X_n > t_n|\Theta=\theta] = \exp\Big(-\theta(\lambda_1 t_1 + \ldots + \lambda_n t_n) \Big).$$

Unconditionally, the X_i are correlated as they depend upon the same random parameter Θ. The joint tf of $\boldsymbol{X}$ is given in terms of the Laplace transform L_{Θ} of Θ by

$$\begin{aligned}\overline{F}_{\boldsymbol{X}}(t_1, \ldots, t_n) &= \int_0^{+\infty} \Pr[X_1 > t_1, \ldots, X_n > t_n|\Theta=\theta] dF_{\Theta}(\theta) \\ &= L_{\Theta}(\lambda_1 t_1 + \ldots + \lambda_n t_n).\end{aligned}$$

For instance, if $\Theta \sim \mathcal{G}am(\alpha, 1)$, the above construction yields a family of multivariate Pareto distributions with joint tf

$$\overline{F}_{\boldsymbol{X}}(t_1, \ldots, t_n) = (1 + \lambda_1 t_1 + \ldots + \lambda_n t_n)^{-\alpha}$$

and with $\mathcal{P}ar(\alpha, 1/\lambda_j)$ marginals. ∇

Remark 7.2.14. It is worth emphasizing that, as explained in Section 1.9, comonotonicity appears as an extreme case of dependence by mixture. ∇

Henceforth, we will also consider the following alternative kind of dependence. Assume that there exists an n-dimensional random vector $\boldsymbol{\Theta}$ such that for each $\boldsymbol{\theta}$ in the support of $\boldsymbol{\Theta}$, the rvs $[X_1|\boldsymbol{\Theta}=\boldsymbol{\theta}]$, $[X_2|\boldsymbol{\Theta}=\boldsymbol{\theta}], \ldots, [X_n|\boldsymbol{\Theta}=\boldsymbol{\theta}]$ are independent and the ith component of $\boldsymbol{X}$ depends on $\boldsymbol{\Theta}$ only through Θ_i, that is, $[X_i|\boldsymbol{\Theta}=\boldsymbol{\theta}]=_d [X_i|\Theta_i=\theta_i]$.

Definition 7.2.15. The n-dimensional random vector $\boldsymbol{X}$ is dependent by multivariate mixture if its joint df can be written as

$$F_{\boldsymbol{X}}(\boldsymbol{x}) = \int_{-\infty}^{+\infty} \cdots \int_{-\infty}^{+\infty} \left(\prod_{i=1}^{n} F_i(x_i|\theta_i) \right) dF_{\boldsymbol{\Theta}}(\boldsymbol{\theta}), \quad \boldsymbol{x} \in \mathbb{R}^n, \tag{7.4}$$

for univariate dfs $F_1(\cdot|\theta_1), \ldots, F_n(\cdot|\theta_n)$ and a multivariate df $F_{\boldsymbol{\Theta}}$. ∇

7.2.4.2 Dependence by mixture and association

As shown by Jogdeo (1978) and Shaked and Spizzichino (1998), dependence by mixture is a positive dependence notion under additional assumptions on the marginals. Specifically, we use the concept of stochastic increasingness introduced in Section 3.3.6.

Property 7.2.16
Let $\boldsymbol{X}$ be an n-dimensional random vector with joint df (7.2). If the $F_i(\cdot|\theta)$ are stochastically increasing in θ for $i=1,2,\ldots,n$, then $\boldsymbol{X}$ is associated.

Proof. Let us define the function h as $h(\theta)=\mathbb{E}[g(\boldsymbol{X})|\Theta=\theta]$. This function is non-decreasing in θ for every non-decreasing g. Indeed, given $\theta \leq \theta'$,

$$[\boldsymbol{X}|\Theta=\theta] =_d \widetilde{\boldsymbol{X}}_\theta = \left(\overline{F}_1^{-1}(U_1|\theta), \overline{F}_2^{-1}(U_2|\theta), \ldots, \overline{F}_n^{-1}(U_n|\theta)\right),$$
$$[\boldsymbol{X}|\Theta=\theta'] =_d \widetilde{\boldsymbol{X}}_{\theta'} = \left(\overline{F}_1^{-1}(U_1|\theta'), \overline{F}_2^{-1}(U_2|\theta'), \ldots, \overline{F}_n^{-1}(U_n|\theta')\right),$$

where $U_1, U_2, \ldots, U_n$ are independent $\mathcal{U}ni(0,1)$ rvs, independent of Θ. It is easy to see that $\Pr[\widetilde{\boldsymbol{X}}_\theta \leq \widetilde{\boldsymbol{X}}_{\theta'}]=1$ by the stochastic increasingness of the $F_i(\cdot|\theta)$ in θ. Hence, Proposition 3.3.86 ensures that $\widetilde{\boldsymbol{X}}_\theta \preceq_{\text{ST}} \widetilde{\boldsymbol{X}}_{\theta'}$. Therefore,

$$\mathbb{E}[g(\boldsymbol{X})|\Theta=\theta] = \mathbb{E}[g(\widetilde{\boldsymbol{X}}_\theta)] \leq \mathbb{E}[g(\widetilde{\boldsymbol{X}}_{\theta'})] = \mathbb{E}[g(\boldsymbol{X})|\Theta=\theta'],$$

whence it follows that h is indeed non-decreasing. Now, given two non-decreasing functions Ψ_1 and Ψ_2, Property 1.8.2(i) allows us to write

$$\begin{aligned}\mathbb{C}[\Psi_1(\boldsymbol{X}), \Psi_2(\boldsymbol{X})] &= \mathbb{E}\Big[\mathbb{C}[\Psi_1(\boldsymbol{X}), \Psi_2(\boldsymbol{X})|\Theta]\Big] \\ &\quad + \mathbb{C}\Big[\mathbb{E}[\Psi_1(\boldsymbol{X})|\Theta], \mathbb{E}[\Psi_2(\boldsymbol{X})|\Theta]\Big].\end{aligned}$$

The first term on the right-hand side is non-negative because of the conditional independence of the X_i (independent rvs are associated by virtue of Property 7.2.7(iv)) and the second can be cast into the form $\mathbb{C}[h_1(\Theta), h_2(\Theta)]$ with non-decreasing h_i; it is thus also non-negative because by Example 7.2.10, a single rv is associated. □

Property 7.2.16 shows which dependence structure arises from a common mixture model provided the conditional marginals satisfy some stochastic monotonicity properties.

Let us now turn to dependence by multivariate mixture. The following result holds in this case, in the same vein as Property 7.2.16.

Property 7.2.17
Let $\boldsymbol{X}$ be an n-dimensional random vector with df (7.4) such that $\boldsymbol{X}$ is stochastically increasing in $\boldsymbol{\theta}$, that is, $[\boldsymbol{X}|\boldsymbol{\Theta}=\boldsymbol{\theta}] \preceq_{\mathrm{ST}} [\boldsymbol{X}|\boldsymbol{\Theta}=\boldsymbol{\theta}']$ holds whenever $\boldsymbol{\theta} \leq \boldsymbol{\theta}'$. If $\boldsymbol{\Theta}$ is associated then $\boldsymbol{X}$ is associated.

Proof. Given two non-decreasing functions Ψ_1 and Ψ_2 mapping $\mathbb{R}^{2n}$ to $\mathbb{R}$, Property 1.8.2(i) allows us to write

$$\mathbb{C}[\Psi_1(\boldsymbol{X},\boldsymbol{\Theta}),\Psi_2(\boldsymbol{X},\boldsymbol{\Theta})] = \mathbb{E}\Big[\mathbb{C}\big[\Psi_1(\boldsymbol{X},\boldsymbol{\Theta}),\Psi_2(\boldsymbol{X},\boldsymbol{\Theta})|\boldsymbol{\Theta}\big]\Big] + \mathbb{C}\Big[\mathbb{E}[\Psi_1(\boldsymbol{X},\boldsymbol{\Theta})|\boldsymbol{\Theta}],\mathbb{E}[\Psi_2(\boldsymbol{X},\boldsymbol{\Theta})|\boldsymbol{\Theta}]\Big].$$

The first term on the right-hand side is non-negative because of the conditional independence of the X_i given $\boldsymbol{\Theta}$ (and the fact that independent rvs are associated). The second term can be written as $\mathbb{C}[h_1(\boldsymbol{\Theta}),h_2(\boldsymbol{\Theta})]$, where $h_\ell(\boldsymbol{\theta}) = \mathbb{E}[\Psi_\ell(\boldsymbol{X})|\boldsymbol{\Theta}=\boldsymbol{\theta}]$, $\ell=1,2$. The stochastic increasingness of $\boldsymbol{X}$ in $\boldsymbol{\theta}$ ensures that h_1 and h_2 are non-decreasing. Hence, the second term is non-negative provided $\boldsymbol{\Theta}$ is associated. Consequently, $\mathbb{C}[\Psi_1(\boldsymbol{X},\boldsymbol{\Theta}),\Psi_2(\boldsymbol{X},\boldsymbol{\Theta})]\geq 0$ and $(\boldsymbol{X},\boldsymbol{\Theta})$ is associated. In particular, $\boldsymbol{X}$ is associated since every subset of associated rvs remain associated by Property 7.2.7(i). This concludes the proof. □

7.2.4.3 Dependence by mixture and MTP_2

Dependence by mixture induces strong positive dependence under additional assumptions on the marginals. Specifically, the likelihood ratio increasingness (or TP_2) property introduced in Section 3.3.11.8 will be used here.

Property 7.2.18
Let $\boldsymbol{X}$ be an n-dimensional random vector with df (7.2). If the $F_i(\cdot|\theta)$ are likelihood ratio increasing in θ for $i=1,2,\ldots,n$, then $\boldsymbol{X}$ is MTP_2.

Proof. It is enough from Proposition 5.3.33 to show that $f_{\boldsymbol{X}}$ is TP_2 in each pair of its variables when the other $n-2$ variables are held fixed. As an illustration, let us fix the values of $x_3,x_4,\ldots,x_n$. The assumption that $[X_1|\Theta=\theta]$ and $[X_2|\Theta=\theta]$ increase in θ in the $\preceq_{\mathrm{LR}}$ sense means that $f_1(t|\theta)$ and $f_2(t|\theta)$ are each TP_2 in t and θ. Now, since the representation

$$f_{\boldsymbol{X}}(\boldsymbol{x}) = \int_{-\infty}^{+\infty}\left(\prod_{i=1}^{n} f_i(x_i|\theta)\right) dF_\Theta(\theta),\quad \boldsymbol{x}\in\mathbb{R}^n,$$

holds, we invoke the basic composition formula of Property 3.3.53 to deduce that $f_{\boldsymbol{X}}$ is TP_2 in x_1 and x_2. □

Example 7.2.19. Let us examine the dependence properties of random vectors $\boldsymbol{X}$ with joint df of the form (4.19). It is easy to see that $\boldsymbol{X}$ admits a pdf of the form (7.2) with conditional df $F_i(x|\theta) = (H_i(x))^\theta$. The $F_i(\cdot|\theta)$ are likelihood ratio increasing. Indeed, denoting the pdf corresponding to the df H_i by h_i, the ratio of the pdfs corresponding to θ and θ' equals

$$\frac{h_i(x)\theta\big(H_i(x)\big)^{\theta-1}}{h_i(x)\theta'\big(H_i(x)\big)^{\theta'-1}} = \frac{\theta}{\theta'}\big(H_i(x)\big)^{\theta-\theta'},$$

which decreases in x if $\theta < \theta'$ (hence the result given in (3.18)). It then follows from Property 7.2.18 that $\boldsymbol{X}$ is MTP_2. ∇

Remark 7.2.20. In particular, Example 7.2.19 shows that Archimedean copulas originating from the frailty construction express strong positive dependence since they are MTP_2. ∇

To end with, let us state the following result, which can be seen as the analogue of Property 7.2.18 for dependence by common multivariate mixture.

Property 7.2.21
Let $\boldsymbol{X}$ be an n-dimensional random vector with df of the form (7.4). If the $F_i(\cdot|\theta)$ are likelihood ratio increasing in θ for $i = 1, 2, \ldots, n$ and $\boldsymbol{\Theta}$ is MTP_2, then $\boldsymbol{X}$ is MTP_2.

Proof. The joint pdf of $\boldsymbol{X}$ can be written as

$$f_{\boldsymbol{X}}(\boldsymbol{x}) = \int_{-\infty}^{+\infty} \cdots \int_{-\infty}^{+\infty} \left(\prod_{i=1}^{n} f_i(x_i|\theta_i)\right) dF_{\boldsymbol{\Theta}}(\boldsymbol{\theta}).$$

Since each $(x_i, \theta_i) \mapsto f_i(x_i|\theta_i)$ is TP_2 by assumption, it follows from Proposition 5.3.33 that the integrand is an MTP_2 function. The composition formula stated in Property 5.3.31 then ensures that $f_{\boldsymbol{X}}$ is also MTP_2, whence the result follows. □

7.2.5 Dependence in the Poisson static credibility model

We are now ready to establish the results in credibility models given earlier.

7.2.5.1 Statements S1–S2 in the Poisson static credibility model

The following result formalizes statements S1 and S2: the increasingness mentioned there is with respect to $\preceq_{\text{LR}}$.

Proposition 7.2.22
In the Poisson static frequency credibility model of Definition 7.2.1,

(i) $[\Theta_i|N_{i\bullet} = n] \preceq_{\text{LR}} [\Theta_i|N_{i\bullet} = n']$ for $n \le n'$;

(ii) $[N_{i,T_i+1}|N_{i\bullet} = n] \preceq_{\text{LR}} [N_{i,T_i+1}|N_{i\bullet} = n']$ for $n \le n'$.

Proof. (i) Denote by $f_\Theta(\cdot|n)$ the conditional pdf of $[\Theta_i|N_{i\bullet}=n]$, $n\in\mathbb{N}$. By virtue of (3.19), we have to show that for any $\theta\leq\theta'$ and $n\leq n'$,

$$\frac{f_\Theta(\theta|n')}{f_\Theta(\theta|n)}\leq\frac{f_\Theta(\theta'|n')}{f_\Theta(\theta'|n)}\Leftrightarrow\frac{f_\Theta(\theta'|n)}{f_\Theta(\theta|n)}\leq\frac{f_\Theta(\theta'|n')}{f_\Theta(\theta|n')}.$$

This result follows from

$$\begin{aligned}\frac{f_\Theta(\theta'|n)}{f_\Theta(\theta|n)}&=\frac{\Pr[N_{i\bullet}=n|\Theta_i=\theta']}{\Pr[N_{i\bullet}=n|\Theta_i=\theta]}\times\frac{f_\Theta(\theta')}{f_\Theta(\theta)}\\&\leq\frac{\Pr[N_{i\bullet}=n'|\Theta_i=\theta']}{\Pr[N_{i\bullet}=n'|\Theta_i=\theta]}\times\frac{f_\Theta(\theta')}{f_\Theta(\theta)}\\&=\frac{f_\Theta(\theta'|n')}{f_\Theta(\theta|n')},\end{aligned}$$

where the inequality follows from the fact that $[N_{i\bullet}|\Theta_i=\theta]$ is increasing in θ for $\preceq_{\text{LR}}$.

(ii) This is a direct consequence of (i) together with Proposition 3.3.54. □

7.2.5.2 Statement S3 in the Poisson static credibility model

Let us now prove that the total claim number $N_{i\bullet}$ of claims made in the past periods and the claim frequency N_{i,T_i+1} for the next coverage period are MTP$_2$. This formalizes statement S3.

Proposition 7.2.23
In the Poisson static frequency credibility model of Definition 7.2.1, $N_{i\bullet}$ and N_{i,T_i+1} are MTP$_2$.

Proof. We have to establish that the function $(n,k)\mapsto\Pr[N_{i\bullet}=n, N_{i,T_i+1}=k]$ is TP$_2$. This is a simple consequence of Property 3.3.53 applied to

$$\Pr[N_{i\bullet}=n, N_{i,T_i+1}=k]=\int_0^{+\infty}\Pr[N_{i\bullet}=n|\Theta_i=\theta]\Pr[N_{i,T_i+1}=k|\Theta_i=\theta]dF_\Theta(\theta).$$

□

Proposition 7.2.23 provides a host of useful inequalities since multivariate total positivity of order 2 is one of the strongest dependence concepts (it implies the weaker conditional increasingness, association and cumulative dependence/positive orthant dependence). In particular, whatever the distribution of Θ_i, the theoretical bonus–malus coefficient $\mathbb{E}[\Theta_i|N_{i\bullet}=n]$ is increasing in n.

7.2.5.3 Serial dependence for claim frequencies in static credibility models

The following result is a direct consequence of Property 7.2.18.

Proposition 7.2.24
In the Poisson static frequency credibility model of Definition 7.2.1, $\boldsymbol{N}_i$ is MTP$_2$.

7.2.6 *Dependence in the Poisson dynamic credibility models*

7.2.6.1 Modelling heterogeneity in the Poisson dynamic credibility models

Let us now supplement assumptions A1 and A2 of Definition 7.2.5 with various structures matching the constraints listed in A2. Model A3 is the classical static credibility model. Models A4–A6 come from Pinquet, Guillén and Bolancé (2001) and Pinquet (2000).

Model A3 As is often done in actuarial science, we could opt for static heterogeneity, that is, $\Theta_t \equiv \Theta$. In this case, we are back at the static credibility model of Definition 7.2.1.

Model A4 Let $\boldsymbol{W} \sim \mathcal{N}or(\boldsymbol{0}, \boldsymbol{\Sigma})$ where $\sigma_{st} = \sigma_W^2 \rho_W(|s-t|)$ with $|\rho_W(h)| \leq 1$, $\rho_W(0) = 1$. The correlation function ρ_W plays a central role in the analysis of the predictive ability of past claims, as shown in Pinquet, Guillén and Bolancé (2001). Now define

$$\Theta_t = \frac{\exp[W_t]}{\mathbb{E}[\exp W_t]} \sim \mathcal{LN}or\left(-\frac{\sigma_W^2}{2}, \sigma_W^2\right), \quad t = 1, \ldots, T_{\max}.$$

Hence, all the $\boldsymbol{\Theta}_i$ have multivariate lognormal distributions.
Note that if the autocorrelation function $\rho_W(h) = 1$ for all h, we have in fact $\boldsymbol{\Theta}_i = (\Theta_i, \ldots, \Theta_i)^t$, with each Θ_i conforming to the lognormal distribution; we thus obtain a special case of model A3.

Model A5 We could further specify model A4 by assuming in addition that $\boldsymbol{W}$ has an autoregressive structure of order 1, that is,

$$W_t = \varrho W_{t-1} + \epsilon_t, \quad t \geq 2,$$

where the errors $\epsilon_t \sim \mathcal{N}or(0, \sigma^2(1-\varrho^2))$ are independent, $|\varrho| < 1$, and $W_1 \sim \mathcal{N}or(0, \sigma^2)$. In this case, $\rho_W(|s-t|) = \varrho^{|s-t|}$ so that the autocorrelation function decreases exponentially with the lag between observations. This specification is particularly appealing for rate-making purposes.

Model A6 This model postulates that there is a static baseline heterogeneity which is perturbated by independent and identically distributed annual effects. Specifically, $\Theta_t = RS_t$ where the S_t are independent and identically distributed, and independent of R, $S_t \sim \mathcal{LN}or(-\frac{\sigma_S^2}{2}, \sigma_S^2)$ and $R \sim \mathcal{LN}or(-\frac{\sigma_R^2}{2}, \sigma_R^2)$. In this case, $\Theta_t \sim \mathcal{LN}or(-\frac{\sigma_R^2+\sigma_S^2}{2}, \sigma_R^2 + \sigma_S^2)$. Therefore in this model the autocorrelation function between the random effects is constant since Property 1.8.2 (i) allows us to write

$$\begin{aligned}\mathbb{C}[\Theta_t, \Theta_{t+h}] &= \mathbb{E}\Big[\mathbb{C}[\Theta_t, \Theta_{t+h}|R]\Big] + \mathbb{C}\Big[\mathbb{E}[\Theta_t|R], \mathbb{E}[\Theta_{t+h}|R]\Big] \\ &= \mathbb{C}\Big[R\mathbb{E}[S_t], R\mathbb{E}[S_{t+h}]\Big] = \mathbb{V}[R].\end{aligned}$$

7.2.6.2 Statement S1 in Poisson dynamic credibility models

We are now ready to state the main result of this section, namely that positive dependence for $\boldsymbol{\Theta}_i$ is transmitted to $\boldsymbol{N}_i$.

Proposition 7.2.25
In model A1–A2 of Definition 7.2.5,

(i) $\boldsymbol{\Theta}_i$ MTP$_2$ $\Rightarrow \boldsymbol{N}_i$ MTP$_2$.

(ii) $\boldsymbol{\Theta}_i$ associated $\Rightarrow \boldsymbol{N}_i$ associated.

Proof. (i) is a straight application of Property 7.2.21; (ii) directly follows from Property 7.2.17. □

Since the type of dependence existing between the N_{it} is induced by the type of dependence existing between the Θ_{it}, as presented in Proposition 7.2.25, it remains to study the dependence structure of the random effects Θ_{it} in models A3–A6. This is done next.

Model A3 Since $\boldsymbol{\Theta}_i$ is comonotonic, it is a fortiori MTP$_2$, so by virtue of Proposition 7.2.25(i) $\boldsymbol{N}_i$ is MTP$_2$ as established in Proposition 7.2.24. Note that $\boldsymbol{N}_i$ is obviously not comonotonic.

Model A4 This model is rather general. Not surprisingly, the type of dependence between the Θ_{it} is determined by the form of the covariance matrix $\boldsymbol{\Sigma}$ of $\boldsymbol{W}$.
In the model combining A1–A2 and A4, the following properties hold:

(i) From Example 5.3.34, we know that $\boldsymbol{W}$ is MTP$_2$ if all the off-diagonal components of the inverse of its covariance matrix $\boldsymbol{\Sigma}$ are non-positive. Since Multivariate total positivity of order 2 is closed under increasing transformation, each $\boldsymbol{\Theta}_i$ is then MTP$_2$. Proposition 7.2.25(i) then indicates that $\boldsymbol{N}_i$ is MTP$_2$.

(ii) We know from Example 7.2.9 that $\boldsymbol{W}$ is associated if all the elements of its covariance matrix are non-negative. Therefore, $\boldsymbol{N}_i$ is associated in this case.

Model A5 In this model, the covariance structure of $\boldsymbol{W}$ is expressed in terms of the autoregressive parameter ϱ. Provided ϱ is non-negative, we get strong positive dependence for the components of $\boldsymbol{N}_i$: specifically, in the model combining A1–A2 and A5, $\varrho \geq 0 \Rightarrow \boldsymbol{N}_i$ MTP$_2$. The elements of $\boldsymbol{\Sigma}$ are given by:

$$\sigma_{tt} = \sigma_W^2, \qquad \sigma_{st} = \sigma_{ts} = \varrho^{|s-t|}\sigma_W^2 \quad \text{for } |s-t| \geq 1.$$

The off-diagonal elements of the matrix $\boldsymbol{R} = \boldsymbol{\Sigma}^{-1}$ are then given by

$$r_{t,t+1} = r_{t+1,t} = -\frac{\varrho}{\sigma_W^2(1-\varrho^2)} \quad \text{for } t = 1, \ldots, T_{\max} - 1$$

and $r_{st} = 0$ for $|s-t| \geq 2$. Therefore, they are all non-positive when $\varrho \geq 0$. Hence $\boldsymbol{W}$ is MTP$_2$. Since the MTP$_2$ property is functionally invariant, $\boldsymbol{\Theta}_i$ is also MTP$_2$ and hence $\boldsymbol{N}_i$ by Proposition 7.2.25(i).

Model A6 Let us now turn to the exchangeable random effects. When the lognormal specification is retained for R_i and the S_{it}, no further conditions are needed for MTP$_2$:

in the model combining A1–A2 and A6, $\boldsymbol{N}_i$ is MTP_2. Let us prove this assertion. The joint pdf of $\boldsymbol{\Theta}_i$ is given by

$$f_{\boldsymbol{\Theta}_i}(\theta_{i1},\ldots,\theta_{iT_i}) = \int_0^{+\infty}\left(\prod_{t=1}^{T_i} f_{S_{it}}\left(\frac{\theta_{it}}{r}\right)\right) f_{R_i}(r)dr. \tag{7.5}$$

Let us show that $f_{S_{it}}(\frac{\theta_{it}}{r})$ is TP_2 in (θ_{it}, r), that is to say, for all $\theta_1 < \theta_2$ and all $r_1 < r_2$ the inequality

$$f_{S_{it}}\left(\frac{\theta_1}{r_1}\right) f_{S_{it}}\left(\frac{\theta_2}{r_2}\right) \geq f_{S_{it}}\left(\frac{\theta_1}{r_2}\right) f_{S_{it}}\left(\frac{\theta_2}{r_1}\right)$$

holds. We therefore have to prove that

$$\exp\left(-\frac{1}{2\sigma_S^2}\left(\left(\ln\frac{\theta_1}{r_1}-\frac{\sigma_S^2}{2}\right)^2+\left(\ln\frac{\theta_2}{r_2}-\frac{\sigma_S^2}{2}\right)^2\right)\right)$$
$$\geq \exp\left(-\frac{1}{2\sigma_S^2}\left(\left(\ln\frac{\theta_1}{r_2}-\frac{\sigma_S^2}{2}\right)^2+\left(\ln\frac{\theta_2}{r_1}-\frac{\sigma_S^2}{2}\right)^2\right)\right),$$

or, equivalently, that

$$-\frac{1}{2\sigma_S^2}\left((\ln\theta_1-\ln r_1)^2+(\ln\theta_2-\ln r_2)^2-(\ln\theta_1-\ln r_2)^2-(\ln\theta_2-\ln r_1)^2\right)\geq 0,$$

which reduces to

$$\frac{1}{\sigma_S^2}(\ln\theta_2-\ln\theta_1)(\ln r_2-\ln r_1)\geq 0.$$

This relation is obviously true. Thus $(\theta_{it}, r)\mapsto f_{S_{it}}(\frac{\theta_{it}}{r})$ is TP_2. The integrand of (7.5) is then MTP_2 in $(\boldsymbol{\theta}_i, r)$, whence it follows that $f_{\boldsymbol{\Theta}_i}$ is MTP_2.

7.2.6.3 Statement S2 in Poisson dynamic credibility models

Let us now prove that policyholders making more claims in the past become more dangerous on unobservable characteristics.

Proposition 7.2.26
In model A1–A2, $[\boldsymbol{\Theta}_i|\boldsymbol{N}_i=\boldsymbol{k}]\preceq_{\mathrm{LR}}[\boldsymbol{\Theta}_i|\boldsymbol{N}_i=\boldsymbol{k}']$ whenever $\boldsymbol{k}\leq\boldsymbol{k}'$ provided $\boldsymbol{\Theta}_i$ is MTP_2.

Proof. The conditional pdf of $\boldsymbol{\Theta}_i$ given $\boldsymbol{N}_i=\boldsymbol{k}$ can be expressed as

$$f_{\boldsymbol{\Theta}_i}(\boldsymbol{\theta}|\boldsymbol{k})=\frac{\Pr[\boldsymbol{N}_i=\boldsymbol{k}|\boldsymbol{\Theta}_i=\boldsymbol{\theta}]f_{\boldsymbol{\Theta}_i}(\boldsymbol{\theta})}{\Pr[\boldsymbol{N}_i=\boldsymbol{k}]}.$$

Let us now consider two claim histories $\boldsymbol{k} \leq \boldsymbol{k}'$ as well as two possible values for the random effects $\boldsymbol{\theta}$ and $\boldsymbol{\theta}'$. Starting from

$$f_{\Theta_i}(\boldsymbol{\theta}|\boldsymbol{k})f_{\Theta_i}(\boldsymbol{\theta}'|\boldsymbol{k}') = \frac{\Pr[\boldsymbol{N}_i = \boldsymbol{k}|\boldsymbol{\Theta}_i = \boldsymbol{\theta}]\Pr[\boldsymbol{N}_i = \boldsymbol{k}'|\boldsymbol{\Theta}_i = \boldsymbol{\theta}']}{\Pr[\boldsymbol{N}_i = \boldsymbol{k}]\Pr[\boldsymbol{N}_i = \boldsymbol{k}']} f_{\Theta_i}(\boldsymbol{\theta})f_{\Theta_i}(\boldsymbol{\theta}')$$

$$= \left(\prod_{t=1}^{T_i} \Pr[N_{it} = k_t|\Theta_{it} = \theta_{it}]\right)\left(\prod_{t=1}^{T_i} \Pr[N_{it} = k'_t|\Theta_{it} = \theta'_{it}]\right)$$

$$\times \frac{f_{\Theta_i}(\boldsymbol{\theta})f_{\Theta_i}(\boldsymbol{\theta}')}{\Pr[\boldsymbol{N}_i = \boldsymbol{k}]\Pr[\boldsymbol{N}_i = \boldsymbol{k}']},$$

we get from the MTP_2 nature of $\boldsymbol{\Theta}_i$ that

$$f_{\Theta_i}(\boldsymbol{\theta}|\boldsymbol{k})f_{\Theta_i}(\boldsymbol{\theta}'|\boldsymbol{k}')$$

$$\leq \left(\prod_{t=1}^{T_i} \Pr[N_{it} = k_t \wedge k'_t|\Theta_{it} = \theta_{it} \wedge \theta'_{it}]\right)$$

$$\times \left(\prod_{t=1}^{T_i} \Pr[N_{it} = k_t \vee k'_t|\Theta_{it} = \theta_{it} \vee \theta'_{it}]\right) \frac{f_{\Theta_i}(\boldsymbol{\theta} \wedge \boldsymbol{\theta}')f_{\Theta_i}(\boldsymbol{\theta} \vee \boldsymbol{\theta}')}{\Pr[\boldsymbol{N}_i = \boldsymbol{k}]\Pr[\boldsymbol{N}_i = \boldsymbol{k}']}$$

$$= \Pr[\boldsymbol{N}_i = \boldsymbol{k} \wedge \boldsymbol{k}'|\boldsymbol{\Theta}_i = \boldsymbol{\theta} \wedge \boldsymbol{\theta}']\Pr[\boldsymbol{N}_i = \boldsymbol{k} \vee \boldsymbol{k}'|\boldsymbol{\Theta}_i = \boldsymbol{\theta} \vee \boldsymbol{\theta}'] \times \frac{f_{\Theta_i}(\boldsymbol{\theta} \wedge \boldsymbol{\theta}')f_{\Theta_i}(\boldsymbol{\theta} \vee \boldsymbol{\theta}')}{\Pr[\boldsymbol{N}_i = \boldsymbol{k}]\Pr[\boldsymbol{N}_i = \boldsymbol{k}']}$$

$$= \frac{\Pr[\boldsymbol{N}_i = \boldsymbol{k}|\boldsymbol{\Theta}_i = \boldsymbol{\theta} \wedge \boldsymbol{\theta}']f_{\Theta_i}(\boldsymbol{\theta} \wedge \boldsymbol{\theta}')}{\Pr[\boldsymbol{N}_i = \boldsymbol{k}]} \times \frac{\Pr[\boldsymbol{N}_i = \boldsymbol{k}'|\boldsymbol{\Theta}_i = \boldsymbol{\theta} \vee \boldsymbol{\theta}']f_{\Theta_i}(\boldsymbol{\theta} \vee \boldsymbol{\theta}'))}{\Pr[\boldsymbol{N}_i = \boldsymbol{k}']}$$

$$= f_{\Theta_i}(\boldsymbol{\theta} \wedge \boldsymbol{\theta}'|\boldsymbol{k})f_{\Theta_i}(\boldsymbol{\theta} \vee \boldsymbol{\theta}'|\boldsymbol{k}'),$$

whence the result follows. □

It is interesting to contrast Proposition 7.2.26 with Proposition 7.2.22(i). Now the $\preceq_{LR}$-increasingness is with respect to to the whole vector $\boldsymbol{N}_i$ and not just to the sum $N_{i\bullet}$ of its components.

7.2.6.4 Statements S3 and S4 in Poisson dynamic credibility models A5–A6

Let us now examine the distribution of the future number of claims N_{iT_i+1} given past claims $\boldsymbol{N}_i$. Model A4 is hardly used to perform prediction on a longitudinal basis. This is due to the fact that the correlation function ρ_W has to be continued beyond the observation period before evaluating experience premiums; see Pinquet, Guillén and Bolancé (2001) for a complete treatment of this subject. In this section, we concentrate on models A5 (with $\varrho \geq 0$) and A6. This ensures that the vector $(\Theta_{i1}, \ldots, \Theta_{iT_i}, \Theta_{iT_i+1})$ is also MTP_2.

Property 7.2.27
In the Poisson dynamic frequency credibility model A1–A2 of Definition 7.2.5 completed by either A5 (with $\varrho \geq 0$) or A6, $[\Theta_{iT_i+1}|\boldsymbol{N}_i = \boldsymbol{k}] \preceq_{LR} [\Theta_{iT_i+1}|\boldsymbol{N}_i = \boldsymbol{k}']$ for all $\boldsymbol{k} \leq \boldsymbol{k}'$.

Proof. Proposition 7.2.26 ensures that under A5 (with $\varrho \geq 0$) or A6,

$$[(\Theta_{i1}, \ldots, \Theta_{iT_i+1})|\boldsymbol{N}_i = \boldsymbol{k}] \preceq_{\mathrm{LR}} [(\Theta_{i1}, \ldots, \Theta_{iT_i+1})|\boldsymbol{N}_i = \boldsymbol{k}']$$

holds whenever $\boldsymbol{k} \leq \boldsymbol{k}'$. Now $\preceq_{\mathrm{LR}}$ is closed under marginalization so that the result is proved. □

We have shown in Property 7.2.27 that a policyholder making more claims in the past will be more dangerous on the unobservable characteristics Θ_{iT_i+1} relating to the year $T_i + 1$. We would now like to establish the same result for the future number of claims.

Property 7.2.28
Under the assumptions of Property 7.2.27, $[N_{iT_i+1}|\boldsymbol{N}_i = \boldsymbol{k}] \preceq_{\mathrm{LR}} [N_{iT_i+1}|\boldsymbol{N}_i = \boldsymbol{k}']$, for all $\boldsymbol{k} \leq \boldsymbol{k}'$.

Proof. This is a direct consequence of Property 7.2.27 together with Proposition 3.3.54. □

7.3 MORE RESULTS FOR THE STATIC CREDIBILITY MODEL

7.3.1 Generalized linear models and generalized additive models

Generalized linear models unify regression methods for a variety of discrete and continuous outcomes. They are presented in Kaas *et al.* (2001, Chapter 8). The basis of GLMs is the assumption that the data are sampled from a one-parameter exponential family of distributions. This happens, for instance, with data conforming to the binomial law, Poisson law, normal law with known variance or gamma law with known dispersion parameter. Specifically, consider a single observation y; GLMs admit a log-likelihood of the form

$$\ell(\eta, \tau; y) = \frac{y\eta - b(\eta)}{\tau} + c(y, \tau), \tag{7.6}$$

where η denotes the canonical parameter and $\tau > 0$ is the dispersion parameter (assumed known). It is easy to see that $\mu = \mathbb{E}[Y] = b'(\eta)$ and $\mathbb{V}[Y] = b''(\eta)\tau = v(\mu)\tau$, where $v(\cdot)$ is called the variance function.

A link function relating the mean μ to the linear predictor is then specified. More precisely, given a p-dimensional vector $\boldsymbol{x}$ of explanatory variables and a vector $\boldsymbol{\beta}$ of regression coefficients, the linear predictor (also called the score) takes the form $\boldsymbol{\beta}^t\boldsymbol{x} = \beta_0 + \sum_{j=1}^{p} \beta_j x_{ij}$; this is then related to the mean by $\boldsymbol{\beta}^t\boldsymbol{x} = a(\mu)$. The function $a(\cdot)$ is called the link function and the special case $a(\mu) = \eta$ is called the canonical link function.

The results established in this section apply directly to more elaborate regression models constructed from the GLM family. A prominent example is furnished by the generalized additive models (GAMs). A standard reference for GAMs is Hastie and Tibshirani (1990). The basis of GAMs is the assumption that the data are sampled from a one-parameter exponential family of distributions with log-likelihood of the form (7.6), as for the GLMs. A link function relating the mean μ to the predictor is then specified. More precisely, given a vector $(\boldsymbol{x}, \boldsymbol{w})$ of explanatory variables, where the components of $\boldsymbol{x}$ are continuous and those of $\boldsymbol{w}$ are further binary covariates (coding categorical explanatory variables), and a vector $\boldsymbol{\beta}$ of regression coefficients, the additive predictor takes the form

$$\sum_{j=1}^{p} \psi_j(x_j) + \boldsymbol{w}^t\boldsymbol{\beta}, \tag{7.7}$$

where $\psi_1(\cdot), \ldots, \psi_p(\cdot)$ are unknown smooth functions of the covariates. The score (7.7) is then related to the mean by a function $a(\cdot)$ called the link function, as for GLMs.

7.3.2 *Some examples of interest to actuaries*

7.3.2.1 Claim frequencies

The Poisson law is particularly suitable for modelling claim counts. In this case, the discrete pdf is written as

$$\exp(-\lambda)\frac{\lambda^y}{y!} = \exp\big(-\lambda + y\ln\lambda - \ln y!\big), \quad y \in \mathbb{N}, \quad \lambda > 0.$$

Identifying this expression with the canonical log-likelihood (7.6) yields $\eta = \ln\lambda$, $b(\eta) = \exp(\eta)$, $c(y, \tau) = -\ln y!$, $\tau = 1$, $a(\xi) = \ln\xi$, $v(\mu) = \mu$.

As the Poisson law falls in the GLM class, the results derived in this section will extend those obtained for the Poisson static credibility model of Definition 7.2.1.

7.3.2.2 Loss ratios

The normal law often provides an appropriate model for loss ratios (i.e., the total claims relating to a risk class or to the whole portfolio, divided by the corresponding pure premium). The associated density function is

$$\frac{1}{\sigma\sqrt{2\pi}}\exp\left(-\frac{1}{2\sigma^2}(y-\mu)^2\right) = \exp\left(\frac{y\mu - \frac{\mu^2}{2}}{\sigma^2} - \frac{1}{2\sigma^2}y^2 - \ln(\sigma\sqrt{2\pi})\right)$$

and we have $\eta = \mu$, $b(\eta) = \eta^2/2$, $\tau = \sigma^2$, $a(\xi) = \xi$, $v(\mu) = 1$, $c(y, \tau) = -\frac{1}{2\sigma^2}y^2 - \ln(\sigma\sqrt{2\pi})$.

7.3.2.3 Claim severities

When the distribution of individual claim severities is of interest, the gamma distribution may provide an acceptable model. In a regression approach, this model is desirable since it falls beyond the scope of GLMs. Moreover, it takes into account the non-negativity and the asymmetry of empirical data. The associated pdf can be written as

$$\begin{aligned}&\frac{1}{\Gamma(\vartheta)}y^{\vartheta-1}\left(\frac{\vartheta}{\mu}\right)^{\vartheta}\exp\left(-\frac{\vartheta y}{\mu}\right)\\&= \exp\left(\vartheta\left(-\frac{y}{\mu} - \ln\mu\right) + (\vartheta-1)\ln y + \vartheta\ln\vartheta - \ln\Gamma(\vartheta)\right), \quad y \in \mathbb{R}^+, \quad \vartheta, \mu > 0,\end{aligned}$$

whence we get $\eta = -1/\mu$, $b(\eta) = \ln(-1/\eta)$, $\tau = 1/\vartheta$, $a(\xi) = -1/\xi$, $v(\mu) = \mu^2$, $c(y, \tau) = (\vartheta - 1)\ln y + \vartheta\ln\vartheta - \ln\Gamma(\vartheta)$. The canonical link imposes restrictions on the regressors $\boldsymbol{\beta}$

to ensure the positivity of the mean μ. Therefore, a log link is often advocated in practice. Moreover, when combined with the Poisson model to represent the total burden of claims relating to an individual policy, the gamma specification with the log link produces a multiplicative pure premium, which is useful in practice.

7.3.3 Credibility theory and generalized linear mixed models

Several extensions of GLMs and GAMs involve models with random terms in the linear predictor; in such a case, we speak of generalized linear mixed models (GLMMs). Given an unobserved random effect (Θ_i, say), the T_i observations $Y_{i1}, Y_{i2}, \ldots, Y_{iT_i}$, relating to the ith policy in year $1, 2, \ldots, T_i$, are assumed to be conditionally independent with means that depend on the linear predictor through a specified link function, have conditional variances that are specified by a variance function, and have a scale factor, in the spirit of (7.6).

Definition 7.3.1. Assume now that n random vectors $\boldsymbol{Y}_1, \boldsymbol{Y}_2, \ldots, \boldsymbol{Y}_n$ of respective dimensions $T_1, T_2, \ldots, T_n$ are observed. Each of the vectors relates to one of the policies in the portfolio and summarizes the past claims history of the contract. The $\boldsymbol{Y}_i$ are mutually independent, but their components may be correlated (because of repeated measures on the same policies). GLMMs rely on the following two assumptions:

A1 Given $\Theta_i = \theta_i$, the responses Y_{it}, $t = 1, \ldots, T_i$, are mutually independent and admit a log-likelihood $\ell(\eta_{it}, \tau; y_{it})$ of the form (7.6) where

$$\mu_{it} = \mu_{it}(\theta_i) = \mathbb{E}[Y_{it}|\Theta_i = \theta_i] \text{ and } v_{it} = v_{it}(\theta_i) = \mathbb{V}[Y_{it}|\Theta_i = \theta_i]$$

satisfy $a(\mu_{it}(\theta_i)) = \boldsymbol{\beta}^t \boldsymbol{x}_{it} + \theta_i$ and $v_{it} = v(\mu_{it})\tau$. The $\boldsymbol{x}_{it}$ are known design vectors, $\boldsymbol{\beta}$ is the vector of unknown regression coefficients, $\boldsymbol{\beta}^t \boldsymbol{x}_{it}$ is the score, $a(\cdot)$ and $v(\cdot)$ are known link and variance functions, respectively.

A2 The random effects $\Theta_1, \ldots, \Theta_n$ are mutually independent with a common underlying distribution.

∇

Henceforth, we restrict our study to the special case of the canonical link function, that is, $a(\mu_{it}(\theta_i)) = \eta_{it}$. This does not represent a real loss of generality (since most results in fact rely on the monotonicity of the function $a(\cdot)$) but facilitates the exposition. Moreover, we treat the $\boldsymbol{\beta}^t \boldsymbol{x}_{it}$ as constants.

The random effects are taken such that

$$\mathbb{E}[\mu_{it}(\Theta_i)] = a^{-1}(\boldsymbol{\beta}^t \boldsymbol{x}_{it}).$$

In particular, if $a(\cdot)$ is the log link, then for the Poisson and the gamma distribution, we obtain $\mathbb{E}[\exp(\Theta_i)] = 1$. This condition is important in actuarial practice. It ensures that the a priori rate-making is correct on average: in every risk class, some policyholders pay too much and subsidize other policyholders who are undercharged, but the company gets enough premium for the whole risk class. Statistically speaking such a condition is often necessary for identifiability.

GLMMs are widely used by actuaries, since they form the basis of credibility theory and bonus–malus systems. Building on Lee and Nelder's (1996) work, Nelder and Verrall (1997) showed how credibility theory can be embedded within the theory of GLMMs. In this context, Y_{it} represents the number or amount of claims made by policyholder i in year t. The random effect Θ_i represents hidden features influencing the risk covered by the insurer.

The following property will be useful in the remainder of our work. It states that in model A1–A2 in Definition 7.3.1, all covariates being observed (fixed), the response is $\preceq_{\mathrm{LR}}$-increasing in the random parameter.

Property 7.3.2
In model A1–A2 of Definition 7.3.1, $[Y_{it}|\Theta_i=\theta_i]$ is increasing in θ_i in the $\preceq_{\mathrm{LR}}$ sense, that is,

$$\theta_i \leq \theta_i' \Rightarrow [Y_{it}|\Theta_i=\theta_i] \preceq_{\mathrm{LR}} [Y_{it}|\Theta_i=\theta_i'] \text{ for any } i \text{ and } t.$$

Proof. Let us denote by $f(\cdot;\eta_{it},\tau)$ the (discrete or continuous) pdf of Y_{it}. The ratio of pdfs of the response has the form

$$\frac{f(y;\eta_{it},\tau)}{f(y;\eta_{it}',\tau)}=\exp\left(\frac{y(\eta_{it}-\eta_{it}')-(b(\eta_{it})-b(\eta_{it}'))}{\tau}\right),$$

which is clearly decreasing in y provided $\eta_{it}\leq\eta_{it}'$. We then get the desired result from (3.18). □

Note that the result of Property 7.3.2 is also valid in the gamma case with a log link.

The next property is the multivariate counterpart of Property 7.3.2. It applies in particular to GLMMs. Henceforth, an inequality between two real vectors is interpreted componentwise.

Property 7.3.3
In model A1–A2 of Definition 7.3.1, $[\boldsymbol{Y}_i|\Theta_i=\theta_i]$ is increasing in θ_i in the $\preceq_{\mathrm{LR}}$ sense, that is,

$$\theta_i \leq \theta_i' \Rightarrow [\boldsymbol{Y}_i|\Theta_i=\theta_i] \preceq_{\mathrm{LR}} [\boldsymbol{Y}_i|\Theta_i=\theta_i'].$$

Proof. Under A1–A2, $[\boldsymbol{Y}_i|\Theta_i=\theta_i]$ is a random vector with independent components. Moreover, by virtue of Property 7.3.2, the stochastic inequalities

$$\begin{aligned}
&[Y_{i1}|\Theta_i=\theta_i] \preceq_{\mathrm{LR}} [Y_{i1}|\Theta_i=\theta_i'],\\
&[Y_{i2}|\Theta_i=\theta_i] \preceq_{\mathrm{LR}} [Y_{i2}|\Theta_i=\theta_i'],\\
&\ldots,\\
&[Y_{iT_i}|\Theta_i=\theta_i] \preceq_{\mathrm{LR}} [Y_{iT_i}|\Theta_i=\theta_i']
\end{aligned}$$

hold for any $\theta_i\leq\theta_i'$. Since a comparison in the multivariate $\preceq_{\mathrm{LR}}$ sense reduces to a componentwise $\preceq_{\mathrm{LR}}$-ranking when both random vectors have independent components, we get that $[\boldsymbol{Y}_i|\Theta_i=\theta_i] \preceq_{\mathrm{LR}} [\boldsymbol{Y}_i|\Theta_i=\theta_i']$ holds provided $\theta_i\leq\theta_i'$, as claimed. □

7.3.4 *Exhaustive summary of past claims*

Since the random effect is constant over time, the age of the claims is not taken into account in the prediction. Technically, this is expressed by the fact that the predictive distribution of Θ_i given the past only depends on the sum $Y_{i\bullet}$ of the Y_{it}, and not on the particular values of the Y_{it}. The following result extends Property 7.2.4 established in the Poisson case to the whole class of GLMs.

Property 7.3.4
In model A1–A2 of Definition 7.3.1, the predictive distribution of Θ_i only depends on $Y_{i\bullet} = \sum_{t=1}^{T_i} Y_{it}$.

Proof. Denote by $f_\Theta(\cdot|\boldsymbol{y}_i)$ the conditional pdf of Θ_i given $\boldsymbol{Y}_i = \boldsymbol{y}_i$ and by $f_{it}(\cdot|\theta_i)$ the conditional pdf of Y_{it} given $\Theta_i = \theta_i$. Then we can write

$$f_\Theta(\theta_i|\boldsymbol{y}_i) = \frac{\left(\prod_{t=1}^{T_i} f_{it}(y_{it}|\theta_i)\right) f_\Theta(\theta_i)}{\int_0^{+\infty} \left(\prod_{t=1}^{T_i} f_{it}(y_{it}|\xi)\right) f_\Theta(\xi) d\xi}.$$

Replacing each pdf involved in this ratio with its actual expression yields

$$f_\Theta(\theta_i|\boldsymbol{y}_i) = \frac{\exp\left(\frac{\sum_{t=1}^{T_i}(y_{it}(\boldsymbol{\beta}^t\boldsymbol{x}_{it} + \theta_i) - b(\boldsymbol{\beta}^t\boldsymbol{x}_{it} + \theta_i))}{\tau}\right) f_\Theta(\theta_i)}{\int_0^{+\infty} \exp\left(\frac{\sum_{t=1}^{T_i}(y_{it}(\boldsymbol{\beta}^t\boldsymbol{x}_{it} + \xi) - b(\boldsymbol{\beta}^t\boldsymbol{x}_{it} + \xi))}{\tau}\right) f_\Theta(\xi) d\xi}$$

$$= \frac{\exp\left(\frac{\theta_i y_{i\bullet} - \sum_{t=1}^{T_i} b(\boldsymbol{\beta}^t\boldsymbol{x}_{it} + \theta_i)}{\tau}\right) f_\Theta(\theta_i)}{\int_0^{+\infty} \exp\left(\frac{\xi y_{i\bullet} - \sum_{t=1}^{T_i} b(\boldsymbol{\beta}^t\boldsymbol{x}_{it} + \xi)}{\tau}\right) f_\Theta(\xi) d\xi}$$

which only depends on $y_{i\bullet}$, and concludes the proof. □

7.3.5 A posteriori distribution of the random effects

Let us now consider the posterior distribution of Θ_i given the observations $Y_{i\bullet} = y_{i\bullet}$. We prove the following result, which basically states that observing large outcomes $Y_{i\bullet}$ increases the unobservable latent variables Θ_i (in the $\preceq_{\mathrm{LR}}$ sense).

Proposition 7.3.5
In model A1–A2 of Definition 7.3.1, $[\Theta_i|Y_{i\bullet} = y_{i\bullet}] \preceq_{\mathrm{LR}} [\Theta_i|Y_{i\bullet} = y'_{i\bullet}]$ whenever $y_{i\bullet} \leq y'_{i\bullet}$.

Proof. We know from Property 7.3.4 that we can express the posterior pdf of Θ_i given $Y_{i\bullet} = y_{i\bullet}$ as

$$f_\Theta(\theta_i|\boldsymbol{y}_i) = \frac{h_1(\boldsymbol{y}_i)h_2(\theta_i)\exp\left(\frac{y_{i\bullet}\theta_i}{\tau}\right) g(\theta_i)}{f(\boldsymbol{y}_i)},$$

where

$$h_1(\boldsymbol{y}_i) = \prod_{t=1}^{T_i} \exp(c(y_{it}, \tau)) \exp\left(\frac{y_{it}\boldsymbol{\beta}^t\boldsymbol{x}_{it}}{\tau}\right)$$

and

$$h_2(\theta_i) = \prod_{t=1}^{T_i} \exp\left(\frac{-b(\theta_i + \boldsymbol{\beta}^t \boldsymbol{x}_{it})}{\tau}\right).$$

For $y_{i\bullet} \leq y'_{i\bullet}$ and $\theta_i \leq \theta'_i$, the inequality

$$f_\Theta(\theta_i|\boldsymbol{y}_i)f_\Theta(\theta'_i|\boldsymbol{y}'_i) \geq f_\Theta(\theta'_i|\boldsymbol{y}_i)f_\Theta(\theta_i|\boldsymbol{y}'_i)$$

holds. Indeed, it reduces to

$$\exp\left(\frac{y_{i\bullet}\theta_i}{\tau} + \frac{y'_{i\bullet}\theta'_i}{\tau}\right) \geq \exp\left(\frac{y_{i\bullet}\theta'_i}{\tau} + \frac{y'_{i\bullet}\theta_i}{\tau}\right)$$
$$\Leftrightarrow (\theta'_i - \theta_i)(y'_{i\bullet} - y_{i\bullet}) \geq 0$$

which is obviously true. □

In a Bayesian framework, it is common to predict Θ_i by means of the posterior mean, that is,

$$\widehat{\Theta}_i(\boldsymbol{y}_i) = \mathbb{E}[\Theta_i | Y_{i\bullet} = y_{i\bullet}].$$

This prediction is optimal in the L_2 sense. Specifically, whatever the function g, the minimum of $\mathbb{E}[(\Theta_i - g(Y_{i\bullet}))^2]$ is obtained with $g^*(y_{i\bullet}) = \mathbb{E}[\Theta_i | Y_{i\bullet} = y_{i\bullet}]$. Proposition 7.3.5 ensures, in particular, that $\widehat{\Theta}_i(y_{i\bullet}) \leq \widehat{\Theta}_i(y'_{i\bullet})$ whenever $y_{i\bullet} \leq y'_{i\bullet}$.

7.3.6 Predictive distributions

The very aim of credibility theory is to predict future claim behaviour. In that respect, predictive distributions are of prime interest: these are the distributions of claim characteristics for next year, given past observations. Looking at Y_{iT_i+1}, we get the following result.

Proposition 7.3.6
In model A1–A2 of Definition 7.3.1, $[Y_{iT_i+1} | Y_{i\bullet} = y_{i\bullet}] \preceq_{\text{LR}} [Y_{iT_i+1} | Y_{i\bullet} = y'_{i\bullet}]$ whenever $y_{i\bullet} \leq y'_{i\bullet}$.

Proof. This is a direct consequence of Proposition 3.3.54 together with Proposition 7.3.5. □

7.3.7 Linear credibility premium

7.3.7.1 General principle

Bayesian statistics offers an intellectually acceptable approach to credibility theory. Bayes revision $\mathbb{E}[\Theta_i | Y_{i\bullet}]$ of the heterogeneity component is theoretically very satisfying but is often difficult to compute (except for conjugate distributions). Practical applications involve computer-intensive methods of Markov chain Monte Carlo type (to perform integration with respect to an a posteriori distribution), making more elementary approaches desirable (so that at least a preliminary approximation to the result can be computed). In that respect, the greatest-accuracy credibility approach initiated by Bühlmann (1970) and presented in Kaas *et al.* (2001, Section 7.2) offers a convenient approximation to more sophisticated credibility premiums. Basically, the actuary still resorts to a quadratic loss function but the shape of the credibility predictor is constrained *ex ante* to be linear in past observations, that is, the predictor $\hat{Y}_{iT_i+1}$ of Y_{iT_i+1} is of the form

$$\hat{Y}_{iT_i+1} = c_{i0} + \sum_{t=1}^{T_i} c_{it} Y_{it}.$$

Specifically, we look for c_{i0} and c_{it}, $t=1, \ldots, T_i$, such that the expected squared difference between Y_{iT_i+1} and its predicted value $\hat{Y}_{iT_i+1}$ is minimum:

$$\Psi(\boldsymbol{c}) = \mathbb{E}\left[\left(Y_{iT_i+1} - c_{i0} - \sum_{t=1}^{T_i} c_{it} Y_{it}\right)^2\right].$$

Equating $\partial\Psi(\boldsymbol{c})/\partial c_{i0}$ to 0 yields

$$c_{i0} = \mathbb{E}[Y_{iT_i+1}] - \sum_{t=1}^{T_i} c_{it}\mathbb{E}[Y_{it}]. \tag{7.8}$$

Next, $\partial\Psi(\boldsymbol{c})/\partial c_{is} = 0$ gives

$$\mathbb{E}[Y_{iT_i+1}Y_{is}] = c_{i0}\mathbb{E}[Y_{is}] + \sum_{t=1}^{T_i} c_{it}\mathbb{E}[Y_{it}Y_{is}],$$

where we insert (7.8) to get

$$\mathbb{C}[Y_{iT_i+1}, Y_{is}] = \sum_{t=1}^{T_i} c_{it}\mathbb{C}[Y_{it}, Y_{is}]. \tag{7.9}$$

In model A1–A2 of Definition 7.3.1, we can write for $s \neq t$, using Property 1.8.2(i),

$$\begin{aligned}\mathbb{C}[Y_{it}, Y_{is}] &= \mathbb{E}\Big[\mathbb{C}[Y_{it}, Y_{is}|\Theta_i]\Big] + \mathbb{C}\Big[\mathbb{E}[Y_{it}|\Theta_i], \mathbb{E}[Y_{is}|\Theta_i]\Big]\\ &= \mathbb{C}[\mu_{it}(\Theta_i), \mu_{is}(\Theta_i)]\end{aligned}$$

whereas, still from Property 1.8.2,

$$\begin{aligned}\mathbb{V}[Y_{is}] &= \mathbb{E}\Big[\mathbb{V}[Y_{is}|\Theta_i]\Big] + \mathbb{V}\Big[\mathbb{E}[Y_{is}|\Theta_i]\Big]\\ &= \tau\mathbb{E}[v_{is}(\Theta_i)] + \mathbb{V}\Big[\mu_{is}(\Theta_i)\Big]\end{aligned}$$

so that (7.9) becomes

$$\mathbb{C}[\mu_{iT_i+1}(\Theta_i), \mu_{is}(\Theta_i)] = \tau c_{is}\mathbb{E}[v_{is}(\Theta_i)] + \sum_{t=1}^{T_i} c_{it}\mathbb{C}[\mu_{it}(\Theta_i), \mu_{is}(\Theta_i)]. \tag{7.10}$$

Let us now examine what we get from (7.10) in three examples of interest.

7.3.7.2 The Poisson case

In this case, we have $\mu_{it}(\theta_i) = \exp(\boldsymbol{\beta}'\boldsymbol{x}_{it} + \theta_i)$, $\tau = 1$ and $v_{is}(\theta_i) = \exp(\boldsymbol{\beta}'\boldsymbol{x}_{is} + \theta_i)$, so that the system (7.10) becomes

$$
\begin{aligned}
&\exp(\boldsymbol{\beta}'\boldsymbol{x}_{iT_i+1})\exp(\boldsymbol{\beta}'\boldsymbol{x}_{is})\mathbb{V}[\exp(\Theta_i)] \\
&\quad = c_{is}\mathbb{E}[\exp(\boldsymbol{\beta}'\boldsymbol{x}_{is} + \Theta_i)] + \sum_{t=1}^{T_i} c_{it}\mathbb{C}[\exp(\boldsymbol{\beta}'\boldsymbol{x}_{it} + \Theta_i), \exp(\boldsymbol{\beta}'\boldsymbol{x}_{is} + \Theta_i)] \\
&\quad = c_{is}\exp(\boldsymbol{\beta}'\boldsymbol{x}_{is}) + \exp(\boldsymbol{\beta}'\boldsymbol{x}_{is})\mathbb{V}[\exp(\Theta_i)]\sum_{t=1}^{T_i} c_{it}\exp(\boldsymbol{\beta}'\boldsymbol{x}_{it}) \\
&\quad \Rightarrow \exp(\boldsymbol{\beta}'\boldsymbol{x}_{iT_i+1})\mathbb{V}[\exp(\Theta_i)] = c_{is} + \mathbb{V}[\exp(\Theta_i)]\sum_{t=1}^{T_i} c_{it}\exp(\boldsymbol{\beta}'\boldsymbol{x}_{it}).
\end{aligned}
$$

This yields $c_{is} = c_i$ for all $s = 1, \ldots, T_i$, and

$$
\begin{aligned}
c_i &= \frac{\exp(\boldsymbol{\beta}'\boldsymbol{x}_{iT_i+1})\mathbb{V}[\exp(\Theta_i)]}{1 + \mathbb{V}[\exp(\Theta_i)]\sum_{t=1}^{T_i}\exp(\boldsymbol{\beta}'\boldsymbol{x}_{it})}, \\
c_{i0} &= \exp(\boldsymbol{\beta}'\boldsymbol{x}_{iT_i+1}) - \frac{\exp(\boldsymbol{\beta}'\boldsymbol{x}_{iT_i+1})\mathbb{V}[\exp(\Theta_i)]}{1 + \mathbb{V}[\exp(\Theta_i)]\sum_{t=1}^{T_i}\exp(\boldsymbol{\beta}'\boldsymbol{x}_{it})}\sum_{t=1}^{T_i}\exp(\boldsymbol{\beta}'\boldsymbol{x}_{it}) \\
&= \frac{\exp(\boldsymbol{\beta}'\boldsymbol{x}_{iT_i+1})}{1 + \mathbb{V}[\exp(\Theta_i)]\sum_{t=1}^{T_i}\exp(\boldsymbol{\beta}'\boldsymbol{x}_{it})}.
\end{aligned}
$$

The Bühlmann linear credibility premium for year $T_i + 1$ thus equals

$$
\exp(\boldsymbol{\beta}'\boldsymbol{x}_{iT_i+1})\frac{1 + \mathbb{V}[\exp(\Theta_i)]\sum_{t=1}^{T_i} Y_{it}}{1 + \mathbb{V}[\exp(\Theta_i)]\sum_{t=1}^{T_i}\exp(\boldsymbol{\beta}'\boldsymbol{x}_{it})}
$$

which appears as the product of the a priori premium $\exp(\boldsymbol{\beta}'\boldsymbol{x}_{iT_i+1})$ and an approximation of the theoretical bonus–malus coefficient $\mathbb{E}[\exp(\Theta_i)|Y_{i1}, \ldots, Y_{iT_i}]$. This approximation possesses a particularly simple interpretation since it entails a malus when $\sum_{t=1}^{T_i} Y_{it} > \sum_{t=1}^{T_i}\exp(\boldsymbol{\beta}'\boldsymbol{x}_{it})$, that is, if the policyholder made more claims than expected a priori.

7.3.7.3 The normal case

In this case, we get $\mu_{it}(\theta_i) = \boldsymbol{\beta}'\boldsymbol{x}_{it} + \theta_i$, $\tau = \sigma^2$ and $v(\theta_i) = 1$, so that the system (7.10) becomes

$$
\mathbb{V}[\Theta_i] = \sigma^2 c_{is} + \mathbb{V}[\Theta_i]\sum_{t=1}^{T_i} c_{it}
$$

whence it follows that $c_{is} = c_i$ for all $s = 1, \ldots, T_i$, and

$$c_i = \frac{\mathbb{V}[\Theta_i]}{\sigma^2 + \mathbb{V}[\Theta_i]T_i},$$

$$c_{i0} = \boldsymbol{\beta}^t \boldsymbol{x}_{iT_i+1} - \frac{\mathbb{V}[\Theta_i]}{\sigma^2 + \mathbb{V}[\Theta_i]T_i} \sum_{t=1}^{T_i} \boldsymbol{\beta}^t \boldsymbol{x}_{it}.$$

The Bühlmann credibility linear premium for year $T_i + 1$ now equals

$$\boldsymbol{\beta}^t \boldsymbol{x}_{iT_i+1} + \frac{\mathbb{V}[\Theta_i]}{\sigma^2 + T_i \mathbb{V}[\Theta_i]} \sum_{t=1}^{T_i} \big(Y_{it} - \boldsymbol{\beta}^t \boldsymbol{x}_{it}\big).$$

This can be seen as a correction of the a priori premium $\boldsymbol{\beta}^t \boldsymbol{x}_{iT_i+1}$ according to the value of the difference $Y_{it} - \boldsymbol{\beta}^t \boldsymbol{x}_{it}$ between the observed outcome and its a priori expectation.

7.3.7.4 The gamma case

In this case, with a log link, we have $\ln \mu_{it} = \boldsymbol{\beta}^t \boldsymbol{x}_{it} + \theta_i$, $\tau = 1/\vartheta$ and $v_{is}(\theta_i) = \exp(2\boldsymbol{\beta}^t \boldsymbol{x}_{is} + 2\theta_i)$. Therefore the system (7.10) becomes:

$$\begin{aligned}
&\exp(\boldsymbol{\beta}^t \boldsymbol{x}_{iT_i+1}) \exp(\boldsymbol{\beta}^t \boldsymbol{x}_{is}) \mathbb{V}[\exp(\Theta_i)] \\
&= \vartheta^{-1} c_{is} \exp(2\boldsymbol{\beta}^t \boldsymbol{x}_{is}) \mathbb{E}[\exp(2\Theta_i)] \\
&\quad + \sum_{t=1}^{T_i} c_{it} \exp(\boldsymbol{\beta}^t \boldsymbol{x}_{it}) \exp(\boldsymbol{\beta}^t \boldsymbol{x}_{is}) \mathbb{V}[\exp(\Theta_i)] \\
&= \vartheta^{-1} c_{is} \exp(2\boldsymbol{\beta}^t \boldsymbol{x}_{is}) \big(\mathbb{V}[\exp(\Theta_i)] + 1\big) \\
&\quad + \exp(\boldsymbol{\beta}^t \boldsymbol{x}_{is}) \mathbb{V}[\exp(\Theta_i)] \sum_{t=1}^{T_i} c_{it} \exp(\boldsymbol{\beta}^t \boldsymbol{x}_{it}).
\end{aligned}$$

It follows that

$$\begin{aligned}
\exp(\eta_{iT_i+1}) \mathbb{V}[\exp(\Theta_i)] = {} & \vartheta^{-1} c_{is} \exp(\boldsymbol{\beta}^t \boldsymbol{x}_{is}) \big(\mathbb{V}[\exp(\Theta_i)] + 1\big) \\
& + \mathbb{V}[\exp(\Theta_i)] \sum_{t=1}^{T_i} c_{it} \exp(\boldsymbol{\beta}^t \boldsymbol{x}_{it}).
\end{aligned}$$

By summing both sides over s we obtain:

$$\sum_{t=1}^{T_i} c_{it} \exp(\boldsymbol{\beta}^t \boldsymbol{x}_{it}) = \frac{T_i \exp(\boldsymbol{\beta}^t \boldsymbol{x}_{it}) \mathbb{V}[\exp(\Theta_i)]}{\vartheta^{-1}\big(\mathbb{V}[\exp(\Theta_i)] + 1\big) + T_i \mathbb{V}[\exp(\Theta_i)]}.$$

This yields

$$c_{is} = \frac{\exp(\boldsymbol{\beta}^t \boldsymbol{x}_{iT_i+1}) \mathbb{V}[\exp(\Theta_i)]}{\exp(\boldsymbol{\beta}^t \boldsymbol{x}_{is})\Big(\vartheta^{-1}\big(\mathbb{V}[\exp(\Theta_i)] + 1\big) + T_i \mathbb{V}[\exp(\Theta_i)]\Big)},$$

$$
\begin{aligned}
c_{i0} &= \exp(\boldsymbol{\beta}^t \boldsymbol{x}_{iT_i+1}) - \frac{T_i \exp(\boldsymbol{\beta}^t \boldsymbol{x}_{iT_i+1}) \mathbb{V}[\exp(\Theta_i)]}{\vartheta^{-1}\big(\mathbb{V}[\exp(\Theta_i)] + 1\big) + T_i \mathbb{V}[\exp(\Theta_i)]} \\
&= \frac{\vartheta^{-1} \exp(\boldsymbol{\beta}^t \boldsymbol{x}_{iT_i+1})\big(\mathbb{V}[\exp(\Theta_i)] + 1\big)}{\vartheta^{-1}\big(\mathbb{V}[\exp(\Theta_i)] + 1\big) + T_i \mathbb{V}[\exp(\Theta_i)]}.
\end{aligned}
$$

Thus the Bühlmann linear credibility premium for year $T_i + 1$ equals

$$
\begin{aligned}
&\frac{\exp(\boldsymbol{\beta}^t \boldsymbol{x}_{iT_i+1})}{\vartheta^{-1}\big(\mathbb{V}[\exp(\Theta_i)] + 1\big) + T_i \mathbb{V}[\exp(\Theta_i)]} \\
&\quad \times \left(\vartheta^{-1}\big(\mathbb{V}[\exp(\Theta_i)] + 1\big) + \mathbb{V}[\exp(\Theta_i)] \sum_{t=1}^{T_i} \frac{Y_{it}}{\exp(\boldsymbol{\beta}^t \boldsymbol{x}_{it})} \right) \\
&= \exp(\boldsymbol{\beta}^t \boldsymbol{x}_{iT_i+1}) \left(1 + \frac{\mathbb{V}[\exp(\Theta_i)]}{\vartheta^{-1}\big(\mathbb{V}[\exp(\Theta_i)] + 1\big) + T_i \mathbb{V}[\exp(\Theta_i)]} \sum_{t=1}^{T_i} \left(\frac{Y_{it}}{\exp(\boldsymbol{\beta}^t \boldsymbol{x}_{it})} - 1 \right) \right).
\end{aligned}
$$

Again this can be seen as a correction of the a priori premium $\exp(\boldsymbol{\beta}^t \boldsymbol{x}_{iT_i+1})$ according to residuals $\frac{Y_{it}}{\exp(\boldsymbol{\beta}^t \boldsymbol{x}_{it})} - 1$.

It is worth mentioning that in the three cases examined above, we have $c_i \geq 0$ and a linear credibility premium of the form $\pi_{\text{cred}} = c_{i0} + c_i Y_{i\bullet}$ (in the gamma case, we work with the auxiliary variable $\frac{Y_{it}}{\mathbb{E}[Y_{it}]}$).

Remark 7.3.7. A disadvantage of the quadratic loss function is that deviations in both directions are punished in the same way. When the new premium amount is fixed by the insurer, two kinds of errors may arise: either the policyholder is undercharged and the insurance company loses its money or the insured is overcharged and the insurer is at risk of losing the policy. In order to penalize large mistakes to a greater extent, it is usually assumed that the loss function is a non-negative convex function of the error. The loss is zero when no error is made and strictly positive otherwise. In most papers, the loss function is taken to be quadratic. Among other choices are absolute loss and quartic loss; see Lemaire and Vandermeulen (1983). Asymmetric loss functions allow actuaries to reduce the maluses obtained with a quadratic loss, maintaining a financially balanced system. A prominent example is obtained with an exponential loss function. Such loss functions were first proposed by Ferreira (1977) and Lemaire (1979) in the classical credibility setting. See Bermúdez, Denuit and Dhaene (2001) and Denuit and Dhaene (2001) for more details. ∇

7.3.7.5 Increasingness in the linear credibility model

The present section aims to show that Bühlmann's premium π_{cred} is indeed a good predictor of future claims characteristics (number or amount) in model A1–A2 of Definition 7.3.1. Basically, we prove that increasing the linear credibility premium (i.e., worsening the claim record of the policyholder) increases the probability of observing more important losses in the future.

The next result shows that Y_{iT_i+1} is indeed increasing in π_{cred}.

Proposition 7.3.8
In model A1–A2 of Definition 7.3.1, $[Y_{iT_i+1}|\pi_{\text{cred}}=p]\preceq_{\text{LR}}[Y_{iT_i+1}|\pi_{\text{cred}}=p']$ whenever $p\leq p'$.

Proof. The result follows directly from Proposition 7.3.6 since

$$\begin{aligned}[Y_{iT_i+1}|\pi_{\text{cred}}=p] &=_d \left[Y_{iT_i+1}\middle|Y_{i\bullet}=\frac{p-c_{i0}}{c_i}\right]\\ &\preceq_{\text{LR}}\left[Y_{iT_i+1}\middle|Y_{i\bullet}=\frac{p'-c_{i0}}{c_i}\right]\\ &=_d [Y_{iT_i+1}|\pi_{\text{cred}}=p'].\end{aligned}$$

□

7.4 MORE RESULTS FOR THE DYNAMIC CREDIBILITY MODELS

7.4.1 Dynamic credibility models and generalized linear mixed models

Let us now consider a vector of random effects instead of a single one. This allows for modelling the dependence in longitudinal studies or the correlation arising from covariates that are omitted or inadequately measured. The motivation for allowing random effects that develop over time is the same as for the Poisson dynamic credibility models.

Definition 7.4.1. Given an unobserved vector of random effects $\boldsymbol{\Theta}_i=(\Theta_{i1},\Theta_{i2}\ldots\Theta_{iT_i})$, say, the T_i observations $Y_{i1},Y_{i2},\ldots,Y_{iT_i}$ relating to the ith subject are assumed to be conditionally independent. The n random vectors $\boldsymbol{Y}_1,\boldsymbol{Y}_2,\ldots,\boldsymbol{Y}_n$ are assumed to be mutually independent, but their components may be correlated (because of repeated measures on the same individuals). Dynamic credibility models built on GLMMs rely on the following two assumptions:

A1 Given $\boldsymbol{\Theta}_i=\boldsymbol{\theta}_i$, the responses Y_{it}, $t=1,\ldots,T_i$, are mutually independent and admit a log-likelihood $\ell(\eta_{it},\tau;y_{it})$ of the form (7.6) where

$$\mu_{it}(\theta_{it})=\mathbb{E}[Y_{it}|\Theta_{it}=\theta_{it}] \text{ and} v_{it}=\mathbb{V}[Y_{it}|\Theta_{it}=\theta_{it}]$$

satisfy $a(\mu_{it}(\theta_{it}))=\boldsymbol{\beta}^t\boldsymbol{x}_{it}+\theta_{it}$ and $v_{it}=v(\mu_{it})\tau$, where $a(\cdot)$ and $v(\cdot)$ are known link and variance functions, respectively.

A2 The vectors of random effects $\boldsymbol{\Theta}_1,\ldots,\boldsymbol{\Theta}_m$ are mutually independent with a common underlying multivariate distribution.

∇

Henceforth, we restrict our study to the special case of the canonical link function, $a(\mu_{it}(\theta_{it}))=\eta_{it}$. This does not really restrict the generality of our results (most of them relying on the monotonicity of the function $a(\cdot)$) but greatly facilitates the exposition. Moreover, we treat $\boldsymbol{\beta}^t\boldsymbol{x}_{it}$ as a constant.

Often, the $\boldsymbol{\Theta}_i$ are assumed to have the multivariate normal distribution $\mathcal{N}or(\boldsymbol{\mu},\boldsymbol{\Sigma})$ with covariance matrix $\boldsymbol{\Sigma}$ featuring the temporal dependence. Classical autoregressive moving average models are often used for $\boldsymbol{\Theta}_i$. Let us describe a couple of examples. The first is the analogue of model A5 in the Poisson dynamic credibility models, whereas the second extends model A6 of the Poisson dynamic credibility models to the GLMM case.

Example 7.4.2. (Dynamic credibility with AR1 random effects). A particularly simple and efficient dynamic credibility model is obtained by assuming that $\boldsymbol{\Theta}_i$ has an autoregressive structure of order 1, that is,

$$\Theta_{it} = \varrho \Theta_{i,t-1} + \epsilon_{it}, \quad t \geq 2,$$

where $\epsilon_{it} \sim \mathcal{N}or(0, \sigma^2(1-\rho^2))$ are independent, $|\varrho| < 1$, and $\epsilon_{i1} \sim \mathcal{N}or(0, \sigma^2)$. In this model, the heterogeneity Θ_{it} for period t is influenced by the preceding period $\Theta_{i,t-1}$ but also has its own characteristics ϵ_{it}. ∇

Example 7.4.3. (Dynamic credibility with exchangeable random effects). Another model (see Pinquet 2000) postulates that there is a static baseline heterogeneity R_i for policyholder i which is perturbed by independent and identically distributed annual effects $S_{i1}, S_{i2}, \ldots, S_{iT_i}$. Specifically, $\Theta_{it} = R_i + S_{it}$ where the S_{it} are independent and identically distributed, and independent of R_i, and they all have normal distributions. ∇

We restrict our attention to these particular cases in this section since they turn out to be the most important for applications. Most results derived in this section nevertheless remain valid for other appropriate choices of distributions.

The following property will be useful in the remainder of this section.

Property 7.4.4
In model A1–A2 of Definition 7.4.1, $[Y_{it}|\Theta_{it} = \theta_{it}]$ is increasing in θ_{it} in the $\preceq_{\text{LR}}$ sense, that is,

$$\theta_{it} \leq \theta'_{it} \Rightarrow [Y_{it}|\Theta_{it} = \theta_{it}] \preceq_{\text{LR}} [Y_{it}|\Theta_{it} = \theta'_{it}] \text{ for any } i \text{ and } t.$$

Proof. The reasoning is similar to that used in the proof of Property 7.3.2. □

The next property is the multivariate counterpart of Property 7.4.4.

Property 7.4.5
In model A1–A2 of Definition 7.4.1, $[\boldsymbol{Y}_i|\boldsymbol{\Theta}_i = \boldsymbol{\theta}_i]$ is increasing in $\boldsymbol{\theta}_i$ in the $\preceq_{\text{LR}}$ sense, that is,

$$\boldsymbol{\theta}_i \leq \boldsymbol{\theta}'_i \Rightarrow [\boldsymbol{Y}_i|\boldsymbol{\Theta}_i = \boldsymbol{\theta}_i] \preceq_{\text{LR}} [\boldsymbol{Y}_i|\boldsymbol{\Theta}_i = \boldsymbol{\theta}'_i] \text{ for any } i.$$

Proof. The proof is similar to that of Property 7.3.3. □

7.4.2 Dependence in GLMM-based credibility models

Our aim is to show that in many cases GLMMs induce positive dependence between the Y_{it}, in the sense that 'large' (or 'small') values of the rvs tend to occur together. This is formally stated in the next result, which uses the increasingness of the conditional distribution in the mixing parameter established in Properties 7.4.4 and 7.4.5.

Proposition 7.4.6
In model A1–A2 of Definition 7.4.1,

(i) $\boldsymbol{\Theta}_i$ associated $\Rightarrow \boldsymbol{Y}_i$ associated;

(ii) $\boldsymbol{\Theta}_i$ $\text{MTP}_2 \Rightarrow \boldsymbol{Y}_i$ MTP_2.

Proof. Implication (i) is a direct consequence of Property 7.2.17 together with Property 7.4.5 (remember that $\preceq_{\text{LR}} \Rightarrow \preceq_{\text{ST}}$). Implication (ii) results from Property 7.2.17 combined with Property 7.4.4. □

Let us now illustrate the usefulness of the results of Proposition 7.4.6 in actuarial problems.

Corollary 7.4.7
If $\boldsymbol{\Theta}_i$ is multivariate normal with covariance matrix $\boldsymbol{\Sigma}$ then Example 7.2.9 ensures that $\sigma_{st} \geq 0$ for all s, t implies that $\boldsymbol{\Theta}_i$ is associated. Then Proposition 7.4.6(i) ensures that in this case $\boldsymbol{Y}_i$ is associated.

Further, provided $\boldsymbol{\Sigma}$ is invertible (denote by $\boldsymbol{R}$ its inverse, i.e., $\boldsymbol{R} = \{r_{st}\} = \boldsymbol{\Sigma}^{-1}$), we know from Example 5.3.34 that $r_{st} \leq 0$ for all $s \neq t$ implies that $\boldsymbol{\Theta}_i$ is MTP_2. Then, Proposition 7.4.6(ii) ensures that $\boldsymbol{Y}_i$ is MTP_2.

Let us now examine the particular cases described in Examples 7.4.2 and 7.4.3.

Example 7.4.8. (Credibility with AR1 random effects). We know from the Poisson dynamic credibility model A5 that $\varrho \geq 0$ implies that $\boldsymbol{\Theta}_i$ is MTP_2, which in turn ensures that $\boldsymbol{Y}_i$ is MTP_2 by virtue of Proposition 7.4.6(ii). ∇

Example 7.4.9. (Credibility with exchangeable random effects). We know from the Poisson dynamic credibility model A6 that $\boldsymbol{\Theta}_i$ (where $\Theta_{it} = R_i + S_{it}$) is MTP_2. In this case, too, $\boldsymbol{Y}_i$ is MTP_2 in view of Proposition 7.4.6(ii). ∇

7.4.3 *A posteriori* distribution of the random effects

Consider the posterior distribution of $\boldsymbol{\Theta}_i$ given the observations $\boldsymbol{Y}_i = \boldsymbol{y}_i$, denoted by $f_{\boldsymbol{\Theta}}(\cdot|\boldsymbol{y}_i)$. Let us prove the following result, which basically states that observing large outcomes $\boldsymbol{Y}_i$ increases unobservable latent variables (in the $\preceq_{\text{LR}}$ sense).

Proposition 7.4.10
In model A1–A2 of Definition 7.4.1, $[\boldsymbol{\Theta}_i|\boldsymbol{Y}_i = \boldsymbol{y}_i] \preceq_{\text{LR}} [\boldsymbol{\Theta}_i|\boldsymbol{Y}_i = \boldsymbol{y}'_i]$ whenever $\boldsymbol{y}_i \leq \boldsymbol{y}'_i$.

Proof. The posterior probability density function of $\boldsymbol{\Theta}_i$ given $\boldsymbol{Y}_i = \boldsymbol{y}_i$ can be written as

$$f_{\boldsymbol{\Theta}}(\boldsymbol{\theta}_i|\boldsymbol{y}_i) = \frac{h_1(\boldsymbol{y}_i)h_2(\boldsymbol{\theta}_i)\left(\prod_{j=1}^{n_i} \exp\left(\frac{y_{ij}\theta_{ij}}{\tau}\right)\right) f_{\boldsymbol{\Theta}}(\boldsymbol{\theta}_i)}{f_{\boldsymbol{Y}}(\boldsymbol{y}_i)}$$

where

$$h_1(\boldsymbol{y}_i)=\prod_{j=1}^{T_i}\exp\left(c(y_{ij},\tau)\right)\exp\left(\frac{y_{ij}\boldsymbol{\beta}^t\boldsymbol{x}_{ij}}{\tau}\right)$$

and

$$h_2(\boldsymbol{\theta}_i)=\prod_{j=1}^{T_i}\exp\left(\frac{-b(\theta_{ij}+\boldsymbol{\beta}^t\boldsymbol{x}_{ij})}{\tau}\right).$$

We must show that for $\boldsymbol{y}_i\leq\boldsymbol{y}_i'$, the inequality

$$f_{\boldsymbol{\Theta}}(\boldsymbol{\theta}_i|\boldsymbol{y}_i)f_{\boldsymbol{\Theta}}(\boldsymbol{\theta}_i'|\boldsymbol{y}_i')\leq f_{\boldsymbol{\Theta}}(\boldsymbol{\theta}_i'\wedge\boldsymbol{\theta}_i|\boldsymbol{y}_i)f_{\boldsymbol{\Theta}}(\boldsymbol{\theta}_i'\vee\boldsymbol{\theta}_i|\boldsymbol{y}_i')$$

holds, which immediately follows from the TP_2 property of the function

$$(y_{ij},\theta_{ij})\mapsto\exp\left(\frac{y_{ij}\theta_{ij}}{\tau}\right)$$

together with Proposition 5.3.33. The proof is now complete. □

In a Bayesian framework, it is common to predict $\boldsymbol{\Theta}_i$ by means of the posterior mean, that is,

$$\widehat{\boldsymbol{\Theta}}_i(\boldsymbol{y}_i)=\mathbb{E}[\boldsymbol{\Theta}_i|\boldsymbol{Y}_i=\boldsymbol{y}_i].$$

Proposition 7.4.10 ensures that $\widehat{\boldsymbol{\Theta}}_i(\boldsymbol{y}_i)\leq\widehat{\boldsymbol{\Theta}}_i(\boldsymbol{y}_i')$ whenever $\boldsymbol{y}_i\leq\boldsymbol{y}_i'$.

7.4.4 Supermodular comparisons

It seems natural to expect that increasing the strength of the positive dependence between the latent Θ_{it} will induce more association between the observed outcomes Y_{it}. This section aims to formalize this intuitive idea. For this purpose, we resort to the supermodular ordering, which will be seen to be an appropriate tool to compare the strength of dependence.

Proposition 7.4.11
In model A1–A2 of Definition 7.4.1, $\boldsymbol{\Theta}_i\preceq_{\text{SM}}\boldsymbol{\Theta}_i'\Rightarrow\boldsymbol{Y}_i\preceq_{\text{SM}}\boldsymbol{Y}_i'$.

Proof. The result follows directly from Property 7.3.2 together with Theorem 4.1(a) in Denuit and Müller (2002). □

Returning to the interpretation of $\preceq_{\text{SM}}$ as a positive dependence order, the statement in Proposition 7.4.11 reads 'more positively dependent Θ_{it} yield more positively dependent Y_{it}, as expected.

Assume that $\boldsymbol{\Theta}_i$ and $\boldsymbol{\Theta}_i'$ both have the multivariate normal distribution, with identical univariate marginals and $\mathbb{C}[\Theta_{is},\Theta_{it}]\leq\mathbb{C}[\Theta_{is}',\Theta_{it}']$ for all $s\neq t$. Then, Theorem 3.13.5 of Müller and Stoyan (2002) ensures that $\boldsymbol{\Theta}_i\preceq_{\text{SM}}\boldsymbol{\Theta}_i'$ and Proposition 7.4.11 in turn yields $\boldsymbol{Y}_i\preceq_{\text{SM}}\boldsymbol{Y}_i'$. The dynamic credibility model thus conforms to intuition: increasing the correlation between each pair of random effects makes the annual claims more dependent.

Let us now examine Example 7.4.2.

Example 7.4.12. (Credibility with AR1 random effects). Since $\mathbb{C}[\Theta_{is}, \Theta_{it}] = \sigma^2 \varrho^{|s-t|}$, Proposition 7.4.11 together with the preceding example ensures that $\varrho \leq \varrho' \Rightarrow \boldsymbol{Y}_i \preceq_{\text{SM}} \boldsymbol{Y}'_i$. In this model, the amount of dependence is thus controlled by the parameter ϱ: a large value of ϱ will increase the importance of past claims history in the determination of future premiums. ∇

7.4.5 *Predictive distributions*

Before studying predictive distributions, let us first examine the monotonicity of a subset of $\boldsymbol{Y}_i$, given the other components.

Proposition 7.4.13
Let $\boldsymbol{Y}_{iJ}$ ($\boldsymbol{Y}_{iK}$) be the random vector with components Y_{ij}, $j \in J$ (Y_{ik}, $k \in K$). In model A1–A2 of Definition 7.4.1, if $\boldsymbol{\Theta}_i$ is MTP_2 then $[\boldsymbol{Y}_{iJ}|\boldsymbol{Y}_{iK} = \boldsymbol{y}_K] \preceq_{\text{LR}} [\boldsymbol{Y}_{iJ}|\boldsymbol{Y}_{iK} = \boldsymbol{y}'_K]$ for any $\boldsymbol{y}_K \leq \boldsymbol{y}'_K \in \mathbb{R}^{\#K}$, for any partition of $\{1, 2, \ldots, T_i\}$ in J and K.

Proof. In view of Proposition 7.4.6(ii), we know that $\boldsymbol{Y}_i$ is MTP_2. Let us denote by $f(\boldsymbol{y}_J|\boldsymbol{y}_K)$ the conditional probability density function of $\boldsymbol{Y}_{iJ}$ given $\boldsymbol{Y}_{iK} = \boldsymbol{y}_K$. We have to prove that

$$f(\boldsymbol{y}_J \wedge \widetilde{\boldsymbol{y}}_J|\boldsymbol{y}_K) f(\boldsymbol{y}_J \vee \widetilde{\boldsymbol{y}}_J|\boldsymbol{y}'_K) \geq f(\boldsymbol{y}_J|\boldsymbol{y}_K) f(\widetilde{\boldsymbol{y}}_J|\boldsymbol{y}'_K)$$

holds for any $\boldsymbol{y}_J, \widetilde{\boldsymbol{y}}_J \in \mathbb{R}^{\#J}$ provided $\boldsymbol{y}'_K \leq \boldsymbol{y}_K$. Since the joint probability density function f of $\boldsymbol{Y}_i$ is MTP_2, we know that

$$f(\boldsymbol{y}_J \wedge \widetilde{\boldsymbol{y}}_J, \boldsymbol{y}_K) f(\boldsymbol{y}_J \vee \widetilde{\boldsymbol{y}}_J, \boldsymbol{y}'_K) \geq f(\boldsymbol{y}_J, \boldsymbol{y}_K) f(\widetilde{\boldsymbol{y}}_J, \boldsymbol{y}'_K)$$

holds, whence the desired inequality follows by dividing each side by $f_K(\boldsymbol{y}_K) f_K(\boldsymbol{y}'_K)$, where f_K is the probability density function of $\boldsymbol{Y}_{iK}$. □

The intuitive explanation behind the results stated in Proposition 7.4.13 is clear: when the components of $\boldsymbol{\Theta}_i$ exhibit strong positive dependence (MTP_2), observing large outcomes for some of the Y_{ij} (those in K) makes the others (those in J) larger (in the $\preceq_{\text{LR}}$ sense).

Let us now apply these results to predictive distributions. The very aim of credibility theory is indeed to predict future claim behaviour. In that respect, predictive distributions are of prime interest: these are the distributions of claim characteristics for next year, given past observations.

If $\boldsymbol{\Theta}_i$ is multivariate normal, provided the covariance matrix $\boldsymbol{\Sigma}$ fulfils the condition of Example 5.3.34 that ensures that $(\Theta_{i1}, \ldots, \Theta_{iT_i}, \Theta_{iT_i+1})$ is MTP_2, we reach the same conclusion as for static credibility models. Again, future claims Y_{iT_i+1} are increasing in the past claims $\boldsymbol{Y}_i$ in the $\preceq_{\text{LR}}$ sense.

Let us now briefly discuss Examples 7.4.2 and 7.4.3.

Example 7.4.14. (Credibility with AR1 random effects). Provided $\varrho \geq 0$, $\boldsymbol{\Theta}_i$ is MTP_2 so Y_{iT_i+1} increases in $\boldsymbol{Y}_i$ in the $\preceq_{\text{LR}}$ sense. ∇

Example 7.4.15. (Credibility with exchangeable random effects). Since $\boldsymbol{\Theta}_i$ is always MTP_2 in this case, the increasingness of the future given the past applies here. ∇

7.5 ON THE DEPENDENCE INDUCED BY BONUS–MALUS SCALES

7.5.1 Experience rating in motor insurance

Rating systems that penalize insureds responsible for one or more accidents by means of premium surcharges (or *maluses*), and that reward claim-free policyholders with discounts (or *bonuses*) are now in force in many countries. Besides encourageing policyholders to drive carefully (i.e., counteracting moral hazard), they aim to better assess individual risks. Such systems are called no-claims discounts, experience rating, merit rating, or bonus–malus systems. They are studied in detail in Kaas *et al.* (2001, Chapter 6); see also Lemaire (1995).

In practice, a bonus–malus system consists of a scale with a finite number of levels, each with its own relative premium. New policyholders enter the scale at a specified level. After each year, the policy moves up or down according to transition rules and to the number of claims at fault. This a posteriori rate-making is a rather efficient way of classifying policyholders according to their risk.

7.5.2 Markov models for bonus-malus system scales

Bonus-malus scales possess a fixed number of levels, $s+1$ say, numbered from 0 to s. A specified level is assigned to a new driver (often according to vehicle use). Each claim-free year is rewarded by a bonus point (i.e., the driver goes one level down). Claims are penalized by malus points (i.e., the driver goes up a certain number of levels each time he files a claim). We assume that the penalty is a given number of classes per claim (k_{pen}, say). After sufficiently many claim-free years, the driver enters level 0 where he benefits from the maximal bonus.

In a commercial bonus–malus system, knowledge of the present level and of the number of claims in the present year suffices to determine the next level. Provided that the annual numbers of claims are independent, this ensures that the system may be represented by a Markov chain: the future (the level for year $t+1$) depends on the present (the level for year t and the number of accidents reported during year t) and not on the past (the complete claim history and the levels occupied in years $1, 2, \ldots, t-1$). Note that fictitious levels sometimes have to be added to fulfil this memorylessness property.

Let us denote by $L_\theta(t)$ the level occupied after t years by a policyholder whose expected annual claim frequency is θ. We then have that

$$\begin{aligned} L_\theta(t) &= \max\left\{0, \min\{L_\theta(t-1) - 1 + N_t \times k_{\text{pen}}, s\}\right\} \\ &= \Psi(N_1, \ldots, N_t) \end{aligned}$$

for some non-decreasing function Ψ, where $N_1, \ldots, N_t$ denote the annual numbers of claims field by this policyholder, which are independently distributed as $\mathcal{P}oi(\theta)$.

The transition matrix $\boldsymbol{M}(\theta)$ associated with the bonus–malus system described above is regular, that is, there exists some integer $\xi_0 \geq 1$ such that all entries of $\{\boldsymbol{M}(\theta)\}^{\xi_0}$ are strictly positive. Consequently, the Markov chain describing the trajectory of a policyholder with expected claim frequency θ accross the levels is ergodic and thus possesses a stationary distribution $\boldsymbol{\pi}(\theta) = (\pi_0(\theta), \pi_1(\theta), \ldots, \pi_s(\theta))^t$; $\pi_\ell(\theta)$ is the stationary probability of a policyholder with mean frequency θ being at level ℓ.

Let us introduce the rv L_θ valued in $\{0, 1, \ldots, s\}$ such that L_θ has distribution $\boldsymbol{\pi}(\theta)$, that is,

$$\Pr[L_\theta = \ell] = \pi_\ell(\theta), \quad \ell = 0, 1, \ldots, s.$$

The variable L_θ thus represents the level occupied by a policyholder with annual expected claim frequency θ once the steady state has been reached.

Let us now pick at random a policyholder from the portfolio that is assumed to be heterogeneous (with respect to annual expected claim frequency), so that the annual expected claim frequency differs from one policyholder to another. Let us denote by Θ the (unknown) annual expected claim frequency of the policyholder selected. The trajectory of this policyholder in the bonus–malus scale is described by the stochastic process $\{L(t), t = 1, 2, \ldots\}$, where $L(t)$ represents the level occupied in year t.

Furthermore, let L be the bonus–malus level occupied by this randomly selected policyholder once the steady state has been reached. The distribution of L can be written as

$$\Pr[L = \ell] = \int_0^{+\infty} \pi_\ell(\theta) f_\Theta(\theta) d\theta. \tag{7.11}$$

7.5.3 *Positive dependence in bonus-malus scales*

Let us start with the following result, which is slightly stronger than Proposition 7.2.24.

Proposition 7.5.1
The random vector $(\Theta, N_1, \ldots, N_T)$ is MTP_2 for any $T \geq 1$.

Proof. The joint pdf for $(\Theta, N_1, \ldots, N_T)$ (with respect to the product measure involving the Lebesgue measure on $\mathbb{R}^+$ and the counting measure on the non-negative integers) is given by

$$\Pr[N_1 = n_1, \ldots, N_T = n_T | \Theta = \theta] f_\Theta(\theta) = \left(\prod_{t=1}^{T} \exp(-\theta) \frac{\theta^{n_t}}{n_t!} \right) f_\Theta(\theta).$$

The result then follows from the fact that the logarithm of the above pdf is supermodular. □

We are now ready to examine the type of dependence existing between the levels occupied in the bonus–malus system.

Proposition 7.5.2

(i) The random vector $(\Theta, L(1), L(2), \ldots, L(T))$ is associated for any $T \geq 1$.

(ii) The random couple $(\Theta, L(t))$ is associated for any t.

(iii) The random couple (Θ, L) is associated.

Proof. We know from Proposition 7.5.1 that $(\Theta, N_1, \ldots, N_T)$ is MTP_2, so that it is also associated. Since non-decreasing functions of associated rvs remain associated, we get (i).

Next, (ii) follows directly from (i) since subsets of associated random vectors remain associated.

Finally, (iii) is a consequence of (ii) since association is preserved under limit with respect to convergence in distribution. □

7.6 CREDIBILITY THEORY AND TIME SERIES FOR NON-NORMAL DATA

7.6.1 The classical actuarial point of view

Actuaries induce serial dependence by letting annual claim characteristics (frequencies or severities) share common random effects. These random effects represent residual heterogeneity: the correlation among annual claim characteristics thus results from omitted explanatory variables and this makes a posteriori corrections of premium amounts necessary. This construction assumes that the dependence is only apparent: if we had complete knowledge about the policyholder then serial correlation would disappear and past claims history would not reveal anything about future accidents.

Until almost the end of the twentieth century, credibility theory largely concentrated on conditional expectations, with particular emphasis on normally distributed processes and linear specifications. When moving beyond conditional expectations, the next step was to consider conditional variance, which has developed a large literature in finance. However, it is most natural to consider the whole conditional distribution and the sequence of predictive distributions. In this respect, the copula construction turns out to be particularly interesting.

7.6.2 Time series models built from copulas

7.6.2.1 Markov processes

Consider an arbitrary state space E, endowed with a sigma-algebra $\mathcal{E}$. The pair $(E, \mathcal{E})$ is a measurable state space. Let us denote by $\mathcal{T} \subseteq \mathbb{R}$ the time space (typically, $\mathcal{T} = \mathbb{N}$ or $\mathcal{T} = \mathbb{R}^+$ in applications).

Definition 7.6.1. A stochastic process $\mathcal{X} = \{X_t, t \in \mathcal{T}\}$ with a measurable state space $(E, \mathcal{E})$ is a Markov process if

$$\Pr[X_{t_k} \in B | X_{t_1}, X_{t_2}, \ldots, X_{t_{k-1}}] = \Pr[X_{t_k} \in B | X_{t_{k-1}}]$$

for all $t_1 < t_2 < \ldots < t_k \in \mathcal{T}$, $k \geq 1$ and $B \in \mathcal{E}$. ∇

7.6.2.2 Copulas and Markov processes

As pointed out by Olsen, Darsow and Nguyen (1996), the key observation is that the derivatives of copulas are related to conditional expectations (see Property 4.2.13).

Let us consider the continuous rvs X_1, X_2 and X_3 with respective dfs F_1, F_2 and F_3. If X_1 and X_3 are conditionally independent given X_2 (think of X_1, X_2 and X_3 as the states occupied at three consecutive instants by the process $\mathcal{X}$) then

$$\Pr[X_1 \leq x_1, X_3 \leq x_3 | X_2 = x_2] = \Pr[X_1 \leq x_1 | X_2 = x_2] \Pr[X_3 \leq x_3 | X_2 = x_2],$$

so that

$$\Pr[X_1 \leq x_1, X_3 \leq x_3] = \int_{-\infty}^{+\infty} \Pr[X_1 \leq x_1 | X_2 = x_2] \Pr[X_3 \leq x_3 | X_2 = x_2] dF_2(x_2).$$

Denoting by C_{ij} the copula for the pair (X_i, X_j), $i < j$, this identity can be restated in terms of copulas as follows:

$$\begin{aligned} C_{13}(F_1(x_1), F_3(x_3)) &= \int_{-\infty}^{+\infty} C_{12}^{(0,1)}(F_1(x_1), F_2(x_2)) C_{23}^{(1,0)}(F_2(x_2), F_3(x_3)) dF_2(x_2) \\ &= \int_0^1 C_{12}^{(0,1)}(F_1(x_1), u_2) C_{23}^{(1,0)}(u_2, F_3(x_3)) du_2 \end{aligned}$$

where

$$C_{ij}^{(0,1)} = \frac{\partial}{\partial u_2} C_{ij}(u_1, u_2) \text{and} C_{ij}^{(1,0)} = \frac{\partial}{\partial u_1} C_{ij}(u_1, u_2).$$

The conditional independence of X_1 and X_3 given X_2 therefore implies the relation

$$C_{13}(u_1, u_3) = \int_0^1 C_{12}^{(0,1)}(u_1, u_2) C_{23}^{(1,0)}(u_2, u_3) du_2, \quad (u_1, u_3) \in [0, 1]^2,$$

between the copulas C_{12}, C_{13} and C_{23}. This leads to a way to state the conditional independence assumption of a real-valued Markov process in terms of the copulas describing the bivariate marginals of the process.

The content of the Chapman–Kolmogorov equations can be stated in terms of the copulas of the process in a particularly simple way.

Proposition 7.6.2
Let $\mathcal{X} = \{X_t, t \in \mathcal{T}\}$ be a stochastic process and let C_{st} denote the copula of X_s and X_t, $s < t \in \mathcal{T}$. The following statements are equivalent:

(i) The transition functions $\Pr[X_t \in B | X_s = x]$, $s \leq t$, satisfy the Chapman–Kolmogorov equations.

(ii) For all $s < u < t$ and for all $(x, y) \in [0, 1]^2$,

$$C_{st}(x, y) = \int_0^1 C_{su}^{(0,1)}(x, t) C_{ut}^{(1,0)}(t, y) dt.$$

A proof of Proposition 7.6.2 is given in Darsow, Nguyen and Olsen (1992). We thus see that copulas capture the dependence structure of real-valued Markov processes in a manner equivalent to that of the Chapman–Kolmogorov equations. Note, however, that they do so without any information about the marginal distributions of the process.

7.6.2.3 Product of copulas and Chapman-Kolmogorov equations

Proposition 7.6.2 motivates the following definition of a product on the set of copulas: for copulas C and $\widetilde{C}$, define

$$C * \widetilde{C}(u_1, u_2) = \int_0^1 C^{(0,1)}(u_1, t)\widetilde{C}^{(1,0)}(t, u_2)dt.$$

The operation $*$ just defined possesses the following properties:

(i) $C * \widetilde{C}$ is a copula;

(ii) $*$ is associative.

Using the $*$ product, condition (ii) of Proposition 7.6.2 can be restated as

$$C_{st} = C_{su} * C_{ut}, \qquad \text{for any } s < u < t.$$

7.6.2.4 Construction of a Markov chain

Let us show how a discrete-time Markov process (i.e., a Markov chain) can be constructed by specifying marginal distributions and copulas. Let $\mathcal{T} = \mathbb{N}$ and construct $\{X_n, n = 1, 2, \ldots\}$ as follows:

1. Assign copulas $C_{n,n+1}$ for the random couple (X_n, X_{n+1}) in any manner.
2. For $k > 1$, define the copula for (X_n, X_{n+k}) as

$$C_{n,n+k} = C_{n,n+1} * C_{n+1,n+2} * \ldots * C_{n+k-1,n+k}.$$

3. Assign continuous marginal dfs F_n to X_n in any manner.
4. Require that the n-dimensional distributions for $n > 2$ satisfy the conditional independence condition for a Markov process.

Observe that the copulas assigned in steps 1 and 2 are those of a Markov process, regardless of what distributions are assigned in step 3 of the construction.

7.6.3 Markov models for random effects

Regarding Poisson dynamic frequency credibility models, specifications A4–A6 in Section 7.2.2 are based on lognormal random effects. Similar specifications have been used in dynamic credibility models based on GLMs. Now, we would also like to be able to specify other distributions for the random effects, such as the gamma law (which facilitates Bayesian analysis of the data). In that respect, the copula construction is of prime interest. In this section, we discuss Markov models for the process $\{\Theta_1, \Theta_2, \ldots\}$ in dynamic credibility models.

By virtue of Sklar's theorem, the joint df H of (Θ_{t-1}, Θ_t) can be represented as

$$\Pr[\Theta_{t-1} \leq \theta_{t-1}, \Theta_t \leq \theta_t] = H(\theta_{t-1}, \theta_t) = C\big(F_\Theta(\theta_{t-1}), F_\Theta(\theta_t)\big),$$

for some copula $C(\cdot, \cdot)$. Note that the stationarity assumption made for the Θ_ts ensures that the copula for the random pair (Θ_{t-1}, Θ_t) does not depend on t. In a constructive approach, inserting any df (e.g., gamma) into some copula $C(\cdot, \cdot)$ (e.g., Clayton, Frank or Gumbel copulas) yields a correlated structure for the Θ_t.

We know from Property 4.2.13 that the conditional df of Θ_t given Θ_{t-1} is given by

$$H(\theta_t|\theta_{t-1}) = \Pr[\Theta_t \leq \theta_t|\Theta_{t-1} = \theta_{t-1}] = C_{2|1}\big(F_\Theta(\theta_t)|F_\Theta(\theta_{t-1})\big)$$

and, if we denote by c the density of the copula C, the conditional pdf of Θ_t given Θ_{t-1} is given by

$$h(\theta_t|\theta_{t-1}) = \frac{\partial}{\partial\theta_t} H(\theta_t|\theta_{t-1}) = c\big(F_\Theta(\theta_{t-1}), F_\Theta(\theta_t)\big) f_\Theta(\theta_t).$$

Bivariate copulas offer a powerful tool to construct autoregressive models for non-Gaussian data. Specifically, selecting some copula C and a marginal df F_Θ, we compute H, and the joint pdf of $\boldsymbol{\Theta}$ is then given by

$$\begin{aligned} f_{\boldsymbol{\Theta}}(\boldsymbol{\theta}) &= f_\Theta(\theta_1)h(\theta_2|\theta_1)\ldots h(\theta_n|\theta_{n-1}) \\ &= \left(\prod_{t=1}^{T} f_\Theta(\theta_t)\right) c\big(F_\Theta(\theta_1), F_\Theta(\theta_2)\big)\ldots c\big(F_\Theta(\theta_{T-1}), F_\Theta(\theta_T)\big). \end{aligned} \tag{7.12}$$

Remark 7.6.3. Note that taking $C(u, v) = \min\{u, v\}$ (i.e., the Fréchet upper bound copula C_U) yields comonotonic random effects, which leads to the static credibility model. ∇

7.6.4 Dependence induced by autoregressive copula models in dynamic frequency credibility models

In the general autoregressive model induced by bivariate copulas C, the dependence structure of $\boldsymbol{Y}_i$ is induced by the properties of C, as expected.

Property 7.6.4
In model A1–A2 of Definition 7.4.1, if the joint pdf of the random effects is of the form (7.12) then $\boldsymbol{Y}_i$ is MTP_2 provided C is TP_2.

Proof. Exploiting the autoregressive of order 1 structure specified in (7.12) yields

$$f_{\boldsymbol{\Theta}_i}(\boldsymbol{\theta}_i) = \left(\prod_{t=1}^{T_i} f_\Theta(\theta_{it})\right) c\big(F_\Theta(\theta_{i1}), F_\Theta(\theta_{i2})\big)\ldots c\big(F_\Theta(\theta_{iT_i-1}), F_\Theta(\theta_{iT_i})\big).$$

If $(u, v) \mapsto c(u, v)$ is TP_2 then $(\theta_{it}, \theta_{it+1}) \mapsto c\big(F_\Theta(\theta_{it}), F_\Theta(\theta_{it+1})\big)$ is also TP_2 so $\boldsymbol{\Theta}_i$ is MTP_2, which concludes the proof. □

Example 7.6.5. Let us give now some prominent examples of copulas that are TP_2 (at least for some values of their parameters), resulting in MTP_2 claim numbers $\boldsymbol{N}_i$:

(i) Frank's copula, TP_2 for $\alpha \geq 0$;

(ii) normal copula, TP_2 for $\alpha \geq 0$;

(iii) Gumbel's copula, TP_2 for $\alpha \geq 1$;

(iv) Clayton's copula, TP_2 for $\alpha > 0$.

∇

7.7 EXERCISES

Exercise 7.7.1. Given $I_1 \sim \mathcal{B}er(q_1)$ and $I_2 \sim \mathcal{B}er(q_2)$, show that the following conditions are equivalent:

(i) $\mathbb{C}[I_1, I_2] \geq 0$;

(ii) $\mathbb{C}[g_1(I_1), g_2(I_2)] \geq 0$ for all non-decreasing g_1 and g_2;

(iii) I_1 and I_2 are associated;

(iv) I_1 and I_2 are CIS.

Exercise 7.7.2. Let $X_1, X_2, \ldots, X_n$ be independent rvs. Let us define the partial sums

$$S_i = \sum_{j=1}^{i} X_j, \quad i = 1, 2, \ldots, n.$$

Show that the vector of the partial sums $(S_1, S_2, \ldots, S_n)$ is associated.

Exercise 7.7.3. Ambagaspitiya (1998) proposed a new family of discrete multivariate distributions representing the number of claims in different classes of business. To be specific, the n-dimensional random vector $\boldsymbol{N}$ is given by

$$\begin{pmatrix} N_1 \\ N_2 \\ \vdots \\ N_n \end{pmatrix} = \begin{pmatrix} a_{11} & a_{12} & \cdots & a_{1k} \\ a_{21} & a_{22} & \cdots & a_{2k} \\ \vdots & \vdots & \ddots & \vdots \\ a_{n1} & a_{n2} & \cdots & a_{nk} \end{pmatrix} \begin{pmatrix} M_1 \\ M_2 \\ \vdots \\ M_k \end{pmatrix},$$

where $a_{ij} \in \mathbb{N}$ for all i and j, and $\boldsymbol{M}$ is a random vector valued in $\mathbb{N}^k$ with independent components. Show that $\boldsymbol{N}$ is associated.

Exercise 7.7.4. Let $\boldsymbol{X}$ and $\boldsymbol{Y}$ be two n-dimensional random vectors with density functions $f_{\boldsymbol{X}}$ and $f_{\boldsymbol{Y}}$, respectively. If $\boldsymbol{X}$ is associated and $f_{\boldsymbol{Y}}(\boldsymbol{x})/f_{\boldsymbol{X}}(\boldsymbol{x})$ is non-decreasing in $\boldsymbol{x}$, show that $\boldsymbol{X} \preceq_{\text{ST}} \boldsymbol{Y}$.

Exercise 7.7.5. Show that the X_i defined in Exercise 5.4.19 are associated.

Exercise 7.7.6. Let Θ be a non-negative rv with positive variance and let Z_1 and Z_2 be independent and identically distributed rvs, independent of Θ. Suppose that $\mathbb{E}[Z_i]=c<0$ and

$$\int_0^{+\infty} z dF_Z(z)=c^+>0.$$

Now, let us define the random couple $\boldsymbol{X}=(X_1, X_2)$ as $X_i=Z_i\Theta$, $i=1,2$. Show that X_1 and X_2 are dependent by mixture but not associated.

Exercise 7.7.7. Let $\boldsymbol{X}$ be dependent by mixture, with $F_i(\cdot|\theta)\equiv F(\cdot|\theta)$. Show, for any function g, that $\mathbb{C}[g(X_i), g(X_j)]\geq 0$.

Exercise 7.7.8. Let Z_1 and Z_2 be two independent risks. Given a positive non-degenerate rv Θ, independent of both Z_1 and Z_2, define

$$X_1=\frac{Z_1}{\Theta} \text{ and} X_2=Z_2\Theta;$$

X_1 and X_2 are obviously dependent by mixture. Show, however, that $X_1^{\perp}+X_2^{\perp}\preceq_{\text{SL},=}X_1+X_2$ cannot hold.

Exercise 7.7.9. In some cases, negative dependence is also of interest in actuarial applications. The random vector $\boldsymbol{X}$ is said to be negatively associated if, for every subset $A\subseteq\{1,2,\ldots,n\}$,

$$\mathbb{C}[\Psi_1(X_i, i\in A), \Psi_2(X_i, i\in \overline{A})]\leq 0$$

whenever Ψ_1 and Ψ_2 are non-decreasing.

(i) Show that a pair $\boldsymbol{X}=(X_1, X_2)$ of rvs is negatively associated if, and only if, the inequality

$$\Pr[X_1\leq x_1, X_2\leq x_2]\leq \Pr[X_1\leq x_1]\Pr[X_2\leq x_2]$$

holds for all $x_1, x_2\in\mathbb{R}$, that is, $\boldsymbol{X}$ is negatively quadrant dependent.

(ii) Show that, for disjoint subsets $A_1, A_2, \ldots, A_m$ of $\{1,2,\ldots,n\}$ and non-decreasing positive functions $\Psi_1, \Psi_2, \ldots, \Psi_m$, if $\boldsymbol{X}$ is negatively associated then

$$\mathbb{E}\left[\prod_{i=1}^m \Psi_i(X_j, j\in A_i)\right]\leq \prod_{i=1}^m \mathbb{E}[\Psi_i(X_j, j\in A_i)].$$

(iii) Show that if $\boldsymbol{X}$ is negatively associated then $\boldsymbol{X}$ is negatively lower orthant dependent and negatively upper orthant dependent, that is, the inequalities

$$\Pr[\boldsymbol{X}\leq \boldsymbol{x}]\leq \prod_{i=1}^n \Pr[X_i\leq x_i] \text{ and } \Pr[\boldsymbol{X}>\boldsymbol{x}]\leq \prod_{i=1}^n \Pr[X_i>x_i]$$

hold for all $\boldsymbol{x}\in\mathbb{R}^n$.

(iv) Show that any subset of negatively associated rvs is negatively associated.

(v) Show that if $\boldsymbol{X}$ has independent components then $\boldsymbol{X}$ is negatively associated.

(vi) Show that if $\boldsymbol{X}$ is negatively associated, $\boldsymbol{Y}$ is negatively associated and $\boldsymbol{X}$ and $\boldsymbol{Y}$ are independent, then $(\boldsymbol{X}, \boldsymbol{Y})$ is negatively associated.

(vii) Let $X_1, X_2, \ldots, X_n$ be independent rvs and suppose that

$$\mathbb{E}\left[\Psi(X_i, i \in A) \middle| \sum_{i\in A} X_i = s\right]$$

is non-decreasing in s for every non-decreasing Ψ and every $A \subseteq \{1, 2, \ldots, n\}$. Show that the conditional distribution of $[\boldsymbol{X} | \sum_{i=1}^n X_i = s]$ is negatively associated for all s.

(viii) Let $X_1, X_2, \ldots, X_n$ be independent rvs with log-concave densities. Show that the conditional distribution of $[\boldsymbol{X}|S = s]$ is negatively associated for all s.

Exercise 7.7.10. A permutation distribution is the joint distribution of the vector $\boldsymbol{X}$ which takes as values all permutations of $\boldsymbol{x}$ with equal probability $\frac{1}{n!}$. Show that every permutation distribution is negatively associated.

Exercise 7.7.11. Recall that $\boldsymbol{X}$ obeys the multinomial distribution with parameters $(n, p_1, p_2, \ldots, p_n)$, with integer $n \geq 1$, $p_i \geq 0$ and $0 < \sum_{i=1}^n p_i < 1$, if

$$\Pr[\boldsymbol{X} = \boldsymbol{x}] = \frac{n!}{x_1!x_2!\ldots x_n!(n - \sum_{i=1}^n x_i)!} \prod_{i=1}^n p_i^{x_i} \left(1 - \sum_{i=1}^n p_i\right)^{n-\sum_{i=1}^n x_i},$$

where $\boldsymbol{x} \in \mathbb{N}^{n+1}$ is such that $\sum_{i=1}^n x_i \leq n$. Show that $\boldsymbol{X}$ is negatively associated.

Exercise 7.7.12. Prove that the rvs X_1 and X_2 of Example 4.1.1 are associated. *Hint*: use Proposition 7.2.7.

Exercise 7.7.13. Show that the order statistics $X_{(1)} \leq X_{(2)} \leq \ldots X_{(n)}$ related to n independent and identically distributed rvs $X_1, X_2, \ldots, X_n$ are associated, whatever the underlying distribution.

Exercise 7.7.14. Let $X_1, X_2, X_3, \ldots$ denote the claims of a collection of risks and let N describe the number of claims. The claim severities are ordered in decreasing size, resulting in $X_{N:1} \geq X_{N:2} \geq \ldots \geq X_{N:N}$. Let $c_1, c_2, c_3, \ldots$ be non-negative constants such that

$$\sum_{i=1}^n c_i y_i \in \left[0, \sum_{i=1}^n y_i\right]$$

holds for all $y_1 \geq y_2 \geq \ldots \geq y_n \geq 0$. In generalized largest claims reinsurance cover, introduced by Kremer (1985, 1998), the claim amount taken by the reinsurer is

$$S_N = \sum_{i=1}^N c_i X_{N:i}.$$

The net premium is $\pi(\boldsymbol{c}) = \mathbb{E}[S_N]$.

(i) Assume the the common df F_X of the X_i is continuous. Show that if

A1 the claim sizes are independent and identically distributed,

A2 the claim frequency N is independent of the claim sizes,

then

$$\pi(\boldsymbol{c}) = \sum_{i=1}^{+\infty} \frac{c_i}{(i-1)!} \int_0^1 F_X^{-1}(p)(1-p)^{i-1} \varphi_N^{(i)}(p)dp, \tag{7.13}$$

where $\varphi_N^{(i)}$ is the ith derivative of the pgf $\varphi_N(s) = \sum_{n=0}^{+\infty} \Pr[N=n]s^n$ of N.

(ii) Show that if A1 is weakened as

A1′ the claim sizes are identically distributed, but possibly dependent,

then

$$\pi(\boldsymbol{c}) \leq \mathbb{E}[X_1]\left(\sum_{m=1}^{+\infty} \frac{c_m}{m} \sum_{n=m}^{+\infty} n\Pr[N=n] \frac{\mathbb{E}[(X_1 - d_{mn})_+]}{\mathbb{E}[X_1]}\right)$$
$$+ \sum_{m=1}^{+\infty} c_m \sum_{n=m}^{+\infty} \Pr[N=n] d_{mn},$$

where the retentions d_{mn} are defined as

$$d_{mn} = F_X^{-1}\left(1 - \frac{m}{n}\right).$$

(iii) Now assume that

$$F_X(x) = 1 - \left(\frac{x}{a}\right)^{-\alpha} \quad \text{for} x \geq a,$$

where $a \geq 0$ and $\alpha > 1$. Show that

$$F_X^{-1}(p) = a(1-p)^{-1/\alpha},$$
$$d_{mn} = a\left(\frac{m}{n}\right)^{-1/\alpha},$$
$$\mathbb{E}[X_1] = a\frac{\alpha}{\alpha - 1},$$
$$\frac{\mathbb{E}[(X_1 - t)_+]}{\mathbb{E}[X_1]} = \left(\frac{t}{a}\right)^{1-\alpha} \frac{1}{\alpha},$$
$$\pi(\boldsymbol{c}) \leq a\left(\sum_{m=1}^{+\infty} \frac{c_m}{m^{1/\alpha}}\right) \mathbb{E}[N^{1/\alpha}] \frac{\alpha}{\alpha - 1} - R,$$

where the remainder term R is given by

$$R = a\left(\sum_{m=1}^{+\infty} \frac{c_m}{m^{1/\alpha}} \sum_{n=1}^{m-1} \Pr[N=n] n^{1/\alpha}\right) \frac{\alpha}{\alpha - 1}.$$

(i) Assume that the evolution of P_t of the Y_i [illegible]. Show that [illegible]

A1 the claim sizes are independent and identically distributed.

A2 the claim frequency N is independent of the claim sizes.

[illegible]

$$[illegible] \quad (7.15)$$

where $\kappa_j^{(i)}$ is the jth cumulant of the [illegible]

(ii) [illegible]

[illegible]

8

Stochastic Bounds on Functions of Dependent Risks

This chapter discusses bounds on functions of correlated risks, with respect to various stochastic orderings. First, a general strategy is proposed for deriving upper and lower stop-loss bounds on directionally convex, increasing functions of possibly dependent risks $X_1, X_2, \ldots, X_n$. Illustrations are presented that involve looking for a bound in the $\preceq_{\mathrm{SL},=}$ sense on the sum $S=\sum_{i=1}^{n} X_i$ of insurance risks whose means and range are known.

Then, we show how to compute bounds on tail probabilities $\Pr[S>s]$, and more generally on $\mathbb{E}[g(S)]$ for monotone, but not necessarily convex functions g. This method will provide bounds in the $\preceq_{\mathrm{ST}}$ sense on S.

8.1 INTRODUCTION

This chapter aims to quantify the possible impact of dependence. To provide a tentative answer to this question, we consider the following simple example. Consider $X_1 \sim \mathcal{E}xp(1)$ and $X_2 \sim \mathcal{E}xp(1)$. We will see further in this chapter that the inequalities

$$\exp(-x) \leq \Pr[X_1+X_2>x] \leq \exp\big(-(x-2\ln 2)_+/2\big) \tag{8.1}$$

hold for all $x\in\mathbb{R}^+$ (and that these bounds are sharp). A direct derivation of the lower bound in (8.1) is easy since we obviously have that $\Pr[X_1+X_2>x]\geq \Pr[X_1>x]$. The other inequality will result from a more general analysis. The inequalities in (8.1) allow us to measure the impact of dependence on tfs. Figure 8.1 (left) displays the bounds (8.1), together with the values corresponding to independence and perfect positive dependence (i.e., $X_1=X_2$). Clearly, the probability that X_1+X_2 exceeds twice its mean (for instance) is significantly affected by the correlation structure of the X_i, ranging from almost 0 to three times the value computed under the independence assumption. We also observe that perfect positive dependence increases the probability that X_1+X_2 exceeds some high threshold compared to independence, but decreases the exceedance probabilities over low thresholds (i.e., the tfs cross once).

Actuarial Theory for Dependent Risks M. Denuit, J. Dhaene, M. Goovaerts and R. Kaas

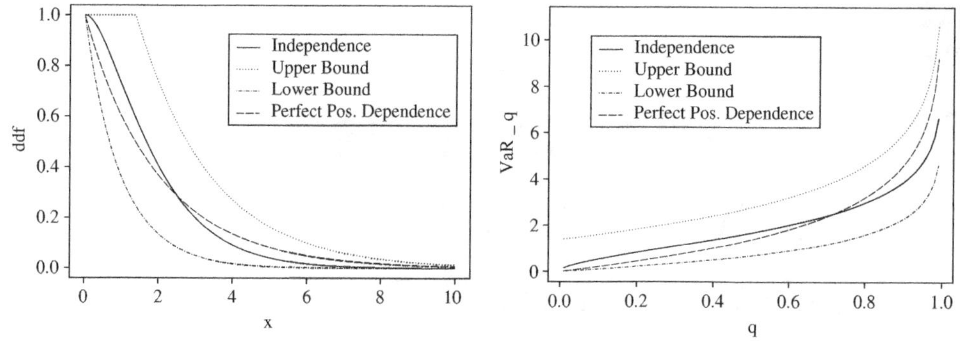

Figure 8.1 Impact of dependence on tfs (left) and VaRs (right) associated with the sum of two $\mathcal{E}xp(1)$ rvs

Another way to look at the impact of dependence is to examine VaRs. For the $\mathcal{E}xp(1)$ rvs introduced above, the inequalities

$$-\ln(1-q) \leq \text{VaR}[X_1 + X_2; q] \leq 2\big(\ln 2 - \ln(1-q)\big) \tag{8.2}$$

hold for all $q \in (0, 1)$. Figure 8.1 (right) displays the bounds (8.2), together with the values corresponding to independence and perfect positive dependence. In this very simple example, we see that the dependence structure may strongly influence the value of exceedance probabilities or VaRs.

Now consider a portfolio consisting of $n \geq 2$ insurance policies and let $X_1, \ldots, X_n$ be the corresponding non-negative claim amounts over a given reference period. There is an abundant literature on the behaviour of the aggregate claim amount $S = X_1 + \ldots + X_n$ in the case where the risks X_i are mutually independent. In this chapter, we will be concerned with the scenario in which these rvs are correlated.

Under the assumption that the marginal df F_i of X_i is known for every $i = 1, \ldots, n$, we know from Proposition 6.3.7 together with Corollary 6.3.10 that the stop-loss premiums for S are maximized when the X_i are comonotonic. Under additional conditions, the dependence structure minimizing the stop-loss premium for S is mutual exclusivity; see Proposition 6.3.8. More generally, comonotonicity and mutual exclusivity give bounds on quantities of the form $\mathbb{E}[g(S)]$ for some monotone convex function g. In this chapter, we show how to determine an upper stop-loss bound on any directionally convex, increasing function $\Psi(X_1, \ldots, X_n)$ of $n \geq 2$ possibly dependent risks in situations where the marginals are either totally or partially known, or even when information may be available about the copula regulating the dependence between the X_i.

We will also derive bounds on quantities of the form $\mathbb{E}[g(S)]$ for some function g that is monotone but not necessarily convex. Such bounds are also of interest to actuaries. Suppose, for example, that an insurer solicits from a reinsurer a stop-loss contract with deductible $d \geq 0$. In the absence of specific information concerning a suspected dependence between the X_i, the reinsurer may then be interested in finding bounds for the probability $\Pr[S > d]$ that an amount $S - d$ must be paid to the ceding company. In such a case, comonotonicity is not helpful, because the indicator function of the set $\{S - d > 0\}$ is non-decreasing but not convex.

As another example, assume the actuary is interested in $\text{VaR}[S;\epsilon]$. In practice, the sum $\sum_{i=1}^{n}\text{VaR}[X_i,\epsilon]$ is usually taken. However, for non-elliptical portfolios, it may be that

$$\sum_{i=1}^{n}\text{VaR}[X_i,\epsilon] < \text{VaR}[S;\epsilon],$$

as demonstrated in Exercises 2.7.5 and 2.7.6. The purpose of the present chapter is to provide the actuary with bounds on $\text{VaR}[S;\epsilon]$ for any probability level ϵ.

In the final part of this chapter, we derive stochastic upper and lower bounds on the present value of a sequence of cash flows, where the discounting is performed under a given stochastic return process.

This chapter is essentially based on the papers by Denuit, Genest & Marceau (1999), Genest, Marceau and Mesfioui (2002), Denuit, Genest and Mesfioui (2004) and Cossette, Denuit and Marceau (2000,2002). Applications are taken from Cossette *et al.* (2001) and Cossette, Denuit and Marceau (2002). Let us also mention the work by Embrechts, Höing and Juri (2003) and Embrechts and Puccetti (2004) focused on VaRs; these authors relaxed some of the continuity assumptions made on Ψ. It is worth mentioning that problems similar to those treated in this chapter have been studied for a long time in probability theory. Bounds for the df of X_1+X_2 were found by Makarov (1981) in terms of generalized inverses. Frank, Nelsen and Schweizer (1987) proved some results exploiting partial knowledge about the type of dependence structure between X_1 and X_2. They also extended Makarov's results to include arbitrary increasing continuous functions Ψ of X_1 and X_2. Williamson and Downs (1990) proved the pointwise best possible nature of the bounds in the two-dimensional case and also developed an algorithm for computing these bounds numerically; see also Williamson (1991).

8.2 COMPARING RISKS WITH FIXED DEPENDENCE STRUCTURE

In this section, we will present some technical results that will be used in this chapter.

8.2.1 The problem

When the dependence structure (i.e., the copula) among risks is fixed, one might think that the riskier are the X_i, the riskier is the aggregate loss S of the portfolio. This conjecture turns out to be true for $\preceq_{\text{ST}}$. But quite surprisingly, it turns out to be false in general, even for $\preceq_{\text{SL}}$. Nevertheless, we will get the desired result under additional conditions on the copula (namely, conditional increasingness).

This problem appears in Muliere and Scarsini (1989) and Scarsini & Shaked (1990) with reference to $\preceq_{\text{ST}}$. Arnold (1987) and Koshevoy and Mosler (1996, 1998) examined similar problems for the Lorenz order and Müller and Scarsini (2001) studied the problem with reference to convex order.

8.2.2 Ordering random vectors with fixed dependence structure with stochastic dominance

Given two random vectors with independent components, $\boldsymbol{X}$ and $\boldsymbol{Y}$ say, we obviously have that

$$X_i \preceq_{\text{ST}} Y_i, \quad \text{for } i = 1, 2, \ldots, n \quad \Leftrightarrow \quad \boldsymbol{X} \preceq_{\text{ST}} \boldsymbol{Y}.$$

In this particular case, multivariate stochastic dominance is thus equivalent to univariate stochastic dominance for all the marginals.

The aim of this section is to prove that in the aforementioned result the crucial assumption is not independence, but rather the fact that the two random vectors have the same dependence structure (i.e., the same copula). Therefore, whenever two random vectors have the same dependence structure, multivariate stochastic dominance conditions may be provided simply by examining the marginal distributions of each of the components of the random vectors. The results presented in this section come from Scarsini (1985) and Müller and Scarsini (2001).

Proposition 8.2.1
Let $\boldsymbol{X} \in \mathcal{R}_n(F_1, F_2, \ldots, F_n)$ and $\boldsymbol{Y} \in \mathcal{R}_n(G_1, G_2, \ldots, G_n)$ be two random vectors having a common copula C (not necessarily unique). Then

$$\boldsymbol{X} \preceq_{\text{ST}} \boldsymbol{Y} \quad \Leftrightarrow \quad X_i \preceq_{\text{ST}} Y_i \quad \text{for } i = 1, 2, \ldots, n.$$

Proof. Since the $\Rightarrow$ part is obvious, we only have to establish the $\Leftarrow$ part. Since $X_i \preceq_{\text{ST}} Y_i$ for every i, we know that $F_i^{-1}(u_i) \leq G_i^{-1}(u_i)$ for all $u_i \in [0, 1]$. Hence, if we let $\boldsymbol{U}$ be distributed as C, then

$$(F_1^{-1}(U_1), F_2^{-1}(U_2), \ldots, F_n^{-1}(U_n)) \leq (G_1^{-1}(U_1), G_2^{-1}(U_2), \ldots, G_n^{-1}(U_n))$$

and thus $\boldsymbol{X} \preceq_{\text{ST}} \boldsymbol{Y}$ by Proposition 3.3.86. □

Note that under the conditions of Proposition 8.2.1, we have in particular that

$$X_i \preceq_{\text{ST}} Y_i \quad \text{for } i = 1, 2, \ldots, n \quad \Rightarrow \quad \sum_{i=1}^{n} \alpha_i X_i \preceq_{\text{ST}} \sum_{i=1}^{n} \alpha_i Y_i$$

whatever $\alpha_1, \ldots, \alpha_n \geq 0$. Hence, univariate stochastic dominance is closed under addition of rvs provided the dependence structure of the summands is identical (and not only for independent summands). This extends Proposition 3.3.17(ii).

8.2.3 Ordering random vectors with fixed dependence structure with convex order

Let us consider two random vectors $\boldsymbol{X}$ and $\boldsymbol{Y}$, such that the components of $\boldsymbol{X}$ are dominated in the convex order by the corresponding components of $\boldsymbol{Y}$. We wish to find conditions under which this implies that any positive linear combination of the components of $\boldsymbol{X}$ is dominated in the convex order by the same positive linear combination of the components of $\boldsymbol{Y}$.

Since a convex function of a positive combination of the components of a vector is directionally convex in the vector, directional convexity becomes an interesting tool for solving the problem described above. A result similar to Proposition 8.2.1 for the convex order only holds if the components of the random vectors are independent (i.e., $C \equiv C_I$). The first counterexample was given by Scarsini (1998). The convex order is thus inappropriate for solving the problem of interest. It is indeed clear that we cannot expect the convex order of the marginals to lead to the convex order for the sum of the components when the components are negatively dependent. In the financial literature this phenomenon is known under the name of 'hedging' risks. Assume that you are the owner of some stock, which yields a random return of X_1. You can diminish your risk by investing in some other risky asset, which is negatively correlated with X_1, for example, a put option for that stock position. Let us assume that this put option yields

$$X_2 = \max\{K - X_1, 0\}$$

and that you have to pay $\mathbb{E}[X_2]$ for this put option. Then we can compare the situation of holding the stock and the amount $\mathbb{E}[X_2]$ in cash (i.e., your portfolio is $\boldsymbol{X} = (X_1, \mathbb{E}[X_2])$) to the situation where you buy the put option (i.e., your portfolio is $\boldsymbol{X}' = (X_1, X_2)$). The portfolio $\boldsymbol{X}'$ is less risky than $\boldsymbol{X}$, namely

$$X_1 + X_2 \preceq_{\mathrm{SL},=} X_1 + \mathbb{E}[X_2],$$

though $\mathbb{E}[X_2] \preceq_{\mathrm{SL},=} X_2$.

Thus, it is clear that we need some notion of positive dependence. The following result, derived by Müller and Scarsini (2001), shows that if we assume the same CI copula for two vectors $\boldsymbol{X}$ and $\boldsymbol{Y}$ whose marginals are ordered in the convex sense, then the directionally convex order holds for the vectors.

Proposition 8.2.2
Let $\boldsymbol{X}$ and $\boldsymbol{Y}$ be n-dimensional random vectors with a common CI copula C and assume that $X_i \preceq_{\mathrm{SL},=} Y_i$ holds for $i = 1, 2, \ldots, n$. Then $\boldsymbol{X} \preceq_{\mathrm{DCX}} \boldsymbol{Y}$.

For a proof, we refer the reader to Müller and Scarsini (2001). These authors showed that the assumption of Proposition 8.2.2 cannot be weakened. Indeed, even under conditional increasingness in sequence, a higher variability for the marginals may lead to a lower variability for the sum of the components.

As a direct consequence of Proposition 8.2.2, we get the following result.

Corollary 8.2.3
Let $\boldsymbol{X}$ and $\boldsymbol{Y}$ fulfil the conditions of Proposition 8.2.2. Then, for all non-negative constants $\alpha_1, \alpha_2, \ldots, \alpha_n$,

$$\sum_{i=1}^{n} \alpha_i X_i \preceq_{\mathrm{SL},=} \sum_{i=1}^{n} \alpha_i Y_i.$$

8.3 STOP-LOSS BOUNDS ON FUNCTIONS OF DEPENDENT RISKS

8.3.1 Known marginals

Assume that upper and lower stop-loss bounds are sought for $\Psi(X_1, \ldots, X_n)$, where $\Psi: \mathbb{R}^n \to \mathbb{R}$ represents an increasing, directionally convex function. The simplest examples of directionally convex, increasing functions are linear combinations

$$\Psi(x_1, \ldots, x_n) = \sum_{i=1}^{n} \alpha_i x_i \text{ with } \alpha_1, \ldots, \alpha_n > 0.$$

Suppose that $F_1, \ldots, F_n$ are known and that, in addition, copulas C^- and C^+ may be found for which

$$C^- \preceq_{\text{SM}} C \preceq_{\text{SM}} C^+. \tag{8.3}$$

Proposition 6.3.9 then implies that

$$\Psi(X_1^-, \ldots, X_n^-) \preceq_{\text{SL}} \Psi(X_1, \ldots, X_n) \preceq_{\text{SL}} \Psi(X_1^+, \ldots, X_n^+) \tag{8.4}$$

whenever $(X_1^-, \ldots, X_n^-)$ and $(X_1^+, \ldots, X_n^+)$ have common univariate marginals $F_1, \ldots, F_n$ but copula C^- and C^+ instead of C.

Proposition 6.3.7 indicates that the Fréchet upper bound C_U constitutes a natural choice for C^+. When the risks X_i are known to be associated in the sense of Definition 7.2.6, Christofides and Vaggelatou (2004) show that an appropriate choice for C^- is the independence copula C_I.

8.3.2 Unknown marginals

8.3.2.1 General strategy

A central question in actuarial science is the construction of *extrema* with respect to some stochastic order relation. Indeed, the actuary sometimes acts in a conservative way by basing his decisions on the least attractive risk that is consistent with the incomplete information available. This can be done by determining in given classes of risks, coherent with the partial known information, the extrema with respect to some stochastic ordering which translates the preferences of the actuary, that is, the 'worst' and the 'best' risk. So given a risk X, many actuarial papers have been devoted to the derivation of lower and upper bounds on quantities of the form $\mathbb{E}[g_0(X)]$, for some given g_0, when X belongs to a class of rvs satisfying certain moment conditions; see Taylor (1977), De Vijlder (1980, 1982, 1983), De Vijlder and Goovaerts (1982, 1983), De Vijlder *et al.* (1984), Goovaerts and De Vijlder (1980), Goovaerts, Haezendonck and De Vijlder (1982), Goovaerts and Kaas (1985), Kaas (1985), Kaas and Goovaerts (1985, 1986a,b,c, 1987), Brockett and Cox (1985), Jansen, Haezendonck and Goovaerts (1986), Heijnen and Goovaerts (1986, 1989) and Heijnen (1990). The solution of these problems was given, in most cases, by atomic random variables with similar structure.

See Denuit, De Vijlder and Lefèvre (1999) for an explanation of this remarkable feature within the framework of the theory of extrema in moment spaces.

Assume now that the marginal dfs of $X_1, \ldots, X_n$ are unknown but that partial information about them allows one to find a lower bound $X^-_{i,\min}$ and an upper bound $X^+_{i,\max}$ in the $\preceq_{SL,=}$ sense on X_i. More precisely, $X^-_{i,\min}$ and $X^+_{i,\max}$ are such that

$$X^-_{i,\min} \preceq_{SL,=} X_i \preceq_{SL,=} X^+_{i,\max}, \text{ for } i = 1, \ldots, n.$$

Suppose, further, that C^- and C^+ involved in equations (8.3) and (8.4) are CI. The independence copula and the Fréchet upper bound clearly meet this requirement, but additional examples include Archimedean copulas obtained from the frailty construction (which are known to be MTP_2 from Example 7.2.19).

Under these conditions on C^- and C^+, a straightforward application of Proposition 8.2.2 yields

$$\Psi\left(X^-_{1,\min}, \ldots, X^-_{n,\min}\right) \preceq_{SL} \Psi\left(X^-_1, \ldots, X^-_n\right) \tag{8.5}$$

and

$$\Psi\left(X^+_1, \ldots, X^+_n\right) \preceq_{SL} \Psi\left(X^+_{1,\max}, \ldots, X^+_{n,\max}\right), \tag{8.6}$$

where $(X^-_{1,\max}, \ldots, X^-_{n,\max})$ has copula C^- and $(X^+_{1,\max}, \ldots, X^+_{n,\max})$ has copula C^+.

A definite advantage of this strategy is that the choice of stop-loss bounds on X_i can then rely on the univariate literature, as will be illustrated in the following section.

8.3.2.2 Bounded risks with given means

Assume that $\mathbb{E}[X_i] = \mu_i$ and $\Pr[0 \leq X_i \leq b_i] = 1$ for known constants μ_i and b_i, $i = 1, 2, \ldots, n$. For simplicity, suppose without further loss of generality that

$$\frac{\mu_1}{b_1} \geq \ldots \geq \frac{\mu_n}{b_n} \geq \frac{\mu_{n+1}}{b_{n+1}} = 0.$$

Then we know from Exercise 3.5.21 that $X_i \preceq_{SL,=} X^+_{i,\max}$, where the df of $X^+_{i,\max}$ is

$$F_{i,\max}(x) = \begin{cases} 0, & \text{if } x < 0, \\ 1 - \frac{\mu_i}{b_i}, & \text{if } 0 \leq x < b_i, \\ 1, & \text{if } x \geq b_i. \end{cases} \tag{8.7}$$

Thus if, for instance, $\Psi(X_1, \ldots, X_n) = X_1 + \ldots + X_n$, one may conclude from (8.4) and (8.6) that

$$S = \sum_{i=1}^{n} X_i \preceq_{SL,=} \sum_{i=1}^{n} F^{-1}_{i,\max}(U) = S_{\max}, \tag{8.8}$$

where $U \sim \mathcal{U}ni(0, 1)$. The next result gives an explicit expression for the df of $S_{\max}$, as well as for its stop-loss transform.

Property 8.3.1
Let us define

$$\mu_i^* = \sum_{j=1}^{i} \mu_j, \quad b_i^* = \sum_{j=1}^{i} b_j, \qquad i = 1, \ldots, n,$$

with $b_0^* = 0$ and $b_{n+1}^* = \infty$. Then,

(i) the df $F_{\max}$ of $S_{\max}$ is given explicitly by

$$F_{\max}(x) = \left(1 - \frac{\mu_i}{b_i}\right) \mathbb{I}[b_{i-1}^* \leq x < b_i^*] \tag{8.9}$$

for $i = 1, \ldots, n+1$.

(ii) the stop-loss premium $\pi_{S_{\max}}(d)$, which constitutes an upper bound on $\pi_S(d)$, is of the form

$$\pi_{S_{\max}}(d) = \left(\mu_n^* - \mu_{i+1}^* + \frac{\mu_{i+1}}{b_{i+1}} (b_{i+1}^* - d)\right) \mathbb{I}[b_i^* \leq d < b_{i+1}^*] \tag{8.10}$$

for $i = 1, \ldots, n-1$.

Proof. To prove (8.9), use the fact that for all $x \geq 0$,

$$\begin{aligned}
F_{\max}(x) &= \Pr\left[\sum_{i=1}^{n} F_{i,\max}^{-1}(U) \leq x\right] \\
&= 1 - \frac{\mu_1}{b_1} + \sum_{i=1}^{n} \Pr\left[b_i^* \leq x \middle| \frac{\mu_{i+1}}{b_{i+1}} \leq 1 - U \leq \frac{\mu_i}{b_i}\right] \times \Pr\left[\frac{\mu_{i+1}}{b_{i+1}} \leq 1 - U \leq \frac{\mu_i}{b_i}\right].
\end{aligned}$$

Since $U \sim \mathcal{U}ni(0, 1)$, this expression amounts to

$$F_{\max}(x) = 1 - \frac{\mu_1}{b_1} + \sum_{i=1}^{n} \left(\frac{\mu_i}{b_i} - \frac{\mu_{i+1}}{b_{i+1}}\right) \mathbb{I}[b_i^* \leq x],$$

which reduces at once to (8.9).

To establish (8.10), observe that for $b_i^* \leq d < b_{i+1}^*$,

$$\pi_{S_{\max}}(d) = \sum_{j=i+1}^{n} (b_j^* - d) \left(\frac{\mu_j}{b_j} - \frac{\mu_{j+1}}{b_{j+1}}\right),$$

which may be rewritten as

$$\begin{aligned}
\pi_{S_{\max}}(d) &= \frac{\mu_{i+1}}{b_{i+1}} b_{i+1}^* + \sum_{j=i+2}^{n} \frac{\mu_j}{b_j} (b_j^* - b_{j-1}^*) - \frac{\mu_{i+1}}{b_{i+1}} d \\
&= \frac{\mu_{i+1}}{b_{i+1}} (b_{i+1}^* - d) + \mu_n^* - \mu_{i+1}^*.
\end{aligned}$$

This concludes the proof. □

8.3.2.3 An application in option pricing

In closing, it should be stressed that while the present approach to determining bounds on a function $\Psi(X_1, \ldots, X_n)$ of non-negative rvs was illustrated here in an actuarial context, it also has obvious applications in finance. For instance, path-dependent options depend on the history of an asset price, not just on its value on exercise. An example is an option to purchase an asset for the arithmetic average value of the asset over the month before expiry. Formally, denoting by X_i the value of some asset at dates t_i, $1 \le i \le n$, the path-dependent option has payoff

$$\max\left(0, -K + \sum_{i=1}^{n} \alpha_i X_i\right), \tag{8.11}$$

where K is the exercise price and α_i is the weight allotted to the value recorded at time t_i. As an additional example, consider an option on an index relating to some stock exchange market. A payoff of the form (8.11) results once again if the index is defined in terms of a basket of leading-firm shares $X_1, \ldots, X_n$, each of which is weighted according to the amount α_i of capital invested.

8.4 STOCHASTIC BOUNDS ON FUNCTIONS OF DEPENDENT RISKS

8.4.1 Stochastic bounds on the sum of two risks

Let us consider the sum $S = X_1 + X_2$ of two possibly dependent risks X_1 and X_2. Following the work of Denuit, Genest and Marceau (1999), we will see that there exist rvs $S_{\min}$ and $S_{\max}$ such that

$$\Pr[S_{\min} \le s] \le \Pr[S \le s] \le \Pr[S_{\max} \le s], \quad s \in \mathbb{R}, \tag{8.12}$$

or, equivalently, such that $S_{\max} \preceq_{\mathrm{ST}} S \preceq_{\mathrm{ST}} S_{\min}$. For such rvs, we have from (3.8) that

$$\mathbb{E}[g(S_{\max})] \le \mathbb{E}[g(S)] \le \mathbb{E}[g(S_{\min})], \tag{8.13}$$

for all non-decreasing functions g, provided that the expectations exist.

For $i = 1, 2$, let X_i represent a risk with df F_i and left limit $F_i^-(s) = \Pr[X_i < s]$ defined for all $s \in \mathbb{R}$. Introduce

$$F_{\min}(s) = \sup_{x \in \mathbb{R}} \max\left\{F_1^-(x) + F_2^-(s-x) - 1, 0\right\} \tag{8.14}$$

and

$$F_{\max}(s) = \inf_{x \in \mathbb{R}} \min\left\{F_1(x) + F_2(s-x), 1\right\}. \tag{8.15}$$

Let us now prove that there exist rvs corresponding to $F_{\min}$ and $F_{\max}$.

Lemma 8.4.1
There exist rvs $S_{\min}$ and $S_{\max}$ such that

$$F_{\min}(s) = \Pr[S_{\min} < s] \quad \text{and} \quad F_{\max}(s) = \Pr[S_{\max} \le s], \qquad s \in \mathbb{R}. \tag{8.16}$$

Proof. It is obvious that $F_{\min}$ and $F_{\max}$ are non-decreasing on their domain, and it follows from a remark by Rudin (1974), p. 39 that $F_{\min}(s)$ is left-continuous while $F_{\max}(s)$ is right-continuous. All that remains to check is that both of these functions have 0 and 1 as their limit as s approaches $-\infty$ or $+\infty$, respectively. This is shown below in the case of $F_{\max}$, the argument for $F_{\min}$ being similar.

To prove that $F_{\max}(s) \to 0$ as $s \to -\infty$, fix $\epsilon > 0$ and choose u_0 such that $F_1(u_0) < \epsilon/2$. Then select s_0 such that $F_2(s_0 - u_0) < \epsilon/2$. Then $F_{\max}(s_0) < \epsilon$ and since this function is non-decreasing, one thus has $F_{\max}(s) < \epsilon$ for all $s \le s_0$.

To handle the case where $s \to \infty$, choose u_1 such that $F_1(u_1) > 1 - \epsilon$. Then pick s_1 such that $F_2(s_1 - u_1) > 1 - \epsilon$. Note that

$$\inf_{u \le u_1} \min\{F_1(u) + F_2(s_1 - u), 1\} \ge F_2(s_1 - u_1) > 1 - \epsilon$$

and that

$$\inf_{u \ge u_1} \min\{F_1(u) + F_2(s_1 - u), 1\} \ge F_1(u_1) > 1 - \epsilon,$$

whence $F_{\max}(s) > 1 - \epsilon$ as well. Since $F_{\max}$ is non-decreasing, the proof is complete. □

As already mentioned, these rvs $S_{\min}$ and $S_{\max}$ whose existence is guaranteed by Lemma 8.4.1 are precisely those for which inequalities (8.12) and (8.13) hold, as implied by the following result.

Proposition 8.4.2
If $S = X_1 + X_2$ and $F_{\min}$ and $F_{\max}$ are defined by (8.14) and (8.15), then

$$F_{\min}(s) \le F_S(s) \le F_{\max}(s), \text{ for all } s \in \mathbb{R}. \tag{8.17}$$

Proof. For arbitrary s and x in $\mathbb{R}$, it is clear that $X_1 > x$ and $X_2 > s - x$ together imply $S > s$, so that

$$F_S(s) \le \Pr[X_1 \le x \text{ or } X_2 \le s - x] \le F_1(x) + F_2(s - x),$$

from which it is obvious that $F_S(s) \le F_{\max}(s)$ everywhere. To show the other inequality, note that

$$\Pr[X_1 < x] + \Pr[X_2 < s - x] - \Pr[X_1 < x, X_2 < s - x] \le 1$$

from which it follows that

$$\max\{F_1^-(x) + F_2^-(s - x) - 1, 0\} \le \Pr[X_1 < x, X_2 < s - x] \le F_S(s),$$

which is the desired result. □

Remark 8.4.3. To see that (8.17) does imply (8.12), and hence (8.13), it suffices to observe that $\Pr[S_{\min} < s + 1/n] \leq \Pr[S \leq s + 1/n]$ for all integers $n \geq 1$, and hence $\Pr[S_{\min} \leq s] \leq F_S(s)$ in the limit. ∇

As a consequence of Proposition 8.4.2, the dfs of $S_{\min}$ and $S_{\max}$ provide the best possible bounds on $S = X_1 + X_2$ in the $\preceq_{\mathrm{ST}}$ sense.

Some illustrations are given below for distributions that are more relevant to actuarial applications.

Example 8.4.4. If $X_i \sim \mathcal{E}xp(\alpha_i)$, $i = 1, 2$, routine calculations show that the df of $S = X_1 + X_2$ is bounded below by a shifted exponential distribution of the form

$$F_{\min} = \tilde{\theta} + \mathcal{E}xp(\alpha_1 + \alpha_2),$$

where $\tilde{\theta} = (\alpha_1 + \alpha_2)\log(\alpha_1 + \alpha_2) - \alpha_1 \log(\alpha_1) - \alpha_2 \log(\alpha_2)$. It is also bounded above by

$$F_{\max} = \mathcal{E}xp(\max\{\alpha_1, \alpha_2\}).$$

∇

Example 8.4.5. If $X_i \sim \mathcal{P}ar(\alpha, \lambda_i)$, $i = 1, 2$, one can check easily that the df is bounded below by a shifted Pareto distribution of the form

$$F_{\min} = \mathcal{P}ar\left(\alpha, \tilde{\lambda}\right) + \tilde{\lambda} - \lambda_1 - \lambda_2,$$

where $\tilde{\lambda} = \left(\lambda_1^{\beta} + \lambda_2^{\beta}\right)^{1/\beta}$ with $\beta = \alpha/(\alpha + 1)$. Likewise,

$$F_{\max} = \mathcal{P}ar\{\alpha, \max(\lambda_1, \lambda_2)\}.$$

Algebraic computation of the bounds when the X_i have different α-values seems intractable. ∇

8.4.2 Stochastic bounds on the sum of several risks

The ideas presented in Section 8.4.1 can be extended without much difficulty to the case of $n \geq 3$ contracts X_i with df F_i and left limit F_i^-, $1 \leq i \leq n$. To be specific, introduce the hyperplane

$$\Sigma(s) = \left\{ \boldsymbol{x} \in \mathbb{R}^n \middle| x_1 + \ldots + x_n = s \right\}$$

and define

$$F_{\min}(s) = \sup_{\boldsymbol{x} \in \Sigma(s)} \max\left\{ \sum_{i=1}^{n} F_i^-(x_i) - (n-1), 0 \right\} \tag{8.18}$$

as well as

$$F_{\max}(s) = \inf_{x \in \Sigma(s)} \min \left\{ \sum_{i=1}^{n} F_i(x_i), 1 \right\}. \tag{8.19}$$

One can then prove the existence of rvs $S_{\min}$ and $S_{\max}$ for which (8.16) continues to hold with these extended definitions of $F_{\min}$ and $F_{\max}$. A straightforward adaptation of the arguments developed in Section 8.4.1 also leads to the following generalization of Proposition 8.4.2.

Proposition 8.4.6
If $S = X_1 + \ldots + X_n$ and $F_{\min}$ and $F_{\max}$ are defined by (8.18) and (8.19), then

$$F_{\min}(s) \leq F_S(s) \leq F_{\max}(s), \text{ for all } s \in \mathbb{R}. \tag{8.20}$$

Remark 8.4.7. Note that while formulas (8.18) and (8.19) each involve an optimum over a hyperplane, they can actually be computed easily by proceeding iteratively, as suggested by Frank, Nelsen and Schweizer (1987). To compute the upper bound $F_{\max} = F_{\max(3)}$ on the distribution of the sum of three contracts, say, one can simply observe that

$$\begin{aligned} F_{\max(3)}(s) &= \inf_{x \in \Sigma(s)} \min \{F_1(x_1) + F_2(x_3) + F_3(x_3), 1\} \\ &= \inf_{x_1 \in \mathbb{R}} \min \left\{F_1(x_1) + F_{\max(2)}(s - x_1), 1\right\} \end{aligned}$$

where

$$F_{\max(2)}(s - x_1) = \inf_{x_2 + x_3 = s - x_1} \min \{F_2(x_2) + F_3(x_3), 1\}.$$

∇

Successive applications of the procedure described in Remark 8.4.7 (with obvious adaptation for $F_{\min}$) lead, for example, to the following extensions of Examples 8.4.4 and 8.4.5.

Example 8.4.8. (Example 8.4.4 continued). Suppose that $X_i \sim \mathcal{E}xp(\alpha_i)$ for $i = 1, 2, \ldots, n$. Then, the df of S is bounded below by a shifted exponential distribution of the form

$$F_{\min} = \tilde{\theta} + \mathcal{E}xp\left(\sum_{i=1}^{n} \alpha_i\right)$$

with

$$\tilde{\theta} = \left(\sum_{i=1}^{n} \alpha_i\right) \log \left(\sum_{i=1}^{n} \alpha_i\right) - \sum_{i=1}^{n} \alpha_i \log(\alpha_i)$$

and

$$F_{\max} = \mathcal{E}xp\Big(\max\{\alpha_1, \ldots, \alpha_n\}\Big).$$

∇

Example 8.4.9. (Example 8.4.5 continued). Suppose that $X_i \sim \mathcal{P}ar(\alpha, \lambda_i)$ for $i = 1, 2, \ldots, n$. Then, the df of S is bounded below by a shifted Pareto distribution of the form

$$F_{\min} = \mathcal{P}ar\left(\alpha, \tilde{\lambda}\right) - \sum_{i=1}^{n} \lambda_i + \tilde{\lambda},$$

with

$$\tilde{\lambda} = \left(\sum_{i=1}^{n} \lambda_i^{\beta} \right)^{1/\beta}$$

and

$$F_{\max} = \mathcal{P}ar\Big(\alpha, \max\{\lambda_1, \ldots, \lambda_n\}\Big).$$

∇

8.4.3 *Improvement of the bounds on sums of risks under positive dependence*

The aim of this section is to describe briefly how it is possible to modify the results of Sections 8.4.1 and 8.4.2 and tighten the bounds on the distribution of an aggregate claim $S = X_1 + \ldots + X_n$ in the presence of additional information concerning the structure of dependence between the terms involved the sum. These developments assume, as before, that the marginal df of each of the individual risks X_i is known.

Concentrating on the case $n = 2$ to start with, suppose, for instance, that X_1 and X_2 are known to be positively dependent, a reasonable assumption in many actuarial applications. A common way of formalizing this hypothesis is to assume that the pair (X_1, X_2) is PQD. The following result shows how it is possible to improve on bounds (8.17) in this case.

Proposition 8.4.10
Let (X_1, X_2) be PQD and $S = X_1 + X_2$. Then

$$F^*_{\min}(s) \leq F_S(s) \leq F^*_{\max}(s) \text{for all } s \in \mathbb{R},$$

with

$$F^*_{\min}(s) = \sup_{x \in \mathbb{R}} \{F_1(x) F_2(s - x)\} \tag{8.21}$$

and

$$F^*_{\max}(s) = 1 - \sup_{x \in \mathbb{R}} \left\{\bar{F}_1(x) \bar{F}_2(s - x)\right\} \tag{8.22}$$

for all $s \in \mathbb{R}$.

Proof. By hypothesis, we have

$$F_1(x)F_2(s-x) \leq \Pr[X_1 \leq x, X_2 \leq s-x] \leq F_S(s),$$

for arbitrary $x \in \mathbb{R}$, which yields the lower bound. Arguing as in the proof of Proposition 8.4.2, we also have

$$F_S(s) \leq \Pr[X_1 \leq x \text{ or } X_2 \leq s-x] = F_1(x) + F_2(s-x) - F_1(x)F_2(s-x)$$

whatever the choice of x, and hence the upper bound obtains. □

Remark 8.4.11. Since it is generally true that

$$\max\{F_1(x) + F_2(s-x) - 1, 0\} \leq F_1(x)F_2(s-x)$$

and

$$F_1(x) + F_2(s-x) - F_1(x)F_2(s-x) \leq \min\{F_1(x) + F_2(s-x), 1\},$$

observe that one must always have

$$F_{\min}(s) \leq F^*_{\min}(s) \leq F_S(s) \leq F^*_{\max}(s) \leq F_{\max}(s).$$

Therefore, the PQD condition leads to sharper bounds. ∇

This section would not be complete without at least a brief mention of a generalization of Proposition 8.4.10 to the case of $n \geq 3$.

Proposition 8.4.12
Let $X_1, \ldots, X_n$ be rvs with dfs $F_1, \ldots, F_n$, respectively. Let $S = X_1 + \cdots + X_n$ and assume that the X_i are POD. Then

$$\sup_{x \in \Sigma(s)} \left\{ \prod_{i=1}^n F_i(x_i) \right\} \leq F_S(s) \leq 1 - \sup_{x \in \Sigma(s)} \left\{ \prod_{i=1}^n \bar{F}_i(x_i) \right\}, \tag{8.23}$$

for $s \in \mathbb{R}$, where $\Sigma(s)$ is defined in the same manner as in Section 8.4.2.

8.4.4 Stochastic bounds on functions of two risks

Assume one wants to get bounds on the df of $\Psi(X_1, X_2)$ in terms of the marginals F_1 and F_2.

Proposition 8.4.13
Given a non-decreasing and continuous function $\Psi: \mathbb{R}^2 \to \mathbb{R}$, let us define for arbitrary s and x in $\mathbb{R}$ the continuous function $\varphi_x: \mathbb{R} \to \mathbb{R}$ by $t \mapsto \varphi_x(t) = \Psi(x, t)$. Then the inequalities

$$F_{\min}(s|\Psi) \leq \Pr[\Psi(X_1, X_2) \leq s] \leq F_{\max}(s|\Psi) \tag{8.24}$$

hold for all $s \in \mathbb{R}$, with

$$F_{\min}(s|\Psi) = \sup_{t_1 \in \mathbb{R}} \max\{F_1(t_1) + F_2(\varphi_{t_1}^{-1+}(s)) - 1, 0\}$$

and

$$F_{\max}(s|\Psi) = \inf_{t_1 \in \mathbb{R}} \min\{F_1(t_1) + F_2(\varphi_{t_1}^{-1+}(s)), 1\}.$$

Proof. It is clear from Lemma 1.5.15 that $X_1 > x$ and $X_2 > \varphi_x^{-1+}(s)$ together imply $\Psi(X_1, X_2) > s$. We then have for any $s \in \mathbb{R}$ that

$$\begin{aligned}\Pr[\Psi(X_1, X_2) \leq s] &\leq \Pr[X_1 \leq x \text{ or } X_2 \leq \varphi_x^{-1+}(s)] \\ &\leq \min\{F_1(x) + F_2(\varphi_x^{-1+}(s)), 1\}.\end{aligned}$$

Therefore,

$$\Pr[\Psi(X_1, X_2) \leq s] \leq \inf_{x \in \mathbb{R}} \min\{F_1(x) + F_2(\varphi_x^{-1+}(s)), 1\},$$

which is the inequality on the right of (8.24). In order to get the one on the left, it suffices to note that for any $s \in \mathbb{R}$,

$$\begin{aligned}\Pr[\Psi(X_1, X_2) \leq s] &\geq \Pr[X_1 \leq x, X_2 \leq \varphi_x^{-1+}(s))] \\ &\geq \max\{F_1(x) + F_2(\varphi_x^{-1+}(s)) - 1, 0\},\end{aligned}$$

and the best lower bound is finally obtained by taking the supremum. □

Remark 8.4.14. It is worth mentioning that $F_{\min}(\cdot|\Psi)$ can be expressed as

$$F_{\min}(s|\Psi) = \sup_{(t_1,t_2) \in \mathbb{R}^2 | \Psi(t_1,t_2)=s} \max\left\{F_1(t_1) + F_2(t_2) - 1, 0\right\}. \tag{8.25}$$

But we cannot say, in general, that

$$F_{\max}(s|\Psi) = \inf_{(t_1,t_2) \in \mathbb{R}^2 | \Psi(t_1,t_2)=s} \min\left\{F_1(t_1) + F_2(t_2), 1\right\}. \tag{8.26}$$

The explanation behind this fact is the following. The condition $\Psi(t_1, t_2) = s$ is equivalent to $\varphi_{t_1}(t_2) = s$, which is the same as

$$\begin{cases} \varphi_{t_1}(t_2) \leq s \\ \varphi_{t_1}(t_2) > s - \epsilon \text{ for all } \epsilon > 0 \end{cases} \Leftrightarrow \begin{cases} t_2 \leq \varphi_{t_1}^{-1+}(s) \\ t_2 > \varphi_{t_1}^{-1+}(s - \epsilon) \text{ for all } \epsilon > 0, \end{cases}$$

according to Lemma 1.5.15, that is,

$$\varphi_{t_1}^{-1+}(s-) \leq t_2 \leq \varphi_{t_1}^{-1+}(s).$$

Now, since $\max\{F_1(t_1) + F_2(t_2), 1\}$ is non-decreasing in (t_1, t_2), it follows that the supremum on the right-hand side of (8.25) is taken at the right endpoint of the interval $[\varphi_{t_1}^{-1+}(s-), \varphi_{t_1}^{-1+}(s)]$ implying the equality in (8.25). However, this reasoning cannot be repeated for the non-decreasing function $\min\{F_1(t_1) + F_2(t_2), 1\}$ for which we have to take the infimum. ∇

Williamson and Downs (1990, Theorem 3) proved the pointwise best possible nature of the bounds in Proposition 8.4.13. In other words, one cannot construct tighter bounds. In the particular case $\Psi(x_1, x_2) = x_1 + x_2$, Proposition 8.4.13 reduces to Proposition 8.4.2.

8.4.5 Improvements of the bounds on functions of risks under positive quadrant dependence

As was the case for sums of correlated rvs, the bounds on the df of $\Psi(X_1, X_2)$ can be improved when the X_i are known to be PQD.

Proposition 8.4.15
Let (X_1, X_2) be PQD with marginals F_1 and F_2. Given a non-decreasing and continuous function $\Psi: \mathbb{R}^2 \to \mathbb{R}$, the inequalities

$$F^*_{\min}(s|\Psi) \leq \Pr[\Psi(X_1, X_2) \leq s] \leq F^*_{\max}(s|\Psi) \tag{8.27}$$

hold for all $s \in \mathbb{R}$, with

$$F^*_{\min}(s|\Psi) = \sup_{t_1 \in \mathbb{R}} \left\{ F_1(t_1) F_2(\varphi_{t_1}^{-1+}(s)) \right\},$$

and

$$F^*_{\max}(s|\Psi) = \inf_{t_1 \in \mathbb{R}} \left\{ F_1(t_1) + F_2(\varphi_{t_1}^{-1+}(s)) - F_1(t_1) F_2(\varphi_{t_1}^{-1+}(s)) \right\}.$$

Again, Williamson and Downs (1990, Theorem 3) proved the pointwise best possible nature of these bounds.

8.4.6 Stochastic bounds on functions of several risks

We now give a multivariate extension of Proposition 8.4.13.

Proposition 8.4.16
Let $\boldsymbol{X}$ be an n-dimensional random vector with marginals $F_1, \ldots, F_n$. Given a non-decreasing and continuous function $\Psi: \mathbb{R}^n \to \mathbb{R}$, let us define for arbitrary $s, x_1, x_2, \ldots, x_{n-1}$ in $\mathbb{R}$ the continuous function $\varphi_{x_1,\ldots,x_{n-1}}: \mathbb{R} \to \mathbb{R}$ by

$$t \mapsto \varphi_{x_1,\ldots,x_{n-1}}(t) = \Psi(x_1, \ldots, x_{n-1}, t).$$

Then the inequalities

$$F_{\min}(s|\Psi) \leq \Pr[\Psi(X_1, \ldots, X_n) \leq s] \leq F_{\max}(s|\Psi) \tag{8.28}$$

hold for all $s \in \mathbb{R}$, with

$$F_{\min}(s|\Psi) = \sup_{(t_1,\ldots,t_{n-1}) \in \mathbb{R}^{n-1}} \max \left\{ \sum_{i=1}^{n-1} F_i(t_i) + F_n(\varphi_{t_1,\ldots,t_{n-1}}^{-1+}(s)) - (n-1), 0 \right\},$$

and

$$F_{\max}(s|\Psi) = \inf_{(t_1,\ldots,t_{n-1})\in\mathbb{R}^{n-1}} \min\left\{\sum_{i=1}^{n-1} F_i(t_i) + F_n(\varphi^{-1+}_{t_1,\ldots,t_{n-1}}(s)), 1\right\}.$$

Proof. It is clear that $X_1 > x_1$, $X_2 > x_2$, ... , $X_{n-1} > x_{n-1}$ and $X_n > \varphi^{-1+}_{x_1,\ldots,x_{n-1}}(s)$ imply $\Psi(X_1,\ldots,X_n) > s$, so that

$$\begin{aligned}
&\Pr[\Psi(X_1,\ldots,X_n) \le s] \\
&\le \Pr[X_1 \le x_1 \text{ or } \ldots \text{ or } X_{n-1} \le x_{n-1} \text{ or } X_n \le \varphi^{-1+}_{x_1,\ldots,x_{n-1}}(s)] \\
&\le \sum_{i=1}^{n-1} F_i(x_i) + F_n(\varphi^{-1+}_{x_1,\ldots,x_{n-1}}(s)),
\end{aligned}$$

whence the right-hand side inequality follows in (8.28). For the left-hand inequality, it suffices to note that

$$\Pr[\Psi(X_1,\ldots,X_n) \le s] \ge \max\left\{\sum_{i=1}^{n-1} F_i(t_i) + F_n(\varphi^{-1+}_{t_1,\ldots,t_{n-1}}(s)) - (n-1), 0\right\},$$

and this completes the proof. □

Remark 8.4.17. We adapt here the comments in Remark 8.4.14 to the multivariate case. The condition $\Psi(t_1,\ldots,t_n) = s$ is equivalent to

$$\begin{cases} \varphi_{t_1,\ldots,t_{n-1}}(t_n) \le s \\ \varphi_{t_1,\ldots,t_{n-1}}(t_n) > s - \epsilon \text{ for all } \epsilon > 0 \end{cases} \Leftrightarrow \begin{cases} t_n \le \varphi^{-1+}_{t_1,\ldots,t_{n-1}}(s) \\ t_n > \varphi^{-1+}_{t_1,\ldots,t_{n-1}}(s-\epsilon) \text{ for all } \epsilon > 0, \end{cases}$$

that is,

$$\varphi^{-1+}_{t_1,\ldots,t_{n-1}}(s-) \le t_n \le \varphi^{-1+}_{t_1,\ldots,t_{n-1}}(s).$$

The supremum over $\{(t_1,\ldots,t_n) \in \mathbb{R}^n | \Psi(t_1,\ldots,t_n) = s\}$ is taken at the right-hand endpoint of the interval $[\varphi^{-1+}_{t_1,\ldots,t_{n-1}}(s-), \varphi^{-1+}_{t_1,\ldots,t_{n-1}}(s)]$, implying that (8.25) readily extends to dimensions 3 or greater as

$$F_{\min}(s|\Psi) = \sup_{(t_1,\ldots,t_n)\in\mathbb{R}^n|\Psi(t_1,\ldots,t_n)=s} \max\left\{\sum_{i=1}^{n} F_i(t_i) - (n-1), 0\right\}.$$

Exactly as in the bivariate case, a representation like (8.26) is in general not valid. ∇

8.4.7 Improvement of the bounds on functions of risks under positive orthant dependence

Now assume that we have at our disposal some partial knowledge of the dependence structure existing between the X_i, namely that they are POD. In such a case, we are in a position to prove the following result, which provides better bounds on the df of $\Psi(X_1,\ldots,X_n)$ than $F_{\min}(\cdot|\Psi)$ and $F_{\max}(\cdot|\Psi)$ in (8.28).

Proposition 8.4.18
Let $\boldsymbol{X}$ be a POD n-dimensional random vector with marginals $F_1, \ldots, F_n$. Given a non-decreasing and continuous function $\Psi: \mathbb{R}^n \to \mathbb{R}$, the inequalities

$$F^*_{\min}(s|\Psi) \leq \Pr[\Psi(X_1, \ldots, X_n) \leq s] \leq F^*_{\max}(s|\Psi) \tag{8.29}$$

hold for all $s \in \mathbb{R}$, with

$$F^*_{\min}(s|\Psi) = \sup_{(t_1,\ldots,t_{n-1})\in\mathbb{R}^{n-1}} \left\{ \prod_{i=1}^{n-1} F_i(t_i) \times F_n(\varphi^{-1+}_{t_1,\ldots,t_{n-1}}(s)) \right\},$$

and

$$F^*_{\max}(s|\Psi) = \inf_{(t_1,\ldots,t_{n-1})\in\mathbb{R}^{n-1}} \left\{ 1 - \prod_{i=1}^{n-1} \overline{F}_i(t_i) \times \overline{F}_n(\varphi^{-1+}_{t_1,\ldots,t_{n-1}}(s)) \right\}.$$

8.4.8 The case of partially specified marginals

Hitherts, we have derived bounds on the df F_S of S assuming that the marginals $F_1, \ldots, F_n$ were completely specified. In this section, we will examine the case where the marginals $F_1, \ldots, F_n$ are unknown but their first few moments (either the mean and variance or the mean, variance and skewness) and upper bound (if any) are given. In order to obtain bounds on F_S, it suffices in fact to bound each F_i with two extremal dfs based on the partial information available about the X_i. To this end, we proceed as in Kaas and Goovaerts (1985).

Consider a non-negative random variable Y for which only the mean μ, and the standard deviation σ are known. Then there exist two dfs, $M^{(\mu,\sigma)}$ and $W^{(\mu,\sigma)}$, say, such that

$$M^{(\mu,\sigma)}(s) \leq F_Y(s) \leq W^{(\mu,\sigma)}(s) \tag{8.30}$$

is verified for all $s \geq 0$. Explicit expressions for the extremal distributions in (8.30) are provided in Table 8.1 (Kaas and Goovaerts 1985, Table 2), where δ_2 stands for the second moment of Y, that is, $\delta_2 = \mathbb{E}[Y^2]$.

Table 8.1 External distributions in (8.30), two moments known, unbounded support

Value of s	$M^{(\mu,\sigma)}(s)$	$W^{(\mu,\sigma)}(s) - M^{(\mu,\sigma)}(s)$
$0 < s < \mu$	0	$\frac{\sigma^2}{(s-\mu)^2+\sigma^2}$
$\mu < s < \frac{\delta_2}{\mu}$	$\frac{s-\mu}{s}$	$\frac{\mu}{s}$
$s > \frac{\delta_2}{\mu}$	$\frac{(s-\mu)^2}{(s-\mu)^2+\sigma^2}$	$\frac{\sigma^2}{(s-\mu)^2+\sigma^2}$

When it is further known that there exists an upper bound b for Y, that is, $\Pr[Y \leq b] = 1$, the extremal distributions in (8.30) can be refined as

$$M^{(\mu,\sigma,b)}(s) \leq F_Y(s) \leq W^{(\mu,\sigma,b)}(s) \tag{8.31}$$

which is verified for all $s \geq 0$. Explicit expressions for these extremal distributions are provided in Table 8.2 (Kaas and Goovaerts 1985, Table 1).

When the skewness γ of Y is also known, tighter bounds $M^{(\mu,\sigma,\gamma)}$ and $W^{(\mu,\sigma,\gamma)}$, say, can be found such that

$$M^{(\mu,\sigma,\gamma)}(s) \leq F_Y(s) \leq W^{(\mu,\sigma,\gamma)}(s) \tag{8.32}$$

is verified for all $s \geq 0$. Explicit expressions for the extremal distributions in (8.32) are provided in Table 8.3 (Kaas and Goovaerts 1985, Table 4), where the following symbols are used: δ_3 stands for the third moment of Y, that is, $\delta_3 = \mathbb{E}[Y^3]$,

$$\beta_1(s) = \frac{\gamma + 3\sigma^2 + \mu^3 - s\delta_2}{\delta_2 - s\mu}, \quad \beta_2(s) = \frac{\delta_2 - \mu s}{\mu - s}$$

Table 8.2 External distributions in (8.31), two moments known, bounded support

Value of s	$M^{(\mu,\sigma,b)}(s)$	$W^{(\mu,\sigma,b)}(s) - M^{(\mu,\sigma,b)}(s)$
$0 < s < \mu - \dfrac{\sigma^2}{b-\mu}$	0	$\dfrac{\sigma^2}{(s-\mu)^2 + \sigma^2}$
$\mu - \dfrac{\sigma^2}{b-\mu} < s < \dfrac{\delta_2}{\mu}$	$\dfrac{\sigma^2 + (\mu - b)(\mu - s)}{sb}$	$\dfrac{\sigma^2 + \mu(\mu - b)}{s(s-b)}$
$s > \dfrac{\delta_2}{\mu}$	$\dfrac{(s-\mu)^2}{(s-\mu)^2 + \sigma^2}$	$\dfrac{\sigma^2}{(s-\mu)^2 + \sigma^2}$

Table 8.3 External distributions in (8.32), three moments known, unbounded support

Value of s	$M^{(\mu,\sigma,\gamma)}(s)$	$W^{(\mu,\sigma,\gamma)}(s) - M^{(\mu,\sigma,\gamma)}(s)$
$0 < s < \alpha_-$	0	$\dfrac{\mu - \beta_2(s)}{s - \beta_2(s)}$
$\alpha_- < s < \dfrac{\delta_2}{\mu}$	$\dfrac{\sigma^2 + (\mu - s)(\mu - \beta_1(s))}{s\beta_1(s)}$	$\dfrac{\sigma^2 + (\mu - \beta_1(s))\mu}{s(s - \beta_1(s))}$
$\dfrac{\delta_2}{\mu} < s < \alpha_+$	$\dfrac{\mu - s}{\beta_2(s) - s}$	$\dfrac{\mu - \beta_2(s)}{s - \beta_2(s)}$
$s > \alpha_+$	$\dfrac{\sigma^2 + (\mu - s)(\mu - \beta_1(s))}{s\beta_1(s)} + \dfrac{\sigma^2 + (\mu - s)\mu}{(\beta_1(s) - s)\beta_1(s)}$	$\dfrac{\sigma^2 + (\mu - \beta_1(s))\mu}{s(s - \beta_1(s))}$

and

$$\alpha_{\pm} = \frac{\delta_3 - \mu\delta_2 \pm \sqrt{(\delta_3 - \mu\delta_2)^2 - 4\sigma^2(\mu\delta_3 - \delta_2^2)}}{2\sigma^2}.$$

As in (8.31), when it is further known that there exists an upper bound b for Y, the extremal distributions in (8.32) can be refined as

$$M^{(\mu,\sigma,\gamma,b)}(s) \le F_Y(s) \le W^{(\mu,\sigma,\gamma,b)}(s) \tag{8.33}$$

which is verified for all $s \ge 0$. Explicit expressions for these extremal distributions are provided in Table 8.4 (Kaas and Goovaerts 1985, Table 3), where the following symbols are used:

$$\zeta = \frac{\gamma + 3\sigma^2 + \mu^3 - b\delta_2}{\delta_2 - b\mu} \text{ and } \beta_2^*(s) = \frac{\gamma + 3\sigma^2 + \mu^3 - (b+s)\delta_2 + bs\mu}{\delta_2 - (b+s)\mu + bs}.$$

Now let μ_i, σ_i and γ_i be the mean, standard deviation and skewness corresponding to F_i, $i = 1, 2, \ldots, n$. From Tables 8.1 and 8.3, we see that

$$M_i(s) \le F_i(s) \le W_i(s), \text{ for } i = 1, 2, \ldots, n, \tag{8.34}$$

where M_i (W_i) stands for either $M^{(\mu_i,\sigma_i)}$ or $M^{(\mu_i,\sigma_i,\gamma_i)}$ (either $W^{(\mu_i,\sigma_i)}$ or $W^{(\mu_i,\sigma_i,\gamma_i)}$). When there exist b_i such that $F_i(b_i) = 1$, $i = 1, 2, \ldots, n$, then (8.34) becomes

$$M_i^{(b_i)}(s) \le F_i(s) \le W_i^{(b_i)}(s), \text{ for } i = 1, 2, \ldots, n, \tag{8.35}$$

where $M_i^{(b_i)}$ ($W_i^{(b_i)}$) stands for either $M^{(\mu_i,\sigma_i,b_i)}$ or $M^{(\mu_i,\sigma_i,\gamma_i,b_i)}$ (either $W^{(\mu_i,\sigma_i,b_i)}$ or $W^{(\mu_i,\sigma_i,\gamma_i,b_i)}$), $i = 1, 2, \ldots, n$. Then

$$\widetilde{F}_{\min}(s) \le F_S(s) \le \widetilde{F}_{\max}(s), \text{ for all } s \ge 0, \tag{8.36}$$

Table 8.4 External distributions in (8.33), three moments known, bounded support

Value of s	$M^{(\mu,\sigma,\gamma,b)}(s)$	$W^{(\mu,\sigma,\gamma,b)}(s) - M^{(\mu,\sigma,\gamma,b)}(s)$
$0 < s < \alpha_-$	0	$\dfrac{\sigma^2 + (\mu - \beta_2^*(s))(\mu - b)}{(s - \beta_2^*(s))(s - b)}$
$\alpha_- < s < \zeta$	$\dfrac{\sigma^2 + (\mu - s)(\mu - \beta_1(s))}{s\beta_1(s)}$	$\dfrac{\sigma^2 + (\mu - \beta_1(s))\mu}{s(s - \beta_1(s))}$
$\zeta < s < \alpha_+$	$\dfrac{\sigma^2 + (\mu - s)(\mu - b)}{(\beta_2^*(s) - s)(\beta_2^*(s) - b)}$	$\dfrac{\sigma^2 + (\mu - \beta_2^*(s))(\mu - b)}{(s - \beta_2^*(s))(s - b)}$
$s > \alpha_+$	$\dfrac{\sigma^2 + (\mu - s)(\mu - \beta_1(s))}{s\beta_1(s)} + \dfrac{\sigma^2 + (\mu - s)\mu}{(\beta_1(s) - s)\beta_1(s)}$	$\dfrac{\sigma^2 + (\mu - \beta_1(s))\mu}{s(s - \beta_1(s))}$

with, for $s \in \mathbb{R}$,

$$\widetilde{F}_{\min}(s) = \sup_{(x_1,x_2,\ldots,x_n)\in\Sigma(s)} \max\left\{\sum_{i=1}^{n} \lim_{k\to\infty} M_i\left(x_i - \frac{1}{k}\right) - (n-1), 0\right\},$$

and

$$\widetilde{F}_{\max}(s) = \inf_{(x_1,x_2,\ldots,x_n)\in\Sigma(s)} \min\left\{\sum_{i=1}^{n} W_i(x_i), 1\right\}.$$

Of course, when there exist b_i such that $F_i(b_i) = 1$, $i = 1, \ldots, n$, M_i and W_i are replaced in the expressions for $\widetilde{F}_{\min}$ and $\widetilde{F}_{\max}$ by $M_i^{(b_i)}$ and $W_i^{(b_i)}$, respectively. If the X_i are POD, then (8.36) is valid with the following improved bounds:

$$\widetilde{F}_{\min}(s) = \sup_{(x_1,x_2,\ldots,x_n)\in\Sigma(s)} \left\{\prod_{i=1}^{n} M_i(x_i)\right\}$$

and

$$\widetilde{F}_{\max}(s) = 1 - \sup_{(x_1,x_2,\ldots,x_n)\in\Sigma(s)} \left\{\prod_{i=1}^{n} (1 - W_i(x_i))\right\}.$$

8.5 SOME FINANCIAL APPLICATIONS

8.5.1 Stochastic bounds on present values

Let V_k be the present value at time 0 of an amount of α_k paid at time k, $k = 1, 2, \ldots$. Denote by F_k the df of V_k. The stochastic discounted value at time 0 of payments α_t made at times $t = 1, 2, \ldots, n$ is then given by

$$Z_n = V_1 + V_2 + \ldots + V_n. \tag{8.37}$$

Consider, for instance, an insurance company facing payments α_t at times $t = 1, 2, \ldots, n$; the present value of these n deterministic payments is given by (8.37).

The V_i involved in (8.37) are obviously correlated, so that the convenient independence assumption for the summands in Z_n is not realistic. As a consequence, an exact expression for the df of Z_n requires knowledge of the joint distribution of the random vector $(V_1, V_2, \ldots, V_n)$, which is in general not available. Goovaerts, Dhaene and De Schepper (2000) proposed to circumvent this problem by approximating Z_n by means of

$$\widetilde{Z}_n = F_1^{-1}(U) + F_2^{-1}(U) + \ldots + F_n^{-1}(U),$$

where $U \sim \mathcal{U}ni(0,1)$ and the F_i^{-1} are the quantile functions associated with the F_i. We obviously have that $\mathbb{E}[Z_n] = \mathbb{E}[\widetilde{Z}_n]$ and we know from Proposition 6.3.7 together with Corollary 6.3.10 that $Z_n \preceq_{\mathrm{SL},=} \widetilde{Z}_n$.

Since Z_n precedes $\widetilde{Z}_n$ in the convex sense, the approximation $\widetilde{Z}_n$ is considered as less favourable by all risk-averse decision-makers, and the method is thus conservative. Moreover, the df of $\widetilde{Z}_n$ admits an explicit expression and is particularly easy to handle.

We aim to provide lower and upper bounds on Z_n in the $\preceq_{\mathrm{ST}}$ sense, using the method described earlier in this chapter. This approach also provides upper and lower bounds on VaRs at different probability levels. Such bounds cannot be obtained with the aid of the convex approximation $\widetilde{Z}_n$. Indeed, there is in general no relation between $\Pr[Z_n \le z]$ and $\Pr[\widetilde{Z}_n \le z]$ (since indicator functions are not convex).

8.5.2 Stochastic annuities

Let δ_s be the force of interest at time s and let the function Y_t denote the force of interest accumulation at time t, that is,

$$Y_t = \int_0^t \delta_s ds.$$

The random present value at time 0 of a payment of 1 monetary unit at time t is given by $\exp(-Y_t)$, $t \ge 0$.

As noticed by Parker (1994b), there are two main approaches to modelling the interest randomness, namely the modelling of Y_t and the modeling of δ_s. In the first approach, we could let Y_t be the sum of a deterministic drift of slope δ and a perturbation modelled by a Wiener process, that is,

$$Y_t = \delta t + \sigma W_t, \quad t \in \mathbb{R}^+, \tag{8.38}$$

where σ is a non-negative constant and $\{W_t, \quad t \in \mathbb{R}^+\}$ is a standardized Brownian motion. In such a case, V_t is lognormally distributed with parameters $-\delta t$ and $\sigma^2 t$. The discounted cash flow Z_n is of the form

$$Z_n = \sum_{i=1}^{n} \exp(-\delta i - X_i),$$

where $X_i \sim \mathcal{N}or(0, i\sigma^2)$ and δ is the expected force of interest. The convex upper bound $\widetilde{Z}_n$ on Z_n obtained by Goovaerts, Dhaene and De Schepper (2000) is

$$\widetilde{Z}_n = \sum_{i=1}^{n} \exp\left(-\delta i - \sigma\sqrt{i}\Phi^{-1}(U)\right), \tag{8.39}$$

where Φ is the df of a standard normal distribution and $U \sim \mathcal{U}ni(0, 1)$. The tf of $\widetilde{Z}_n$ then follows from

$$\Pr[\widetilde{Z}_n > x] = 1 - F_{\widetilde{Z}_n}(x) = \Phi(\nu_x),$$

with ν_x the root of the equation

$$\sum_{i=1}^{n} \alpha_i \exp(-\delta i - \sqrt{i}\sigma\nu_x) = x.$$

Figure 8.2 shows the functions $F_{\min}$ and $F_{\max}$ involved in Proposition 8.4.13. Between them is the approximation $F_{\widetilde{Z}_n}$ of the unknown F_{Z_n} for $n = 10$, $\delta = 0.08$ and $\sigma = 0.02$. Figure 8.4

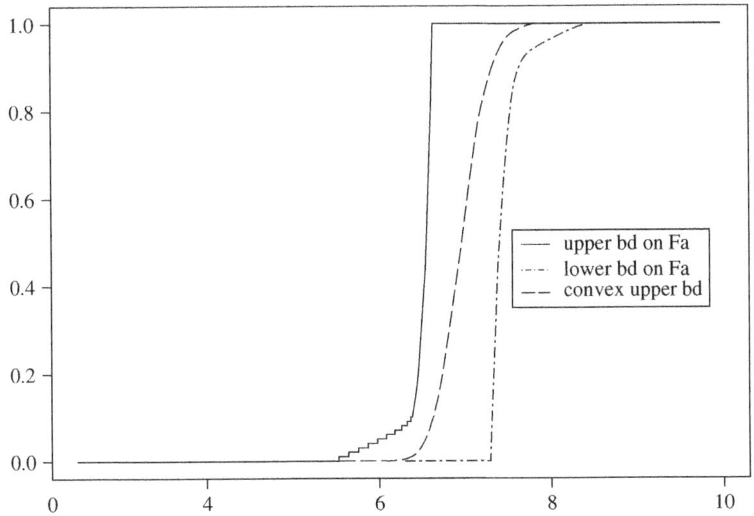

Figure 8.2 Graph of the bounds in Proposition 8.4.13 and cumulative distribution function of $\tilde{Z}_{10}$ for (8.38) with $\delta = 0.08$ and $\sigma = 0.02$

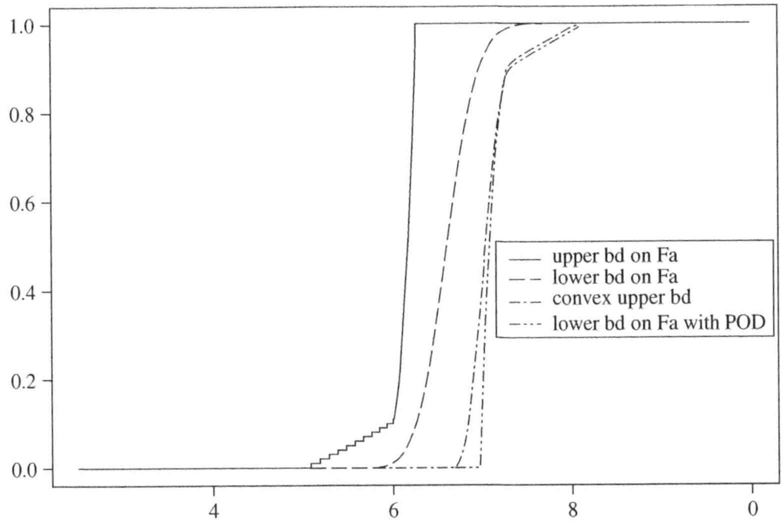

Figure 8.3 Graph of the bounds (8.23) and cumulative distribution function of $\tilde{Z}_{10}$ for (8.38) with $\delta = 0.08$ and $\sigma = 0.02$

shows the same functions for $n = 20$. Comparing the df of the convex approximation (8.39) with the stochastic bounds of Proposition 8.4.13, we see from Figures 8.2 and 8.4 that (8.39) lies in the very middle of the admissible region bordered by $F_{\min}$ and $F_{\max}$. This indicates that (8.39) is reasonable. In Figures 8.3 and 8.5, we further assume that the V_i are POD and we compute the improved bounds furnished in Proposition 8.4.12. Only the lower bound is improved. Indeed, both upper and lower bounds on the distribution of a sum of rvs are improved when the supports of the random variables are of the form $[a_i, b_i]$ with

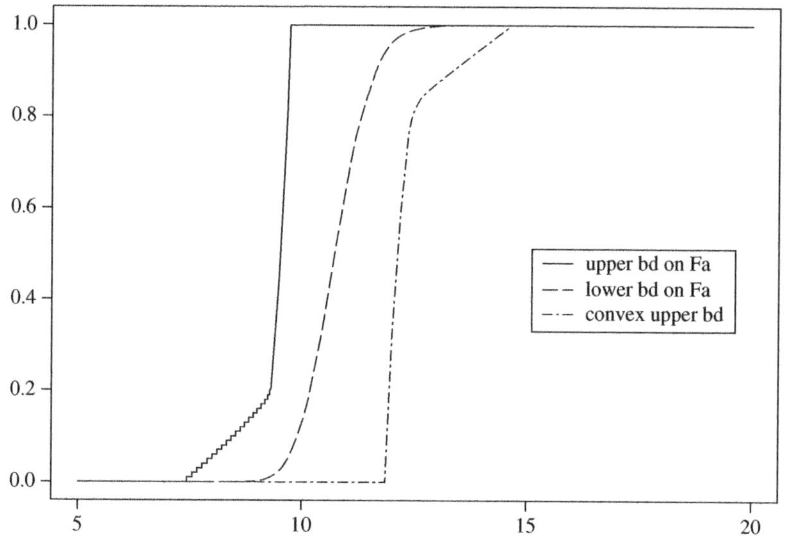

Figure 8.4 Graphs of the bounds in Proposition 8.4.13 and cumulative distribution function of $\tilde{Z}_{20}$ for (8.38) with $\delta = 0.08$ and $\sigma = 0.02$

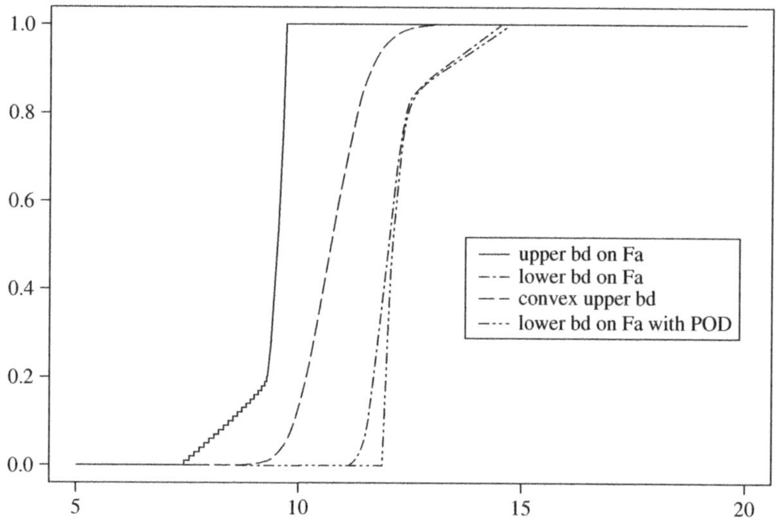

Figure 8.5 Graphs of the bounds (8.23) and cumulative distribution function of $\tilde{Z}_{20}$ for (8.38) with $\delta = 0.08$ and $\sigma = 0.02$

$-\infty < a_i < b_i < +\infty$. If b_i is equal to $+\infty$, only the lower bound will be improved with the POD assumption. In our examples, the rvs are lognormally distributed with supports corresponding to $[0, +\infty)$. If, as in Goovaerts and Dhaene (1999), δ_t is defined by a Cox–Ingersall–Ross model, then Y_t will be strictly positive, $V_t = \exp(-Y_t)$ will take values between 0 and 1, and therefore upper and lower bounds on the distribution of Z_t will have been improved.

A second approach to modelling interest randomness is to model δ_s. For instance, the force of interest can be defined by the differential equation

$$d\delta_t = -\alpha(\delta_t - \delta)dt + \sigma dW_t, \tag{8.40}$$

with non-negative constants α and σ, and with initial value $\delta_0 = \delta \geq 0$; $\{\delta_t, t \geq 0\}$ is thus an Ornstein–Uhlenbeck process. The force of interest accumulation function $\{Y_t, t \geq 0\}$ is therefore a Gaussian process with mean function

$$t \mapsto \mu_t = \delta t + (\delta_0 - \delta)\frac{1-\exp(-\alpha t)}{\alpha}$$

and autocovariance $(s, t) \mapsto \mathbb{C}[Y_s, Y_t] \equiv \omega(s, t)$, where

$$\omega(s,t) = \frac{\sigma^2}{\alpha^2}\min(s,t) + \frac{\sigma^2}{2\alpha^3}\{-2 + 2\exp(-\alpha s) + 2\exp(-\alpha t) \\ - \exp(-\alpha(t-s)) - \exp(-\alpha(t+s))\};$$

see Parker (1994a, Section 6). Then,

$$Z_n = \sum_{i=1}^{n} \exp(-Y_i),$$

where Y_i is a normal rv with mean μ_i and variance $\omega(i, i)$. In such a case, the convex upper bound $\widetilde{Z}_n$ follows from Goovaerts, Dhaene and De Schepper (2000)

$$\widetilde{Z}_n = \sum_{i=1}^{n} \exp\left(-\mu_i - \sqrt{\omega(i,i)}\Phi^{-1}(U)\right),$$

where $U \sim \mathcal{U}ni(0, 1)$. Figure 8.6 shows the bounds on the cumulative df of Z_{10} in (8.40) with $\delta = 0.06$, $\delta_0 = 0.08$, $\alpha = 0.3$ and $\sigma = 0.01$, together with the cumulative df of $\widetilde{Z}_{10}$. Figure 8.8 shows the same bounds for Z_{20}. The comments inspired by Figures 8.2 and 8.4 still apply. In Figures 8.7 and 8.9, we assume that the V_i are POD. Again, the improvement with POD is moderate.

8.5.3 *Life insurance*

Consider a temporary life annuity issued to an individual aged x with curtate future lifetime K, and write $\Pr[k < K \leq k+1] = {}_{k|}q_x$ and $\Pr[K > n] = {}_n p_x$. We assume that K is independent of the random discount factors $V_1, V_2, V_3, \ldots$. The net single premium relating to this contract is given by

$$a_{x;\overline{n}|} = \mathbb{E}[a^\circ_{x;\overline{n}|}],$$

with

$$a^\circ_{x;\overline{n}|} = \begin{cases} 0 & \text{if } K = 0, \\ Z_K, & \text{if } K = 1, \ldots, n-1, \\ Z_n, & \text{if } K \geq n, \end{cases}$$

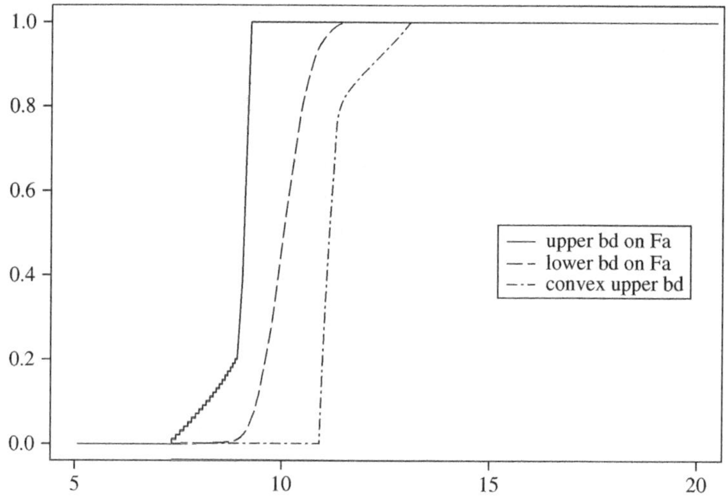

Figure 8.6 Graphs of the bounds in Proposition 8.4.13 and cumulative distribution function of $\tilde{Z}_{10}$ for (8.40) with $\delta = 0.06$, $\delta_0 = 0.08$, $\alpha = 0.3$ and $\sigma = 0.01$

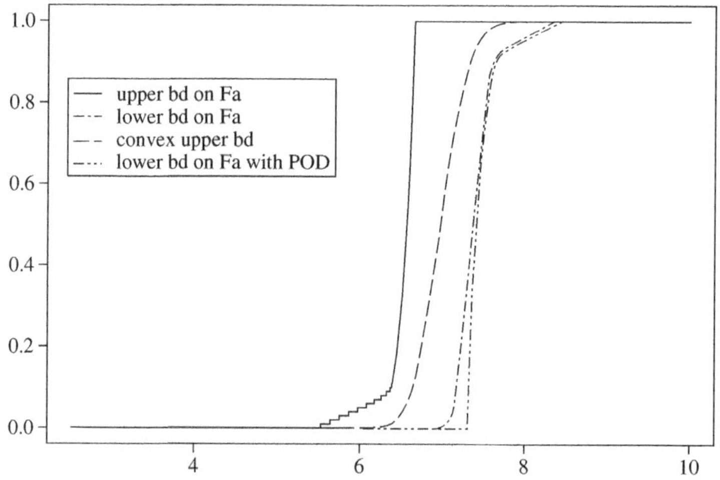

Figure 8.7 Graphs of the bounds (8.23) and cumulative distribution function of $\tilde{Z}_{10}$ for (8.40) with $\delta = 0.06$, $\delta_0 = 0.08$, $\alpha = 0.3$ and $\sigma = 0.01$

where Z is defined as in (8.37). By conditioning on K, the net single premium relating to such a contract is

$$a_{x;\overline{n}|} = \sum_{k=1}^{n-1} \mathbb{E}[Z_k]_{k|}q_x + \mathbb{E}[Z_n]_n p_x.$$

The cumulative df of $a^{\circ}_{x;\overline{n}|}$ is also obtained by conditioning on K:

$$\Pr[a^{\circ}_{x;\overline{n}|} \leq y] = q_x + \sum_{k=1}^{n-1} \Pr[Z_k \leq y]_{k|}q_x + \Pr[Z_n \leq y]_n p_x.$$

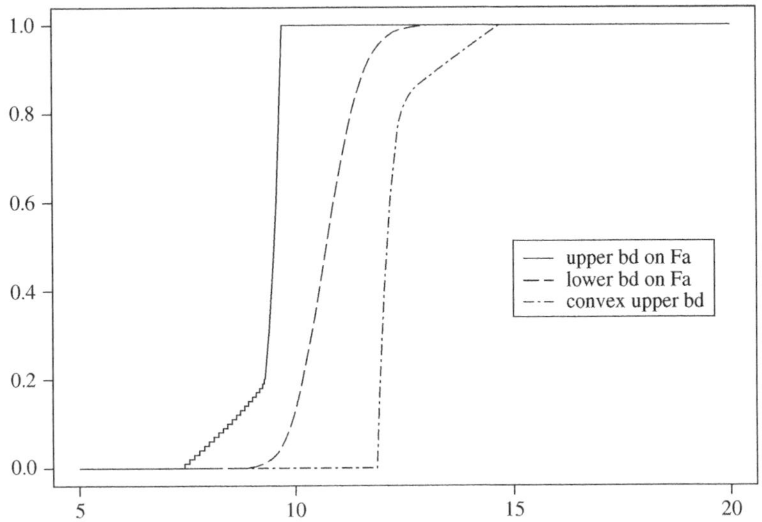

Figure 8.8 Graphs of the bounds in Proposition 8.4.13 and cumulative distribution function of $\tilde{Z}_{20}$ for (8.40) with $\delta = 0.06$, $\delta_0 = 0.08$, $\alpha = 0.3$ and $\sigma = 0.01$

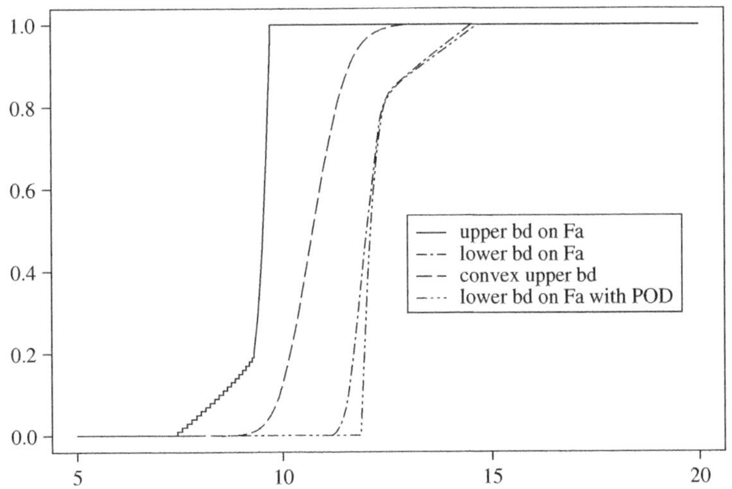

Figure 8.9 Graphs of the bounds (8.23) and cumulative distribution function of $\tilde{Z}_{20}$ for (8.40) with $\delta = 0.06$, $\delta_0 = 0.08$, $\alpha = 0.3$ and $\sigma = 0.01$

No explicit expression exists for $\Pr[a^{\circ}_{x;\overline{n}|} \leq y]$, but using the approach developed above allows us to find stochastic dominance bounds on $a^{\circ}_{x;\overline{n}|}$. Figure 8.10 plots the bounds on $\Pr[a^{\circ}_{x;\overline{n}|} \leq y]$ for an individual aged 45 for model (8.38) with $\delta = 0.08$ and $\sigma = 0.02$. Figure 8.11 does the same for (8.40) with $\delta = 0.06$, $\delta_0 = 0.08$, $\alpha = 0.3$ and $\sigma = 0.01$. For these numerical illustrations, we used the standard mortality table (Makeham model) given in Bowers *et al.* (1997). The bounds in Figures 8.10 and 8.11 give a good idea of the danger inherent in the stochastic interest rate combined with the stochastic mortality. Let us mention that the convex approximation of Goovaerts, Dhaene and De Schepper (2000) also applies in this situation.

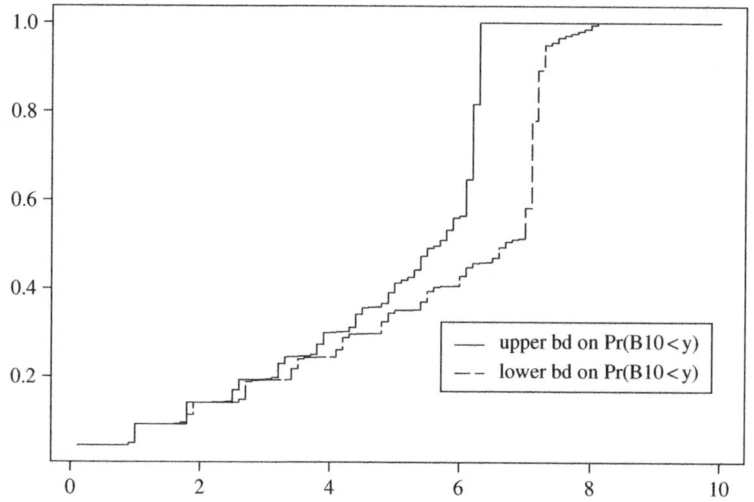

Figure 8.10 Bounds on $\Pr[a^{\circ}_{\overline{x;10|}} \le y]$ for $x = 45$ and (8.38) with $\delta = 0.08$ and $\sigma = 0.02$

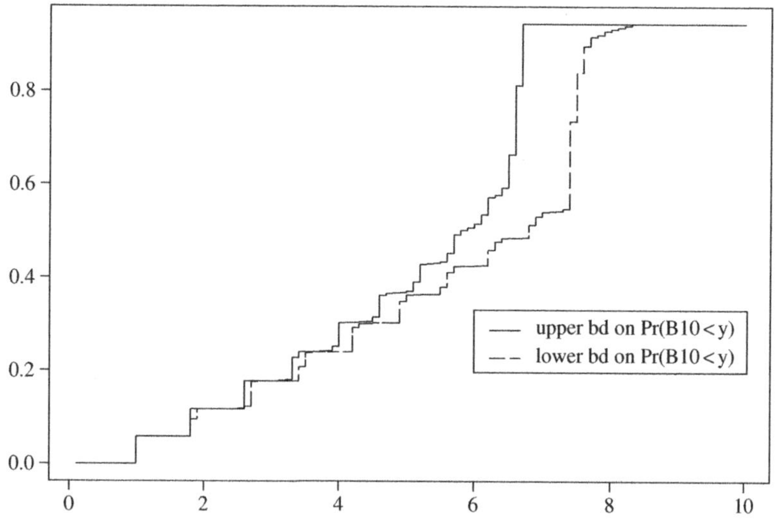

Figure 8.11 Bounds on $\Pr[a^{\circ}_{\overline{x;10|}} \le y]$ for $x = 45$ and (8.40) with $\delta = 0.06$, $\delta_0 = 0.08$, $\alpha = 0.3$ and $\sigma = 0.01$

8.6 EXERCISES

Exercise 8.6.1. Show that if $X_i \preceq_{\mathrm{SL},=} Y_i$, for $i = 1, 2, \ldots, n$, implies $\mathbb{E}[g(\boldsymbol{X})] \le \mathbb{E}[g(\boldsymbol{Y})]$ for all comonotone random vectors $\boldsymbol{X}$ and $\boldsymbol{Y}$, then g is directionally convex.

NB. This result establishes a sort of inverse of Proposition 8.2.2 that holds for comonotonic random vectors. Since comonotonicity is the strongest possible notion of positive dependence, this shows that the directionally convex order is the strongest conclusion that one can expect in Proposition 8.2.2.

Exercise 8.6.2. Let X_1 and X_2 be $\mathcal{U}ni(0,1)$ rvs. Compute $F_{\min}$ and $F_{\max}$ as in Proposition 8.4.2.

Exercise 8.6.3. Consider Weibull rvs $\mathcal{W}ei(\lambda_i, \alpha_i, \theta_i)$ with df

$$F_i(x) = 1 - \exp\left(-\left(\frac{x-\theta_i}{\alpha_i}\right)^{\lambda_i}\right), \quad x \geq \theta_i$$

and parameters $\theta_i \in \mathbb{R}$, $\alpha_i > 0$ and $\lambda_i > 0$. In the special case where $\lambda_1 = \ldots = \lambda_n = \lambda$, show that

$$F_{\max} = \mathcal{W}ei\left(\lambda, \max\{\alpha_1, \ldots, \alpha_n\}, \sum_{i=1}^{n} \theta_i\right).$$

Note that no explicit expression can be derived for $F_{\min}$, however.

Exercise 8.6.4. Let X_1 and X_2 be $\mathcal{N}or(0, \sigma^2)$ rvs. Compute $F_{\min}$ and $F_{\max}$ as in Proposition 8.4.2.

Exercise 8.6.5. Proposition 8.4.13 is easily adapted to monotone functions Ψ. Show that under the assumptions of Proposition 8.4.13 with Ψ non-decreasing in the first argument and non-increasing in the second argument, the bounds in (8.24) become

$$F_{\min}(s|\Psi) = \sup_{t_1 \in \mathbb{R}} \left\{F_1(t_1) - \min\left\{F_1(t_1), F_2(\varphi_{t_1}^{-1}(s))\right\}\right\},$$

and

$$F_{\max}(s|\Psi) = \inf_{t_1 \in \mathbb{R}} \left\{1 + F_1(t_1) - \min\left\{F_1(t_1), F_2(\varphi_{t_1}^{-1}(s))\right\}\right\}.$$

Exercise 8.6.6. Show that if Ψ is decreasing, (8.24) becomes

$$1 - F_{\max}(-s| - \Psi) \leq \Pr[\Psi(X_1, X_2) \leq s] \leq 1 - F_{\min}(-s| - \Psi).$$

Exercise 8.6.7. Show that the results of Proposition 8.4.16 can be adapted to functions Ψ non-increasing in some of their arguments and non-decreasing in the others.

9

Integral Orderings and Probability Metrics

In this chapter, integral stochastic orderings and corresponding probability metrics are studied. Several applications in risk management are described. Integral orderings are generated by classes of measurable functions and can be seen as the common opinion shared by categories of decision-makers, in the framework of expected utility theory. Probability metrics measure distances between probability distributions. They can be used to quantify the impact of dependence between risks on various functionals. The actual computation of probabilistic distances will be much facilitated when specific stochastic orderings are known to hold.

9.1 INTRODUCTION

The notion of distance found new life in probability in the form of metrics in spaces of rvs and their probability distributions. The study of limit theorems (among other questions) made it necessary to introduce functionals evaluating the nearness of probability distributions in some probabilistic sense. The use of metrics in many problems is connected with the following fundamental question: 'Is the proposed stochastic model a satisfactory approximation to the real model, and if so, within what limits?'

In this chapter, we focus on probability metrics that have proved their usefulness in actuarial sciences, mainly in the context of risk theory (essentially the approximation of the individual model by its collective analogue). For a thorough presentation of probability metrics, we refer the interested reader to Rachev (1991).

We will be mainly interested in integral probability metrics. Specifically, we will see that such metrics are closely related to integral stochastic orders. These orderings are obtained by requiring that expectations of functions in a given class are ordered. Several stochastic order relations examined so far are of this form. Let us mention $\preceq_{ST}$ generated by the class of non-decreasing functions, $\preceq_{SL}$ by the class of non-decreasing and convex functions and $\preceq_{SL,=}$ by the class of convex functions. It will be seen that many interesting results connect integral stochastic orderings to probability metrics defined with the help of similar classes of functions. Specifically, once appropriate stochastic order relations hold, the computation of probabilistic distance becomes straightforward.

Actuarial Theory for Dependent Risks M. Denuit, J. Dhaene, M. Goovaerts and R. Kaas

Probability metrics can also be used to evaluate the impact of dependence in a given stochastic model, compared to independence. Typical situations where independence may be questioned include policies covering natural disasters, such as hurricanes, tornadoes or floods, where risks located in the same geographical area will be subject to the same catastrophes, and policies covering a group of individuals, such as a household or the staff of important companies. For insurance policies compensating the losses incurred by insured people, the occurrences of claims could be strongly dependent (think of floods or earthquakes in fire insurance) while the dependence among the claim amounts is often much weaker. Although it might be possible for a catastrophe to affect just one economic agent in theory, the more common scenario is that one event affects many economic agents. This might be through some type of contagion or via geographical proximity. Applying results derived for probabilistic distances, we will be in a position to construct bounds for the distance between the total numbers of claims in the original model and under a standard independence assumption. These bounds are effective, that is, easily computable and reasonably small when the dependence is weak; see Lefèvre and Utev (1998), Boutsikas and Koutras (2000) and Denuit, Lefèvre and Utev (2002).

As far as applications are concerned, we will examine the distances between the individual and collective models of risk theory. These models are thoroughly discussed in Kaas *et al.* (2001, Chapters 2 and 3). With this application in mind, we will pay attention in particular to the computation of various distances between $\mathcal{B}er(q)$ and $\mathcal{P}oi(\lambda)$ distributions.

9.2 INTEGRAL STOCHASTIC ORDERINGS

9.2.1 Definition

Integral stochastic orderings are defined by comparing expectations of test functions, as shown in the following definition.

Definition 9.2.1. Consider two rvs X and Y. The integral stochastic ordering $\preceq_*$ corresponding to the class $\mathcal{U}_*$ of functions is defined by

$$X \preceq_* Y \Leftrightarrow \mathbb{E}[g(X)] \leq \mathbb{E}[g(Y)] \text{ for all } g \in \mathcal{U}_*, \tag{9.1}$$

provided that the expectations exist. ∇

Whitt (1986) introduced the notion of *integral stochastic orderings* for relations defined by (9.1). In the literature, various properties of these orderings have been given, mostly on a case-by-case basis. Nevertheless, Marshall (1991) and Müller (1997a) provide some understanding of how some of these properties arise directly as consequences of conditions satisfied by the underlying class $\mathcal{U}_*$. The definition (9.1) of integral stochastic orderings is closely related to expected utility theory, relating g to some utility function u.

9.2.2 Properties

9.2.2.1 Integral orderings and generating classes of functions

A noteworthy feature of the integral stochastic orderings $\preceq_*$ is that many of their properties can be obtained directly from conditions satisfied by the underlying class of functions $\mathcal{U}_*$.

This approach offers an opportunity for a unified study of the various orderings, and provides some insight into why some of the properties do not hold for all stochastic orderings.

Of course, there may be different classes of functions which generate the same integral stochastic order. To check whether the stochastic inequality $X \preceq_* Y$ holds, it is desirable to have 'small' generators, whereas 'large' generators are of interest in applications. From an analytical point of view, this involves restricting $\mathcal{U}_*$ to a dense subclass of it, or replacing $\mathcal{U}_*$ with its closure with respect to some appropriate topology (e.g., the topology of uniform convergence). Müller (1997a, Theorem 3.7) solved the problem of characterizing the largest generator. Broadly speaking, the maximal generator of an integral stochastic ordering is the closure (in some appropriate topology) of the convex cone spanned by $\mathcal{U}_*$ and the constant functions. Henceforth, we denote by $\overline{\mathcal{U}}_*$ the maximal generator of $\preceq_*$.

Translated into an expected utility context, the minimal generator is the set of all decision-makers who lead those in the maximal generator in the following sense. If all the individuals whose utility function belongs to the minimal generator agree on a comparison between X and Y then all those with utility in $\overline{\mathcal{U}}_*$ systematically join them.

9.2.2.2 Properties of the integral ordering

In order to be useful in applications, stochastic order relations should possess at least some of the following properties.

(i) Shift invariance: if $X \preceq_* Y$ then $X+c \preceq_* Y+c$ for any constant c.

(ii) Scale invariance: if $X \preceq_* Y$ then $cX \preceq_* cY$ for any positive constant c.

(iii) Closure under convolution: given X, Y and Z such that Z is independent of both X and Y, if $X \preceq_* Y$ then $X+Z \preceq_* Y+Z$.

(iv) Closure with respect to weak convergence: if $X_n \preceq_* Y_n$ for all $n=1,2,\ldots$ and X_n (Y_n) converges in distribution to X (Y) then $X \preceq_* Y$.

(v) Closure under mixing: if $[X|Z=z] \preceq_* [Y|Z=z]$ for all z in the support of Z, then $X \preceq_* Y$ also holds unconditionally.

9.2.2.3 Corresponding properties of the generating class of functions

A common feature of the integral stochastic orderings is that many of the above properties are consequences of the structure of the generating class of functions, as shown in the next result.

Property 9.2.2
Let $\preceq_*$ be defined as in (9.1). Then,

(i) $\preceq_*$ is shift-invariant provided $g \in \mathcal{U}_* \Rightarrow g_c \in \overline{\mathcal{U}}_*$ where $g_c(x)=g(x+c)$;

(ii) $\preceq_*$ is scale-invariant provided $g \in \mathcal{U}_* \Rightarrow g_c \in \overline{\mathcal{U}}_*$ where $g_c(x)=g(cx)$;

(iii) $\preceq_*$ is closed under convolution provided $g \in \mathcal{U}_* \Rightarrow g_c \in \overline{\mathcal{U}}_*$ where $g_c(x)=g(x+c)$;

(iv) $\preceq_*$ is closed with respect to weak convergence provided there exists a generator consisting of bounded continuous functions;

(v) closure under mixing holds for any integral stochastic order!

Note that the same condition on the elements of $\mathcal{U}_*$ that leads to (i) also gives (iii). This can be seen as follows. From (i), we have that

$$X \preceq_* Y \Rightarrow X + z \preceq_* Y + z \text{ for any } z \in \mathbb{R}.$$

Therefore, given Z independent of X and Y, we get from (v) that

$$X \preceq_* Y \Rightarrow X + Z \preceq_* Y + Z. \tag{9.2}$$

9.2.2.4 Stability under convolution and compounding for integral orderings

Note that many other properties follow from Property 9.2.2, such as closure under compounding, for instance. This is formally stated in the next result.

Property 9.2.3
Let $X_1, X_2, X_3, \ldots$ and $Y_1, Y_2, Y_3, \ldots$ be two sequences of independent rvs such that $X_i \preceq_* Y_i$ for every i. If $\preceq_*$ is closed under convolution then

(i) $\sum_{i=1}^n X_i \preceq_* \sum_{i=1}^n Y_i$ for any integer n;

(ii) $\sum_{i=1}^N X_i \preceq_* \sum_{i=1}^N Y_i$ also holds, where the integer-valued variable N is independent of the X_i and the Y_i.

Proof. To establish (i), note that $X_1 + \ldots + X_{n-1} + X_n \preceq_* X_1 + \ldots + X_{n-1} + Y_n$ and proceed iteratively (without loss of generality, we may assume the the X_i and Y_j are mutually independent).

Turning to (ii), from (i) we have of course that

$$\left[\sum_{i=1}^N X_i \middle| N = n\right] \preceq_* \left[\sum_{i=1}^N Y_i \middle| N = n\right] \text{ for all } n = 1, 2, \ldots.$$

The result then follows from closure under mixing. □

9.3 INTEGRAL PROBABILITY METRICS

9.3.1 Probability metrics

Probability metrics measure the closeness between rvs. They are defined next.

Definition 9.3.1. A functional d mapping a couple of rvs (X, Y) to $\overline{\mathbb{R}}^+ = \mathbb{R}^+ \cup \{+\infty\}$ is said to be a probability metric if it possesses the following three properties: for all rvs X, Y and Z defined on the same probability space,

(i) $\Pr[X=Y]=1 \Rightarrow d(X,Y)=0$;

(ii) $d(X,Y)=d(Y,X)$;

(iii) $d(X,Y) \leq d(X,Z)+d(Z,Y)$.

∇

Since the value of d may be infinite, property (iii) in Definition 9.3.1 means that only one of the two terms in the right-hand side has to be infinite if the left-hand side of the inequality is infinite.

9.3.2 Simple probability metrics

If the value of $d(X,Y)$ is uniquely determined by the marginal distributions of X and Y, the probability metric d is said to be simple. In this case, we sometimes write $d(F_X, F_Y)$ instead of $d(X,Y)$. This is formally stated in the next definition.

Definition 9.3.2. A functional d is said to be a simple probability metric if it possesses properties (ii)–(iii) in Definition 9.3.1, with (i) replaced with $X =_d Y \Rightarrow d(X,Y)=0$. ∇

Note that the value of $d(X,Y)$ is uniquely determined by the marginal distributions F_X and F_Y of X and Y, so that

$$d(X,Y)=d(\widetilde{X},\widetilde{Y}) \text{ for all } (\widetilde{X},\widetilde{Y}) \in \mathcal{R}_2(F_X,F_Y).$$

9.3.3 Integral probability metrics

Important examples of simple probability metrics are the integral probability metrics defined as follows.

Definition 9.3.3. An integral probability metric is defined for a pair of rvs X and Y as

$$d_*(X,Y)=\sup_{g \in \mathcal{U}_*} \left| \mathbb{E}[g(X)] - \mathbb{E}[g(Y)] \right| \tag{9.3}$$

where $\mathcal{U}_*$ is some set of measurable functions $g: \mathbb{R} \to \mathbb{R}$. ∇

Note the strong similarity between integral stochastic orderings defined by (9.1) and integral probability metrics of the form (9.3). This apparent analogous structure will be exploited further to derive powerful results in the same vein as those obtained by Lefèvre and Utev (1998) and Boutsikas and Vaggelatou (2002).

Several metrics considered in this chapter are of integral type. Specifically, we will obtain the total-variation distance by taking $\mathcal{U}_*$ to be the class of indicator functions $\mathbb{I}[A]$ of all the (measurable) subsets A of the real line $\mathbb{R}$; see Section 9.4. The Kolmogorov distance will be obtained by taking $\mathcal{U}_*$ to be the class of all indicator functions $\mathbb{I}[(t,+\infty)]$ of the regions

$(t, +\infty)$; see Section 9.5. The stop-loss distance will be obtained by taking the supremum of the absolute difference between the stop-loss premiums associated with the two claim amounts; see Section 9.7. Stop-loss distances have found many applications in actuarial science; see Gerber (1979, 1984) and De Pril and Dhaene (1992).

Besides integral probability metrics, we will also use integrated (or cumulated) probability metrics. These metrics serve as upper bounds for the corresponding integral probability metrics. They also possess convenient mathematical properties that make them easy to compute. Metrics of this type include the Wasserstein distance (studied in Section 9.6) and the integrated stop-loss metric (studied in Section 9.8).

It is worth mentioning that the distances recalled above have been extended to classes of stop-loss and total-variation distances of various degrees, which can be found in Rachev and Rüschendorf (1990) and Denuit and Van Bellegem (2001). In particular, discrete distances suitable for evaluating the closeness of integer-valued rvs are defined in Denuit, Lefèvre and Utev (2002) and have proved their usefulness in various problems encountered in actuarial risk theory.

9.3.4 *Ideal metrics*

9.3.4.1 Definition

A useful class of metrics studied in this chapter is the class of ideal metrics, defined below. This class is convenient for the study of functionals of sums of independent rvs.

Definition 9.3.4. A metric d is said to be s-ideal if it possesses the following two properties:

(i) Regularity property: for any rvs X, Y and Z such that X and Y are independent of Z, $d(X+Z, Y+Z) \leq d(X, Y)$.

(ii) Positive homogeneity property: for any rvs X and Y and for any positive constant c, $d(cX, cY) = c^s d(X, Y)$.

∇

Condition (i) of Definition 9.3.4 is quite intuitive: it means that it is more difficult to discriminate between $X+Z$ and $Y+Z$ than between X and Y (adding Z to X and Y makes them more similar and results in a smaller distance).

9.3.4.2 Invariance under translation

A simple consequence of the regularity property is the invariance of the metric d under constant translation of the rvs, as stated next.

Property 9.3.5
Let d be an s-ideal metric. For any constant $a \in \mathbb{R}$ and any random variables X and Y,

$$d(X+a, Y+a) = d(X, Y).$$

Proof. Condition (i) of Definition 9.3.4 immediately gives, for $Z = a$,

$$d(X + a, Y + a) \le d(X, Y). \tag{9.4}$$

On the other hand, substituting $X + a$ and $Y + a$ for X and Y, respectively, the same condition (i) yields, with $Z = -a$,

$$d(X, Y) \le d(X + a, Y + a), \tag{9.5}$$

whence the result follows by combining (9.4) and (9.5). □

Adding the same constant to X and Y thus does not modify their distance; this is appealing for actuaries since adding a constant does not increase or decrease the dangerousness of the situation faced by the insurer. In the framework of expected utility theory, this also allows us to set the initial wealth to 0 provided this wealth is deterministic.

9.3.4.3 Subadditivity of ideal metrics

Another consequence of the regularity property in Definition 9.3.4 is the subadditivity of the ideal metric d.

Property 9.3.6
Let d be an s-ideal metric. Given two collections $\{X_1, X_2, \ldots, X_n\}$ and $\{Y_1, Y_2, \ldots, Y_n\}$ of independent rvs and positive constants $c_1, c_2, \ldots, c_n$, we have that

$$d\left(\sum_{i=1}^{n} c_i X_i, \sum_{i=1}^{n} c_i Y_i\right) \le \sum_{i=1}^{n} c_i^s d(X_i, Y_i).$$

Proof. Since the metric d is s-ideal it suffices to prove that if $\{X_1, X_2, \ldots, X_n\}$ and $\{Y_1, Y_2, \ldots, Y_n\}$ are two collections of independent rvs then

$$d\left(\sum_{i=1}^{n} X_i, \sum_{i=1}^{n} Y_i\right) \le \sum_{i=1}^{n} d(X_i, Y_i). \tag{9.6}$$

Let us establish this result by a recursive argument. Inequality (9.6) obviously holds for $n = 1$. Now, assume it is valid for k and let us prove it for $k + 1$. Applying (i) in Definition 9.3.4 yields

$$d\left(\sum_{i=1}^{k+1} X_i, \sum_{i=1}^{k} Y_i + X_{k+1}\right) \le d\left(\sum_{i=1}^{k} X_i, \sum_{i=1}^{k} Y_i\right) \le \sum_{i=1}^{k} d(X_i, Y_i)$$

and

$$d\left(\sum_{i=1}^{k} Y_i + X_{k+1}, \sum_{i=1}^{k+1} Y_i\right) \le d(X_{k+1}, Y_{k+1}),$$

so that we get by the triangle inequality

$$d\left(\sum_{i=1}^{k+1} X_i, \sum_{i=1}^{k+1} Y_i\right) \leq d\left(\sum_{i=1}^{k+1} X_i, \sum_{i=1}^{k} Y_i + X_{k+1}\right)$$
$$+d\left(\sum_{i=1}^{k} Y_i + X_{k+1}, \sum_{i=1}^{k+1} Y_i\right)$$
$$\leq \sum_{i=1}^{k} d(X_i, Y_i) + d(X_{k+1}, Y_{k+1}),$$

and this concludes the proof. □

9.3.5 Minimal metric

With each metric d we can associate the functional

$$\widehat{d}(X, Y) = \inf_{(\widetilde{X},\widetilde{Y})\in\mathcal{R}_2(F_X,F_Y)} d(\widetilde{X}, \widetilde{Y}).$$

It is possible to prove that the functional $\widehat{d}$ is a simple metric. Such a metric is called minimal with respect to d. The idea of minimal metrics goes back to the work of Kantorovitch in the 1940s on the transportation problems of linear programming. Such metrics have been found independently by many authors. They are connected with the useful method of coupling. Distances for such metrics are often hard to compute, but it is easy to give upper bounds attained by at least one joint probability distribution.

9.3.6 Integral orders and metrics

As pointed out by Lefèvre and Utev (1998), integral stochastic orderings and probability metrics are closely related. This fact can be exploited to get interesting results. Specifically, let us consider the integral stochastic ordering $\preceq_*$ generated by the class $\mathcal{U}_*$ of measurable functions through (9.1). Associated with $\preceq_*$ there is a probability metric d_* of the form (9.3). With this choice, the following desirable result holds.

Property 9.3.7
Let us consider a metric d_* of the form (9.3) and an ordering $\preceq_*$ of the form (9.1). Given the rvs X, Y and Z such that $X \preceq_* Y \preceq_* Z$, we have $d_*(X, Y) \leq d_*(X, Z)$.

Proof. It suffices to write

$$d_*(X, Y) = \sup_{g\in\mathcal{U}_*} |\mathbb{E}[g(X)] - \mathbb{E}[g(Y)]|$$
$$\leq \sup_{g\in\mathcal{U}_*} |\mathbb{E}[g(X)] - \mathbb{E}[g(Z)]| = d_*(X, Z),$$

where the inequality follows from the ordering of X, Y and Z, which ensures that for any $g \in \mathcal{U}_*$, $0 \leq \mathbb{E}[g(Y)] - \mathbb{E}[g(X)] \leq \mathbb{E}[g(Z)] - \mathbb{E}[g(X)]$. □

The intuitive result contained in Property 9.3.7 highlights the duality between metrics (9.3) and orders (9.1); it plays an important role in many theoretical developments, even though it is not always explicitly stated.

9.4 TOTAL-VARIATION DISTANCE

9.4.1 Definition

In this section, we examine the total-variation metric, which has been applied in several instances in the actuarial literature. Our definition differs slightly from the classical one (by a constant factor, in fact).

Definition 9.4.1. The total-variation distance between two random variables X and Y, denoted by $d_{\text{TV}}(X, Y)$, is given by

$$d_{\text{TV}}(X, Y) = \int_{-\infty}^{+\infty} |dF_X(t) - dF_Y(t)|.$$

∇

In the light of Definition 9.4.1, d_{TV} turns out to be an L_1-distance between pdfs. It is easy to verify that d_{TV} is 0-ideal. For integer-valued rvs M and N, Definition 9.4.1 obviously reduces to

$$d_{\text{TV}}(M, N) = \sum_{k=0}^{+\infty} \big| \Pr[M = k] - \Pr[N = k] \big|.$$

The following example shows how d_{TV} can be calculated.

Example 9.4.2. Let $I \sim \mathcal{B}er(q)$ and $N \sim \mathcal{P}oi(\lambda)$. Let us examine different cases:

(i) If $\lambda \geq -\ln(1-q)$, then

$$\begin{aligned} d_{\text{TV}}(I, N) &= 1 - q - \exp(-\lambda) + |\lambda \exp(-\lambda) - q| + \sum_{k=2}^{+\infty} \Pr[N = k] \\ &= 2 - 2\exp(-\lambda) - q - \lambda \exp(-\lambda) + |\lambda \exp(-\lambda) - q| \\ &= 2\Big(1 - \exp(-\lambda) - \min\{q, \lambda \exp(-\lambda)\}\Big). \end{aligned}$$

(ii) If $\lambda \leq -\ln(1-q)$, then $\exp(-\lambda) \geq 1 - q$ so that

$$d_{\text{TV}}(I, N) = \exp(-\lambda) - 1 + q + |\lambda \exp(-\lambda) - q| + 1 - \exp(-\lambda)(1 + \lambda).$$

Note that

$$\exp(-\lambda) + \lambda \exp(-\lambda) < 1$$

so that

$$1 - q + \lambda \exp(-\lambda) < 1 \quad \text{since} \exp(-\lambda) > 1 - q.$$

It then follows that $q > \lambda \exp(-\lambda)$ so that, finally,

$$d_{\mathrm{TV}}(I, N) = 2\Big(q - \lambda \exp(-\lambda)\Big).$$

∇

9.4.2 Total-variation distance and integral metrics

The following result gives the connexion between d_{TV} and the standard variation distance, which considers the supremum of the difference between the probability masses given to some random event.

Property 9.4.3
Given two rvs X and Y, $d_{\mathrm{TV}}(X, Y)$ can be represented as

$$d_{\mathrm{TV}}(X, Y) = 2 \sup_A \Big| \Pr[X \in A] - \Pr[Y \in A] \Big|.$$

Proof. Let us start from

$$\begin{aligned}\int_{-\infty}^{+\infty} \Big| dF_X(t) - dF_Y(t) \Big| &= \int_{-\infty}^{+\infty} \Big(dF_Y(t) - dF_X(t) \Big) \\ &\quad + 2\int_{-\infty}^{+\infty} \Big(dF_X(t) - dF_Y(t) \Big)_+ \\ &= 2\int_{-\infty}^{+\infty} \Big(dF_X(t) - dF_Y(t) \Big)_+.\end{aligned}$$

This implies that for any A,

$$\begin{aligned}\int_{-\infty}^{+\infty} \Big| dF_X(t) - dF_Y(t) \Big| &= 2\int_{\{t\in\mathbb{R} | dF_X(t) > dF_Y(t)\}} \Big(dF_X(t) - dF_Y(t) \Big) \\ &\geq 2\Big(\Pr[X \in A] - \Pr[Y \in A] \Big),\end{aligned}$$

with equality for $A = \{t \in \mathbb{R} | dF_X(t) > dF_Y(t)\}$. Hence,

$$\sup_A \Big\{ \Pr[X \in A] - \Pr[Y \in A] \Big\} = \frac{1}{2} \int_{-\infty}^{+\infty} \Big| dF_X(t) - dF_Y(t) \Big|.$$

This yields the assertion. Indeed, since the equality

$$\begin{aligned}&\Big| \Pr[X \in A] - \Pr[Y \in A] \Big| \\ &\qquad = \max\Big(\Pr[X \in A] - \Pr[Y \in A], \Pr[X \in \overline{A}] - \Pr[Y \in \overline{A}] \Big)\end{aligned}$$

holds for any A, the absolute values may be omitted and

$$\sup_A \Big\{ \Big| \Pr[X \in A] - \Pr[Y \in A] \Big| \Big\} = \sup_A \Big\{ \Pr[X \in A] - \Pr[Y \in A] \Big\}.$$

□

Property 9.4.3 pinpoints a practical actuarial use of the total–variation distance. Assume that the actuary approximates the rv X of interest by a simpler one, Y say. If he computes the probability of the event A with the aid of Y, then $\Pr[X \in A]$ satisfies

$$\Pr[Y \in A] - \frac{1}{2} d_{\mathrm{TV}}(X, Y) \leq \Pr[X \in A] \leq \Pr[Y \in A] + \frac{1}{2} d_{\mathrm{TV}}(X, Y).$$

9.4.3 Comonotonicity and total-variation distance

The following result plays a central role in the study of the total-variation distance.

Property 9.4.4
If X and Y are two rvs defined on the same probability space, then

$$d_{\mathrm{TV}}(X, Y) \leq 2\Pr[X \neq Y].$$

Proof. We have for any A that

$$\Pr[X \in A] = \Pr[X \in A, X = Y] + \Pr[X \in A, X \neq Y]$$

and also that

$$\Pr[Y \in A] = \Pr[Y \in A, X = Y] + \Pr[Y \in A, X \neq Y].$$

By subtraction, we see that

$$\begin{aligned} \Big|\Pr[X \in A] - \Pr[Y \in A]\Big| &= \Big|\Pr[X \in A, X \neq Y] - \Pr[Y \in A, X \neq Y]\Big| \\ &\leq \Pr[X \in A, X \neq Y] + \Pr[Y \in A, X \neq Y] \\ &\leq \Pr[X \neq Y], \end{aligned}$$

whence the result follows from Property 9.4.3. □

Using Property 9.4.4, the problem of finding a sharp upper bound for the total-variation distance between X and Y can be reduced to the problem of constructing a joint distribution for X and Y which minimizes $\Pr[X \neq Y]$ or, equivalently, which maximizes $\Pr[X = Y]$.

Let us examine the following example, where the upper bound in Property 9.4.4 is attained when X and Y are comonotonic.

Example 9.4.5. Let $I \sim \mathcal{B}er(q)$ and $N \sim \mathcal{P}oi(q)$. If we take N and I comonotonic, that is, $(N, I) =_d (F_N^{-1}(U), F_I^{-1}(U))$ for $U \sim \mathcal{U}ni(0, 1)$, we get

$$\begin{aligned} \Pr[I = N] &= \Pr\left[F_I^{-1}(U) = F_N^{-1}(U)\right] \\ &= \int_0^{1-q} du + \int_{\exp(-q)}^{\exp(-q)(1+q)} du \\ &= 1 - q + \exp(-q)q, \end{aligned}$$

so that

$$\Pr[I \neq N] = q\Big(1 - \exp(-q)\Big).$$

Now we know from Example 9.4.2 that $d_{\rm TV}(I, N) = 2q(1 - \exp(-q))$ so that

$$d_{\rm TV}(I, N) = 2\Pr[I \neq N],$$

whence it follows that for the Poisson–Bernoulli couple with identical means,

$$d_{\rm TV}(F_I^{-1}(U), F_N^{-1}(U)) = 2\Pr[F_I^{-1}(U) \neq F_N^{-1}(U)].$$

∇

9.4.4 Maximal coupling and total-variation distance

A random couple (X^*, Y^*) is said to be the $d_{\rm TV}$-maximal coupling of (X, Y) if $(X^*, Y^*) \in \mathcal{R}_2(F_X, F_Y)$ and (X^*, Y^*) achieves the upper bound of Proposition 9.4.4, that is,

$$d_{\rm TV}(X^*, Y^*) = 2\Pr[X^* \neq Y^*].$$

For the Bernoulli-Poisson couple, the maximal coupling (I^*, N^*) is the comonotonic version of (I, N), as shown in Example 9.4.5.

In general, however, the maximal coupling is not given by the upper Fréchet bound. The problem of finding a maximal coupling for two arbitrary integer-valued random variables N and M was solved by Wang (1986).

9.5 KOLMOGOROV DISTANCE

9.5.1 Definition

One of the most popular metrics is the Kolmogorov (or uniform) metric based on the well-known Kolmogorov–Smirnov statistic (associated of the goodness-of-fit test of that name), defined as follows.

Definition 9.5.1. The Kolmogorov distance $d_{\rm K}$ between the rvs X and Y is given by

$$d_{\rm K}(X, Y) = \sup_{t \in \mathbb{R}} |\overline{F}_X(t) - \overline{F}_Y(t)|.$$

∇

The practical use of $d_{\rm K}$ is obvious. Assume that the actuary bases his computations on the rv Y, simpler than the 'true' rv X. He has at his disposal the following margin on the probability that X exceeds any threshold t:

$$\Pr[Y > t] - d_{\rm K}(X, Y) \leq \Pr[X > t] \leq \Pr[Y > t] + d_{\rm K}(X, Y).$$

Let us now compute the distance between the Bernoulli and the Poisson distributions.

Example 9.5.2. Let us consider $I \sim \mathcal{B}er(q)$ and $N \sim \mathcal{P}oi(\lambda)$. If $q \leq \lambda < -\ln(1-q)$, then

$$d_K(N, I) = \max\left\{\exp(-\lambda) - 1 + q, 1 - (1+\lambda)\exp(-\lambda)\right\}.$$

The case $\lambda \geq -\ln(1-q)$ will be treated in Example 9.5.5. ∇

9.5.2 Stochastic dominance, Kolmogorov and total-variation distances

It is easily checked that d_K is 0-ideal. The stochastic ordering associated with d_K is $\preceq_{ST}$; by virtue of Property 9.3.7 we have that

$$X \preceq_{ST} Y \preceq_{ST} Z \Rightarrow d_K(X, Y) \leq d_K(X, Z).$$

Let us now examine the relationship between d_{TV} and d_K; the following result is an immediate consequence of Property 9.4.4 since $\overline{F}_X(t) = \Pr[X \in (t, +\infty)]$.

Property 9.5.3
Given two rvs X and Y, we have that $d_K(X, Y) \leq d_{TV}(X, Y)$.

9.5.3 Kolmogorov distance under single crossing condition for probability density functions

Let us now examine the consequence of a ranking in the $\preceq_{ST}$ sense between rvs whose distance has to be evaluated. The following result is due to Lefèvre and Utev (1998).

Proposition 9.5.4
If $X \preceq_{ST} Y$ and $S^-(dF_X - dF_Y) \leq 1$ then $d_{TV}(X, Y) = 2d_K(X, Y)$.

Proof. The result is obvious when $S^-(dF_X - dF_Y) = 0$, so that we only have to consider the situation $S^-(dF_X - dF_Y) = 1$. Let t_0 be such that $dF_Y(t) - dF_X(t) \leq 0$ for $t \leq t_0$ and $dF_Y(t) - dF_X(t) \geq 0$ for $t \geq t_0$. Therefore,

$$\begin{aligned} d_{TV}(X, Y) &= \int_{-\infty}^{+\infty} |dF_X(t) - dF_Y(t)| \\ &= \int_{-\infty}^{t_0} \Big(dF_X(t) - dF_Y(t)\Big) + \int_{t_0}^{+\infty} \Big(dF_Y(t) - dF_X(t)\Big) \\ &= 2\int_{t_0}^{+\infty} \Big(dF_Y(t) - dF_X(t)\Big) \\ &= 2\Big(\overline{F}_Y(t_0) - \overline{F}_X(t_0)\Big) \leq 2d_K(X, Y). \end{aligned}$$

On the other hand, since $X \preceq_{\text{ST}} Y$ we obtain

$$\begin{aligned}
2d_{\text{K}}(X, Y) &= 2\sup_{t\in\mathbb{R}} \left\{\overline{F}_Y(t) - \overline{F}_X(t)\right\} \\
&= 2\sup_{t\in\mathbb{R}} \left\{\int_t^{+\infty} \left(dF_Y(x) - dF_X(x)\right)\right\} \\
&= \sup_{t\in\mathbb{R}} \left\{\int_{-\infty}^{t-} \left(dF_X(x) - dF_Y(x)\right) + \int_t^{+\infty} \left(dF_Y(x) - dF_X(x)\right)\right\} \\
&\leq \sup_{t\in\mathbb{R}} \left\{\int_{-\infty}^{t-} \left(dF_X(x) - dF_Y(x)\right)\right\} + \sup_{t\in\mathbb{R}} \left\{\int_t^{+\infty} \left(dF_Y(x) - dF_X(x)\right)\right\} \\
&= \int_{-\infty}^{t_0-} \left(dF_X(x) - dF_Y(x)\right) + \int_{t_0}^{+\infty} \left(dF_Y(x) - dF_X(x)\right) \\
&= d_{\text{TV}}(X, Y),
\end{aligned}$$

which leads to the desired result. □

Let us now apply Proposition 9.5.4 to compute Kolmogorov distances in several particular cases of interest.

Example 9.5.5. Let us consider $I \sim \mathcal{B}er\,(q)$ and $N \sim \mathcal{P}oi\,(\lambda)$. If $\lambda \geq -\ln(1-q)$ then $S^-(\Pr[I=k] - \Pr[N=k]) = 1$ so that Proposition 9.5.4 applies. Hence, Example 9.4.2 allows us to write

$$\begin{aligned}
d_{\text{K}}(N, I) &= \tfrac{1}{2} d_{\text{TV}}(N, I) \\
&= 1 - \exp(-\lambda) - \min\{q, \lambda\exp(-\lambda)\}.
\end{aligned}$$

∇

9.6 WASSERSTEIN DISTANCE

9.6.1 Definition

Dobrushin (1970) used a characteristic of proximity of two probability distributions that he called the Wasserstein distance. This distance, also known as the Dudley or Kantorovitch distance, is defined as follows.

Definition 9.6.1. Given two rvs X and Y, the Wasserstein distance d_{W} is defined as

$$d_{\text{W}}(X, Y) = \int_{-\infty}^{+\infty} \left|\overline{F}_X(t) - \overline{F}_Y(t)\right| dt.$$

∇

For two integer-valued rvs X and Y, it is clear from Definition 9.6.1 that the Wasserstein distance d_{W} can be cast into the form

$$d_{\text{W}}(X, Y) = \sum_{j=0}^{+\infty} \left|\overline{F}_X(j) - \overline{F}_Y(j)\right|.$$

The information provided by d_W completes that contained in d_K. It gives an indication of the total deviation of F_X from F_Y in a situation where the actuary replaces the df F_X by a simpler one, F_Y say.

Example 9.6.2. Let us consider $I \sim \mathcal{B}er(q)$ and $N \sim \mathcal{P}oi(\lambda)$. If $q \leq \lambda < -\ln(1-q)$ then

$$\begin{aligned} d_W(I, N) &= \overline{F}_I(0) - \overline{F}_N(0) + \sum_{j=1}^{+\infty} \overline{F}_N(j) \\ &= q - (1 - \exp(-\lambda)) + \lambda - (1 - \exp(-\lambda)) \\ &= q + \lambda - 2(1 - \exp(-\lambda)). \end{aligned}$$

The case $\lambda \geq -\ln(1-q)$ will be treated in Example 9.6.4. ∇

9.6.2 Properties

9.6.2.1 Wasserstein distance is an ideal metric

Note that the Wasserstein distance, unlike the total-variation and Kolmogorov distances, is not preserved under changes of scales. In fact, if X and Y are real-valued rvs then $d_W(cX, cY) = c d_W(X, Y)$ for any $c > 0$. So the Wasserstein distance d_W is 1-ideal.

9.6.2.2 Wasserstein distance and stochastic dominance

Even if d_W does not strictly fall under the conditions of Property 9.3.7, we still have that

$$X \preceq_{ST} Y \preceq_{ST} Z \Rightarrow d_W(X, Y) \leq d_W(X, Z)$$

since the inequalities $0 \leq \overline{F}_Y(t) - \overline{F}_X(t) \leq \overline{F}_Z(t) - \overline{F}_X(t)$ are satisfied for all $t \in \mathbb{R}$. Note, moreover, that d_W is easily obtained when X and Y are ordered in the $\preceq_{ST}$ sense, as shown in the next result.

Property 9.6.3
Given two risks X and Y, if $X \preceq_{ST} Y$ then $d_W(X, Y) = \mathbb{E}[Y] - \mathbb{E}[X]$.

Proof. This simply comes from

$$d_W(X, Y) = \int_0^{+\infty} \left(\overline{F}_Y(t) - \overline{F}_X(t)\right) dt = \mathbb{E}[Y] - \mathbb{E}[X],$$

by Property 1.6.6. □

Let us now apply Property 9.6.3 to compute the Wasserstein distance between the Poisson and the Bernoulli distributions.

Example 9.6.4. Let us consider $I \sim \mathcal{B}er(q)$ and $N \sim \mathcal{P}oi(\lambda)$ with $\lambda \geq -\ln(1-q)$. In this case, the dfs of I and N never cross and $I \preceq_{ST} N$ holds. Property 9.6.3 allows us to write $d_W(I, N) = \lambda - q$. ∇

9.6.3 Comonotonicity and Wasserstein distance

We summarize in the next results the main properties of the Wasserstein distance.

Proposition 9.6.5

(i) Given two rvs X and Y,

$$d_W(X,Y) = \min_{(\widetilde{X},\widetilde{Y})\in\mathcal{R}_2(F_X,F_Y)} \mathbb{E}\big[|X-Y|\big] = \mathbb{E}\big[|F_X^{-1}(U)-F_Y^{-1}(U)|\big].$$

(ii) For integer-valued rvs M and N,

$$d_{TV}(N,M) \le 2 d_W(N,M);$$

for continuous random variables X and Y, $d_W(X,Y)$ and $d_{TV}(X,Y)$ are in general not comparable.

Proof. (i) Proposition 6.2.12 together with Property 6.2.8 ensures that for $U \sim \mathcal{U}ni(0,1)$, the stochastic inequality

$$\mathbb{E}\Big[|\widetilde{X}-\widetilde{Y}|\Big] \ge \mathbb{E}\Big[|F_X^{-1}(U)-F_Y^{-1}(U)|\Big]$$

holds for any $(\widetilde{X},\widetilde{Y}) \in \mathcal{R}_2(F_X,F_Y)$. Now we can write

$$\begin{aligned}\mathbb{E}\Big[|F_X^{-1}(U)-F_Y^{-1}(U)|\Big] &= \int_0^1 |F_X^{-1}(p)-F_Y^{-1}(p)|dp \\ &= \int_{-\infty}^{+\infty} |\overline{F}_X(t)-\overline{F}_Y(t)|dt\end{aligned}$$

where we recognize the Wasserstein distance $d_W(X,Y)$.

(ii) This comes from the fact that for integer-valued rvs M and N,

$$\Pr[X\neq Y] = \Pr\big[|X-Y|\ge 1\big] \le \mathbb{E}\Big[|X-Y|\Big]$$

so that

$$\begin{aligned}d_{TV}(X,Y) &= 2 \min_{(\widetilde{X},\widetilde{Y})\in\mathcal{R}2(F_X,F_Y)} \Pr[X\neq Y] \\ &\le 2 \min_{(\widetilde{X},\widetilde{Y})\in\mathcal{R}_2(F_X,F_Y)} \mathbb{E}\Big[|X-Y|\Big] = 2d_W(X,Y),\end{aligned}$$

where the last equality follows from (i). □

Remark 9.6.6. It is worth mentioning that, by virtue of Proposition 9.6.5(i), d_W coincides with the Gini measure of discrepancy, widely used in the economics literature. ∇

9.7 STOP-LOSS DISTANCE

9.7.1 Definition

In the actuarial literature, models are often compared by finding bounds for differences in probabilities, that is, (integrated) differences between their respective pdfs or dfs. This is the way it is done in probability theory, allowing one to build on all the mathematical results found there. However, this approach is often questionable when tackling insurance problems. Instead, the focus should be on the resulting premiums, in particular stop-loss premiums. The reason for this is obvious: small variations in the probabilities of events hardly ever influence the decision made by insurance management. Any difference between calculated premiums, however, will be directly visible. For more details on this issue, we refer the reader to Kaas (1993). Gerber (1979) defined the stop-loss distance as follows.

Definition 9.7.1. Given two rvs X and Y, the stop-loss distance d_{SL} is defined as

$$d_{\mathrm{SL}}(X,Y)=\sup_{t\in\mathbb{R}}|\pi_X(t)-\pi_Y(t)|.$$

∇

9.7.2 Stop-loss order, stop-loss and Wasserstein distances

It is easy to check that d_{SL} is 1-ideal. The stochastic ordering associated with d_{SL} is the stop-loss order $\preceq_{\mathrm{SL}}$. We have that

$$X\preceq_{\mathrm{SL}}Y\preceq_{\mathrm{SL}}Z\Rightarrow d_{\mathrm{SL}}(X,Y)\leq d_{\mathrm{SL}}(X,Z).$$

Let us now examine the relationship between d_{SL} and d_{W}.

Property 9.7.2
Given two rvs X and Y, we have that $d_{\mathrm{SL}}(X,Y)\leq d_{\mathrm{W}}(X,Y)$.

Proof. It suffices to write

$$\begin{aligned} d_{\mathrm{SL}}(X,Y) &= \sup_{t\in\mathbb{R}^+}\left|\int_t^{+\infty}\left(\overline{F}_X(x)-\overline{F}_Y(x)\right)dx\right| \\ &\leq \sup_{t\in\mathbb{R}^+}\int_t^{+\infty}\left|\overline{F}_X(x)-\overline{F}_Y(x)\right|dx \\ &= \int_0^{+\infty}\left|\overline{F}_X(x)-\overline{F}_Y(x)\right|dx=d_{\mathrm{W}}(X,Y), \end{aligned}$$

which concludes the proof. □

9.7.3 Computation of the stop-loss distance under stochastic dominance or dangerousness order

Lefèvre and Utev (1998) derived the following elegant formulas which make the computation of d_{SL} particularly easy when some $\preceq_{\mathrm{ST}}$ or $\preceq_{\mathrm{D}}$ ranking is known to hold.

Property 9.7.3
For two rvs X and Y,

(i) if $X \preceq_{\text{ST}} Y$ then $d_{\text{SL}}(X,Y) = \mathbb{E}[Y] - \mathbb{E}[X]$;

(ii) if $X \preceq_{\text{D}} Y$ then $d_{\text{W}}(X,Y) = 2d_{\text{SL}}(X,Y) + \mathbb{E}[X] - \mathbb{E}[Y]$.

Proof. (i) Invoking Proposition 3.3.9, we see that the supremum in d_{SL} is attained for $t=0$ when $X \preceq_{\text{ST}} Y$, which yields $d_{\text{SL}}(X,Y) = \mathbb{E}[Y] - \mathbb{E}[X]$.

(ii) Let t_0 be such that $\overline{F}_Y(t) \leq \overline{F}_X(t)$ for $t \leq t_0$ and $\overline{F}_Y(t) \geq \overline{F}_X(t)$ for $t \geq t_0$. We proceed as in the proof of Proposition 9.5.4. Specifically, let us first note that

$$
\begin{aligned}
d_{\text{W}}(X,Y) &= \int_{-\infty}^{+\infty} \left|\overline{F}_Y(t) - \overline{F}_X(t)\right| dt \\
&= \int_{-\infty}^{t_0-} \left(\overline{F}_X(t) - \overline{F}_Y(t)\right) + \int_{t_0}^{+\infty} \left(\overline{F}_Y(t) - \overline{F}_X(t)\right) dt \\
&= 2\int_{t_0}^{+\infty} \left(\overline{F}_Y(t) - \overline{F}_X(t)\right) dt + \mathbb{E}[X] - \mathbb{E}[Y] \\
&= 2\left(\pi_Y(t_0) - \pi_X(t_0)\right) + \mathbb{E}[X] - \mathbb{E}[Y]
\end{aligned}
$$

Also, $\pi_Y(t) - \pi_X(t)$ is maximal at $t = t_0$, since $\frac{d}{dt}\left(\pi_Y(t) - \pi_X(t)\right) = F_Y(t) - F_X(t)$. This yields the desired result. □

Note that when $X \preceq_{\text{ST}} Y$, Properties 9.6.3 and 9.7.3 indicate that d_{W} and d_{SL} coincide and reduce to the difference of the associated means. Let us now investigate some particular cases where Property 9.7.3 applies.

Example 9.7.4. Suppose that $[N|\Theta_1 = \theta] \sim \mathcal{P}oi(\theta)$ and $[M|\Theta_2 = \theta] \sim \mathcal{P}oi(\theta)$. If $\Theta_1 \preceq_{\text{ST}} \Theta_2$ then $N \preceq_{\text{ST}} M$ and Property 9.7.3(i) yields

$$
d_{\text{W}}(N,M) = d_{\text{SL}}(N,M) = \mathbb{E}[\Theta_2] - \mathbb{E}[\Theta_1].
$$

Note that in this case,

$$
d_{\text{W}}(N,M) = d_{\text{SL}}(N,M) = d_{\text{W}}(\Theta_1, \Theta_2) = d_{\text{SL}}(\Theta_1, \Theta_2).
$$

∇

Example 9.7.5. Let M be distributed according to a mixture of Poisson-distributions and let N be Poisson distributed with mean $\mathbb{E}[M] = \mathbb{E}[\Theta] = \theta$. Then it is well known that $N \preceq_{\text{D},=} M$, so that

$$
d_{\text{W}}(N,M) = 2d_{\text{SL}}(N,M).
$$

Therefore, if we are able to compute $d_W(N, M)$, we will get $d_{SL}(N, M)$ from the last identity. To compute d_W, let k_0 be such that $\Pr[N>j]\geq \Pr[M>j]$ for $j\leq k_0$ and $\Pr[N>j]\leq \Pr[M>j]$ for $j\geq k_0+1$. Then

$$\begin{aligned} d_W(N, M) &= 2\sum_{j=k_0+1}^{+\infty}\Big(\Pr[M>j]-\Pr[N>j]\Big)\\ &= 2\sum_{j=0}^{k_0}\Big(\Pr[N>j]-\Pr[M>j]\Big). \end{aligned}$$

∇

Example 9.7.6. Let $I\sim \mathcal{B}er\,(q)$ and $N\sim \mathcal{P}oi\,(\lambda)$. Consider the following cases:

(i) If $\lambda\geq -\ln(1-q)$ then $I\preceq_{ST}N$, so that Property 9.7.3 yields

$$d_W(I, N)=d_{SL}(I, N)=\lambda-q.$$

(ii) If $q<\lambda<-\ln(1-q)$, then $\mathbb{E}[I]<\mathbb{E}[N]$ and $I\preceq_D N$, so that Property 9.7.3 yields

$$d_{SL}(I, N)=\frac{d_W(I, N)-q+\lambda}{2}.$$

Hence, Example 9.6.2 gives $d_{SL}(I, N)=\lambda+\exp(-\lambda)-1$.

∇

9.8 INTEGRATED STOP-LOSS DISTANCE

9.8.1 Definition

In Goovaerts *et al.* (1990, Section III.1), the integrated difference in stop-loss premiums is used to measure the distance between two non-negative rvs with finite variances. The integrated stop-loss distance has been used by Kaas (1993) and by Kaas, Van Heerwaarden and Goovaerts (1994). This distance is defined as follows.

Definition 9.8.1. Given two rvs X and Y, the integrated stop-loss distance d_{ISL} is given by

$$d_{ISL}(X, Y)=\int_{-\infty}^{+\infty}\Big|\pi_X(t)-\pi_Y(t)\Big|dt.$$

∇

9.8.2 Properties

The distance d_{ISL} has the following properties.

Proposition 9.8.2
Given two risks X and Y,

(i) if $X\preceq_{SL}Y$ then $d_{ISL}(X, Y)=\frac{1}{2}(\mathbb{E}[Y^2]-\mathbb{E}[X^2])$;

(ii) if $X\preceq_{SL,=}Y$ then $d_{ISL}(X, Y)=\frac{1}{2}(\mathbb{V}[Y]-\mathbb{V}[X])$.

Proof. For (i), it suffices to write

$$d_{\mathrm{ISL}}(X,Y)=\int_0^{+\infty}\Big(\pi_Y(t)-\pi_X(t)\Big)dt=\frac{1}{2}\mathbb{E}[Y^2]-\frac{1}{2}\mathbb{E}[X^2].$$

To get (ii), it suffices to note that $\mathbb{E}[Y^2]-\mathbb{E}[X^2]=\mathbb{V}[Y]-\mathbb{V}[X]$ when $\mathbb{E}[Y]=\mathbb{E}[X]$. □

Example 9.8.3. Let us compute the integrated stop-loss distance between an rv and its mathematical expectation. Consider the rvs $X=\mu$ and Y such that $\mathbb{E}[Y]=\mu$. Proposition 9.8.2(ii) yields

$$d_{\mathrm{ISL}}(X,Y)=\frac{1}{2}\mathbb{V}[Y]$$

since $X\preceq_{\mathrm{SL},=}Y$ holds, so that the identity

$$\frac{1}{2}\mathbb{V}[Y]=\int_0^{\infty}\big(\pi_Y(t)-(\mu-t)_+\big)dt$$

is valid. ∇

Example 9.8.4. Let $I_1,I_2,\ldots,I_n$ be independent Bernoulli rvs with means $q_1,q_2,\ldots,q_n$. Let $I_\bullet=I_1+I_2+\ldots+I_n$ and $q_\bullet=q_1+q_2+\ldots+q_n$. Let N be Poisson-distributed with mean $q_\bullet$. Then $I_\bullet\preceq_{\mathrm{SL},=}N$, and Proposition 9.8.2(ii) yields

$$d_{\mathrm{ISL}}(N,I_\bullet)=\frac{1}{2}\big(\mathbb{V}[N]-\mathbb{V}[I_\bullet]\big)=\frac{1}{2}\sum_{j=1}^{n}q_i^2.$$

In particular,

$$d_{\mathrm{TV}}(N,I_\bullet)\le 2d_{\mathrm{W}}(N,I_\bullet)\le\sum_{j=1}^{n}q_i^2$$

where the first inequality comes from Proposition 9.6.5(ii). We also have that

$$\max\Big\{d_{\mathrm{K}}(N,I_\bullet),\ d_{\mathrm{SL}}(N,I_\bullet)\Big\}\le\frac{1}{2}\sum_{j=1}^{n}q_i^2.$$

∇

Example 9.8.5. Let us elaborate on Example 9.8.4. The total number of policies producing claims is denoted by $I_\bullet(\boldsymbol{q})$, with $\boldsymbol{q}=(q_1,q_2,\ldots,q_n)$, to make apparent the dependence upon the q_i. Kim and Makowski (1999) derived the following result: given the vectors $\boldsymbol{p}$ and $\boldsymbol{q}$ in $[0,1]^n$,

$$\boldsymbol{p}\preceq_{\mathrm{MAJ}}\boldsymbol{q}\Rightarrow I_\bullet(\boldsymbol{p})\preceq_{\mathrm{SL},=}I_\bullet(\boldsymbol{q}).$$

Therefore, if $\mathbf{p}\preceq_{\mathrm{MAJ}}\mathbf{q}$, then

$$\begin{aligned}d_{\mathrm{ISL}}\big(I_\bullet(\boldsymbol{p}),I_\bullet(\boldsymbol{q})\big)&=\frac{1}{2}\Big(\mathbb{V}[I_\bullet(\boldsymbol{q})]-\mathbb{V}[I_\bullet(\boldsymbol{p})]\Big)\\&=\frac{1}{2}\sum_{i=1}^{n}\Big(q_i(1-q_i)-p_i(1-p_i)\Big)=\frac{1}{2}\sum_{i=1}^{n}\Big(p_i^2-q_i^2\Big).\end{aligned}$$

∇

9.8.3 Integrated stop-loss distance and positive quadrant dependence

Let (X, Y) be PQD and let us denote by $(X^{\perp}, Y^{\perp})$ an independent version of (X, Y). We know from Proposition 5.3.9 that $X + Y \preceq_{SL,=} X^{\perp} + Y^{\perp}$ so that

$$d_{ISL}(X+Y, X^{\perp}+Y^{\perp}) = \frac{1}{2}\Big(\mathbb{V}[X+Y] - \mathbb{V}[X^{\perp}+Y^{\perp}]\Big) = \mathbb{C}[X, Y].$$

The integrated stop-loss distance between a sum of two PQD risks and the sum of independent risks with the same marginal distributions reduces to the covariance between these risks.

Example 9.8.6. Consider an insurance company with aggregate claim S. The company is asked to bear an additional risk X. If S and X are mutually independent, the impact of adding X to the portfolio is often considered to be neutral. If X and S are PQD then $X^{\perp} + S^{\perp} \preceq_{SL,=} X + S$ so that the situation is more dangerous than under independence. Then

$$d_{ISL}(X^{\perp} + S^{\perp}, X + S) = \mathbb{C}[X, S].$$

The covariance thus plays an important role. Moreover, under the postive quadrant dependence assumption for X and S, we know that

$$\mathbb{C}[X, S] = 0 \Leftrightarrow X \text{ and } S \text{ are independent} \Leftrightarrow d_{ISL}(X^{\perp} + S^{\perp}, X + S) = 0$$

and

$$\begin{aligned}\mathbb{C}[X, S] = \mathbb{C}[F_X^{-1}(U), F_S^{-1}(U)] &\Leftrightarrow X \text{ and } S \text{ are comonotonic}\\ &\Leftrightarrow d_{ISL} \text{ is maximal.}\end{aligned}$$

∇

9.8.4 Integrated stop-loss distance and cumulative dependence

Proposition 9.8.2 is useful if we want to measure the impact of the dependence among the correlated risks $X_1, X_2, \ldots, X_n$. Assume that the structure of dependence of the X_i is such that one of the stochastic inequalities

$$\sum_{i=1}^{n} X_i^{\perp} \preceq_{SL,=} \sum_{i=1}^{n} X_i \text{ or } \sum_{i=1}^{n} X_i \preceq_{SL,=} \sum_{i=1}^{n} X_i^{\perp} \tag{9.7}$$

holds. This is the case, for instance, if $\boldsymbol{X}$ is CD or associated. We then have

$$\begin{aligned}d_{ISL}\left(\sum_{i=1}^{n} X_i, \sum_{i=1}^{n} X_i^{\perp}\right) &= \frac{1}{2}\left|\mathbb{V}\left[\sum_{i=1}^{n} X_i\right] - \mathbb{V}\left[\sum_{i=1}^{n} X_i^{\perp}\right]\right|\\ &= \frac{1}{2}\left|\sum_{i,j} \mathbb{C}[X_i, X_j]\right| = \left|\sum_{i<j} \mathbb{C}[X_i, X_j]\right|.\end{aligned}$$

Now the integrated distance between the sums of positively correlated risks $\sum_{i=1}^{n} X_i$ and the sum $\sum_{i=1}^{n} X_i^{\perp}$ of their independent counterparts is given by the sum of the covariances between every pair of correlated risks.

Example 9.8.7. Let I_i be the indicator of the event 'policy i produces at least one claim during the reference period'. Classically, the I_i are assumed to be mutually independent in the individual risk model. Of course, the independence hypothesis is not always reasonable. Therefore, we now suppose that the indicators $I_1, I_2, \ldots, I_n$ may be correlated. Henceforth, the superscript $\perp$ will always indicate that the corresponding quantity is embedded in a model where the independence assumption holds. Thus, $I_\bullet^{\perp} = I_1^{\perp} + I_2^{\perp} + \ldots + I_n^{\perp}$ denotes the number of policies yielding claims under the independence assumption. We denote by $\boldsymbol{I}$ the random vector $(I_1, I_2, \ldots, I_n)$, and by $\boldsymbol{I}^{\perp}$ the independent version $(I_1^{\perp}, I_2^{\perp}, \ldots, I_n^{\perp})$.

Following Goovaerts and Dhaene (1996), let us consider a portfolio consisting of $m+n$ life insurance policies providing a death benefit. There are m couples (wife and husband) in the portfolio. They are represented as $(I_i, \widetilde{I}_i)$, $i = 1, 2, \ldots, n$, where I_i $(\widetilde{I}_i)$ is the indicator of the event 'the wife (husband) of the ith couple dies during the period'. Hence,

$$I_\bullet = \sum_{i=1}^{m} (I_i + \widetilde{I}_i) + \sum_{i=m+1}^{n} I_i.$$

All the indicators are independent, except for the coupled risks. Now, assume that the kind of dependence between the components of the $(I_i, \widetilde{I}_i)$ is such that $I_\bullet^{\perp} \preceq_{\text{SL},=} I_\bullet$. For instance, let us propose, following Cossette, Gaillardetz, Marceau and Rioux (2002), the model

$$\begin{cases} I_i = \min\{J_i + K_i, 1\}, \\ \widetilde{I}_i = \min\{\widetilde{J}_i + K_i, 1\}, \end{cases}$$

where $J_1, J_2, \ldots, J_m, \widetilde{J}_1, \widetilde{J}_2, \ldots, \widetilde{J}_m, K_1, K_2, \ldots, K_m$ are independent (see Example 7.2.8). Then K_i can be thought of as the indicator of an event killing both spouses. In this case $(I_i, \widetilde{I}_i)$ is known to be associated so that $I_\bullet^{\perp} \preceq_{\text{SL},=} I_\bullet$ does indeed hold. It suffices in fact for the random couples $(I_i, \widetilde{I}_i)$ to be PQD; indeed, in this case,

$$(I_i, \widetilde{I}_i) \text{ PQD} \Rightarrow I_i^{\perp} + \widetilde{I}_i^{\perp} \preceq_{\text{SL},=} I_i + \widetilde{I}_i \text{ and hence } I_\bullet^{\perp} \preceq_{\text{SL},=} I_\bullet,$$

from the closure of $\preceq_{\text{SL},=}$ under convolution. Then,

$$d_{\text{ISL}}(I_\bullet^{\perp}, I_\bullet) = \sum_{i=1}^{m} \mathbb{C}[I_i, \widetilde{I}_i] \leq \sum_{i=1}^{m} \sqrt{q_i(1-q_i)\widetilde{q}_i(1-\widetilde{q}_i)}.$$

∇

Example 9.8.8. Suppose that $Y \sim \mathcal{E}xp(1/\theta)$. If $Y_1, Y_2, \ldots, Y_n$ are independent copies of Y, then

$$W_n = \frac{2}{\theta} \sum_{i=1}^{n} Y_i$$

is distributed according to a chi-square distribution with $2n$ degrees of freedom (denoted by χ^2_{2n}). In practice, the assumption of exponentiality is only an approximation; it is therefore interesting to examine the quality of the χ^2_{2n} approximation for W_n. For this purpose, let us consider

$$Z_n = \frac{2}{\theta}\sum_{i=1}^{n} X_i,$$

where the X_i are harmonic new worse than used in expectation, that is, $X_1 \preceq_{\mathrm{SL},=} Y_1$. From this stochastic inequality, we immediately get that

$$d_{\mathrm{ISL}}(X_1, Y_1) = \frac{1}{2}\left(\mathbb{V}[X_1] - \theta^2\right).$$

Therefore,

$$d_{\mathrm{ISL}}(W_n, Z_n) = \frac{4}{\theta^2} n d_{\mathrm{ISL}}(X_1, Y_1) = 2n\left(\frac{\mathbb{V}[X_1]}{\theta^2} - 1\right).$$

In the light of this result, we see that the quality of the approximation of Z_n by W_n is determined by the coefficient of variation of X_1 (the quantity in brackets representing the difference between the coefficients of variation of X_1 and Y_1). ∇

9.9 DISTANCE BETWEEN THE INDIVIDUAL AND COLLECTIVE MODELS IN RISK THEORY

9.9.1 Individual model

The individual model is presented in detail in Kaas *et al.* (2001, Chapter 2). Consider a portfolio consisting of n policies oberved during a given reference period (one year, say). To each contract is associated an indicator I_i for the event 'policy i produces at least one claim during the reference period', $i = 1, 2, \ldots, n$; $I_i \sim \mathcal{B}er(q_i)$. The number of policies producing claims is denoted by $I_\bullet$ and is given by $I_\bullet = I_1 + I_2 + \ldots + I_n$.

Risk i produces a claim amount X_i during the reference period. Traditionally, the individual risks $X_1, X_2, \ldots, X_n$ are assumed to be mutually independent. The aggregate claims of the portfolio during the reference period are denoted by

$$S_{\mathrm{ind}} = X_1 + X_2 + \ldots + X_n,$$

where the subscript 'ind' refers to the individual model. It is common to represent each X_i as

$$X_i = I_i V_i = \begin{cases} V_i, & \text{if } I_i = 1, \\ 0, & \text{if } I_i = 0, \end{cases}$$

$i = 1, 2, \ldots, n$, where V_i is the total claim amount produced by risk i (when at least one claim has been filed).

9.9.2 Collective model

The individual model is of primary importance for rate-making on an individual basis. However, it is not convenient when calculations have to be caried out at the portfolio level.

Therefore, it is customary to resort to an approximation of the individual model. A number of approximations for S_{ind} are provided in the actuarial literature; see Kaas and Gerber (1994) and Kaas *et al.* (2001 Chapter 3), as well as the references therein.

The classical collective approximation to the individual model can be seen as a two-stage procedure. We first approximate X_i by $\widetilde{X}_i$ defined as

$$\widetilde{X}_i = \sum_{k=1}^{N_i} V_{i;k},$$

where $N_i \sim \mathcal{P}oi(\lambda_i)$ and is independent of the $V_{i;k}$, $k = 1, 2, \ldots$, these rvs being independent copies of V_i. Then, we define S_{coll} as

$$S_{\text{coll}} = \sum_{i=1}^{n} \widetilde{X}_i = \sum_{i=1}^{n} \sum_{k=1}^{N_i} V_{i;k} =_d \sum_{i=1}^{N_\bullet} Y_i$$

where $N_\bullet \sim \mathcal{P}oi(\lambda)$ with $\lambda = \sum_{i=1}^{n} \lambda_i$ and the Y_i are independent with common df $\frac{1}{\lambda} \sum_{i=1}^{n} \lambda_i \Pr[X_i \leq x | X_i > 0]$.

There are two standard choices for the λ_i. The first is $\lambda_i = q_i$, for which

$$\mathbb{E}[I_i] = \mathbb{E}[N_i] \text{ for } i = 1, 2, \ldots, n \Rightarrow \mathbb{E}[I_\bullet] = \mathbb{E}[N_\bullet].$$

The mean number of policies producing claims is identical in the individual and the collective models. The second standard choice is

$$\begin{aligned} \lambda_i = -\ln(1 - q_i) &\Leftrightarrow \exp(-\lambda_i) = 1 - q_i \\ &\Leftrightarrow \Pr[N_i = 0] = \Pr[X_i = 0], i = 1, 2, \ldots, n. \end{aligned}$$

In this case, the no-claims probabilities are equivalent in the collective and individual models for each policy. Similarly, at the portfolio level, we have $\Pr[N_\bullet = 0] = \Pr[I_\bullet = 0] \Leftrightarrow \Pr[S_{\text{coll}} = 0] = \Pr[S_{\text{ind}} = 0]$.

9.9.3 Distance between compound sums

Let us now examine the distance between two compound sums with identically distributed summands. This kind of result will play a central role in the analysis of the individual and collective models of risk theory.

Proposition 9.9.1
Let N and M be integer-valued rvs and let $\{X_1, X_2, X_3, \ldots\}$ and $\{Y_1, Y_2, Y_3, \ldots\}$ be two sequences of independent and identically distributed risks. The rvs M and N are independent of the X_i and of the Y_i. Let us define

$$S_N = \sum_{i=1}^{N} X_i \text{ and } S_M = \sum_{i=1}^{M} X_i.$$

Then the following inequalities hold: $d_{\text{TV}}(S_N, S_M) \leq d_{\text{TV}}(N, M)$, $d_{\text{K}}(S_N, S_M) \leq d_{\text{K}}(N, M)$, $d_{\text{W}}(S_N, S_M) \leq \mathbb{E}[X_1] d_{\text{W}}(N, M)$ and $d_{\text{SL}}(S_N, S_M) \leq \mathbb{E}[X_1] d_{\text{SL}}(N, M)$.

Proof. To get the inequality for d_{TV}, it suffices to write

$$d_{\mathrm{TV}}(S_N, S_M) = \int_0^{+\infty} \left| \sum_{n=0}^{+\infty} \Big(\Pr[N=n] - \Pr[M=n] \Big) \right| d\Pr[S_n \leq t]$$
$$\leq \sum_{n=0}^{+\infty} \Big| \Pr[N=n] - \Pr[M=n] \Big| = d_{\mathrm{TV}}(N, M).$$

Let us now examine the corresponding inequality for the Kolmogrov distance. Conditioning again on the number of claims N and M allows us to write

$$\begin{aligned}
&d_{\mathrm{K}}(S_N, S_M) \\
&= \sup_{t\in\mathbb{R}^+} \left| \sum_{n=0}^{+\infty} \Big(\Pr[N=n] - \Pr[M=n] \Big) \Pr[S_n > t] \right| \\
&= \sup_{t\in\mathbb{R}^+} \left| \sum_{n=0}^{+\infty} \Big(\Pr[N>n] - \Pr[M>n] \Big) \Big(\Pr[S_{n+1} > t] - \Pr[S_n > t] \Big) \right| \\
&\leq \sup_{t\in\mathbb{R}^+} \left\{ \sum_{n=0}^{+\infty} \Big| \Pr[N>n] - \Pr[M>n] \Big| \Big(\Pr[S_{n+1} > t] - \Pr[S_n > t] \Big) \right\} \\
&\leq \sup_{t\in\mathbb{R}^+} \left\{ \sup_{n\in\mathbb{N}} \Big| \Pr[N>n] - \Pr[M>n] \Big| \sum_{n=0}^{+\infty} \Big(\Pr[S_{n+1} > t] - \Pr[S_n > t] \Big) \right\} \\
&= \sup_{n\in\mathbb{N}} \Big| \Pr[N>n] - \Pr[M>n] \Big| = d_{\mathrm{K}}(N, M),
\end{aligned}$$

as desired.

For the Wasserstein distance,

$$\begin{aligned}
&d_{\mathrm{W}}(S_N, S_M) \\
&= \int_0^{+\infty} \left| \sum_{n=0}^{+\infty} \Big(\Pr[N=n] - \Pr[M=n] \Big) \Pr[S_n > t] \right| dt \\
&= \int_0^{+\infty} \left| \sum_{n=0}^{+\infty} \Big(\Pr[N>n] - \Pr[M>n] \Big) \Big(\Pr[S_{n+1} > t] - \Pr[S_n > t] \Big) \right| dt \\
&\leq \int_0^{+\infty} \sum_{n=0}^{+\infty} \Big| \Pr[N>n] - \Pr[M>n] \Big| \Big(\Pr[S_{n+1} > t] - \Pr[S_n > t] \Big) dt.
\end{aligned}$$

Invoking Property 1.6.6 allows us to write

$$\begin{aligned}
d_{\mathrm{W}}(S_N, S_M) &\leq \sum_{n=0}^{+\infty} \Big| \Pr[N>n] - \Pr[M>n] \Big| \Big(\mathbb{E}[S_{n+1}] - \mathbb{E}[S_n] \Big) \\
&= \mathbb{E}[X_1] d_{\mathrm{W}}(N, M),
\end{aligned}$$

as desired.

To end with, let us consider the stop-loss distance between S_N and S_M. We first write the difference between the stop-loss transforms associated with S_N and S_M as

$$\begin{aligned}
&\mathbb{E}[(S_N - t)_+] - \mathbb{E}[(S_M - t)_+] \\
&= \sum_{n=0}^{+\infty} \Big(\Pr[N > n] - \Pr[M > n]\Big)\Big(\mathbb{E}[(S_{n+1} - t)_+] - \mathbb{E}[(S_n - t)_+]\Big) \\
&= \sum_{n=0}^{+\infty} \Big(\pi_N(n) - \pi_M(n)\Big)\Big(\mathbb{E}[(S_{n+2} - t)_+] - 2\mathbb{E}[(S_{n+1} - t)_+] + \mathbb{E}[(S_n - t)_+]\Big).
\end{aligned}$$

Hence, taking the supremum over t gives

$$\begin{aligned}
d_{\mathrm{SL}}(S_N, S_M) &\leq \sup_{n\in\mathbb{N}} \Big|\pi_N(n) - \pi_M(n)\Big| \\
&\quad \sup_{t\in\mathbb{R}^+} \left\{\sum_{n=0}^{+\infty} \Big(\mathbb{E}[(S_{n+2} - t)_+] - 2\mathbb{E}[(S_{n+1} - t)_+] + \mathbb{E}[(S_n - t)_+]\Big)\right\} \\
&= d_{\mathrm{SL}}(N, M) \sup_{t\in\mathbb{R}^+} \mathbb{E}[(S_1 - t)_+] \\
&= \mathbb{E}[X_1] d_{\mathrm{SL}}(N, M),
\end{aligned}$$

where the last equality follows from the decreasingness of the stop-loss transform of X_1. □

It is worth stressing that the characteristics of the risks do not appear in the upper bound for d_{TV} and d_{K}, whereas their expected value is involved in the upper bound for d_{W} and d_{SL}.

9.9.4 Distance between the individual and collective models

Let us now apply Proposition 9.9.1 to measure the closeness between the individual and collective models. Let d_* be one of the distances d_{TV}, d_{K}, d_{W} or d_{SL}. The semi-additivity of d_* yields

$$d_*(S_{\mathrm{ind}}, S_{\mathrm{coll}}) \leq \sum_{i=1}^{n} d_*(X_i, \widetilde{X}_i).$$

Then Proposition 9.9.1 yields

$$d_*(X_i, \widetilde{X}_i) \leq d_*(N_i, I_i) \text{ for } i = 1, 2, \ldots, n,$$

for d_{TV} and d_{K}, so that the inequality

$$d_*(S_{\mathrm{ind}}, S_{\mathrm{coll}}) \leq \sum_{i=1}^{n} d_*(N_i, I_i)$$

holds in this case. On the other hand, we have that

$$d_*(X_i, \widetilde{X}_i) \leq \mathbb{E}[V_i] d_*(N_i, I_i) \text{ for } i = 1, 2, \ldots, n,$$

for d_{W} and d_{SL}, leading to the inequality

$$d_*(S_{\mathrm{ind}}, S_{\mathrm{coll}}) \le \sum_{i=1}^{n} \mathbb{E}[V_i] d_*(N_i, I_i).$$

Let us now summarize our results about the total-variation distance between the individual and collective models of risk theory. The results below are direct consequences of the bounds on $d_*(S_{\mathrm{ind}}, S_{\mathrm{coll}})$ established above, together with our detailed study of the distance between the Bernoulli and Poisson distributions.

Proposition 9.9.2

(i) If $\lambda_i \ge -\ln(1-q_i)$ for $i = 1, 2, \ldots, n$, then

$$d_{\mathrm{TV}}(S_{\mathrm{ind}}, S_{\mathrm{coll}}) \le 2\sum_{i=1}^{n}\Big(1 - \exp(-\lambda_i) - \min\{q_i, \lambda_i \exp(-\lambda_i)\}\Big),$$

$$d_{\mathrm{K}}(S_{\mathrm{ind}}, S_{\mathrm{coll}}) \le \sum_{i=1}^{n}\Big(1 - \exp(-\lambda_i) - \min\{q_i, \lambda_i \exp(-\lambda_i)\}\Big),$$

$$d_{\mathrm{W}}(S_{\mathrm{ind}}, S_{\mathrm{coll}}) = d_{\mathrm{SL}}(S_{\mathrm{ind}}, S_{\mathrm{coll}}) = \sum_{i=1}^{n} \mathbb{E}[V_i](\lambda_i - q_i).$$

(ii) If $q_i \le \lambda_i < -\ln(1-q_i)$ for $i = 1, 2, \ldots, n$, then

$$d_{\mathrm{TV}}(S_{\mathrm{ind}}, S_{\mathrm{coll}}) \le 2\sum_{i=1}^{n}\Big(q_i - \lambda_i \exp(-\lambda_i)\Big),$$

$$d_{\mathrm{K}}(S_{\mathrm{ind}}, S_{\mathrm{coll}}) \le \sum_{i=1}^{n} \max\Big\{q_i - 1 + \exp(-\lambda_i), 1 - \exp(-\lambda_i)(1+\lambda_i)\Big\},$$

$$d_{\mathrm{W}}(S_{\mathrm{ind}}, S_{\mathrm{coll}}) \le \sum_{i=1}^{n} \mathbb{E}[V_i]\Big(q_i + \lambda_i - 2(1 - \exp(-\lambda_i))\Big),$$

$$d_{\mathrm{SL}}(S_{\mathrm{ind}}, S_{\mathrm{coll}}) \le \sum_{i=1}^{n} \mathbb{E}[V_i]\Big(\lambda_i - 1 + \exp(-\lambda_i)\Big).$$

Remark 9.9.3. When $\lambda_i = q_i$, Gerber (1984) proved that

$$d_{\mathrm{TV}}(S_{\mathrm{ind}}, S_{\mathrm{coll}}) \le 2\sum_{i=1}^{n} q_i^2. \tag{9.8}$$

This is a direct consequence of the inequality stated for d_{TV} in Proposition 9.9.2(ii), by noting that $\exp(-q_i) > 1 - q_i$. ∇

The next property examines $d_{\mathrm{ISL}}(S_{\mathrm{ind}}, S_{\mathrm{coll}})$. Note that in this case, we obtain an exact expression $\lambda_i \ge q_i$.

Property 9.9.4
If $\lambda_i \ge q_i$ holds for all i, then

$$d_{\mathrm{ISL}}(S_{\mathrm{ind}}, S_{\mathrm{coll}}) = \sum_{i=1}^{n}\Big((\lambda_i - q_i)\mathbb{E}[V_i^2] + \frac{1}{2}(\lambda_i^2 - q_i^2)(\mathbb{E}[V_i])^2\Big) + \sum_{i<j}\Big(\lambda_i\lambda_j - q_i q_j\Big)\mathbb{E}[V_i]\mathbb{E}[V_j].$$

Proof. If $\lambda_i \geq q_i$ holds for all i, then we know that $I_i \preceq_{\rm SL} N_i$ which in turn implies $X_i \preceq_{\rm SL} \widetilde{X}_i$ and $S_{\rm ind} \preceq_{\rm SL} S_{\rm coll}$. Hence, Proposition 9.8.2 allows us to write

$$
\begin{aligned}
d_{\rm ISL}(S_{\rm ind}, S_{\rm coll}) &= \frac{1}{2}\Big(\mathbb{V}[S_{\rm coll}] - \mathbb{V}[S_{\rm ind}] + (\mathbb{E}[S_{\rm coll}])^2 - (\mathbb{E}[S_{\rm ind}])^2\Big) \\
&= \frac{1}{2}\left(\sum_{i=1}^n (\mathbb{V}[\widetilde{X}_i] - \mathbb{V}[X_i]) + \sum_{i=1}^n\sum_{j=1}^n \mathbb{E}[\widetilde{X}_i\widetilde{X}_j] - \sum_{i=1}^n\sum_{j=1}^n \mathbb{E}[X_iX_j]\right) \\
&= \frac{1}{2}\sum_{i=1}^n\Big((\lambda_i - q_i)\mathbb{V}[V_i] + (\mathbb{E}[V_i])^2(\lambda_i - q_i(1-q_i))\Big) \\
&\quad + \frac{1}{2}\sum_{i=1}^n\Big(\mathbb{E}[\widetilde{X}_i^2] - \mathbb{E}[X_i^2]\Big) + \sum_{i<j}\Big(\mathbb{E}[\widetilde{X}_i]\mathbb{E}[\widetilde{X}_j] - \mathbb{E}[X_i]\mathbb{E}[X_j]\Big) \\
&= \frac{1}{2}\sum_{i=1}^n\Big((\lambda_i - q_i)\mathbb{V}[V_i] + (\mathbb{E}[V_i])^2(\lambda_i - q_i(1-q_i))\Big) \\
&\quad + \frac{1}{2}\sum_{i=1}^n\Big(\mathbb{E}[\widetilde{X}_i^2] - \mathbb{E}[X_i^2]\Big) + \sum_{i<j}\Big(\mathbb{E}[\widetilde{X}_i]\mathbb{E}[\widetilde{X}_j] - \mathbb{E}[X_i]\mathbb{E}[X_j]\Big) \\
&= \sum_{i=1}^n\Big((\lambda_i - q_i)\mathbb{E}[V_i^2] + q_i^2(\mathbb{E}[V_i])^2\Big) \\
&\quad + \frac{1}{2}\sum_{i=1}^n\Big((\lambda_i^2 - q_i^2)(\mathbb{E}[V_i])^2\Big) + \sum_{i<j}\Big(\lambda_i\lambda_j - q_iq_j\Big)\mathbb{E}[V_i]\mathbb{E}[V_j] \\
&= \sum_{i=1}^n\Big((\lambda_i - q_i)\mathbb{E}[V_i^2] + \frac{1}{2}(\lambda_i^2 - q_i^2)(\mathbb{E}[V_i])^2\Big) \\
&\quad + \sum_{i<j}\Big(\lambda_i\lambda_j - q_iq_j\Big)\mathbb{E}[V_i]\mathbb{E}[V_j],
\end{aligned}
$$

as claimed. □

9.9.5 Quasi-homogeneous portfolios

Let us now examine the situation where the portfolio is quasi-homogeneous, that is,

$$V_1 =_d V_2 =_d V_3 =_d \cdots =_d V_n \equiv_d V.$$

Thus, the portfolio is homogeneous with respect to claim amounts (that have the same distribution for all the policyholders) but heterogeneous with respect to claim occurrences, with different occurrence probabilities $q_1, \ldots, q_n$ for the policyholders. In this case, it is clear that we can represent $S_{\rm ind}$ and $S_{\rm coll}$ as

$$S_{\rm ind} = \sum_{i=1}^{I_\bullet} Z_i \text{ and } S_{\rm coll} = \sum_{i=1}^{N_\bullet} Z_i \tag{9.9}$$

where the Z_i are independent and distributed as V, $N_\bullet = \sum_{i=1}^n N_i$. Michel (1987) proved that in the quasi-homogeneous model

$$d_{TV}(S_{ind}, S_{coll}) \leq \frac{2}{\lambda}\sum_{i=1}^n q_i^2 \tag{9.10}$$

when $\lambda_i = q_i$, which is an improvement of Gerber's bound (9.8) if $\lambda > 1$.

We can now derive upper bounds for the various distances between S_{ind} and S_{coll} in the quasi-homogeneous model. The first step involves applying Proposition 9.9.1 to (9.9).

Proposition 9.9.5
In the quasi-homogeneous case, we have

$$\begin{aligned} d_{TV}(S_{ind}, S_{coll}) &\leq d_{TV}(N_\bullet, I_\bullet), \\ d_{K}(S_{ind}, S_{coll}) &\leq d_{K}(N_\bullet, I_\bullet), \\ d_{W}(S_{ind}, S_{coll}) &\leq \mathbb{E}[V] d_{W}(N_\bullet, I_\bullet), \\ d_{SL}(S_{ind}, S_{coll}) &\leq \mathbb{E}[V] d_{SL}(N_\bullet, I_\bullet). \end{aligned}$$

The subadditivity of these metrics allows us to majorize $d_*(N_\bullet, I_\bullet)$ by $\sum_{i=1}^n d_*(I_i, N_i)$. This takes us back to Proposition 9.9.2. Another possibility involves working on $d_*(N_\bullet, I_\bullet)$ directly. This distance has been examined by many authors, and we summarize their main findings next.

In the particular case $\lambda_i = q_i$, many bounds for $d_{TV}(N_\bullet, I_\bullet)$, $d_K(N_\bullet, I_\bullet)$ and $d_W(N_\bullet, I_\bullet)$ are available in the literature (see Barbour, Holst and Janson 1992). We list some of them in Table 9.1. In this table, $q_{max} = \max_{1 \leq i \leq n} q_i$, $q_\bullet = \sum_{i=1}^n q_i$, $q_\bullet^{(2)} = \sum_{i=1}^n q_i^2$, $\theta = q_\bullet^{(2)}/q_\bullet$,

$$a = \left\lfloor q_\bullet + \frac{1}{2} + \sqrt{q_\bullet + \frac{1}{4}} \right\rfloor \text{ and } b = \left\lfloor q_\bullet + \frac{1}{2} - \sqrt{q_\bullet + \frac{1}{4}} \right\rfloor.$$

Table 9.1 Some bounds on the distance d_{TV}, d_K, or d_W between $I_\bullet$ and $N_\bullet$ when $\lambda_i = q_i$ for $i = 1, 2, \ldots, n$

Distance	Upper bound
d_{TV}	$2q_\bullet^{(2)}$
d_{TV}	2.1θ
	provided $q_{max} \leq 1/4$
d_{TV}	$2(1-\exp(-q_\bullet))\theta$
d_{TV}	$q_\bullet^{(2)} \exp(-q_\bullet)\left(\frac{q_\bullet^{a-1}(a-q_\bullet)}{a!} + \frac{q_\bullet^{b-1}(q_\bullet-b)}{b!}\right) + \frac{(2\theta)^{3/2}}{1-\sqrt{2\theta}}$ provided $\theta < 1/2$

(*continued overleaf*)

Table 9.1 *(continued)*

Distance	Upper bound
d_{TV}	$2\frac{\theta\exp(-2q_{\max})}{\sqrt{2\pi}(1-2\theta\exp(2q_{\max})}$ provided $\theta<\exp(-2q_{\max})/2$
d_{TV}	$q_\bullet^{(2)}\exp(-q_\bullet+2q_{\max})\left(\frac{q_\bullet^{a-1}(a-q_\bullet)}{a!}+\frac{q_\bullet^{b-1}(q_\bullet-b)}{b!}\right)$ $+2\frac{(\theta\exp(2q_{\max}))^2}{1-\theta\exp(2q_{\max}))}$ provided $\theta<\exp(-2q_{\max})/2$
d_K	$\frac{1}{2}q_\bullet^{(2)}$
d_K	$\frac{q_\bullet^{(2)}}{2}\exp(-q_\bullet)\max\left\{\frac{q_\bullet^{a-1}(a-q_\bullet)}{a!},\frac{q_\bullet^{b-1}(q_\bullet-b)}{b!}\right\}+\frac{1+\sqrt{\pi/2}}{2}\frac{\theta^{3/2}}{1-\sqrt{\theta}}$ provided $\theta<1$
d_K	$\frac{\sqrt{e}(1+\sqrt{\pi/2})}{2\sqrt{2\pi}}\frac{\theta\exp(2q_{\max})}{1-\theta\exp(2q_{\max})}$ provided $\theta<\exp(-2q_{\max})/2$
d_K	$\frac{q_\bullet^{(2)}}{2}\exp(-q_\bullet+2q_{\max})\max\left\{\frac{q_\bullet^{a-1}(a-q_\bullet)}{a!},\frac{q_\bullet^{b-1}(q_\bullet-b)}{b!}\right\}$ $+\frac{\sqrt{e}(1+\sqrt{\pi/2})}{4\sqrt{\pi}}\frac{(\theta\exp(2q_{\max}))^2}{1-\theta\exp(2q_{\max})}$ provided that $\theta<\exp(-2q_{\max})/2$
d_W	$q_\bullet^{(2)}\exp(-q_\bullet)\frac{q_\bullet^{[q_\bullet]}}{[q_\bullet]!}+\frac{2\sqrt{q_\bullet}(2\theta)^{3/2}}{1-\sqrt{2\theta}}$ provided $\theta<1/2$
d_W	$-\frac{1}{2}\frac{\sqrt{eq_\bullet}}{\sqrt{2\pi}}\ln(1-2\theta\exp(2q_{\max}))$ provided $\theta<\exp(-2q_{\max})/2)$
d_W	$q_\bullet^{(2)}\exp(-q_\bullet+2q_{\max})\frac{q_\bullet^{[q_\bullet]}}{[q_\bullet]!}-\frac{1}{2}\frac{\sqrt{eq_\bullet}}{\sqrt{2\pi}}\Big(\ln(1-2\theta\exp(2q_{\max}))+2\theta\exp(2q_{\max})\Big)$

9.9.6 Correlated risks in the individual model

Assume that the X_i are correlated in such a way that (9.7) holds. We then get from the triangle inequality that

$$d_{ISL}(S_{ind}, S_{coll}) \le d_{ISL}(S_{ind}, S_{ind}^{\perp}) + d_{ISL}(S_{ind}^{\perp}, S_{coll})$$
$$= \left|\sum_{i<j}\mathbb{C}[X_i, X_j]\right| + \frac{1}{2}\sum_{i=1}^{n}(\mathbb{E}[V_i])^2 q_i^2.$$

9.10 COMPOUND POISSON APPROXIMATION FOR A PORTFOLIO OF DEPENDENT RISKS

9.10.1 Poisson approximation

9.10.1.1 Poisson law of small numbers

One of the oldest limit theorems of probability is the Poisson 'law of small numbers'. In its simplest form, it states that $\mathcal{Bin}(n, q)$ converges to $\mathcal{Poi}(\lambda)$ as $n\to+\infty$ if $q=\frac{\lambda}{n}$ for some

$\lambda > 0$. The Poisson law of small numbers is a central principle in actuarial science where the Poisson distribution is often the candidate for fitting claim frequencies. In 1975 a new technique was introduced, the Chen–Stein method, which makes it possible to estimate the accuracy of the Poisson approximation in a wide range of situations including a possible dependence among the Bernoulli summands.

9.10.1.2 Chen-Stein method

Chen (1975) proposed an original method for Poisson approximation, inspired by Stein's (1972) work in the context of the central limit theorem for dependent summands.

Property 9.10.1
If $Z \sim \mathcal{P}oi(\lambda)$, then

$$\mathbb{E}\Big[\lambda g(Z+1) - Zg(Z)\Big] = 0 \tag{9.10}$$

for any bounded function $g: \mathbb{N} \to \mathbb{R}$.

Proof. We have that

$$\begin{aligned}
\mathbb{E}[Zg(Z)] &= \sum_{k=0}^{+\infty} kg(k)\Pr[Z=k] \\
&= \sum_{k=1}^{+\infty} g(k)\exp(-\lambda)\frac{\lambda^k}{(k-1)!} \\
&= \lambda \sum_{k=0}^{+\infty} g(k+1)\Pr[Z=k] = \lambda\mathbb{E}[g(Z+1)],
\end{aligned}$$

so (9.10) follows. □

Moreover, given $Z \sim \mathcal{P}oi(\lambda)$, any function $f: \mathbb{N} \to \mathbb{R}$ for which $\mathbb{E}[f(Z)] = 0$ can be written as

$$f(j) = \lambda g(j+1) - jg(j)$$

for a bounded function $g: \mathbb{N} \to \mathbb{R}$. So, there is a sort of reciprocal to Property 9.10.1. This yields the following characterization of the Poisson distribution.

Proposition 9.10.2
Let Z be an integer-valued rv. Then (9.10) holds for every bounded function $g: \mathbb{N} \to \mathbb{R}$ if, and only if, $Z \sim \mathcal{P}oi\,(\lambda)$.

Similarly, given an integer-valued rv M, if $\mathbb{E}[\lambda g(M+1) - Mg(M)] \approx 0$ holds for all g then M is nearly $\mathcal{P}oi\,(\lambda)$. It is often easier to establish this fact than to directly estimate the difference between $\mathbb{E}[f(M)]$ and the same expectation computed for the $\mathcal{P}oi\,(\lambda)$ distribution.

The argument then runs as follows. For any $A \subseteq \mathbb{N}$, a function $g_{\lambda,A}: \mathbb{N} \to \mathbb{R}$ is constructed to solve the equation

$$\lambda g_{\lambda,A}(j+1) - j g_{\lambda,A}(j) = \mathbb{I}[j \in A] - \Pr[Z_\lambda \in A], \quad j \in \mathbb{N}, \tag{9.11}$$

where $Z_\lambda \sim \mathcal{P}oi(\lambda)$. The value $g_{\lambda,A}(0)$ is irrelevant and is conventionally taken to be 0; the solution to (9.11) is then easily obtained recursively, starting from $j=0$. Thus, for any integer-valued rv M, we get

$$\Pr[M \in A] - \Pr[Z_\lambda \in A] = \mathbb{E}\Big[\lambda g_{\lambda,A}(M+1) - M g_{\lambda,A}(M)\Big] \tag{9.12}$$

so that $d_{\mathrm{TV}}(M, Z_\lambda)$ can be found provided the right-hand side of (9.12) can be uniformly estimated for all the $g_{\lambda,A}$.

9.10.1.3 Poisson approximation to the sum of independent Bernoullis

Let us apply this method to independent indicator summands $I_1 \sim \mathcal{B}er(q_1), I_2 \sim \mathcal{B}er(q_2), \ldots, I_n \sim \mathcal{B}er(q_n)$. Thus $M = \sum_{i=1}^n I_i$, and define $M_{-i} = \sum_{j \neq i} I_j$. Then, for any function $g: \mathbb{N} \to \mathbb{R}$

$$\mathbb{E}[I_i g(M)] = E[I_i g(M_{-i}+1)] = q_i \mathbb{E}[g(M_{-i}+1)] \tag{9.13}$$

because of the independence assumption between I_i and M_{-i}. From (9.13), it follows that

$$\mathbb{E}[\lambda g(M+1) - M g(M)] = \sum_{i=1}^n q_i \Big(\mathbb{E}[g(M+1)] - \mathbb{E}[g(M_{-i}+1)]\Big).$$

Since M and M_{-i} are equal unless $I_i = 1$, which occurs with probability q_i, it becomes clear that

$$\Big|\Pr[M \in A] - \Pr[Z_\lambda \in A]\Big| \leq 2 \sup_{j \geq 1} |g_{\lambda,A}(j)| \sum_{i=1}^n q_i^2$$

and

$$\Big|\Pr[M \in A] - \Pr[Z_\lambda \in A]\Big| \leq \sup_{j \geq 1} |g_{\lambda,A}(j+1) - g_{\lambda,A}(j)| \sum_{i=1}^n q_i^2.$$

All that remains is to compute bounds for the suprema involved in these expressions; such bounds are given in the next result; for a proof, see Barbour, Holst and Janson (1992, p. 7).

Property 9.10.3
If $g_{\lambda,A}$ solves (9.11), then

$$\sup_{j \geq 1} |g_{\lambda,A}(j)| \leq \min\{1, \lambda^{-1/2}\}$$

and

$$\sup_{j \geq 1} |g_{\lambda,A}(j+1) - g_{\lambda,A}(j)| \leq \frac{1 - \exp(-\lambda)}{\lambda} \leq \min\{1, \lambda^{-1}\}.$$

From Property 9.10.3 we get

$$d_{\mathrm{TV}}(M, Z_\lambda) \le \frac{1-\exp(-\lambda)}{\lambda} \sum_{i=1}^{n} q_i^2 \le \min\{1, \lambda^{-1}\} \sum_{i=1}^{n} q_i^2. \tag{9.14}$$

To end with, let us mention that

$$\frac{1}{\lambda} \sum_{i=1}^{n} q_i^2 = \frac{\sum_{i=1}^{n} q_i^2}{\sum_{i=1}^{n} q_i} \le \max q_i$$

obviously holds; this shows that $d_{\mathrm{TV}}(M, Z_\lambda)$ is governed by $\max q_i$.

Remark 9.10.4. We might be tempted to approximate $I_\bullet = \sum_{i=1}^{n} I_i$ by a mixture of Poisson distributions, M say, in such a way that

$$\mathbb{E}[I_\bullet] = \mathbb{E}[M] \text{ and } \mathbb{V}[I_\bullet] = \mathbb{V}[M] \tag{9.15}$$

both hold. However, this is not possible since, for $B \sim \mathcal{B}in(n, q_\bullet/n)$ and $N_\bullet \sim \mathcal{P}oi(q_\bullet)$ with $q_\bullet = \sum_{i=1}^{n} q_i$, we know that

$$I_\bullet \preceq_{\mathrm{SL},=} B \preceq_{\mathrm{SL},=} N_\bullet$$

indicating that

$$\mathbb{V}[I_\bullet] \le \mathbb{V}[B] = \frac{q_\bullet(1-q_\bullet)}{n} \le \mathbb{V}[N_\bullet] = q_\bullet$$

so that for any non-degenerate Poisson mixture M with mean $q_\bullet$, $q_\bullet < \mathbb{V}[M]$. It is thus impossible to approximate $I_\bullet$ by a mixture of Poisson distributions in such a way that (9.15) holds. ∇

9.10.1.4 Poisson approximation for sums of dependent indicators

Consider now the case where the I_i are correlated, and define the rvs

$$Q_i = q_i(I_1, \ldots, I_{i-1}) = \Pr[I_i = 1 | I_1, \ldots, I_{i-1}], \quad i = 2, \ldots, n.$$

By convention, $Q_1 = q_1$. We then have the next result, due to Serfling (1975).

Proposition 9.10.5
Let $I_1, I_2, \ldots, I_n$ be dependent Bernoulli rvs and $I_1^*, I_2^*, \ldots, I_n^*$ be independent Bernoulli rvs with respective means $q_1^*, q_2^*, \ldots, q_n^*$. Then,

$$d_{\mathrm{TV}}\left(\sum_{i=1}^{n} I_i, \sum_{i=1}^{n} I_i^*\right) \le \sum_{i=1}^{n} \mathbb{E}[|Q_i - q_i^*|].$$

Proof. Let us construct $I_1, I_2, \ldots, I_n$ and $I_1^*, I_2^*, \ldots, I_n^*$ on a common probability space. Explicitly, we must construct a sequence $I_1^*, I_2^*, \ldots, I_n^*$ of independent Bernoulli rvs and a sequence of correlated Bernoulli rvs having the joint distribution which is determined by the set of quantities q_1 and

$$q_i(x_1, \ldots, x_{i-1}) = \Pr[I_i = 1 | I_1 = x_1, \ldots, I_{i-1} = x_{i-1}], \quad i = 2, \ldots, n$$

for $x_j = 0$ or 1, $j = 1, \ldots, i-1$. Introduce a sequence $U_1, \ldots, U_n$ of independent $\mathcal{U}ni(0, 1)$ rvs and set

$$I_i^* = \mathbb{I}[U_i \leq q_i^*], \quad i = 1, 2, \ldots, n.$$

Moreover, set $I_1 = \mathbb{I}[U_1 \leq q_1]$, and, for $i = 2, \ldots, n$,

$$I_i = \mathbb{I}[U_i \leq q_i(I_1, \ldots, I_{i-1})].$$

It is clear that the I_i and I_i^* described above fulfil the requirements. Further,

$$\Pr[I_i \neq I_i^*] = \mathbb{E}\Big[\Pr[I_i \neq I_i^* | I_1, \ldots, I_{i-1})\Big] = \mathbb{E}\Big[|q_i(I_1, \ldots, I_{i-1}) - q_i^*|\Big],$$

which concludes the proof. □

If we choose $q_i^* = \mathbb{E}[Q_i]$, we get with $N \sim \mathcal{P}oi(\lambda)$, where $\lambda = \sum_{i=1}^n \mathbb{E}[Q_i]$,

$$\begin{aligned} d_{\mathrm{TV}}(I_{\bullet}, N) &\leq d_{\mathrm{TV}}(I_{\bullet}, I_{\bullet}^{\perp}) + d_{\mathrm{TV}}(I_{\bullet}^{\perp}, N) \\ &\leq \sum_{i=1}^{n} \Big((\mathbb{E}[Q_i])^2 + \mathbb{E}\big[|Q_i - \mathbb{E}[Q_i]|\big] \Big). \end{aligned}$$

Note that the q_i^* may be chosen arbitrarily. For instance, if we aim to minimize $\mathbb{E}|Q_i - q_i^*|$, we take q_i^* to be the median of Q_i instead of $q_i^* = \mathbb{E}[Q_i]$. We refer the reader to Vellaisamy and Chaudhuri (1996, 1999) for related results.

9.10.2 *Dependence in the quasi-homogeneous individual model*

In this section we will continue to work within the framework of Michel's (1987) 'quasi-homogeneous' portfolio but without assuming the mutual independence of the risks involved. We will adhere to the assumption $\lambda_i = q_i$ for all i and we denote by λ the sum of the λ_i.

9.10.2.1 The Chen–Stein method

Henceforth, we will relax the independence assumption and suppose that the conditional claim amounts V_i are mutually independent but not assume that the indicators I_i are mutually independent. The assumption retained in this section states that the dependence between the individual risks is caused by the dependence between the indicators.

For a portfolio of insurance policies that provide a fixed amount if a claim occurs, the conditional claim amounts are deterministic so that the assumption made above holds in this case. For a portfolio of insurance policies which compensate the loss incurred after a claim, it will often be the occurrences of claims that will be more or less strongly dependent, while the dependence of the conditional claim amounts will be much weaker. Hence, in this case the above assumption will often offer a first attempt to describe the dependence between the risks. In what follows, we will consider a portfolio which is quasi-homogeneous in the sense that the conditional claim amounts V_i all have the same distribution.

We know from Proposition 9.9.5 that the inequality $d_{\text{TV}}(S_{\text{ind}}, S_{\text{coll}}) \leq d_{\text{TV}}(I_\bullet, N_\bullet)$ is valid, so that we only have to deal with $d_{\text{TV}}(I_\bullet, N_\bullet)$ to get an upper bound for $d_{\text{TV}}(S_{\text{ind}}, S_{\text{coll}})$.

For each I_i, $i = 1, 2, \ldots, n$, we now define the set of dependence $B_i \subset \{1, 2, \ldots, n\}$ such that I_j is independent of I_i if and only if $j \notin B_i$. Further, define

$$b_1 = \sum_{i=1}^{n} \sum_{j \in B_i} q_i q_j \tag{9.16}$$

and

$$b_2 = \sum_{i=1}^{n} \sum_{i \neq j \in B_i} \mathbb{E}[I_i I_j]. \tag{9.17}$$

The following result can be found in Chen (1975).

Property 9.10.6
We have that

$$d_{\text{TV}}(I_\bullet, N_\bullet) \leq 2(b_1 + b_2)\frac{1 - \exp(-\lambda)}{\lambda}$$

A more general version of this result appears in Arratia, Goldstein and Gordon (1990). In the following theorem we show that the Chen–Stein method can also be useful in individual risk theory. It is a direct consequence of Property 9.10.6.

Proposition 9.10.7
In the quasi-homogeneous case, the inequality

$$d_{\text{TV}}(S_{\text{ind}}, S_{\text{coll}}) \leq 2(b_1 + b_2)\frac{1 - \exp(-\lambda)}{\lambda}$$

holds, where $\lambda = \sum_{i=1}^{n} q_i$, and b_1 and b_2 are defined by (9.16) and (9.17) respectively.

The bound presented in Proposition 9.10.7 will work best for dealing with local dependence, corresponding to situations in which the sets of dependence B_i have only a few elements so that b_1 and b_2 are small.

Remark 9.10.8. Let us now look at the special case where the X_i are mutually independent. We find that $B_i = \{i\}$, $i = 1, 2, \ldots, n$, and hence $b_1 = \sum_{i=1}^{n} q_i^2$, $b_2 = 0$, so that we obtain from Proposition 9.10.7 that

$$d_{\text{TV}}(S_{\text{ind}}, S_{\text{coll}}) \leq 2 \sum_{i=1}^{n} q_i^2 \frac{1 - \exp(-\lambda)}{\lambda}. \tag{9.18}$$

If $\lambda < 1$ we have

$$d_{TV}(S_{ind}, S_{coll}) \leq 2\sum_{i=1}^{n} q_i^2$$

which is a special case of (9.8). For $\lambda > 1$ we have from (9.18) that

$$d_{TV}(S_{ind}, S_{coll}) \leq \frac{2}{\lambda}\sum_{i=1}^{n} q_i^2,$$

which is (9.10). ∇

Example 9.10.9. Consider a portfolio consisting of $m+n$ life insurance policies providing a death benefit. There are m couples (wife and husband) in the portfolio and all death benefits are equal to 1 (which means that in fact we are looking at the total number of deaths during the reference period). Then we can write the aggregate claims as

$$S_{ind} = \sum_{i=1}^{m}(X_i + X_i') + \sum_{i=m+1}^{n} X_i.$$

We assume that all risks are mutually independent, except for the 'coupled' risks. This means that the only dependence that occurs is the dependence between the risks of a wife and her husband.

The sets of dependence are then given by $B_i = B_i' = \{i, i'\}$, $i = 1, 2, \ldots, m$, $B_i = \{i\}$, $i = m+1, \ldots, n$, and hence

$$\lambda = \sum_{i=1}^{m}(q_i + q_i') + \sum_{i=m+1}^{n} q_i,$$

$$b_1 = \sum_{i=1}^{m}(q_i + q_i')^2 + \sum_{i=m+1}^{n} q_i^2,$$

$$b_2 = 2\sum_{i=1}^{m}\left(q_i.q_i' + \mathbb{C}[X_i, X_i']\right).$$

From Proposition 9.10.7 we find the following error bound for the (compound) Poisson approximation of this portfolio:

$$d_{TV}(S_{ind}, S_{coll}) \leq \frac{2}{\lambda}\left(\sum_{i=1}^{m}\left((q_i + q_i')^2 + 2q_i q_i' + 2\mathbb{C}[X_i, X_i']\right) + \sum_{i=m+1}^{n} q_i^2\right). \tag{9.19}$$

We denote Michel's upper bound (9.10), which is valid under the independence assumption, by

$$M = \frac{2}{\lambda}\left(\sum_{i=1}^{m}(q_i^2 + q_i'^2) + \sum_{i=m+1}^{n} q_i^2\right).$$

Hence, from (9.19) we find

$$d_{\text{TV}}(S_{\text{ind}}, S_{\text{coll}}) \leq M + \frac{4}{\lambda}\sum_{i=1}^{m}\Big(2q_i q_i' + \mathbb{C}[X_i, X_i']\Big). \tag{9.20}$$

If we do not have any information about $\mathbb{C}[X_i, X_i']$ then we can use the following upper bound for this covariance:

$$\begin{aligned}\mathbb{C}[X_i, X_i'] &= \sqrt{q_i(1-q_i)q_i'(1-q_i')}\, r_{\text{P}}(X_i, X_i') \\ &\leq \sqrt{q_i(1-q_i)q_i'(1-q_i')}\end{aligned}$$

In order to establish the effect on the bound of introducing dependence into the portfolio, assume that all claim probabilities are of the same order – say, all are equal to q. Then we find $\lambda = (m+n)q$ and $M = q$, so that (9.20) becomes

$$d_{\text{TV}}(S_{\text{ind}}, S_{\text{coll}}) \leq M + \frac{4m}{m+n}\Big(2q + (1-q)\, r_{\text{P}}(X_i, X_i')\Big), \tag{9.21}$$

which shows that increasing the relative number of couples or increasing the correlation coefficients will lead to an increased bound.

As a numerical illustration consider the case where $q \leq \frac{10}{11}$ and

$$\Pr[X_i' = 1 \,|\, X_i = 1] = 1.1 \times q\,.$$

This means that

$$r_{\text{P}}(X_i, X_i') = 0.1 \times \frac{q}{1-q}.$$

Further, let $\frac{m}{m+n} = 5\,\%$, which means that $10\,\%$ of the portfolio consists of couples. Then we find from (9.21) that

$$d_{\text{TV}}(S_{\text{ind}}, S_{\text{coll}}) \leq 2.42 \times q,$$

which indicates that the bound is increased by $\pm\ 20\,\%$ if $10\,\%$ of the portfolio consists of couples with dependent risks and if the mortality rate of a person is increased by $10\,\%$, given the mortality of his spouse during the reference year. ∇

To end with, let us mention the work by Genest, Marceau and Mesfioui (2003) containing nice illustrations of the compound Poisson approximation for portfolios with correlated risks.

9.11 EXERCISES

Exercise 9.11.1. Consider a family $\{X_\theta,\ \theta \in \mathcal{S}\}$, $\mathcal{S} \subseteq \mathbb{R}^+$, of rvs indexed by a single parameter θ, and let X_Θ represent a mixture of the X_θ, that is,

$$F_{X_\Theta}(x) = \int_0^{+\infty} F_{X_\theta}(x)\, dF_\Theta(\theta), \quad \theta \in \mathbb{R}^+.$$

Prove that

$$d_{\mathrm{TV}}(X_{\Theta_1}, X_{\Theta_2}) \leq d_{\mathrm{TV}}(\Theta_1, \Theta_2). \tag{9.22}$$

It is worth mentioning that the result contained in Proposition 9.9.1 can be considered as a particular case of (9.22) since a random sum is a mixture of deterministic sums S_n.

Exercise 9.11.2. (Distance between mixtures). Show that $d_{\mathrm{K}}(X_{\Theta_1}, X_{\Theta_2}) \leq d_{\mathrm{K}}(\Theta_1, \Theta_2)$ provided $\{X_\theta, \ \theta \in \mathcal{S}\}$ is stochastically increasing in θ, that is, $X_\theta \preceq_{\mathrm{ST}} X_{\theta'}$ whenever $\theta \leq \theta'$.

Exercise 9.11.3. Let X, Y and Z be three rvs such that $X \preceq_{\mathrm{ST}} Y \preceq_{\mathrm{ST}} Z$ holds, and let $S^-(dF_Y - dF_X) \leq k-1$. Show that

$$d_{\mathrm{TV}}(X, Y) \leq k d_{\mathrm{K}}(X, Y) \leq k d_{\mathrm{K}}(X, Z) \leq k d_{\mathrm{TV}}(X, Z).$$

Exercise 9.11.4. Let us consider the independent rvs $I_1 \sim \mathcal{B}er\,(q_1),\ I_2 \sim \mathcal{B}er\,(q_2),\ \ldots,\ I_n \sim \mathcal{B}er\,(q_n)$. Let us also consider the independent rvs $N_1 \sim \mathcal{P}oi\,(\lambda_1),\ N_2 \sim \mathcal{P}oi\,(\lambda_2),\ \ldots,\ N_n \sim \mathcal{P}oi\,(\lambda_n)$.

(i) Show that if

$$\lambda_i \geq -\ln(1-q_i) \text{ for } i = 1, 2, \ldots, n,$$

then $I_\bullet \preceq_{\mathrm{ST}} N_\bullet$ and $S^-(dF_{N_\bullet} - dF_{I_\bullet}) \leq n$.

(ii) Deduce that

$$d_{\mathrm{K}}(I_\bullet, N_\bullet) \leq d_{\mathrm{TV}}(I_\bullet, N_\bullet) \leq n d_{\mathrm{K}}(I_\bullet, N_\bullet).$$

Exercise 9.11.5. Let X and Y be two finite-mean rvs such that $\mathbb{E}[X] \leq \mathbb{E}[Y]$. Show that $X \preceq_{\mathrm{ST}} Y$ if, and only if, $d_{\mathrm{W}}(X, Y) = \mathbb{E}[Y] - \mathbb{E}[X]$.

Exercise 9.11.6. Let X, Y and Z be two rvs with finite expectations such that $X \preceq_{\mathrm{SL}} Y \preceq_{\mathrm{SL}} Z$. If $S^-(F_X - F_Y) \leq k-1$, show that

$$d_{\mathrm{W}}(X, Y) \leq k d_{\mathrm{SL}}(X, Y) \leq k d_{\mathrm{SL}}(X, Z) \leq k d_{\mathrm{W}}(X, Z).$$

References

Abdous, B., Genest, C., and Rémillard, B. (2004). Dependence properties of meta-elliptical distributions. In *Statistical Modeling and Analysis for Complex Data Problems* (eds P. Duchesne and B. Rémillard). Kluwer, Dordrecht, pp. 1–15.

Acerbi, C. (2002). Spectral measures of risk: A coherent representation of subjective risk aversion. *Journal of Banking and Finance* **26**, 1505–1518.

Acerbi, C., and Tasche, D. (2002). On the coherence of expected shortfall. *Journal of Banking and Finance* **26**, 1487–1503.

Albrecher, H., and Boxma, O.J. (2003). A ruin model with dependence between claim sizes and claim intervals. *Insurance: Mathematics & Economics* **35**, 245–254.

Albrecher, H., and Teugels, J.L. (2004). Exponential behavior in the presence of dependence in risk theory. EURANDOM Research Report 2004–042.

Alzaid, A.A. (1988). Mean residual life ordering. *Statistical Papers* **29**, 35–43.

Alzaid, A., Kim, J.S., and Proschan, F. (1991). Laplace ordering and its applications. *Journal of Applied Probability* **28**, 116–130.

Ambagaspitiya, R.S. (1998). On the distribution of a sum of correlated aggregate claims. *Insurance: Mathematics & Economics* **23**, 15–19.

Arnold, B.C. (1987). *Majorization and the Lorenz Order: A Brief Introduction*. Springer-Verlag, New York.

Arratia, R.A., Goldstein, L., and Gordon, L. (1990). Poisson approximation and the Chen–Stein method. *Statistical Science* **5**, 403–434.

Arrow, K.J. (1974). *Essays in the Theory of Risk-Bearing*. North-Holland, New York.

Artzner, P., Delbaen, F., Eber, J.-M., and Heath, D. (1999). Coherent risk measures. *Mathematical Finance* **9**, 203–228.

Averous, J., and Dortet-Bernadet, J.-L. (2004). Dependence for Archimedean copulas and ageing properties of the generating function. *Sankhyā*, in press.

Baccelli, F., and Makowski, A.M. (1989). Multidimensional stochastic ordering and associated random variables. *Operations Research* **37**, 478–487.

Barbe, P., Genest, C., Ghoudi, K., and Rémillard, B. (1996). On Kendall's process. *Journal of Multivariate Analysis* **58**, 197–229.

Barbour, A.D., Holst, L. and Janson, S. (1992). *Poisson Approximation*. Oxford University Press, Oxford.

Barlow, R.E., and Proschan, F. (1975). *Statistical Theory of Reliability and Life Testing – Probability Models*. Holt, Rinehart and Winston, New York.

Barrett, G., and Donald, S. (2003). Consistent tests for stochastic dominance. *Econometrica* **71**, 71–104.

Barrois, T. (1834). *Essai sur l'Application du Calcul des Probabilités aux Assurances contre l'Incendie*. Daniel, Lille.

Bartoszewicz, J. (1986). Dispersive ordering and the total time on test transformation. *Statistics & Probability Letters* **4**, 285–288.

Bartoszewicz, J. (1995). Stochastic order relations and the total time on test transform. *Statistics & Probability Letters* **22**, 103–110.

Bassan, B., Denuit, M., and Scarsini, M. (1999). Variability orders and mean differences. *Statistics & Probability Letters* **45**, 121–130.

Bäuerle, N. (1997). Inequalities for stochastic models via supermodular orders. *Communications in Statistics – Stochastic Models* **13**, 181–201.

Bäuerle, N., and Müller, A. (1998). Modeling and comparing dependencies in multivariate risk portfolios. *ASTIN Bulletin* **28**, 59–76.

Bäuerle, N., and Müller, A. (2004). Stochastic orders and risk measures: Consistency and bounds. Manuscript.

Bäuerle, N., and Rolski, T. (1998). A monotonicity result for the work-load in Markov-modulated queues. *Journal of Applied Probability* **35**, 741–747.

Belzunce, F. (1999). On a characterization of right spread order by the increasing convex order. *Statistics & Probability Letters* **45**, 103–110.

Bermúdez, L, Denuit, M., and Dhaene, J. (2001). Exponential bonus-malus systems integrating a priori risk classification. *Journal of Actuarial Practice* **9**, 84–112.

Bernoulli, D. (1738). Specimen theoriae novae de mensura sortis. *Commentarii Academiae Scientiarum Imperialis Petropolitanae*, **5**, 175–192. (Translated as 'Expositions of a new theory on the measurement of risk' in *Econometrica* **22**, 23–46.)

Bickel, P.J., and Lehmann, E.L. (1979). Descriptive statistics for nonparametric models. IV. Spread. In *Contributions to Statistics* (ed. J. Jurečková). Academia, Prague, pp. 33–40.

Black, F., and Scholes, M. (1973). The pricing of options and corporate liabilities. *Journal of Political Economy* **81**, 637–654.

Boland, P.J., Proschan, F., and Tong, Y.L. (1992). A stochastic ordering of partial sums of independent random variables and of some stochastic processes. *Journal of Applied Probability* **29**, 645–654.

Borch, K. (1961). The utility concept applied to the theory of insurance. *ASTIN Bulletin* **1**, 245–255.

Borch, K. (1974). *The Mathematical Theory of Insurance*. D.C. Heath and Co., Lexington, MA.

Borch, K. (1990). *Economics of Insurance*. North-Holland, Amsterdam.

Boutsikas, M.V., and Koutras, M.V. (2000). A bound for the distribution of the sum of discrete associated or negatively associated random variables. *Annals of Applied Probability* **10**, 1137–1150.

Boutsikas, M.V., and Vaggelatou, E. (2002). On the distance between convex-ordred random variables, with applications. *Advances in Applied Probability* **34**, 349–374.

Bowers, N.L., Gerber, H.U., Hickman, J.C., Jones, D.A., and Nesbitt, C.J. (1997). *Actuarial Mathematics*. Society of Actuaries, Itasca, IL.

Brockett, P.L., and Cox, S.H. (1985). Insurance calculation using incomplete information. *Scandinavian Actuarial Journal*, 94–108.

Brouhns, N., and Denuit, M. (2003). Actuarial modelling of longitudinal claims data through GAMM's: Some methodological results. *German Actuarial Bulletin* **26**, 25–39.

Bühlmann, H. (1960) *Austauschbare stochastische Variabeln und ihre Grenzwertsätze*. University of California Publications in Statistics, Vol. 3, No. 1. University of California Press, Berkeley.

Bühlmann, H. (1970). *Mathematical Methods in Risk Theory*. Springer-Verlag, New York.

Bühlmann, H. (1980). An economic premium principle. *ASTIN Bulletin* **11**, 52–60.

Bühlmann, H., Gagliardi, B., Gerber, H., and Straub, E. (1977). Some inequalities for stop-loss premiums. *ASTIN Bulletin* **9**, 75–83.

Cambanis, S., Huang, S., and Simons, G. (1981). On the theory of elliptically contoured distributions. *Journal of Multivariate Analysis* **11**, 368–385.

Cambanis, S., Simons, G., and Stout, W. (1976). Inequalities for $\mathcal{E}(X, Y)$ when the marginals are fixed. *Zeitschrift für Wahrscheinlichkeits theorie und Verwandte Gebiete* **36**, 285–294.

Capéraà, P., and Genest, C. (1993). Spearman's rho is larger than Kendall's tau for positively dependent random variables. *Journal of Nonparametric Statistics* **2**, 183–194.

Carrière, J. (1994). Dependent decrement theory. *Transactions of the Society of Actuaries* **46**, 45–74.

Carrière, J. (2000). Bivariate survival models for coupled lives. *Scandinavian Actuarial Journal*, 17–32.

Carrière, J.-F., and Chan, L.K. (1986). The bounds of bivariate distributions that limit the value of last-survivor annuities. *Transactions of the Society of Actuaries* **38**, 51–74 (with discussion).

Carter, M., and Van Brunt, B. (2000). *The Lebesgue–Stieltjes Integral. A Practical Introduction*. Springer-Verlag, New York.

Cebrian, A., Denuit, M., and Scaillet, O. (2004). Testing for concordance ordering. *ASTIN Bulletin* **34**, 151–173.

Chang, C.-S., Chao, X.L., Pinedo, M., and Shanthikumar, J.G. (1991). Stochastic convexity for multidimensional processes and its applications. *IEEE Transactions on Automatic Control* **36**, 1347–1355.

Chateauneuf, A., Cohen, M., and Meilijson, I. (1997). Comonotonicity, rank-dependent utilities and a search problem. In *Distributions with Given Marginals and Moment Problems* (eds. V. Beněs and J. Štěpán). Kluwer Academic Publishers, Amsterdam.

Chen, L.H.Y. (1975). Poisson approximation for dependent trials. *Annals of Probability* **3**, 534–545.

Cherubini, U., Luciano, E., and Vecchiato, W. (2004). *Copula Methods in Finance*. John Wiley & Sons, Ltd, Chichester.

Choquet, G. (1963). Les cônes convexes faiblement complets dans l'analyse. In *Proceedings of the International Congress of Mathematicians*, Stockholm, pp. 317–330.

Chow, Y.S., and Teicher, H. (2003). *Probability Theory. Independence, Interchangeability, Martingales*. Springer-Verlag, New York.

Christofides, T. C., and Vaggelatou, E. (2004). A connection between supermodular ordering and positive/negative association. *Journal of Multivariate Analysis* **88**, 138–151.

Clayton, D.G. (1978). A model for association in bivariate life tables and its application in epidemiological studies of familial tendency in chronic disease incidence. *Biometrika* **65**, 141–151.

Cohen, A., and Sackrowitz, H.B. (1995). On stochastic ordering of random vectors. *Journal of Applied Probability* **32**, 960–965.

Colangelo, A., Scarsini, M., and Shaked, M. (2004). Some positive dependence stochastic orders. *Canadian Journal of Statistics*, in press.

Cook, R.D., and Johnson, M.E. (1981). A family of distributions for modelling non-elliptically symmetric multivariate data. *Journal of the Royal Statistical Society Series B* **43**, 210–218.

Cossette, H., Denuit, M., Dhaene, J., and Marceau, E. (2001). Stochastic approximations for present value functions. *Bulletin of the Swiss Association of Actuaries*, 15–28.

Cossette, H., Denuit, M., and Marceau, É. (2000). Impact of dependence among multiple claims in a single loss. *Insurance: Mathematics & Economics* **26**, 213–222.

Cossette, H., Denuit, M., and Marceau, E. (2002). Distributional bounds for functions of dependent risks. *Bulletin of the Swiss Association of Actuaries*, 45–65.

Cossette, H., Gaillardetz, P., Marceau, É., and Rioux, J. (2002). On two dependent individual risk models. *Insurance: Mathematics & Economics* **30**, 153–166.

Cossette, H., Landriault, D., and Marceau, É. (2003). Ruin probabilities in the compound Markov binomial model. *Scandinavian Actuarial Journal*, 301–323.

Cossette, H., and Marceau, É. (2000). The discrete-time risk model with correlated classes of business. *Insurance: Mathematics & Economics* **26**, 133–149.

Daduna, H., and Szekli, R. (1996). A queueing theoretical proof of increasing property of Polya frequency functions. *Statistics & Probability Letters* **26**, 233–242.

Dardanoni, V., and Forcina, A. (1999). Inference for Lorenz curve orderings. *Econometrics Journal* **2**, 48–74.

Darsow, W.F., Nguyen, B., and Olsen, E.T. (1992). Copulas and Markov processes. *Illinois Journal of Mathematics* **36**, 600–642.

Davidson, R., and Duclos, J.Y. (2000). Statistical inference for stochastic dominance and for the measurement of poverty and inequality. *Econometrica* **68**, 1435–1464.

Davis, H., and Feldstein, M. (1979). The generalized Pareto law as a model for progressively censored survival data. *Biometrika* **66**, 299–306.

De Pril, N., and Dhaene, J. (1992). Error bounds for compound Poisson approximation of the individual risk model. *ASTIN Bulletin* **22**, 135–148.

De Vijlder, F.E. (1980). An illustration of the duality technique in semi-continuous linear programming. *ASTIN Bulletin* **11**, 17–28.

De Vijlder, F.E. (1982). Best upper bounds for integrals with respect to measures allowed to vary under conical and integral constraints. *Insurance: Mathematics & Economics* **1**, 109–130.

De Vijlder, F.E. (1983). Maximization, under equality constraints, of a functional of a probability distribution. *Insurance: Mathematics & Economics* **2**, 1–16.

De Vijlder, F.E., and Goovaerts, M.J. (1982). Upper and lower bounds on stop-loss premiums in case of known expectation and variance of the risk variable. *Bulletin of the Swiss Association of Actuaries*, 149–164.

De Vijlder, F.E., and Goovaerts, M.J. (1983). Maximization of the variance of a stop-loss reinsured risk. *Insurance: Mathematics & Economics* **2**, 75–80.

De Vijlder, F.E., Goovaerts, M.J., Haezendonck, J., and Garrido, J. (1984). Bornes pour des espérances sous des contraintes d'égalité. *Bulletin de l'Association Royale des Actuaires Belges* **78**, 29–44.

Denuit, M. (1997). A new distribution of Poisson-type for the number of claims. *ASTIN Bulletin* **27**, 229–242.

Denuit, M. (1999). The exponential premium calculation principle revisited. *ASTIN Bulletin* **29**, 215–226.

Denuit, M. (2000). Stochastic analysis of duplicates in life insurance portfolios. *German Actuarial Bulletin* **24**, 507–514.

Denuit, M. (2001). Laplace transform ordering of actuarial quantities. *Insurance: Mathematics & Economics* **29**, 83–102.

Denuit, M. (2002). S-convex extrema, Taylor-type expansions and stochastic approximations. *Scandinavian Actuarial Journal*, 45–67.

Denuit, M., De Vijlder, F.E., and Lefèvre, C. (1999). Extremal generators and extremal distributions for the continuous *s*-convex stochastic orderings. *Insurance: Mathematics & Economics* **24**, 201–217.

Denuit, M., and Dhaene, J. (2001). Bonus-malus scales using exponential loss functions. *German Actuarial Bulletin* **25**, 13–27.

Denuit, M., and Dhaene, J. (2003). Simple characterizations of comonotonicity and counter-monotonicity by extremal correlations. *Belgian Actuarial Bulletin* **3**, 22–27.

Denuit, M., Dhaene, J., Le Bailly de Tilleghem, C., and Teghem, S. (2001). Measuring the impact of a dependence among insured lifelengths. *Belgian Actuarial Bulletin* **1**, 18–39.

Denuit, M., Dhaene, J., and Ribas, C. (2001). Does positive dependence between individual risks increase stop-loss premiums? *Insurance: Mathematics & Economicx* **28**, 305–308.

Denuit, M., Genest, C., and Marceau, É. (1999). Stochastic bounds on sums of dependent risks. *Insurance: Mathematics & Economics* **25**, 85–104.

Denuit, M., Genest, C., and Marceau, É. (2002). Criteria for the stochastic ordering of random sums, with actuarial applications. *Scandinavian Actuarial Journal*, 3–16.

Denuit, M., Genest, C., and Mesfioui, M. (2004). Stop-loss bounds on functions of possibly dependent risks in the presence of partial information on their marginals. Discussion Paper 04–08, Institut de Statistique, Université Catholique de Louvain, Louvain-la-Neuve, Belgium.

Denuit, M., Goderniaux, A.-C., and Scaillet, O. (2004). A Kolmogorov-type test for the right-spread and excess-wealth orders against parametric alternatives. Working Report, Institut des Sciences Actuarielles, Université Catholique de Louvain, Louvain-la-Neuve, Belgium.

Denuit, M., and Lambert, Ph. (2001). Smoothed NPML estimation of the risk distribution underlying bonus-malus systems. *Proceedings of the Casualty Actuarial Society* **88**, 142–174.

Denuit, M., and Lambert, Ph. (2005). Constraints on concordance measures in bivariate discrete data. *Journal of Multivariate Analysis*, **93**, 40–57.

Denuit, M., Lefèvre, C., and Mesfioui, M. (1999). A class of bivariate stochastic orderings with applications in actuarial sciences. *Insurance: Mathematics & Economics* **24**, 31–50.

Denuit, M., Lefèvre, C., and Scarsini, M. (2001). On *s*-convexity and risk aversion. *Theory and Decision* **50**, 239–248.

Denuit, M., Lefèvre, C., and Shaked, M. (1998). The *s*-convex orders among real random variables, with applications. *Mathematical Inequalities and Applications* **1**, 585–613.

Denuit, M., Lefèvre, C., and Shaked, M. (2000a). On the theory of high convexity stochastic orders. *Statistics & Probability Letters* **47**, 287–293.

Denuit, M., Lefèvre, C., and Shaked, M. (2000b). Stochastic convexity of the Poisson mixture model, with applications in actuarial sciences. *Methodology and Computing in Applied Probability* **2**, 231–254.

Denuit, M., Lefèvre, C. and Shaked, M. (2000c). On *s*-convex approximations. *Advances in Applied Probability* **32**, 994–1010.

Denuit, M., Lefèvre, C., and Utev, S. (1999a). Generalized stochastic convexity and stochastic orderings of mixtures. *Probability in the Engineering and Informational Sciences* **13**, 275–291.

Denuit, M., Lefèvre, C., and Utev, S. (1999b). Stochastic orderings of convex/concave-type on an arbitrary grid. *Mathematics of Operations Research* **24**, 835–846.

Denuit, M., Lefèvre, C., and Utev, S. (2002). Measuring the impact of dependence between claims occurrences. *Insurance: Mathematics & Economics* **30**, 1–19.

Denuit, M., and Müller, A. (2002). Smooth generators of integral stochastic orders. *Annals of Applied Probability* **12**, 1174–1184.

Denuit, M., Purcaru, O., and Van Keilegom, I. (2004). Bivariate archimedean copula modelling for loss-ALAE data in nonlife insurance. Discussion Paper 04–23, Institut de Statistique, Université Catholique de Louvain, Louvain-la-Neuve, Belgium.

Denuit, M., and Scaillet, O. (2004). Nonparametric tests for positive quadrant dependence. *Journal of Financial Econometrics* **2**, 422–450.

Denuit, M., and Van Bellegem, S. (2001). On the stop-loss and total variation distances between compound sums. *Statistics & Probability Letters* **53**, 153–165.

Denuit, M., and Vermandele, C. (1998). Optimal reinsurance and stop-loss order. *Insurance: Mathematics & Economics* **22**, 229–233.

Deprez, O., and Gerber, H.U. (1985). On convex principles of premium calculation. *Insurance: Mathematics & Economics* **4**, 179–189.

Deshpande, J.V., and Kochar, S.C. (1983). Dispersive ordering is the same as tail-ordering. *Advances in Applied Probability* **15**, 686–687.

Dhaene, J., and Denuit, M. (1999). The safest dependence structure among risks. *Insurance: Mathematics & Economics* **25**, 11–21.

Dhaene, J., Denuit, M., Goovaerts, M.J., Kaas, R., and Vyncke, D. (2002a). The concept of comonotonicity in actuarial science and finance: Theory. *Insurance: Mathematics & Economics* **31**, 3–33.

Dhaene, J., Denuit, M., Goovaerts, M.J., Kaas, R., and Vyncke, D. (2002b). The concept of comonotonicity in actuarial science and finance: Applications. *Insurance: Mathematics & Economics* **31**, 133–161.

Dhaene, J., and Goovaerts, M.J. (1996). Dependency of risks and stop-loss order. *ASTIN Bulletin* **26**, 201–212.

Dhaene, J., and Goovaerts, M.J. (1997). On the dependency of risks in the individual life model. *Insurance: Mathematics & Economics* **19**, 243–253.

Dhaene, J., Goovaerts, M.J., and Kaas, R. (2003). Economic capital allocation derived from risk measures. *North American Actuarial Journal* **7**, 44–59.

Dhaene, J., Vanneste, M., and Wolthuis, H. (2000). A note on dependencies in multiple life statuses. *Bulletin of the Swiss Association of Actuaries*, 19–34.

Dionne, G., and Vanasse, C. (1989). A generalization of actuarial automobile insurance rating models: the negative binomial distribution with a regression component. *ASTIN Bulletin* **19**, 199–212.

Dionne, G., and Vanasse, C. (1992). Automobile insurance ratemaking in the presence of asymmetrical information. *Journal of Applied Econometrics* **7**, 149–165.

Dobrushin, R.L. (1970). Prescribing a system of random variables by conditional distributions. *Theory of Probability and Its Applications* **15**, 458–486.

Doksum, K. (1969). Star-shaped transformations and the power of rank tests. *Annals of Mathematical Statistics* **40**, 1167–1176.

Drouet-Mari, D., and Kotz, S. (2001). *Correlation and Dependence*. Imperial College Press, London.

Dyckerhoff, R., and Mosler, K. (1997). Orthant orderings of discrete random vectors. *Journal of Statistical Planning and Inference* **62**, 193–205.

Efron, B. (1965). Increasing properties of Pölya frequency functions. *Annals of Mathematical Statistics* **36**, 272–279.

Embrechts, P., Höing, A., and Juri, A. (2003). Using copulae to bound the value-at-risk for functions of dependent risks. *Finance & Stochastics* **7**, 145–167.

Embrechts, P., Lindskog, F., and McNeil, A. (2003). Modelling dependence with copulas and applications to risk management. In *Handbook of Heavy Tailed Distributions in Finance* (ed. S. Rachev). Elsevier, Amsterdam, pp. 329–384.

Embrechts, P., McNeil A., and Straumann, D. (2002). Correlation and dependency in risk management: Properties and pitfalls. In *Risk Management: Value at Risk and Beyond* (eds M. Dempster and H. Moffatt). Cambridge University Press, Cambridge.

Embrechts, P., and Puccetti, G. (2004). Bounds on value-at-risk. Technical Report, Department of Mathematics, ETHZ, Switzerland.

Esary, J.D., and Proschan, F. (1972). Relationship among some concepts of bivariate dependence. *Annals of Mathematical Statistics* **43**, 651–665.

Esary, J. D., Proschan, F., and Walkup, D. W. (1967). Association of random variables with applications. *Annals of Mathematical Statistics* **38**, 1466–1474.

Fagiuoli, E., Pellerey, F., and Shaked, M. (1999). A characterization of the dilation order and its applications. *Statistical Papers* **40**, 393–406.

Fahmy, S., Proschan, F., Pereira, C., and Shaked, M. (1982). The influence of the sample on the posterior distribution. *Communications in Statististics – Theory and Methods* **11**, 1757–1768.

Fang, K.T., Kotz, S., and Ng, K.W. (1990). *Symmetric Multivariate and Related Distributions*. Chapman & Hall, London.

Feller, W. (1966). *An Introduction to Probability Theory and its Applications*. John Wiley & Sons, Inc., New York.

Fernandez-Ponce, J.M., Kochar, S.C., and Muñoz-Perez, J. (1998). Partial orderings of distributions based on right-spread functions. *Journal of Applied Probability* **35**, 221–228.

Ferreira, J. (1977). Identifying equitable insurance premiums for risk classes: an alternative to the classical approach. Lecture presented at the 23th international meeting of the Institute of Management Sciences, Athens, Greece.

Finkelshtain, I., Kella, O., and Scarsini, M. (1999). On risk aversion with two risks. *Journal of Mathematical Economics* **31**, 239–250.

Fishburn, P.C. (1964). *Decision and Value Theory*. John Wiley & Sons, Inc., New York.

Fishburn, P.C. (1982). *The Foundations of Expected Utility*. Reidel, Dordrecht.

Föllmer, H., and Schied, A. (2002). Convex measures of risk and trading constraints. *Finance and Stochastics* **6**, 429–447.

Fortuin, C.M., Kastelyn, P.W., and Ginibre, J. (1971). Correlation inequalities on some partially ordered sets. *Communications in Mathematical Physics* **22**, 89–103.

Frahm, G., Junker, M., and Szimayer, A. (2003). Elliptical copulas: applicability and limitations. *Statistics & Probability Letters* **63**, 275–286.

Frank, M.J. (1979). On the simultaneous associativity of $F(x, y)$ and $x + y - F(x, y)$. *Aequationes Mathematicae* **19**, 194–226.

Frank, M.J., Nelsen, R.B., and Schweizer, B. (1987). Best-possible bounds on the distribution of a sum – a problem of Kolmogorov. *Probability Theory and Related Fields* **74**, 199–211.

Fréchet, M. (1951). Sur les tableaux de corrélation dont les marges sont données. *Annales de l'Université de Lyon, Sect. A* **14**, 53–77.

Fréchet, M. (1958). Remarques au sujet de la note précédente. *Comptes Rendus de l'Académie des Sciences de Paris* **246**, 2719–2720.

Frees, E.W. (2003). Multivariate credibility for aggregate loss models. *North American Actuarial Journal* **7**, 13–27.

Frees, E.W., Carrière, J.F., and Valdez, E. (1996). Annuity valuation with dependent mortality. *Journal of Risk and Insurance* **63**, 229–261.

Frees, E.W., and Valdez, E.A. (1998). Understanding relationships using copulas. *North American Actuarial Journal* **2**, 1–25.

Genest, C. (1987). Frank's family of bivariate distributions. *Biometrika* **74**, 549–555.

Genest, C., Ghoudi, K., and Rivest, L.-P. (1995). A semiparametric estimation procedure of dependence parameters in multivariate families of distributions. *Biometrika* **82**, 543–552.

Genest, C., Ghoudi, K., and Rivest, L.-P. (1998). Discussion of the paper by Frees and Valdez. *North American Actuarial Journal* **2**, 143–149.

Genest, C., Quessy, J.-F., and Rémillard, B. (2004). Goodness-of-fit procedures for copula models based on the probability integral transformation. Manuscript.

Genest, C., and MacKay, J. (1986a). The joy of copulas: Bivariate distributions with uniform marginals. *American Statistician* **40**, 280–283.

Genest, C., and MacKay, R.J. (1986b). Copules archimédiennes et familles de lois bidimensionnelles dont les marges sont données. *Canadian Journal of Statistics* **14**, 145–159.

Genest, C., Marceau, É., and Mesfioui, M. (2002). Upper stop-loss bounds for sums of possibly dependent risks with given means and variances. *Statistics & Probability Letters* **57**, 33–41.

Genest, C., Marceau, É, and Mesfioui, M. (2003). Compound Poisson approximation for individual models with dependent risks. *Insurance: Mathematics & Economics* **32**, 73–91.

Genest, C, and Rivest, L.-P. (1993). Statistical inference procedures for bivariate archimedean copulae. *Journal of the American Statistical Association* **88**, 1034–1043.

Genest, C., and Rivest, L.-P. (2001). On the multivariate probability integral transformation. *Statistics & Probability Letters* **53**, 391–399.

Gerber, H.U. (1979). *An Introduction to Mathematical Risk Theory*. Huebner Foundation Monograph **8**. S.S. Huebner Foundation, Philadelphia.

Gerber, H.U. (1980). Credibility for Esscher premiums. *Bulletin of the Swiss Association of Actuaries*, 307–312.

Gerber, H.U. (1981a). The Esscher premium principle: A criticism. Comment. *ASTIN Bulletin* **12**, 139–140.

Gerber, H. (1981b). On the probability of ruin in an autoregressive model. *Bulletin of the Swiss Association of Actuaries*, 213–219.

Gerber, H. (1982). Ruin theory in the linear model. *Insurance: Mathematics & Economics* **1**, 177–184.

Gerber, H.U. (1984). Error bounds for the compound Poisson approximation. *Insurance: Mathematics & Economics* **3**, 191–194.

Gerber, H.U., and Jones, D. (1975). Credibility formulas of the updating type. *Transactions of the Society of Actuaries* **27**, 31–52.

Gerber, H.U., and Shiu, E.S.W. (1994). Option pricing by Esscher transforms. *Transactions of the Society of Actuaries* **46**, 99–191 (with discussion).

Goovaerts, M.J., and De Vijlder, F.E. (1980). Upper bounds on stop-loss premiums under constraints on claim size distributions as derived from representation theorems for distribution functions. *Scandinavian Actuarial Journal*, 141–148.

Goovaerts, M.J., De Vijlder, F., and Haezendonck, J. (1982). Ordering of risks: a review. *Insurance: Mathematics & Economics* **1**, 131–163.

Goovaerts, M.J., De Vijlder, F.E., and Haezendonck, J. (1984). *Insurance Premiums: Theory and Applications*. North-Holland, Amsterdam.

Goovaerts, M.J., and Dhaene, J. (1996). The compound Poisson approximation for a portfolio of dependent risks. *Insurance: Mathematics & Economics* **18**, 81–85.

Goovaerts, M.J., and Dhaene, J. (1999). Supermodular ordering and stochastic annuities. *Insurance: Mathematics & Economics* **24**, 281–290.

Goovaerts, M., Dhaene, J., and De Schepper, A. (2000). Stochastic upper bounds for present value functions. *Journal of Risk and Insurance* **67**, 1–14.

Goovaerts, M.J., Haezendonck, J., and De Vijlder, F.E. (1982). Numerical best bounds on stop-loss premiums. *Insurance: Mathematics & Economics* **1**, 287–302.

Goovaerts, M.J., and Kaas, R. (1985). Application of the problem of moment to derive bounds on integrals with integral constraints. *Insurance: Mathematics & Economics*, **4**, 99–111.

Goovaerts, M.J., Kaas, R., Van Heerwaarden, A.E., and Bauwelinckx, T. (1990). *Effective Actuarial Methods*. North-Holland, Amsterdam, New York, Oxford, Tokyo.

Goovaerts, M.J., Kaas, R., Dhaene, J., and Tang, Q. (2003). A unified approach to generate risk measures. *ASTIN Bulletin* **33**, 173–191.

Goovaerts, M.J., Van den Borre, E., and Laeven, R.J.A. (2004). Manageing economic and virtual economic capital within financial conglomerates. *North American Actuarial Journal*, in press.

Gouriéroux, C., Laurent, J.-P., and Scaillet, O. (2000). Sensitivity analysis of values at risk. *Journal of Empirical Finance* **7**, 225–245.

Gumbel, E.J. (1960). Bivariate exponential distributions. *Journal of the American Statistical Association* **55**, 698–707.

Gupta, A.K., and Varga, T. (1993). *Elliptically Contoured Models in Statistics*. Kluwer Academic Publishers, Amsterdam.

Hardy, G.H., Littlewood, J.E., and Pólya, G. (1934). *Inequalities*. Cambridge University Press, Cambridge.

Hastie, T., and Tibshirani, R. (1990). *Generalized Additive Models*. Chapman & Hall, London.

Heijnen, B. (1990). Best upper and lower bounds on modified stop-loss premiums in case of known range, mode, mean and variance of the original risk. *Insurance: Mathematics & Economics* **9**, 207–220.

Heijnen, B., and Goovaerts, M.J. (1986). Bounds on modified stop-loss premiums in case of unimodal distributions. *Bulletin de l'Association Royale des Actuaires Belges* **80**, 53–62.

Heijnen, B., and Goovaerts, M.J. (1989). Best upper bounds on risks altered by deductibles under incomplete information. *Scandinavian Actuarial Journal*, 23–46.

Heilmann, W.R. (1983). Characterizations of claim distributions by reliability techniques. *German Actuarial Bulletin* **16**, 13–19.

Heilmann, W.-R. (1985). Transformations of claim distributions. *Bulletin of the Swiss Association of Actuaries*, 57–69.

Heilmann, W.-R. (1986). On the impact of independence of risks on stop loss transforms. *Insurance: Mathematics & Economics* **5**, 197–199.

Heilmann, W.-R., and Schröter, K. J. (1991). Orderings of risks and their actuarial applications. In *Stochastic Orders and Decision under Risk* (eds K. Mosler and M. Scarsini), IMS Lecture Notes – Monograph Series **19**. Institute of Mathematical Statistics, Hayward, CA, pp. 157–173.

Hennessy, D.A., and Lapan, H.E. (2002). The use of Archimedean copulas to model portfolio allocations. *Mathematical Finance* **12**, 143–154.

Hesselager, O. (1995). Order relations for some distributions. *Insurance: Mathematics & Economics* **16**, 129–134.

Höffding, W. (1940). Masstabinvariante Korrelationstheorie. *Schriften des Mathematischen Instituts und des Instituts für Angewandte Mathematik der Universität Berlin* **5**, 179–233.

Holley, R. (1974). Remarks on the FKG inequalities. *Communications in Mathematical Physics* **36**, 227–231.

Hougaard, P. (1986). A class of multivariate failure time distributions. *Biometrika* **73**, 671–678.

Huang, C., and Litzenberger, R.H. (1988). *Foundations for Financial Economics*. Prentice Hall, Englewood Cliffs, NJ.

Hürlimann, W. (1998). On best stop-loss bounds for bivariate sums by known means, variances and correlation. *Bulletin of the Swiss Association of Actuaries*, 111–134.

Hutchinson, T.P., and Lai, C.D. (1990). *Continuous Bivariate Distributions, Emphasising Applications*. Rumsby Scientific, Adelaide.

Jansen, K., Haezendonck, J., and Goovaerts, M.J. (1986). Upper bounds on stop-loss premiums in case of known moments up to the fourth order. *Insururance: Mathematics & Economics* **5**, 315–334.

Jewitt, I. (1989). Choosing between risky prospects: The characterization of comparative static results and location independent risks. *Management Science* **35**, 60–70.

Joag-Dev, K. (1990). Conditional negative dependence in stochastic ordering and interchangeable random variables. In *Topics in Statistical Dependence* (eds H.W. Block, A.R. Sampson and T.H. Savits), IMS Lecture Notes –Monograph Series **16**. Institute of Mathematical Statistics, Hayward, CA, pp. 295–298.

Joe, H. (1990). Multivariate concordance. *Journal of Multivariate Analysis* **35**, 12–30.

Joe, H. (1993). Parametric families of multivariate distributions with given marginals. *Journal of Multivariate Analysis* **46**, 262–282.

Joe, H. (1997). *Multivariate Models and Dependence Concepts*. Chapman & Hall, London.

Jogdeo, K. (1978). On a probability bound of Marshall and Olkin. *Annals of Statistics* **6**, 232–234.

Johnson, N.L., and Kotz, S. (1992). *Distributions in Statistics: Discrete Multivariate Distributions*. John Wiley & Sons, Inc., New York.

Jorion, P. (2000). *Value at Risk*. McGraw-Hill, New York.

Kaas, R. (1985). *Bounds and Approximations for some Risk Theoretical Quantities*. Doctoral thesis, Universiteit van Amsterdam.

Kaas, R. (1993). How to (and how not to) compute stop-loss premiums in practice. *Insurance: Mathematics & Economics* **13**, 241–254.

Kaas, R., and Gerber, H.U. (1994). Some alternatives for the individual model. *Insurance: Mathematics & Economics* **15**, 127–132.

Kaas, R., and Goovaerts, M.J. (1985). Bounds on distribution functions under integral constraints. *Bulletin de l'Association Royale des Actuaires Belges – Koninklijke Vereniging der Belgische Actuarissen* **79**, 45–60.

Kaas, R., and Goovaerts, M.J. (1986a). Bounds on stop-loss premiums for compound distributions. *ASTIN Bulletin* **16**, 13–17.

Kaas, R., and Goovaerts, M.J. (1986b). Best bounds for positive distributions with fixed moments. *Insurance: Mathematics & Economics* **5**, 87–92.

Kaas, R., and Goovaerts, M.J. (1986c). Extremal values of stop-loss premiums under moment constraints. *Insurance: Mathematics & Economics* **5**, 279–283.

Kaas, R., and Goovaerts, M.J. (1987). Unimodal distributions in insurance. *Bulletin de l'Association Royale des Actuaires Belges* **81**, 61–66.

Kaas, R., Goovaerts, M.J., Dhaene, J., and Denuit, M. (2001). *Modern Actuarial Risk Theory*. Kluwer Academic Publishers, Dordrecht.

Kaas, R., and Hesselager, O. (1995). Ordering claim size distributions and mixed Poisson probabilities. *Insurance: Mathematics & Economics* **17**, 193–201.

Kaas, R., Van Heerwaarden, A.E., and Goovaerts, M.J. (1994). *Ordering of Actuarial Risks*. CAIRE Education Series. CAIRE, Brussels.

Kamae, T., Krengel, U., and O'Brien, G.L. (1977). Stochastic inequalities on partially ordered spaces. *Annals of Probability* **5**, 899–912.

Karamata, J. (1932). Sur une inégalité relative aux fonctions convexes. *Publications Mathématiques de l'Université de Belgrade* **1**, 145–148.

Karlin, S. (1968). *Total Positivity*. Stanford University Press, Stanford, CA.

Karlin, S., and Novikoff, A. (1963). Generalized convex inequalities. *Pacific Journal of Mathematics* **13**, 1251–1279.

Karlin, S., and Rinott, Y. (1980). Classes of orderings of measures and related correlation inequalities. I. Multivariate totally positive distributions. *Journal of Multivariate Analysis* **10**, 467–498.

Kelker, D. (1970). Distribution theory of spherical distributions and location-scale parameter generalization. *Sankhyā* **32**, 419–430.

Kemperman J.H. (1977). On the FKG-inequality for measures on a partially ordered space. *Indigationes Mathematicae* **39**, 311–331.

Kestemont, R.-M., and Paris, J. (1985). Sur l'ajustement du nombre de sinistres. *Bulletin of the Swiss Association of Actuaries*, 157–163.

Kim, Y.B., and Makowski, A.M. (1999). Stochastic comparison results for non-blocking switches with output queueing. *Communications in Statististics – Stochastic Models* **15**, 161–180.

Kimberling, C.H. (1974). A probabilistic interpretation of complete monotonicity. *Aequationes Mathematicae* **10**, 152–164.

Kimeldorf, G., and Sampson, A.R. (1975). Uniform representation of bivariate distributions. *Communications in Statistics* **4**, 617–627.

Kimeldorf, G., and Sampson, A.R. (1978). Monotone dependence. *Annals of Statistics* **6**, 895–903.

Kimeldorf, G., and Sampson, A.R. (1987). Positive dependence orderings. *Annals of the Institute of Statistical Mathematics* **39**, 113–128.

Kimeldorf, G., and Sampson, A.R. (1989). A framework of positive dependence. *Annals of the Institute of Statistical Mathematics* **41**, 31–45.

Klefsjö, B. (1983). A useful ageing property based on the Laplace transform. *Journal of Applied Probability* **20**, 615–626.

Klugman, S.A., Panjer, H.H., and Willmot, G.E. (1998). *Loss Models: From Data to Decisions*. John Wiley & Sons, Inc., New York.

Klugman, S.A., and Parsa, R. (1999). Fitting bivariate loss distributions with copulas. *Insurance: Mathematics & Economics* **24**, 139–148.

Konijn, H.S. (1959). Positive and negative dependence of two random variables. *Sankhyā* **21**, 269–280.

Koshevoy, G., and Mosler, K. (1996). The Lorenz zonoid of a multivariate distribution. *Journal of the American Statistical Association* **91**, 873–882.

Koshevoy, G. A., and Mosler, K. (1997). Multivariate Gini indices. *Journal of Multivariate Analysis* **60**, 252–276.

Koshevoy, G., and Mosler, K. (1998). Lift zonoids, random convex hulls and the variability of random vectors. *Bernoulli* **4**, 377–399.

Kotz, S., Balakrishnan, N., and Johnson, N.L. (2000). *Continuous Multivariate Distributions*. John Wiley & Sons, Inc., New York.

Kremer, E. (1985). Finite formulae for the premium of the general reinsurance treaty based on ordered claims. *Insurance: Mathematics & Economics*, **4**, 233–238.

Kremer, E. (1998). Largest claims reinsurance premiums under possible claims dependence. *ASTIN Bulletin*, **28**, 257–267.

Kusuoka, S. (2001). On law invariant coherent risk measures. *Advances in Mathematical Economics* **3**, 83–95.

Laeven, R.J.A., and Goovaerts, M.J. (2004). An optimization approach to the dynamic allocation of economic capital. *Insurance: Mathematics & Economics*, **35**, 299–320.

Landsberger, M., and Meilijson, I. (1990). Lotteries, insurance and star-shaped utility functions. *Journal of Economic Theory* **52**, 1–17.

Landsberger, M., and Meilijson, I. (1994a). The generating process and an extension of Jewitt's location independent risk concept. *Management Science* **40**, 662–669.

Landsberger, M., and Meilijson, I. (1994b). Comonotone allocations, Bickel–Lehmann dispersion and the Arrow–Pratt measure of risk aversion. *Annals of Operations Research* **52**, 97–106.

Landsman, Z.M., and Valdez, E.A. (2003). Tail conditional expectations for elliptical distributions. *North American Actuarial Journal*, **7**(4), 55–71.

Langberg, N.A. (1988), Comparison of replacement policies, *Journal of Applied Probability* **25**, 780–788.

Lee, A.J. (1993). Generating random binary deviates having fixed marginal distributions and specified degree of association. *American Statistician* **47**, 209–215.

Lee, Y., and Nelder, J.A. (1996). Hierarchical generalized linear models (with discussion). *Journal of the Royal Statistical Society Series B* **58**, 619–678.

Lefèvre, C., and Utev, S. (1998). On order-preserving properties of probability metrics. *Journal of Theoretical Probability*. **11**, 907–920.

Lehmann, E.L. (1955). Ordered families of distributions. *Annals of Mathematical Statistics* **26**, 399–419.

Lehmann, E.L. (1959). *Testing Statistical Hypotheses*. John Wiley & Sons, Inc., New York.

Lehmann, E.L. (1966). Some concepts of dependence. *Annals of Mathematical Statistics* **37**, 1137–1153.

Lemaire, J. (1979). How to define a bonus-malus system with an exponential utility function. *ASTIN Bulletin* **10**, 274–282.

Lemaire, J. (1995). *Bonus-Malus Systems in Automobile Insurance*. Kluwer Academic, Boston.

Lemaire, J., and Vandermeulen, E. (1983). Une propriëtë du principe de l'espérance mathématique. *Bulletin Trimestriel de l'Institut des Actuaires Français*, 5–14.

Levy, H. (1992). Stochastic dominance and expected utility: Survey and analysis. *Management Sciences* **38**, 555–593.

Li, D.X. (2000). On default correlation: A copula function approach. *Journal of Fixed Income* **9**, 43–54.

Lin, G.D. (1994). On a probabilistic generalization of Taylor's theorem. *Statistics & Probability Letters* **19**, 239–243.

Lindvall, T. (1992). *Lectures on the Coupling Method*. John Wiley & Sons, Inc., New York.

Machina, M.J., and Pratt, J.W. (1997). Increasing risk: Some direct constructions. *Journal of Risk and Uncertainty* **14**, 103–127.

Makarov, G. D. (1981). Estimates for the distribution function of a sum of two random variables when the marginal distributions are fixed. *Theory of Probability and its Applications* **26**, 803–806.

Marshall, A.W. (1991). Multivariate stochastic orderings and generating cones of functions. In *Stochastic Orders and Decision under Risk* (eds K.C. Mosler and M. Scarsini). IMS Lecture Notes – Monograph Series **19**. Institute of Mathematical Statistics, Hayward, CA, pp. 231–247.

Marshall, A.W. (1996). Copulas, marginals, and joint distributions. In *Distributions with Fixed Marginals and Related Topics*(eds L. Rüschendorf, B. Schweizer and M.D. Taylor). IMS Lectures Notes – Monograph Series **28**. Institute of Mathematical Statistics, Hayward, CA, pp. 213–222.

Marshall, A.W., and Olkin, I. (1979), *Inequalities: Theory of Majorization and Its Applications*, Academic Press, New York.

Marshall, A.W., and Olkin, I. (1988). Families of multivariate distributions. *Journal of the American Statistical Association* **83**, 834–841.

Massey, W.A., and Whitt, W. (1993). A probabilistic generalization of Taylor's theorem. *Statistics & Probability Letters* **16**, 51–54.

Meester, L. E., and Shanthikumar, J. G. (1993), Regularity of stochastic processes: A theory based on directional convexity, *Probability in the Engineering and Informational Sciences* **7**, 343–360.

Michel, R. (1987). An improved error bound for the compound Poisson approximation. *ASTIN Bulletin* **17**, 165–169.

Milgrom, P., and Weber, R.J. (1982). A theory of auctions and competitive bidding. *Econometrica* **50**, 1089–1122.

Mosler, K.C., and Scarsini, M. (1993). *Stochastic Orders and Applications, a Classified Bibliography*. Springer-Verlag, Berlin.

Muliere, P., and Scarsini, M. (1989). A note on stochastic dominance and inequality measures. *Journal of Economic Theory* **49**, 314–323.

Müller, A. (1996). Ordering of risks: A comparative study via stop-loss transforms. *Insurance: Mathematics & Economics* **17**, 215–222.
Müller, A. (1997a). Stochastic orderings generated by integrals: A unified study. *Advances in Applied Probability* **29**, 414–428.
Müller, A. (1997b). Stop-loss order for portfolios of dependent risks. *Insurance: Mathematics & Economics* **21** 219–223.
Müller, A. (2000). On the waiting times in queues with dependency between interarrival and service times. *Operations Research Letters* **26**, 43–47.
Müller, A., and Pflug, G. (2001). Asymptotic ruin probabilities for risk processes with dependent increments. *Insurance: Mathematics & Economics* **28**, 381–392.
Müller, A., and Scarsini, M. (2000). Some remarks on the supermodular order. *Journal of Multivariate Analysis* **73**, 107–119.
Müller, A., and Scarsini, M. (2001). Stochastic comparison of random vectors with a common copula. *Mathematics of Operations Research* **26**, 723–740.
Müller, A., and Scarsini, M. (2004). Archimedean copulae and positive dependence. *Journal of Multivariate Analysis*, in press.
Müller, A., and Stoyan, D. (2002). *Comparison Methods for Stochastic Models and Risks*. John Wiley & Sons, Ltd, Chichester.
Munoz-Perez, J. (1990). Dispersive ordering by the spread function. *Statistics & Probability Letters* **10**, 407–410.
Munoz-Perez, J., and Sanchez-Gomez, A. (1990). A characterization of the distribution: The dispersion function. *Statistics & Probability Letters* **10**, 235–239.
Nelder, J.A., and Verrall, R.J. (1997). Credibility theory and generalized linear models. *ASTIN Bulletin* **27**, 71–82.
Nelsen, R.B. (1996). Nonparametric measures of multivariate association. In *Distributions with Fixed Marginals and Related Topics* (eds L. Rüschendorf, B. Schweizer and M.D. Taylor) IMS Lectures Notes – Monograph Series, **28**. Institute of Mathematical Statistics, Hayward, CA, pp. 223–232
Nelsen, R.B. (1999). *An Introduction to Copulas*. Lecture Notes in Statistics No. 139. Springer-Verlag, New York.
Nelsen, R.B., Quesada-Molina, J., Rodriguez-Lallena, J., and Ubeda-Flores, M. (2004). Best-possible bounds on sets of bivariate distribution functions. *Journal of Multivariate Analysis* **90**, 348–358.
Newman, C. (1984). Asymptotic independence and limit theorems for positively and negatively dependent random variables. In *Inequalities in Statistics and Probability* (ed. Y.L. Tong). IMS Lecture Notes **5**, Institute of Mathematical Statistics, Hayward, CA, pp. 127–140.
Norberg, R. (1989). Actuarial analysis of dependent lives. *Bulletin of the Swiss Association of Actuaries*, 243–254.
Oakes, D. (1989). Bivariate survival models induced by frailties. *Journal of the American Statistical Association* **84**, 487–493.
Oja, H. (1985), Ordering of distributions, partial. In *Encyclopedia of Statistical Sciences*, Vol. 6 (eds S. Kotz and N.L. Johnson). John Wiley & Sons, Inc., New York, pp. 490–494.
Olsen, T.E., Darsow, W.F., and Nguyen, B. (1996). Copulas and Markov operators. In *Distributions with Fixed Marginals and Related Topics*. (eds L. Rüschendorf, B. Schweizer and M.D. Taylor) IMS Lecture Notes – Monograph Series **28**. Institute of Mathematical Statistics, Hayward, CA, pp. 244–259.
Overbeck, L. (2000). Allocation of economic capital in loan portfolios. In *Measuring Risk in Complex Systems* (eds. J. Franke, W. Härdle, and G. Stahl). Springer-Verlag, New York.
Panjer, H.H. (ed.) (1998). *Financial Economics, with Applications to Investments, Insurance and Pensions*. Actuarial Foundation, Schaumburg, IL.
Parker, G. (1994a). Limiting distribution of the present value of a portfolio. *ASTIN Bulletin* **24**, 47–60.
Parker, G. (1994b). Two stochastic approaches for discounting actuarial functions. *ASTIN Bulletin* **24**, 167–181.
Pellerey, F., and Semeraro, P. (2003). A positive dependence notion based on the supermodular order. Working Paper, Dipartimento del Politecnico di Torino, Italy.
Pham, T.G., and Turkkan, N. (1994). The Lorenz and the scaled total-time-on-test transform curves: a unified approach. *IEEE Transactions on Reliability* **43**, 76–84.
Pinquet, J. (1997). Allowance for cost of claims in bonus-malus systems. *ASTIN Bulletin* **27**, 33–57.

Pinquet, J. (2000). Experience rating through heterogeneous models. In *Handbook of Insurance* (ed. G. Dionne). Kluwer Academic, Boston.

Pinquet, J., Guillén, M., and Bolancé, C. (2001). Allowance for the age of claims in bonus-malus systems. *ASTIN Bulletin* **31**, 337–348.

Pitt, L.D. (1982). Positively correlated normal variables are associated. *Annals of Probability* **10**, 496–499.

Poon, S., Rockinger, M., and Tawn, J. (2004). Extreme-value dependence in financial markets: Diagnostics, models and financial implications. *Review of Financial Studies*, **17**, 581–610.

Pratt, J. W. (1964). Risk aversion in the small and in the large. *Econometrica* **32**, 122–136.

Preston, C.J. (1974), A generalization of the FKG inequalities, *Communications in Mathematical Physics* **36**, 233–241.

Purcaru, O., and Denuit, M. (2002a). On the dependence induced by frequency credibility models. *Belgian Actuarial Bulletin* **2**, 74–80.

Purcaru, O., and Denuit, M. (2002b). On the stochastic increasingness of future claims in the Bühlmann linear credibility premium. *German Actuarial Bulletin* **25**, 781–793.

Purcaru, O., and Denuit, M. (2003). Dependence in dynamic claim frequency credibility models. *ASTIN Bulletin* **33**, 23–40.

Quiggin, J.P. (1982). A theory of anticipated utility. *Journal of Economic Behavior and Organization* **3**, 323–343.

Rachev, S.T. (1991). *Probability Metrics and the Stability of Stochastic Models*. John Wiley & Sons, Ltd, Chichester.

Rachev, S.T., and Rüschendorf, L. (1990). Approximation of sums by compound Poisson distributions with respect to stop-loss distances. *Advances in Applied Probability*, **22**, 350–374.

Ribas, C., Goovaerts, M.J., and Dhaene, J. (1998). A note on the stop-loss preserving property of Wang's premium principle. *Bulletin of the Swiss Association of Actuaries*, 237–241

Roberts, A.W., and Varberg, D.E. (1973). *Convex Functions*. Academic Press. New York.

Roëll, A. (1987). Risk aversion in Quiggin and Yaari's rank-order model of choice under uncertainty. *Economic Journal* **97**, 143–159.

Rootzén, H., and Klüppelberg, C. (1999). A single number cannot hedge against economic catastrophes. *Ambio-Royal Swedish Academy of Science* **8**, 550–555.

Ross, S.M. (1983). *Stochastic Processes*. John Wiley & Sons Inc., New York.

Rudin, W. (1974). *Real and Complex Analysis*, 2nd edn. McGraw-Hill, New York.

Rychlik, T. (1992). Stochastically extremal distributions of order statistics for dependent samples. *Statistics & Probability Letters* **13**, 337–341.

Rychlik, T. (1994). Distributions and expectations of order statistics for possibly dependent random variables. *Journal of Multivariate Analysis* **48**, 31–42.

Scaillet, O. (2000). Nonparametric estimation and sensitivity analysis of expected shortfall. *Mathematical Finance* **14**, 115–129.

Scarsini, M. (1984). On measures of concordance. *Stochastica* **8**, 201–218.

Scarsini, M. (1985). Stochastic dominance with pair-wise risk aversion. *Journal of Mathematical Economics* **14**, 187–201.

Scarsini, M. (1998). Multivariate convex orderings, dependence, and stochastic equality. *Journal of Applied Probability* **35**, 93–103.

Scarsini, M., and Shaked, M. (1990). Stochastic ordering for permutation symmetric distributions. *Statistics & Probability Letters* **9**, 217–222.

Scarsini, M., and Shaked, M. (1996), Positive dependence orders: A survey. In *Athens Conference on Applied Probability and Time Series I: Applied Probability* (eds C.C. Heyde, Y.V. Prohorov, R. Pyke, and S.T. Rachev). Springer-Verlag, New York, pp. 70–91.

Schechtman, E., and Yitzhaki, S. (1999). On the proper bounds of the Gini correlation. *Economics Letters* **63**, 133–138.

Schmeidler, D. (1989). Subjective probability and expected utility without additivity. *Econometrica* **57**, 571–587.

Schmid, F., and Trede, M. (1998). A Kolmogorov-type test for second-order stochastic dominance. *Statistics & Probability Letters* **37**, 183–193.

Schmidt, U. (1998). *Axiomatic Utility Theory under Risk*. Lecture Notes in Economics and Mathematical Systems **461**. Springer-Verlag, Berlin.

Schweder, T. (1982). On the dispersion of mixtures. *Scandinavian Journal of Statistics* **9**, 165–169.

Schweizer, B., and Sklar, A. (1983). *Probabilistic Metric Spaces*. North-Holland, Amsterdam.
Serfling, R. J. (1975). A general Poisson approximation theorem. *Annals of Probability* **3**, 726–731.
Shaked, M. (1982). Dispersive ordering of distributions. *Journal of Applied Probability* **19**, 310–320.
Shaked, M., and Shanthikumar, J.G. (1988). Stochastic convexity and its applications. *Advances in Applied Probability* **20**, 427–446.
Shaked, M., and Shanthikumar, J.G. (1990). Multivariate stochastic ordering and positive dependence in reliability theory. *Mathematics of Operations Research* **15**, 545–552.
Shaked, M., and Shantikumar, J.G. (1994). *Stochastic Orders and Their Applications*. Academic Press, New York.
Shaked, M., and Shanthikumar, J.G. (1997). Supermodular stochastic orders and positive dependence of random vectors. *Journal of Multivariate Analysis* **61**, 86–101.
Shaked, M., and Shanthikumar, J.G. (1998). Two variability orders. *Probability in the Engineering and Informational Sciences* **12**, 1–23.
Shaked, M., Shanthikumar, J.G., and Tong, Y.L. (1995). Parametric Schur convexity and arrangement monotonicity properties of partial sums. *Journal of Multivariate Analysis* **53**, 293–310.
Shaked, M., and Spizzichino, F. (1998). Positive dependence properties of conditionally independent random lifetimes. *Mathematics of Operations Research* **23**, 944–959.
Shaked, M., and Tong, Y.L. (1985). Some partial orderings of exchangeable random variables by positive dependence. *Journal of Multivariate Analysis* **17**, 333–349.
Shanthikumar, J.G., and Yao, D.D. (1991). Bivariate characterization of some stochastic order relations. *Advances in Applied Probability* **23**, 642–659.
Shih, J.H., and Louis, T.A. (1995). Inferences on the association parameter in copula models for bivariate surival data. *Biometrics* **51**, 1384–1399.
Shih, W.J., and Huang, W. (1992). Evaluating correlation with proper bounds. *Biometrics* **48**, 1207–1213.
Simon, H.A. (1957). *Models of Man, Social and Rational. Mathematical Essays on Rational Human Behavior in a Social Setting*. John Wiley & Sons, Inc., New York.
Sklar, A. (1959). Fonctions de répartition à *n* dimensions et leurs marges. *Publications de l'Institut de Statistique de Paris* **8**, 229–231.
Stein, C. (1972). A bound for the error in the normal approximation to the distribution of a sum of dependent random variables. In *Proceedings of the Sixth Berkeley Symposium on Mathematical Statistics and Probability* (eds L. LeCam, J. Neyman and E.L. Scott), Vol. 2. University of California Press, Berkeley, pp. 583–602.
Stoyan, D. (1983). *Comparison Methods for Queues and Other Stochastic Models*. John Wiley & Sons, Ltd, Chichester.
Strassen, V. (1965). The existence of probability measures with given marginals. *Annals of Mathematical Statistics* **36**, 423–439.
Straub, E. (1971). Applications of reliability theory to insurance. *ASTIN Bulletin* **6**, 97–107.
Sugden, R. (1997). Alternatives to expected utility theory: Foundations and concepts. In *Handbook of Utility Theory* (eds S. Barberà, P.J. Hammond, and C. Seidl) Kluwer, Boston.
Sundt, B. (1988). Credibility estimators with geometric weights. *Insurance: Mathematics & Economics* **7**, 113–122.
Szegö, G. (ed.) (2004). *Risk Measures for the 21st Century*. John Wiley & Sons Ltd, Chichester.
Szekli, R. (1995). *Stochastic Ordering and Dependence in Applied Probability*. Lecture Notes in Statistics Number 97. Springer-Verlag, New York.
Szekli, R., Disney, R.L., and Hur, S. (1994). MR/G/1 queues with positively correlated arrival stream. *Journal of Applied Probability* **31**, 497–514.
Tasche, D. (2000). Conditional expectation as quantile derivative. Technical Report, Zentrum Mathematik (SCA), TU München, Germany.
Tawn, J.A. (1997). Bivariate extreme value theory. *Biometrika* **75**, 397–413.
Taylor, G.C. (1977). Upper bounds on stop-loss premiums under constraints on claim size distribution. *Scandinavian Actuarial Journal*, 94–105.
Tchen, A.H. (1980). Inequalities for distributions with given marginals. *Annals of Probability* **8**, 814–827.
Thistle, P.D. (1993). Negative moments, risk aversion, and stochastic dominance. *Journal of Financial and Quantitative Analysis* **28**, 301–311.
Tong, Y.L. (1990). *The Multivariate Normal Distribution*. Springer-Verlag, New York.

Tong, Y.L. (1994). Some recent developments on majorization inequalities in probability and statistics. *Linear Algebra and Its Applications* **199**, 69–90.

Tremblay, L. (1992). Using the Poisson inverse Gaussian distribution in bonus-malus systems. *ASTIN Bulletin*, **22**, 97–106.

Trowbridge, C.L. (1989). *Fundamental Concepts of Actuarial Sciences.* Actuarial Education and Research Fund, Itasca, IL.

Tsanakas, A., and Desli, E. (2003). Risk measures and theories of choice. *British Actuarial Journal* **9**, 959–981.

Valdez, E. (2001). Bivariate analysis of survivorship and persistency. *Insurance: Mathematics & Economics* **29**, 357–373.

Valdez, E., and Dhaene, J. (2004). Bounds for sums of non-independent log-elliptical random variables. Technical Report, University of New South Wales, Australia.

Van Heerwaarden, A.E., and Kaas, R. (1992). The Dutch premium principle. *Insurance: Mathematics & Economics* **11**, 129–133.

Van Heerwaarden, A.E., Kaas, R., and Goovaerts, M.J. (1989). Properties of the Esscher premium calculation principle. *Insurance: Mathematics & Economics* **8**, 261–267.

Vaz de Melo Mendes, B., and Martins de Souza, R. (2004). Measuring financial risks with copulas. *International Review of Financial Analysis* **13**, 27–45.

Veinott, R. (1965). Optimal policy in a dynamic, single product, non-stationary, inventory model with several demand classes. *Operations Research* **13**, 761–778.

Vellaisamy, P., and Chaudhuri, B. (1996). Poisson and compound Poisson approximation for random sums of random variables. *Journal of Applied Probability* **33**, 127–137.

Vellaisamy, P., and Chaudhuri, B. (1999). On compound Poisson approximation for sums of random variables. *Statistics & Probability Letters* **41**, 179–189.

Von Neumann, J., and Morgenstern, O. (1947). *Theory of Games and Economic Behavior*, 2nd edn. Princeton University Press, Princeton, NJ.

Walhin, J.-F., and Paris, J. (1999). Using mixed Poisson processes in connection with bonus-malus systems. *ASTIN Bulletin* **29**, 81–99.

Wang, S. (1995). Insurance pricing and increased limits ratemaking by proportional hazard transforms. *Insurance: Mathematics & Economics* **17**, 43–54.

Wang, S. (1996). Premium calculation by transforming the layer premium density. *ASTIN Bulletin* **26**, 71–92.

Wang, S. (1998). Aggregation of correlated risk portfolios: Models and algorithms. *Proceedings of the Casualty Actuarial Society*, **85**, 848–939.

Wang, S. (2000). A class of distortion operators for pricing financial and insurance risks. *Journal of Risk and Insurance* **67**, 15–36.

Wang, S. (2002). A universal framework for pricing financial and insurance risks. *ASTIN Bulletin* **32**, 213–234.

Wang, S., and Dhaene, J. (1998). Comonotonicity, correlation order and stop-loss premiums. *Insurance: Mathematics & Economics* **22**, 235–243.

Wang, W., and Wells, M.T. (2000). Model selection and semiparametric inference for bivariate failure-time data. *Journal of the American Statistical Association* **95**, 62–72.

Wang, Y.H. (1986). Coupling methods in approximations. *Canadian Journal of Statistics* **14**, 69–74.

Whitmore, G.A. (1970). Third-degree stochastic dominance. *American Economic Review* **60**, 457–459.

Whitt, W. (1979). A note on the influence of the sample on the posterior distribution. *Journal of the American Statistical Association* **74**, 424–426.

Whitt, W. (1982). Multivariate monotone likelihood ratio and uniform conditional stochastic order. *Journal of Applied Probability* **19**, 695–701.

Whitt, W. (1985). Uniform conditional variability ordering of probability distributions. *Journal of Applied Probability* **22**, 619–633.

Whitt, W. (1986). Stochastic comparisons for non-Markov processes. *Mathematics of Operations Research* **11**, 608–618.

Wilfling, B. (1996). Lorenz ordering of power-function order statistics. *Statistics & Probability Letters* **30**, 313–319.

Williamson, R.C. (1991). An extreme limit theorem for dependency bounds of normalized sums of random variables. *Information Sciences* **56**, 113–141.

Williamson, R.C., and Downs, T. (1990). Probabilistic arithmetic I: Numerical methods for calculating convolutions and dependency bounds. *International Journal of Approximate Reasoning* **4**, 89–158.

Willmot, G.E. (1987). The Poisson-inverse Gaussian distribution as an alternative to the negative binomial. *Scandinavian Actuarial Journal*, 113–127.

Wirch, J.L., and Hardy, M.R. (1999). Distortion risk measures: Coherence and stochastic dominance. Working Paper, Department of Statistics and Actuarial Science, University of Waterloo, Canada.

Xu, K., Fisher, G., and Willson, D. (1996). Testing first- and second-order stochastic dominance. *Canadian Journal of Economics* **29**, s526–s564.

Yaari, M.E. (1987). The dual theory of choice under risk. *Econometrica* **55**, 95–115.

Yanagimoto, Y., and Okamoto, M. (1969). Partial orderings of permutations and monotonicity of a rank correlation statistic. *Annals of the Institute of Statistical Mathematics* **21**, 489–506.

Yuen, K.C., and Guo, J.Y. (2001). Ruin probabilities for time-correlated claims in the compound binomial model. *Insurance: Mathematics & Economics* **29**, 47–57.

Zehnwirth, B. (1981). The Esscher premium principle: A criticism. *ASTIN Bulletin* **12**, 77–78.

Index

Association 316–19, 321, 326, 341, 345, 350–2

Blomqvist's correlation coefficient 261

Coherent risk measure 65, 91, 93
Common mixture model 49, 320
  see also Dependence by mixture
Comonotonicity 49–50, 56, 63, 68, 90, 96, 109, 136, 165–6, 205, 227, 228, 247, 251, 253, 279, 295, 302, 320, 326, 356, 382, 395, 400, 405
  see also Fréchet bounds
Completely monotone function 35, 140, 141, 229, 230
  see also Stochastic complete monotonicity
Conditional increasingness in sequence 274–6, 278, 281, 319, 350, 359
Conditional tail expectation 72, 73–4, 76–7, 94
Conditional value-at-risk 72–3, 74
Convex order 149–82, 184–5, 187, 267–9, 271, 272–3, 290, 291, 303, 351, 358–9, 361–3, 375, 382, 403–7
Copula 191–243, 249, 255, 258, 266, 275, 292, 346–50, 358–60
  Archimedean 218–25, 229–41, 242, 243, 257, 276, 292–3, 305, 323
  Clayton 205, 210–13, 219, 222, 224, 228, 229, 238, 243, 257, 350
  co- 215–16
  dual 215
  elliptical 210
  Farlie–Gumbel–Morgenstern 249, 282
  Franck 205–7, 212, 219, 229, 238–41, 350
  Fréchet bounds 196, 202, 214–15, 216, 218, 219, 223, 227, 242, 246, 256, 260, 261–2, 295, 360
  Gaussian, *see* Normal distribution
  Gumbel 238, 282, 350
  Joe 238, 242
  Marshall–Olkin 198, 202–3, 218, 279
  normal 207–8, 212–13, 218, 228, 279, 283, 350
  Pareto 196, 215
  Student 208–10, 229, 243
  survival 213–15, 216
Correlation order 287–95, 305
Countermonotonicity 51, 55, 56, 247, 251, 253, 295
  see also Fréchet bounds
Cumulative dependence 272–3, 319, 405

Dangerousness order 158–61, 401–2
Dependence by mixture 320–3, 351
DFR 31, 33, 118–19, 126, 142, 166
Dilation order 186–7
Directionally convex
  function 179–80, 356, 359, 360, 382
  order 180, 181–2, 298, 359, 383
Dispersive order 133–7, 148, 185, 187
Distorted expectation theory 84–95, 112–13, 152–4
DMRL 33, 127, 166, 174

Economic capital 66, 69, 70, 77, 294
Elliptical distribution 41–8, 357
  see also Copula; Elliptical distribution
Esscher
  premium, *see* Esscher, risk measure
  risk measure 82–4, 99
  transform 83–4, 130–1
Expected remaining lifetime, *see* Mean-excess, function
Expected shortfall 73, 74, 93, 99, 175–6
Expected utility theory 77–84, 87–8, 107, 110–12, 140, 151–2, 177–8
Exponential premium 139

Failure rate, *see* Hazard rate
Force of mortality, *see* Hazard rate
Fréchet bounds 49–50, 51–5, 57, 250, 256, 259, 260, 263, 279, 290, 298
  see also Comonotonicity; Copula; Countermonotonicity; Fréchet bounds

Actuarial Theory for Dependent Risks M. Denuit, J. Dhaene, M. Goovaerts and R. Kaas

Gini's correlation coefficient 260

Hazard rate
  function 30–1, 33, 34, 124–5, 135, 139
    see also DFR; IFR
  order 123–7, 136, 174, 183

IFR 31, 33, 118–19, 124, 126, 133, 142, 166, 185
IMRL 33, 127, 166, 186
Increasing convex order, *see* Stop-loss, order
Integral probability metric 388–93
Integral stochastic ordering 106–8, 386–8, 392
Integrated stop-loss distance 403–7, 411, 414

Kendall's rank correlation coefficient 253–7, 259, 262–4, 266–7, 279, 292, 297, 304
Kolmogorov distance 396–8, 408–14, 422

Laplace
  order 137–42
  transform 34–6, 138, 220, 230, 320
Law of large numbers 24, 163
Likelihood ratio
  increasingness 131–2, 168, 322, 323, 332, 340
  order 123, 127–33, 143–4, 148, 183–4, 187, 240, 276, 277, 314, 323, 327–9, 333, 334, 339, 341, 343
Lorenz order 169–71

Majorization 171–3, 300–2, 404
Mean-excess
  function 32–3, 34, 73, 119, 174
  order 173–4, 185
  see also DMRL; IMRL
Moment generating
  function 36–7
  order 139, 142, 274
Multivariate total positivity of order 2 – MTP_2 276–8, 322–4, 326–8, 341, 343, 345, 349
Mutual exclusivity 51–5, 57, 356

NBU 119, 142
NBUE 119–20, 142
Normal distribution 38–41, 42, 43, 45, 46, 68, 71–2, 95, 234, 248, 266, 276, 278, 318, 325, 339, 341–3
  see also Copula; Normal distribution
NWU 119, 142
NWUE 119–20, 142

Orthant orders 143, 145–6, 288, 296, 304

Pearson's correlation coefficient 247–53, 257, 266–7, 279, 292, 297, 304, 421
Positive orthant dependence 273–4, 319
Positive orthant dependence order 304, 368, 371–2, 375
Positive quadrant dependence 265–74, 280–3, 289, 318, 319, 367–8, 370, 405, 406
Positive stop-loss dependence 270–1
Probability generating function 35, 141, 353
Prudence order 271

Quantile function 17–20, 56, 67, 109, 135, 240–1
  see also Value-at-risk

Right-spread order 175–8
Risk-adjusted capital 66
Risk aversion 80–1, 82, 86–7, 151–2, 154, 177–8

Solvency capital, *see* Economic capital
Spearman's rank correlation coefficient 257–9, 266–7, 279, 292, 297, 304
Spectral risk measure 88
Spherical distribution 46–8
Stationary renewal distribution 34, 119–20, 127, 142, 166–7, 184, 185
Stochastic complete monotonicity 141
Stochastic dominance 108–48, 157, 166–7, 182, 265, 269, 273, 274–5, 281–2, 305, 350, 358, 363–75, 397, 399, 401–2, 422
Stochastic increasing convexity 167–9
Stochastic increasingness 120–2, 183, 321, 322, 422
Stop-loss
  dependence, *see* Positive stop-loss dependence
  distance 401–3, 408–14
  order 149–82, 184–5, 187, 270–1, 291, 299, 304, 360, 401, 403, 422
  premium 29–30, 32, 34, 70, 75, 97, 110, 149, 356, 362
  transform, *see* Stop-loss, premium
Student distribution 45–6
  see also Copula; Student distribution
Supermodular
  function 131, 179–80, 277, 289, 345
  order 295–303, 305, 342, 360

Tail dependence 217–18, 242, 243
Tail value-at-risk 72–7, 92–3, 98, 291
Total positivity of order 2 – TP_2 276–7, 342
  see also Likelihood ratio, increasingness
Total-variation distance 393–6, 397, 400, 404, 408–14, 419–21, 422

Value-at-risk 67–72, 87, 89–90, 92, 95, 96, 97, 108–9, 130, 134–5, 169, 184, 240–1

Wang risk measure 88–95, 126, 166
Wasserstein distance 79, 398–400, 401, 402, 404, 408–14, 422

Zero-utility premium 81–2, 88–9

Printed and bound by CPI Group (UK) Ltd, Croydon, CR0 4YY
23/04/2025
14660952-0005